AFRICAN EVANGELICALISM AND THE TRANSFORMATION OF AFRICA

Race, Religion, and Politics Series

Edited by Terrence L. Johnson

Recently Published Titles

"My Faith in the Constitution Is Whole":
Barbara Jordan and the Politics of Scripture
Robin L. Owens

AFRICAN EVANGELICALISM AND THE TRANSFORMATION OF AFRICA

JACOB K. OLUPONA, EDITOR

GEORGETOWN UNIVERSITY PRESS / WASHINGTON, DC

Library of Congress Cataloging-in-Publication Data

Names: Olupona, Jacob K. (Jacob Kẹhinde), 1951– editor.
Title: African evangelicalism and the transformation of Africa /
    [edited by] Jacob K. Olupona.
Description: Washington, DC : Georgetown University Press, [2025] |
    Includes bibliographical references and index.
Identifiers: LCCN 2024020686 (print) | LCCN 2024020687 (ebook) |
    ISBN 9781647125509 (hardcover) | ISBN 9781647125516 (paperback) |
    ISBN 9781647125523 (ebook)
Subjects: LCSH: Evangelicalism—Africa, Sub-Saharan. | Pentecostalism—Africa,
    Sub-Saharan. | Christianity—Africa, Sub-Saharan.
Classification: LCC BR1642.A357 A38 2025 (print) | LCC BR1642.A357 (ebook) |
    DDC 276.7—dc23/eng/20241107

LC record available at https://lccn.loc.gov/2024020686
LC ebook record available at https://lccn.loc.gov/2024020687

♾ This paper meets the requirements of ANSI / NISO Z39.48-1992 (Permanence of Paper).

26 25   9 8 7 6 5 4 3 2 First printing

Printed in the United States of America

Cover design by Brad Norr
Interior design by Westchester Publishing Services

This volume is dedicated to pioneering African scholars in
Evangelical Christianity research:

Kwame Bediako (1945–2008)
Ogbu Kalu (1942–2009)
John S. Mbiti (1931–2019)
Lamin Sanneh (1942–2019)
Andrew Walls (1928–2021)

And in loving memory of our colleague and fellow traveler
David D. Daniels III (1954–2024)

CONTENTS

Introduction

Jacob K. Olupona

Evangelical Christianity is manifesting into a strong presence on the African continent, perhaps more than in any other place in the world.[1] Given the increased adherence to Evangelical Christianity, it is clear that Christianity in its Evangelical form is exercising significant influence in virtually all spheres of life. Hence, it is important that we ask questions about the ways in which Evangelical Christianity is defining nations and peoples' identities, and also about how it affects participation in politics and public life. For example, how does Evangelical Christianity shape African Christian practices and theology? What is its influence on the African public sphere, notably, the media, popular culture, civil society, and economic activities of contemporary Africa? How does African Evangelicalism differ from Evangelical Christianity in other parts of the world? Given the fact that African Evangelical Christianity travels from the continent to the West (a phenomenon that I call "reverse mission"), it plays a decisive role in global Christianity. This book will examine the Evangelical Christian experience as it defines the religious identities and lived practices of Africans.

BACKGROUND

As suggested by Peter Berger, "society is a dialectic phenomenon in that it is a human product, and nothing but a human product, that yet and continuously acts back upon its producer."[2] For this reason, we will attempt to examine these religious phenomena in the context of their origin and history, function, and substantive essence, without subjecting them to only one of these three elements of inquiry. Very deliberately and provocatively, this research is not framed in juxtaposition to Pentecostalism, which has certainly received more than its share of attention in contemporary scholarship from Africa. Rather, it emanates from the basic observation throughout the continent, where Evangelicalism has grown significantly. So, whereas one can argue that all Pentecostals in contemporary Africa are Evangelicals, not all Evangelical churches and movements consider themselves to be Pentecostals. The basic premise, however, is that African Protestant Christianity in all its forms is essentially Evangelical in its practices, social engagement, devotional lives, attitudes to politics, and so on. The missionary churches of the nineteenth century, the African Independent Churches of the early twentieth century, and Pentecostal Charismatic Christianity of the twenty-first century all exhibit features that are traceable to the central tenets and structures of Evangelicalism. Our work will attempt to explain different manifestations and forms of Evangelical phenomena without labeling one as less authoritative and authentic than the other. In other words, Christianity in Africa by its very nature, tone, and identity is primarily Evangelical. It is this unique story of African Christianity that spurs this work.

We also begin on another premise: the overemphasis on Pentecostalism as a rubric for studying modern African Christianity has marginalized what should have become a robust inquiry into the real situation of contemporary African Christians and their faith practices. This exclusivity affects a large portion of Christian practices, denominational affiliations, and sectarian groupings that, excluded from the rubric of Pentecostalism, cease to exhibit their own identity. The question here is the following: How can we include the traditional mission churches, the independent African Church, and the normative Pentecostal Charismatics in explaining the different manifestations and forms of Evangelicalism? Let us take the case of African indigenous churches (AIC) that dominated the socioreligious scene in the mid-twentieth century, when the mission churches were thought to be in decline and the Pentecostals as we know them today were not yet fully birthed. The rationale for the breakaway of the AIC was their concern for Evangelicalism, their belief that the mission churches that preceded them were not spiritually "hot" enough to withstand the vagaries of life in Africa then. The AIC's newfound life included fervent prayer, miracles, signs, and wonders that were some of the core elements constituting the beginnings and growth of Evangelical Christianity in Africa.

What binds the three main religious groups (Christianity, Islam, and Indigenous Religion) together is the dominance of African cosmology, particularly the perceived reality of the active spiritual world, which is often viewed in negative terms by the Christian denominational institutions. The need for the latter to respond to these active agents through the adoption of Christian symbols, rituals, and morality is part of the driving force underlying Evangelical Christianity. We must ask what the implications of this Evangelical fervor are for the revival of neotraditional religious practices, the phenomenal growth of radical Islam in Africa, and Muslim-Christian relations, particularly at a time when the Islamic Reformist movement has become totally intolerant of other traditions outside its fold. Indeed, the strength and the phenomenal growth of Evangelical Christianity particularly in the last few decades have engendered a negative reaction from radical Islam. Adherents of radical Islam believe that Christianity is infringing on the house of Islam through its stringent evangelization, particularly in predominantly Muslim regions, such as the Sahel region of the Chad, Niger, northern Nigeria, Burkina Faso, and Mauritania.

The centrality of religion in African affairs—political, economic, cultural, and ideological concerns—has raised the stakes for Evangelical Christianity, which has inevitably become the official face of the Christian Church in Africa today. The key questions this research intends to ask are (among others): What influence have the African religious worldview and cosmology in their local and global contexts exerted on the emergence and formation of Evangelical Christianity in Africa? What are the social, political, and economic influences and contexts that drive Evangelical spirituality? How does religious citizenship, particularly Christianity identity and citizenship, affect church state relations?

UNIQUE ANGLES

The influence of Evangelical Christianity on African societies has not attracted much attention from scholars of Christianity in Africa. Although some works have focused on the influence of Western Evangelicals on African Christianity in recent years, this project will challenge some of the findings in these works, particularly those that contend that Evangelicalism emerged from and is sustained by Euro-American missionary influence on Africa.[3] Africa has always been at the center of religious conversation. Despite this fact, there has been no comprehensive theoretical, empirical, and ethnographic work on African Evangelicalism across the continent. Only a few works—including Terence Ranger's 2008 edited volume, *Evangelical Christianity and Democracy in Africa*[4]—have focused specifically on African Evangelicals, but this literature is not comprehensive and has not accurately represented the influence of African Christianity in contemporary society. This creative research will therefore bring to light deep aspects of the cultural, social, political, economic, and moral compass of Evangelicals throughout Africa.

By focusing on an Evangelical tapestry that runs through the length and breadth of African Christianity since its beginning in the missionary movements of the nineteenth century, to its presence and triumphant claims in the twenty-first century in the Pentecostal Charismatic Movement, this collaborative research project will explore several critical issues that will enable us to map the contours of African Christian identities in contemporary Africa. Analyzed in the context of the emergence of modern African states and societies since the nineteenth century, we will critically analyze how Evangelical Christianity has consistently transformed the inner core of religious and spiritual life throughout the African continent. The significance of this religious phenomenon in many African communities will inevitably be analyzed in the context of the emergence of the colonial state at the turn of the twentieth century as well as the challenges inherent in the experience of African societies with the imposition of a largely weak postcolonial state that has consistently exhibited growing statism, neopatrimonialism, and neoliberal globalism.

Consequently, Christian Evangelicalism will be analyzed in the context of the complex political, social, and economic transformations that have engulfed African states throughout the colonial and postcolonial periods. In this context, Evangelical Christianity is not only at the core of a moral framework for the articulation of religious life but also fundamental to the myriad conditions that define the aspiration of the masses of local people in contemporary African societies. Accordingly, this study of Evangelical Christianity will focus on the explicitly religious way this phenomenon encapsulates political, social, and economic experiences in modern African societies.

Another major concern of this project is the discourse on a concrete definition, nomenclature, and analytical clarification of the varieties of Protestant Christianity in Africa. What is Evangelical Christianity in the African context? And how does it differ from other labels such as Pentecostal and Charismatic Christianity? What approaches and methodological considerations will provide genuine and in-depth answers to the central questions relating to forms of Christian identity and citizenship in Africa? Here in this work, we are concerned with the real-life situation of African peoples, their religious belongingness, and their lived religious practices in both pre- and postcolonial periods. Our work will deviate from scholarship that continues to compartmentalize people and traditions into structures that may be heuristically appropriate for academic exercise and intellectual discourse but that do not, in reality, tally with how Africans engage these traditions, profess their religious identities, and live their religious and devotional lives; or with the ways and manners of practice that emphasize forms of plurality of values, spirituality, and inclusiveness that are uncommon in other parts of the world. The urgency for a new paradigm and research agenda cannot be overemphasized. At the core of this interdisciplinary, collaborative research is the need to understand the dynamics of the African spirit world: the cosmology and the ontological status that forms the bedrock of concerns for human wholeness in Evangelical theology and praxis. Evangelicalism is not only a denominational term but also a way of being religious that is discernible in all the three forms of Evangelical Christian religious traditions in Africa.

In short, this research project will explore how Evangelical Christianity has formed one of the most important and pervasive religious movements that has swept through African societies since the emergence of mission Christianity at the beginning of the nineteenth century to the present period. It evolved from mission Christianity, and African-initiated churches and the contemporary Pentecostal movement, and it has grown exponentially during the political upheavals of the postcolonial era, notably in the context of the uncertainties, instability, and disruptions of a neopatrimonial and neoliberal postcolonial state and society. In this context, this research project will also underscore how critical connections between Evangelical Christianity and the material conditions of local people reveals a dialectical process between temporal and transcendence, local and global, engaging major themes that are emblematic of the rapidly changing conditions in African societies.

CONTRIBUTIONS TO THIS VOLUME

This project offers a timely response to the sparse ethnographic and historical and critical analyses of African Evangelicalism, and more specifically responds to the following shortcomings. First, the few existing works focus on Evangelicalism in specific contexts, for instance, in relation to democracy or development, but fail to pay sufficient attention to the broad influence of the movement. Second, many of the works are limited to specific topics and features of Evangelical religion as well as individual case studies, such as Ghana, Nigeria, Zimbabwe, South Africa, and so on. While such issue-specific and country-focused work is important to the study of Evangelical Christianity, a larger framework is crucial to better capture the expansive scope of this far-reaching religious phenomenon in contemporary African states and history. Third, current works take a narrow view of Evangelicalism as a subset of Christianity distinct from other branches such as Catholicism or mainline Protestantism but inclusive of various Pentecostal and Charismatic churches. Given the prominence of churches that explicitly claim to be Evangelical in their teachings, mission statements, and sometimes even their names, it is understandable that scholars assume that Evangelicalism includes only such churches. Yet, a closer exploration of African Christianity clearly reveals that the practices and ethos of Evangelicalism operate far beyond these denominations and are pervasive in both ancient and contemporary African Christianity. Indeed, it is notable that Evangelical theological practices and strategies were essential to the transformative impact of early mainline mission Christianity in African societies starting at the beginning of the nineteenth century.

The most notable recent work in this area has been Ogbu Kalu's 2008 book *African Pentecostalism: An Introduction*,[5] which addresses the nuances of Pentecostal theology in the African context. Kalu's book does a good job of introducing scholars to how the confluence of African indigeneity and the mysticism of African Pentecostal theology have merged to create an interesting blend of both worldviews and social constructions. However, as I observed earlier, several continent-specific volumes have engaged how different Evangelical praxes present themselves in different parts of the globe. As is well known, Pentecostalism and Evangelicalism (while often considered synonymously) are different iterations of a prevailing religiosity, one that we now broadly construe as Evangelicalism. So, whereas Kalu's book addresses Pentecostalism specifically, and its theological representations across the continent, this volume will take his work to the next step to more deeply engage with this phenomenon. For example, scholars interested in Evangelicalism would be right to question whether all African Evangelicals are in fact Pentecostal. Or, alternatively, whether all African Pentecostalism are Evangelical. In Africa, some forms of Catholicism carry Pentecostal / Charismatic traits while maintaining a truly Catholic identity. Noting this ambiguity, this research project will engage this complicated question within Africa's influential Catholic movement since the imposition of colonialism at the beginning of the twentieth century.

Given the deep evocative dimensions of the spiritual in African Christian religious practices, it is essential to carefully explore the complex connections between Evangelical Christianity in African societies and indigenous cosmologies and worldviews. This research project will thus seek to show how Christian Evangelicalism might be connected both to the early and to the contemporary African Christian worldview, particularly because it resonates with some of the deeply held indigenous beliefs and practices. Going against the suggestion that modern prominence of the movement in Africa is a response to the American religious influence on the content, this project reveals inherent connections between a traditional African worldview and contemporary forms of Christianity, an approach that demands deep familiarity not only with African Christianity but also African indigenous beliefs and practices. Bringing into focus continuity and uninterrupted progression, the project also challenges previous claims that contemporary forms of African Evangelicalism, such as Pentecostal and Charismatic Christianity, represent a total break with the past.[6] Considering these factors, a new theoretical framework is timely for the study of Evangelicalism in all its forms and manifestations in African societies.

This book is divided into four parts. "Part I: Subjectivity and the Political" addresses questions of governance in Nigeria through the lens of Evangelical Christianity. "Part II: Embodiment, Gender, and Identity" looks closely at how the categories of gender and sexuality intersect with religion. "Part III: African Traditional Religion and Interfaith Relations" examines religious pluralism, civic religion, and the influence of indigenous religious traditions. "Part IV: Global / Transnational Christianity and Mission" concludes this work with an analysis of how Evangelical Christianity in Africa shapes and is shaped by Christianity worldwide.

Part I begins with chapter 1, "Governance as Trauma in Nigeria: Turning Evangelicalism into Pentecostal Incredible," by Dr. Nimi Wariboko, asking how Christianity in Africa can move beyond its origins of trauma and despair. This chapter addresses Evangelicalism's potential to foster a common life in Nigerian despite the problems of postcoloniality. Wariboko grounds his argument in the idea of "Governance-as-Trauma," which is the notion that bad government in Nigeria has traumatized common life there and distorted the nation's collective memory. For the past sixty years, the postcolonial state has inflicted historical, structural, and microtrauma on the average Nigerian citizen. This immoral governance constitutes what Wariboko calls the "postcolonial incredible." The postcolonial incredible destabilizes social cohesion and replaces good governance with perpetual crisis and corruption that becomes normalized. This chapter describes how Evangelical Christianity in Nigeria responds to this postcolonial incredible by establishing the church parallel to the developmental state. Second, Evangelical Christians respond with a Pentecostal epistemology that seeks to make sense of the absurd and incredible by turning to the spirit.

This spiritual response leads Wariboko to make the argument that the emerging Pentecostal epistemology in Nigeria rejects modernist and rationalist thinking. Wariboko argues that this Pentecostal epistemology challenges Christianity and its moral claims, making Pentecostalism a subversive theology. The "pentecostal incredible," he explains, embraces emotion over reason and seeks short-term success instead of a genuine, long-lasting connection with God. Wariboko describes the Pentecostal faith as an anxiety response to the existential crises brought about by the postcolonial incredible. The pentecostal incredible encourages believers to focus on themselves and pursue a personal freedom, which Wariboko sees as a false freedom that further estranges Christians from divine freedom. This chapter demonstrates how the pentecostal incredible sheds light on the reality of despair and bad governance in Nigeria. To reconcile the pentecostal incredible with Christian theology, Wariboko develops a radical theology of the "chaosmosic" life. His radical theology recenters the centrality of the promise in Christianity and urges Nigerians to take more seriously the task of promise keeping in politics and common life.

In chapter 2 "Evangelical Christianity and Politics in Africa: A New Map for an Old Terrain," Rev. Dr. Esther E. Acolatse analyzes the three main phases of Evangelical Christianity in Africa and interrogates American Evangelical Christianity. She primarily argues that Evangelical Christianity has become increasingly popular and relevant in Africa because it effectively caters to the psychospiritual attitudes of many Africans. However, Acolatse notes the linguistic limits and shortcomings of African Evangelical Christianity, raising the question of how transformative Evangelical Christianity really is. She makes the distinction between "Global Christianity," the European political enterprise that interpreted the Bible as inspiration and justification for colonialism, and "World Christianity," which recognizes that Christianity is practiced differently around the world and that there is no nation or culture that has a monopoly on Christianity. Because Europeans used Christianity to exercise control in Africa during colonialism, African nations' response to the colonial legacy inevitably involves a religious historical reckoning.

Acolatse traces this history by starting with the phase of individual conversion in Africa that breaks with the tradition of communal practices. Following this phase of conversion and Evangelical organizations working with more traditional denominations, the Evangelical movement elevated the pastor to a role of authority that in many instances gave the pastors and churches a political platform. In analyzing Evangelicalism's relationship with indigenous religious traditions, Acolatse concludes that the form and function of Evangelical Christianity in Africa are counter to African philosopholinguistic culture. Despite its rapid growth, Evangelical Christianity does not venture into the public political discourse as much as it could. This chapter argues that if Evangelical Christianity wants to take up a larger role in the public arena, it must learn and employ common sayings and proverbs practiced by the rich African linguistic traditions. Last, Acolatse advises that Evangelical Christianity can be more African if it adopts a hermeneutic grounded in African philosophical and linguistic traditions. These traditions provide unique forms of speaking and meaning making, such as the deep narratives of African myths. Acolatse concludes with a hopeful message that both the Bible and African traditions can inform Evangelical Christianity in the future.

Chapter 3, "Ethiopian Evangelicals and Politics: Polite Distance or Keen Interest?," by Dr. Tibebe Eshete, investigates Evangelical Christianity in Ethiopia and how it has become a major political force. Evangelical Christians now constitute 20 percent of Ethiopia's population, a significant increase from just 5 percent in 1980. Although the local slang term *Pente* refers to all protestant Christians in the country, Eshete makes clear that Evangelical Christianity consists of different denominations and varies by region. Pente developed as a shorthand for Pentecostals, who in their early history sought to distance themselves from the political arena and focus on personal spirituality. However, the rise of neo-Charismatic churches in major cities in Ethiopia has propelled Evangelical Christians into the public sphere. Eshete attributes this shift partly to the work and writings of Ethiopian theologian and general secretary of the Ethiopian Evangelical Church Gudina Tumsa. Gudina preached that Evangelicals, like all Christians, ought to be concerned with the plight of the poor and act on behalf of the oppressed. Furthermore, Gudina pioneered "holistic ministry" in Ethiopia, urging the church to meet the spiritual and material needs of congregants and their communities. Eshete's analysis of Gudina offers a refreshing and critical analysis of this pivotal theologian and his theories around Evangelical Christianity.

In addition to Gudina's theology, Eshete argues that the Revolution of 1974 ushered in a new and more public-facing role for Evangelical Christians. The revolution granted citizens new freedoms and thus created more room for Evangelical congregations to grow. At the same time the new Marxist government's attempts to challenge Christian churches represented a common struggle that in many ways unified the diverse group of Evangelical Christians in Ethiopia. Eshete demonstrates how we can understand the tribulations and growth of Evangelical Christianity in Ethiopia through their relations with national politics. In 2005 young Evangelicals supported the opposition party the Coalition for Unity and Democracy (CUD) to protect the country and Constitution from one-party rule. Though many young Evangelicals were active in this political movement, the Evangelical church as a whole condemned this activity, representing the paradoxical relationship Evangelical Christians had with political activism. Eshete carefully traces this complex history to help us better understand the growing political involvement of different denominations, such as the Pentecostals with their recent power ministry and the recent election of Abiy Ahmed, an Evangelical Christian, as prime minister. This chapter provides key insights into the history and politics of Evangelical Christianity in Ethiopia and its implications for the country's future religious and social landscapes.

In chapter 4, "Governing Religious Life in Idi Amin's Uganda," Dr. Derek R. Peterson explores how the work of renowned Kenyan philosopher John Mbiti shaped the former president of Uganda Idi Amin's policies around religion and African culture. Peterson makes this connection by focusing on Mbiti's tenure at Makerere University in Uganda, where he taught and researched between 1964 and 1974. In addition to his frequent publications in the famous *Transition* magazine, Mbiti published the book *African Religions and Philosophy*, which explores the systemic thinking and beliefs shared among African religions.[7] Mbiti's publications gained the attention not only of scholars but also of government officials. Shortly after General Idi Amin took power in Uganda in 1971, he reached out to Professor Mbiti at Makerere University to inquire about a possible Ministry of Religious Affairs. Peterson masterfully explains how Mbiti's research into African religions provided the moral and philosophical backbone to Amin's cultural work and analyzes Mbiti's initial letter supporting the Ministry of Religious Affairs. Mbiti was thrilled at the prospect of this new initiative that sought to use religion as a tool for peacekeeping, public dialogue, and national unity. For its first major challenge the Department of Religious Affairs helped unify the fraying Anglican Church of Uganda and in doing so proved that politics can reduce religious disagreements.

However, Peterson explains that this Christian unification came at a cost. Amin's government persecuted religious dissenters and regulated Charismatic churches. These Evangelical Christians threatened the social order and religious dogma, making them public enemies in Amin's eyes. Therefore, the government formally banned Evangelical denominations such as Pentecostal Churches that undermined religious syncretism. After the government closed these Evangelical churches, the mainline Anglican Church pursued religious consolidation by inviting these former Pentecostal churches to join their congregations. While Peterson explains that Mbiti certainly did not envision or support this religious persecution, his ideas about a unified and whole African religious life were misused to limit the religious freedom of those outside the accepted religious order. Peterson notes that Mbiti did speak out against Libyan dictator Muammar Gaddafi's plan to make Uganda a Muslim state. Mbiti's sermon on the need for Christians and Muslims to coexist in Africa made him a political target of Amin's regime and forced Mbiti to flee Uganda. Peterson concludes with a warning for us to learn from the example of Amin and not confuse calls for cultural unity with authoritarianism.

In Chapter 5, "Are You Ready to Hear?": Politics, Prophecy, and Practical Theology in Malawi," Dr. Blair D. Bertrand draws on the discipline of practical theology to analyze the role of religious prophets in African politics. Bertrand employs Richard Osmer's equilibrium model to construct a practical theology that takes political prophecies seriously. This chapter explains how practical theology's methodology can help both social scientists and theologians better understand how prophetic utterances in the Pentecostal and Charismatic traditions relate to politics, specifically their influence on the 2020 Malawian election. Evangelical prophets claimed to predict President Lazarus Chakwera, a Pentecostal theologian, winning the highly contested election. Bertrand argues that the skeptics and social scientists, who were quick to dismiss these prophecies, operate on the assumption that prophetic predictions are invalid because they do not believe in an omniscient or omnipotent God. To grapple seriously with these prophecies as truth claims, Bertrand uses the lens of practical theology. Bertrand offers a meta-theory analysis, a prophetic sermon in a Malawi church that made predictions about the 2019–20 election.

Bertrand brackets his own presuppositions and questions whether researchers can fully understand the prophecies if they do not recognize the prophet's theology. He raises a concern about how ethnographers, sociologists, and researchers in general misinterpret and fail to understand the complexities of those who hold different and oftentimes irreconcilable beliefs. Bertrand explains how practical theology gives us the tools and framework to interpret the prophecy about Malawi election in more complete and authentic ways. Practical theology can help us explore the theological doctrines behind the prophecy and reflect on its ethical implications. Furthermore, practical theology can provide examples of past best practices to reform and rethink the congregation's social values and relationship with God. Bertrand ends this chapter and with it the first part of this book with a plea for epistemic humility. He notes that because the prophet and the congregation in Malawi believe these prophecies to be the truth, he ought to approach these prophecies from a place of faith and humility, which lends itself to the discipline of practical theology.

Part II begins with chapter 6, Dr. Yolanda Covington-Ward's "Embodiment and Evangelical Christianity: Missions, Prophets, and Bodies in Post-Colonial Democratic Republic of Congo." Covington-Ward explores the role of the body in Evangelical Christianity in the Democratic Republic of Congo. For this study, Covington-Ward looks at how a number of Evangelicals and prophets in the rural town of Luozi speak about how Christians should deal with the past and their views on embodiment. She analyzes this Evangelical discourse in the Congo through her interviews and observations of the community. This chapter draws on prophets' personal narratives to emphasize the importance of connecting with the past through dreams, which raises an important question in Evangelical Christianity of whether believers should tap into visions as a spiritual practice. Covington-Ward analyzes this debate and other disagreements within Evangelical churches such as whether trembling is a divine or demonic practice. In doing so, she corrects a scholarly overemphasis on Pentecostalism and instead takes a more holistic and balanced approach to studying Evangelical Christianity in Africa.

Covington-Ward details her thorough fieldwork in Luozi, which serves as an excellent example for any researcher interested in ethnographic work in rural areas in Africa, especially in Democratic Republic of Congo. She contextualizes her interviews with prophets with the rich tradition of spiritual healers and prophets in Congolese history. Not only does Covington-Ward analyze the discourse around dreams in Evangelical Christianity, but she also adds to and reshapes the discourse through her interviews. She incorporates key quotes from her interviews, as well as her own insights about how Evangelical Christians in Luozi interpret encounters with the Holy Spirit. This chapter complicates and deepens Evangelical discourse by destabilizing popular assumptions about embodiment. While the common discourse among Evangelical Christians in Africa sees trembling as an embodiment of evil, the folks in Luozi interviewed by Covington-Ward consider trembling a vital part of their conversion to a prophetic church or to prophetic work. Covington-Ward concludes this chapter by explaining how the prophets she interviewed do not fit neatly into the dominant categories used to describe Christianity in Africa. That is, the religious activities of these Christians were not perfect indicators of their religious identities. In this provocative and well-researched study, Covington-Ward uses the conversion story of four prophets in Luozi to reframe the discourse on embodiment within Evangelical Christianity in Africa.

In chapter 7, "Women's Evangelical Revolutions in Northern Nigeria," Dr. Shobana Shankar analyzes the religious significance of the diaries of some of 276 Nigerian schoolgirls kidnapped by Boko Haram in 2014.

Specifically, Shankar looks at the Christian underpinnings of the girls' writings about refusing marriage and slavery under Boko Haram. Their diaries reveal key insights into the Christianity and lives of women in Northern Nigeria, who live in a predominantly Muslim society. Shankar studies how Christianity and gender intersect in Northern Nigeria and informs the schoolgirls' narratives. To provide a historical background to these diaries, Shankar traces how Protestant Evangelical Christianity in Northern Nigeria developed into what she calls a "female religion." The girls wrote about how Boko Haram used physical and phycological torture to force them to convert to Islam and marry Muslim men. Shankar also takes into account the writings of Sufi women when reflecting on the gender and religious dynamics of the diaries.

Shankar examines how a nineteenth-century social revolution in Northern Nigeria propelled by women like Nana Asma'u ushered in new conceptions of Muslim womanhood. Asma'u formed female organizations that drew attention to women's presence in public spaces. Parallel to this history, Shankar explains how even after emancipation from the British, Christianity became the popular religion among slave girls and women in Northern Nigeria. Not only did Christianity denote a lower social status there, but Western Christian missionaries also limited the rights of women within the church, making Christian women in Nigeria "doubly marginalized." The missionaries discouraged women who converted to Christianity from marrying Muslim men. Education for Christian women became a way to delay marriage or even escape from an unpleasant marriage. Given this history, Shankar argues that the Chibok girls' refusing to convert and marry embodies a rich tradition of Christianity for women in Northern Nigeria. Their resistance to Boko Haram emerges in the form of diaries and status as schoolgirls put on full display how Christian women use education as a tool for protection and social advancement. Shankar offers a powerful analysis of how Boko Haram's kidnapping of the schoolgirls reflects issues of gender and religious oppression that have long characterized social history in Northern Nigeria.

Chapter 8, "Weddings Are Not a Sexy Affair! Youth Sexuality, Embodiment, and Moral Imaginaries in a Neo-Pentecostal Church in Kenya," by Dr. Damaris Seleina Parsitau, explores how the Ministry of Repentance and Holiness (MRH) in Kenya teaches youth about gender, sex, and sexuality. Parsitau positions this ministry within the context of a growing youth population in Kenya, many of whom consider faith to be an important part of their lives and turn to Pentecostal churches for guidance. By preaching about intimacy and youth issues, Pentecostal churches have begun to shape youth perceptions and practices in regard to relationships and reproduction.

Parsitau interviewed thirty-five young church members and ex-members who are part of the MRH University's Students Outreach Program. Based on this ethnographic research, this chapter examines how the Pentecostal discourses shape and challenge "moral imaginaries and gendered sexualities." Specifically, Parsitau analyzes how Prophet David Owuor at the MRH preaches about gender and sexuality to youth. Prophet Owuor's sermons often emphasize his belief that any type of sex outside of a heterosexual marriage is a sin punishable by death. Parsitau explains how purity culture and holy thoughts are key elements of MRH's public theology.

This emphasis on Christian purity depicts women as temptations, and Prophet Owuor therefore instructs women to dress modestly to avoid luring men. Parsitau makes the apt comparison between the MRH's preaching about sexual purity and the Evangelical Movement in the 1970s United States that placed the responsibility of sexual morality entirely on women. Furthermore, MRH seeks to control the media its followers consume, regulating what type of music they listen to and TV shows or movies they watch. While Owuor claims Kenyan churches have neglected the youth, Parsitau points out that many churches in Kenya have youth ministries. Parsitau uses direct quotes from Owuor's sermons to trace how he teaches youth about sins of premarital sex. Additionally, this chapter details how MRH controls many aspects of their members' lives, such as pregnancy and HIV testing. Parsitau makes the convincing case that young people need true sex education instead of the hysterical and extreme lessons around sex espoused by Owuor and MRH. From her interviews, Parsitau learns that many of the young members joined the Ministry of Repentance and Holiness because they feared contracting HIV and wanted spiritual guidance on how to navigate intimacy. The young members largely embrace Owuor's idea that Kenya needs a future generation of moral and holy leaders. This chapter provides an inside look into how a Pentecostal church in Kenya exercises rigid control over young people and their views on sex, sexuality, and health.

In Chapter 9, "'A Mightier Power': Women and Gender Construction in the *African Challenge*, 1951–1961," Dr. Andrew E. Barnes interprets articles from the Christian magazine the *African Challenge* that concern the role of Christian women in newly independent African Nations. The *African Challenge* was edited entirely by African Christians and was part of a coalition of Evangelical churches in West Africa, making it a valuable primary source for examining the ideas and attitudes of Evangelical Christians in Africa during the mid-twentieth century. Breaking from the simple narrative that Christian missions colonized the African psyche, this chapter explores how African Christians decided what lessons and practices from the Western missionaries should stay, be adopted, or be left in the past. Barnes notes that these articles written by and for women for the most part affirmed the views of the male-dominated editorial staff of the *African Challenge*. This chapter does a good job of noting the complexity of publishing articles about the role of women. At first the *African Challenge* would publish articles on the same page written by women with contrasting perspectives on how Christian women should embrace their freedom and religion. Ultimately, Barnes describes how the male audience grew to resent any space the magazine gave to women and women's issues.

Barnes prefaces his analysis of these articles written by Christian women with a discussion of the history, purpose, and religious messaging of the *African Challenge*. He draws on excerpts from the articles to highlight their key themes such as maternal activism at home and abroad. Maternal activism advocated for African mothers to pursue healthy child-rearing practices and not listen solely to missions or the government. Barnes acknowledges the progress the *African Challenge* made by giving women the opportunity to write about their faith and their articles prominent space throughout the magazine. This chapter demonstrates how the *African Challenge* sought to portray women's domestic duties as an Evangelical pursuit of God's wish for women to work in the homes. Barnes analyzes the response to the articles from both men and women who took issue with the strong emphasis on child rearing. Barnes also covers a variety of different series run by the magazine about gender roles within households. He makes the compelling historical argument that the debates about gender found in the pages of the *African Challenge* in the 1950s precede and anticipate the tension about gender roles in Western Evangelical circles in the 1970s and 1980s. This chapter explains the nuance of articles written by African Evangelical women and their cultural context.

To begin part III of this volume, "African Traditional Religion and Interfaith Relations," Dr. Katrien Pype examines Pentecostal market radio in Kinshasa, the capital of the Democratic Republic of Congo. Chapter 10, "Awakening the Market: Small Pentecostal Genres and Religious Accommodation in Kinshasa," presents a religious tension between the Pentecostal radio station at the Marché Kato market in Kinshasa and the nearby mosque that did not want to hear this evangelizing radio during their Friday prayer. Pype draws on a collection of ethnographic data she gathered visiting marketplaces in Kinshasa to analyze genres of radio such as quizzes and dilemma tales. This research shapes understandings of Pentecostal publics and religious pluralism. Pype explains how Pentecostalism has rapidly grown by repackaging Christian motifs as lines in popular culture and music. This chapter introduces public markets as origin points for Christian Evangelism and Evangelical preachers gaining an audience. Pype observes that many Muslim vendors will listen to the Pentecostal radio for moral lessons and tune out the spiritual instruction. She also notes how the Evangelical animateurs must work hard to win attention in the public and religiously diverse marketplace.

Pype describes the practical functions of radio and the Pentecostal programming as well. This chapter reports on how important the calls to collect money for fueling the generators are. Pype categorizes these calls for fuel, quizzes, and shouts of born-again Evangelical Christians as small, discursive genres of Pentecostal radio. She argues that these small genres generate small acts among Christians in the market who can express their Evangelical faith through small donations or quickly shouting religious language. In contrast to small genres that elicit faith responses, the genre of the *dilemme* transcends religious lines. Pype convincingly argues that these dilemme stories represent the "moral middle" of Evangelical media in the markets by presenting interesting tales about choice. She analyzes an exciting excerpt from a dilemme performance and demonstrates how the story and the Evangelical animateur engage the audience irrespective of their religious background. This chapter offers a thorough analysis of how genres of Evangelical radio form a variety of Pentecostal publics in the markets of Kinshasa.

In chapter 11, "'Let Us Offer Thanks for the Nation of Ghana': Indigenous Harvest Festival as a Civil Ceremony of Thanksgiving," Dr. Mariam Goshadze explores how the Christian Council of Ghana brokered peace between the Ga people and Evangelical Christians. Goshadze takes a nuanced approach to *Hɔmɔwɔ*-Thanksgiving, an annual festival hosted by churches since 2015 as an interfaith initiative. She recognizes how the festival celebrates the indigenous traditions of the Ga people. At the same time, this chapter notes that understanding the Hɔmɔwɔ-Thanksgiving festival as a cultural event obscures and dilutes the sacred Ga religious cosmology. To contextualize this festival, Goshadze offers a brief and informative history of interfaith relations in Ghana. She explains how Pentecostal / Charismatic churches upset the peaceful relationship between Christianity and indigenous religions by verbally demeaning practitioners of traditional religions. Goshadze interviewed Reverend Dr. Kwabena Opuni- Frimpong, who served as the general secretary of the Christian Council of Ghana and developed the festival. Opuni-Frimpong sees the Hɔmɔwɔ-Thanksgiving festival as a way to impart moral wisdom and solve pressing issues.

From the perspective of the state, the modern Hɔmɔwɔ-Thanksgiving celebration is a sign of "progress" and "cultural enhancement." Goshadze makes clear that although it seeks to be a nationwide festival, the Hɔmɔwɔ-Thanksgiving is celebrated by only a number of mainline Christian churches. These churches host the festival not only to foster better interfaith relations but also to expose those practicing traditional religion to Christianity. In this sense the Hɔmɔwɔ-Thanksgiving festival is a form of Evangelism cloaked in culture and interreligious understanding. Goshadze carefully explores the Christian influences on the festival, such as the church's attempt to merge the pantheon of Ga deities into a singular god. However, this chapter makes clear that the churches consulted with the chief of Osu throughout the whole process, and the Ga traditional community is overall pleased with the festival and its work toward interfaith peace. Most Evangelical Christian churches do not hold the Hɔmɔwɔ-Thanksgiving festival, because they see the embrace of traditional religious practices as antithetical to their Christian faith and ultimately a futile compromise. Goshadze concludes that the primary goal of the Hɔmɔwɔ-Thanksgiving festival is to build peace and understanding between the Evangelical Christians and Ga people who believe in traditional religion.

Chapter 12, "'I Am a Witch for Jesus!': Confronting Ritual Praxis, Symbolic Violence, and Trauma in African Evangelical Pentecostalism," by Dr. Afe Adogame, interrogates the connection between religion and crime in the context of Evangelical Christian rituals. Adogame analyzes a notorious incident at the Pentecostal megachurch Living Faith Church Worldwide (LFCW), Winners Chapel International, where Pastor David Oyedepo slapped a female congregant after she proclaimed, "I am a witch for Jesus." This chapter explains that Oyedepo, along with many African Evangelicals, regard witchcraft as Satanic, evil behavior that must be conquered through spiritual practices. Adogame's major contribution here is his theorizing on religion and crime, a growing and important field in sociology of religion and criminology. In a comprehensive literature review, Adogame covers current scholarship that often sees religious activity as a crime deterrent and points to the lack of research on how religious leaders commit crimes against their congregants. For an example of such crimes, this chapter explores the academic reports and church policies and history concerning the cases of clerical Child Sexual Abuse within the Catholic Church.

Adogame argues that ministers sexually abuse children in other Christian denominations throughout the entire world, so it is not just a Catholic issue. To explore how religion and crime are related in the African context, Adogame brings up the history of European missions committing crimes against indigenous religions and burning their sacred objects. This chapter examines religion and crime through the lens of gender, analyzing why women are usually the victims of these crimes committed by religious leaders. In the final sections, Adogame discusses how moral panic theory and social capital theory can shed light on the problem of religious leaders committing crimes and escaping serious accountability. He explains how these crimes are fueled by the government and media, fostering moral panic about a particular group that then permeates the public consciousness. Some Evangelical pastors contribute to and sustain moral panic around traditional religious rituals by demonizing them in their sermons. Adogame uses social capital theory to emphasize the strong connections churches build as well to demonstrate how these strong connections can be misused to exclude others. This chapter provides a close look into the theories and research that help explain the relatedness of religion, crime, deviant behavior, and trauma.

In chapter 13, "Some Thoughts on Evangelical Christianity in Africa and the Diaspora," I look specifically at how African immigrant religious communities in the West are slowly shaping the religious landscapes in the United States and Europe. This chapter explores how African Evangelicals in their new homes engage in civil discourse around belonging, citizenship, and immigrant identity. These African Evangelical churches in the West reflect a concept I coined called "reverse mission." The reverse mission refers to how in contrast to the European missionaries evangelizing Africa, African Evangelicals are now "taking the Gospel back" to the West. For example, the largest Protestant religious congregation in Europe is the Embassy of the Blessed Kingdom in Kiev, Ukraine, pastored by the Nigerian preacher Sunday Adelaja. I situate African immigrant religion within the multireligious society of the United States and its connection to the law and the state. After fleeing oppression in their home countries, many African immigrants find refuge and community in the African Christian churches in the United States. I argue that in this era of globalization, we must understand African congregations abroad as important aspects of the African religious experience. Additionally, I explore the political significance of prayer and urge scholars to take prayer's meaning, history, and context seriously. I also raise the question of how African Evangelicals in the United States may influence American Evangelicals. Last, I explore why a good number of African Evangelicals in the United States voted for President Trump. This chapter analyzes how African churches are influencing the Western religious landscape and ideas around citizenship and immigration.

In chapter 14, "African Evangelical Politics in Global Perspective," Paul Freston compares the growth and nature of African Evangelical Christianity with Evangelical Christianity in South America. This fruitful and generative comparison sheds light on how Evangelicals in Africa negotiate their faith and politics in the public sphere. Freston explores global Pentecostalism through the lens of Evangelical Christianity to destabilize American-centric views of Evangelical Christianity. His close reading of polling data and the attitudes of Evangelicals illuminates how the complexities of Evangelical Christianity play out on the world stage, particularly regarding the Middle East and Islam. Freston draws on the case of Pentecostalism in Brazil to sketch the state and possible future directions of Pentecostals' relationship with civil society in Nigeria. Freston depicts how Pentecostalism in Brazil has often codified corruption with large Pentecostal denominations naming the "official" candidates. Freston outlines how Evangelical politics fit into Nigeria's religious diversity and explores the implications of "Islamized Pentecostalism" in the country. Last, Freston traces the social, ideological, and theological limits of Pentecostal politics.

Chapter 15, " 'Africa . . . Leads the Way': Kwame Bediako's Understanding of the Remaking of Christian Theology," by Dr. Tim Hartman, explores the life and intellectual legacy of Ghanaian theologian Kwame Bediako. Bediako argues that Christendom worldwide can learn from the example of Christianity in Africa, which understands Christianity within the context of religious pluralism. Bediako believed that Christians should be able to read the Bible in their native tongue and that Christianity was indigenous to Africa. The central argument is that given the growing number of Christians in the Global South, scholars of religious studies need a new, post-Christendom theological framework. Bediako knew that Christianity could not have only one geographic center or universal meaning. Rather, Christianity had to be understood as a global phenomenon with different meanings dependent on social context. Bediako challenged the term "postcolonial theology," urging Africans to remember their precolonial, indigenous wisdom. He reimagined theology as less of a story about European Christian history and more of an exploration of the ongoing development of Christianity in the Global South. Drawing attention to the deep theological resources of African religions and how African theology can shape theological thinking worldwide, he argued that African theology raises new methods, questions of identity, and the tension between new and old in religious discourse. The emphasis on identity takes seriously the connection between theology and the theologian. Bediako insisted that academic theology should start at the grassroots level. Hartman's analysis of Bediako's theology offers an interesting look into African religious thought and the future of world Christianity.

In the final chapter, 16, "Evangelical Transformation and Transnationalism in Africa," Dr. Stephen Offutt explores the common building blocks of

African Evangelicalism and how they manifest in all corners of the continent. He argues that although African Evangelicalism consists of diverse groups in different geographic areas, they all share social structures and cultural content. To highlight these shared building blocks of African Evangelicalism, Offutt examines five case studies of how African Evangelicalism cultivate transnational networks. The first set of case studies explores the development of Evangelical Churches Winning All (ECWA) in Nigeria and the Africa Gospel Church (AGC) in Kenya. Offutt explains how these networks of churches serve as hubs for community service. For example, the ECWA operates many hospitals, schools, and banks for the surrounding communities. The chapter traces how the Sudan Interior Mission (SIM) builds transnational networks to finance and support these two churches and their community outreach efforts. The second set of case studies looks at Calvary Missions (CARPO), a Pentecostal in Nigeria that addresses food insecurity and spreads the Gospel, and Faith Ministries, a Charismatic movement in Zimbabwe. Offutt explains how CARPO missionaries and members of Faith Ministries establish congregations throughout the world, such as in the United Kingdom. The last case study describes how Evangelical churches partner with nongovernmental organizations (NGOs). Specifically, this section talks about the relationship between the Evangelical Covenant Church (ECC) and World Vision, the largest Christian NGO in the world. Offutt explores the implications of these two American-based organizations working in Africa and current efforts that try to give the communities in Africa more agency in this philanthropic work. This concluding chapter shows the complexity and diversity of African Evangelical congregations and their transnational networks.

This volume offers a cutting-edge exploration of African Evangelicalism and how it is transforming Africa and shaping Christianity around the world. From accounts of Pentecostal radio in the markets of Kinshasa to an analysis of how Evangelical youth in Kenya navigate their faith and relationships, this work contains exciting and robust ethnographic studies. This collection displays the myriad ways Evangelical Christianity is shaping African society and how long-standing African traditions interact with Evangelical Christianity. In addition to ethnographic research, this book carefully interrogates the theology and theologians that reconceptualized Christianity and religious pluralism in Africa. I hope the readers enjoy these enlightening chapters written by the world's leading experts on religious studies, African Christianity, political science, sociology, and international affairs.

NOTES

1. Because Evangelical Christianity is an evolving and dynamic category, the different authors in this volume may approach its meaning and orthography differently.
2. Peter Berger, *The Sacred Canopy: Elements of a Sociological Theory of Religion* (New York: Anchor Books, 1967), 3.
3. Julie Hearn, "The 'Invisible' NGO: US Evangelical Missions in Kenya: Christian and Islamic Non-Governmental Organisations in Contemporary Africa," *Journal of Religion in Africa* 32, no. 1 (2002): 32–60; Katharina Hofer, "The Role of Evangelical NGOs in International Development: A Comparative Case Study of Kenya and Uganda," *Afrika Spectrum* 38, no. 3 (2003): 375–98; Asteris Huliaras, "The Evangelical Roots of US Africa Policy," *Survival (London)* 50, no. (2008): 161–82, https://doi.org/10.1080/00396330802601917.
4. T. O. Ranger, *Evangelical Christianity and Democracy in Africa* (Oxford: New York: Oxford University Press, 2008).
5. Ogbu Kalu, *African Pentecostalism: An Introduction* (1st ed; Oxford: Oxford University Press, 2008).
6. *Economist*, "Halleluja! The Rise of Pentecostalism Could Change the Face of Kenya," July 20, 2006.
7. John Mbiti *African Religions and Philosophy* (Garden City, NY: Anchor Books, 1970).

PART I

Subjectivity and the Political

CHAPTER 1

Governance as Trauma in Nigeria

Turning Evangelicalism into Pentecostal Incredible

Nimi Wariboko

Epistemology is the worm at the heart of the apple of African Christianity and its commons. The commons is the plumb line of the morality of African Christianity. In the commons, believers themselves—instead of doctrine and devotion—have become the display (or declaration) of Christ, not however, as believers but as the mode of manifestation of the ethicoepistemological correlation (or constitution) of self and world (or community). This worm has many friends. Together, they are deforming the apple.

Can Christianity exist without a viable commons? Will African Christianity continue to flourish if its foundations are increasingly displaced by trauma, desperation, and despair? Is Nigerian Christianity in good health when its common life in Christ is governed by deformed reason, nonreason, or emotionalism? Can Christianity thrive in a culture where there is little or no commitment to making and keeping the kind of promises that sustain social fabrics? Responding to these questions about the commons will move us away from evaluating the success of evangelicalism in Nigeria by narrowly focusing on church attendance, growth of believers, vibrancy of deliverance ministries, or number of churches. The narrow focus often hides the deformities that attend to the life of the commons (political, epistemological, ethical, etc.) or to the dynamics of Christ and the common life in the country.

This chapter examines the deformities of evangelicalism in Nigeria and how this sickness has shaped the commons of Christian life in the country. Our thesis is that we will have a better grasp of the prospects of evangelicalism if we focus on the kind of common life it has fashioned under the pressure of the predicament of postcoloniality. Of course, this is not the only way to decipher the future of Nigerian evangelical Christianity, but it is a good way to arrive at an unvarnished diagnosis of Nigerian Christianity. Though our examination starts with an evaluation of the diseased, crisis-ridden commons in which Nigerian Christians practice their faith, it concludes that the illness is not a sickness unto death.

Governance-as-trauma is the ground, the commons indeed, of Christian life in Nigeria. Governance, just like the daily existential condition, is an incredible phenomenon, a situation of perpetual crisis, crisis-as-norm. Christianity in the country is a struggle to survive the perpetual trauma of national political governance. Caught in this agonistic struggle, Christianity (especially its Pentecostal variant) has become part of what the Nigerian scholar Tejumola Olaniyan, calls the "postcolonial incredible." "The incredible is not simply a breach but an outlandish infraction of 'normality' and its limits."[1] I will transform Olaniyan's postcolonial incredible into the "pentecostal incredible."

There are many Pentecostals—certainly not all of Nigerian Pentecostals—who claim to have direct insight into God's mind with the idea that this divinity demands critical resistance to current society's knowledge systems and habitus. This God, they believe, often asks his followers to perform psychotic-delirious actions to prove their faith. The pentecostal incredible is not simply a breach but an outlandish infraction of "reason" and Christian "normativeness" and their limits. These three "powers" bombard the average Nigerian Pentecostal. First governance—metaphor for disaster of faith (in nationhood)—attacks her; then the postcolonial incredible—a metonym for disaster of faith (in normality); finally, disaster of faith itself attacks as the pentecostal incredible. In this chapter, we will analyze how Christianity / Pentecostalism participates in the reign of the incredible in Nigeria. I will conclude our discussion with a section that lays out the likely principles that might inform a radical Christian political theology that can meaningfully prepare Nigerian citizens and state to respond to the reticulated operations of the three forms of disaster. This will include a discourse on the act of making and keeping promises to counter the uncertainties caused by these disasters. The goal is to nudge Nigerians to begin the process of healing the deformities of their variety of Christianity.

THE NATURE OF GOVERNANCE IN NIGERIA

Governance in Nigeria is a state of government autosuspension.[2] Government is in force only in the form of its absence, nonpresence, or suspension.

Governance is a civil war within the body politic, holding the people into a life consecrated to death. In this marginal position, the traditional distinction between the past (future) and the present has disappeared. The two have contracted into one intense moment of precariousness.

The whole idea of bad governance abolishing the past and future—and only the present remaining—can also be accessed through the lens of trauma from the standpoint of the victims of traumatic governmentality. Trauma studies have demonstrated that the effects and memories of the past are always present in ways that suggest the past (though not technically abolished as a temporal event) is totally displaced into the present. The now of the past is (persists in) the now of the present. The past memory in its ongoingness and perpetual return rebirths itself, escapes its temporal identity, and operates as the present. Traumatic events that remain continue with the victims, who do not recognize or respect temporal segmentation between past and present. The experience of the aftermath of a traumatic event marks future and present as unbounded, just as life and death blur into one another as death-in-life in the reliving of the event. Amid trauma or unconcluding remains of a traumatic event, conceiving the future seems impossible. The overwhelming event that keeps returning and impacting the present continues into the future. The precipitating event that is "always here" with the victim in the present makes it difficult to conceive of a future life or flow of time apart from the sufferer's reality, the categories of the pain and after-living of the violence.[3]

Trauma has the capacity to unbound time segments because it "is not located in the past but instead is located in the gap between the occurrence of the traumatic event and a subsequent awakening to it. The suffering does not lie solely in the violence of trauma's impact (in its happening) but in the ways in which that happening, that occurrence, was not known or grasped at that time."[4] What I am saying is this: bad governance as a traumatic affliction on the people of Nigeria (might have) shrunk their temporal segments into only a painful present, a traumatic middle that appears ever immobile. The suffering of bad governance does not go away. The violence of bad governance does not only reduce temporality, but its immediacy also shrinks social worlds in ways that shed light on the "lotus-flower world" of most Nigerians.[5] The enormity of pain and agony of torture and trauma often serves to focus victims' minds on the self, the contours of their bodies, cutting off connections to larger social relationships and resulting in the production of atomized individuals and the fragmentation of society.[6]

Governance in Nigeria is not the ordering of resources, human lives, social conditions, and juridical-political rules for human flourishing but the disorganization and dislocation of life within life, that is, the penetration of death into life. Governance is keeping the nation in the zone of indistinction between life and death. It is maintaining Nigeria as a *camp* of living dead, life-in-death.

Governance as Trauma

Nigeria is an ever-present *now* of suffering, an eternal now of perpetual curse. Governance is the site where temporality, the people, and their history come undone. This arises from the trauma that governance has visited upon the people. One of the definitions of traumatic event is that it is a happening that overwhelms the epistemological ballast, or exceeds the conceptual-linguistic determinations, or surpasses the range of human experience such that it cannot be easily grasped or integrated into a person's or group's knowledge system or identity. Either because the event, like the primal ("original") one, occurs frequently or because images and fragments of it keep intruding into the present, the survivors of trauma tend to organize their lives around *this* present period of the pervading intrusions. Trauma alters the time of survivors, or at least their relationships to time. The past stays in the present; the present is a churning of lived and expected traumatic experiences. The past claws the future into the present. The gravitational force of the excessive weight of the traumatic event that lingers into the present bends the future into the present—the future is a reenactment of the invaded, intensified present, a kind of mathematical squaring of the "primal" period. Put differently, the future is only an awakening to an earlier experience. Commenting on Freud's work on trauma on World War I veterans, Shelly Rambo writes that the trauma they experienced "is not located in the past but instead is located in the gap between the occurrence of the traumatic event and a subsequent awakening to it. The suffering does not solely lie in the violence of trauma's impact (in its happening) but in the ways in which that happening, that occurrence, was not known or grasped at that time."[7]

To better grasp governance as a source of traumatic events or as the prime unyielding traumatic event on Nigerians, let us examine two basic types of trauma: historical and structural. The First World War is a historical trauma, a punctual, monumental event or series of past events that overwhelm the psyche, identity, or interpretative schema of the shell-shocked veterans. Structural trauma, according to Dominick LaCapra, "is not an event but the anxiety-producing condition of possibility related to the potential for historical traumatization."[8] We pivot to the special case of Nigeria by adding a third category that combines both historical and structural traumas into a devilish brew, "microtrauma." This trauma is not a result of a single event of magnitude and horror but relentless micro daily events that produce anxiety related to the potential for shattering cessation of existence, quite possibly from sudden devastating illness, increased poverty, terror, vulgarity of power, or death. This is a daily, constant, ongoing exposure to heightened vulnerability that can disable or terminate physical, psychic, or social lives. The vulnerability—contingent, dispersed, and all-pervading—can suddenly become materialized absolute disaster "anytime, anywhere, by any means, and for any reason."[9] When daily living conditions, the encompassing environment of everyday life, is a pressure cooker of arbitrary microaggressions and microattacks, then the citizens are dying by a thousand cuts that never stop bleeding. This trauma is delivered in the fashion of constant drops of water that crack a rock.

The average Nigerian citizen is plunged into all three types of trauma, and these attacks have been going on for about sixty years of the postcolonial state. Under these awful conditions of constantly battling historical, structural, and microtypes of trauma, the subjective perception of the victims of bad governance is bound to change. If we are to borrow Hannah Arendt's word from a very different context, I will describe the "present" in which the Nigerian victims of trauma-giving governance live with these words. Ordinarily, time is a flow of uninterrupted succession, a continuum; but in Nigeria it is broken in the middle, at the point where the traumatized citizens are imprisoned, at the point where their socioeconomic development is in standstill. And this standpoint "is not the present as we usually understand it but rather a gap in time" that constant bad governance, its abolishing of the past and future, keeps in existence.[10] Only because the postcolonial state inserts bad governance into the time of Nigerians and only to the extent that the state stands its ground does time exhaust itself into fatigued time and fatigue of time. The pain of the past is turning and turning in a widening vortex, the present cannot hear the past; things fall apart; the present cannot move and mere anarchy is the center. Now a blues-dimmed, incredible-laced tide is loosed, and everywhere confusion breaks the bone of time and change. Time has lost its forward-propelling motion. This is the traumatizing truth of governance in Nigeria. It is this existential condition in which the past and the future seem to have been erased, in which categories of time are rendered inoperative, that I have named as the "eternal now of perpetual curse."

The eternal now is precisely neither time nor eternity, and it dwells paradoxically within time and timelessness while belonging to neither. Time no longer governs the rhythm of development; it is a pure manifest and acts as an incubus. Time, as having severed the nexus between human activities and transformation of society, becomes only the tormenting pure noise of clocks, chronometers, tower bells, and aches—all sounds of the echo chamber of a gigantic torture apparatus. In this perverse state, the present deepens anomie, ensures futility, and resists redemption. Time itself is an anomic figure. Time is a prime *homo sacer* in Nigeria: it can be killed but never sacrificed to produce justice or socioeconomic transformation.

NATURE OF THE POSTCOLONIAL INCREDIBLE

Unbearable poverty. Excruciating suffering.[11] Unyielding trauma. Postcolonial incredible.[12] Power vulgarity. These are some of the morbid symptoms or effects of governance in Nigeria, the choking string of unutterable treason of the nation's depraved ruling class. In front, Nigerians see only immiseration; in back, they have experienced sixty years of deprivation; on the right, they face unending corruption; on the left, they witness the all-pervasive anomie; and at the center, Nigerians see nothing but a black hole. Governance in Nigeria is a storm blowing out of the people's patrimony, a destructive wild wind that spreads doom and gloom across the regions, piling ruin upon ruin, wreaking havoc on the ethics and morals of society.

Between 1960 and 2019, the nature of governance has drastically changed for the worse. In the mid-1960s, when the five army majors struck in a coup d'etat and overthrew the civilian government of Prime Minister Tafawa Belewa, governance had perhaps three possibilities: it could represent an uncomplicated embodiment of the citizens' hope for their socioeconomic uplift, an uncomplicated embodiment of corruption, or the uncertainty of part good and part corruption. Now we have only two options: sociopathic corruption or the uncertainty of whether corruption is going to treat the citizens with divine or demonic impunity. Chris Abani, in his novel *GraceLand*, captures something about this shift in the nation's morality in a dialogue between the protagonist Elvis Oke and his friend Redemption.[13] In the 1960s, when the characters were younger, the movies had three archetypes: John Wayne, the ur-character for uncomplicated goodness; the Actor, always part villain and part hero; and the Bad Guy, the embodiment of malicious evil. By the early 1980s, things had changed, the movies had changed, mirroring the changes in scale of corruption and anomie in the country. To Elvis, this was all confusing until Redemption explained: "Now dere is only Bad Guy and Actor. No more John Wayne."[14]

This novel portrays the nihilism that has settled on Nigerians as the certainties that constitute the "fence" of the ethical domain of a society are gone. The word "ethics" comes from ethos, which in its etymology means the "fence" that keeps animals within their protective pen or "dwelling," and by extension the "cement" or bonds that hold a society together.[15] Within the limits of the fence, a society seeks harmony, the harmony of ethos, the congruence between the character (way of life) of the individuals, and the community's moral values. The moral institutions of the community work to translate the fence, the domain of moral values, into the bonds of the community, co-belonging. They transform the law (norms, *nomos*) into its spirit, that is, the individual internalization of the expectations and requirements of the law. In *GraceLand*'s Nigeria there is a break in the ethos, a rupture in the specific mode of being together. The pathway between moral principles of a people and their ensuing concrete mode of existence or way of being has been forgotten. Ethics, or the harmony of ethos, today amounts to a dissolution of forms of practices and discourses into corruption. A new "ethics" has emerged insofar as we understand ethics as "the kind of thinking in which an identity is established between an environment, a way of being and a principle of action."[16] In *GraceLand*'s Nigeria—wracked as it is by corruption, nihilism, and anomic repercussions of the civil war—the ethical options presented to the sixteen-year-old Elvis for self-formation and socialization as he enters adulthood are severely limited. His possible ethical turns are a series of specific conjunctions of the Colonel (murderous agent or face of the postcolonial state), the King (a corrupt beggar who aspires to transform the system and avenge what was done to him during the civil war, 1967–70), and Redemption (a man with an unbelievable ability to function, to survive, and to eke out a living from the deadly jaws of corrupt agents of the state). More important, in this novel we see Nigeria as a place in which hopes for and narratives of national economic development have been abandoned, where grotesque and obscene displays of necropower pass for the height of human civilization, and existential nihilism protrudes as the wet blanket spread by what goes for governance over the citizens. Things that happen do not make sense. Ambulances do not carry sick people to hospitals but carry dead people for a fee as part of elaborate funeral processions. In one of the most moving scenes in the novel, Elvis has gone home after being tortured by the state, the Colonel, to discover that his Maroko ghetto in Lagos megacity has been razed by the government; in the process, his father has died. He rakes through the rubble where their house stood with his bare hands to find the body. A soldier discovers what he is doing and stops him, threatening to kill him. "If you annoy me I will kill you and add you to your father." The soldier will only let him take the body for a fee, a bribery. When Elvis responds that he has no money, the soldier replies, "No what? Get out of here." He immediately "descended on Elvis and pounding him repeatedly with his rifle butt. Elvis stumbled away. The tears that wouldn't come for his father streamed freely now as he felt worthless in the face of blind, unreasonable power. He could return later, when it was dark, but he knew the body would be gone."[17] This scene broke my heart. Governance is all about humiliating the people and generating confusion all over the country.

Governance in Nigeria is the "pitiless incubus that feeds on [citizens'] most valuable possession, dreams, which it endlessly defers and derides."[18] The words between the quotation marks were actually used to describe the city of Lagos, the commercial hub of Nigeria. The disposition to see Lagos, or parts therein, as metonyms for the whole country is an old practice of scholars and artistes of Nigeria. Fela Anikulapo-Kuti in his song "Confusion Break Bone" compares the absolute chaos of Ojuelegba, a street in Lagos, to Nigeria.

I sing about one street for Lagos	I sing about a street in Lagos
Dem call am Ojuelegba	They call it Ojuelegba
I think e compare how Nigeria be	I compare it to Nigeria
One crossroad in the center of town	
Chorus: Larudu repeke	
For Ojuelegba	At Ojuelegba
Moto dey come from east	Vehicles approach from east
Motor come from west	From west
Motor come from north	From north
Motor come from south	From south
And policeman no dey for center	And no policeman to direct the traffic
No confusion be that oh-o	The result is utter confusion!
Chorus: Pafuka na quench	It is utter confusion[19]

Governance in Nigeria is like the traffic at Ojuelegba, a permanent state of crisis, anomie that replaces or ruptures normality.[20] Governance is a national terrorism of power, and the exercise of this power is very arbitrary. This arbitrariness defines the present Nigerian postcolonial state. As Achille Mbembe puts it, "What distinguishes our age from the previous ages, the breach over which there is apparently no going back is existence that is contingent, dispersed, but reveals itself in the guise of arbitrariness and the absolute power to give death anytime, anywhere, by any means, and for any reason."[21]

Why do the governed accept such confusion and arbitrariness as governance, exercise of power, and sovereignty? From the perspective on Nigeria given to us by Abani's *GraceLand*, we infer that there are many forces or factors at work that we cannot fully account for in this chapter. We would like to focus on only one of them: the postcolonial incredible. Tejumola Olaniyan describes the reign of the incredible in these words:

> The "incredible" inscribes that which cannot be believed; that which is too improbable, astonishing, and extraordinary to be believed. The incredible is not simply a breach but an outlandish infraction of "normality" and its limits. If "belief," as faith, confidence, trust, and conviction, underwrites the certainty and tangibility of institutions and practices of social exchange, the incredible dissolves all props of stability, normality, and intelligibility (and therefore of authority) and engenders social and symbolic crisis. . . . A presupposed interregnum that increasingly threatens to become the norm, a norm with a rapidly consolidating hierarchy of privileges feeding on and dependent on the crisis for reproduction.[22]

The reign of the incredible is not transitional as Fela might have thought when he resisted it with his full vigor; it is a permanent state in Nigeria. It is the form the unfolding of Nigeria's history has taken at the moment. In this condition of the incredible, governance renders and heightens the vulnerability of citizens. The enormity of pain and agony of the incredible scale of social anomie, not unlike torture and trauma, often serves to focus victims' minds on the self, the survival of their bodies and pursuit of daily bread, desiccating social relations and fragmenting society that lead to the production of atomized individuals.[23] It appears that instead of generating the wherewithal to defeat the incredible, most Nigerian citizens have accepted not to challenge it. Elvis finds it irritating that his friends accept the condition of anomie, or even funny that some even feed from it or contribute to it in their own small ways. He cries, "That is the trouble with this country. Everything is accepted. No dial tones or telephones. No stamps in post offices. No electricity. No water. We just accept."[24] It is easy to see this hapless acceptance of the reign of the incredible by the citizens as a case of passive nihilism, an acceptance of the dissolution of meaning or sense in the way life hangs together in Nigeria. But we should not yield to such an easy conclusion. There is a certain soteriology of ambiguity, a dialectic, a juxtaposition of opposites to it. On the one hand, there is a definite sense of loss of meaning, a sense that the country has lost something meaningful or desirable, something important for human flourishing. On the other, there is a conviction that it is important for some citizens to pursue and create alternative situations that might redeem the nation from the reign of the postcolonial incredible. The tension is between a realization that all might have been lost and that there is still a meaning or credible existence that transcends the chaos and arbitrariness of the postcolonial incredible.

The weight of governance-as-trauma and the postcolonial incredible has a devasting effect on the common life. The disorder has created the informalization of the common life. The common life is so poorly institutionalized that much of it takes place through informal channels of relations, not able to rise above and beyond religious, ethnic, and regional cleavages. It is not public and supracommunal. The common life has not been structurally differentiated from patrimonial, ethnic, clientelistic networks, and other particularistic domains. The common life is informalized to the extent that it thrives by evading the predatory state and its functions, striving to create parallel organizations for dealing with arbitrary violence. It is informalized to the extent that it is an instrumentalization of disorder. The logics, causalities, and rationalities of the informal common life resist the order that founds or sustains the common life—and benefits from disorder. The informal common life is, indeed, not a commons but a kind of national life that operates at the interstices of existing ethnic, religious, social, economic, and political networks. Its informality should not be all too surprising to scholars familiar with state, politics, and society in Africa. As Patrick Chabal and Jean-Pascal Daloz argue in their book *Africa Works*, the state in Africa is also beholden to similar networks and domains. Politics, according to them, is also informalized. The defense and promotion of the common good of the nation—the sine qua non of the common life—are all too often done through personalized and particularistic channels.[25]

An adequate understanding of informalization should be the point of departure for theorizing evangelicalism or crafting a political theology of the common life for Nigerian Christians. This point of departure is unlikely to intersect with most political theologies of the common life.[26] In the regnant political theologies, the dominant understanding of the common life is situated between a highly institutionalized state and mass society, individuals separated from ethnic and infrainstitutional dynamics and whose collective identification as citizens is not contingent. But what happens to the common life when the state is not strongly institutionalized; when citizens' collective identification is contingent, precarious, and uncertain; and when there is no crosscutting notion of common good?

Another implicit assumption of the regnant models of the common life is that it operates on the basis of horizontal links between citizens. Self-defined citizens claiming political equality gather to pursue shared goals; men and women act in concert to create and sustain the power that they need to effect change in public policy. But in African nations or societies where vertical links (connections with ethnic, patrimonial, and similar groups) are relatively more important than horizontal ones, the common life has to be informalized. What is therefore more important to theologize is not the formal political configurations or visible institutions of the common life but the subterranean roots of entanglements engendered by disorder, factional struggles, and uncertainty that are at work. To further elucidate this disorder, let us now turn to the pentecostal incredible, which has developed as a response of a segment of evangelical Christians to the postcolonial incredible and governance-as-trauma.

Evangelicalism as Response to Postcolonial Incredible

There are two types of responses to the postcolonial incredible and traumatic governance that are observable in evangelical Christianity in Nigeria, especially in Pentecostal Christianity. First, the church as / *is* state, a developmental state. Big Pentecostal denominations see themselves as agents of economic development in their local communities, a ministate providing infrastructure and acting as owners of for-profit corporations generating revenues for development projects.[27] Pentecostal pastors who are well connected to the state use the state security apparatus to discipline erring members.

Second, it takes the form of "It does not make sense, but it makes spirit" to explain the unexplainable or affirm what a preexisting community fund of knowledge, justificatory system, and cultural logic will not accept. This form seems like a yielding to the loss of meaningful rationality or intelligibility provoked by the daily assaults from governance-as-trauma. I have called this orientation the "pentecostal hypothesis," a conjecture to explain some surprising or wished-for facts about reality on the part of Pentecostals.[28] The pentecostal hypothesis is the capacity to resist conventional wisdom in social actions. Daily Pentecostals deploy or enact this capacity through the use of the formula "It does not make sense, but it makes spirit" in their decision-making processes. The epistemological here is not about the *that* of knowing but the *how* (the performative dimension) of knowing, which is affective, emotive, and embodied practice. The resort to alternate ways of knowing and being should not be interpreted as only a resistance to modernity or a penchant for occult knowledge but as one way of coping with the trauma of governance, which has removed or is constantly displacing, desiccating the coordinates of phenomenological reality.

The formula, "it does not make sense, but it makes spirit" is ambiguous; that is, it is both constructive and destructive in its operation as an epistemological guide to everyday life or adaptation to governance-as-trauma. In my book *Pentecostal Hypothesis*, I focus primarily on its constructive effect on pentecostal spirituality, decision making, and social ethics. In the next section, "The Nature of the Pentecostal Incredible," I will more closely examine its destructive effect on Nigerian Pentecostal Christians' ways of thinking, explaining, and talking about the world, common life, and human flourishing.

If the postcolonial incredible is the reality of the actual everyday existence of Pentecostals, then the pentecostal incredible is the "abstract" spectral logic of Nigerian Pentecostals that determines their interpretation, engagement / confrontation with, and adaptation to the postcolonial incredible. The pentecostal incredible is the mad metaphysical dance of Reason in blessed indifference to common standards of justification and acceptability.[29] Solipsistic Reason enthralled by the superego to enjoy is in a Dionysian revel, having rejected any Master-Signifier to impose some order on its obscene dance. This Reason is limitless, shattering the coordinates of our finite knowledge system with its excess. The pentecostal incredible is Reason that contains the infinite—so, at least, the limitless desire for miracles and the extraordinary lead many Pentecostal Christians to believe. All these pose a threat, not only to human flourishing but also to the polity.

The following discussion will demonstrate that we cannot adequately grasp the common life in a democratic plurality if we ignore the epistemological issues about the disconcerting matter of the pentecostal incredible. The epistemological is political, but it does not get much traction in the scholarship on political theology. We should not dismiss the matter of the pentecostal incredible in Christian political theology with the usual academic sleight of hand that shoos away African issues or particularity as too foreign to Western universalism. It is not enough to say all the forms of violence emanating from governance-as-trauma, postcolonial incredible, and pentecostal incredible are all too peculiar to Africa. Let us not even think that we are once again dealing with the tragic or basket case of the otherized continent. We are not permitted to dismiss the uncomfortable triage of forms of violence as a peculiar pentecostal mess. What if, on the contrary, the gesture of refusal of "respectable" reason, the violent rejection of a Master-Signifier (be it from religion within bounds of reason, orderly religion, or rationalistic theology) is the innermost logic, conviction, or stance of religion (Christianity)? Have Nigerian Pentecostals not exposed the gap between the story Christian theologians tell themselves about their faith and what Christians are doing, on the one hand, and the intimate experiences of those who sincerely hold to the (spectral) logic of Christianity as if their lives depend on it, on the other? The question that stares at us in the West is: How do we fully assume the consequences of the three forms of violence in our Christian political theology?

What we have described as the pentecostal incredible should not be construed as a tension between the good pentecostal life and its bad, excretable sibling. What provokes the crisis of the pentecostal incredible is nothing other than the intensity of pentecostal life. Spiritual learning, an integral part of pentecostal life, allows people to put divine powers, the numinous to use, to connect things without understanding how they fit together. (Hence, they can say it does not make sense, but it makes spirit.) Pentecostals do not always need to know how things, laws, or nature work. They take complexity and unpredictability of the world into their account of the world without taking principles and physical laws as seriously as the rest of the world. Sidestepping the principles and laws in the name of spiritual insight is one way they deal with the complexity and unpredictability of their worlds.

What is happening under the name of the pentecostal incredible might not be a tension between superstitious belief and "good" theology. It is a tension between two aspects of Christian theology. The force of academic theology is confronted with the nature of religion at its purest, the logic of submission to an unseen power, of ruthless intervention of the divine Real, generated by the libidinal investment and the excessive enjoyment of believers.[30] This is where I think Fyodor Dostoevsky got it wrong in *The Brothers Karamazov*: "If God doesn't exist, then everything is permitted."[31] Under the regime of the pentecostal incredible, because God exists everything is permitted, even psychotic-delirious acts: lying down to eat grass like animals in the open fields, beating innocent infants deemed witches or wizards, spouting baleful speeches, male pastors giving women deep kisses in the mouth to transfer anointing to them, male pastors placing their hands over vulvae against the thin layer of dresses to cast out the "spirits of fornication," and pastors anointing their members with minerals (soda: coke, Fanta). The only justification one needs for these unusual actions is the claim that one is acting at the behest of God's will, one directly knows what God wants. This is so "since clearly a direct link to God justifies [their] violation of any 'merely human' constraints and considerations" and reason.[32]

In these lights, the acts of the pentecostally incredible Christian constitute not only a thaumaturgical suspension of the epistemological but also the religious suspension of the ethical. When faith dovetails or dissolves into "just believe or love God and do whatever you perceive God wants or what will bring you prosperity and increased anointing," without reference to any external standards, as the pentecostal incredible indicates, then the political commons is in potential danger. "In the absence of any ethical standards external to your belief in and love for God, the danger is always lurking that you will use your love of God as the legitimization of the most horrible deeds."[33]

Not to put an excellent point on the pentecostal incredible, and to be fair to the Pentecostals twinned in its complex web, we need to bring another thought into our discourse. Is the whole matter concerning the belief system of the pentecostally incredible Christians not a baroque, extravagant critique of Christianity (religion) itself? Is modern Christianity, Christianity in the so-called polished, varnished, and stately uppity circles not sustained by obscene superego supplements? We all know what the Bible and the accumulated wisdom of the Christian faith say about God, supernatural magic, unscientific knowledge, talking donkeys, erotic spirits, and so on. But we have taught ourselves not to take them seriously. We say: "You want to practice Christianity in the twenty-first century? Okay, these are the injunctions and prohibitions on how not to take the Bible and God seriously." The Cinderella-Pentecostals did not get the memo on the unwritten rules, winks, hints, suppressed amusements, the expected habit of indifference; and they take the Bible and its ideological edifice seriously and literally. Precisely, is their habit of ignoring how things actually function in polite circles not a critique of mainstream Christianity? They have not changed the text of the Bible but have only ignored the obscene virtual supplement of the in-group, intervened in the virtual unwritten shadow of Enlightenment Christianity of rationalism and skepticism.[34]

THE NATURE OF PENTECOSTAL INCREDIBLE

What do you do when you confront the common life in the nation as a *now* of perpetual curse? How do you think if you are an African Pentecostal theologian like me contemplating this thought: It seems the Pentecostal brain has fallen under the claptrap of thaumaturges? Miracle workers now control the brain's neural processes of Pentecostals. And you are asking yourself, "Am I a witness to a form of collective possession that will require collective deliverance (exorcism) as the appropriate form of treatment," to parse Cheryl Kirk-Duggan's words?[35] O wretched man that I am! Who will help me make sense of all this?

The ground, the common ground, has collapsed, shifted from ground to *Ungrund*, the groundless ground. The common ground has become "chaosmos," waiting and awaiting for new molding or divergences. The ground that is the common of human intelligence and the shared world of understanding has folded, crumbled, or deformed into a pathless desert. The ground of common knowledge, the world of appearances, has now shifted into the *underground* of knowledge, the "night of the world," primordial underworld of spirits, the self-determining, self-grounding intelligence; displaced into the uncertainty that precedes the will-to-know arousing itself into shared knowledge, to parse Jacob Boehme.

We are witnessing the unraveling of the very structure of shared understanding that makes thought possible. The very foundationless foundation that organizes thought or defines the episteme of a people who live in a particular common has shifted. The psychic abyss that grounds thought, modernist rationality that inheres between reason and desire, thought and unthought, known and unknown, is being eviscerated. For instance, thought and unthought, reason and nonsense, blend into ideas and actions that shatter the coordinates of preexisting knowledges. This shaking is regarded as divine. This happens as the abyss is celebrated as the Spirit, or the womb of the spirit. The knowledge from this womb is an *alienated* knowledge, cut off from common structures of shared understanding, from the ground of knowledge. Hence, the knowledge is more volitional than rational. Alienation is here celebrated as divine, holy, and renewing of the mind. This alienated knowledge desires itself and longs for recognition; regarding itself as the glory of God, it aspires to cover the face of the earth as water covers the sea.

Is the knowledge engendered by the demotic energy of the pentecostal incredible rational or irrational? The pentecostal incredible is the law of "unlawing." It is the unmooring of rationality without the burden of irrationality;[36] it is a capability that can undo authoritative societal principles and regulations by faithful obedience to an authority beyond the strictures, strength, and structures of rationality and irrationality. Here knowledge is neither rational or irrational; it folds and unfolds, swirls and staggers with experiential, subversive possibilities made graspable or legible by the Spirit. In this space of the Spirit, the likelihood of discovery of shared meaning and justificatory warrants with those who do not self-identify as Pentecostals dwindles. This is so because what was formerly an agonistic religious-knowledge posture that recognizes differences and conflicts between church and world becomes an antagonistic stance that absolutizes difference, fiercely rejecting any dialogic practices of an epistemological common life. The *ecstatic reason* of pentecostal incredible has elevated itself to the realm of the infinite, considers itself a manifestation of the divine or an embodiment of divine mystery. It presumably comes down from heaven. In the non-Sartrean world of Nigerian Pentecostalism, hell is not just the other person but the reason that cannot contain the infinite.

What we are witnessing in Nigeria or Africa is a chaotic liquefaction of current existing modernist patterns of knowledge and belief. If in the past the processes of capitalist modernization and the rise of Pentecostalism caused an epistemic crisis and rupture in traditional patterns of episteme (knowledge), today Pentecostalism has opened up a battlefront against the modernist, rationalistic framework for determining human flourishing or comprehending the nature and meaning in religious, economic, and political life. This is a different form of epistemic crisis and rupture. The emerging troubling Pentecostal knowledge system is occupying a territory in African modernity that renders the continental structures of knowledge production, public reasoning, and justificatory warrants vulnerable. This is not a rupture with the past but rupture with the present by impregnating the present with the seeds of disavowed flotsams of knowledge from bygone era. Pentecostalism, through the "work" of the Holy Spirit, opens the present time to and breathes into it the duress of the past. Shared rationality existing across church-world distinction, across Pentecostal and non-Pentecostal cultures, has been roasted in the crucibles of divine activity that only Pentecostals can see, hear, or access.

Epistemology is the act of not just to know but to know in concert with others. So epistemology always coheres or belongs to a group of people. Epistemology is consensual; it is a social practice. The pentecostal incredible appears where epistemology is threatened in ways that signal its disappearance as shared practice within a community, the unraveling of the old consensus that opens space for new a paradigm or consensus. The incredible may transform into a new consensual epistemology through its capacity of "violence" to create a new concert of knowing.

It is also important to mention that the incredible is simultaneously included and excluded from consensual epistemology. Wherever it first emerges, its engagement in "violence" does not exclude it or its advocates from participating in consensual epistemology. Those given to the incredible daily engage with the extant consensual epistemology, working well within its parameters, its legitimized ends and justifications, while simultaneously practicing violence on the consensual system of rationality. This apparent disorder, this chaotic epistemology, signals the oncoming reordering of a group's consensus. With the increasing acceptance of the disorder by rising number of members of the community, it is almost impossible to say where epistemology ends and the incredible begins. The Nigerian Christian community as a whole is at this inflection point.

The evaluation of the truth value of ordinary statements in the country is also at an inflection point. Under the pressure of the incredible, evaluation of human speech undergoes deep changes. A speaker is not adjudged by whether her speech is correct or incorrect but rather by whether it is effective or not. This is at the root of the axiom: it does not make sense, but it makes spirit. When the concern is over sense, the focus on an utterance is on truth and error as determined by scientific, aesthetic, communal criteria. But there is a slight shift with the pivot to the spirit. The Pentecostals are here concerned with the difference between truth and lying (empty) words. Words lie, not because they are in error but because they cannot accomplish what they promise; they are empty of the inner strength and truth to produce what they imply. They are empty because they did not make things happen, or they did not accomplish what they promised.[37] They are empty because words and deeds are disconnected. They are empty because words do not establish the reality they declare.

In the Pentecostal circle, there is supposed to be not much of a difference between these two statements that ordinarily bother other Christ-believers: (a) in the beginning was the Word, and (b) in the beginning was the Deed. In the beginning was the "Deed" because deeds were utterances; you declare a thing, and it is established for you (Job 22:28). " 'Let there be light,' and there was light" (Genesis 1:3). Deeds are themselves words coming alive. So the criterion of speech is not necessarily whether it is true or not. A speaker can make very silly statements, but if there is the belief that his / her foolish statements can be transformed into beneficial deeds, then he / she is hailed as a true man or woman of God. There is another layer to this religious obscurantism. Often the so-called men and women are still taken seriously after their words have repeatedly failed to translate into deeds. Why? It is because of what anthropologist Robin Horton calls "converging causal sequences."[38] Many Pentecostals will not dump a particular man or woman of God as long as they still believe in the overall efficacy of the worldview that underlines and energizes their incredible epistemology.

Is the pentecostal incredible only a matter of epistemology? It is not so much an epistemological failure or crisis as it is an appetitive problem, disordered seeking of emotional energy, disordered desire for the miraculous. It is, indeed, a moral problem, the failure to properly control or regulate desire. It could be regarded as an epistemological crisis or problem of rationality only to the extent that we focus on the distinct ability of human beings to control their desires through the exercise of reason, as Aristotle taught us. But the same Aristotle regards the failure to regulate the appetitive as a moral failure and the ability to control desires as moral, desire-regulating virtue. The pentecostal incredible is a habitual tendency of some Pentecostals to say, act, react, or feel in ways that are inappropriate to *lawing* in order to benefit from the contingency of an expect-a-miracle.

There is also something subversive about the pentecostal incredible. Pentecostals have developed ways of separating biblical stories, words, and practices from their conventional, orthodox, or historic meanings and putting them into quite different uses. They play with and manipulate images in the Bible. In their meetings and gatherings, they appear to publicly confirm the legitimacy of the Bible, and its overwhelming influence on their lives, but they are also carving out avenues of escape from its strict, confining conventions. Under the cover of the Bible, they poach Christianity of meanings, forcefully integrating it into different kinds of imagery (which now highlights that of Christ believers grazing grass, pastors acquiring jets to soar into the sky, heartless pastors capturing spoils from the poor, and hoarding largesse of the devil) and saturating it with terminologies of power, prosperity, and profit. Above all, the pentecostal incredible is an economy of damage. Or more precisely, it founds a site for spiritual enjoyment, space for exaggerated faith, spiritual extravagance at the very moment that it paves a road to the damage of Christianity, a pathway for death of faith, a byway to loss of limits. Many theologians claim it is silliness dressed in the mantle of religion and the loss of sense of proportion garbed in the majesty of Holy Ghost's *kavod* and power.

Indeed, everyday pentecostal theology is a subversive theology within Christian theology—a sort of a bare, naked theology. It is a theology that does not have the protection of rationality but is exposed to the violence of rationality, the heteronomous force of modernist all-encompassing rationality. Its pariah status is such that as a theology it can be "killed" (condemned) by anyone, dismissed, disposed, or ignored by any academy theologian as bunkum, but it can never be critiqued, engaged *as* theology. This theology is carefully considered, tracked, branded, profiled—while being denied the status of a theology, refused the academic status accorded to other theologies. The incredible theology appears not even as a polemical argument of the stately theological academy to assert its difference from it. The incredible is abjected from the universal grammars of theology.

But here I am willing to engage it and bring it into conversation with mainstream theology. In the last thirteen years, I have studied and written theologies in ways that probe its established properties, extending and stretching it from the main roads to the byways. As expected, after my doctoral degree, I wrote standard-issue stuff—still ensconced in mainstream predominant theology (e.g., see my 2008 *God and Money*[39]). Later, I went into everyday theologies and microtheologies, attempting to liberate theology from its stately uppity form (e.g., see my 2018 *The Split God*[40]). In this essay, I may have gone beyond theology to what is neither theological nor untheological. It is nontheological. Nontheological does not negate a predicate but affirms a nonpredicate. Untheological negates or attempts to negate academic theology, whereas predicate is asserted in the case of nontheological, which undermines the distinction between academic and not-academic theology, academic and everyday theology. The theology of the pentecostal incredible opens a new space beyond academic theology and its negation or resistance. Stating that everyday theology is untheological means simply that it is external to academic theology and resists it, while nontheological means something thoroughly different, namely, that it is neither theological nor not-theological "but marked by a terrifying excess which, although negating what we understand" as theology is inherent to being theological.[41]

How do we theorize or theologize this space, this uncanny space, the site of disorder? Political theology is often about order, about God / Christ and common life. Scholarships in political philosophy, political theology, and social sciences, for that matter, are too oriented to order, to how to create order and sustain order. Now there is nothing fatally flawed with this orientation to academic inquiry. My only concern is that it often takes our eyes away from the irruptions and disruptions that are part of every order, from the disorders that sustain orders, and from places and peoples who have only perpetual disorder, ruptures, and fragility to contend with 24 / 7 as their form of common life. How do we make sense of the disorder that is the common life in Africa, and how do we understand it in the light of Pentecostal Christian experiences?

Instead of talking about Christ and the common life, about Christ and order, let us talk about Christ and the *chaosmosic* life. Is Christ only God of the cosmos (common life, organized life), or is he also Lord of the life on the verge of chaos and cosmos? Please note that I am not championing disorder as the locus classicus of political theology but instead to draw our attention to places in the world where theology cannot proceed from the presupposition of preexisting order that needs to be Christically transformed. I only want us to think with those who live in disordered situations, which are the order and command of their precarious lifeworlds. I am not here to celebrate those radical theologians and philosophers who live in ordered, *manicured* societies and dream of exploding their inherited order of being and privileges to initiate something new. I am thinking of radical thoughts, new ways of relating Christ to the common life in societies that are already uprooted and always uprooting—radical in the old sense of life, lifeworld whose roots are upended. I am thinking of infusing Christian political theology with the kind of radical energy that will upend its theorized foundations.

In the next section, I will engage the works of theologian Luke Bretherton to enable us to figure out how to think of Christian political theology in the light of the pentecostal incredible. What kind of principles or perspectives should concern us if we are interested in crafting an *everyday theology of chaosmosic* life? If we think together the everyday sociality of pentecostal practices (which includes the domain of the pentecostal incredible) and the chaos that not only defines (condition) but also seems to sustain many postcolonial societies in which embodied pentecostal praxis is embedded, then we are likely to improve our understanding of the life and growth of Pentecostalism and political theology.

THE PENTECOSTAL INCREDIBLE AS A SOURCE OF RADICAL POLITICAL THEOLOGY

In his new book, *Christ and the Common Life: Political Theology and the Case for Democracy*, Luke Bretherton makes a solid, incisive case for democracy as a critical concept and veritable practice under Christian political theology. He brings together democracy (that affirms plurality, distinct identities, and traditions) and Christian theology under the rubric of what he calls a "common-life framework," which is a methodology, a form of discipline, and a vision for life in Christ.[42] "The common-life framework is distinct from either identity politics or multicultural approaches because recognition and respect are not given simply by dint of having a different culture or identity; recognition is conditional upon contributing to and participating in shared, reciprocal, common work."[43]

Indeed, the core achievement of the book is to contest the received meaning of political theology and successfully launch an expanded, inclusive, accessible—yet rigorous—definition and meaning of Christian political theology. In this way, Bretherton's book generates a more vibrant sense of what political theology is and the good that it can do toward advancing human flourishing. I also read his book as oriented toward order. His book is an attempt to describe, analyze how the order of common life in Europe and America can be sustained or understood in the light of Christian theology.

Besides, Bretherton's book is focused on societies that have rich democratic practices. This is not the case in Nigeria. Thus, as African theologian Elias Kifon Bongmba argues, the issue of recovering or founding of the common political life needs a democratic base as a point of departure.[44] We are going to argue that the recovery or founding of a democratic base might not be enough to deliver the postcolonial African state from the grip of the pernicious triune powers of governance-as-trauma, postcolonial incredible, and the pentecostal incredible. We are running ahead of ourselves. Let us turn to the fundamental question that is supposed to drive the conversation in this section of our chapter.

How does Bretherton's book help us think about Christian political theology in light of the pentecostal incredible? How do we make sense of his book given that we critiqued Christian political theology for the presupposition of preexisting order that needs to be Christically transformed? I want us to use his book to think with and against him, to grope for the kind of new political theology that can take as its point of departure people who live in disordered situations. I want us to follow a trail of his thought as it folds, enfolds, and unfolds implicitly through his book. This is to say, I want us to read Bretherton to isolate the key breakthrough of his thought in this book as it relates to the notion of the pentecostal incredible interlaced with Christ and the common life.

Let me begin by stating that I know that Bretherton wrote his book for communities in North America and Europe. But I want to examine the applicability of its ideas to the Nigerian situation I have described. The great solution that Bretherton's scintillating book suggests for Nigeria amid the triumvirate of governance-as-trauma, the postcolonial incredible, and the pentecostal incredible is the combination of the virtue of tolerance and efficient administration and coordination of interests—all as undergirded by a Christian commitment to democracy.[45] Alas, something does not quite fit. Democracy is not big enough; there just ain't enough material in it, in the Western capital-parliamentary size-five democratic dress to fit the Nigerian body of size twenty.[46] It is emancipatory politics that can only provide ample material to sew a dress that will cover the nakedness of the current extensive necropolitical "democratic" flesh of Nigeria. Alas, Bretherton's book evades discussing emancipation, political struggle, and armed revolutionary struggle to overturn a ruling, oppressive class. Cannot the common life in Christ be engendered by emancipatory violence ("divine violence" as per Walter Benjamin)? The reader may be bristling at this question.[47]

I agree with her that this question is the wrong one to ask, because it is not within the purview of Bretherton's book. At the heart of the book is a conception of politics as a problem of intolerance and quest for human flourishing, not the problem of the absence of the egalitarian logic in the distribution of places and roles, fundamental wrong and capitalist exploitation, and the relevant quest for human flourishing. To think politics in the way Bretherton has done is to engage in "culturalization of political theology": political theology as a theorization of harmonious living into different ways of life. We need a "politicization of political theology," that is, political theology as a theorization of emancipatory politics.[48] What Nigeria needs today is a political theology that is *creatively destructive* and *constructive*. At the dimension of creative destruction, it must accent the politics of emancipation (rupture, radical politics of equalitarianism) as a new foundation for human flourishing. At the dimension of construction, it must show us what kind of radical social ethics can prepare ordinary citizens to disrupt the transfer of fragility from capitalist markets and other devastating social forces to them and make themselves "antifragile."[49]

Christian political theology needs the ethics of antifragility. Antifragility is not the opposite of fragility; it goes beyond resilience or robustness. A fragile system breaks under stress, disorders, or volatility. An antifragile system not only withstands shocks, stress, disorder, uncertainty, and volatility but also benefits from them. The ethics of antifragility is about developing the capability in the citizenry to resist the fragility of socioeconomic life imposed upon citizens, even as they learn to deploy their resistance toward their own human flourishing. The combined weight of governance-as-trauma, postcolonial incredible, and pentecostal incredible has rendered the life and livelihood of ordinary citizens fragile. Nigeria needs a political theology that can demonstrate how ordinary citizens can build an antifragile social ethics capable of resisting these triune powers to promote freedom and human flourishing. The good news is that Nigerian Christians, after years of relentless bombardments by the triumvirate of powers, have fashioned, in pragmatic terms, such a political theology.[50] How else do you think they have been surviving the bombardments?

What we need now are scholars to investigate and adequately articulate it, that is, theologize their (citizens') experiences in coping with and evading the combined working of the three insidious powers. This is a task most suitable for only those who can craft a political theology within the framework of disruptive grace, virtue as an irruptive actualization of human potentialities, and unfinishable commons.[51] Among other things, this will be a theology that thoughtfully considers the possibility of the impossible in the way life hangs together in the commons. Those Christians living in an abyss of governance-as-trauma require an "impossible theology" that can conceptualize a commons that allows human creativity and freedom to manifest, disrupts the hierarchical distribution of places, and makes spaces for persons to resist obstacles to human flourishing creatively. We need to liberate political theology from its excessive concern with order and good citizenry to serve as a liberatory principle for interrogating all extant social organizations in the name of a better future.

All these concerns summon us to meditate on radical political theology. In this case, a theology is radical, in a certain given sense, if it focuses on how politics works in chaosmosic life rather than explaining why or how it does not. Such a radical theology involves research that seeks to uncover how African nations marked by pentecostal incredible and postcolonial incredible work, rather than showing how they differ from the logic and dynamic of so-called well-ordered ("politically developed," "spiritually matured") nations. It means we have to stop thinking that Pentecostals qua Pentecostals have an inherent character flaw that traps them in backward logic and keeps their political spiritualities from aiding Africa's political development. The so-called trap of the *incredibles* are escapable and are not destiny. The task before us now is to show how they can be turned into elements of radical politics.

The Pentecostal Incredible and Existential Anxiety

I want to turn now to insights from Tillichian philosophical theology to deepen our understanding of the postcolonial incredible as we move closer to the kind of radical politics and theology I have in mind. Governance-as-trauma constitutes the structure of reality, the objective condition that Nigerians face daily. For the sake of our analysis, the postcolonial incredible could be considered the rational structure of the mind grasping this reality. It is the attempt of subjects living in a certain reality to actualize themselves by its demands. It is the subjective condition, a response to or acceptance of the objective condition. These two factors (governance-as-trauma and the postcolonial incredible) have created the condition of meaninglessness. The pentecostal incredible is the spiritual-existential distortion of both of them.[52] It is the rise of antirational forces when governance and the other incredible have destroyed the formal structures of reason. It distorts the manifestation of the depth of reason, ontological reason; this is the reason that can properly point us to the determination of the proper ends of the human sociality that is Nigeria. These are ends that should point Nigerians beyond the existing forms of their human sociality, to move their gaze further beyond themselves. Ontological reason is the search for fulfillment, representing an inescapable moral call on Nigerians to deepen and widen their being, to move toward ultimate meaning and significance. Ontological reason is the longing for the source of all meaning, the driving force toward the good itself.[53] The dominance of the pentecostal incredible distorts the manifestation of ontological reason, the rational structure of reason in two ways. It rises and fills the "vacuum" created by the dual forces of traumatic governance and the postcolonial incredible with not just empty sentimentality but emotionalism that is destructive of the structure of reason, the "formal structure of the mind which enables it to grasp and transform reality."[54] It is an attack on formal reason, or whatever it is left of it or reappears from its ruins.

Emotionalism is a reaction against the formalism of reason. The formalism of reason aims only to grasp reality but not shape it and does not express any spiritual life (substance). Hence, it is seen as destructive of spiritual life.[55] Formal reason neither seeks "a truth which is present in spite of the infinity of theoretical possibilities" nor "a good which is present in spite of the infinite risk."[56] Emotionalism is a reaction against formal reason, reason that absolutizes itself. Such a reason is demonic in the Tillichian sense. But the reaction to it in the form of the emotionalism of the pentecostal incredible is similarly demonic. Emotionalism turns into destructive irrationalism when it is without rational structure, when it champions "reason" that sacrifices its formal structure and attendant critical power. As Paul Tillich is wont to put it:

Emotion is powerless without intellectualism . . . if it remains mere emotion. But, although powerless over reason, it can have great power of destruction over the mind, personally and socially. Emotion without rational structure (in the sense, of course, of ontological reason) becomes irrationalism. And irrationalism is destructive in two respects. If it attacks formalized reason, it must have some rational content. This content, however, is not subject to rational criticism and gets its power from the strength of the emotion that carries it. It is still reason, but irrationally promoted reason, and therefore blind and fanatical. It has all the qualities of the demonic, whether it is expressed in religious or secular terms. If, on the other hand, irrationalism empties itself of any content and becomes mere subjective feeling, a vacuum is produced, into which distorted reason can break without a rational check.[57]

The pentecostal incredible is not just faith or emotion but emotion without rational structure, a destructive irrationalism. With its "rational irrationalism" it distorts the manifestation of the depth of reason, the rational structure of reason that expresses itself in the objective-subjection condition. All these conceptualizations do not mean that faith itself does not include nonrational elements, but it is not identical to nonrationalism. In the same vein, faith has a rational character, though it is not identical to rationalism. It transcends both the rational and nonrational elements of believers' being.[58]

What may seem to the casual observer as a display of faith by Pentecostal Christians is not necessarily faith per se. It is a mere traditional attitude to use God to fulfill wishful thinking for one's purposes and to manage (caulk) the wounds of existence. The faith that is born or engendered by the pentecostal incredible is not a movement toward something of ultimate concern, ultimate meaning and significance. The faith acts, which are directed toward success, do not express a longing, dynamic reunion with God; they are only giving ultimacy to preliminary concerns. Paul Tillich might say that this is a faith that has not "conquered its demonic-idolatrous possibilities"[59] He goes on to add that an "idolatrous faith is by necessity fanatical. It must repress the doubts which characterize the elevation of something preliminary to ultimacy."[60]

We cannot adequately understand the link between the pentecostal incredible and faith if we do not grasp how the distorted faith is, at some level, a reaction to existential crisis, precisely anxiety. The pentecostal incredible is some intriguing combination of faith (not-faith) and existential anxiety. At one level, some might interpret the incidence of the pentecostal incredible as a careful attempt of religion to provide a meaning framework for its adherents amid the blows of the bad governance and postcolonial incredible. It is, instead, a display of the anxiety of meaninglessness, a lashing out, and floundering in the sea of postcolonial disorder. The Nigerian postcolony (in its nightmarish mixture of governance-as-trauma and postcolonial incredible) threatens citizens' ontic self-affirmation, relatively in terms of vulnerability to disaster, the sheer contingency of catastrophe, the irrationality, the impenetrable darkness of arbitrariness of exercise of power, absolutely in terms of death.[61] It threatens citizens' "spiritual self-affirmation, relatively in terms of emptiness, absolutely in terms of meaninglessness."[62] It threatens citizens' moral "self-affirmation, relatively in terms of guilt [self-implicature in societal rut], and absolutely in terms of condemnation [disgust at self and awareness of non-acceptance or seemingly insurmountable nausea]."[63] The postcolony is a symbol of nonbeing, threatening individual and social existence of the nation.

The faith that is engendering the pentecostal incredible speaks to "anxiety" in the classical philosophical (existentialism) sense of the word. Anxiety is an existential response to the threat or menace of nonbeing. The forms this anxiety takes in the postcolony are devastating threats of emptiness and meaninglessness, and haunting proximity and heightened vulnerability to sudden death or disability. The threat of nonbeing—particularly contingent, dispersed, all-pervading—can become, at any time, for no apparent reason, and anywhere, materialized absolute disaster. Pentecostals as participants in "being" within the matrix of governance-as-trauma and the postcolonial incredible have distorted faith as a response to the naked terror of nonbeing. For them, faith is not the state of being ultimately concerned with God— Jesus Christ as the ground of being. Faith is not the state of being grasped by the ultimate—"being-itself." Faith is not the state of being grasped by a seriousness that infinitely transcends the self. Nigerian Pentecostals in a state of being grasped by the power of bad governance and the postcolonial incredible seek to affirm themselves by surrendering the "self" to what they believe are sudden irruptions of the powers of being-itself that might be answers to preliminary concerns of life in the postcolony. Faith (as in chasing after miracles and disavowal of reason or "reasonable faith") is a management tool as much as the distracting consumer culture or ever-rising productivity is at other climes, lands, and times.

In the polarity between self and world (world as fabricated or articulated by governance-as-trauma and the postcolonial incredible), Pentecostals have developed an existential response by fixating on self-formation, technologizing or weaponizing faith in a desperate and often futile attempt to take the peculiar anxiety of the Nigerian postcolony into the courage to be. The pentecostal incredible as compulsive self-affirmation, self-indulgence, and fanatical self-surrender is actually an expression of "the noncreative courage to be as oneself."[64]

What kind of noncreative courage is this? It is what I would call thaumaturgical conformism. In particular, how does it deal with the anxieties in the postcolony? For thaumaturgical conformism, the essence of a person is her miracle-existence. A person is what she makes of herself. Moreover, the courage to be oneself is the courage to make of herself what miracle she wants.[65] Pentecostalism is existentialist, a hidden existentialism in plain sight. Without intending to turn over Jean-Paul Sartre in his grave, I can say that in Pentecostalism, "the essence of woman is her existence." In the reign of the pentecostal incredible—under the hammer of despair and anxiety of meaninglessness—Nigerian Pentecostals do not believe that there is an essential nature, a fixed nature of a person, "except in the one point that [she] can make of [herself] what [she] wants."[66] The Pentecostal creates what she is. "The essence of [her] being—the 'should-be,' 'the ought-to-be—is not something which [she] finds; [she] makes it."[67] Nigerian Pentecostals may talk about existence as working out destinies given by God. In reality, this mystical concept of being or existence has no real significance in the way they desperately seek to make themselves and existence into miracles. They work as if nothing is given to them (including the structures of reality) to determine their creativity. To put it differently, they pursue their existence without mystical restriction. They work to make themselves what they want and only read their "essences" from what they make of themselves.

The desperate desire to escape the suffocating, hope-dashing, and death-dealing environment of the postcolony has driven the Pentecostal to consider his life as a mere possibility that he can mold as he wills. He fills it with contents, orientation, and rejections of whatever catches his fancy to reject in the hope of preserving his freedom. These contents have turned out to enslave him and drive him to the loss of the true freedom he aspires. The courage to be oneself, the courage to take existence upon oneself, and make oneself into what one wants has become under the psychologically destructive hammer of the pentecostal incredible fanatic-neurotic reaction against structures of reality and reason. Faith as an existential acceptance of an order, potential site transcending the sordid experiences of the postcolony, has devolved into faith as an "in spite of" structures of rationality and reality. Faith as a desire for safety has become an infinite leap into dogmatic certitude of miracles in which the special meaning of one's life is believed to be embodied or revealed. This faith does not really reveal the special or secret meaning of life. At best, it reveals the state of being grasped by the reality and power of the Nigerian postcolony.[68]

The pentecostal incredible is revelation. It is an exposition of Nigerian social existence as it is. It is an honest identification of a sociality in which the structures of reality and categories of causality have lost their validity.[69] And this is true not only of Nigeria but also of other societies. The pentecostal incredible is a silent energy coiled at the base of every common life, waiting to be awakened in order to threaten social bonds and structures of reality and mind. The common life, the so-called center of intersubjective existence, is inhabited by the incredible, its truly existential double. Common life is the institutionalization of trust at the community's level, sociality. Common life flourishes when the members of the community are grasped and attuned with their "being-with." The grasping and attunement are always penetrated by elements of doubt, awareness of uncertainty, elements of insecurity. When the community is regarded by its members as meaningful and powerfully relevant to their existence, the element of doubt, insecurity, or uncertainty is taken into the common life as an act of courage, the courage to belong. But when there is an anxiety of meaninglessness, when the common life as a union of power (dynamics) and meaning for its members is broken, then the incredible breaks open. The incredible belongs to the dynamics of the common life. Where there is a community, there is the tension between participation and separation. Without the element of separation, without individuals or parts, the community will be a single, simple thing, and there will be no participation by the parts in it. Out of the elements of participation is the common life, and out of the element of separation is the incredible or the paradox of chaos of common life.[70]

From the preceding, it is wrong to think that the emergence of the pentecostal incredible is an phenomenon accidental to Nigeria's common life, something we can chalk up to peculiarities of African existence. We want to argue that one cannot adequately understand the common life of any society if we ignore the crucial link between common life and what we are naming in this chapter as the pentecostal incredible. Nigerian Pentecostalism may embody it but is not limited to it.

A THEOLOGY OF CHAOSMOSIC LIFE

The task of this last section is to develop a radical theology of the chaosmosic life as an additional address to the urgent matter of the pentecostal incredible. First, I hope that such a theology might be able to reunite the form and emotion of reason. This is a problematic issue to theorize or theologize. The problem of the incredible is not a stand-alone one. We cannot simply solve it by "reforming" religion, that is, Pentecostalism. The problematic religion that births the cleavage in emotion is fostered by the peculiar human conditions of the postcolony. Thus, our primary focus should be on transforming the postcolony. Second, I hope to also address the anxiety of meaninglessness through emancipatory politics that seeks to transform the postcolony. Thus, the possibility of transforming religion must be brought together with the possibility (or impossible possibility) of transforming the postcolony.

Alas, proposing solutions to address the pentecostal incredible is wickedly difficult. In order to raise or transform people who take the structures of rationality seriously and have creative responses to existential anxiety, there must be good laws and ethos—societal transformation—in the postcolony. For how else can we form well-formed Pentecostals or Nigerians? The problem is: Where will be the good ethos in the absence of good people, well-formed citizens? This is an enigmatic paradox. How does a religion that has been corrupted by the "incredibles," anarchic waywardness, raise virtuous "remnants" in large numbers to transform its people and their ethos? (Is it only God that can save us? Let us leave this question or response to the paradox to the theologians and here focus on political theoretical solution.)

What are the sources of legitimation of the common life in Christ? Is it only order, the rule of law, reign of reason, on the one hand, or irruptions, popular sovereignty, and dominance of will (enthusiasm), on the other hand, that constitute the common life in Christ, or both? Before we respond to this question, let us note one point: in seeking a solution to the plight of the pentecostal incredible in the church and in society, we must be careful not to conclude that opposing the pentecostal incredible with rationalism is adequate. It is also not enough to oppose the incredible with the common life, ordered life, trust. As already noted, the incredible, strictly speaking, is the immanent otherness of the common life. The incredible exposes the common life to deny and negate it. The trust, rationality of the common life, tries to suture parts and tears in the fabric of the community, but the incredible increases the tears, lacerations, wounds, the ruptures in and of social existence. The incredible is the spasm, surplus of excitement and violence of trust, exposing it for its inherent otherness.

The point of contact between the incredible (a form of nihilism) and the common life (community) is Promise. Fear (of insecurity, uncertainty) with its power of nothing is the premise of nihilism. But fear, as Thomas Hobbes informs us, drives toward hope, the state of the community, peaceful coexistence. Community is a response and safeguarding of promise, that is, the human desire and activities providing, as Arendt teaches us, an island of certainty amid uncertainty and unpredictability. Promise is the concept or vision of "sharing with," a gift to be made, always a lack, not a possession or expropriation. It always consists of the other—what is to come—and is inhabited by the absence of a realization, substance, a presence. It intimates a mode of being. It is a relation that draws the individuals of a community from the abyss of incalculability, insecurity, and unpredictability with a line "which traversing them, alters them: it is the 'with,' the 'between,' and the threshold where they meet in a point of contact that brings them into relation with others."[71] In a sense, promise is the "no-thing" of the jug, the void, the emptiness that holds the contents we pour into the vessel. Just as the void does the holding for the vessel, as Martin Heidegger teaches us, promise does the community's holding. The void is the "essence" of the jug. The void is the nonthing of the thing as vessel. The nothing, nonpresence of the promise is the "essence" of the community as the void is to the holding vessel, the void of our "sharing with," "being-with." Promise constitutes not only the point of resistance against the destructive force of the incredible ("the nonthing," the power of nothing), the vortex of nullity, but also the reserve of meaningful existence ("the thing," the being-with of common life).[72] Promise, theorized in this way, is a likely solution to the disasters of faith (lack of trust, confidence). We stated earlier that the average Nigerian is encumbered and bombarded by three disasters. There is the disaster of faith in nationhood (that is the name for governance-as-trauma), the disaster of faith in normality (also known as the postcolonial incredible), and the disaster of faith in God (what we have named as the pentecostal incredible).

Our task now is to bring together the incredible and the common life in a unitary thought, seeing in the dynamics of the pentecostal incredible not an insurmountable obstacle to the common life in Christ "but instead the occasion for a new way of thinking" about the common life in Christ.[73] This is to say we will attempt to think of promise as constitutive of both, the incredible and the common life. Promise is what the two have in common. Promise is their premise and protention. Christ is the premise and protention of the common life. Christ *is* promise. Christ is the grand promise. Christ is the void of the communal vessel that holds its being-with, sharing-with but also the content that we pour or that flows into the void; and he is the jug itself. It is in this multiplicity and complexity of Christic functioning that we have the jug, the gathering together, called Christ and the common life. Alternatively, it is where we can find a new bearing to theorize Christ and the common life as a radical theology.[74]

Christ, his promises, are yea and amen. If we took Friedrich Nietzsche's point that only free persons can promise, then Christ is the freest person. If the essence of personhood is promise, as Nietzsche implies, it means we cannot fully understand who Christ is if we consider him apart from his ability to keep his promises, to provide an island amid ambiguities and uncertainties, and to remain faithful to himself as the ultimate promise keeper. Through keeping his promises, Jesus identifies himself as the one who is, who was, and who is to come. Jürgen Moltmann is very clear about the place of promise in Christianity. Yahweh is the God of promise, and Christianity (as well the religion of Israel, Judaism) is a religion of promise. The promise is always in contradiction to the present, historical reality. It overflows reality with surfeit of possibilities, and points believers to the not-yet.[75]

One veritable lens to examine the incredibles in Nigeria is through the lens of promise. The ocean of uncertainty that breeds the pentecostal incredible cannot be divorced from decades of broken promises by the state and from the experiences of citizens growing up in communities and institutions where promises are not the islands of certainty amid oceans of unpredictability and uncertainties. Church leaders do not keep promises, the state does not even offer any guarantee in the form of promises, and communities abort promises and even dismantle the premises of promises in their own disarray. Even God, if we are to believe the Pentecostals, does not keep promises with regard to respecting the integrity of the physical laws of the universe, and certainly regards the laws of reason as abyss of uncertainty and unpredictability. Promises do sustain social fabrics—and even religion or faith. But this is one lesson Nigerians (Nigerian leaders) seem to have conveniently forgotten.

Thus, the first step toward tackling the issue of the incredibles is the restoration of promise, a turn to commitment to promises as the premise of political togetherness and politics. More than ever before, Nigerians need a full-blooded commitment to promise keeping as the basic covenant of their being-with and sharing-with with one another. It is here that we must turn to Arendt. In her book *The Human Condition*, she associates keeping promises with political action.[76] Arendt holds that the normal ordinary practice of promising, keeping promises, becomes an extraordinary act in times of transitions or exceptional circumstance.[77] The reign of the incredibles with its deep alienation from scientific reason certainly qualifies as a context of exception. The simple act of making and keeping promises conveys social existence as not mercurial or ruptural but as governed by norms and rationality. In its simplicity, keeping promises appears as rebuttal to the notion of ruptural, mercurial willful God who is deemed the agent that anchors the pentecostal incredible, the fabulous deeds of faith. It is also a rebuttal to the *everything-scatter-scatter* logics of the postcolonial incredible.

The pentecostal incredible as a response to the postcolonial incredible is complicit in the generation and sustenance of a world of lawlessness where simple promises that sustain political togetherness are not kept. Promise as a political tool suspends the "logics of rule-exception" in which both the postcolonial incredible and the pentecostal incredible are stuck.[78] This is not the whole story. In their logics of exception, in their inclination to the perpetual suspension of reason or ordinary lawfulness of daily existence, Pentecostals and indeed Nigerians are seeking the promises that can heal their wounds of existence. They are seeking actors, institutions, and governments that can keep promises that relate to mere life and promises that attend to more life. Though Nigerians are grasping for both types of promises with passionate intensity in the "widening gyres" of postcoloniality that have unleased anarchy upon their world, they are indeed seeking the second coming of Promise. Things fell apart long ago in the "blood-dimmed tide" of governance-as-trauma and when the ceremony of innocent promises that marked the birth of an independent nation on October 1, 1960, drowned in chaos soon after. Inevitably, a second hope is at hand.[79] They are thirsting for the promise of life and life more abundantly. The real revelatory power of the incredibles is the laying bare of the Nigerians' orientation to promise amid the widening gyre of the madness of postcoloniality. Where do we begin to discern the magic of the second coming of Promise?

The magic of the incredibles does not lie in the grasping of their time in widening gyres but in their potentialities. Their magic is not in the despotic grip on the necks of their subjugated subjects experiencing them as mysterium tremendum of irrationality but in their *mysterium fascinans* of promise. The magic of the incredibles does not cohere in their disruption of reason but in their ability to make the unmasking of the extraordinary rottenness of Nigeria's constituting structures and abiding ethos as ordinary occurrences.

It is in these recognitions that we should venture to discern the emergence of the *Incredible Man/Woman* from the fashioning of the incredibles. In the very thesis of the dialectics of incredibles there is an antithesis, which might "create" the Incredible Man/Woman as a synthesis. In the fashioning of the incredibles there is the (unintended) crafting of a subjectivity that refuses to harmonize the plurality and multiplicity of epistemologies so as to appear enlightened; there is a disciplining that resists the urge to close off alternate ways of being by identifying with hegemonic ideas but accepts self-ill-fittedness in the regnant practices of modernity. The incredibles, as we have earlier described them, are not reducible to the abnormal or the strange "but instead are the excess, the ill-fitted, the remainder, that which escapes and resists the standard frame of" modernism's ways of knowing.[80] A person who has imbibed the subjectivity forged by the incredibles is potentially a subject with dissonant impulses. This is a person who is sensitive to excess, inconsistencies, and remainders of any structures of existence and is willing to expose the rifts and fissures of ordinary life for the sake of an agonistic common life. He or she is a kind of ideal man (woman) but unlike those citizens of *perfect virtue* who want to stabilize social systems. He or she is the subject (looking to *virtùi* and not to virtue) who wants to disrupt the systems, to overcome old relations and create new realities.[81] What can this possibly mean for politics? What does it mean for a person fashioned in an atmosphere of the incredibles to want to initiate something new in his or her society? What does it mean to consider the "antiethical" world of the incredibles as transformable into sites of revolutionary (subversive) power? Such a person has to locate politics at sites that aspire to generate alternative practices and has to be inclined to treat the agnostic ill-fittedness of Pentecostal subjectivity as resistance to identifying "politics with administration and treat juridical settlement as the task of politics. . . . [But rather] see politics as a disruptive practice that resists the consolidations and closures of administrative and juridical settlement for the sake of the perpetuity of political contest."[82] Does this mean that all structures must be constantly contested and perpetually repoliticized? Political theorist Bonnie Honig clarifies this point for us: "To affirm the perpetuity of contest is not to celebrate a world without points of stabilization [or for that matter irrationality]; it is to affirm the reality of contest, even within ordered setting, and to identify the affirmative dimensions of contestation. It is to see that the always imperfect closure of political space tends to engender remainders and that, if those remainders are not engaged, they may return to haunt and destabilize the very closures that deny their existence."[83] Will the Incredible Man or Woman ever emerge? I cannot believe it, but I must believe it. It is crucial at this juncture of our discussion to remind ourselves of Arendt's insight that human beings always have the capacity to act, to start something new, even in the unlikeliest of circumstances. Arendt writes:

> The life span of man running toward death would inevitably carry everything human to ruin and destruction if it were not for the faculty of interrupting it and beginning something new, a faculty which is inherent in action like an ever-present reminder that men, though they must die, are not born in order to die but in order to begin. . . . The miracle that saves the world, the realm of human affairs, from its normal, "natural" ruin is ultimately the fact of natality, in which the faculty of action is ontologically rooted. It is, in other words, the birth of new men and the new beginning, the action they are capable of by virtue of being born.[84]

This is the promise of human social existence, the potentiality of a people breaking out of the chain of events that has ensnared them. The promise of the Nigerian situation and its *plural* Pentecostals, each of whom can initiate something new, acquire new perspectives, should not be ignored. The emergence of men and women, acting in concert, who are capable of new actions will not fit a predictable model if we believe as Arendt that the supreme capacity of human beings as a plurality of distinct, unique individuals is to begin. There is hope in any polity, according to her, because new people are continually added to the plurality and are capable of new beginnings. The new people coming into the world are capable of interrupting the ongoing social processes, initiating the miracle of beginnings in the apparently inexorable chain of events set in motion by the incredibles. Promise—yea, mutual promise—is not only an embodiment of human natality and the miracle of new beginnings but also a reminder of them in the haphazard contingency of the Nigerian postcolony. The incredibles are not the last words; promise is.

NOTES

1. Tejumola Olaniyan, *Arrest the Music!: Fela and His Rebel Art and Politics* (Bloomington: Indiana University Press, 2004), 2.
2. This section is a slightly revised version of portions of chap. 4 of Nimi Wariboko, *Ethics and Society in Nigeria: Identity, History, and Political Theory* (Rochester, NY: University of Rochester Press, 2019), 73–97.
3. Shelly Rambo, *Spirit and Trauma: A Theology of Remaining* (Louisville, KY: Westminster John Knox Press, 2010).
4. Rambo, *Spirit and Trauma*, 20.
5. Wariboko, *Ethics and Society in Nigeria*, 19–34.
6. William T. Cavanaugh, *Torture and Eucharist* (Malden, MA: Blackwell, 1998).
7. Rambo, *Spirit and Trauma*, 20.
8. Dominick LaCapra, *Writing History, Writing Trauma* (Baltimore: Johns Hopkins University Press, 2001), 82.
9. Achille Mbembe, *On the Postcolony* (Berkeley: University of California Press, 2001), 13.
10. Hannah Arendt, *Between Past and Future: Eight Exercises in Political Thought* (New York: Penguin Books, 1968), 11.
11. This section is a slightly revised version of portions of chapter 4 of Wariboko, *Ethics and Society in Nigeria*, 73–97.
12. Olaniyan, *Arrest the Music!*, 90.
13. This way of linking the dialogue to the moral situation of Nigeria was inspired by Hugh Hodges, "No, This Is Not Redemption: The Biafra War Legacy in Chris Abani's *GraceLand*," in *Writing the Nigeria-Biafra War*, ed. Toyin Falola and Ogechukwu Ezekwem (New York: James Currey, 2016), 380–99.
14. Chris Abani, *GraceLand* (New York: Farrar, Straus and Giroux, 2004), 147, 190.
15. Paul L. Lehman, *Ethics in a Christian Context* (Eugene, OR: Wipf and Stock, 1998), 24–25.
16. Jacques Rancière, *Dissensus: On Politics and Aesthetics*, ed. and trans. Steven Corcoran (London: Continuum, 2010), 184.
17. Abani, *GraceLand*, 306.
18. Olaniyan, *Arrest the Music!*, 90.
19. Olaniyan, *Arrest the Music!*, 96.
20. Olaniyan, *Arrest the Music!*, 96.
21. Mbembe, *On the Postcolony*, 13.
22. Olaniyan, *Arrest the Music!*, 2.
23. Cavanaugh, *Torture and Eucharist*.
24. Abani, *GraceLand*, 58.
25. The concept and discussion that follow were inspired by Patrick Chabal and Jean-Pascal Daloz, *Africa Works: Disorder as Political Instrument* (Oxford: James Currey, 1999).

26. See Luke Bretherton, *Christ and the Common Life: Political Theology and the Case for Democracy* (Grand Rapids, MI: Eerdmans Publishing, 2019).
27. Nimi Wariboko, "Pentecostal Paradigms of National Economic Prosperity in Africa," in *Pentecostalism and Prosperity: The Socio-economics of the Global Charismatic Movement*, Christianities of the World 1, ed. Amos Yong and Katy Attanasi (New York: Palgrave Macmillan, 2012), 35–59.
28. See Nimi Wariboko, *The Pentecostal Hypothesis: Christ Talks, They Decide* (Eugene, Or: Cascade Books, 2020).
29. Slavoj, Žižek, *Violence: Six Sideways Reflections* (New York: Picador, 2008), 12–13.
30. Žižek, *Violence*, 96, inspired this way of expressing my ideas.
31. Fyodor Dostoyevsky, *The Brothers Karamazov*, trans. Constance Garnett (New York: Lowell Press), https://www.gutenberg.org/cache/epub/28054/pg28054-images.html.
32. Žižek, *Violence*, 136.
33. Žižek, *Violence*, 137.
34. Žižek, *Violence*, 170–71 inspired this paragraph, and I have borrowed his phrasing to express my ideas here in ways that he might not agree with.
35. Cheryl Kirk-Duggan, *Exorcizing Evil: A Womanist Perspective on the Spirituals* (Maryknoll, NY: 1997), 132.
36. We will come back to this claim and reassess it. We will do so in the subsection where I discuss Paul Tillich's theorization of reason and emotionalism in Christian faith.
37. Richard K. Fenn, *Liturgies and Trials: The Secularization of Religious Language* (Oxford: Basil Blackwell, 1982), 71–78.
38. Robin Horton, *Patterns of Thought in Africa and the West: Essays on Magic, Religion and Science* (Cambridge: Cambridge University Press, 1993), 239.
39. Nimi Wariboko, *God and Money: A Theology of Money in a Globalizing World* (Lanham, MD: Lexington Books, 2008).
40. Nimi Wariboko, *The Split God: Pentecostalism and Critical Theory* (Albany: SUNY University Press, 2018).
41. Slavoj Žižek, *Less Than Nothing: Hegel and Shadow of Dialectical Materialism* (London: Verso, 2012), 166.
42. Luke Bretherton, *Christ and the Common Life: Political Theology and the Case for Democracy* (Grand Rapids, MI: William B. Eerdmans Publishing Company, 2022), 54.
43. Bretherton, *Christ and the Common Life*, 455.
44. Elias K. Bongmba, "What Has Kinshasa to Do with Athen? Methodological Perspective on Theology and Social Sciences in Search for a Political Theology" in *Faith in African Lived Christianity*, ed. Karen Lauterbach and Mika Vähäkangas (Leiden, Netherlands, Brill, 2019), 195–223, quotation from 213.
45. For an excellent critique of the kind of Bretherton's approach to political theory that emphasizes administration and coordination of interests rather than the irruptions and disruptions of politics, see Bonnie Honig, *Political Theory and the Displacement of Politics* (Ithaca, NY: Cornell University Press, 1993).
46. Here I am alluding to Delores S. Williams, "The Color of Feminism or Speaking the Black Woman Tongue," In *Feminist Theological Ethics: A Reader*, ed. Lois K. Daly (Louisville, KY: Westminster John Knox Press, 1994), 42–58.
47. Bretherton has responded to some of these issues in response to my essay for a symposium on his book published by Syndicate, an online academic discussion forum: https://syndicate.network/symposia/theology/christ-and-the-common-life/.

48. Slavoj Žižek, *Violence*, 140. See also Honig, *Political Theory*.

49. See Nimi Wariboko, *Economics in Spirit and Truth: A Moral Philosophy of Finance* (New York: Palgrave Macmillan, 2014) for detailed explanation of this ethics.

50. This is not to say that the version they have worked out is exactly benefiting them; nonetheless it is a starting point for academic study.

51. Nimi Wariboko, *The Pentecostal Principle: Ethical Methodology in New Spirit* (Grand Rapids, MI: Eerdmans, 2012), 3–4, 25–26, 151–54; and Wariboko, *Economics in Spirit and Truth*, xvi, 166.

52. Existential distortion is a distortion that penetrates into and impacts the very existence of human beings or nations. See Paul Tillich, *Dynamics of Faith* (New York: Perennial Classic, 2001), 13.

53. Paul Tillich, *Systematic Theology*, vol. 1: *Reason and Revelation, Being, and God* (Chicago: University of Chicago Press, 1951), 72–77.

54. Tillich, *Systematic Theology*, 1: 72.

55. Tillich, *Systematic Theology*, 1: 90–92.

56. Tillich, *Systematic Theology*, 1: 93.

57. Tillich, *Systematic Theology*, 1: 93.

58. Tillich, *Dynamics of Faith*, 7.

59. Tillich, *Dynamics of Faith*, 133.

60. Tillich, *Dynamics of Faith*, 133.

61. Paul Tillich, *The Courage to Be* (New Haven, CT: Yale University Press, 2014), 39.

62. Tillich, *The Courage to Be*, 39.

63. Tillich, *The Courage to Be*, 39.

64. Tillich, *The Courage to Be*, 139.

65. Tillich, *Courage to Be*, 138.

66. Tillich, *Courage to Be*, 138.

67. Tillich, *Courage to Be*, 138.

68. This paragraph was inspired by Tillich, *Courage to Be*, 141.

69. Tillich, *Courage to Be*, 136.

70. This paragraph is indebted to Tillich, *Dynamics of Faith*, 21–24.

71. Roberto Esposito, *Communitas: The Origin and Destiny of Community* (Stanford, CA: Stanford University Press, 2010), 139. I have with infinite liberty transposed Esposito's word about community to serve my purpose about promise.

72. Esposito, *Communitas*, 136–39, inspired this paragraph, both the ideas and their phrasing.

73. Esposito, *Communitas*, 137.

74. I have manipulated Esposito's ideas about community to make my point here. See Esposito, *Communitas*, 136–39.

75. Jürgen Moltmann, *Theology of Hope* (Minneapolis: Fortress Press, 1993), 94–143.

76. Hannah Arendt, *The Human Condition*, 2nd ed. (Chicago: University of Chicago Press, 1998).

77. Bonnie Honig, *Emergency Politics: Paradox, Law and Democracy* (Princeton, NJ: Princeton University Press, 2009), 83–103.

78. Honig, *Emergency Politics*, 94.

79. Please pardon my excessive allusions to William Butler Yeat's poem "The Second Coming."

80. Bonnie Honig, *Political Theory and the Displacement of Politics* (Ithaca, NY: Cornell University Press, 1993), 194.

81. For the difference between virtue and *virtùi*, see Honig, *Political Theory*, 1–17.

82. Honig, *Political Theory*, 2.

83. Honig, *Political Theory*, 15.

84. Arendt, *Human Condition*, 246–47.

Evangelical Christianity and Politics in Africa

A New Map for an Old Terrain

Esther E. Acolatse

It is arguable that politics and the spread of the Gospel went hand in glove with the colonization of Africa as well as in its return to Christianity,[1] especially with the nineteenth- and early twentieth-century-missionary movement from Europe and the Americas. Both in colonial and postcolonial times, Christianity has been a visible part of African sociopolitical existence. It has, however, taken on a more prominent role through its Evangelical strand of the faith, which is fast becoming the official face of the Christian Church in Africa today. This continent-wide phenomenon deserves attention because of what that space now portends not only for the church worldwide but what implications it holds for shaping political will and thus economic and social reality globally. In this chapter, I trace the history of Evangelical Christianity through what I note as its three main phases, with special attention to the third phase (which includes Neo-Pentecostals / Independent Charismatic Churches). I probe Evangelical Christianity's strong ties to American Evangelicalism with what I see as its bibliolatry and tendency to be unnuanced in its hermeneutics, which it deems biblical purity, and address its limits in providing a public theology capable of contributing to the creation of a civil society in Africa. Ultimately, I argue that Evangelical Christianity in its current form enjoys the goodwill of the people because its biblical hermeneutics and practice tap into the psychospiritual sensibilities of African peoples as it draws heavily on their religiocultural tropes, and thus has come to stay. Nevertheless, even now, it is proving ineffectual in the public space for making the moral change that will create the kind of civil society that Africa needs to flourish because it ignores what I see as an essential part of African culture—its broad and deep linguistic register and pluriform ways of broaching issues (pithy sayings, proverbs, parables, paradoxes, etc.). All culture is carried on language—*langue*—and nowhere more than in African philosopholinguistic expression is this observed. If current Independent Evangelical Charismatic Christianity will draw not just on the psychospiritual wellspring but also the philosopholinguistic underpinnings of African sociocultural existence,[2] it will be able to provide a more nuanced approach to apprehension of Scriptures that are more germane to African culture, and add needed depth to deliberations that can be carried out in African linguistic vein, thus making Evangelical Christianity a better contender in the public arena.

EVANGELICAL CHRISTIANITY IN AFRICA: RETROSPECT AND ASSESSMENT OF A BURGEONING LIVED RELIGION

Evangelical Christianity, especially its ultra-Right and uber-conservative branch with its deep political agenda, is under scrutiny in America from within its own ranks as well as from others antithetical to its ways of expressing Christianity. Its theological claim to rightly interpreting the Bible, which is seen as the rulebook not only for Christians but for the whole earth, its insistence that morality be checked at its bar of interpretation, and its fight to affect everything from geopolitics to the most mundane issues of life at the individual and corporate levels are in question. The overt and covert control of the political life by Evangelical leaders in America, which they ascribe to the will of God based in their interpretation of Scriptures, as well as the biblicism and sometimes bibliolatry with which they camouflage what is clearly their need to rule the nation from the pulpit as well as the corridors of power,[3] have found their way into the nation-states of Africa. Much of this influence comes through the Evangelical / Charismatic and Pentecostal churches,[4] many of whom borrow from the hermeneutical method and liturgical book of American Evangelicalism. Ironically, the leaders of many of these African Churches are now founders of megachurches in Europe and the Americas, and thus African Evangelical faith is on the move to subtly shape political power in the West.[5]

There is no doubt that religious revival in all forms is on the rise in Africa and that attention needs to be paid to what it portends for global social reality, especially in our day of mass migrations of people across the globe. It is a reality, for all paying attention, that Evangelicalism is becoming the new global unifying force of many peoples, with Africa as its epicenter because of the attested rise of Christianity on the continent.[6] Africa's position deserves attention because of what it now portends not only for the church worldwide but what implications it holds for shaping political will and thus economic and social reality. One has only to turn to the various national and public events to understand the import of this phenomena across the continent. Ministers of state are commonly flagged by clergy at such national events. Many of these clergy are founders of these new Charismatic / Evangelical churches with branches in Europe and America and who, for good or ill—especially with their assumed status as those who also live in foreign lands (lands that continue to be viewed as more developed and hence better)—usually jockey with those in political office for prominence on public platforms. In this regard, rather than emulate the characteristics of the one who calls them to be pastor, to feed sheep, and tend lambs, they join the political elite in forming their own elite groups within the fraternity of clergy. From one prophet to another and from prophecy to prophecy, many declare winners and losers of referendums and ingratiate themselves with the political elite. When that happens, they lose the much-needed prophetic edge to challenge and admonish when the political leaders corrupt the political office and defraud citizens by making government coffers their private funds.[7]

The question that needs addressing: Why has Evangelicalism taken center stage in the political arena in African in unprecedented forms, and why does the entanglement seem to be accommodated and even sought after by political leaders?[8] Why, for instance, would Christians demand that Parliament or other civil spaces be shorn of artifacts they consider demonic or question why Christianity is even at the center of governance in a pluralistic nation? What is the relationship between public spaces and Christians so that there is the need to demand that the space be kept as Christian, with the result that, by various rituals including spiritual warfare, Christians claim a location and even a whole nation for God.[9] The answer lies partly in African traditional ways of governing, which have always included a deep spiritual guiding principle for chieftains and even the military. The chieftaincy and attendant governance, along with military ranks, have always been fortified by the powers of the priesthood, and in this case is not unlike what pertained in biblical accounts, whether they be of Israel or of surrounding nations.[10]

CHRISTIANITY AND POLITICS AND AFRICA IN MISSIONARY AND POSTMISSIONARY TIMES

There is no doubt that politics and the spread of the Gospel moved in step with the colonization of Africa as well as in its return to Christianity, especially with the nineteenth- and early twentieth-century missionary movement from Europe and the Americas. It is arguable that politics cannot be extricated entirely from the Christianity, since the liberative ethos of the Scriptures leads in that direction. The Scriptures are enshrined with political moments, the prime example being Israel's release from bondage and the less overt ones being Jesus's confrontation of the religious and political powers of his day insofar as they curtailed freedom of people. The Kingdom of God includes not just the economics (*oikonomia*) but the politics of God, in which is encapsulated God's love and justice. Instead of a kingdom that allows the fringes of society to be bought to the center, freed, shored up, and empowered for joyful living, we find one of separating the marginalized and so-called weak nations with the very Gospel, in many instances, used in aid of subjugating and denigrating African peoples to serve the exploitative agenda of powerbrokers in Europe. The ways the political dimension strong-armed and distorted the evangelizing missions of the church is evidenced in fallout of the partitioning of Africa, a partitioning that took no notice of existing groups and carved out the continent in ways that forced people of different nations and differing cultures into current nation-states. The numerous civil wars and the ongoing intertribal skirmishes that rear themselves, especially in sub-Saharan Africa, are but moments of the disastrous effect and extent of the political agenda that marched along the propagation of the Gospel.[11] Global Christianity was the result of missionary efforts in that era, an attempt to make Christianity wear European garb everywhere, and in Africa the pushback is the disenchantment with missionary Christianity and the birth of the African Initiated or Instituted Churches, with the current Independent Evangelical Charismatic Churches as a form of protest to Global Christianity. Global Christianity, as Lamin Sanneh notes, is that Christianity embroiled with the political agenda of Euro-America and the extension of Western Christendom, as opposed to World Christianity, where the Gospel is experienced and expressed in multiple and various ways in every part of the world.[12] In this way World Christianity is authentic biblical Christianity, with the changing face of the same Gospel in every locale.[13]

CHRISTIANITY AND POLITICS IN THE POST-INDEPENDENT ERA

Much as we need to move beyond the simplistic missionary as villain and indigenous as victim model that has plagued how the eighteenth-to-twentieth-century missionary movements in Africa have been viewed, the fact remains that Africa lost more than it gained in the forced encounter with the West and that Christianity was partly used to pave the way for conquest and pillaging. Africa also lost in the way that ministers who worked with the missionaries came under suspicion as collaborators with missionaries and colonial powers. Such suspicion no doubt undermined and discredited the mainline churches and their pastors with a double-pronged effect. In the first place it affected the propagation of the Gospel and contributes in a certain measure to the disregard for trained clergy and rise of minimally and untrained pastor / prophets in the church currently. Second, the fallout is demonstrated in the spate of deconversions evidenced in the change of Christian names back to indigenous names witnessed continentwide.[14] Today, whether African nation-states are truly independent and whether we can even speak of post-independence in relation to former European colonizers are open to debate. At the least we can agree on attempts at postcolonizing lived reality, and religion is at the pinnacle of such lived reality. The various attempts at contextualization and enculturation and Africanizing Christianity are indications of postcolonial attempts on the religious front. While some nation-states have to a large extent attempted to transcend their colonial past, many in fits and starts,[15] and yet many more are still controlled financially by former colonizers,[16] we find that the blend of politicoreligious ethos that Euro-American missionary Christianity brought remained in more covert ways. For example, several civil unrests and political destabilizations, and some coup d'états,[17] were purported to be instigated by Euro-American political will, and sometimes even funded by Euro-American powers. In the midst of what is clearly the Western world's complicity in African political affairs, public ceremonies to celebrate establishment of new governments, even military nondemocratic ones, included church services and or religious services and more recently representatives of Traditional Religionists and Islam. There is an at-homeness, so to speak, of the religious and especially Christianity in the political even in post-independent Africa.

EVANGELICALS IN THE POLITICAL AND SOCIAL SPHERE: TWO MOMENTS OF A MOVEMENT

As is now obvious, Evangelical presence in the African sociopolitical sphere has a long history embedded in the geopolitical and religious history of the Euro-American colonization of Africa, a colonizing process that was based in the so-called Doctrine of Discovery,[18] itself a theological treatise about power relations and power distances among and between nations used to justify past colonization and seizures and acquisitions of other peoples' lands. It is plausible that Africa has had what I can term two moments of Evangelical presence in Africa. One moment, with its ecumenical ethos that primarily fostered Scripture-centric Christianity starting with the various parachurch organizations that still dot the continent, grew out of the form of protestant religion that had sprung up in Britain since the 1730s.[19] I speak here of the child evangelism movement,[20] which sought to inculcate faith in the young and operated within the primary schools and church Sunday schools by way of Christian education; the Scripture Union,[21] which was focused mainly in the secondary institutions and inculcated in teenagers the reading and studying of the Bible and weekly fellowships usually under the guidance of a teacher staff in the school; and the Intervarsity Christian Fellowship,[22] Campus Crusade for Christ,[23] and Navigators,[24] each of which operated at the tertiary level of many campuses continentwide.

The distinctive feature about the abovementioned evangelical organizations is their cooperation with the mainline churches in discipling and evangelizing (sometimes reevangelizing)[25] church members rather than in competition with them for membership, which we see more often in the second phase of Evangelicalism in Africa. The emphasis on individual conversion and the conversion narrative that attends their history could be seen as counterintuitive to an African collectivistic and communalistic ethos and even the biblical approach to salvation as that which also and perhaps more so accrues to peoples, families, and clans (cf. the story of Cornelius and his household in Acts 10).

The general mark of this first phase, which it shares with the second moment of Evangelicalism, is the felt kinship among the group signified by calling each other "brother and sister" so that within the African sociocultural milieu there were clearly, in a spiritual sense, insiders and outsiders based on the felt sense of relationship with God through Christ and the new birth. But how that new kinship is navigated differs within and without the ecclesial space, affecting people at the individual levels as well as spilling over into the public political sphere.

During this first phase, there is the understanding at the organic and clearly visceral level of what it means to be the body of Christ, a kind of oneness with Christ into which all who are "born again" are incorporated. It is this understanding that produces the basic fundament of Pentecostal anthropology in which new bodies are produced in the Spirit and thus allows for the kind of "creation of specific kinds of subjects and bodies" as essential "to the making of a body politic."[26] Further, the kind of translocal tributaries formed, with what is in a real sense a body politic, explains the intra- and international political influences attested in Evangelicalism and African politics today.[27] It is a psychospiritual reality that transcends logic and operates in the suprarational realm, what in Pentecostal parlance is described as "making spirit" even if it does not make rational sense. We can partially account for the kind of influence that pastors in the second phase of Evangelical presence wield over members of their congregations continentwide and even in diaspora, which often defies logic, to utilizing this basic Pentecostal belief in the work of the Spirit that transcends normal sense. In Wariboko's observation: "The *circuits of control* between micro and macro are a variety of techniques of interpretation, politics of interpretative license, and power / knowledge networks. . . . The body is political, it is the anchor point of spiritual knowledge and the dense transfer point for relations of power for the defense of and resistance to society."[28] In addition, there is also strong allegiance on the part of members of these churches to their pastors. Pastors in a sense act as co-mediators with Christ and in many instances may be said to usurp the place of Christ in the affection of many. The double identity of pastors in this case and the often-subtle assumption that they may wield more power than Jesus for access to God are common.[29] This notion is not only embedded in the minds of individuals but also seems lodged in the national psyche of most nations touched by the current Pentecostal-Charismatic prophetic movement. From the playground to the political arena, from cradle to grave, consultations and oracles abound. The heightened need to "see" ahead, sometimes with the good intention of living in tune with God, causes even national leaders to consult these prophets and men of God about elections, their personal lives, and especially about their opposition. National sports are predicted to the exact moments of the winning goal.[30] The causes and sources of infertility and death are usually ascribed, through word of knowledge, to family members. It would not be lost on Africans familiar with the pool of proverbs what the referent is here,[31] and at once we observe the psychospiritual and sociocultural forces at work in such predictions and understand why such credibility is easily accorded the predictions. The roots are already in the social imaginary.

The influence of these pastors shifts back and forth from the individual, to the corporate body, into the public political body. The way Neo-Pentecostal Evangelical Christians read their lives spills over into the public arena and so the belief in the Christian as embattled, and the need to be vigilant and to fight "principalities and powers," is transposed unto the nations (often conceived as Christian, sometimes described with theocratic language), which become sites of conflict for territorial spirits.[32] Fundamental to this process is the understanding of the body as the site of the work of the Spirit, and even though sometimes it is unclear what spirit is involved the need to "see" ahead is directed by the word of knowledge from "pastor co-mediators" with Christ, who may also be influenced in multiple ways within and without, through the tributaries of the Evangelical stream (alluded to earlier in the chapter) and often mainly from the American Evangelical fountainhead. The cognitive religious premises that undergird electoral voting decisions follow the same patterns and are often driven by a Western agenda. In fact, we see the influence and effect of globalization during elections in the United States, when African Evangelicals channel American right-wing Evangelical conspiracy theories and propaganda via various social platforms. The candidate in question to be voted into political office must subscribe at least in word, to the conservative Evangelical reading of the Scriptures about homosexuality and sanctity of life in utero. I find that these days African Evangelicals are as vested in the outcome of the elections especially in the United States as much as, if not more than, in their own countries.

AFRICAN INDIGENOUS SYSTEMS AS THE BASIS FOR ITS FLOURISHING EVANGELICALISM

It is arguable that Independent Evangelical Charismatic churches, along with the theology that is birthed and the practices that emanate from the churches, flourish largely due the religiocultural and psychospiritual antecedents of African life. Especially in its worship and governance, which includes its military force, in selecting leaders for the various positions and in how the chosen occupy and function in the positions, there is always the mystical element in the rituals that stamp the approval and support of the gods on the selected leaders. When it comes to governance through traditional chieftaincy, however, authority is conferred by the will of the people, and even in what is assumed to be a patriarchal culture the power of the female through the Queen Mother, as the case may be among some tribes, is formidable. I have argued elsewhere for how the Independent Evangelical Charismatic pastors deploy the African chief / king and subjects' relationship to relate to their congregants. Therefore I contend that, in some cases, condemnations of the pastoral authority they wield over their flock reflect a misunderstanding of these cultural cues.[33] The demonization of African Traditional Religion, especially by Evangelical Christianity, which claims biblical purity and orthodoxy, makes it difficult to see the differentiation in unity between African Traditional Religions and the culture in which they are embedded. Ironically, while conflating the cultural and the religious moments of African Traditional Religion and then seemingly repudiating the traditional religion, Evangelical Christianity at the same time embraces a Christianity that is clothed in western garb, which it then reclothes in a semblance of African religious practices. The result of this modern syncretism, as witnessed in many church gatherings, is an enchanted atmosphere where pastors sometimes utilize what is at best a caricature of African spirituality and its place in the social imaginary. Key is the prophetic element, which is akin to divination. And yet ritual purity that attends divination and the role of the diviner in African Traditional Religion is clearly missing when one hears of the many escapades of these prominent Evangelical pastors, not to mention a criterion of being Evangelical as tied to conduct and character.[34] As Ogbu Kalu says largely of Pentecostalism in Africa, which we can apply to the Evangelical Charismatic stream:

> The movement . . . is a response to the deep-level challenge of the eco-theater, applying the pneumatic resources of biblical theology . . . within African maps of the universe. . . . They have exploited the elasticity in the African worldview, its capacity to make room within its inherited body of traditions for new realities, which though seemingly from outside, come in to fulfill aspirations with the tradition, and then, to offer quite significantly the basis of self-understanding within the tradition.[35]

Yet, it is more than the individual benefits of finding a spiritual home,[36] a place where one's soul language, as it were, is spoken that keeps people—including many across all professions, top government officials, and the uber-rich—populating these churches. Amid the rich lifestyle that accompanies the Prosperity Gospel ethos is the clear social and economic changes the churches offer depressed communities.[37] Many of these churches have development projects that attempt to improve and enrich lives and step into the gap left by government. It is a mixed bag of goods in all ways, and while we may find some aspects of the expression worrisome,[38] and even down-right bizarre bordering on abuse,[39] some not even recognizable as Christian in any form except in minimal aspects of liturgy,[40] this is a form of Christianity that has come to stay and is gaining much ground and many followers. It is already the face of Christianity in Africa and will soon be the identity and character of the Christian faith as we know it. A critical look at the growth of Evangelical Christianity on the continent and the tributaries that it continues to spread in diaspora shows that African Christianity is poised to be at the vanguard of the faith for a long time to come.[41] That being the case (and the numbers point in that direction), and knowing from the church's history that theology is born and directed from the flourishing center of the faith, the church in its catholicity needs to pay attention to the African Church as determinant of her future in doctrine and practice. We need not look far back in history to understand both the importance of Africa for World Christianity and the way she can sway serious theological will as demonstrated by the fracture of the Anglican Communion a few years ago.

If there is any credence accorded the insights I have brought up about the importance of African Christianity not just for the continent but for World Christianity, if the church in Africa is going to be writing the theology for the direction of the Global Church, if its theology, character, and identity are to be forged in African soil, then it will no doubt carry African psychospiritual and sociocultural experience, much the same way as the Bible and the Gospels themselves portray. In each culture the Scriptures and the Gospel have worn the cultural garb of the soil in which they take root. The Messiah of Israel becomes the Lord of Gentile lands. In this case, the language helps to carry the message within the new receiving culture so it makes sense within that culture, allowing the unimpeded expansion of the Gospel. Language is the vehicle of culture and a vehicle of what sets a culture apart from other cultures. My experience on the ground in many of the Evangelical churches is that even when the mother tongue is used, there is a simplistic thinking and utilization of language and in the way texts (that are more at home in Afro-Mediterranean soil) are parsed, interpreted, and practiced that is antithetical to African philosopholinguistic culture.

THE PROMISE OF AFRICAN PHILOSOPHOLINGUISTIC CULTURE FOR EVANGELICALISM

It is an understatement that the fastest-growing Independent Evangelical Charismatic faith in Africa is almost tepid in the public square (in spite of the vibrancy of church services), and I think it is such because it follows the white North American Evangelical agenda in the way it speaks into the political arena. It is in many ways instrumentalizing the faith, an approach that is not only un-African but also neither biblical nor credal. It is often constricted by the way in which interpretation is done inside the thought patterns of a language that is not one's mother tongue, and so the necessary imagery that should be spontaneously evoked to aid meaning is lost. The result is unnuanced thinking about what the Bible says and means, even in the religious, that when transported into the public arena has no teeth.

Yet even in everyday parlance, Africans think and wield words in complex forms, and we observe this more today captured in traditional songs. From cradle songs to battle cries and funeral dirges, we encounter a blend of pithy sayings, proverbs, myths, and legends tightly held together in a paradoxical form. This way of framing thought, to be almost obtusely leaning toward opacity, is an invitation to think deeply, to enter and transcend the speakers' frame of reference (fusing of horizons a la Hans-Georg Gadamer) and to understand (literally stand under), thereby learn—that is, to produce at the least a relatively permanent change in behavior potential. If African Evangelicalism is to make inroads in the moral sphere, it needs to speak in ways that invite people to think in life-shaping ways rather than what currently seems like prepackaged sound bites of another culture quoted in African flavor.[42] African philosopholinguistic registers are all about seeing the tangible and feeling out, intuiting the intangible elements of lived experience. It is to know with one's gut, a bodily way of knowing, what the Ewe-Fon of West Africa name as *se le lame* (hear twice in the body). This level of attunement to one's body requires silence and the quiet space in which to engage. Often music, pentatonic polyrhythmic percussion (with its intended effect on the brain) is the medium for traversing the liminal space between this world and the world of spirits. It is not a noisy filler that seems to inhabit many an ecclesial space currently. What has become noise pollution in many church gatherings and evangelistic crusades prevents people from using their bodily ways of knowing and thus all their senses in worship, even though bodies are moving more than in the past in mainline churches.

TOWARD AN EFFICIENT EVANGELICAL CHRISTIAN IDENTITY AND POLITICAL WILL IN AFRICA

Altogether, what is becoming increasingly clear at least by the preceding analysis is that the face of African Christianity has not transcended its cultural moment and thus light and salt that are capable of bending moral will by political process in Africa because it has not in a deep sense become truly African. In the next few pages, I will attempt to craft what I hope will contribute to the pot of ideas on how African Christianity can be authentically African as well as credal and what it can offer World Christianity, especially since currently the eyes of the faithful globally are on the African Church for its future. Much of what I raise and adduce may have no citation or need one as it comes from familiarity with traditional ways of being and an insider's intuitive awareness and observations that have more credibility, I think, than that accorded participant-observers. A great deal has already been provided in the literature on African Christianity about the psychospiritual and sociocultural antecedents in its rapid growth. Not enough or no real attention has been paid to what I now consider the most pertinent aspect of the African cultural distinctive, namely, its philosopholinguistic traditions. It is to these sources I now turn in order to resource African Evangelical Charismatic-Pentecostal theology and the churches it grows so that its theology experience and expression of the faith may carry a mark of an African identity rather than an imitation of foreign sociolinguistic structures in African garb. I will be drawing largely on the philosopholinguistic traditions of West Africa particularly, the Ewe-Fon and Yoruba, with whom I am familiar and related.

The fact that language matters has already been established. But coupled with the fact that we are dealing with a religion of texts (OT, NT, and some and other literature that mediates the two) means that words matter and how we spin words matters especially in delivering what is claimed as revealed truth. The ineffability of the encounter with the divine in revelation prohibits concrete definite proclamations, which have become the centerpiece of much prophetic preaching and word of knowledge in African Churches today. The examples in the Bible themselves point in the direction of the word of God being spoken in ways that are at once sure yet tentative, multilayered, and even opaque, inviting indwelling to be fully absorbed and thus revealed almost piecemeal. Such is the way (and this is attested of all peoples in sub-Saharan Africa) of mature speech, the combination of pithy sayings, proverbs, and allusions to historical and especially migration history and how that have formed a people. To overhear the elders in council is to be enthralled by the way they wield language as a juggler might throw his instruments. It is a thing of beauty but above all the invitation to think deeply and to crave and to be at peace with the tension of the paradoxical moment. The meaning stretches endlessly and brings forth even more new ideas. Even at play, when drumming and dancing take center stage, one encounters in the call-response pattern of the accompanying singing, lyrics that have multiple levels of meaning for learning and enjoyment. There is no space in African culture that does not lend itself to this form of speech pattern in address. And no more than in the religious space and ritual is it most palpable. In fact, so intent is the culture to eschew the kind of complacency and lazy thinking that can emanate from single-level meaning in speech that there is a god dedicated to disrupting the forced unity of thought that can be entrenched in peoples.

Among the Ewe-Fon and the Yoruba of West Africa is a god who resides at the threshold of homes. Never in or quite out, this god appropriately occupies the liminal space between inside and outside. It always ensures that those who enter and leave pay attention where they step. Myth and folklore have rendered this god called Legba / Elegba,[43] the god of conflict and confusion,[44] because of the god's penchant for disrupting perfectly peaceful and joyful moments by walking through a crowd wearing a cap with a different color on each side. While the crowd is busy arguing which color the cap was, the god saunters away with a smile, its nefarious deed done. I want to claim for that god not so much the role of conflict maker but the role of the one who occupies the much-needed space of drawing people back from simplistic thinking, who invites a look at both sides of an issue and who helps people insist that one viewpoint does not provide absolute knowledge. At the least it makes one pause and proceed cautiously but, most important, give consideration to the other, with the art of aesthetic persuasion, before a matter is settled, if people are to live in true harmony.

And yet the African Church has lost the edge of this vital distinction that could benefit its experience and expression of the Christian faith because it will help it avoid what I observe as the simplistic unnuanced interpretation of Scripture and its theology that produces a tepid faith in spite of the outward fervor. In fact, the external trappings in the form of whipping people up to frenzy in song and sometimes bizarre behavior,[45] the uber-emotionalism— as the Akan Twi phrases it *akɔm kɔ ama ato / aka ntwitwaho*—leads to a loss of the spirit of prophecy, and what remains is the gyration. Empty of substance, one overperforms the effects of the spirit.

PROSPECTS FOR A NEW EVANGELICALISM IN AFRICA: A TENTATIVE PROPOSAL

It cannot be overstated that the future of the church dwells partially in the churches in Africa. Therefore, what happens in the church in Africa ought to concern all the faithful. If the religious sphere affects all aspects of life, then it stands to reason that what happens in this space be regarded as what is vital globally, and we have already alluded to the reach of African Independent Evangelical Charismatic churches. No doubt the African Evangelical churches have something to offer the World Church. But first it must attend to what I see as its current bane. What will rescue Evangelical Christianity in Africa from the trappings that encase the Evangelicalism we now witness in the West, where a part of the Evangelical church that is following scriptural purity and strictures of narrow interpretation enters the political arena with the one- or two-issue arsenal and hopes to bend political will without effecting moral change? I propose a return to the philosopholinguistic fountain of its culture. It is this thick language with its deep structures and multilayered meaning in which Africans are versed that would be so crucial and helpful in the hermeneutical project of expression of the African Christian Theology that might ensure its stability and its major contribution to the future of World Christianity.

My proposal seems idealistic perhaps, and one drawback is the power distance between pastors and parishioners, which is itself a large part of the problem, since it requires that parishioners and lay Christians challenge the sometimes warped and naive interpretations they receive from the pulpit. The kind of misplaced adoration that attends attitude to pastors makes such a move almost sacrosanct. But there is hope in that the Bible as well as African traditional systems offer examples on approaches in such a situation. When a child learns to wash her hands well, she can dine with king, coupled with the fact that proper authority is always conferred by the people. From the Bible, the example of the Berean Christians, whom Paul commends on their noble-mindedness for checking their Scriptures to make sure his teaching was in line with the ancient texts, is a good place to start (Acts 17:10–15).

NOTES

The term "Evangelical" itself is a contested category given its history and its differing expressions in the various lands of its sojourn beginning with its birth in Britain in the eighteenth century. Nevertheless, they are general characteristics that continue to render the term useful in theological and religious discussions. See Fisher, 181–213.

1. No one needs reminding today that Christianity predated the missionary movement of the nineteenth and twentieth centuries in Africa. North Africa and even parts of sub-Saharan Africa had known Christianity and even Judaism in the past. What we see now described as African Christianity rising is what has been appropriately interpreted as an

Afro-Asiatic religion that made its rounds in other parts of the world and is now return-ing home. See Jenkins, *The Next Christendom*.

2. In the African landscape all the categories are troubled, and to use just one descrip-tor does not suffice for accommodating the forms of ecclesiology one witnesses on the ground. For church hierarchy/structure, liturgy, teaching, and practice lack the clear distinction among the strands that make up the current independent charismatic Evan-gelical Churches and parachurch organizations that dot the sub-Saharan landscape. Each new evolution of an existing church indicates that soon this trichotomous descrip-tor might not be able to bear the strain.

3. The Fellowship or the Family is a Christian organization geared toward Christians is the public arena and provides a space for decision makers to share in Christian practices. A recent documentary uncovers the indoctrination as well as the political agenda of its founder and leaders. They are better known, since Eisenhower's time, for the Yearly Prayer Breakfast. See https://thefellowshipfoundation.org/history/ for more informa-tion on their activities and political reach.

4. I use the multiple descriptors because Evangelical in its truer sense does not quite cap-ture the faith as expressed on the continent. The fourfold characteristics of Evangelical faith, what David Bebbington has proposed as "biblicism, crucicentrism, conversion-ism, and activism," seem more germane to many mainline churches on the continent than to those identified as Evangelical. In agreement with Terrence O. Granger and Paul Gifford, who makes this observation, I opt for the rather loose Independent Evangeli-cal/Charismatic, a catchall that nevertheless seems more apt. See their full argument in Granger, 1–6.

5. Here I refer to the ways in which what is preached in the pulpit in these more conserva-tive Evangelical churches shapes the political will of the people in deciding which way to vote in official elections and how that decision impacts who occupies political office and thus influences not just national but global affairs.

6. Jenkins, *The Next Christendom*; Jenkins, *The New Faces of Christianity*.

7. A week does not go by in the media without one African politician or Evangelical pastor rumored to have involvement in one corrupt deal or another on the continent. It is usu-ally more newsworthy when the politician claims to be an Evangelical Christian, garners following and votes, and fails to live up to Christian ethical codes. A case in point is the Zambian president. See Phiri, 401–28.

8. Various predictions during elections across the region, with prophets predicting differ-ent winners and losers, come to mind here. See Ilo; Adefisoye, 25–37.

9. A group of Christian intercessors led by Emeka Nwakpa started spiritual warfare prayers for spatial healing. See Lawson and Nwakpa.

10. The story of Israel's deliverance from Egypt is a key moment in which the powers of the gods of both nations through their priest enable their leaders to show prowess in contesting each other.

11. We are by no means unmindful of the work of missionaries who stood up to heads of civil services and were sometimes penalized by the withholding of funds and support. The story of Jacobus Capitein provides an example. See Kpobi.

12. In Lamin Sanneh's view Western Christendom has a monolithic view of the expression of Christianity. In contrast, World Christianity is spontaneous belief and lived religion that are of and from the periphery. And yet, as Jenkins points out, this distinction is

rather difficult to maintain due to the very nature of globalization in our day. The distinction nevertheless has merit and bears acknowledging.

13. The Jerusalem Church was not the Corinthian Church as witnessed in Acts and the First Epistle to the Corinthians, for example. The confrontation between Peter and Paul at the first Church Council bears witness (Acts 15).

14. For example, many Africans dropped the Anglo baptismal names and took indigenous African names or indigenized their Anglo names. For example, East African writer James Ngugi, famed for *A Grain of Wheat*, becomes Ngũgĩ wa wa Thiong'o.

15. These would be mainly the countries of the former British Empire, for whom independence came relatively earlier and would be more facile; Ghana and Nigeria are prime examples.

16. These would be mainly the Francophone countries and some of those colonized by Belgium, the former with its system of assimilation and the latter with its inhumane practices that have left an indelible mark.

17. A prime example is that of the overthrow of Nkrumah of Ghana because of the assumption that Ghana was shifting from a nonaligned to pro-Soviet stance during the height of the Cold War. Nkrumah's suspicion of CIA involvement in his overthrow was borne out later in a report by CIA intelligence officer John Stockwell. See excerpts from BBC World News.

18. The Doctrine of Discovery was the spiritual, political, and legal justification behind the papal bulls that allowed for the seizures of lands not inhabited by Christians beginning in the fifteenth century.

19. See Bebbington, 31–55.

20. The Child Evangelism Fellowship, founded by Jesse Irvin Overholtzer in 1937, self-describes as a fellowship of born-again Christians who aim at discipling boys and girls for faithful living in the local church. For more information, see https://www.cefonline .com/about/history/, accessed August 6, 2020.

21. The Scripture Union started in the UK and has a history dating to 1867; it aimed at providing Bible training for children through various activities especially through Bible study, for which it provided written devotionals. See https://scriptureunion.org/about -us/, accessed August 6, 2020, for more information on aims and mission.

22. As the name suggests, the Intervarsity Christian Fellowship gathers mainly born-again Christians on campuses worldwide for fellowship and evangelism in many forms. See more information about the organization, history mission, and aims at https:// intervarsity.org/about-us, accessed August 6, 2020.

23. The Campus Crusade, now known as Cru for short, founded by Bill Bright in 1951, seeks to connect people with Christ in tertiary institutions worldwide. See more information about the organization, historical mission, and aims at https://www.cru.org/us /en/about.html, accessed August 6, 2020.

24. The Navigators, founded in 1933 by a young Californian lumberyard worker, Dawson Trotman, aim at forming disciples on a person-to-person basis and through small study fellowships worldwide. See more information about the organization, historical mission, and aims at https://www.navigators.org/about/, accessed August 6, 2020.

25. The various evangelistic crusades, revivals, and especially the famed Jesus Marches and Dawn Broadcasts on and off campus that Christian fellowships hold several times a year, are one such example.

26. Wariboko, 113, citing Stoler, 12.
27. See, for example, Smith, 235–44; Illesanmi; and Olupona.
28. Wariboko, 114. Here he is drawing generally on Foucault and especially Stoler.
29. Vhumani, 1–10.
30. For example, recent FIFA (international governing body of association football) and T.B. Joshua predictions, Ghanaian elections, and pronouncements by the Ghanaian pastor who was predicting deaths of prominent leaders including the chief imam's death.
31. "An insect can only sting if it is already in your cloth" goes one such proverb that is used to explain why witchcraft cannot affect a person unless there are witches in their home or family.
32. Daniel's dream in which he prays and is told by an angel the answer was delayed by the "prince of the air of Persia" is a key verse for such belief and practice (Daniel 10:12).
33. Acolatse, "Pastoral Authority and Responsibility," 15–29.
34. Holiness and ritual purity are aspects of the African Traditional priest as well as distinctive of the identity of the Evangelical. For the latter, see Riche, 247–60.
35. Kalu, 152.
36. Pobee.
37. The crusades that are accompanied by clothing drives, church buildings that double up as a place to hold basic school education, and wells/bore holes to provide potable water and various free health clinics are but a few of the development projects that many of the Evangelical churches take on.
38. See Acolatse, *For Freedom or Bondage?*
39. The media coverage of some South African pastors abusing their congregations provides such examples: https://www.dailymail.co.uk/news/article-2537053/Lawn-Christians-South-African-preacher-makes-congregation-eat-GRASS-closer-God.html; https://www.google.com/search?client=firefox-b-d&sxsrf=ALeKk0274y78-2cyjiYHdZ9AUplaafHb9w:1599517243831&q=pastor+tells+congregation+to+strip&sa=X&ved=2ahUKEwiDqoWJitjrAhUihHIEHU_WDOAQ1QIoAnoECAsQAw&biw=1280&bih=607.
40. I refer here to the more contemporary Christian music genre, often dubbed praise and worship songs, which started in the Evangelical circles in the West popularized by recording companies, such as Intergrity Music, and made their way to African churches.
41. See Illesanmi; and a response by Olupona.
42. The question of whether we are entering a theocracy and whether in a religiously plural culture we should be considering Christianity as a force that should have public role and shape politics is perhaps to be engaged in the public arena.
43. As migrations occur among peoples, the name has changed with each new dialect of the language. Variations include Eshuelegba, Esuelegbara, and in Latin America Elegua.
44. There is a place Lagos Island that embodies this god, who is thought to be called Ojuelegba, and there one finds the meeting of five roads that has no traffic signals and is the center where all migrants from various parts congregate, forcing people to embrace complexities that enrich their lives. See Bibi Bakare-Yusuf and Jeremy Weate, 318–40.
45. These range from pastors beating or stomping on church members as the congregation looks on, to pastors bathing in mud while fully clothed as an indication of being anointed by God.

BIBLIOGRAPHY

Acolatse, Esther. "Pastoral Authority and Responsibility: An African Traditional Leadership Model for Church Governance and Functioning." In *Pastoral Care, Health, Healing, and Wholeness in African Contexts: Methodology, Context, and Issues*, edited by E. Y. Lartey and Tapiwa Mucherera. Vol. 1. Eugene, OR.: Wipf and Stock Publisher, 2017, 15–29.

———. *For Freedom or Bondage? A Critique of African Pastoral Practices*. Grand Rapids, MI: William B. Eerdmans, 2014.

Adefisoye, Taiwo O. "Prophesying or Prophelying: Prophets, Prophetic Punditry in the 2015 General Elections in Nigeria." *International Journal of Case Studies* 6, no. 3 (March 2017): 25–37.

Bakare-Yusuf, Bibi, and Jeremy Weate. "Ojuelegba: the Sacred Profanities of a West African Crossroad." In *Urbanization and African Cultures*, edited by Toyin Falola and Steven J. Salms. Durham, NC: Carolina Academic Press, 2005, 318–40.

BBC World News. "Four More Ways the CIA Has Meddled in Africa." Accessed July 29, 2020. Accessed July 29, 2020. https://www.bbc.com/news/world-africa-36303327.

Bebbington, David. "The Nature of Evangelical Religion." In *Evangelicals: Who they Have Been, Are Now, and Could Be*, edited by Mark Noll et al. Grand Rapids, MI: Wm. B. Eerdmans, 2019, 31–55.

Fisher, Linford. "Evangelicals and Unevangelicals: The Contested History of a Word." In *Evangelicals: Who They Have Been, Are, Now, and Could Be*. Grand Rapids, MI: Wm. B. Eerdmans, 2019, 181–213.

Granger, Terrence O., ed. *Evangelical Christianity and Democracy in Africa*. Oxford: Oxford University Press, Electronic Source, May 2008.

Illesanmi, Simeon. "From the Periphery to the Center: Pentecostalism Is Transforming the Secular State in Africa." *Harvard Divinity Bulletin* 35, no. 4 (Autumn 2007). Accessed July 9, 2024. https://bulletin.hds.harvard.edu/from-periphery-to-center/ and https://bulletin.hds.harvard.edu/on-africa-a-need-for-nuance/.

Ilo, Stan Chu. "Prophetic Predictions and Politics in Africa." https://opinion.premiumtimesng.com/2016/03/01/171450-2/.

Jenkins, Philip. *The Next Christendom: The Coming of Global Christianity*. London: Oxford University Press, 2011.

———. *The New Faces of Christianity: Believing the Bible in the Global South*. Oxford University Press, 2006.

Kalu, Ogbu U. "*Sankofa*: Pentecostalism and African Cultural Heritage." In *Emerging Pentecostal Theologies in Global Contexts*, edited by Veli-Matti Kärkkäinen. Grand Rapids: MI.: Wm. B Eerdmans Publishing, 2009, 135–52.

Kpobi, David Nii Anum. *The Saga of a Slave: Jacobus Capitein of Holland and Elmina*. Accra: Sub-Saharan Publishers, 2002.

Lawson, Beatrice, and Emeka Nwakpa. *Redeeming the Land: Interceding for the Nations*. Accra: Africa Christian Press, 1998.

Olupona, Jacob. "On Africa, a Need for Nuance: Responding to Simeon Ilesanmi." *Harvard Divinity Bulletin* 35, no. 4 (Autumn 2007).

Phiri, Isabel Apawo. "President Frederick J. T. Chiluba of Zambia: The Christian Nation and Democracy." *Journal of Religion in Africa* 33, no. 4 (2003): 401–28. Accessed September 7, 2020. http://www.jstor.org/stable/1581750.

Pobee, John "African Instituted (Independent) Churches." AIC in *Dictionary of the Ecumenical Movement*. Geneva: World Council of Churches and Grand Rapids, MI: Wm. Eerdmans, 2002, 5–12.

Riche, Toni. "Azusa-era Optimism: Bishop J. H. King's Pentecostal Theology of Religions as a Possible Paradigm as a Possible Paradigm for Today," *Journal of Pentecostal Theology* 14, no. 2 (2006): 247–60.

Sanneh, Lamin O. *Translating the Message: The Missionary Impact on Culture*. 2nd, rev. and exp. ed. Maryknoll: Orbis Books, 2009.

Smith, M. P. "Transnational Urbanism Revisited." *Journal of Ethnic and Migration Studies* 31 (2): 235–44.

Stoler, Ann Laura. *Carnal Knowledge and Impartial Power: Race and the Intimate in Colonial Rule*. Berkeley: University of California Press, 2010.

Vhumani, Magezi and Collium Banda. "Competing with Christ? A Critical Christological Analysis of the Reliance on Pentecostal Prophets in Zimbabwe." *In die Skriflig* ISSN (online) 2305–0853, 51, no. 2 (2017): 1–10.

———. *Nigerian Pentecostalism*. Rochester, NY: University of Rochester Press, 2014.

CHAPTER 3

Ethiopian Evangelicals and Politics

Polite Distance or Keen Interest?

Tibebe Eshete

GENERAL BACKGROUND

Ethiopian evangelical churches are among the fastest growing in the world. Ethiopia has the third-largest Christian population in sub-Saharan Africa. As recently as 1980, Protestant evangelicals accounted for less than 5 percent of the population, but today they make up nearly 20 percent (and 30 percent of the country's Christians). Considering demography alone, Ethiopian evangelicals are thus in a position to make an enormous impact on their nation. The evangelical churches in Ethiopia are of relatively recent origins compared to that of the existence of the Ethiopian Orthodox Church (EOC). Though several attempts were made to introduce the Protestant Christian faith in the nineteenth century, the heyday of the missionary enterprise in Ethiopia was during the reign of Emperor Haile Selassie. In 1928 Dr. Thomas Lambie, who was originally from a Reformed background and later became part of the Sudan Interior Mission (SIM), came to Ethiopia to begin mission work in the southern part of the country. The fruits of his work contributed to the rise of the Kale Heywet Church, which has nearly 9 million members. The Lutherans also made significant inroads in the southwestern part of Ethiopia, and their missionary activities eventually led to the emergence of the Ethiopian Evangelical Church Mekane Yesus (EECMY), or Mekane Yesus Church (MYC), which is believed to have a membership of close to 6 million people. Other missionary groups from the United States, Britain, Switzerland, Germany, and Norway also contributed considerably to the extension of the Protestant faith. Most of the missionary activity lay in the south and southwestern parts of Ethiopia, where the presence of the EOC was not strongly felt and in areas where the traditional form of religions and Islam were dominant. According to the Mission Decree of 1944, the missionaries were legally restricted from propagating any other message apart from preaching the Gospel. Of course, they used the establishment of schools and clinics as vehicles for spreading the faith. It is noteworthy that the missionaries who came to Ethiopia did not come mainly from a Reformed background promoting social engagements or what was then known as social gospel. The SIM, for instance, maintained a conservative theology of proclaiming the Gospel and showed modest interest in terms of addressing social and economic concerns publicly. In an interview conducted several years ago, I asked a village chief in southern Ethiopia, which is naturally endowed with resources but inhabited by a poverty-ridden people: "Does not the gospel tackle the issue of poverty?" His automatic and candid response was *yehis alberalenem*, "we had no revelation on this matter." One of my informants shared with me how he apparently struggled with the leadership of a church, one of the largest denominations in Ethiopia, in his attempt to expand the scope the church's services in the area of social and economic justice. He faced vehement resistance from other leaders in seeking to introduce various urban-based ministries, such as small-scale microfinancial institutions targeting the poor, in his capacity as the head of the Department for Holistic Ministry.[1]

The evangelical enterprise received a new lease on life in the 1960s, with the outburst of a national youth revival in the form of Pentecostalism. Ethiopian Pentecostals broke new grounds on multiple levels and brought the Protestant faith to a visible space, unlike the missionaries who were operating among ethnic groups in rural areas.

The current popular appellation of the term *Pente*, referring to all the denominations of various Protestant backgrounds in Ethiopia, is too confusing to be employed in any scholarly work without major qualifications. The designation *Pente* has morphed into a generic label for all non-Orthodox and non-Catholic Christians in Ethiopia, as if they form a monolithic block. Its derogatory origin continued to lend movements associated with the term a negative countercultural image that contained "foreign elements" (i.e., foreign roots) and that, above all, clashed with national loyalties. Consequently, its adherents were depicted in the prevalent public optic as followers of something amounting to a cultic practice.

The term came into popular usage for the first time in the late 1960s in the aftermath of an episode in Debre Zeit.[2] Soon the incident became an issue in the media that referred to the new expression of faith as a *Pente* and an unknown religion (*Yaltaweke Addis Haymanot*).[3] It was the media and other social forums that brought the term into popular parlance. Though the term *Pente* was originally designed to connote a derogatory meaning by way of allusion to the new "religious outsiders," with the growth of the ecclesial bodies falling under this name it has become a convenient umbrella term for all Protestant groups, although the element of stigma has not completely gone.

This is a phenomenon that has unfolded uniquely in Ethiopia and that has no equivalence elsewhere in Africa. Members of the burgeoning new movements introduced concepts such as *dageme ledet* (born again) and *getan mekebel* (trusting / receiving Jesus), which were unfamiliar in the theological terrain of the preexisting form of Christianity. Coupled with their aggressive missionizing energy, known as *memesker*, to draw people to their faith based on convictions and personal grounds, these members aroused suspicion from the public as pioneers of a countercultural religious movement.

Since most of those who launched the movement were young people, mainly from urban areas—and came from the rising elite, colleges, and high schools—they lent a national visibility to a religious phenomenon that was unfolding largely in rural parts of the country. The Christian faith that western Protestant missionaries introduced in the rural regions of Ethiopia was denominationally divided and not identified by a single name. It was during the day of the *Derg* that the name *Pente* started to be used as generic tag to mark various evangelical groups in Ethiopia. It should be noted that the term *Pente* is a shortened reference to the Pentecostal faith experience, the most salient aspect being speaking in tongues as evidence of the "baptism of the Holy Spirit."[4] Consequently, the lumping of all Protestant groups under the same category does not suggest that they share the same doctrinal convictions.

Through their early history Ethiopian Pentecostals maintained a narrow outlook on the Gospel that discouraged public engagements. Their exclusive stress on holiness, piety, and purity was meant to separate (*meleyet*) them from the "world" and barred them from having a sound theology of engagement in the sociopolitical sphere of the country. Engaging the world, it was feared, would lead to a contaminating influence upon their religious lives. In their worldview conversion requires a bridge-burning process (meleyet), by which believers live at a remove from the "unholy world" and demonstrate their identity as transformed beings. Until recently the leaders of Mulu Wongel Church, the first independent Pentecostal church in Ethiopia, were reluctant to be involved in social and economic development programs. They assumed that such engagement would have corrosive effects and lead to unneeded entanglements, hampering the mission of spreading the Gospel.

The church was also socially conservative. An example of this is the church's position regarding the ordination of women. Although most of its founding members came from the rising elite, who held high social and political status, for most of its history the Mulu Wongel Church has maintained the position of not ordaining women and not placing them in key leadership roles.

It is against this background that I will discuss the issue of the evangelical church with respect to its engagement in the public realm. I employ the term "evangelical" as a generic or umbrella term for churches in Ethiopia outside the EOC and the Catholic Church insofar as they share many features despite denominational differences. Consequently, the use of the word "evangelical" in this chapter implicitly assumes the reference to the local term *Pente*.

EVANGELICAL CHRISTIANS AND THE PUBLIC SPACE TO 1974

The evangelical / Pentecostal movement has gone through several phases of transformation or mutation since its appearance in the 1960s. Nowadays, Pentecostalism expresses itself in several shapes and shades of color. It is becoming one of the most visible and robust expressions of the evangelical Christian faith in Ethiopia. It is attracting the youth and the middle class, and consequently its members and leaders reflect this demography. As pointed out, a pietistic attitude emphasizing the separation between the spiritual and the secular realm and the consequent recalcitrance to get involved in public affairs historically characterized the Ethiopian Pentecostal movement. This apolitical stand was reinforced by the narrative and self-representation of the movement, emphasizing the memory of the persecution suffered under the Derg and the resulting conception of politics and public affairs as two separate spheres. Crossing the line of the religious into the political space was considered entering a dangerous zone and was seen by some as tantamount to engaging in a sinful persuasion. The conventional dictum "Poletika ena electric beruke new"—literally, distance yourself from politics as much as you do from electricity—has been the mantra of many evangelical Christians. In the last few years, this position has been increasingly challenged by a "theological" shift promoting a holistic approach to social salvation and calling on evangelical Christians to become actively involved in the public arena in order to have an impact in bringing transformation to the country at all possible levels.

Taking advantage of the climate of religious freedom, a new strain of Pentecostalism dubbed as an independent or neocharismatic movement with high profiles in major towns is emerging in Ethiopia. The neocharismatic churches established in strategic locations and affluent residential quarters of the capital city are increasingly drawing in youth and urging them to "occupy" the secular space. Their leaders are calling for a more visible and prominent presence of Christians in sociocultural arenas and to actively engage in the political affairs of the nation. It is interesting to note that the new Pentecostal thrust is thriving in the contradictory sociopolitical reality of Ethiopia, where there is religious freedom unparalleled in the history of the nation and growing political dissatisfaction in the ethnically driven and divisive policy of the current government, not to mention the escalating nature of class polarization and rampant corruption. The level of disorientation in the country is the context in which these churches thrive, for they promise to provide transcendental leverage to overcome the fractured sense of identity.

Evangelical churches in Ethiopia are increasingly becoming cognizant of the call of the church as it is boldly written in Scripture. The mission of the church is to serve those who live under the bondage of oppression. This includes those who are under the yolk of both spiritual and physical captivities. The teaching of Christ in Luke 4:18 is relevant here:

> The Spirit of the Lord is upon Me,
> Because He anointed Me to preach the gospel to the poor.
> He has sent Me to proclaim release to the captives,
> And recovery of sight to the blind,
> To set free those who are oppressed.

Most church leaders in contemporary Ethiopia believe that the church exists to accomplish this liberating mission of Jesus Christ. Apparently, evangelical churches in Ethiopia have not developed a systematic and contextualized theology of public engagement to serve as guidepost to inform both thought and practice. Hence there have been many instances that caught the evangelical churches in Ethiopia by surprise and thrust them into the quagmire of political turmoil, often with disastrous consequences. Under these circumstances, some of the churches' leaders have not only been rashly entangled in politics but also risked their lives while responding to the immediate situation without the benefit of relayed wisdom.[5]

A good example of this is the case of Rev. Gudina Tumsa. Unprepared for the challenges of the 1974 Revolution, the Ethiopian evangelical church experienced a monumental trial. To address the new critical development, interested church leaders began to meet to reflect on the evolving political dynamics and come up with a consensus. The group reached the understanding that the evangelical church must demonstrate concern regarding the issue of "social salvation" in the context of the changing dynamics of the Ethiopian Revolution. The group felt that the church should present a relevant message to the Ethiopian people in their new existential dilemmas.[6] The move was definitely mingled with guilt as to the lack of action in the past and was also a call for inclusion as actors in the new reality of Ethiopia. Gudina was part of this group. From a historical perspective it appears that he carried on with this message with both fervor and in more practical ways.

In February 1975 and 1976, Qes Gudina Tumsa, an Ethiopian evangelical who served as the general secretary of the Ethiopian Evangelical Church Mekane Yesus, together with the World Lutheran Federation (WLF) took the novel initiative of organizing a series of ecumenical colloquiums at Mekane Yesus Seminary on the theme of Christianity and socialism. Leaders of the various Christian groups from the Ethiopian Orthodox, Catholic, and Protestant Churches, as well as select staff members from parachurch organizations like the Radio Voice of the Gospel, were invited to attend the seminar for the purposes of reflecting on new developments in the country and what it means to be Christians in the context of the revolution. The seminar was also intended to help Christians be conversant with pertinent issues of the times in order to prepare them for constructive dialogue with the state-sponsored revolutionary ideology of scientific communism.

During the seminar Gudina outlined the basic ingredients of socialism and compared them with Christianity. He concluded that the evangelical church ought to know about the basics of this ideology and that it should essentially be sympathetic to the plight of the poor and the oppressed, the social categories for which the revolution was making a strong appeal. The seminar expressed its support for change and welcomed the opportunities that the new situation offered for bringing this change about in Ethiopia. It also underscored the fact that a socially responsible church might invalidate much of the religious criticism of socialism. Gudina stressed that the church could not afford to be ignorant of some of the basic issues that the revolution had raised, such as equality, justice, freedom, and the dismantling of oppressive structures. Yet, he also clearly spelled out that the Christian approach and the road map chartered by socialism in Ethiopia were two entirely different routes. According to some informants who participated in the seminar, the inclination of Gudina and the WLF was to move the evangelical churches in the direction of the revolution so as to demonstrate sympathy to the cause of the people and provide critical solidarity with the state.[7] The approach was premised on the claim that the revolution created a new moment in Ethiopia's history for the church to demonstrate its social concerns and engage the broader public in practical ways.[8] This seminar was unprecedented in the history of the church, for social, ideological, and political issues had rarely been discussed openly among leaders. Thus a new conversation began.

Gudina could be credited for articulating valid theological positions concerning the role of the church in society and the relationship between church and state, even though it was, at least in part, dictated by the newly evolving political circumstances in Ethiopia. In the Pastoral Letter of March 1975, which is a prime example of his social-ethical reflections, he stated that the church was willing to promote efforts to address the issue of poverty and social justice and appreciated the new government's measures to that effect. It noted, however, that ideologies could not be a substitute for faith and should not be viewed as absolutes. The letter affirmed that the church's complete allegiance is due to God and God alone.[9] The pastoral letter was not an endorsement of the Derg's power but a voice from the margin, acknowledging the new political trend and revealing a desire to be involved as a participatory agent in the course of rebuilding the nation. In short, it provided the template for a theology of love and justice where justice, human rights, and the rule of law are its core commitments and ideals.[10]

As the only theologian of national standing, Gudina stood in the gap to provide ecumenical guidance for the various churches in Ethiopia. As the secretary of Meserete Kristos Church (MKC), he played a noteworthy role in conveying the message of unity and the need for establishing an interdenominational platform at this critical juncture for the history of the church and the nation at large. He was instrumental in setting up the Council for the Cooperation of Churches in Ethiopia (CCCE), known locally as Yemetebaber Gubae, in 1976. The founding members of the CCCE were the Ethiopian Orthodox Church, Ethiopian Catholic Church, and various representatives from evangelical churches such as Kale Hiwot Church, EECMY, and Mulu Wongel Church. The hope was that the CCCE would help Christians work in unison to promote social change in Ethiopia considering the new political development in the country. It was aimed at assisting the church to engage more actively using the rights guaranteed in the new Constitution and secure a meaningful space to preach the Gospel.[11] In a way, the CCCE was a creative effort pioneered by evangelicals to save the image of the church that had already been tainted in the past by its lack of involvement in social and national issues. It was also meant to serve as a platform to withstand the rising propaganda of the communist state against the church. It was also an ingenious response to the burning question of the church: How should the church survive, operate, and serve in a socialist state?

CCCE was an ecumenical forum that was created to draw together various Christian groups with the intent of creating a shared basis and corporate voice for faith groups in the new political reality of Ethiopia in which communism was gaining ascendance.[12] For Gudina, the more unified the church, the more it would be able to both maintain its autonomy and independence as well as reduce the chances for the state to divide and weaken the church and its leadership. Rev. Gudina, who came from a new tradition that had combined deep theological reflection with informed political convictions, was elected as its first chairman and worked to foster cooperation and harmony between the Orthodox Church and the Catholic Church.

Serving in this capacity in revolutionary Ethiopia proved to be challenging. Gudina had to walk the dangerous and fine line between faith and politics. Coming from the peripheral regions where the evangelical faith had thrived, Gudina was sensitive to both the needs of socially and politically sidelined people to whom the revolution appealed as well as the sanctity of the church. He tended to show guarded support to the state by means of critical dialogue, as the revolution sought to address structural issues like land redistribution and the ending of ethnic marginalization. Though he sought to come up with a new dispensation that considered the new political developments, he became very critical of the regime and distanced himself from it as it increasingly assumed a more totalitarian stance under Marxism. Gudina's attempt to establish a common front of Christians to fault the regime on moral and ideological grounds was not well received. The regime perceived Gudina's efforts as a threat. His towering influence and unflinching defense of the faith made him an obvious target of the military rulers. In 1979, failing to co-opt him, the military junta ultimately took Gudina's life. His execution by a corrupt government has led some to view him as modern-day Christian martyr. Some have even dubbed him as the Dietrich Bonhoeffer of Ethiopia, though the comparison might be unwarranted.

As far as the issue of martyrdom is concerned, many who knew and followed the circumstances of his death are convinced that he died conscious of the inevitable. If martyrdom means submitting oneself to suffering and ultimately giving up one's life for higher cherished religious beliefs or political convictions, then Gudina is a qualified martyr. In fact, as early as 1976 he conveyed the conviction that if responsible Christian commitment demands the sacrifice of one's life, then let it be so. Paul Wee cites the following observations from Gudina's work on the role of Christians in a given society: "A responsible Christian does not aggravate any situation and thereby court martyrdom. . . . to be a Christian is not to be a hero to make history for oneself. A Christian goes as a lamb to be slaughtered only when he / she knows that this is in complete accord with the will of God who has called him to his service."[13] It is remarkable that Gudina declined to accept the escape that was masterfully arranged involving President Julius Nyrere of Tanzania and acting president of the WLF, Bishop Josiah Kibira. Though his release was obtained through the intervention of Nyrere, the plan to remove him and rescue his life failed because of his refusal to cooperate. He emphatically and unequivocally told those involved in the plan that he would not betray his nation and his church in times of crisis. Oberkirchenrat Krause, who was part of this team, offered this remembrance on Gudina's response:

> What now followed had never happened before in our friendship. He yelled at me and said: "Here is my church and my congregation. How can I, as a church leader, leave my flock at this moment of trial? I have again and again pleaded with my pastors to stay on." He then quoted 2 Cor. 5:15: Christ died for all that those who live should no longer live for themselves but for him who died for them and was raised again.[14]

In his last paper on the role of a Christian in society, he wrote: "In my opinion a Christian has to make a choice only when he / she is faced with the demand not to confess Christ as Lord and when he / she is denied the right to teach in his name (Acts 4:16–20). Many things were considered 'adiaphora' by the Early Church. But when it concerned the denial of the Person of Christ as the Lord, the believers preferred physical death to earthly life and went for martyrdom."[15] It is also important to note that the EOC, which had millions of followers and was still in a position of exerting a measure of influence, virtually kept silent regarding the death of its religious partner as a champion of the Christian faith and unity. There was not a single statement that came from EOC leaders concerning an important ally in the faith who was murdered in such an undignified manner by an evil regime.

Gudina needs to be credited on other counts, too. Coming from an area that has experienced religious persecutions and some form of political marginalization, his Christian ministry was laden with political commitments. While studying in the United States during the Civil Rights Movement, he became more attuned to political, social, and cultural issues and returned home with a heightened civic consciousness and a renewed sense of the church's mission. He sought to translate his understanding of the mission of the church and took steps to prepare both himself and his church for critical social engagements. Gudina made a vital contribution to the church by launching the notion of "holistic ministry" that seeks to expand the church's mission by addressing the physical and spiritual needs of humanity. His notion of "serving the whole person" was developed in order to better connect the Gospel message to the diversity of human needs, spiritual, physical, social, and so on. Holistic ministry was a concept that called the church to live up to the full expectations of the mission of Jesus. For all but the MYC, it was a new idea among the evangelical churches in Ethiopia, whose theological premises and practical variables seem to lack clarity and solidity.

According to Gudina, holistic ministry entails more than occasionally sponsoring a program. It goes beyond short-term, relief-oriented aid. Holistic ministry, if embraced and incorporated within the church, means modeling God's concern for the total well-being of persons and communities. It means an incarnational lifestyle of integrity, compassion, commitment, and more. It means sharing the good news both for this life and for the life after death. In other words, proclamation of salvation should encompass the vision of a transformed social order that includes the healing of broken social relationships, a concern for the nation, and the proper nurturing of the environment, to cite just a few cases. The comprehensive formulation of a holistic mission of the church is a major task that awaits future leaders and theologians of the evangelical churches in Ethiopia.

Gudina's role during the period of the Ethiopian revolution was highlighted because of both of his towering voice, being uniquely situated regarding his theological training at this time, and the leadership and influence that he exhibited. However, there were other voices or expressions of discursive engagement that should be accounted for. These are voices that indirectly engaged the political space through the medium of music as a form of protest. There were many songs composed during the revolution with messages intended to uplift the sovereignty of God and challenge, or so it appears, the assumptions behind so-called scientific socialism and the litany of slogans that promoted atheism. "Denke new lene geta" (He / God is awesome to me) by Tamirat Haile, "Zingero Aydelehum" (I am not an ape / monkey) by Derege, "Keber yegebahal" (Glory be unto You) by an unknown composer, "Semay zufanu new" (The Heaven is his Throne) by Geja choir, and "Akil dama" (Bemoaning the bloodshed of the civil strife and war) (by an unknown artist) are a few examples.[16]

Tesfaye Gabiso's songs give expression to a sense of joyous defiance. They used biblical narratives and allusions, highlighting refusal to submit before a human-made object, and conveyed the message of triumphing through trials, even if it meant passing through fires.[17] Tamirat Haile's music defended the eternal value of biblical truth and contained powerful messages that warned people not to be beguiled by the passing fads of the day. "Dinq qal" (Amazing Word) was composed and sung in response to attacks against the Bible.[18] Tamrat Welba's song, "Bewengel alafrem" (I am not ashamed of the Gospel), was also sung to reassure Christians that the Bible contained the eternal power of God. The gospel songs produced during the time of the military regime mostly stressed steadfastness, courage, and firmness in the faith. The song "Getachen new kehulum belay" (Our Lord is above all things), based on John 3:31, was written in 1978 in response to the slogan "the revolution is above everything." The song "Egziabher yemesgen kemilut honenal" (We are amongst those praising Thee), was sung to counter the new style of socialist greeting (*enkuan deresen*) that was being gradually promoted by party officials and their cronies, particularly political cadres operating at the local levels. There was significant growth in the number of artists writing songs about trials, agony, and assurance of victory. The closure of churches and the disbanding of their musical choirs paved the way for the proliferation of soloists.[19] As one prominent church elder commented, "The mouth opened more when it was stifled more, the more the voice was muted, the more the spirit shouted."[20] Hymns produced during the revolution by composers and singers, either in band or in solo form, stressed themes such as firmness, faithfulness, hope, courage, and the like. Scholars have rarely given attention to demonstrations of dissent couched in religious terms like these, focusing rather on the discursive interrogation of hegemonic and dictatorial narratives.

The songs may not have been composed to intentionally sound political, but according to King Dunway, "music may be said to be political when its lyrics or melody evoke or reflect a political judgment by the listener."[21] As Roberta King points out, "among their multiple functions, songs provide opportunities for processing life's vagaries, difficulties and daily interactions."[22] Most of the songs composed during the days of the revolution were generated by the climate of the time, addressing politics and making political judgments. The choice of themes and the ability of the composers to identify and apply biblical verses to defend their faith and obliquely critique Marxist ideology clearly testify to the level of sophistication and the intellectual dimension of their protest. Hence, gospel songs formed potent expressions of a vocal variant of struggle against a hegemonic ideology, short of violence. These subtle, civilized forms of ideological engagement have been overlooked in contexts where brute force was employed. However, they deserve more attention, especially within the discourse of public theology.

Gospel songs that derived from experiences of suffering not only provided solace and comfort from God but became the chief avenues by which the evangelical church assumed its indigenous identity.[23] In this respect gospel songs can be referred to as voices from the margin. Overall, the resistance of evangelical Christians can be described as nonviolent and based on the logic of absolute faith in biblical truth, which runs counter to the logic of dialectical materialism. However, as church leaders admit, this position has not been expressed in solid theological articulations. The firm stand taken by evangelical Christians not to yield to the state-sponsored ideology and the tenacity with which they held biblical truth to be the supreme guide for their lives, along with their fearless determination to share their faith to / with others, sometimes at huge personal cost, were forms of resistance, indirectly contributing to the attrition and the bankruptcy of the state and its ideology. Gospel music, while once limited to select groups, has become part of the larger public culture in Ethiopia, lending evangelicalism the public face by which it is known.

Since the fall of the military regime, the evangelical church has been experiencing unparalleled growth. Ethiopian society has witnessed a second major decentering phenomenon besides the Revolution of 1974, with far more social and political ramifications. The new federal form of government introduced by the rulers of the Ethiopian People's Revolutionary Front (EPRDF), who replaced the previous regime, was founded on an ethnic-political calculus. Though it attempted to redress some structural imbalances, the sudden implementation of an ethnic-oriented sociopolitical order had the unintended consequence of causing psychic disorientations and questioning of identity that led to a variety of bewildering experiences. This effect can be attributed both to the novelty of the political arrangement and to the disequilibrium it generated for societal structures and relations that have existed among Ethiopians for centuries. The explosion of the pursuit of identity that has plagued the nation is an important context within which one should view the current surge of growth in the evangelical church and the new political coloring that this church is assuming.

The freedom obtained in Ethiopia following the deposition of the military rulers has allowed substantive growth. Although the expansion of the Evangelical faith is taking place across the board, its new members are largely coming from the urban youth, who are being drawn to the movement for several reasons, including the charismatic nature of the movement in particular; the preaching and worship styles; the applications of innovative forms of modern gospel music that stress themes of praise, victory, and a sense of activism—these all constitute major attractions. This is a crucial demographic scenario, if not a significant shift, with implications that need to be taken seriously considering both the current situation and the future trajectories of the evangelical churches in Ethiopia. It has to be underscored that freedom did not bring merely blessings to the evangelical churches in Ethiopia. With freedom also came a reconfiguring of identity, partly associated with the ethnic-based political order but also from denominational fractures. The formidable challenge that evangelical churches commonly faced under the Marxist government provided the means for unity that was indispensable for survival. The newly found freedom, however, is testing the Evangelical church in a different way, presenting a potential challenge that has renewed the call for discernment and accentuated the need to learn from lessons of the past.

NEW STRAINS OF ACTIVISM: POST-DERG DEVELOPMENTS

This piece would be amiss if it did not include a discussion, even if in a cursory manner, of the parliamentary election of May 15, 2005, and the involvement of evangelical Christians who sided with the opposition party, the Coalition for Unity and Democracy (CUD, also known as Kinijit). Kinijit was formed by four newly organized political parties in 2004 with the aim of securing victory over the ruling party backed by the state. It consists of the All Ethiopian Unity Party (AEUP), the Ethiopian Democratic League (EDL), the Ethiopian Democratic Unity Party-Medhin (EDUP-M), and the Rainbow Alliance / Movement for Democracy and Social Justice (RAMDSJ). The organization contains constituents with differing views regarding economic and political management, ranging from social democrats to economic liberals. A few evangelical Christians, most of them young but also more seasoned members and prominent church leaders like Million Belete, joined the opposition party in the hopes of creating a voice in the democratic process. Moreover, they came alongside other fellow Ethiopians in order to end a one-party-dominated political system that espoused an ill-planned, ethnic-based federal system of government that may lead to the balkanization of Ethiopia. They perceived a need in Ethiopia for the full recognition of the rule of law and respect for the implementation of democratic rights as stipulated in the Constitution.

Some of the young people who became involved in the opposition party include Birtukan Mideksa, a former judge who currently serves as head of Ethiopia's Election Board, and Muleneh Eyuel, an economist who became the secretary of CUD and later joined the Ginbot 7 Movement for Justice, as well as Tariku Belay, Seleshi Bekele, and many others. Most of these young political actors started their movement at Sunday group gatherings, usually after Sunday church services, to discuss topics such as reason and faith, democracy and justice, and matters pertaining to the calling of Christians in relation to society and politics.

The political activists conducted their meetings in one of the coffee houses in Bole area. The main reason for this venue was that participating denominations—such as the International Evangelical Church (IEC), Barabbas, and the Crusaders—did not have an open platform within their respective churches. Though they belonged to different denominations, beginning in 2001–02 young people from these groups used their professional ties and educational connections to establish an informal network. They discussed key issues of the country with intensity and passion and brainstormed ideas of how they could meaningfully engage and contribute toward the creation of a just democratic order in Ethiopia. They concluded that evangelical Christians should not be bystanders and onlookers of the degenerating politics in Ethiopia but rather should take a stand and become active participants—no matter the costs. Their goal was to serve as "force multipliers" and contribute their share to bring about transformation.

It was incumbent upon these young actors, they believed, to "influence" society and the public square in tangible ways, investing it with Christian values that stress purity, integrity, transparency, and servanthood. The groups considered various options including the creation of political parties as Christians, which was found to be unviable as the Constitution does not allow the creation of political parties along religious lines. This was also not a pragmatic approach, since it would limit their scope of involvement in terms of addressing the whole Ethiopian community. Hence, they decided to join the opposition group, with whom they shared common interests and entered in the campaign for election.

Informants point out that they were initially attracted to a small political organization, the EDL, led by Dr. Alemayehu Aredo, in which they could leverage their impact. It is tempting to speculate that they might have placed greater expectations on the rapidly growing evangelical Christian population, whose societal influence was on the rise. As is well known, the election, which was the first of its kind in the nation's history, was rigged by the government. Leaders of the opposition group faced imprisonment. The evangelical Christians who ventured into the new political experiment suffered doubly: ill-treatment by the state and their own churches.

What is very intriguing is that the evangelical church at large condemned and openly reprimanded those who participated in the 2005 election, for they had crossed the red line by going beyond the turf of the church. The Sunday groups were mostly young, educated men in their early twenties and able to capitalize on their college connections to initiate a new political conversation in the country. Most of its members came from the newly emerging church fellowship that contained a heavy foreign influence and presence.[24]

It has to be noted that the new strain of activism that led to the breaking of glass ceilings by evangelical Christians unfolded in the context of the harsh political realities of Ethiopia, where ethnic politics was sapping the energy of the people and corruption was becoming glaringly rampant. It also came out of the deep conviction that the evangelical church had stayed within its four-wall confines for too long, while the "world" around it was in great distress. The activists were seeking to launch a new conversation for evangelical Christians to heighten their social obligations by extricating themselves from the limiting binary outlook of us-versus-them. They were responding to the call of the creation of a just political order in the country as Christians informed by their evangelical Christian perspective of "being salt and the light" to society.

Interestingly, as noted earlier, they were joined in their new crusading efforts by some senior members of the evangelical church like Million Belete. Million is a well-known church leader from the Mennonite tradition. In a recent interview Million related to me that he had a firm conviction that Ethiopian evangelicals need to participate in the political affairs of the nation. He developed a concept paper based on the Bible that supports his stance. He considered prominent characters like David and Daniel whose stories as political figures are well recorded in the Bible. He also consulted books on how evangelical Christians actively participated in politics and was particularly impressed by the observation of a prominent South African church leader who commented that politics are not dirty; rather, what makes politics dirty are politicians.[25]

As he began to share his ideas with several church leaders, the conviction came to him that he should practice what he had been teaching in the pulpit. This meant that though in his seventies, he could still be a good example for fellow evangelicals, young and old, to be actively engaged in politics and become catalysts of change in their society.[26] The Ethiopian evangelicals who participated in the election of 2005 broke new ground by challenging the prevalent notion of *menfesawinet* (a spiritualist) that saw the "world," particularly politics, as the polar of opposite of the doctrine of born-again Christianity.

Contemporary Ethiopia has witnessed the rise of a bewildering variety of new religious movements that are becoming increasingly vocal in the public space. The proliferation of Pentecostal movements, specifically those that heavily emphasize power ministry and that are garnering more and more attention in society, calls for critical reflection in connection to the study of evangelical Christians in the public square in Ethiopia. It is hard to subsume the various expressions of the movement into one category and place them under a single phenomenological narrative. Most of the leaders of the new movement have television channels that used to transmit sermon messages and display acts of miraculous healing. An intriguing feature of this development is the amazing speed with which these movements have flourished. Over (merely) the last five years, these ministries have seen a surge in popularity.

The teachings of these Pentecostal pastors stress the need for impacting the world in word and deed, living by example—although this claim could be dubious—and planting seeds of righteousness in society by making deep and strategic inroads in all sectors of the public square. The intent is to infiltrate the public domain with resolve by establishing close links with associations, like the Ethiopian Christian Graduates Fellowship, or other profession-based associations, and create networks with influential political and business groups. Virtually, all the main independent and neocharismatic churches—such as Beza International Church, City of Refugee (formerly You-Go City) Church, Presence TV, Unic / Unique 7000, Exodus—have established their own fellowships that target business and professional communities. The new Pentecostal groups rationalize that their involvement in business and political sectors is necessary in order to "occupy" the socioeconomic space and use it as a radiating spot of Christian values. They strongly believe that this form of engagement by Christians is of great importance to end the pervasive nature of corruption in Ethiopia. They organize national prayer convocation days for church leaders framed around key national issues like political and economic corruption, the decline of moral values in the nation, and growing manifestations of degenerated social and cultural practices such as increasing rates of drug use among youth. A characteristic feature of these convocations are the unabashed pronouncements on matters like rebuking generational curses, poverty, ethnic discords, and the prophesying of the advent of glorious days for Ethiopia. The leaders frequently invoke biblical verses such as II Chronicles 7:14, Psalm 68:31, and II Corinthians 10:5–7 to frame their messages in lieu of the need to wage or engage in spiritual warfare and the call for national salvation. The leaders of these new churches believe that the socioeconomic and political problems in Ethiopia are not merely products of historical realities and constructed material conditions. They posit that these problems are also shaped by invisible dark forces, hence their emphasis in a higher dimension of engagement through what they call spiritual warfare in order to redeem the past, rescue people from bondage, and bring about new life in the present.

PROPHECY AS VEILED POLITICS: VOICES FROM THE MARGIN

There are now public utterances made by some religious figures in Ethiopia referring directly to the past and future political landscape of the nation. A

YouTube video concerning Prime Minister Dr. Ahmad recently went viral. It claimed that a prophetess by the name Bertukan gave a prophecy about five years earlier that Ahmad would be the PM of Ethiopia. She made the statement in a small congregation when he was not a well-known figure. I draw attention to this event because it indicates a significant phenomenon in evangelical social engagement; namely, it shows an area where some evangelical Christians in Ethiopia make their voices heard and their presence felt in the political cartography of the nation with the claimed authority of divine revelation. This is not unique to Ethiopia. For instance, self-described prophet Dr. Akwasi Agyemang Prempeh created a stir in Ghana on New Year's Day by predicting that the incumbent president, John Mahama, would win the November 2016 election. His prediction was, of course, welcomed and widely publicized by the ruling party. Though much to his chagrin, it did not come true.

In this respect it is germane to note the prophecy of Rev. Sarka Belina, a man from an Oromo ethnic origin and with a Lutheran church background. According to Qes Belina, following earnest petitions for unity and peace for his nation, which he had been undertaking since 1977, God answered his prayer in 2002 while in Hermannsburg, Germany. Belina claims that God appeared to him one morning at 3 A.M. Just as God revealed the Ten Commandments to Moses in the form of a tablet, so did God reveal to Belina the future of Ethiopia in the form of TV movie captions. Belina claims that God revealed to him the successive events that were to unfold in Ethiopia in the coming decades, telling Belina that Ethiopia would return to her former glory and that its previous administrative organization of fourteen provinces that included Eritrea would be restored.

The vision he saw consisted of three scenes. The first scene was about Eritrea, Tigray, Gondar, and Wallo. These areas are to become the industrial backbone of Ethiopia. Scene 2 dealt with Bale, Arsi, Shawa, and Gojjam and the agricultural products they would produce to feed the empire. In scene 3, God revealed that Hararhge, Sidamo, Wallaga, Gamo-Gofa, and Illu Babor would produce abundant fruits, tea, coffee, and spice. This means that the northern provinces would develop technologically but the people of southern and southwestern Ethiopia and others would flourish as strong agricultural societies. He also claims that God has shown him the places where rich mineral and oil deposits are located. According to the prophecy, the first ten years would be a period of agony, turmoil, and challenging times; the second ten years would be a time for the settlement of 100 years' worth of accumulated problems; and the last ten years would be meant as a time for the eradication of 500 years' worth of problems when the nation would see unprecedented economic social and technological development, much to the surprise of the world. Visitors would come to Ethiopia from across the globe to witness these amazing events. The children of Ethiopia, who are scattered throughout the world, would return home to enjoy a secure life. The prediction affirms that within this thirty-year period, Ethiopia's economic level of development would be equal to Japan's current economic status. There are many evangelical Christians who take this prophecy seriously and are incurably optimistic about the future of Ethiopia. In fact, some even tend to interpret the unfolding of current developments in Ethiopia alongside the prophecy of Rev. Belina.[27]

There are also emerging prophetic voices in contemporary Ethiopia whose representatives are making bold statements publicly condemning the ethnicization of politics and religion. These voices openly fault the rulers for their lack of transparency and accountability. They strongly warn political and church leaders that the nation is on the verge of disaster unless change takes place through actions and behavior rooted in the fear of God. One such voice is the Rev. Dr. Tolesa Gudina, a theologian and pastor of a megachurch in Atlanta, Georgia. Rev. Tolesa has been organizing prayer convocations in Ethiopia on the themes of national repentance, public harmony, and reconciliation for several years. He has arranged crusades and revival conferences at the nation's stadium in Addis Ababa and in other major cities in the country in association with local churches. Though he comes from the Oromo ethnic background, like the late Gudina, he places strong emphasis on national unity in his message, namely, the identity of all the people regardless of their ethnic origins as Ethiopians. Above all, Rev. Tolesa urges evangelical Christians in Ethiopia to stress their heavenly citizenship as people belonging to the Kingdom of God and to reflect that in their daily lives, vocations, and characters. He frequently travels to Ethiopia to meet people in leadership positions at the national and regional level and holds prayer gatherings with them for providential wisdom and guidance as they lead a complex nation with multilayered problems. I happened to witness one of these meetings personally when I was invited by Tolesa to visit the palace of the late Ethiopian president, Mr. Girma Wolde-Giorgis, in 2003 while on a research trip.

Tolesa has made several public appearances on one of the newly emerging and highly popular Christian TV media outlets, known as Elshaddai Television Network. In a speech he delivered last year during the Ethiopian new year's celebration, he bemoaned the collapse of a cherished national ethos and attributed the current leadership crisis to a character anomie and declining moral values. In his public pronouncement he claimed to receive fresh revelation from God concerning the causes of disharmony and corruption in Ethiopia as well as its marred image, both nationally and internationally, and a way forward for the nation. Rev. Tolesa claims that God spoke to him while he was visiting the headquarters of the African Union with a call to tell the Ethiopian people that the glory of the nation had departed as a result of the ignoble treatment of the late emperor Haile Selassie and the circumstances around his political fallout. Whatever the misgivings, the emperor represented a father figure for Africa and Ethiopia. As a long-reigning and older monarch, he should have received a respectable burial treatment. He called the nation to repentance before God in order to restore Ethiopia to its former glory. Tolesa noted that remedying the gross error of the past and redeeming the future for the sake a speedy national recovery would entail the following: the erection of Haile Selassie's statue in front of the headquarters of the African Union (AU) headquarters and the establishment of a Pan-African University bearing his name that will serve as a center to draw students and scholars from across Africa. Tolesa emphatically told his audience that his ideas were not products of a well-planned theoretical discourse coming from a contemplative mind but revelations received directly from God through the Holy Spirit in the form of a series of visions. The erection of a statue at the AU headquarters was accomplished on February 10, 2019.

Rev. Tolesa has become increasingly vocal in challenging the government in Ethiopia for not being good stewards of its authority and power. He has not spared the church and its leadership for failing to be prophetic in the midst of escalating social anarchy and violence and for not standing as unified body. In his most recent public discourse, weeks before the election of Dr. Abiy Ahmed, he boldly charged the church for its apathetic position while the nation faces serious challenges, notably the threat of an imminent civil war with catastrophic results. He pleaded with Ethiopians to recall what happened during the days of the Ethiopian Revolution, when citizens perished in tens of thousands as an important reminder that silence is not an option.

Tolesa is emerging as a new voice in the nation who is heard by many, including nonevangelical Christians. Lending credibility to his message is his consistency as a strong social critic of social injustice and moral degeneration, often at the risk of his own life. To the evangelical community his message is clear: maintain proper balance between servanthood, service, and stewardship. He insists that the church should not just be preparing its members for the eternal life that comes after death. More than this, it is important that the church should be cognizant of the fact that members need peace, safety, prosperity, and protection here on earth. The church cannot stay passive when the poor are oppressed and injustice exists. He noted that the role of the church is far greater than conducting funeral services when citizens are slaughtered by the tyrant government. Moreover, as a public, visible figure Gudina has both fans and detractors. Many of the latter come from his own Oromo group, for Tolesa's stance on national unity does not gel well with their separatist agenda.

CONCLUDING REMARKS

Ethiopia has recently elected a new prime minister, a committed evangelical Christian from a Muslim background. He is young and well educated and has renewed a sense of hope in the nation. Though he comes from an Oromo ethnic background, he is receiving loud praises and support across the board for publicly embracing and campaigning for national unity, reconciliation, and peaceful development. Surprisingly, he is embraced by EOC members, Muslims, and secular communities in Ethiopia, including diasporic opposition groups, though this situation remains in flux. While he is a member of the Mulu Wongel Pentecostal Church, he does not appear to play this (church) card in his public discourse and in delivering messages as the PM of the nation.

Most evangelical Christians see the new political developments as a kairos moment and watch the changing dynamics with a heightened sense of optimism, claiming that a new era is dawning in their country. There are some signs that evangelical Christians and the church they represent are making their presence felt in celebrating and giving voice to the fact that Ethiopia has a Pente PM. At the same time, others openly call for caution and advise Christians to show greater resolve against making sudden efforts to garner more attention.

The church in Ethiopia needs to respond to poverty and structural and sociopolitical injustices. It should serve as a catalyst in impacting the culture that fosters vile attitudes like greed, hatred, and the stereotyping of minority ethnic or occupational groups. Evangelical Christians, despite their sporadic efforts to engage society, are found lacking in the development of a strategic, systematic, and contextualized plan for public participation. It appears that their track record in this regard is poor and that action is long overdue. Despite the claim of numerical growth, of which the evangelical church is humbly proud, its influence as a transforming agent and a prophetic voice is skin deep. Given their dramatic expansion and their ethnic diversity, as well as their youthful demographic profile, Ethiopian evangelicals are in a position to make an enormous impact on their nation and the continent in the coming decades.

A factor with the potential to limit this impact, however, may be certain aspects of the Ethiopian evangelical worldview. Ethiopian evangelicals in the past have tended to hold a dualistic worldview, that is, a vision that separates reality into two fundamentally distinct categories: holy and profane, sacred and secular. Consequently, this view entails avoiding a meaningful integration of the two layers of life at the individual and social level. The dualistic position can be traced historically to the influence of the EOC that also holds this view, from the pietistic theology evangelical Christians received from Protestant missionaries who saw the world in a binary dichotomy, and also from the experience of persecution under the Derg that created mistrust toward the state and politics. These factors may account for the minimal involvement of evangelical Christians in Ethiopia in the past. There are some signs of change associated with the reconfigured self-understandings among the youth and educated Ethiopians that stem from their own experiences in troubling political contexts as well as the impact of globalization, especially the impact of technology and the new ways of communication. But as the old adage has it, habits do not die easily, and the older outlook may still serve as a drag inhibiting the full participation of evangelical Christians in the social and political life of the country. All things considered, it looks like the attitude of evangelical Christians in the past can be characterized as that of distant interest and polite distance, although the new political environment in Ethiopia may drastically change this posture.

NOTES

1. Interview, Pastor Mesfin Gutu, May 3, 2018.
2. Many informants agree that they do not recall the term *Pente* being used for any religious group prior to the Debre Zeit incident of 1967. Doctor Tilahun Adera, one of the active participants of the Pentecostal faith in Haile Selassie University in 1966, recalls that university students, opposed to their movement, continued to refer to them as followers of anti-Mary or simply as simpleton idealist believers. Informant: Tilahun Adera.
3. "Be-Debre Zeit ketema lijochena welagoch tegachu," *Addis Zemen* 27, no. 826 (September 19, 1967): 1. According to the report, the "unknown religion" was started a year before the incident took place by three young men and enlisted more than 200 people in the town alone. Their sudden rise and increase in membership coupled with rumors of "vulgar" practices, including promiscuous sex under the guise of night prayers, set the context for the attack. According to *Addis Zemen*, more than 6,000 people were involved in the assault. Informants: Melese, Debebe, and Assefa.

4. It is very hard to come up with a uniform definition of Pentecostals. W. J. Hollenweger, a noted scholar in the field, defined Pentecostals this way: "all groups who profess at least two religious crisis experiences (1. baptism or rebirth; 2 baptism of the Spirit), the second being subsequent and different from the first one, and the second, usually, but not always, being associated with speaking in tongue." W. J. Hollenweger, *The Pentecostals* (Minneapolis: Augsburg, 1972), xix. Ethiopian Pentecostals are in agreement that the term refers to those Christians who express the power and presence of the Holy Spirit and the gifts of the Spirit directed toward effectively witnessing to Jesus Christ as Lord and Savior. Most Pentecostals embrace the view that the baptism of the Holy Spirit comes subsequent to conversion. Though there is no unanimity, speaking in tongues is considered to be the chief indication of the infilling of the Spirit and a mark of being a true Christian. In addition to the baptism of the Holy Spirit, Pentecostals believe that nine biblical gifts of the Spirit: "the word of wisdom, the word of knowledge, the gift of faith, the gifts of healing, the gift of miracles, the gift of prophesy, the gifts of discerning spirits, the gifts of tongues and the gifts of interpretation of tongues are available today" to those Christians who earnestly seek them. David E. Harrel, *All Thing Are Possible* (Bloomington: Indiana University Press, 1975), 11–12.

5. For more detail, see Donald Donham, *Marxist Modern* (Berkley: University of California Press, 1999).

6. Daniel Fite, "The Challenge of Denominational Conflict in the Context of the Ethiopian Evangelical Churches" (senior essay, Mekane Yesus Seminary, Addis Ababa, 2001), 19.

7. Informants: Shiferaw, Wubshet, Herui, etc. See also, Gudina Tumsa Foundation, "The Initial Response to the Revolution: Documents of the Rev. Gudina Tumsa and the Mekane Yesus Church from the First Phase of the Revolution," 1974–75, in *Church and Society: Lectures and Responses. Second Missiological Seminar 2003, on the Life and Ministry of Gudina Tumsa, General Secretary of the Ethiopian Evangelical Church Mekane Yesus (EECMY) (1966–1979)* (Hamburg, Germany: WDL-Publishers, 2010), 12.

8. Perhaps if this line had been pursued, the likely outcome would have been something akin to the Three Self Patriotic Movement of China. Informants: Wubshet, Hiruie (Herui) Tsige Abebe Mesfin, and others. Wubshet is of the opinion that there were many evangelical Christians who joined the revolution innocently as an opportunity to show solidarity with and do something for the poor but lost their ways in the maze. Examples cited were Temesgen Madebo, Ergete Madebo, Tsion Dessie, Petros Wandano, and Semon Galero.

9. For the full content of the letter, see H. E. Emmanuel Abraham and Rev. Gudina Tumsa, "Pastoral Letter: The Evangelical Church Mekane Yesus in the Ethiopian Revolution," *Witness and Discipleship* (Addis Ababa: Gudina Tumsa Foundation, 2003), 77–80. Gudina later refined his thought when he developed his indigenous theology of "holistic ministry," where he challenged the Ethiopian churches to rise to the challenge of addressing the entire human, spiritual and physical. He insisted that African Christianity should develop a political theology relevant to the African people. He firmly believed that such a theology should never take the place of the Gospel of Jesus Christ. For more, see Gudina Tumsa, memorandum, August 1975, quoted in O. M. Edie, *Revolution and Religion in Ethiopia* (Oxford: James Currey, 2000), 119.

10. His thoughts might have been strongly influenced by Reinhold Niebuhr and Dietrich Bonhoeffer.

11. Informants: Hiruye, Berhanu, Debela, and others.
12. According to Gudina, the word "ecumenical" describes the common strategy of the churches in working together to further causes of common interest. It also describes two or more churches of the same confessional faith family or various denominations with different confessional backgrounds. Gudina set up CCCE under a principle stressing unity outlined in the Gospel of John chapter 17:21–22. Debela Birri, "Rev Gudina Tumsa and the Ecumenical Movement of the 1970's," in *The Life and Ministry of Rev. Gudina Tumsa*, ed. Gudina Tumsa Foundation (Addis Ababa: Gudina Tumsa Foundation, 2001), 130. In essence, Gudina was taking on the mantle of the evangelical pioneers who struggled for the formation of the evangelical alliance, which could not materialize for lack of a clear theological framework of ecumenism and due to the unwillingness of the missionaries to see the fruition of the project.
13. Paul Wee "Dietrich Bonhoeffer and Gudina Tumsa: Shaping the Church's Response to the Challenges of Our Day," in *Church and Society: Lectures and Responses. Second Missiological Seminar 2003, on the Life and Ministry of Gudina Tumsa, General Secretary of the Ethiopian Evangelical Church Mekane Yesus (EECMY) (1966–1979)*, ed. Gudina Tumsa Foundation (Hamburg, Germany: WDL-Publishers, 2010), 15. It is interesting to note that Bonhoeffer put the same in a more laconic way: "When Christ calls a man, he bids him come and die." Quoted from Bonhoeffer's *The Cost of Discipleship*, in Wee, "Dietrich Bonhoeffer and Gudina Tumsa," 17.
14. Wee, 22.
15. Øyvind Eide, *Revolution and Religion in Ethiopia: Growth and Persecution of the Mekane Yesus Church, 1974–86* (Oxford: James Currey, 2000), 179.
16. Taken from recorded cassette songs and personal interviews.
17. Lila W. Balisky, "Theology in Song: Ethiopia's Tesfaye Gabbiso," *Missiology: An International Review* 4 (October 1997): 452–53.
18. Personal collection of Tamrat's songs.
19. Alemayehu H / Gabriel and Atalay Alem, "Yemezmur Agelgloxtena Yewengel Serchit," (manuscript, 1997), 6.
20. Informant: Shiferaw.
21. Quoted in Reuben Makayiko Chriambo, " 'Mzimu wa Soldier': Contemporary Popular Music and Politics in Malawi," in *A Demography of Chameleons*, ed. Harri Englund (Blantyre, Malawi: Christian Literature Association, 2002), 118.
22. Roberta King, *Music in the Life of the African Church* (Waco, TX: Baylor University Press, 2008), 120.
23. For the general expansion of Pentecostalism in other denominations, see Taye Abdisa, "The Pentecostal Movement Development and the Rise of the Charismatic Movement in Ethiopia" (senior essay, Mekane Yesus Seminary, 1977).
24. The story of the participation of evangelical Christians in Ethiopia in the election of 2005 awaits a serious future investigation.
25. For further details, see his recent book, Million Belete, *Tewestaye* (Addis Ababa: Raeye Publishers, 2018), 240–47.
26. Interview, Million Belete, June 26, 2018.
27. For more on this, see the manuscript "Yekefta zemen beIypia." Belina later wrote his vision in a book as a blueprint as well as to serve as a document for the next generation. Bethel TV Channel Worldwide, *Reverend Belina Sarka in Bethphage International Church* (YouTube video), https://www.youtube.com/watch?v=Ic52Rj2ANNk

CHAPTER 4

Governing Religious Life
in Idi Amin's Uganda

Derek R. Peterson

John Mbiti died in 2019 at the age of eighty-seven. His 1969 book *African Religions and Philosophy* set the parameters for a whole field of scholarly inquiry: it showed that African philosophical and religious traditions were consistent and sensible and that they could be understood as an integrated system, rather than as superstition.[1] The eulogies have—rightly—been full of praise. Kenyan president Uhuru Kenyatta hymned him as "a role model and an ambassador of the Kenya brand abroad"; while Raila Odinga, sometime leader of the opposition, described his book as "an eye-opener and ground-breaking work."[2]

The praise from Kenya's leading public figures makes it easy to ignore the fact that Mbiti's scholarly career was largely defined in Uganda, not Kenya. He was appointed lecturer at Makerere University in Kampala in 1964 and taught there until 1974. Prof. Mbiti composed his scholarly work in a place and a time at which political authorities were consolidating the religious field, closing down avenues of dissent, and imposing conformity on religious life and in the political world. Mbiti was not involved in the suppression of dissident religions, and he could not have foreseen the purposes to which his theological thought would be put. The ideas he pioneered, however, helped make the government of religious life thinkable. His scholarship made it appear as though Africans—their outward diversity notwithstanding—were unified in their devotion to a shared set of religious ideas. For the men who governed Idi Amin's Uganda, the idea of "African Traditional Religion" was a template from which to work. It was a license to organize and consolidate the cultural field. It was one of an ensemble of ideas and institutions that allowed the Amin government to distinguish authentic from inauthentic forms of cultural life.

When Idi Amin came to power in 1971, Ugandans found themselves, all at once, positioned on the front line of the global war against racism, imperialism, and apartheid. New bureaucratic institutions were set up to regulate the production of culture. Religion had to be reoriented. The space for dissident forms of Christianity and Islam was radically narrowed. Pentecostals, Baha'is, Adventists, and other nonconformists were imprisoned, their property was seized, and their religious lives were foreclosed. It was part of a process by which political life was evacuated of competition and loyalties were centered around the president.

THE MAKING OF AFRICAN TRADITIONAL RELIGION

At the time of his appointment at Makerere University, Mbiti was already an accomplished writer, with a PhD from Cambridge University and an impressive scholarly and political network.[3] He had published his first book, *Mūtūnga na Ngewa Yake* ("Mutunga and His Story"), in 1954; in 1955 he had published a kiKamba translation of Robert Louis Stevenson's *Treasure Island*.[4] These and other early works of translation gave Mbiti a vocation as a spokesman for African language and cultures. In 1959 he presented a paper on Kamba-language literature at the Second Congress of Negro Writers and Artists in Rome, the most important transnational collective of African, Caribbean, and African American writers and artists at the time. The paper was later published in the *negritude* journal *Présence Africaine*.[5]

Makerere University was at that time full of creative, politically engaged scholars. At the center of it was *Transition* magazine, edited by Rajat Neogy with the assistance of the political scientist Ali Mazrui, the Nigerian poet Christopher Okigbo, and others. The magazine published short stories from the South African writer Bessie Head, essays from Wole Soyinka, fiction from Paul Theroux, and philosophy from Okot p'Bitek. Makerere lecturers were regular contributors to *Transition*. Among them was Fred Welbourn, whose 1961 book *East African Rebels* had powerfully argued for the political rationality of dissident Christian movements.[6] Another contributor was Bethwell Ogot, who was at the time of Mbiti's appointment revising the book that would be published as *History of the Southern Luo*.[7] All of these scholars were public figures, and all of them saw themselves as contributing toward the building of a specifically African university, furnished with a curriculum that responded to the priorities of the age.

Mbiti published two works in *Transition* during those years. His second poem, "The Snake Song," went as follows:

> I have neither legs nor arms
> But I walk on my belly
> And I have
> Venom, venom, venom!
>
> I have neither bows nor guns
> But I flash fast my tongue
> And I have
> Venon, venom, venom!
>
> I have neither radar nor missiles
> But I stare with my eyes
> And I have
> Venom, venom, venom![8]

There is a lovely creativity about this poem. Here Mbiti felt free to experiment, try on authorial voices that were not his own, and invest unlikely characters with voice and meaning. It must have been a source of wonder and enjoyment at a time when so much serious work had to be done.

Professor Mbiti published his *African Religions and Philosophy* in 1969.[9] The book was composed to fulfill Mbiti's obligations to an academic discipline that was, under his stewardship, coming into view. Here there was no space for experimentation with literary voice. He wrote it as a course of lectures on African religions, the first of its kind in Makerere's curriculum. The book laid out, in chapter after chapter, a systematic theology for African traditional religion. Their outward diversity notwithstanding, Mbiti argued, African religions shared an underlying structure: a veneration for the divine, a sacred sensibility, rituals, an awareness of evil, an account of creation. The book was a work of huge ambition, a powerful argument for the intellectual integrity of a religious system.

In his own time Mbiti's account of traditional religion was subject to a scathing criticism from his colleague, the anthropologist and poet Okot p'Bitek, whose *African Religions in Western Scholarship* was published in 1970.[10] Okot argued that Mbiti and other scholars had forced the changeable dynamics of African religious practice into the foreign categories of western theology. "The African deities of these books, clothed with the attributes of the Christian God, are, in the main, creations of the students of African religions," he wrote.[11] Mbiti surely knew of Okot's criticism, but he chose to make no public response.[12] The same year that Okot's criticism was published Mbiti brought out his second book, *Concepts of God in Africa*.[13] The book was based on the premise—as stated by Mbiti—that "there is but One Supreme God." For Mbiti it was essential that African religions be grasped systematically. In Kampala, he offered regular lectures to Anglican priests-in-training on the subject "Traditional Religion and Christianity." His scholarly work was an aspect of his larger vocation: he was opening up paths of comparison and dialogue between Christianity and African religions.

REGULATING CULTURAL LIFE

In January 1971 General Amin overthrew Milton Obote and became president of the Second Republic of Uganda. Amin came to power at the head of what he called a "government of action." Matters that had formerly stood outside government's attention were, quite suddenly, targeted. Programs of action were launched to address hitherto unremarkable issues. Everywhere there were campaigns, as ordinary people were drafted to serve in projects conceived at the center. The Keep Uganda Clean campaign, launched in 1973, was meant to cleanse Uganda both of dirt and of moral turpitude. The penal code was rewritten, making it a criminal offense to beg for alms, play games of chance in public, or behave in a "disorderly or indecent manner in any public place."[14] Ugandans were obliged to clean up city streets on a mandated schedule. Meanwhile, the Double Production campaign, launched in 1971, required farmers to dramatically expand the scale of their cultivation. The campaign's advocates saw themselves as clear-sighted pioneers, manfully pushing Uganda's agriculture forward. "We are now engaged in a dynamic programme to ensure that the standard of living for our people in the countryside is improved," wrote one local government officer. "We have the land and the brains. What we need now is determination and will power. CHESTS FORWARD, HEADS UP AND MOVE STRAIGHT TO THE FARMER."[15]

There was particularly urgent work to do in the domain of culture and religion. The call for cultural recovery was widely articulated across the African continent in the 1970s. It was the decade of *authenticité*, the ideology of cultural self-assertion propounded by the dictator of Zaire, Mobutu Sese Seko. Zairians adopted new African names to replace European names; and European attire was discouraged in favor of authentically African styles.[16]

Mobutu's cultural program attracted interest and support in Uganda. "The Europeans came with their intention to confuse the masses they were leading. They wanted to feel great and superior by getting Africans to accept their names," wrote an editorialist in the *Voice of Uganda*. "What is wrong with calling yourself Rubanga, Twenomujuni, Mirembe etc.?"[17] In 1972 the Amin government summarily banned the wearing of miniskirts. The matter had been discussed at the highest levels. At an early meeting of Amin's cabinet the minister of culture and community development warned that miniskirts had "spread throughout the country very fast to the extent of threatening or even signaling the extinction of our National dresses. These dresses are a source of scandal, they encourage crime and they are not in the interest of our culture."[18] Shortly after miniskirts were banned, the Amin government prohibited the growing of bushy beards and the wearing of long hair by men. Government blamed "foreign hippies" for all manner of criminal behavior, including printing counterfeit money, kidnapping, and assassination.[19] In 1974 the president banned the wearing of wigs. The wigs that Ugandan women craved, said President Amin, were "made by the callous imperialists from human hair mainly collected from the unfortunate victims of the miserable Vietnam war." They made "our women look unAfrican and artificial."[20]

It was the role of government bureaucrats to ensure that the struggle against colonial culture was fought and won. New departments, new ministries, and new bureaucracies came, quite suddenly, into being. They claimed the custodianship of categories of people and arenas of cultural life that had never before been subject to regulation. In every district, county, and parish the Amin government established "culture committees" to carry out the work of preservation. "We cannot afford to watch our Culture rot or die a gradual death when we ourselves are able people," a culture officer in the west of the county told an audience in 1971.[21] Each committee was to be chaired by the local chief; the vice-chair was to be an "elderly and influential person who has an interest in cultural affairs."[22]

The space for improvisation was strictly constrained. Under government oversight cultural practices were made into routines that could be practiced and mastered. Everywhere there were inventories, standards, and routines. In 1972 the culture officer in southern Uganda prepared an assessment of the dancing traditions of Kigezi and Ankole Districts.[23] The report began with "Kikiga" dance, the tradition of the "Bakiga tribes." The dance was said to vary in instrumentation and melody in different parts of the district, but "what is in common is that it is danced by jumping and hitting the group very hard with one's feet." It was important to be exact, to bring the performance up to standard. In 1977 government sent out a team to carry out training programs in Uganda's remote provinces.[24] The aim was to improve the standard of local dancing groups, to "show that the nation is determined not to lose such an important aspect of our culture." The Heart Beat of Africa—Uganda's national dance troupe—was revived in 1974, when the troupe's artistic director toured the country selecting leading dancers from each district.[25] Once recruited, the fifty dancers took up residence in Kampala, where they were trained in the standardized repertoire: from Acholi, the Otole, Bwola, and Araka-Oraka dances; from Kigezi, the Intole, Batwa, and Katiguriro dances; from Bugisu, the Imbalu, Mwaga, and Ifumbo dances.[26]

Traditional music was likewise subject to regimentation and oversight. The Ministry of Education introduced "African Traditional Folk Songs" into the repertoire for school music festivals in 1973. The guidelines given to adjudicators set out the criteria: performers were evaluated according to "tone (appropriate, traditional tone)," "diction and rhythm (time keeping, freedom, steadiness)," "costume," and "authenticity."[27] Within a year the composer Cosma Warugaba had written a series of short operas, plays, and songbooks for sale to music teachers. Warugaba reminded educators that "it is you, and no other, to promote, improve, and propagate your own culture. Your music is just as good as any other and can be used, with pride, in churches, concert halls, dance halls, at international gatherings etc." His song book was eighty pages long and featured sixteen tunes.[28]

In this way dance, music, and other performance traditions were remodeled and made into routines. They could furnish the elements of a national curriculum. In 1971 Uganda Television launched a new program titled *Our Heritage,* which was meant to display "cultural dances, indigenous handcrafts, indigenous customary ceremonies, traditional music etc." Each district was invited to select three indigenous dances to be televised, and performers were to wear "uniform costumes."[29] At regular intervals culture officers organized seminars to tutor local performers on the elements of Uganda's standard dances. A 1978 seminar for cultural leaders promised to "embrace all aspects of our culture, i.e. drama, music, story telling, and carving." A substantial part of the conference was spent on the "improvement of our dances," and there were instructors from the Heart Beat of Africa troupe on hand to offer direction.[30]

That is what Amin's war against colonial culture entailed: the creation of new bureaucracies to coordinate the production of traditional culture. That is how performance genres got defined, how dance and music were lifted out of the dynamic world and rendered into routines, how human creativity was hemmed in by rules and standards. It was also how some people became experts, authorities in their field.

REGULATING RELIGION

At the time Amin came to power, Mbiti was professor and head of the Department of Religion at Makerere University. A scant two weeks after the coup, President Amin's secretary wrote to Mbiti and other church leaders to ask for their views on a new initiative: a Ministry of Religious Affairs, with political and administrative powers over religious organizations. "What field of responsibility would the Ministry or Department cover in relation to religious affairs?" the secretary asked. "Do you seriously think that there is a need for such a Ministry?"[31]

Mbiti was thrilled at the prospect. In six typed pages he laid out, in numbered paragraphs, a series of justifications for government supervision over religious life.[32] Uganda had known too much religious conflict, Mbiti wrote. "Some of the conflicts took on political forms, others tribal, some even had backing from outside countries." The new ministry would reduce conflict between religions through "reconciliation, mediation, or even the use of governmental powers." Moreover it would allow for easier coordination between different service agencies. While universities could enable dialogue in small-scale settings, "the practical meaning of dialogue would best be achieved under governmental initiative, supervision, and encouragement." There were organizational reasons for the new bureaucracy, too: Mbiti hoped it might provide accountants for parishes struggling with their finances.

The most remarkable part of Professor Mbiti's letter came under point 10, where he set out a theological rationale for the government of religious life. "African traditional life does not have a division between 'secular' and 'sacred', between what is religious and what is not," he argued. "The division of life into 'religious' and 'secular' compartments was imported into Africa from Europe" under colonial government. Mbiti argued that "this division has greatly undermined and ignored a basic African philosophy in which the universe and the whole of life are conceived religiously, and in which the spiritual realities and physical realities are only two dimensions of the same basic concept of existence." Mbiti was cribbing—almost word for word—from his 1969 book *African Religions and Philosophy*.[33] It is "unnatural for African people to be made to live this divided life," he wrote in his letter to Amin, "and we have to safeguard against such a division." Europe and America had already paid the price for their secularism: the evidence could be seen in the "rebellion of their young people against authority, tradition, and so on."

Professor Mbiti was confident that Amin's government could mend the division between the sacred and the secular. The new Department of Religious Affairs would be a concrete symbol and expression of the basic African philosophy which sees the whole of life as a deeply religious experience. In setting up this ministry, Uganda would be reasserting a profoundly African heritage which our colonial past has eclipsed and in many ways undermined seriously. . . . [It would] be an exciting platform where the religious heritage, values, commitments and sacrifices of the different religious traditions can be pooled together and better utilized for the good of the nation.

That is where Mbiti's religious thought led him. Working from a theological position that asserted that African religions were—or ought to be—unified in their consonance with ancestral tradition, Mbiti saw in Amin's administration a vehicle by which to bring dissension, argument, and debate to an end. Here was an opportunity for unification.

Mbiti had reason to be worried about Christian unity. The Anglican Church—called the Church of Uganda—was in those tumultuous days consumed by a vexing and divisive argument over ethnicity.[34] The nub of the dispute was Namirembe Cathedral, at the historic center of the kingdom of Buganda. Buganda was in colonial times the foremost Anglican society in Africa. Its ruling aristocracy—who controlled most of the kingdom's best land—were Anglicans, and the cathedral at Namirembe had been built in the early twentieth century through their exertions.[35] In 1966 Prime Minister Milton Obote—determined to build up power in his own hands—had sent in the army to crush the king's palace. Thereafter the kingdom was abolished. That very year, as the Buganda kingdom met its political demise, the Church of Uganda enthroned a new archbishop, the first African to occupy the position. He was Rev. Erica Sabiti, from Ankole, in southwest Uganda. For Christians of Buganda the imposition of a cultural outsider as their bishop was a source of alarm. "Buganda has been oppressed too much and has suffered so terribly, both politically and now in the Church they helped to build, maintain, and undeniably spread throughout Uganda," wrote a clergyman in a panicked letter.[36] Buganda's ruler, the kabaka, had been sent into an ignominious exile by President Obote. For Ganda Anglicans the elevation of Archbishop Sabiti was a further form of cultural and political degradation. Buganda had "struggled for years to retain her identity through her unselfish services, hospitality, [and] the missionary spirit and zeal," wrote the clergyman. Sabiti's election as bishop undermined this historical legacy. "The other members of our church outside Buganda are slowly but steadily converging on Buganda to swallow it up," he wrote. "This is not the fair reward of our grandparents' sacrifices."

The tensions dividing the Church of Uganda were at the forefront of public life when Amin came to power. On January 23, 1971—two days before the coup—the diocese of Namirembe had resolved to secede from the rest of the Church of Uganda; and on January 31—six days after the coup—Bishop Sabiti was forcibly turned away from the cathedral. Fliers were circulated around Kampala condemning the archbishop; and Sabiti's representative was blocked from entering Namugongo, where clergy where celebrating Uganda Martyr's Day.[37] Early in March Amin's government organized the repatriation of the remains of Mutesa, Buganda's king, who had died in exile in London. The body was laid in state at Namirembe Cathedral. Bishop Sabiti had to ask President Amin for security guards in order to attend the service. He told Amin that he had received several letters "threatening to fall on me and knock me down and trample me to death."[38]

The Amin government established the Department of Religious Affairs in April 1971. Its secretary, Mr. Ntende, had his office in the western wing of the Parliament building. Ntende's first act was to organize a conference to iron out differences within the Church of Uganda. It was convened in Kabale, in southern Uganda, in May. President Amin dedicated his opening speech to emphasizing the need for unity. "This government believes that religion must be a source of togetherness—that kind of unity and fraternity must pervade not just the limits of the ranks of those who believe that religion, but also embrace all peoples," he said.[39] Uganda's army—by bringing Amin to power—had "set the stage" for a "permanent return to a sense of Unity, Liberty and Freedom in Uganda." It was the responsibility of leaders in government and in the church to "ensure that all Ugandans are truly united."[40] Bishop Sabiti agreed: in his opening remarks he assured the president that "religion has a vital role to play in the creation of stable conditions so that men and women might have an opportunity to enjoy life to the fullest."[41]

Over the course of Amin's first year in office Uganda's government organized, funded, and hosted several conferences meant to resolve the divisions in the Church of Uganda. It was President Amin's abiding preoccupation. Matters came to a head in the last days of November 1971, when the Anglican Diocese in west Buganda announced that it intended to secede from the Church of Uganda to form its own, independent Anglican church.[42] Four days later the diocese of Namirembe—at the very center of the Buganda kingdom—announced its intention join the secession. The day following these announcements, President Amin called all of the Church of Uganda bishops and their diocesan councils to Kampala. They convened in the International Conference Centre. President Amin's cabinet ministers were in attendance. "My sorrow knows no bounds," Amin told the bishops in his opening remarks.[43] "If these two dioceses were allowed to separate, there might be a further break up into small, ineffective units.... It could have very harmful and great effects in the unity of this country." It was a "tremendous security risk." Amin accused the bishop of Namirembe—Dunstan Nsubuga—of "showing utter contempt to me personally and his attitude, and that of his supporters, is close to that of a traitor." He threatened to evict Nsubuga from Namirembe Cathedral.

The churchmen got the message. The administrator who took notes reported that Amin had "made it clear that there must be an end to all nonsense of secession and to the confusing of Christians in the country."[44] The following day the bishops of the Church of Uganda resolved their disagreement. Namirembe Cathedral was to be independent of any diocese; and both Archbishop Sabiti and Namirembe's bishop would have their thrones there. Mr. Ntende—the government's secretary of religious affairs—thought "it would be the understatement of the year if I said that I am overwhelmed" by the positive outcome of the conference.[45] Archbishop Sabiti described what had happened in that conference hall as a religious awakening. "Walls of division were collapsing, feelings of hatred, anger and suspicion were being replaced by love and trust, smiles replaced hardness in people's hearts, hands were waved in joy across the hall," he hymned.[46] It was a decidedly rosy account of a meeting that had been—by all indications—extraordinarily tense.

The Amin government's project of religious unification was thereby welded to the consolidation of political life. Here was a new bureaucracy—the Department of Religious Affairs—that was empowered to monitor religious organizations and suppress conflict. It was one of a number of new government bodies that worked to regulate and control cultural life, buttress hierarchies of authority, suppress deviance and dissidence, and impose unity.

IMPOSING ORDER

The imposition of order within the Christian church went hand in hand with the persecution of opposition. Churches and religious bodies that espoused idiosyncrasy and charisma were rendered illegal, and religious life was forcibly consolidated under government supervision.[47]

The Uganda government's campaign against religious dissent was by no means new. Colonial Uganda was built upon the administrative architecture of the Buganda kingdom, and in the early twentieth century Anglican and Catholic administrators from Buganda had gone out to newly conquered provinces to set up local governments on behalf of the British.[48] Proud Ganda chiefs regarded unorthodox Christian churches with suspicion. In the 1910s and 1920s the Anglican establishment had been horrified by the "Church of God Who Can Do All Things." The new church's members regarded disease as an act of providence and refused to take medicine. In 1929 the dissident church was forcibly suppressed by the Buganda establishment, and its leaders were sent into exile.[49] By 1957 colonial officials were convinced that "small missionary sects," especially those led by Americans, were dangerous: their leadership was uncertain, and African Christians were given undue powers over the leadership of the church.[50] In 1961 the Anglican bishop warned government about Canadian missionaries who had set up a tent at Makerere, holding open-air services attended by hundreds of people. They claimed to be able to cure blindness and other afflictions. "We have quite enough with the Roman Catholics and Moslems here," wrote Uganda's governor, "and don't want any other sects, especially of the American hot-gospel variety."[51]

Why did colonial authorities—and, later, the leaders of postcolonial Uganda—regard charismatic Christianity with suspicion? Evangelical and charismatic Christianity posed a mortal challenge to the architecture of government. Converts unsettled the hierarchies of families, communities, and polities. They pushed against the geographic enclosures and social routines that organized public life, challenging orthodoxies in the social order. In 1960 a man named Kener Koular—an employee of the weaving department at a textile company—wrote to Uganda's governor reporting that he had personally composed a new edition of the Christian Bible.[52] Mr. Koular's new Bible encouraged readers to "adopt a form of government more suitable to Uganda and which will be the best of all governments in Africa." He also hoped to "create new kinds of work which have not been done anywhere in African states like Sudan, Congo Nigeria. . . . this will bring Uganda to the top in every respect—wisdom, method of working, economy and politics." It is not clear what Koular's revised Bible consisted of. A government official who met with him reported Koular possessed "several names of his own imagining," and the Bible he had composed contained "very strange illustrations."[53] Koular had made several copies, handwritten, for distribution. The official reported that the passages he had seen contained attacks on the senior management at the company where he worked.

Koular was one of a great number of people who pursued idiosyncratic or partisan ways of engaging with the Bible. In his recomposition of Christian texts he found means of challenging managerial authority over technology and time. Other charismatic thinkers found in their expansive Christianity a license to conceive of an altogether new polity. On October 20, 1963, at 7:30 P.M., a young man named John Egesa was coming from a service at a Catholic church when an angel appeared, bathed in light and standing ten feet from the ground.[54] The angel gave Egesa and his friend a document—fifteen chapters long—that revealed the existence of a "lost country" called Eligonea. The angel instructed Egesa and his colleague to take the message to Ugandan prime minister Obote, Julius Nyerere—the president of Tanzania—and to the Catholic archbishops of Uganda and Tanzania. Egesa had tried several times to see Milton Obote, but on every occasion his request had been refused. According to Egesa, the angel Gabriel himself had sought an audience with government officials: he visited Sudan, Congo, Kenya, and South Rhodesia, carrying news of the newly uncovered land. Thereafter he went to Obote's office, then to the director of planning and housing, the Central Police Station, and the Ministry of Internal Affairs. Everywhere he was turned away. At the request of a government officer—who had been assigned to look into the matter—Egesa typed up a report on these events and titled it "A Direct Miracle from a Spirit who Claimed to be an Angel." The dutiful official concluded that "the alleged story appears to be an imaginary one."[55] But Egesa was insistent: he had in his possession a sealed envelope that, he said, could only be opened in the presence of Obote, Nyerere, and several bishops.

For Egesa and Koular—as for others working within this expansive, charismatic, idiosyncratic tradition of Christian life—the canon was not closed. It could be amended, rewritten, translated, or added to. That is what they both were doing: bringing new texts to light, expanding what could be said and imagined on the basis of Christian scripture. In the years right around Uganda's independence, there was a proliferation of new Bibles and a multiplication of angels. Even as African politicians gained control over the instruments of governance, people like Egesa were pushing at the geographical boundaries that defined new states. With the angel Gabriel leading the way, Egesa was disinvesting from the locality in which he lived. His was a pan-African Christianity, a Christianity that was directed toward another homeland, wherever it was.

For orthodox believers this expansive, deterritorialized Christianity was offensive. It rubbed against the attachments—to ancestry, to family, to convention, to locality—that conventional religions valued. Many nonconformists severed their connections with kith and kin. They saw themselves as sojourners, citizens of another world, disconnected from their obligations to relatives. Others fastened whole ways of life on idiosyncratic readings of the Bible.[56] All of this activity horrified defenders of tradition and custom. Their patriotic efforts to protect kith and kin were the impetus for conservative reform. Family life, that is, was the forum where the social dangers of non-conformity were made clear. Family life—the place where intimate relations were tested, strained, and broken—was also the engine for the production of outrage.

That is why the government of Amin came to regard Pentecostals and other religious nonconformists as enemies of good order. In May 1972 a man named Paul Kadoma wrote to the Indian religious teacher Charan Singh to complain that his wife had "unilaterally decided to break my family so as to follow your religion irrespective of what may befall the children."[57] Singh was the head of a religious organization—called the Radha Soami Satsang Beas—based in Lahore.[58] Under the influence of Singh's disciples, Mr. Kadoma's wife had become a vegetarian. For Mr. Kadoma it undermined culture itself. "Meat is a staple food here," he argued, and "eating it is very much serious in my country. . . . You can imagine the feeling and gravity of this situation." Two weeks later Mr. Kadoma—increasingly incensed about his vegetarian wife—wrote to an Anglican priest describing how Singh's disciples had been passing "confusing books and teachings" to his wife.[59] Singh's disciples had threatened to kill him by magic, and, he said, "I am now living a miserable life with my children while my wife is being paraded everywhere by these people." He was sure that Singh's followers possessed a "special magic to hypnotize or attract people they want."

At the end of June 1972 Mr. Kadoma—convinced that his wife was "3 / 4 mad"—wrote to Amin to ask him to make the Radha Soami Satsang Beas illegal in Uganda.[60] The "unity, love, respect and freedom of our families have been very much interfered with by confusing agents" of Singh's religion, he complained, for "they have no respect for families let alone husbands." Under the influence of drugs, women who joined Singh's disciples "appear to be hypnotized and they become stubborn, unruly, half mad, and disrespectful to whatever the husband might advise." Women who followed Singh would "leave their homes on Sunday in the morning against the wish of the husbands and . . . return home late any time they please." Kadoma insisted that Radha Soami Satsang Bear presented an existential threat to civil and political order: if the religion were not banned immediately, Uganda would "face the same situation as Zambia," where the rebellious church of Alice Lenshina had mounted an insurrection against the government.[61] He wanted this "alien religion banned before it brings bloodshed and destroys our cherished families beyond repair."

Kadoma was uniquely extravagant in his paranoia about his wife's vegetarianism, but his anxiety was shared by many men and women who found themselves confronting relatives who refused to play their part in the performance of family duty. Dissident converts—whether to an aesthetic Hindu tradition or to evangelical Christianity—disregarded the obligations that custom and tradition imposed, challenging husbands' and fathers' control over their time, labor, and loyalty.

I am not certain that Amin read Kadoma's letters. I do know that he—like the political leaders who came before him—thought religious idiosyncrasy was dangerous. Amin was perplexed by the fissiparous nature of Christian leadership: over the course of his first years in office he had long conversations with Bishop Sabiti, asking why Christians parceled themselves into small groups.[62] In 1973 government outlawed several religious denominations that were thought to be inimical to good order. Among them were the United Pentecostal Churches, the Jehovah's Witnesses, Legio Maria, and the Pentecostal Assemblies of God.[63] In 1975 the list was expanded to include the Quakers and several evangelical organizations based in America.[64] And in 1977 twenty-seven religious organizations were banned, among them the Baha'is, the Baptists, the Holy Ghost Church of East Africa, the Dini ya Roho, and the Nomiya Luo Church.[65] Their buildings were seized by government, and their leaders were forbidden to preach or carry out services.

By the late 1970s the religious field had been consolidated under the management of three institutions: the Anglican Church, the Catholic Church, and the Muslim Supreme Council. All of this was full of violence, as people of conviction were made to bend the knee to government mandates. The Deliverance Church, for instance, had been founded by a small group of charismatic preachers in 1971. They were noisy and demonstrative. "The time is drawing nearer and nearer to His second coming and we must compel people to enter the kingdom of God while there is still time," wrote their leader. "Let us paint for them a horrible picture of hell so that we wanted them of the danger of rejecting the Lord Jesus."[66] The church's musical ensemble was called the "Explosion Choir." In April 1978 Uganda's vice president heard the noisy congregation at worship and ordered the church disbanded. Amin's men shot up the building and interned 200 people who had gathered there. The congregants were held in the cells of the notorious State Research Bureau, where they were beaten and tortured for two months.[67]

More often the consolidation of religious life was unspectacular and mundane. There were bureaucratic questions to resolve. The foreclosure of so many churches left hundreds of buildings unoccupied. Local government authorities took custody of these buildings and allocated them to organizations that could claim them for the public interest. All of this change required a great amount of wrangling. In Bwera, on the border with Congo, the Seventh-Day Adventists had built an impressive center: there was a church building, a school, houses for teachers and for the pastors, and a great amount of equipment. After the Adventist Church was banned in 1977, local authorities deliberated for months over the disposition of the buildings. The pastor and his family stayed in the parish house, looking after the church buildings and—after dark—convening clandestine services in the bush for church members.[68] Matters came to a head in February 1978, when the government chief arrived at the church and gave the pastor fourteen days to vacate the premises. He told the pastor that "his private worship had been reported and was known to the CID, the State Research Bureau and the Intelligence sections."[69] It was a dire warning. The pastor hastily handed over the keys to the buildings.

For the leadership of the established churches—the Anglicans in particular—all of this upheaval presented an opportunity for expansion. In the months following the closure of Pentecostal and evangelical churches Bishop Sabiti carried on a campaign to persuade their members and their leadership to join the Anglican Church. "We have the same Bible, the same savior and we are admitted into his church through baptism by water," he told the bishop of one of the banned churches. "Why don't we ignore the other small differences and come together?"[70] Several Protestant churches did, in fact, come into the Anglican Church in those years. "Instead of going on celebrating anniversaries for this church or for that church, there is one church of the Lord and that is the church of the saved people," Sabiti told the leader of a banned denomination.[71]

Here was a new regime of governance. Everywhere new bureaucracies were springing up to manage, regulate, and control the dynamics of cultural life. In religious life, too, there were new managers. The Amin government sublet the oversight of dissident and nonconformist Christianity to establishment churches. For Anglicans like Bishop Sabiti it was an occasion for ecumenism. Even as dissident churches were being forcibly suppressed and rendered illegal, the theology of ecumenical solidarity enjoyed a newfound relevance in Christian life.[72]

CHURCH AND STATE

In the archives of the Church of Uganda there is a file full of scraps of paper.[73] On each of them there is a numbered list of names. They are the names of Anglicans who were murdered by Amin's men. Each of the lists is headed with the name of the diocese from which the deceased came. None of the lists are typed, and each is written in a different hand. They appear to have been jotted down toward the middle of 1979, a few months after Amin's government was overthrown. Were the lists composed to furnish material for a memorial project? Or—as seems likely—were they created at the spur of the moment, as a group of Christians talked about loved ones they had lost? Were they an aide-mémoire for a priest leading in prayer?

In the week immediately following the coup that brought Amin to power there was a pogrom in the army, as soldiers from Lango—Milton Obote's home area—were singled out and subjected to awful violence. A newspaper reporter who toured the barracks heard that Amin had ordered the execution of Langi soldiers holding a rank above corporal.[74] In Gulu, where the Uganda air force was headquartered, the reporter estimated that 100 soldiers were killed; in Kampala 114 soldiers were executed. In April Archbishop Sabiti and other Anglican bishops had lodged a protest with President Amin against these indiscriminate killings. Two army chaplains had disappeared, and "many people have been killed, many are missing, many are in fear of death, and many others are in detention," wrote the bishops.[75] "We beg you to consider what is happening in the country and use your authority to put a stop to what we believe to be an evil in the sight of God." They asked Amin's government to publish the names of people detained in custody and to make investigations into the many deaths.

Over the course of the 1970s a great many people died, far more than those listed on the papers in the church archives. Among the most eminent of them was Erica Sabiti's successor, Archbishop Janani Luwum. At a show trial convened in February 1977 Luwum was accused—falsely—of plotting to import weapons and overthrow Amin's government. He was tortured and murdered later that day.[76] In the wake of the archbishop's murder, government officials were quick to call comity between church and state. The district commissioner in one provincial town noted that "the mass had developed fear of attending church services [and instead were] exiling themselves and starting spreading rumours against their motherland." He advised priests of the church to "concentrate on preaching the word of God, pray for peace rather than dangerous weapons."[77] Later that year one of Uganda's most autocratic officials spoke before an Anglican audience. "Let the church become instrumental in the development of nations," he said. "Let division be a background to help the government mould people into good citizens."[78]

What did Christians hear in government officials' calls for unity and solidarity? Even in the wake of the archbishop's murder—even at a time when thousands of people were being imprisoned, tortured, and murdered— there were reasons for optimism. Even after the cataclysmic events of 1977, some high-minded people saw in Amin's regime an opportunity to suppress the petty divisions and antagonisms that partitioned religious life.

Eighteen months after the archbishop's death an Anglican priest in western Uganda opened up a colloquy with a government official named Cypriano Mutahigwa. Mutahigwa was a person of consequence in local life. In colonial times he had been a member of a committee that promoted literature in the Rutooro language; in the 1960s he had served Milton Obote's government as a chief. By 1978—when the parish priest wrote to him— he was an assistant district commissioner in the government of Amin. The priest was sure that "all governing authorities were instituted by God," but it seemed to him that Mutahigwa was uniquely determined, as the priest put it, to "develop the spiritual realm, as this obviously has been a source for your being and all that you have."[79] Mutahigwa responded by laying out a theological justification for government work. If a "Christian society is to be effective in faith," there must be "true and brotherly cooperation" among its leaders, he wrote. God

> offers to us the possibility of bringing about the required significant mutual esteem, respect and love of one another; and thus reproducing Christ's image in society we are leading rather than demonstrating unnecessary separation and disregard. In so doing, we render a valuable spiritual and social health to our country by assisting it to achieve the goals of a perfect society. . . . If we want progress and faith to continue among our people of God we are leading, separation should be stamped out in the strongest terms, but truly united in Christ.[80]

I have no reason to think that either Cypriano Mutahigwa or the priest were insincere. Their theological thinking was animated by a sincere sense of possibility. At a time when—for many people—public life was full of terror and death, Mutahigwa could imagine a "perfect society," where government and church worked in harmonious concord to reproduce Christ's image in the social order. Like other earnest people, he could find theologically sound reasons to promote a close relationship between church and state. Here there were no grounds for suspicion, for resistance, or for dissent.

That very year the Amin government had launched a nationwide campaign to raise funds for the construction of a new high-rise building—called Church House—in Kampala. It was occasioned by the centenary of Anglican missionaries' arrival in Uganda. The government bureaucracy was put in the service of the fundraising campaign, and officials were given the task of collecting funds from businesses and civic organizations in their localities.

Each province was given a financial target to meet. An array of unlikely organizations were dragooned to contribute. In one province the Uganda Revenue Authority, a dairy farm, an oil company, several tea estates, and the Muslim community made donations.[81] The Catholic Diocese was likewise obliged to contribute.[82] In another place fundraisers encouraged donations by organizing a tug-of-war between Anglican clergymen and officials of local government.[83] The culminating event in the fundraising campaign came in September, when representatives of all of these organizations were obliged to appear at the Anglican cathedral to present their offerings.

Church House was not actually built during the presidency of Amin. The building—now named Janani Luwum Church House—was completed in 2018 and opened in a public ceremony involving Uganda's prime minister.[84] It is a sixteen-story high-rise, positioned in the center of the city. The building is an enduring monument to the murdered archbishop. It is also a memorial to an enduring alliance. The financial beginnings for the building lie in the months immediately following Archbishop Luwum's murder, when Amin's government mobilized Ugandans to contribute toward its construction. The campaign was, surely, an apology, a political strategy to palliate the outrage that many people felt. It was also a sincere work of theological justification, growing out of the historical alliance between the Uganda government and the Anglican Church. Even in those dark and dangerous years, it was possible for some earnest Christians to see that Amin's government was working toward the perfection of the social order.

READING JOHN MBITI

In those vexed and dangerous days a great many Makerere scholars left Uganda, seeking refuge in other places. The eminent political scientist Ali Mazrui fled to my institution, the University of Michigan, where he was to become a leading interpreter of African and African American history. Mbiti remained at his post in Makerere. In 1971 he published *New Testament Eschatology in an African Background,* and in the years that followed he brought out several other works: translations of *African Religions and Philosophy* in French and German; an edition of the inaugural lecture he gave when he was made professor; a book about love and marriage; and another about prayer and African religion.[85] The early years of Amin's regime were the most productive phase of Mbiti's scholarly career.

Academic vocations have their own momentum. Even as the world around him fell apart, Mbiti continued to pursue his scholarly program. In the first months of 1973 Mbiti gave a series of lectures at universities and seminaries in the United States. In none of the several lectures did Mbiti speak about Amin, about the campaign against Pentecostals and other evangelical Christians, or about the people who had died in the hands of the Ugandan state. It must have been a conscious strategy. Everywhere he spoke about the happy convergence between Christianity and African tradition. "Christianity and traditional African religion are in accord in many areas," he told an audience in Pittsburgh. "Churches are developing their own sense of independent judgment and control."[86] Early in May he was at the San Francisco Theological Seminary. "Christianity, from ancient orthodox forms to nouveau workshop based on spontaneity and exuberance, is thriving in Africa," he told the audience. African heritage "really prepared the groundwork for the Christian message to be heard and accepted."

This outpouring of theological writing supplied material for a curriculum that Prof. Mbiti and other members of the Department of Religious Studies and Philosophy launched in those years. There was a traveling seminar—called the "Seminar on Religion and Culture in Africa"—organized through Makerere's extramural education unit and convened in several provinces around Uganda.[87] The aim, wrote one of the tutors, was to "address itself to the African traditional religious beliefs and practices and their impact on and interactions with Revealed Religions, namely Christianity and Islam." The curriculum took up different aspects of the scholarly work in which Prof. Mbiti was engaged. There was a unit "African Concepts of God," derived from the book that Prof. Mbiti had published in 1970.[88] There was another unit "Spirits and the Spirit World in Africa"; and a third, "The Meeting of Christianity with African Religion and Culture." In the places where it was convened, government officials shared the platform with Makerere lecturers. There was much about religious life on which they could agree. "A true African can never imagine life without God," the curriculum averred. The curriculum was an expansion on the foundational work that Professor Mbiti was doing to define the elements of religion that were shared across Uganda's disparate religious landscape.

On March 4, 1974, the Libyan dictator Muammar Gaddafi made a state visit to Uganda. A crowd of several thousand people greeted him at the airport, and Amin called him the "most revolutionary leader in the world."[89] Over the course of three days Gaddafi spoke before large audiences, calling on Uganda's Muslims to seize the opportunity that was before them. The time had come to spread Islam to every part of the world, he said. There was "no doubt that God wanted Islam to progress in Uganda because he had chosen a dynamic leader like General Amin to lead the people."[90] "If you do this,"

Gaddafi said, "I assure you that we in Libya will stand by you and support you." At a private meeting Gaddafi asked Amin's Christian cabinet ministers to leave the room, then presented Amin with a written agreement. It was a promissory note, obligating Amin to eliminate Christianity from Uganda. Amin refused to sign. Later, he told his cabinet ministers about the offer that Gaddafi had made.[91]

Shortly after Gaddafi's departure Professor Mbiti delivered a sermon before a packed audience at the chapel of Makerere University. Had he heard news of Gaddafi's plan to turn Uganda into an Islamic state? His sermon was a refutation of Gaddafi's religious program. "Christianity and Africa have fallen in love with each other, and intend to live in the bonds of a lifelong marriage," he said. "Christianity is here to stay."[92] The sermon was an act of great courage. It made Mbiti into a target of Amin's men. Later that month Professor Mbiti—doubtless fearing for his life—left Uganda. On March 31 he was in California, where he spoke at the University of the Redlands.[93] Thereafter he moved to Geneva and took up the directorship of the Ecumenical Institute of the World Council of Churches. He was to spend the remainder of his life in Switzerland.

The first essay that Professor Mbiti wrote after coming to Geneva, titled "The Future of Christianity in Africa," came out in 1978.[94] It was sunnily optimistic. A great many "prophets of doom have spoken about either a complete extinction of Christianity in Africa or a substantial reduction of its presence there," wrote Mbiti. In fact the religion was growing at a rapid pace—5 percent per year. He attributed this rate of growth to the new liberties of independent Africa, for the end of colonialism had "restored human dignity to African peoples both in secular life and the Church." Mbiti lamented the many divisions among African Christians. He was sure that the "Church is disfigured by these divisions, which constitute a real insult to our Lord Jesus Christ." But he applauded the growing "spirit of ecumenism." In many places, he noted, churches were being made to unite by African governments, "which will increasingly see denominational differences as working against national unity."

Nowhere in his essay did Mbiti write about the dangers that he had personally faced as one of the leading spokesmen for Uganda's Christianity. He did not write about Janani Luwum, archbishop of Uganda, who had died a dehumanizing death just a year before Mbiti's essay was published. Neither did he write about the bloody consequences of Amin's campaign against charismatic and evangelical churches. The African Christianity about which Mbiti wrote was a depoliticized abstraction, disconnected from the real world of conflict and terror. In a similar manner African traditional religion was abstracted out of the circumstances of its making. Forged in the context of Uganda's cultural politics of the 1960s and '70s, "African Traditional Religion" was one of an ensemble of standardized forms that helped the Amin government regiment the cultural field. Through the publications of Professor Mbiti—its leading theologian—African traditional religion made its way into the canon, where it could furnish scholars with a conceptual apparatus with which to work.

How ought we remember Mbiti? He was one of the architects of the curriculum of multiculturalism. Working from Kampala, he helped to define a whole world of ritual and thought. It is right that he should be honored and celebrated, for his work greatly enabled a more respectful, more sympathetic, and more systematic engagement between religious traditions.

And yet, in our own time, it is important to remember how quickly calls for cultural integrity can become engines for nativism and intolerance. From his lecture hall at Makerere John Mbiti conjured up a religious order in which people fit seamlessly into a theological system that governed their thought and dictated their dispositions. Mbiti's view of African religious life—as integrated, whole, and all embracing—made nonconformists seem to be opponents of good order. By drawing attention to the unity that is underneath outward diversity, Professor Mbiti's work unintentionally offered a theological framework for the Amin government's coercive program of religious consolidation.

NOTES

1. John Mbiti, *African Traditions and Philosophy* (London: Heinemann, 1969).
2. "President Kenyatta Mourns Renowned Scholar Prof. Mbiti," *Nation*, October 8, 2019.
3. Mbiti's biography appears in Jacob Olupona, "A Biographical Sketch," in *Religious Plurality in Africa: Essays in Honour of John S. Mbiti*, ed. Olupona and Sulayman S. Nyang (Berlin: de Gruyter, 1993), 1–10.
4. John Mbiti, *Mūtūnga na Ngewa Yake* (London: Thomas Nelson and Sons, 1954); Mbiti, *Kithamani kya uthwi* (Kampala: Nairobi Printers, 1955).
5. Mbiti, "Reclaiming the Vernacular Literature of the Akamba Tribe," *Présence Africaine* 24–25 (1959): 244–61.
6. Fred Welbourn, *East African Rebels* (London: SCM Press, 1961).
7. Bethwell Ogot, *History of the Southern Luo* (Nairobi: East African Publishing House, 1967).
8. John Mbiti, "The Snake Song," *Transition* 27 (1966): 49.
9. Mbiti, *African Traditions*.
10. Okot p'Bitek, *African Religions in Western Scholarship* (Kampala: East African Literature Bureau, 1970), 80.

11. Latter-day criticism has largely followed Okot's lead. See Rosalind Shaw, "The Invention of 'African Traditional Religion,'" in *Religion* 20 (1990): 339–53; Paul Landau, "'Religion' and Christian Conversion in African History: A New Model," *Journal of Religious History* 23 (1) (February 1999): 8–30; and Derek R. Peterson and Darren Walhof, eds., *The Invention of Religion: Rethinking Belief in Politics and History* (New Brunswick, NJ: Rutgers University Press, 2002).

12. Frederick Hale, "A Ugandan Critique of Western Caricatures of African Spirituality: Okot p'Bitek in Historical Context," *Journal for the Study of Religion* 21, no. 2 (2008): 19–31.

13. John Mbiti, *Concepts of God in Africa* (London: SPCK, 1970).

14. Alicia Decker, "Idi Amin's Dirty War: Subversion, Sabotage, and the Battle to Keep Uganda Clean, 1971–1979," *International Journal of African Historical Studies* 43, no. 3 (2010): 489–513.

15. Kasese DA "Boma" file, regional agriculture officer to all Saza chiefs, March 15, 1971.

16. See, among other works, Kenneth Adelman, "The Recourse to Authenticity and Negritude in Zaire," *Journal of Modern African Studies* 13, no. (1975): 134–39; and Sarah Van Beurden, *Authentically African: Arts and the Transnational Politics of Congolese Culture* (Athens: Ohio University Press, 2015).

17. Editorial letter, *Voice of Uganda* 1, no. 3 (December 5, 1972).

18. Uganda District Archives OP Confidential Collection 31/06, cabinet memorandum 119, "Mini Dresses," June 1, 1971.

19. British NA FCO 31/1234, Hyde, High Commission, to East Africa Department, July 7, 1972.

20. "Decree Bans Women's Wigs and Trousers," *Voice of Uganda* 1, no. 365 (February 5, 1974).

21. Kasese DA "Boma" file, Culture Officer, Toro, to County Chiefs, March 19, 1971.

22. Kabale DA Comm. Dev. 21, "Cultural Activities" file. John Tumusiime to all county chiefs, July 4, 1972.

23. Kabale DA Comm. Dev. 20, "Dances" file: "Brief Note on Filming in Ankole and Kigezi Districts," n.d. (but 1972).

24. Jinja DA Comm. Dev. 5, file 15, P.S., Ministry of Culture and Community Development, to all provincial governors, April 15, 1977.

25. Kabale DA Comm. Dev. 17, "Festivals and Competitions" file, meeting of culture officers, July 25, 1974.

26. Kabale DA Comm. Dev. 21, "Culture Activities" file, E. Galabuzi-Mukasa, national coordinator, to all culture officers, August 16, 1974.

27. Kabale DA Comm. Dev. 20, "Music" file, Ministry of Education, Uganda Schools Music Festival, guide for adjudicators, 1973.

28. Kabale DA "Misc." file (uncatalogued), C. Warugaba circular to head teachers, November 6, 1974.

29. Kasese DA "Boma" file, culture officer, Toro and Bunyoro, to all county chiefs, October 14, 1971.

30. Bundibugyo DA box 521, "Rural Development" file, Culture Office, Toro, Rwenzori, and Semuliki, to P.S., Ministry of Culture and Community Development, April 20, 1978.

31. Church of Uganda archives (hereafter CoU) ABP 42/4, J. Okodoi to the archbishop, Church of Uganda, February 12, 1971.

32. CoU ABP 42/4, John Mbiti to J. Okodoi, February 17, 1971.

33. Mbiti, *African Religions*, 3–4.

34. Akiiki B. Mujaju, "The Political Crisis of Church Institutions in Uganda," *African Affairs* 75, no. 298 (January 1976): 67–85.

35. Neil Kodesh, "Renovating Tradition: The Discourse of Succession in Colonial Buganda," *International Journal of African Historical Studies* 34, no. 3 (2001): 511–41; Derek R. Peterson, *Ethnic Patriotism and the East African Revival: A History of Dissent* (Cambridge: Cambridge University Press, 2012), chap. 4.

36. CoU ABP V General file 43/1, Rev. A. M. Kasozi to Amin, September 30, 1971.

37. British NA FCO 31/1066, high commissioner to East Africa Department, June 17, 1971.

38. CoU ABP 42/4, Sabiti to P.S., Office of the President, 19, March 1971.

39. CoU PS II 91/1, Speech by H. E. President Amin on the occasion of meeting the leaders of the Church of Uganda, April 26, 1971.

40. CoU Provincial Secretary II 75/3, Conference of Religious Leaders, speech by H. E. the president, May 19, 1971.

41. CoU ABP V General file 42/4, speech of welcome given by His Grace the Archbishop of Uganda to H. E. the president, May 1971.

42. CoU ABP V General File 43/1, E. Kamya, E. Sendiwala, and others to Archbishop Sabiti, November 17, 1971.

43. CoU ABP V General File 43/1, address of H. E. the president of Uganda to the bishops of the Church of Uganda, November 26, 1971.

44. CoU PS II General file 75/3, report on the Conference of Bishops and Diocesan Councils, November 29, 1971.

45. CoU PS II General file 75/3, report on the Conference of Bishops and Diocesan Councils, November 29, 1971.

46. CoU ABP V General File 43/1, Sabiti, circular letter, December 3, 1971.

47. See M. Louise Pirouet, "Religion in Uganda under Idi Amin," *Journal of Religion in Africa* 11, no. 1 (1980): 13–29.

48. Andrew Roberts, "The Sub-imperialism of Buganda," *Journal of African History* 3, no. 3 (November 1962): 435–50.

49. Derek R. Peterson, "The Politics of Transcendence in Colonial Uganda," *Past and Present* 230 (February 2016): 197–225.

50. Kabarole DA box 581, "Missions" file, P.S., Ministry of Social Services, to all permanent secretaries, May 30, 1957.

51. British NA FCO 141/18252, Leslie Brown to governor, February 7, 1961.

52. Jinja DA Community Development 3/9, Kener Koular to governor of Uganda, November 15, 1960.

53. Jinja DA Community Development 3/9, D.C. Busoga to permanent secretary, Ministry of Local Government, December 21, 1960.

54. Jinja DA ADM Complaints 13/7, John Egesa, "A Direct Miracle," n.d. (March 1965).

55. Jinja DA ADM Complaints 13/7, district commissioner, Busoga to permanent secretary, Office of the Prime Minister, April 6, 1965.

56. Derek R. Peterson, *Ethnic Patriotism and the East African Revival: A History of Dissent* (Cambridge: Cambridge University Press, 2012).

57. CoU ABP General File 59/2, P. Kadoma to Mr. Charan Singh, May 22, 1972.

58. The website of Radha Soami Satsang Beas is www.rssb.org; accessed March 18, 2020.

59. CoU ABP General File 59/3, Kadoma to Rev. John, Makindye, Kampala, June 5, 1972.

60. CoU ABP General File 59/3, Paul Kadoma to Idi Amin, June 27, 1972.

61. See David Gordon, *Invisible Agents: Spirits in a Central African History* (Athens: Ohio University Press, 2012), chap. 4 to 6.

62. CoU ABP V General file 69/5, Sabiti to Mr. S. Mungoma, September 19, 1973.

63. Kabarole DA box 382, file 2, minister of internal affairs, Penal (Unlawful Societies) Order, May 31, 1973.

64. Kabarole DA box 382, file 4, Unlawful Society Declaration order, February 21, 1975.

65. Kabarole DA box 382, file 3, D.C. Toro to all county chiefs, October 18, 1977.

66. CoU ABP General File 69/5, Stephen Mungoma, "The Challenge of the Year," n.d. (but 1975).

67. Dan Wooding and Ray Barnett, *Uganda Holocaust: They Faced Amin's Terror Machine Undaunted* (London: Pickering and Inglis, 1972), 23–32.

68. Kabarole DA box 382 folder 2, Y. Musane to D. C. Rwenzori, August 16, 1978.

69. Kabarole DA box 382 folder 2, Y. Mukirane to D. C. Rwenzori, June 27, 1978.

70. CoU ABP V General file 69/5, Sabiti to Rev. Edward Ssebowa, September 13, 1973. In an essay about Christian division in Kenya, John Mbiti argued that "denominationalism and its proliferation . . . are the product of human selfishness and weakness. . . . [However] the essentials of the Christian faith have remained intact, so that the causes and the fact of denominational division are fundamentally peripheral to, and not essential of, the Christian faith which is otherwise grounded on Jesus Christ who is himself unchangeable and indivisible." Mbiti, "Diversity, Divisions and Denominationalism," in *Kenya Churches Handbook: The Development of Kenyan Christianity*, ed. David Barrett et. al. (Kisumu, Kenya: Evangel Publishing House, 1973), 144–52.

71. CoU ABP V General file 69/5, Sabiti to S. Mungoma, September 19, 1973.

72. J. J. Carney, "The Politics of Ecumenism in Uganda, 1962–1986," *Church History* 86, no. 3 (September 2017): 765–95.

73. CoU ABP General file 27/2.

74. "The Bloody Facts of Uganda Coup," *Times of Zambia*, February 10, 1971.

75. CoU ABP V General file 42/4, Bishops of the Church of Uganda to Idi Amin, April 26, 1971.

76. Margaret Ford, *Even unto Death: The Story of Uganda Martyr Janani Luwum* (Elgin, IL: David Cook Publishing, 1978); Emmanuel Kalenzi Twesigye, "Church and State Conflicts in Uganda: President Idi Amin Kills the Anglican Archbishop," in *Religion, Conflict, and Democracy in Modern Africa: The Role of Civil Society in Political Engagement*, ed. Samuel K. Elolia (Eugene, OR: Pickwick Publications, 2012), 151–99; Zac Niringiye, *The Church in the World: A Historical-Ecclesiological Study of the Church of Uganda* (Carlisle, UK: Langham Partnership, 2016), chap. 5; Kevin Ward, "Archbishop Janani Luwum: The Dilemmas of Loyalty, Opposition and Witness in Amin's Uganda," in *Christianity and the African Imagination*, ed. David Maxwell and Ingrid Lawrie (Leiden, Netherlands: Brill, 2002), 199–224.

77. Kabarole DA box 382 file 2, Juma Aiga, address to religious leaders, February 28, 1977.

78. Kabarole DA box 382 file 2, Alex Owuor, speech on the centenary of the Church of Uganda, June 30, 1977.

79. Kabarole DA box 382, file 3, parish priest Humura to A. D. C., Kyaka District, September 12, 1978.

80. Kabarole DA box 382, file 3, Cypriano Mutahigwa to parish priest, Humura, October 25, 1978.

81. Kabarole DA box 382 file 2, governor of Western Province, list of contributors toward the construction of Church House, August 17, 1978.

82. Kabarole DA box 382, file 2, provincial executive secretary to bishop of Rwenzori, August 17, 1978.

83. Bundibugyo DA box 513, "Celebrations, Ministry of Information," file D. C. Semuliki to heads of department, May 23, 1978.

84. "Church House Handed Over to Ntagali," *New Vision*, June 14, 2018, https://www.newvision.co.ug/new_vision/news/1479703/church-house-handed-ntagali.

85. John Mbiti, *New Testament Eschatology in an African Background* (New York: Oxford University Press, 1971); Mbiti, *Love and Marriage in Africa* (London: Longman, 1973); Mbiti, "Death and the Hereafter in the Light of Christianity and African Religion: An Inaugural Lecture," Department of Religious Studies and Philosophy, Kampala, 1974; Mbiti, *The Prayers of African Religion* (London: SPCK, 1975).

86. "Christian Faith Gains in Africa with Freedom," *Pittsburgh Press*, March 22, 1973.

87. Kabarole DA box 382, file 2, P. Wangola, resident tutor, Makerere University, to governor, Western Province, April 22, 1974.

88. Mbiti, *Concepts of God in Africa* (London: SPCK, 1970).

89. "Red Carpet Welcome for Libyan Leader," *Voice of Uganda* 1, no. 388 (March 4, 1974).

90. "Libyan Leader Ends Historic Visit," *Voice of Uganda* 1, no. 390 (March 6, 1974).

91. Library and Archives of Canada, RG 25 10849 20-UGDA-1-3, vol. 6, high commissioner to Ottawa, June 4, 1975.

92. Ford, *Even unto Death*, 65–66.

93. "U of R Culture Week Starts with Speech Today," *San Bernardino County Sun*, March 28, 1974.

94. John Mbiti, "The Future of Christianity in Africa," *CrossCurrents* 28, no. 4 (Winter 1978–79): 387–94.

CHAPTER 5

"Are You Ready to Hear?"

Politics, Prophecy, and Practical Theology in Malawi

Blair D. Bertrand

INTRODUCTION: "CAN YOU HEAR WHAT I'M SAYING?"

On June 10, 2020, Malawi held an almost unprecedented election.[1] Earlier, in February, the High Court of Malawi had overturned the results from the previous election, held on May 21, 2019.[2] In this ruling not only did the incumbent, Peter Mutharika, and the Democratic Progressive Party (DPP) have their victory ruled invalid, but the court also made a constitutional interpretation saying that the condition of victory was not a simple first-past-the-post (i.e., plurality) but rather a fifty-plus-one majority. The second election looked much different from the first. This time, the second- and third-place candidates from the first election rallied a number of other smaller parties, including former president Joyce Banda's People's Party, to win fifty plus one on the first ballot. Getting to this point was quite difficult politically and, for a country as impoverished as Malawi, stretched scarce resources. Nevertheless, the population responded and rose to the challenge with little violence. That is not to say there wasn't violence, but compared to other countries that attempted similar feats, such as Kenya in 2017, Malawians proceeded decently and in good order.[3] Popular Western and African news reports rightly announced a truly historic event, and Malawians were justifiably proud of their accomplishment.

The fact that the eventual victor, Lazarus Chakwera, is a Pentecostal pastor and professor should garner academic attention but, perhaps, not for readily apparent reasons.[4] Places like neighboring Zambia, who has had a shift toward pentecostal political leadership, have come under needed critical scrutiny.[5] It should follow that scholars from various disciplines, within and without Malawi, will provide some of the same kind of scrutiny. The fact that such a unique election provides material for disciplines like anthropology, political science, and sociology is common sense. What is less obvious is that theology has something to offer to our understanding of Malawian politics in 2019–20.

Absent from much of the discussion of the rise of pentecostals in African politics are the specific claims that they make. When prominent prophets such as Shepherd Bushiri or TB Joshua make statements pertaining to Malawi, it is front-page news.[6] News outlets report, as objective fact, that Bushiri made accurate predictions about the 2019 Malawian elections and subsequent court case.[7] According to the news, the "leader of the Enlightened Christian Gathering church (ECG) had successfully predicted that President Peter Mutharika would retain power and preside over a minority government but the opposition and activists would challenge the results and protests."[8] Skeptics will quickly point out that in this case Bushiri's predictions are too vague and commonsensical to constitute real and true prophecy. Pentecostals could also doubt Bushiri but on different grounds. Christians have ways and means of determining whether a prophecy is true or false. They could test Bushiri's statements using criteria from their own theological commitments.

The difference between the skeptic and the pentecostal Christian, and this is the crux of my argument, is that the skeptic dismisses prophetic claims based on the a priori assumption that no prophetic claim can be true or false because there is a priori no God that can or does speak in human history. The pentecostal Christian can dismiss this particular prophetic claim because there are criteria that measure the veracity or falsehood of whether or not a particular speech act is from God. The speaker, the prophet, and the receivers, as well as the congregation and in this case the nation of Malawi, all understand the prophetic utterance as potentially true, whereas the skeptic can only understand the prophet to be speaking objective lies.

The only context in which this truth claim can make sense as a truth claim is theological because that is the main criteria that prophet and congregation use to gauge truth. Pentecostals have distinctive understandings of how the Holy Spirit acts in everyday life, including politics, and these understandings find their rationale within a larger theological interpretation of reality. Like the skeptic, other disciplines might be able to interpret these claims, perhaps explain them to a large extent, but they fail to take these claims as they are intended. African pentecostals intend these claims as being true representations of the way that God acts in the world. At best, academics from disciplines other than theology can take these claims "as if" they are true, but for those making the claims there is no doubt or tentativeness. There is no as-if nature to a prophet; there is only the bold claim that he or she speaks for God. For African pentecostals, God can and does willfully act within history as a personal agent.

This chapter uses Richard Osmer's equilibrium model of practical theology as a heuristic to show how theology might make a significant contribution to our understanding of pentecostal politics.[9] To anchor this metatheoretical analysis I use a very small example, a prophet preaching and exhorting his congregation with specific references to the 2019–20 Malawian election. The prophet begins his 7-minute, 50-second exhortation with the question, "Let me tell you as a church, as a church, are you ready to hear?" to which the church enthusiastically responds, "YES!"[10] The question seems as valid to ask of academics. Can we hear the prophet as he intends, or are we limited to imposing our own, Western, categories of understanding?

THE DESCRIPTIVE TASK: BLIND TO DIVINE ACTION

If this were an essay based in the social sciences, it would more than likely begin with an exemplary anecdote drawn from more extensive fieldwork. This narrative would introduce the reader to the main conclusion emerging from the data. A rationale for how and why the researcher went about gathering data would follow. This rationale would also include a certain amount of self-reflexivity, locating the researcher in relation to the subjects. Finally, the researcher would give a more extensive account of their fieldwork before proceeding to interpret that data. This description would not be neutral. Rather, it would be shaped by the disciplinary focus of the researcher. A political scientist would point to political details, an anthropologist to cultural, and so on. The disciplinary focus would shape the narrative, the rationale, the self-reflexivity, and the research program in general.

In this particular case, I would present a particularly interesting or illustrative moment from the prophet speaking. I would then justify why I chose this prophet or how this prophet fits into a larger research program. I would want to show that studying prophets is relevant to understanding contemporary Malawian politics. My place in this research, recognizing my outsider status to both Central Africa (I'm Canadian) and to this particular worshipping community (I'm Reformed, not pentecostal) would give the reader some sense of my biases but also the ethics of trying to avoid imposing those presuppositions upon the researched subject. Finally, I would give a fulsome description of how this particular prophet fits within the larger context.[11]

This way of presenting research fits easily within Richard Osmer's sketch of how practical theologians go about their work. In his writings on the field of practical theology, Osmer has striven for a "'reflective equilibrium': looking across a field at a certain point in time and articulating what we have in common, as well as our differences."[12] In his *Practical Theology: An Introduction*, Osmer points to four tasks, sometimes called moments, that all practical theologians, regardless of other methodological commitments, undertake when they go about their work: descriptive, interpretive, normative, and pragmatic. His goal in writing *Practical Theology* was not to proscribe but rather describe, to move toward a reflective equilibrium rather than establishing the superiority of any one methodology. A particular practical theologian will go about these four tasks differently, but all practical theologians hold these four tasks in common.

These are held in common because they stem from four basic questions that practical theologians attempt to answer:

> What is going on? (descriptive-empirical)
> Why is this going on? (interpretive)
> What ought to be going on? (normative)
> How might we respond? (pragmatic)[13]

Osmer contends that which question instigates an investigation is immaterial, although many academic practical theologians in conversation with social sciences begin with the descriptive. For instance, the most prominent academic Pentecostal practical theologian, Mark J. Cartledge, self-identifies as an empirical practical theologian.[14] By definition, Cartledge begins with Osmer's definition of the descriptive: "gathering information that helps us discern patterns and dynamics in particular episode, situations or contexts."[15]

Sociologist Gerardo Marti has a similar understanding of the empirical moment in relation to theology, in his case using ethnography from within his discipline of sociology. Specifically writing about how theologians (he does not make a distinction between systematic, historical, or practical theologians, although he cites practical theologians most often) might appropriate ethnography with integrity, Marti advocates for "found" versus "imposed" theologies.[16] Ethnography, a kind of "immersive, observational methodology," can help theologians by "grasping contemporary and 'real world' dynamics found in local social situations and structures."[17] This immersive experience with "patterned knowledge and systematic observation" contrasts with "armchair commentary" based on "anecdote and speculation."[18] The main danger with practical theologians using ethnography, and by extension most empirical research methods, is that "the insights generated by participant observation are constantly at risk of personal presumptions and variously asserted 'truths,' especially when researchers enter the field of observation with strongly held convictions and compelling worldviews."[19] The kind of bracketing that ethnographers do in order to see and hear their subjects as they really are is impossible to achieve when strongly held beliefs, in this case normative theological presuppositions, are at work. Marti offers a number of tools for practical theologians so that they can bracket out those distorting assumptions.[20] Osmer and Cartledge, both members of the by-invitation-only International Association of Practical Theology, would agree that practical theologians should heed Marti's warnings and take his advice concerning methodology.

At the same time, Marti invites conversation, and I think that an empirical description of the prophet's utterances from a practical theology perspective offers some counterpoints and caveats to Marti's one-sided discussion. Rightfully so, Marti offers no warnings to sociologists attempting to do theology, but that begs the question, "Are there not dangers inherent in studying a prophet's speech that are theological in nature?" Two seem germane. The first has to do with the personal involvement of the prophet along with their congregation and the nature of knowledge.[21] If they follow Marti's advice, practical theologians, like sociologists, will by definition miss the prophetic utterance as a truth claim upon the hearer's life. The ethnographer participant / observer has bracketed out the normative value of the words for their own life. They create a distance where they are neither fully naive participant or critical observer but in doing so miss the full knowledge of the participant.[22] When the prophet says, "Are you ready to hear" the participant / observer can say "Yes" but only on the condition that anything that the prophet says does not have a claim on his or her life. But if this is true, have they really heard what the prophet has to say? This tentativeness is in contradiction to how the prophet actually intends the speech and in contrast to how the congregation hears the words. The participant / observer can say "Yes" but only on their own terms, not those of the prophet or the congregation. This does not mean that the researcher must impose a theology on the prophet. Quite the opposite. If the researcher cannot submit to the theology of the prophet, can they really hear what the prophet has to say?[23]

Second, and ironically, is the fact that while Marti warns theologians against imposing assumptions on subjects, sociology's assumptions go unexamined and are therefore imposed without comment. To be fair, Marti's article is short, and he is writing about a specific and real danger facing practical theologians. But perhaps because he is looking from sociology to theology, he misses a significant shortcoming in sociology. Because sociology takes human belief and practices as its object of study, and only human belief and practices, it brackets out a critical component of the episode, situation, or context under study, namely, the divine. Marti rightly warns, "Students, pastors, and theologians who seek to use ethnography should be urged to remember that our observations are guided by our theories. Theory is essentially the sharpening of our observations to pay attention to what we would otherwise ignore"[24] but does not address the fact that sociology uses theories just as much as theology. Sociology theoretically assumes that all human belief and behavior can be explained as products of human belief and behavior. There is no theoretical room for God as an agent. There can be belief in God, but there can be no God as God at work.

In general, the prophet's claims constitute a significant lacuna for sociology. He claims that God is active in human history, a claim that social science cannot recognize as a valid claim unto itself. More specifically, this prophet makes six explicit claims related to God's agency in the world ("God assigned me again to pray," "God had already chosen a leader," "The grace of God is not with you," "God is going to a side," "God showed me," "The hand of God is with you"), and two implicit claims ("I am given that authority" and "'O God, when is this thing going to come?' I saw 2050"). As well, the prophet claims that the Devil also can and is acting in human history: "The Devil is penetrating in order to destroy so that the election on the 25th should not happen." All told, there are nine claims to divine or transcendent agency. At issue in the empirical is not the veracity of these claims, that might need to wait until Osmer's normative moment, but the very ability to see a thing as it is in itself. Marti and other social scientists rightly eschew a naive essentialism that believes bracketing can reveal something in its essence. Marti argues that by bracketing out presuppositions, the researcher can truly be surprised by their findings. Except, by bracketing out God, social scientists avoid any kind of divine surprise.[25]

THE INTERPRETIVE TASK: HUMILITY, FALLIBILISM, AND PERSPECTIVE

The differences between social science and practical theology in relation to the phenomena of prophecy take on more importance because of the cross-cultural nature of contemporary academic work. History reveals that when we cannot see something for what it is, we interpret it negatively. For example, take the work of J. D. Y Peel in *Religious Encounter and the Making of the Yoruba*.[26] Peel's main object of study is the encounter between religions: Christianity and various forms of belief / practice found where Yoruba people live. To see these encounters, Peel draws on the written archives of the Christian Missionary Society (CMS), but he does so with a hermeneutic of suspicion. The story of an encounter retold from one perspective can hardly give a full picture of what really happened. Examples of obvious prejudice such as calling *orisa* priests "deceivers of the people" do not concern Peel as much as other more subtle dangers. The "real challenge is to allow for the effects of the missionaries' selective interest in what they saw, the rubrics governing their reportage, and the psychological, even ontological, assumptions that lay behind them."[27] Each of these challenges (selective interests, rubrics, and assumptions) are all part of the empirical moment.

Osmer argues that all practical theologians must interpret their empirical findings. This is no different, in almost all ways, from what a scholar like Peel must do. Peel begins with his primary sources, the journals and other writings of CMS missionaries, and then must interpret them. The interpretive moment, for Osmer, is when the practical theologian "draw[s] on theories of the arts and sciences to understand and respond to particular episodes, situations, or contexts."[28] Using interdisciplinary methods, a practical theologian tries to answer the question "Why is this going on?" In Peel's case he does not have direct access to either the religious perspective of the evangelical missionaries nor the religious encounters they participated in. Peel's interpretive work is doubled by this dilemma. First, he must determine the interests, rubrics, and assumptions at work in the accounts that he has. This is an interpretive work in its own right that is informed by but not determined by the actual subject he wants to study. Second, he must analyze and understand the episodes, situations, and contexts of religious encounter in light of that interpretation. There is a double interpretation going on, first of understanding the missionaries then understanding the religious encounters.

What he finds is that the missionaries did not have a concept of "culture" at hand. They were not interested in the beliefs or practices of others, because they did not assume that those beliefs and practices formed a larger whole called culture. From the missionary's perspective, the religious encounter was not so much a clash of civilizations as it was skirmishes between particular "Christian" and "heathen" beliefs and practices. With no vision of the whole, missionaries could not appreciate the people that they encountered in all of their complexity. This is one reason they left no anthropological accounts of the people they encountered but instead scattered observations germane to their pragmatic interests. Peel attributes this perspective to a "mix of individualism and Christian universalism, underpinned by associationist psychology."[29] When Peel turns to philosophy (individualism), theology (Christian universalism), and psychology (associationist), he enters into an interdisciplinary conversation that illuminates and interprets his empirical findings.

Over the course of his book Peel makes extensive use of a wide variety of interpretive lenses, all to great effect. This kind of multiplicity leads to an agreement, at least theoretically, with Osmer, who advocates for a fallibilist and perspectival understanding of interpretation. By fallibilist, Osmer means "an awareness that the theories constructed by human reason offer an approximation of the truth, not truth itself."[30] No one perspective captures the fullness of truth inherent in any empirical finding necessitating multiple perspectives. By perspectival, Osmer means that "theories construct knowledge from a particular perspective, or position."[31] Truth is contextual and has a discernible immanent logic. The brilliance of a scholar like Peel is to illuminate another's perspective sufficiently to allow someone who does not share it to understand the immanent logics that propel it forward.

In the case of our prophet speaking about the Malawian elections, social science can interpret his words in illuminating ways. For instance, even a cursory interpretation reveals why the prophet favors Chakwera and Chilima over Mutharika. At one point the prophet locates himself in Zambia. The former Malawian president Bakili Muluzi, a Muslim, is "causing confusion in Malawi." The prophet wants "you people here in Zambia" to understand that there is an anarchy in Malawi. He claims to be "one nation" with sisters and brothers in Malawi based, in part, on "a common language that is Nyanja." Mutharika does not listen to the prophet and therefore contributes to the anarchy; Chakwera and Chilima listen to "men of God," and therefore God is on their side. The northern part of Malawi bordering Zambia, an area closely associated with Chakwera's Malawi Congress Party (MCP), is very rich, whereas the southern part, associated with Mutharika's DPP, will suffer because the north will secede. Rhetorically the prophet contrasts the constellation of Christian / northern Malawi / Chakwera / obedience / riches against Muslim / southern Malawi / Mutharika / disobedience / poverty. Each of the terms in the contrast lend themselves to social scientific interpretation.

The danger is that the researcher will mistake reasonable interpretations for the truth. Peel's research demonstrates a humility necessitated by the subject matter. The Yoruba people and their experience were discounted by the Christian missionaries because those missionaries lacked the interpretive imagination to do anything but impose their categories on the people they encountered. This is the colonial gaze at work, forcing the subject to conform to alien expectations that privilege the researcher. Just because we can explain the prophet by using academic interpretive tools does not mean that we have captured the fullness of meaning inherent in this episode. The very fact that various disciplines may make sense of this episode suggests a surplus of meaning not captured by any one discipline. Osmer and Peel would both advocate for a certain humility based on the fallibilism of human knowledge and the various perspectives at work within each subject researched.

THE NORMATIVE TASK: WHAT IS AND WHAT OUGHT TO BE

If there is a unique contribution that practical theology can make to understanding an episode like a prophet speaking about the Malawian election, it is here in the normative task. Theology makes the claim that there is an "ought" in every situation, episode, or context. This normative claim to something right and, by implication, something wrong is sometimes explicit but oftentimes implied. In his basic primer on practical theology Osmer portrays the normative task in three ways: theological, ethical, and best practices. The first, theological interpretation, is perhaps what people most commonly associate with the norm and is what is clearly in Marti's sights: "The use of theological concepts to interpret episodes, situations, and contexts, including those in which we are actors."[32] Mark Cartledge's proposals that Pentecostal practical theology "should develop a deeper and more critical dialogue with systematic theology and an engagement with the full range of theological loci" and "pay specific attention to the theological theme of soteriology" are good examples of this approach.[33] The second, the ethical approach, takes "ethical principles, rules, and guidelines" derived from theological commitments, perhaps "love" or "justice" or "liberation," and interprets an episode in that light.[34] Cartledge is likely correct in suggesting that the liberation theology stream of practical theology most closely resembles this approach and also that it is quite limited within pentecostal circles.[35] The third, best practices, revolves around the coinherence of practice and beliefs. Pentecostal philosopher James K. A. Smith's work draws on this norm when it advocates for a close connection between practice and belief.[36]

If we take our prophet and his words about the Malawi election, Osmer gives us at least three viable paths to understanding what norms are at play and perhaps more difficult to determine, what norms should be in play. The first, theological interpretation, begins with what doctrines might help make sense of the episode. At least two jump out: pneumatology and providence. Pneumatology provides an understanding of what ways the Holy Spirit might or might not be acting in a given situation. A whole host of questions open up such as, When the prophet claims that God gave him a vision in prayer, is this an actual theological possibility? What is the nature of the Spirit? And the list goes on. Likewise, the doctrine of providence can help in understanding the claims that God has chosen a particular leader. More generally, how does God's will come into effect within time and space?

Ethical reflection is another possible avenue. Joel Robbins gives a good example of this kind of interpretation.[37] At first glance his assessment of older interactions between the prosperity "gospel" and theologians and anthropologists falls into an ethical category. He notes that both anthropologists and theologians have had a negative assessment of the prosperity gospel as it has manifested in Africa. Theologians see heresy that leads to impoverishment of everyday believers, and anthropologists connect it to repugnant traditional forms of economic oppression. In both cases there is an ethic at work: humans cannot condone oppressing another for selfish gain. This assessment is true but inadequate for Osmer or for Robbins. This older view, one that Robbins sees as dissipating, "makes no attempt to reckon with the specificities of the prosperity gospel as an outgrowth of the Christian tradition and as a faith that both leaders and followers are highly committed to seeing as still within its borders."[38] In other words, it makes no attempt to really hear the episode on its own terms nor interpret it as fully as might be.

Interestingly, since the prophet I've been addressing here comes from Zambia, Robbins points to the work of Naomi Haynes on the Zambian copper belt as a new movement forward. Haynes focuses on the power of hierarchical relationships within the church. These kinds of relationships offend an ethic of egalitarianism but, in her account, point to a number of other viable ethics.[39] In Robbins's words, "prosperity here is not the fulfillment of selfish, neo-liberally informed individual desires for material goods for their own sake, but instead, as Haynes puts it, a relationally expansive kind of advancement that puts Copperbelt prosperity churches at the center of people's efforts to build community during materially difficult times."[40] There could be good or bad forms and practices of hierarchy using the ethic already at work within these communities. Haynes work points to an ethical reflection that is grounded in the empirical and interpretive moments. It is not imposed but arises from the research.

The final category, what Osmer has labeled as "best practices," has two parts. The first is offering "a model of good practice from the past or present with which to reform a congregation's present actions."[41] Because he is more interested in normative reflection, he turns to the second without too much discussion of this aspect. The second is to "generate new understandings of God, the Christian life, and social values beyond those provided by the received tradition."[42] An example of this part from our prophetic speech could be the emphasis on order. Among many sins that the prophet could call out, he focuses on anarchy and the violence that follows from it. Clearly there is an ethic of order at work here, and theological reflection could determine the contours of that ethic. A strict law-and-order ethic often is not actually ethical. Instead, it masks evil power dynamics in a cloak of respectability. At the same time, the experience of everyday Malawians during the leadup to the second election was one of uncertainty. This uncertainty exacerbated an already-precarious economic situation. Is it inconceivable that God could desire order for those facing significant economic uncertainty?

Whichever path a practical theologian takes, they can go to places that social scientists cannot. Robbins notes that even when an anthropologist has ethical qualms about a situation, in this case a church espousing a prosperity gospel, they will receive little help from the conventions of the discipline. In good anthropological fashion, Robbins studies theologians who do make normative judgments. The first attribute he notes is that theologians assume a "stance of humility."[43] This humility is not debilitating as it might be in an anthropologist. While he does not explicitly point to the fallibilism and perspectivalism that Osmer does, it is not wild conjecture to suggest that a practical theologian who is self-reflective will be circumspect in their pronouncements. In his survey of various theological approaches to the prosperity gospel, two come to the fore. The first measures the actual words against the biblical record. Careful examination of a shared authority leads to a correction. The second is what I call the "fruits" test. For the Gospel to be good news, it must be good news for people today. Does the prosperity gospel bring salvation to people? If not, then it is a distortion of the true Gospel and must be corrected.

THE PRAGMATIC TASK: WHAT NEXT?

Correction arising from a norm implies some kind of pragmatic action. This is Osmer's final task: "forming and enacting strategies of action that influence events in ways that are desirable."[44] Applying this norm could be in the form of "models of practice" that set out a kind of ideal picture of how to go about doing things. Or it could be developing "rules of art" that can guide the skillful implementation of an action. If social science has corollary practices for the empirical and interpretive tasks, the only corollary practice for the pragmatic would be some form of advocacy research. The goal is not just to understand the world but to change it, albeit with change determined by the dynamic relationship between context and God's ongoing action in the world.

There are very definite limits to these models and rules of art, imposed both by the episode, situation, or context and by the theological norms guiding the reflection. In relation to the specific prophet in question, I cannot determine whether our Zambian prophet is a false one or not. When he throws back the accusations that he is false prophet and points to the fulfillment of his previous prophecies as authoritative claims, I could try to verify whether, objectively speaking, he did or did not say this or that and whether this or that did or did not happen. However, to do so would be holding the prophet to criteria not his own and not from within his theological world. Skeptics have been pursuing this avenue of verification for centuries. It is the starting assumption of all social science: that because there is no God there can be no true prophecy.

Instead, I must begin from a place of epistemic humility. The prophet claims to speak truth. His congregation claims to hear truth. Large swaths of Malawian society hear truth in prophetic utterances. This is not *argumentum ad populum*. It is a recognition that many see truth where I cannot, and so, because of my commitment to that community and to the enterprise of theology in general, I will begin from a place of faith rather than doubt. Hearing this truth is difficult. First, I am not a charismatic theologian who entered into the situation in such a way that I could potentially hear the word of God. I have some access to the episode—it came to me via WhatsApp—but I am not of the context. I must recognize the great distance between "to" and "of" a context. Second, there are rules of art inherent to the pentecostal theological tradition that I am not part of. My own theological tradition, which is broadly Reformed, has a different understanding of prophecy than does the pentecostal. Consequently, my goal in this chapter has been to open the way for a pentecostal practical theologian to enter into larger conversations about the role of God in Malawian politics, not to determine whether or not God's hand was on Chakwera or there are riches in northern Malawi.

So then, what use is there in asking a question about prophecy and politics in Malawi? The importance is threefold. First, theological interpretation raises important questions for the Malawian community hearing this prophecy. Pentecostal pneumatology understands that the Holy Spirit falls on all flesh, not just on the prophet. The hearers of the prophecy are also empowered by the

Holy Spirit to hear the word of God. How can a congregation discern whether and in what way the Holy Spirit is present when a prophet speaks? The question that the prophet begins with, "Are you ready to hear?," is also the scriptural question put to the community. The Bible tells the pentecostal community that those who have eyes will see and ears will hear.[45] By indirectly citing Scripture, the prophet is making the claim that his words are as authoritative as the Bible because they are from God. So, the pentecostal community needs to discern, to test the words of the prophet, against something. In biblical terms they must know the voice of their shepherd, but that can't be the prophet's responsibility since it is the prophet's words that they are to test. They need models to emulate and rules of art to guide their faithful discernment.

Second, the theological claims made by the prophet are similar to claims made by those in other contexts, namely, North America. Scholars such as André Gagné trace the connections between neocharismatics and right-wing politics; it is not just Africa that has a confluence of prophecy and politics.[46] Is it possible that this obscure Zambian prophet speaking about a "shithole" (quoting Donald Trump) African country could teach Western Christians something about how God acts in the world?

Finally, proposing models to emulate or rules of art to follow is important because the prophet just might actually be speaking the word of God. There may be lies and obfuscations and outlandish claims, but there might also be truth and clarity and principles to live by. Millions of Malawians gain value from prophecies just like these, and it may be that they are receiving more than what social scientists can tell us. Practical theologians are under no illusions that a great many prophets are charlatans and hucksters, false prophets who fleece the sheep for their own gain. Yet, because the practical theologian begins from a stance of theological humility with an eye to act in the world, they hold out hope that the prophet might be able to do what he or she claims, namely, speak the words of God. The truth is a pearl of great value, worth selling everything else to hold.[47] Or, to bring in another biblical parable, there are many weeds in the field but there is also wheat.[48] Is it not worth attempting to find the wheat among the weeds? When the prophet asks, "Are you ready to hear?" is it not hopeful and possibly good to unreservedly answer "Yes"?

APPENDIX A: TRANSCRIPTION OF PROPHET X

Let me tell you as a church, as a church, are you ready to hear? [*calls of Yes*]. Are you ready? Let me tell you. There are terrible things happening in

Malawi. Which you people here, you don't know. But in the Spirit we[49] know because God has assigned me here to pray for Malawi. And God has assigned me again to pray for Zambia. And God assigned me again to pray for Tanzania and some other countries. Malawi is slowly deteriorating into a civil war. Mark my words, Malawi is deteriorating into a civil war just because of politics. Malawians you are killing your brothers, you are killing your sisters. Nonsense. Why can't you just say no? Say no to such things.

I have a vision as I was praying for Malawi. I have a vision where people started knifing one another, killing one another, because of political game. The former president of Malawi, Bakili Muluzi, must sit down, stop campaigning. He is causing confusion in Malawi. He is causing confusion [unclear] him. He must sit down. He is causing anarchy,[50] causing confusion, in that nation, which you people here in Zambia will hear shortly. He must sit down. Malawi, we've got our sisters, our brothers, Malawi and ourselves, yes, one nation. We have got a common language that is Nyanja, and we don't want our brothers and sisters to suffer.

Now, for the president of Malawi I also tell him without fear. And I will tell him because I am given that authority to speak to the presidents and I don't fear when I speak, "Your time is over. Just start thinking of how to pack and start off to go to the airport and think of going back." And for the running mate who is Atupele Muluzi, he is being used as a conduit, as a conduit of anarchy, as a conduit of destroying his own brothers and sisters. Now he is one of the brothers and sisters, [*unclear*], he is now using Islam to contradict Christianity. This will not work in Malawi. [*calls of Amen*]. This will not work in Malawi.

This will not work, and as I say now [as] I said before, that in Malawi God had already chosen a leader; I said it even last year, I said it even before last year, that the leader in Malawi has already been chosen. And I told you, Peter Mutharika, president of Malawi, I said, "Do not take this matter to court. Because the minute you take this matter to court no one is going to hear you because the favor and the grace of God is not with you." But he didn't listen. They started calling me, "False prophet! False prophet!" And he took the matter to court. When the matter went to court, ALL his cases he has never won any.

Are you aware? Do you remember my prophecy? [*calls of Yes*] I warned him. I said, "Do not take this matter in the way. Just accept the defeat and let the winner take over in order to avoid anarchy, in order to avoid people dying." But now, our brothers, our sisters are killing each other in Malawi. And for this blood is counted on the head of President Peter Mutharika.[51] President Peter Mutharika you still have some days, some weeks as a president, please, please, think, think. Bring peace to the nation of Malawi.

[*clapping*] Think. Think, God is going to a side, God is not at your side at all. I warned you and you didn't listen. I told you but you could not listen to me. And now what is next? Next is death on you. Next is death on you. You are carrying the blood of so many people who are dying right now.

And the message for Saulos Chilima, I said to the [*unclear*]. Because a person who had thought that he could not listen to men of God, a person who thought he could not listen to the prophets that He gave to Malawi, Saulos Chilima obeys and he humbled himself. He humbled himself and he is working with Chakwera. And you'll be the president of Malawi. Saulos Chilima, you are destined to be the president of Malawi and Dr. Chakwera, you are the president of Malawi. No matter what. No matter what. For you, Malawi, if Dr. Chakwera is not the president you will never see peace. So be careful if and when you go to election. Be careful, who you choose.

Then the final message I want to tell the people of Malawi is that Malawi is a very rich country. Start exploiting.[52] Start exploiting. There is, [*aside, "What do we call this?"*], oil. Oil which comes from Lake Tanganyika,[53] up to somewhere Salima? [*not clear of the place*], is there? There is oil in Malawi, which is there, so Chakwera when you become a president, exploit this. In Malawi there is gold. Malawi is sitting on gold but they can't see. But God showed me, to say that this country is sitting on gold. In Malawi there is ruby, but they don't know. God showed me. In Malawi, there is uranium, but they don't know. Malawi is sitting on uranium. Malawi is not a poor country. More especial from the northern part of Malawi. Northern part of Malawi is not poor. All these things are based in the north and part of the central region. [*calls of Amen*]. Hallelujah. [*calls of Amen*].

Are you getting me [*unclear*]. [*calls of Yes*]. Remember whatever I tell you, you should be writing. Because it will come to pass. I said, I prayed this, "O God, when is this thing going to come?" I saw 2050. 2050. Let them keep note properly because in the near future, in 2075, if they are not careful, northern part of Malawi will declare as a state. They will start fighting; it will separate from the entire Malawi because it will have gold, it will have diamond, it will have uranium, it will have oil, and it will be the richest part of Malawi. So please stop this anarchy. Work together. Love one another so that the riches and resources should be distributed accordingly to the nation of Malawi [*applause*]. As for Chakwera, God is with you. The hand of God is with you. Nothing is going to happen. Just tighten your security. For Chilima, tighten your security. For Mtambo, tighten your security. Do not allow the Devil to penetrate. The Devil is penetrating in order to destroy so that the election on the 25th should not happen. They want to buy time, but it is not going to be so. Whatever has been said has said in Jesus name. Amen.

NOTES

1. For an example of the popular press using the term "historic," see "After Historic Election."
2. Potani, Madise, and Kapindu.
3. For an example of the violence that did occur, see "Another Firebomb Targets Malawi's HRDC Protest Leader | Africa Times," August 22, 2019, https://africatimes.com/2019/08/23/another-firebomb-targets-malawis-hrdc-protest-leader/.
4. Chakwera is part of a self-identified Pentecostal denomination. When appropriate I use "Pentecostal" in its capitalized form to indicate a specific self-identified group. The word "pentecostal" with a lowercase *p* indicates a larger group of Christians who may or may not self-identify as Pentecostal. I include Pentecostals, charismatics, the majority of African indigenous churches (AIC), and a good number of evangelicals within this designation. The nomenclature is notoriously difficult, and by casting a very broad net I am signaling that making distinctions between these groups is less important for this essay than pointing to those Christians who practice and believe in charismatic gifts as a common and popular expression of their faith. I am making a broad theological designation between secessionists and nonsecessionists rather than a sociological or historical distinction. For more on this decision, see Jamie Smith, *Thinking in Tongues.*
5. For an example of a critical approach to prophetism and the neo-Pentecostal shift in Zambian politics, see Teddy Sakupapa, "Prophets in the Zambian/African Context"; and Sakupapa, "Christianity in Zambia," 758–65.
6. "Prophet Tb Joshua Releases 2020 Prophecy."
7. Stephen Ellis and Gerrie ter Haar do offer a nuance to claims of objectivity within newspapers (and by extension their internet presence): "By comparison with what is taught in US schools of journalism, African newspapers in general are extremely casual about establishing hard facts. They cannot be regarded as reliable sources of factual information or as journals of record other than in a few cases. African newspapers are, in fact, better considered as written forms of *radio trottoir* than as vehicles for rigorous reporting. If they are read with this caveat and considered as a privileged point of access to public debates in Africa, they can be treasure-houses of information." Stephen Ellis and Gerrie ter Haar, 467–71.
8. "Malawi Will Burn."
9. I make a distinction between various kinds of theology. When I say "practical theology," I mean those theologians who identify as operating within the academic subdiscipline of practical theology rather than systematic or historical theologians.
10. For a transcription of this recorded event, see appendix A. Further quotes are taken verbatim from this transcript.
11. For a good example of this kind of presentation, see pt. 1, "African Pentecostalism in Context" of Anderson, *Spirit-Filled World*, 3–80.
12. Osmer, "Consensus and Conflict in Practical Theology," 233. For Osmer's thinking on practical theology in general, see the appendix in Osmer, *The Teaching Ministry of Congregations,* Osmer, *Practical Theology*; and Osmer and Nel, "Practical Theology," 7.
13. Osmer, *Practical Theology,* 4.
14. Each of these book-length projects explicitly uses "empirical" in the title or series name: Cartledge, *Charismatic Glossolalia: An Empirical-Theological Study*; Cartledge,

Practical Theology: Charismatic and Empirical Perspectives; and Cartledge, *Testimony in the Spirit: Rescripting Ordinary Pentecostal Theology*, Explorations in Practical, Pastoral, and Empirical Theology. Cartledge also intentionally engages with the groundbreaking work of van der Ven, *Practical Theology: An Empirical Approach*.

15. Osmer, *Practical Theology*, 4.

16. Marti, 157–72.

17. Marti, 158.

18. Marti, 158.

19. Marti, 159.

20. A good example of this kind of approach is adopted by Ellis and ter Haar. They note that "the main feature of the Intellectualist approach is its propensity to consider statements on religious matters in the first instance in the believers' own terms before attempting to translate these into a vocabulary more appropriate to other branches of learning." For Ellis and ter Haar, "it is most important to note that this does not imply that an analyst shares the religious beliefs of the people she or he studies; it implies only that the observer suspends judgement by allowing believers (in this case Africans) the right to express matters in the terms they think appropriate." They adopt this approach. See Ellis ter Haar, 268–72.

21. Here I am drawing on a much larger argument found in Polanyi.

22. Christian philosopher James Smith makes much of the category of "testimony" when arguing for a pentecostal contribution to epistimology. His argument draws on some of the same sources as I do here but adds the role of narrative in our knowing. His argument is that "against the Enlightenment ideal of the impersonal, impartial, abstract 'knower,' pentecostalism affirms an affective, involved, confessing knower who 'knows that she knows that she knows' because of her story, because of a narrative, she can tell about a relationship with God." Smith, *Thinking in Tongues*, pt. 295.

23. At another point Smith argues that if we want to understand pencostalism, and that would include the prophet and their congregation, "and not just working with the ideas of a pentecostal theology, then such a philosophy must be pursued from within a web of worship practices that inform and inculcate a pentecostal worldview." Smith, *Thinking in Tongues*, pt. 530.

24. Marti, 169.

25. Smith claims that "it is an essential feature of pentecostal belief and practice to be open to God's surprises, [and] this presupposes a sense that the universe and natural world must also remain open systems." The argument I am making is that social science remains open only to human, or immanent, activity and not divine, transcendent, activity. Smith, *Thinking in Tongues*, 1569.

26. Peel.

27. Peel, 12.

28. Osmer, *Practical Theology*, 83.

29. Peel, 12.

30. Osmer, *Practical Theology*, 83.

31. Osmer, *Practical Theology*, 83.

32. Osmer, *Practical Theology*, 131.

33. Cartledge, *The Mediation of the Spirit*, secs. 4277–82.

34. Osmer, *Practical Theology*, 147.

35. Cartledge, *The Mediation of the Spirit*, pt. 524. It is also a possibility that the liberation stream, with its focus on orthopraxis, could easily fit within the best practices category as well. The lines between these various kinds of interpretation are not hard and fast.
36. This is the approach clearly advocated in relation to pentecostal spirituality in Smith, *Thinking in Tongues*. More generally, see Smith's three-part series *Cultural Liturgies*: vol. 1, *Desiring the Kingdom: Worship, Worldview, and Cultural Formation*; vol. 2, *Imagining the Kingdom: How Worship Works*; and vol. 3, *Awaiting the King: Reforming Public Theology*.
37. Robbins.
38. Robbins, 24.
39. The groundbreaking work of Peter Ekeh comes to mind in relation to the idea of viable alternatives to Western ethics at work, often hidden, within African societies. See Ekeh, "Colonialism and the Two Publics in Africa," 91–112, and Ekeh, "Afterword," 219–32.
40. Robbins, 26.
41. Osmer's book aims at congregations, but really he means any episode or context. Osmer, *Practical Theology*, 152.
42. Osmer, *Practical Theology*, 152.
43. Robbins, 29.
44. Osmer, *Practical Theology*, 176.
45. See Isaiah 6:10, Jeremiah 5:21, Ezekiel 12:2, Matthew 13:15, Acts 28:27, and Romans 11:8 for examples. There is almost always a note of judgment implied when people do not see or cannot hear, adding urgency to the need to train congregations how to see and hear.
46. Gagné.
47. See Matthew 13:44–45.
48. See Matthew 13:24–30.
49. It is clear from watching the video that the prophet is simply confusing the singular and plural first-person pronouns here. The "we" is not inclusive of those gathered but rather the prophet himself. Nor should this be interpreted as some kind of royal we.
50. The prophet consistently clips the ending off of "anarchy" so it sounds like "anarch." Context dictates which word I use in the transcription.
51. Through most of the address the prophet is speaking generally to the gathered congregation. At this point, though, he turns directly to the camera phone recording and breaks the fourth wall by speaking directly to President Mutharika.
52. It is not clear whether the prophet is saying, "exploit" or "explore." The transcription indicates that I favor "exploit," but there is a possibility that it is "explore."
53. It is not clear why the prophet mentions Lake Tanganyika in a prophecy directed to Malawi, since it is not within Malawian borders. It is more likely that the prophet means Lake Malawi, which forms the northeastern border of Malawi.

BIBLIOGRAPHY

"After Historic Election, What Next for Malawi?" Accessed August 21, 2020. https://www .aljazeera.com/news/2020/06/historic-election-malawi- 200626070010661.html.

Anderson, Allan Heaton. *Spirit-Filled World: Religious Dis/Continuity in African Pentecostalism*. Charis Christianity & Renewal Interdisciplinary Studies. London: Palgrave Macmillan, 2018.

Cartledge, Mark J. *Charismatic Glossolalia: An Empirical-Theological Study.* Ashgate New Critical Thinking in Theology and Biblical Studies. Surrey, UK: Ashgate, 2002.

———. *The Mediation of the Spirit: Interventions in Practical Theology.* Pentecostal Manifestos. Grand Rapids, MI: Eerdmans, 2015.

———. *Practical Theology: Charismatic and Empirical Perspectives.* Studies in Charismatic and Pentecostal Issues. London: Paternoster, 2003.

———. *Testimony in the Spirit: Rescripting Ordinary Pentecostal Theology.* Explorations in Practical, Pastoral, and Empirical Theology. Surrey, UK: Ashgate, 2010.

Ekeh, Peter P. "Afterword: Note on 'Colonialism and the Two Publics in Africa: A Theoretical Statement.'" In *Reclaiming the Human Sciences and Humanities through African Perspectives,* edited by Helen Lauer and Kofi Anyidoho, 1:219–32. Lego-Accra, Ghana: Sub-Saharan Publishers, 2012.

———. "Colonialism and the Two Publics in Africa: A Theoretical Statement." *Comparative Studies in Society and History* 17, no. 1 (January 1975): 91–112.

Ellis, Stephen, and Gerrie ter Haar. *Worlds of Power: Religious Thought and Political Practice in Africa.* New York: Oxford University Press, 2004.

Gagné, André. *Ces évangéliques derrière Trump: Hégémonie, démonologie et fin du Monde.* Geneva: Labor et Fides, 2020.

Malawi 24. "Malawi Will Burn—Bushiri | Malawi 24—Malawi News." *Malawi 24* (blog), January 27, 2020. https://malawi24.com/2020/01/27/malawi-will-burn-bushiri/.

Marti, Gerardo. "Found Theologies versus Imposed Theologies: Remarks on Theology and Ethnography from a Sociological Perspective." *Ecclesial Practices* 3 (2016): 157–72.

Osmer, Richard Robert. "Consensus and Conflict in Practical Theology: Reflections." In *Consensus and Conflict: Practical Theology for Congregations in the Work of Richard R. Osmer,* edited by Blair D. Bertrand, Kenda Creasy Dean, Amanda Drury, and Andrew Root, 213–37. Eugene, OR: Pickwick Publications, 2019.

———. *Practical Theology: An Introduction.* Grand Rapids, MI: Eerdmans, 2008.

———. *The Teaching Ministry of Congregations.* Louisville, KY: Westminster John Knox Press, 2005.

Osmer, Richard Robert, and Malan Nel. "Practical Theology: A Current International Perspective." *HTS Teologiese Studies / Theological Studies* 2, no. 67 (2011): 7.

Peel, J. D. Y. *Religious Encounter and the Making of the Yoruba: African Systems of Thought.* Bloomington: Indiana University Press, 2000.

Polanyi, Michael. *Personal Knowledge: Towards a Post-Critical Philosophy.* London: Psychology Press, 1998.

Potani, Kamanga, Tembo Madise, and Kapindu [Tembo J, Kamanga J, Potani J, Kapindu J, and Madise J]. Constitutional Reference No.1 of 2019. High Court of Malawi, February 3, 2020.

"Prophet Tb Joshua Releases 2020 Prophecy: No Change in Malawi, 'Lord Will Humble Us.'" Accessed August 27, 2020. https://www.nyasatimes.com/prophet-tb-joshua-releases-2020-prophecy-no-change-in-malawi-lord-will-humble-us/.

Robbins, Joel. "World Christianity and the Reorganization of Disciplines: On the Emerging Dialogue between Anthropology and Theology." In *Faith in African Lived Theology: Bridging Theological and Anthropological Perspectives,* edited by Karen Lauterbach and Mika Vähäkangas. Vol. 35. Global Pentecostal and Charismatic Studies. Boston: Brill, 2019.

Sakupapa, Teddy. "Christianity in Zambia," In *Anthology of African Christianity,* edited by Phiri, Isabel Apawo et al, 758–65. 1517 Media, 2016. *JSTOR.* Accessed 14 July 2024. https://doi.org/10.2307/j.ctv1ddcqdc.

———. "Prophets in the Zambian / African Context: A Survey from an Ecumenical Perspective." *Prophecy Today: Reflections from a Southern African Context, Special edition of Word and Context Journal* (2016): 113–28.

Smith, James K. A. *Awaiting the King: Reforming Public Theology.* Vol. 3. *Cultural Liturgies.* 3 vols. Grand Rapids, MI: Baker Academic, 2017.

———. *Desiring the Kingdom: Worship, Worldview, and Cultural Formation.* Vol. 1. *Cultural Liturgies.* 3 vols. Grand Rapids, MI: Baker Academic, 2009.

———. *Imagining the Kingdom: How Worship Works.* Vol. 2. *Cultural Liturgies.* 3 vols. Grand Rapids, MI: Baker Academic, 2013.

———. *Thinking in Tongues: Pentecostal Contributions to Christian Philosophy.* Kindle. Pentecostal Manifestos. Grand Rapids, MI: Eerdmans, 2010.

Ven, Johannes van der. *Practical Theology: An Empirical Approach.* Leuven, Belgium: Peeters Press, 1998.

PART II

Embodiment, Gender, and Identity

Embodiment and Evangelical Christianity

Missions, Prophets, and Bodies in Post-Colonial Democratic Republic of Congo

Yolanda Covington-Ward

INTRODUCTION

Sometime in 2002 Mama Mazola, lay in her bed in Luozi and began to dream. In her dream, she saw herself in Bas-Fleuve, near Boma and next to the Congo River. At the waterside she saw two men: Tata Simon Kimbangu, dressed in a white *pagne* (a cotton wrapper) and a top, and Tata Joseph Kasa-Vubu, also dressed in all white but in pants and a shirt. "They are together even today," she said. They told her that their country, Bas-Congo, would not see many wars. They told her to walk through bushes of thorns, and at first she refused, saying that she would be hurt. They reassured her that she would not be harmed, and she did as they said and was not hurt by the thorns. She followed the men, and suddenly they were at Mpioka, and then crossed the Congo River to arrive at Luozi. The men told her that they were giving her the power to heal in the name of Jesus Christ, and then they left. All of sudden, when Mama Mazola was in her bed in Luozi, her entire body began to vigorously tremble. "People thought I was crazy," she said, and she uncategorically refused to heed the call, this embodied call, to become a prophet. "I didn't want to work with the Holy Spirit or wear the white robes," she said. She tried to ignore what was happening and continued to cross the Congo River to sell small goods on the other side. Each time she crossed the river to sell, she wouldn't sell anything. Her lack of business success was being caused by her refusal to heed the call to work with the Holy Spirit. She eventually sought help and healing from Mama Tatu, a prophetess on the other side of the Congo River, but the trembling returned when she stood in a line with others in order to give an offering to the prophetess. She began to work with Mama Tatu, and Mama Mazola herself began to have visions and prophesize as well. Eventually people came to Mama Mazola in her compound for prophecies and healing. Once, filled with the Holy Spirit, she turned and pointed to the road outside her compound. "Look! There is Tata Simon Kimbangu in a limousine." Others present, who had also received the Holy Spirit, claimed to see him as well.[1]

* * *

I start with the story in order to illustrate the confluence of dreams and embodiment in modern-day spiritual practices and conversion narratives of BisiKongo people in the Lower Congo who have been spiritually called to be *bangunza,* or prophets. Mama Mazola's experience of being spiritually called to work with the Holy Spirit was clearly predicated upon connections to the past. More specifically, these connections are to past prophets, especially Tata Simon Kimbangu, who in 1921 led what Robert H. C. Graham, a British Baptist Missionary Society missionary, called, "the most remarkable movement the country has ever seen."[2] Kimbangu's religious movement, which started in mid-March in 1921 and has been called the Kimbanguist or *kingunza* movement, had a lasting impact on the religious landscape of the Lower Congo from the colonial period until the present day.

In this chapter, I argue that several characteristics that defined the colonial-era kingunza movement, notably, visions and spirit-induced trembling (*zakama*), continue to have salience in modern-day religious practice, especially for becoming an *ngunza,* or prophet, or being engaged in forms of religious practice in prophetic churches. However, these experiences are not usually welcome in Pentecostal contexts. Evangelical Christianity is growing exponentially throughout Africa, especially through Pentecostal and Charismatic movements, transforming communities and relationships in many different ways. However, certain discourses and practices that are championed by some evangelical Christians—especially Pentecostal Christians—clash or differ considerably with evangelical African Initiated Churches (AICs). This chapter examines conflicting discourses around individual Christian relationships with the past and interpretations of embodiment in several churches located in the rural town of Luozi in the westernmost province of the Democratic Republic of Congo. One of the most prominent themes defining Pentecostal discourse in Africa is that of converts needing to break their ties with the past, including cultural practices, beliefs, and, even in some cases, their families and clans. Yet, in many AICs throughout the Lower Congo region, connections with the past through visions and dreams of a MuKongo prophet named Simon Kimbangu are key to personal spiritual callings and to one's calling to join particular churches. Similarly, while uncontrolled embodied trembling is defined as "demonic" in certain Pentecostal spaces, many AICs in these same communities define it as evidence of contact with the Holy Spirit. Using participant observation and interviews with four individuals in Luozi, the Democratic Republic of Congo, who have been called to prophetism in different ways and who belong to various Protestant churches (or none at all), I seek to broaden the discourse on the lived experience of what it means to be a Christian in the Lower Congo while probing the politics of belonging that shape the local religious landscape. Overall, this essay offers considerations of how the deep and meaningful histories of Kongo-centered religious movements in the region have shaped evangelical Christianity in Luozi.

This chapter seeks to answer several questions: What does a scholarly overemphasis on Pentecostalism elide in regard to understanding contemporary evangelical African Christianity? How does a focus on spiritual practice, relationality and intersubjectivity, and embodiment shift our focus? And how does centering practice reshape how we view the importance of institutional affiliations for Christian identities? This work is important for pushing against the domination of academic literature on African Christianity by studies of Pentecostal Churches while seeking to expand our definition of evangelical Christianity, as religious life in other types of Christian churches (and even outside of church contexts) remains important for many people across Africa.

EVANGELICAL CHRISTIANITY IN AFRICA

While exact definitions of evangelical Christianity are intensely debated, an oft-cited and useful set of characteristics emerges from the work of David Bebbington based on his study of evangelical Christianity in Great Britain.[3] Paul Freston summarizes these characteristics as "conversionism (emphasis on the need for change of life), activism (emphasis on evangelistic and missionary efforts), biblicism (a special importance attributed to the Bible, though not necessarily the fundamentalist shibboleth of 'inerrancy') and crucicentrism (emphasis on the centrality of Christ's sacrifice on the cross)."[4] Freston argues further for not limiting our understanding of evangelical Christianity based on self-labeling but to look instead at churches that meet the criteria. Taking such an approach would allow the inclusion of many AICs, which he admits may "come into a broad evangelical category."[5] Thus, evangelical Christianity can include "some of the historic Protestant mission churches; the so-called African Initiated Churches; and the new pentecostal movements."[6] Indeed, in his own study of Kenyan evangelical churches, John Karanja pushes for an even more expansive understanding of evangelicalism that "embraces all Protestant Christians" based on the observation that "the founders of all Kenyan Protestant churches came from an evangelical background."[7] For the churches I examine here, the same logic applies, as all of the founders were shaped by membership in churches that emerged from evangelical perspectives in Christianity. This chapter examines distinctions between how different Kongo churches emerging from the evangelical tradition wrestle with embodiment and dreams.

THE PENTECOSTAL-CHARISMATIC SHIFT?

Pentecostal Christianity is one point along the evangelical Christian continuum. Yet, Pentecostal Christianity receives excessive attention currently in scholarly studies of the last two decades or so. In her 2004 review article, Birgit Meyer describes a large shift in studies of Christianity in Africa from African Independent/Initiated Churches (AICs) to what she calls Pentecostal-Charismatic Churches (PCCs), which have exhibited tremendous growth over the last few decades, not just in Africa but also in Asia and Latin America. One of the most prominent themes defining both evangelical and Pentecostal discourse in Africa is that of converts needing to break their ties with the past, including cultural practices, beliefs, and, even in some cases, their families and clans. While both Ruth Marshall's work on Pentecostal churches in Nigeria and Katrien Pype's research in the Democratic Republic of Congo examine rupture to some extent, Meyer's research on Pentecostalism in Ghana extensively conceptualizes ruptures with the past as a precondition for self-identification as a modern Christian.[8]

According to Meyer, Pentecostal churches share certain features such as baptism in the Holy Spirit, speaking in tongues, divine healing, an emphasis on personal prayers, similar liturgy, discourses on the Devil and demons, and rituals of deliverance to exorcise such demons.[9] To be freed from these demons, however, one must turn to the past in order to find the "occult sources" of your troubles in the present.[10] Meyer thus sees deliverance rituals as subverting "the bonds created and protected by the collective worship of particular gods as well as the bonds between relatives. This is a distinctive feature of Pentecostalism. Whereas traditionally the fight against evil is to a large extent focused on the restoration of bonds between people . . . Christian deliverance basically unties them."[11]

Meyer's observations on ruptures with the past have been very productive for studies of Pentecostalism in Africa more generally. However, in a recent essay entitled "Past Pentecostalism," Matthew Engelke cautions that rupture as a concept may not capture the full complexity of the choices people make as African Pentecostals or as those of other Christian denominations. "Breaking with the past," he writes, "is not only the erasure of a tradition but the inscription of another."[12] With every rupture, there is always realignment, meaning a reimagining and reconfiguration of a particular history and your relationship to it. Another major point that he makes is that while studies of Pentecostal and Charismatic churches have come to dominate the academic literature on Christianity in Africa more recently, large segments of populations across the continent continue to attend and support a broad swathe of Christian churches, including mainline churches emerging from European missions as well as AICs. Engelke thus argues for the need to look past the privileging of Pentecostalism in order to capture the diversity and complexity of Christian religious experiences in Africa.

In his book *Faith in Flux: Pentecostalism and Mobility in Rural Mozambique*, Devaka Premawardhana also makes the point that rupture is not, in fact, very new for some communities like in Lichinga, Mozambique, where he conducted his research. In his own work, he seeks to "render rupture less exceptional, to see Pentecostal conversion at least potentially—and certainly in what I witnessed—as a mundane extension of an already convertible way of being. Conversion, so understood, is less a matter of continuity *or* change than of the continuity *of* change."[13] It is at this juncture that I seek to enter the discussion. Like both Engelke and Premawardhana, I believe that the experiences of people both in and outside of AICs continue to provide lessons and challenges from which scholars studying African Christianity can benefit. Moreover, the association that is often made of AICs with "tradition" or a static approach to religion belies the continuity of change that enables AICs to continue to address contemporary everyday challenges for their church members. In fact, many AICs developed out of explicit African desires to dictate the terms of their own worship experiences and lives as Christians. Mainline Protestant churches founded by missionaries themselves followed a set of practices aimed at disrupting cultural behaviors and beliefs. In the Lower Congo, for instance, Swedish missionaries in the late nineteenth century passed multiple resolutions to target and eradicate certain cultural practices among the Kongo population, such as the following in 1894: "Old customs, habits and conceptions, such as dance, all forms of idolator feasts, hair cutting feasts, funeral feasts, gun-salutes and wailing for the deceased, together with the drinking of palm-wine at such feasts, and at palavers, should be vigorously opposed and exterminated."[14] All of this history shows that Pentecostal and larger evangelical approaches seek to disconnect African Christians from their pasts in myriad ways.

LUOZI AND ITS RELIGIOUS LANDSCAPE

I conducted ethnographic research and interviews for this chapter during a return trip to the Congo in 2010, where I was based in Luozi. Before this, I lived in Congo (in both Kinshasa and Luozi) from 2005–06, working on my dissertation. Luozi is a small town of about 14,000 people in a rural part of Kongo Central Province located on the northern bank of the Congo River. Most people make a living there by farming only or by combining agricultural cultivation with other jobs. People often leave Luozi in search of employment and opportunity in the larger cities in Kongo Central Province or in Kinshasa, the capital city. There are a number of churches there whose histories date back to the colonial period mainly, with some others having been created post-independence.

The Communauté Évangélique au Congo (CEC) is a mainline Protestant church founded by Swedish missionaries from the Swedish Mission Covenant Church (a Swedish reformed church with origins in the Lutheran Church of Sweden). Founded in Congo in 1881 by Swedish missionaries, it became autonomous and led by Congolese in 1961, a year after the country gained independence. This church seems to be the largest in terms of membership and has a steady flow of Swedish missionaries who continue to come there. Many of the attendees are of higher socioeconomic status and / or educational status. Paroisse Notre-Dame de Fatima is a Catholic church that was established there in 1948. It is the other large church in the area, although it does not have as much land or resources as the CEC Church. The Kimbanguist Church was the third-largest church in Luozi when I conducted my research. Yet, it is commonly recognized as the largest AIC in the world, first receiving formal recognition in 1959 and growing out of the religious movement that Simon Kimbangu started in 1921. Its members do an excellent job of raising their own funds for construction, for schools, and for other activities. The Kimbanguist Church was started by the sons of Simon Kimbangu. The Dibundu dia Mpeve Nlongo mu Afelika (DMNA) or Communauté de Saint Esprit en Afrique (CSEA) (in English, Church of the Holy Spirit in Africa), was founded in February 1961 by Masamba Esaie. He was imprisoned in 1952 due to being a prophet during the kingunza movement, was sent to a penal labor camp, and was released right before independence (Covington-Ward 2016, 108).[15] He separated from the mainline Protestant church in 1961 after its members couldn't accept the form of worship that he wanted to practice, which included embracing spirit-induced trembling. The DMNA Church is often called the bangunza (prophets') church; it is much smaller than the other churches. Nsinga wa Yenge is a newer AIC founded in 2001. The founder of Nsinga wa Yenge, Papa Nsimba, was formerly a member of the mainline Protestant church in Luozi as well. There are other small churches too, including the Salvation Army Church.

PROPHETS IN KONGO THOUGHT

One of the important themes across the narratives that we will explore is the experiences people have that indicate to them that they have been called to be prophets or to work with prophets. All of my interviewees were already Christians when they received these callings. Thus, first I explore the activities and characteristics that define a person as prophet more broadly and more specifically in a Kongo context. While the Greek concept of prophet was someone who spoke on behalf of a deity or god, and the Hebrew idea was someone who was a mouthpiece for the Supreme Being, they both shared the basic tenet that a prophet was someone able to communicate with and pass on a message from the supernatural realm.[16] The prophet (or ngunza) is one of the three most important recurring figures in Kongo culture and history, along with the chief (*mfumu*) and the priest / healer / ritual specialist (*nganga*).[17] How is a prophet defined in Kongo thought? Ngunza is a KiKongo word that means "messenger of a chief," "protector of the clan," "clairvoyant," or "prophet-healer."[18] Another term associated with prophetism is *kimbikudi*. "*Kimbikudi* is the art of premonition, that is, the art of seeing the future through a vision, a dream, or a state of ecstasy. The principal function of this institution is to predict the future, to divine, to assess in the sense of advising and blessing the people."[19] In fact, the KiKongo terms *ngunza*, *ntumwa*, and *mbikudi*, were all used by the indigenous Kongo population to refer to Simon Kimbangu during his time of spiritual activity, and meant "the hero, the messenger, and the visionary and came directly from the Kongo ethos."[20] Like other words in KiKongo, moreover, these same terms were being appropriated by European missionaries in the Lower Congo to translate Christian concepts. *Ngunza* was the term used by Protestant missionaries to describe Christian prophets in the Bible. So, while the indigenous Kongo population had referred to certain individuals as prophets before the arrival of Europeans, Christian evangelization added another characteristic to these figures—their relationship to a Christian God. This shows the dynamic interaction between precolonial Kongo and European Christian ideas and vocabulary, an interaction that impacted and defined Kimbangu's movement.[21]

Anthropologist Wyatt MacGaffey has observed that the modern ngunza is "defined in Kongo popular consciousness by his exercise of healing powers in the public interest."[22] He has also investigated the multiple ways in which the term *ngunza* was used in the Lower Congo in the mid-twentieth century, concluding that it describes any healer or diviner who appears to be using Christian ritual, religious groups that developed on the north bank of the Congo River whose name is generally a variation of Dibundu dia Mpeve ya Nlongo (DMN), and one chosen individual in each generation through whom the power of God is manifested.[23] Thus, altruistic healing, divination, blessing, and prophecy are key attributes of Kongo prophets. Moreover, the term *ngunza* is not necessarily limited to describing one major prophet but rather is applied widely, encompassing many individuals who are engaged in prophetic activities. Using such a Kongo culturally contextualized concept of prophet allows us to see that for centuries in the Kongo region many individuals have held positions of spiritual authority and have been engaged in prophetic activities.

DREAMS, VISIONS, AND CONNECTIONS WITH THE PAST

First, I would like to consider the comparative significance of dreams and visions. During the precolonial period, examples abound of the importance of visions and dreams in the spiritual life of people in and around what was then the Kongo Kingdom, located in and near modern-day Lower Congo. Dona Beatrice was a young woman who fell gravely ill, became possessed by the spirit of Saint Anthony, and told others that she had been charged with the mission of restoring the Kongo Kingdom. Deriving authority from her recovery from a debilitating sickness, being possessed by a Catholic saint, and having continuous spiritual revelations and dreams, Dona Beatrice's growing power threatened not only the Catholic missionaries stationed in the area but also claimants to the throne of king. She was burned alive at the stake as a heretic on July 2, 1706.[24] Yet, illness itself was often seen as a calling to become an nganga, especially if the illness was seen to have spiritual causes. This association ties to larger cultural conceptions of being called to prophetism that developed in later centuries.

Before the start of his religious movement in 1921, Prophet Simon Kimbangu himself claimed to have experienced certain visions. Kimbangu apparently had a vision in 1917 or 1918 that evidenced his calling to preach. In 1920 his town Nkamba was made into an official substation of the Baptist Missionary Society Wathen mission station, and Kimbangu asked the local church elders if he could be the evangelist for Nkamba. While they agreed, other people at Nkamba did not support him, and the position was given to his stepbrother instead. After this devastating setback, Kimbangu went home to pray. Kongo chroniclers of the movement describe what Kimbangu himself explained happened next: "Then I had a dream and God said to me, 'I have heard your prayer; people think you need the spirit to do my work but I will give you something even greater.' I took no notice of this. But from day to day I heard a voice that told me I would do the work of Peter and of John. I would be an apostle." Kimbangu's visions continue the Kongo tradition of continuous revelation—revelatory dreams and visions thought to originate in the spirit world. Such beliefs and practices have been documented back to the precolonial Kongo Kingdom from even the early years of the kingdom converting to Christianity in 1491.[25] These practices existed in Kongo religion before Christianity and continued after the conversion to Christianity.

In modern-day Lower Congo, dreams and visions continue to play a major role in people's spiritual experiences. However, in the larger evangelical discourse, dreams and visions may be seen as negative aspects that hold you back as a Christian. For example, in Birgit Meyer's study of Pentecostalism in Ghana, people seeking deliverance at one church were asked to complete a questionnaire that focused specifically on visions and dreams, including whether people heard voices, smelled strange things, or other types of phenomena.[26] Affirmative answers signified the presence of demonic spirits that needed to be exorcised, and born-again Christians in this context were told to remain continually vigilant against such forces in their lives, the origins of which could often be traced to their family or ancestors. While dreams and visions were also highly significant for interviewees in Luozi, their interpretation of the meaning of such events differs considerably from evangelical and Pentecostal ideas. Tata Makiadi, a man in his fifties who initially was a member of the mainline CEC Protestant Church in Luozi, explains the role of visions in his later religious conversion to the DMNA Church.

> At the age of three, in my home village, it was a big day, it was extremely
> warm, I was alone outside and I looked towards the cemetery, I saw
> many people . . . in the cemetery. I saw many people dressed in white.
> I didn't know what it was. I didn't say anything to either my mother or
> my father. . . . I think three or two weeks passed. . . . I was there again,
> during the day, mother left for the fields, father left for the fields. . . .
> I saw people descending, two people, dressed in white, they began to
> play with me. Me, I thought my friends could see them, they couldn't
> see them, only I could see them. After some time, they are lost. These
> are the things that remain imprinted in my head.[27]

Tata Makiadi referred to this experience as a "calling" and like others I interviewed, he initially tried to ignore it. Kongo cosmological symbolism and
larger connections to the past are also inferred in this vision. The unknown
beings that he saw were dressed in white (*mpemba*), the color of the land of
the dead in Kongo cosmology.[28] Their initial appearance in the village ceme-
tery also has significance, as this is the place where ancestors have been laid
to rest. While these otherworldly beings were not named or people he recognized, "these people I saw," he asserts, "were people of God."[29]

Mama Kudada, another interviewee I spoke with in 2010, also describes
the importance of a vision in impacting her decision to join the DMNA
Church. A short, slender woman in her late thirties, demure and bit reserved,
she becomes more animated when she discusses one particular vision.
"When I was born, my mother had me baptized in the Catholic Church."
She was raised on a Catholic mission in another part of Luozi territory, but
her life was completely changed when she underwent her confirmation ceremony as a teen.

> When I approached the alter, when my turn arrived because we were
> in a line, he [the bishop] threw ashes on us. These ashes had an inde-
> scribable odor. I immediately noticed something in me. . . . When
> the bishop touched my forehead with the oil, I noticed something
> had happened in me; a big change as if I saw a big, ferocious animal at
> the alter that was going to devour me, immediately I fled the church.
> I trembled, I couldn't see anyone around me.[30]

She then explained that the Holy Spirit had descended into her, and it was
this experience that led her to eventually become a member of the DMNA
Church. Here, Mama Kudada's vision of a ferocious animal contrasts with
the visions of Tata Makiadi and Mama Mazola. Rather than seeing ancestors

or godly beings, she had a terrifying vision that caused her to flee the Catholic Church. Although she first received the Holy Spirit in the context of this confirmation ceremony, she did not interpret this as a sign that she should remain in the Catholic Church. Rather, not long after her vision, she decided to become a member of the DMNA Church.

Yet another interviewee reiterated the importance of visions by not only laying out a life history of dreams and visions but also making connections with Prophet Simon Kimbangu. Papa Nsimba was a member of the mainstream CEC Protestant Church in Luozi. Inspired to do the work of God since 1970, he was a member of the church until he was excommunicated in 2000, founding his own church in 2001.

> It was a Sunday, me, I didn't go to the church there, Protestant, when I was sitting under the mango tree, I met someone who was sent to tell me, you are excommunicated from the church . . . why? What had I done? Oh, you are too stubborn. Stubborn in what? . . . the pastor had denounced this matter, the church was panicking. The church was divided in two parts, this should not be done, me, I said fine, I cannot do otherwise, I prayed with other people, I received a dream, I saw the prophet Simon Kimbangu, you are free now, but go and found a church called Nsinga wa Yenge. And this church even today, the people regret my leaving.[31]

Here, Papa Nsimba bases the decision to start his own church on the directives of Prophet Simon Kimbangu. Interestingly, he was excommunicated because of engaging in prophetic activities within the CEC Church community, which included sharing his dreams about Kimbangu, praying for others, and in some instances healing others. Here is a clear clash between the hierarchy and power structure of the CEC Church and visions and dreams of Kongo ancestors like Simon Kimbangu. Moreover, connecting the founding of his church with the prophet lends spiritual legitimacy that acts as a valuable currency in a religious landscape in which missionary-founded churches wield considerable power and influence.

Yet, his vision of Simon Kimbangu was not his first one. Indeed, Papa Nsimba outlines a history of dreams and visions since childhood that indicated that he should be a prophet:

> In 1969, I received a dream that I should be baptized, I was baptized, then at that time, I went into fourth grade . . . it was December 24, I received another dream that . . . I was encircled by small

angelic children, they threw pebbles to me. Then, on the 24th around 2 P.M. . . . I looked at the sky here, I saw some clouds, then there was a small rainstorm during which ice fell, but it only lasted five minutes. . . . I had the inspiration . . . and then it was the 25th, we left for the church with people from the village, they began to say to us, this child has received a spiritual gift now. Monday, I heard a voice that said Go to Ntoto Ndombe, there is a child about to die there. . . . I asked the question, My God of mine, I don't know this work that I must now do? You must leave, I am with you. When I met the sick person, he was really in a coma. . . . I laid my hands on him, get up, you have to make something for him to eat. They made a small soup, he ate, he lived eight years.[32]

Here the dreams and visions that Papa Nsimba had repeatedly as a child (of angelic children, an unlikely natural phenomenon, and hearing the voice of God) led to him eventually healing another child of his illness. He emphasized that it was this sequence of visions and the resulting healing activities in which he engaged that convinced him to become a prophet later in life. Papa Nsimba founded his own prophetic church Nsinga wa Yenge in 2001.

Coming back to the many visions of Mama Mazola, which I discussed at the start of the presentation, her visions were actually of recognizable people who many BisiKongo consider to be among the ancestors of Kongo people; Prophet Simon Kimbangu and Joseph Kasa-Vubu, first president of independent Congo and leader of the Alliance of Bakongo (Alliance des Bakongo; ABAKO) nationalist movement for independence. Like Tata Makiadi, Mama Mazola saw them dressed in white, although, notably, Kimbangu is wearing a white pagne, perhaps referencing a style of dress for men that was more common in the precolonial era, while Kasa-Vubu wears white pants. In addition, the fact that she sees them at the waterside and then crosses the river with them is significant, as water is seen in Kongo cosmology as the boundary between the land of the living and that of the dead. The constant visions, especially of Kimbangu, seem to represent a sanctioning of Mama Mazola's gifts and abilities as a prophet, especially in regard to continuing the legacy of Prophet Kimbangu. Mama Mazola's visions evidence a connection to past great ancestors who have issued this calling for her to engage in prophetic activities. Moreover, Mama Mazola's vision of Simon Kimbangu in a limousine challenges the notion promoted in Pentecostal discourse that one must break with the past in order to become modern. Her experience echoes that of many others who have been inspired by visions of Kimbangu from 1921 to the present, and seeing Kimbangu in a limousine on the red dirt roads of Luozi demonstrates that the past can indeed make itself relevant in modern times. In all, these four different narratives of the role of visions in conversion demonstrate the continued salience of visions and dreams for non-Pentecostal African Christians in ways that affirmatively draw on rather than divorce people from the past.

EMBODIED CALLINGS: THE IMPORTANCE OF TREMBLING

Zakama, or trembling, is an embodied practice that has particular salience in the Lower Congo. In fact, the most notable ritual practice of Simon Kimbangu's colonial-era movement was the embodiment of spiritual power through trembling. During the precolonial era, trembling was used by *banganga* (traditional healers / diviners) in the healing of sick patients and for divination purposes, representing the physical possession of the body by spiritual beings and forces. In his analysis of trends in Kongo religious thought before, during, and after European colonialism, renowned anthropologist John Janzen associates trembling with the concept of *mpeve* and its relevance for spiritual belief and action: "*Mpeve* specified the vital principle or attribute of every individual. Its verbal root, *veeva*, meant to blow, to breathe, or implied the breeze responsible for the fluttering of a cloth or flag. . . . But the interior manifestation of *mpeve* in Kongo thought is trembling, ecstatic manifestation accompanied usually by glossalalia and exorbited eyes."[33]

In the larger discourse of Pentecostalism, trembling is not usually a sign of the Holy Spirit; rather, it is a sign of demonic possession.[34] In other studies of Pentecostal and Neo-Pentecostal churches in Africa such as in the Full Gospel Bible Fellowship Church in Dar-es-Salaam, Tanzania, trembling and shaking often occur during exorcisms, when what are believed to be evil spirits are leaving the body.[35] In contrast, in the narratives of my interviewees, sudden, unexpected trembling played a huge role in their conversion to either a prophetic church or individual activity as a prophet. These experiences of embodied trembling (zakama) themselves serve as the call to do prophetic work. Tata Makiadi explains that he first embodied the presence of the Holy Spirit through trembling at a huge revival (*nsikumusu*) put on by the Communauté Evangélique du Zaïre (CEZ) Protestant Church in 1974: "In 1971, I was baptized, but this day, I saw a certain power that descended into me but I didn't know how to make it appear. . . . in 1974, in the middle of prayer, it was there that I began to tremble . . . , in a big meeting . . . at Nkundi that they called *nsikumusu*. . . . It was there that

I trembled for the first time. People said to me, oh, you will be *ngunza*, a prophet."[36] At this revival sponsored by the mainline Protestant church in the area, other attendees interpreted Tata Makiadi's sudden trembling as a sign that he would become a prophet. While his vision occurred much earlier in his life, it was in fact the trembling that acted as an embodied signifier of the presence of the Holy Spirit and a calling to engage in the activities of prophets. This experience greatly impacted his decision to leave the CEZ Church and join the DMNA Church in Luozi. Notable also is that others in his church recognized the meaning of this trembling, even as it went against the dictates of the church itself. Here they are making sense of his experience within a larger context of prophetism in which zakama plays a central role in this area.

Similarly, as already mentioned in Mama Kudada's narrative of conversion, she began to tremble when she fled the alter in the Catholic Church. For Mama Mazola as well, her trembling began after her first dream of Prophet Simon Kimbangu and Joseph Kasa-Vubu. Her narrative of how she eventually accepted this embodied calling to become a prophet was built around a number of visions and experiences of intense bodily trembling. Before she fully accepted the spiritual call she had received, she tried to ignore it and just go on with daily life, trying unsuccessfully to sell her goods across the Congo River. After a number of unsuccessful trips, she had another dream in which Tata Simon Kimbangu appeared again, this time chastising her: "You don't listen to the Holy Spirit? You don't want to work with the Holy Spirit?" Her body began to tremble again, and she screamed out the name of Jesus. People came running into her compound to help her, but she told them not to touch her. Not long after, she went to the river to fetch some water, but each time she tried to pick up the container to put it on her head, it fell down. Another woman at the river helped her to carry the water, and when they arrived at Mama Mazola's compound, she began to tremble again. She began to run all around Luozi, eventually jumping from a bridge into the Luozi River, causing alarm and panic in the town. A group of students tried to help her from the river, and she told them not to touch her. She then began to preach the word of God all throughout the streets of Luozi, finally starting to accept her embodied call to be an ngunza.

Mama Mazola's story places zakama at the center of her experience of conversion to kingunza. While her first experiences of the trembling occurred after dreams, eventually the trembling started to overtake her in daily life, when she was not dreaming. Her insistence that she not be touched is also a characteristic that existed among former prophets during the colonial era. Like Tata Makiadi and Mama Kudada, Mama Mazola did not seek to receive the Holy Spirit; in fact, she wanted nothing to do with it. Moreover, while none of the interviewees fell sick before trembling, the pattern of being called through their bodies clearly relates to what John Janzen has written about as spiritual calls that were seen as signs that people should be initiated as prophets or banganga.[37] However, the uncontrollable and unexpected trembling present in all of these narratives reveals the import of this particular form of embodiment for encouraging the practice of a particular form of Christianity in this area. All of this reported experience shows that centering studies of African Christianity on lived experience and more specifically on the body and embodiment offers a lens that may reveal beliefs and practices that are critical to forms of intersubjectivity that define one's Christian identity in particular ways.

CONVERSION EXPERIENCES, PROPHETISM, AND RELIGIOUS INSTITUTIONS

My last intervention here is to suggest that we reexamine the usefulness of some of the categories that are imposed on Christianity on Africa and remain aware of the fluidity of categories and how they may not fully capture the everyday realities. In his book *Faith in Flux: Pentecostalism and Mobility in Rural Mozambique*, Devaka Premawardhana questioned some of the assumptions behind the idea of a Pentecostal explosion by making the point that "religious identity is an imperfect indicator of religious activity."[38] Using his own ethnographic research in Lichinga, Mozambique, he convincingly shows that people who call themselves Pentecostals draw on multiple types of spiritual practices, Pentecostal and non-Pentecostal, in navigating their quotidian worlds. In the case of my interviewees in Congo, one could in fact say the inverse: "Religious activity is an imperfect indicator of religious identity." While all of my interviewees share similar conversion experiences grounded in prophetism in which a connection to past Kongo ancestors is centered, as well as an embodied experience that includes vigorous trembling, they all moved between churches in their searches to accommodate and nurture their prophetic gifts. Tata Makiadi moved from the CEC Church to the DMNA Church; Mama Kudada left the Catholic Church for the DMNA Church as well. Papa Nsimba left the CEC Church to found his own church, Nsinga wa Yenge in 2001. Yet, Mama Mazola's story, because it was more recent at the time of the interview, was even more telling. Mama Mazola was a member of the Kimbanguist Church in Luozi, a church founded by the sons of Simon Kimbangu, where now trembling is not encouraged or allowed by average churchgoers. The pastor of the local Kimbanguist Church and other church members came to visit Mama Mazola after she had begun preaching in the streets. This was also after she had gone for two weeks without eating and drinking, as she "could not take the odor of food." They tried to convince her to go to Nkamba, the town where Simon Kimbangu's movement began in 1921, now seen as a sacred place for Kimbanguists and other Kongo churches alike. She told them, "How can I go to Nkamba? I am weak, I haven't eaten, and God has given me permission to heal and bless people." They told her if she continued, then they were done with her. She is no longer welcome in the Kimbanguist Church. She thus occupies an undefined space in the religious landscape, as she remains unaffiliated with any church. Yet, she receives people in her compound and is now seen as a prophet by the larger community. How, then, do we classify her religious practice? Moreover, women are not allowed to heal in Kimbanguist churches or in most DMNA (Church of the Holy Spirit) churches in the Lower Congo, all institutions who place their origins in the 1921 movement of Tata Simon Kimbangu. This official prohibition contradicts the fact that during the many decades of the kingunza movement, there were many women who were also prophets.[39] For Mama Mazola, then, accepting this spiritual gift from the ancestors moved her beyond the walls of religious institutions and thus allowed her to breach standard protocol in relation to the roles of women in these other Kongo-led churches.

Questions such as these reveal the complexity of religious affiliation that may not necessarily be captured by labels such as AIC, mainline churches, or PCC. The spiritual practices that she shared—dreams and visions, and spirit-induced trembling—led her to a lack of affiliation with religious institutions. This predicament suggests that belonging needs to be reconsidered not on the basis of churches—buildings, hierarchies, infrastructure—but rather on the basis of shared spiritual experiences. A focus on the microinteractions between individuals and the spiritual realm rather than on the macrostructures of religious institutions allows us to reimagine the religious landscape in the Lower Congo while also seeing the potential limitations of institutional categories.

Moreover, for Mama Mazola, heeding the call to become a prophet was also a form of self-making that remains embedded within a larger shared intercorporeal and intersubjective experience. In a town where the missionary-founded churches are the largest, are the most prestigious, and have the most resources and power, choosing to establish one's own *lumpangu* (enclosure) is one that can lead to a lot of conflict with existing religious institutions. Yet,

Mama Mazola, and the members of her community, place themselves within a preexisting yet continuously recurring tradition of Kongo prophetism that is reinforcing one's connection to the past rather than emphasizing the rupture with the past privileged in Pentecostal discourse.

CONCLUSION

In closing, I have used these four narratives of conversion to prophetism to show that while important for understanding African Christianity, Pentecostal discourse has limitations in its applicability and usefulness. Visions and dreams, connections with the past (and with particular ancestors), and embodiment through spirit-induced trembling have vastly different meanings and uses for bangunza in modern-day Lower Congo. One of the larger takeaway points is that the specific local contexts must be taken into account when examining how people engage with and understand their own (and their community's) relationship to Christianity. In this particular region of Kongo Central, the long history of prophetism has a direct impact on how people understand what it means to be Christian. A second point is that attention to the body and embodiment plays a central role in how people in Luozi experience the Holy Spirit in their everyday lives. Last, institutional affiliations may not always capture what is actually happening on the ground in terms of how people engage with the spiritual realm as Christians in the Congo. Recognition and validation of their experiences by those around them, even if these experiences are not supported by religious institutions, are incredibly significant for shaping Kongo Christian identities in Luozi.

NOTES

1. Interview, July 31, 2010, Luozi.
2. Graham."
3. Bebbington.
4. Freston, 2.
5. Freston, 3.
6. Cruz e Silva, 166.
7. Karanja, 68.
8. Marshall; Pype, 280–310; Birgit Meyer, "'Make a Complete Break with the Past,'" 316–49; Meyer, *Translating the Devil*; Meyer, "Christianity in Africa," 447–74.
9. Meyer, "'Make a Complete Break with the Past,'" 321.
10. Meyer, "'Make a Complete Break with the Past,'" 328.
11. Meyer, "'Make a Complete Break with the Past,'" 338.
12. Engelke, 179.

13. Premawardhana, 8.
14. Axelson, 285.
15. Covington, *Gesture and Power*, 108.
16. Baum.
17. MacGaffey, *Custom and Government in the Lower Congo.*
18. Kimpianga Mahaniah, 90–93.
19. Mahaniah, 89.
20. Mahaniah, 93.
21. Mahaniah, 90–93.
22. MacGaffey, "Cultural Roots of Kongo Prophetism," 179.
23. MacGaffey, "The Religious Commissions of the BaKongo," 28; MacGaffey, *Modern Kongo Prophets.*
24. Thornton.
25. Thornton, 257.
26. Meyer, "'Make a Complete Break with the Past,'" 348.
27. Interview, July 19, 2012, Luozi.
28. Janzen, "Deep Thought," 106–39; A. kia Bunseki-Lumanisa, *N'Kongo ye nza yakun'zungidila*; MacGaffey, *Religion and Society in Central Africa.*
29. Interview, July 19, 2010, Luozi.
30. Interview, July 26, 2010, Luozi.
31. Interview, July 25, 2010, Luozi.
32. Interview, July 25, 2010, Luozi.
33. Janzen, "The Tradition of Renewal in Kongo Religion," 107.
34. Interview, Tata Makiadi, July 19, 2010, Luozi.
35. Dilger, 71.
36. Interview, July 19, 2010, Luozi.
37. Janzen.
38. Premawardhana, 10.
39. Yolanda Covington-Ward, "'Your Name is Written in the Sky,'" 317–46.

BIBLIOGRAPHY

Axelson, Sigbert. *Culture Confrontation in the Lower Congo: From the Old Congo Kingdom to the Congo Independent State with Special Reference to the Swedish Missionaries in the 1880's and 1890's.* Stockholm: Gummessons, 1970.

Baum, Robert. "Prophecy: African Prophetism." In *Encyclopedia of Religion.* 2nd ed., edited by Lindsay Jones. Detroit: Macmillan Reference, 2005, 7442–45.

Bebbington, David W. *Evangelicalism in Modern Britain: A History from the 1730s to the 1980s.* London: Routledge, 1989. ProQuest Ebook Central. http://ebookcentral.proquest.com/lib/pitt-ebooks/detail.action?docID=179445.

Covington-Ward, Yolanda. *Gesture and Power: Religion, Nationalism, and Everyday Performance in Congo.* Durham, NC: Duke University Press, 2016.

———. "'Your Name Is Written in the Sky': Unearthing the Stories of Kongo Female Prophets in Colonial Belgian Congo, 1921–1960." *Journal of Africana Religions* 2, no. 3 (2014): 317–46.

Cruz e Silva, Teresa. "Evangelicals and Democracy in Mozambique." In *Evangelical Christianity and Democracy in Africa*, edited by Terence Ranger. Oxford: Oxford University Press, 2008, 161–89.

Dilger, Hansjörg. "Healing the Wounds of Modernity: Salvation, Community and Care in a Neo-Pentecostal Church in Dar Es Salaam, Tanzania." *Journal of Religion in Africa* 37 (2007): 59–83.

Engelke, Matthew. "Past Pentecostalism: Notes on Rupture, Realignment, and Everyday Life in Pentecostal and African Independent Churches." *Africa* 80, no. 2 (2010): 177–99.

Freston, Paul. *Evangelicals and Politics in Asia, Africa and Latin America*. Cambridge: Cambridge University Press, 2001. ProQuest Ebook Central. http://ebookcentral.proquest.com/lib/pitt-ebooks/detail.action?docID=259864.

Graham, R. H. C. "The Prophets: The Remarkable Movement in Lower Congo." *Missionary Herald*, October 1921.

Janzen, John. "Deep Thought: Structure and Intention in Kongo Prophetism, 1910–1921." *Social Research* 46, no. 1 (1979): 106–39.

———. "Kongo Religious Renewal: Iconoclastic and Iconorthostic." *Canadian Journal of African Studies* 5, no. 2 (1971): 135–43.

———. *The Quest for Therapy in Lower Zaire*. Berkeley: University of California Press, 1978.

———. "The Tradition of Renewal in Kongo Religion." In *African Religions: A Symposium*, edited by Newell S. Booth Jr. New York: Nok Publishers, 1977, 69–115.

Karanja, John. "Evangelical Attitudes towards Democracy in Kenya." In *Evangelical Christianity and Democracy in Africa*, edited by Terence Ranger. Oxford: Oxford University Press, 2008, 67–93.

Kia Bunseki-Lumanisa, A. Fu-Kiau. *N'Kongo ye nza yakun'zungidila; nza-Kôngo / Le Mukongo et le monde qui l'entourait* (The MuKongo and the world that surrounds him). French Translation by Zamenga Batukezanga. Kinshasa: Office National de la recherche et de développement, 1969.

Kimpianga, Mahaniah. *La maladie et la guérison au Milieu Kongo*. Kinshasa: Éditions Centre de Vulgarisation Agricole, 1982.

MacGaffey, Wyatt. "Cultural Roots of Kongo Prophetism," *History of Religions* 17, no. 2 (1977): 177–93.

———. *Custom and Government in the Lower Congo*. Berkeley: University of California Press, 1970.

———. *Modern Kongo Prophets: Religion in a Plural Society*. Bloomington: Indiana University Press, 1983.

———. *Religion and Society in Central Africa: The BaKongo of Lower Zaire*. Chicago: University of Chicago Press, 1986.

———. "The Religious Commissions of the BaKongo," *Man* 5, no. 1 (1970): 27–38.

Marshall, Ruth. *Political Spiritualities: The Pentecostal Revolution in Nigeria*. Chicago: University of Chicago Press, 2009.

Meyer, Birgit. "Christianity in Africa: From African Independent to Pentecostal-Charismatic Churches." *Annual Review of Anthropology* 33 (2004): 447–74.

———. "'Make a Complete Break with the Past.' Memory and Post-colonial Modernity in Ghana." *Journal of Religion in Africa* 48, no. 3 (1998): 316–49.

———. *Translating the Devil: Religion and Modernity among the Ewe in Ghana*. Trenton, NJ: Africa World Press, 1999.

Premawardhana, Devaka. *Faith in Flux: Pentecostalism and Mobility in Rural Mozambique.* Philadelphia: University of Pennsylvania Press, 2018.

Pype, Katrien. "Confession cum Deliverance: In / Dividuality of the Subject among Kinshasa's Born-Again Christians." *Journal of Religion in Africa* 41 (2011): 280–310.

Thornton, John. 1998. *The Kongolese Saint Anthony: Dona Beatriz Kimpa Vita and the Antonian Movement, 1684–1706.* Cambridge: Cambridge University Press.

CHAPTER 7

Women's Evangelical Revolutions in Northern Nigeria

Shobana Shankar

INTRODUCTION

The abduction of 276 girls from their school in the town of Chibok in northeastern Nigeria by the terrorist group Boko Haram on October 14, 2014, shocked the world. Though Boko Haram had before carried out similar kidnappings of both females and males (mostly young) and continues to do so, the Chibok girls garnered the attention of international figures like Michelle Obama, Obiageli Ezekwesili, and many lesser-known activists who organized mass public protests and other campaigns to pressure Nigerian leaders to secure the girls' release.[1] Over the last six years, the escape of some of the girls and the release of over 100 of them through negotiations between the Nigerian government and Boko Haram have kept steady attention on the Chibok girls and the broader situation of girls and women in relation to Boko Haram. They have been the subject of media articles and shows, books, and a 2018 feature-length film *Stolen Daughters*, produced jointly by the BBC and HBO.[2]

A significant but, arguably, underappreciated element of the Chibok saga is the diary keeping of girls who endured life under Boko Haram. In 2017 writer, journalist, and researcher Adaobi Tricia Nwaubani, a reporter for the BBC and location producer for *Stolen Daughters*, described what she learned from Chibok survivor Naomi Adamu, who kept secret writings along with a few other girls in exercise notebooks given to them by their captors "for the Koranic classes they were made to attend."[3] Along with the important details related by Adamu from her diary to Nwaubani and the mother of Sarah Samuel, Adamu's classmate who was still in captivity,[4] other writings also provided valuable and harrowing information to the makers of *Stolen Daughters*, Karen Edwards and producer Sasha Achilli. Lines read from the diary of an unnamed girl in the film reveal the terrifying psychological torment the Boko Haram captors inflicted on the girls: "One day they asked us to write down our names. We didn't know why they needed the list. They continued to bring different people to talk to us about the importance for us to get married. We remained adamant about not getting married. To those of us who refused, they said, "we will give you the real Boko Haram 'treatment.' " The film does not elaborate on what this girl witnessed as the "treatment" for those who refused to convert but instead shows the devastating account of Habiba, a girl abducted at fifteen and forced to become a "wife." She said she did not like her "husband" but only lived with him out of fear: "He looked like a hyena that eats people. I didn't love him because he was a murder." She escaped, two months pregnant, and lives as a "Forgotten Girl" in Maiduguri. It is from Naomi Adamu's diary that we learn details of the treatment of those who refused "marriage" and conversion:

> Then they came to us and said, "Those who are Muslim, it is time for prayer." After they had prayed, [they said], "Those who are Muslim, let them be on one side and those who are Christian let them too be on one side."
>
> Then we saw jerrycan in the car so we thought it was petrol. Then they said, "Who and how many of you will turn to Muslim." So many of us, because of fear, some of us stand up and went inside. So [they said], "The rest that remain you want to die, is that why you don't want to be Muslim? We are going to burn you . . ." Then they give us that jerrycan which we thought it was petrol. It is not petrol; it is water.[5]
>
> Adamu compared the treatment of the non-converts to slavery: "Every day, they beat us. They tell us to marry and if you refuse, they will beat you. We will wash cloth, fetch water, do everything for their wives. We were slaves."[6] Another girl, Leah Sharibu, who was captured from Dapchi with 109 other girls and 1 boy, in February 2018 was not released with others because "she refused to accept Islam."[7] Her father said, "I am feeling fantastic because she did not deny Christ as her personal savior."[8]

Naomi Adamu's father told Adaobi Tricia Nwaubani that he was not surprised that his daughter kept a journal, for she "was always reading."[9] In 2018, a young adult novel, *Buried beneath the Baobab Tree*, written by Nwaubani about the Chibok girls' experiences highlighted the dreams of education that girls like Naomi lost. But Nwaubani also saw the diaries as a way for Naomi to remember and hold on to her past that was slipping away, citing this line: "My father's name is Samuel and my mother's name is Rebecca." Forgetting former lives was a clear pattern in survivors' testimonies in *Stolen Daughters* and other accounts—Boko Haram terrorists wanted precisely to destroy the abductees' past. Another significance of the diary writing lies in the traditions of witnessing and testifying in which these Christian girl-writers wrote. Adamu herself said she wrote for her family—her brothers, sisters, and parents—to "see it." She does not say more about what she wanted them to see, but her suffering, especially for keeping her faith, is one very clear revelation. Naomi's words convey the sense of a Christian stalwart in the face of great persecution.

Until now, all of the diaries by Boko Haram's captives that have been shared publicly appear to have been written by Christian girls. This is not to say that Muslim girls or boys have not kept accounts of their experiences. And it is not to ignore Boko Haram's Muslim victims, a point that is underscored here for those who decry claims of the terrorists' targeting of Christians as repoliticizing religion. But, given what the girls' diaries reveal, it is hard to overlook the use of religious differentiation and denigration as calculated Boko Haram strategies. It is equally hard to ignore the "politicization" of religious difference in the discourses of "marriage" and "slavery." The meaning to Christian Northern Nigerians of the refusal of marriage by such young and vulnerable women, written down with great care, deserves attention.

These Northern Nigerians' firsthand accounts provide glimpses of a Christian female identity, which I use as a starting place to bring greater focus to the religious lives of Christian girls and women in a predominantly Muslim society. Victimization by Boko Haram—even if these women were not the "majority" of those abducted or those whose lives have been otherwise upended—brought Northern Nigerian Christian women into a spotlight that they had arguably never occupied. In contrast to a great deal of scholarly interest in Muslim Northern Nigerian women's history, very few researchers have considered the history of Christian women— an invisible group within a religious minority—in Northern Nigeria as worthy of deeper exploration.[10] Of the growing number of studies on Christianity in Northern Nigeria, most written since Christian-Muslim tensions began to increase in the 1990s, very few pay attention to women or gender dynamics.

The Chibok girls' diaries suggest that it is time to address this sorely neglected topic. One reason that scholars should be interested is that Christian Northern Nigerian women have produced their own narratives. In a remarkable parallel, the writings of Muslim Northern Nigerian women, particularly Nana Asma'u, the daughter of Shehu Usman 'dan Fodio, leader of the Sokoto jihad in the nineteenth century, have also been found in this same region and have captivated scholars.[11] These writings cover many topics, from honoring women's piety to celebrating the wartime victories of the Sufi reformers over their opponents; they demonstrate the possibilities of Muslim women's leadership in religious life and their importance in the wider community. The modes of Muslim women's expression—poetry and exegesis—may be different from those of Christian women, but, for now, we still do not have any research into Christian education or cultural expression of Northern Nigerian women, as we find with Muslim women. If great differences exist in the religious activities and expectations of Muslim and Christian women, could we learn more about the nature of cultural and social difference in Northern Nigerian society?

Research on Islam among Northern Nigerian women has yielded provocative and often unexpected insights about broader society. Added to historical research showing Sufi women's distinct piety in the nineteenth and twentieth centuries, Muslim women's activities in education, law, and social welfare have emerged as important spheres in the aftermath of the declaration of shari'a law in all or parts of twelve states in the north of Nigeria since 1999.[12] Fatima Adamu has analyzed women's centrality in the regulation of public morality through an incident in 2004, when the government of Kano State, the largest in Northern Nigeria, attempted to ban the use of motorcycle taxis for women.[13] The move was intended to appease those who supported the increased separation of men and women as part of shari'a implementation. In addition to adding public buses reserved for women, the state imported 500 rickshaws from India to serve as cheap alternatives, which were stenciled with the words "Be Pious." When the *hisba*, or volunteer morality police corps, attempted to punish women riders and motorcycle drivers who defied the use of these state transports, conflicts broke out. Adamu aptly notes that "the redefinition of the role of women in relation to public morality" could have profound impacts on gender relations more broadly, particularly in the private realm, where male relatives could feel more emboldened to "monitor, 'protect' and curtail the behaviour of junior women."[14] At the same time, women themselves have resisted infringement on their movements and their involvement in social life.

Indeed, the many gendered layers of and experiences of religious reformism in Northern Nigeria have, at turns, scared and confused observers, particularly westerners who fear "radicalism" in Africa's most populous nation with a northern border on the Sahel. The adultery convictions and proposed stoning of Safiatu Hussein and Amina Lawal in the earlier years of shari'a implementation shocked international observers, but just a few years later the *New York Times* painted the Kano ban on women on motorcycles as "a distinctly Nigerian compromise between the dictates of faith and the chaotic realities of modern life."[15] In 2007, A *Washington Post* article featured a sentiment from Northern Nigerians themselves: "Nigerians say the strictest interpretation of sharia runs counter to their culture. Keeping women behind doors and out of sight, or cloaking them in fabric, is a foreign idea in Nigeria, where women play leading roles in economic life."[16] Professor Mustapha Ismail, founder of the Centre of Human Rights in Islam in Kano and an Arabist scholar who helped defend several women in high-profile shari'a court cases, has had Muslim and Christian women seek his legal aid in order to take cases to shari'a courts or with community-level hisba negotiators.[17]

Given that Muslim and Christian women in Northern Nigeria do not conform to expectations, their histories merit more intensive and comparative investigation. To that end, this chapter has two interrelated purposes. First, it provides a deeper historical examination of Northern Nigerian Christianity as a female religion. It highlights key areas in which Christianity connected to and challenged some fundamental social norms in the region. The focus here is on Protestant evangelical Christianity, which arrived in Northern Nigeria through the work of African, European, and American missionaries from the nineteenth century. Throughout the broader history of Christian missions in the region, the most relevant point for the purposes of this essay is that reformist Islam being the basis of power—political, cultural, social, and economic—in the northernmost areas of what became the British Protectorate of Northern Nigeria had major consequences for the religious development of the region, consequences that continue to play out today. The British banned Christian missions in certain parts of the protectorate and encouraged them in others, albeit by trying to control foreign missionaries and Nigerian converts with a heavy hand.[18] Christianity became strongest among communities where Islam had not been a major religion and, in many cases, where antagonism toward the predominantly Muslim Hausa and Fulani ethnic elites stemmed from older histories of slave raiding, ethnic conflicts, and political disagreements.[19] Christian subjectivity understood in the experience of slavery as voiced by the Chibok girls therefore has a historical resonance but so too does the girls' resistance to Muslim conversion. It reveals a Christian honor, demonstrated here amid attempts at forced conversion, which needs to be unpacked.[20]

Given that Christianity in Northern Nigeria is inextricable from Islam in many ways, the second goal of this chapter is to examine interreligious relations through the lives of girls and women. The Chibok girls' experiences reveal the reality of religious competition and coerced conversion as gendered lived experiences, and here I seek to place this dynamic in a historical cultural framework by asking: Why do Muslim-Christian tensions play out on female bodies in Northern Nigeria? And to go further, when girls and women are at the center of religious conflicts, how do we understand the priority placed on marriage, labor, or learning and literary activities as social expressions of piety, if we consider Sufi women's writings along with those of Christian Boko Haram survivors? The work of political scientist Hilary Matfess on Muslim women survivors of Boko Haram—including escapees and willing vigilantes who remain with the group—allows us to compare women's voices across religious differences and see a commonality, a desire for identity. Identity may be defined not only by a confessional mode but also a social, even a familial, presence. Matfess's research in Nigeria and other countries suggests that the rising costs of marriage hampering young men and women to become independent from their families may be fueling alienation and even violence.[21] While an in-depth analysis of this finding in relation to Northern Nigeria is impossible to accommodate in this article, this perspective suggests a common basis with other research on Christian-Muslim relations in Southern Nigeria and world Christianity more broadly.[22] In arguing that world Christianity is a women's movement, Dana Robert writes about the "costs" of conversion that once held more women back from Christianity or made their conversions individual affairs rather than familial or social movements: the potential loss of marital or other familial stability and the difficulty of subsistence without male income.[23] But Christianity's "liberative potential"—as a source of solidarity, healing, and positions of leadership—still won over women, even when men might eventually resume dominance in the faith. While Robert's demographic concern about women in Christianity may not be as relevant for the case of the Christian minority in Northern Nigeria, her points about what shapes pious identity appear to be driving, at least in some measure, female identification in Christian-Muslim dynamics in Northern Nigeria.

A REVOLUTION IN THE MAKING? WOMEN IN ISLAMIC REFORM

Several observers, notably white women, in Northern Nigeria during the era of British colonial rule (ca. 1900–60) wondered whether women would ever recognize their oppression and rise up. Writing from Ilorin Province, a largely Muslim region situated in the south of the Northern Provinces, Sylvia Leith-Ross, lady superintendent of education, noted that Muslim women seemed content with their lives.[24] She found no tradition of female Islamic scholarship as in other parts of Northern Nigeria, and women seemed more interested in business. She recommended that the colonial government not change "until the women cry out for it."[25] Voicing a similar idea of Muslim women's complacency just a few years later, Dame Margery Perham, a historian and political observer, visited a school for elite Muslim girls in Katsina and "felt like a wild bird indeed, looking in that cage."[26] The British administrator consoled her, "They like it all right. They don't know anything else," but Perham hoped for a better future instead: "I wondered how long it would take them to cross over to where I stood, and remembered with a more instructed satisfaction what the Emancipation which happened of late in Turkey."[27] With the then recent secularization of law and women's suffrage movement after the fall of the Ottoman Empire, Turkey seemed like a good comparison.

Yet it can be argued that Northern Nigeria had experienced a women's revolution a century earlier, during the era of the Fulani jihad, and was indeed undergoing another perhaps quieter but no less dramatic upheaval with the conversion of girls and women to Christianity from the early 1900s. Both transformations occurred in the status of non-Muslim women, who were practitioners of indigenous religions before the nineteenth century, and then of Christianity with the arrival of missions.

Even before the nineteenth century, we know that interactions between Muslim and non-Muslim women occurred in the domestic spaces of elite women, particularly of the Muslim royalty, where slavery brought girls and women of different social status and religious backgrounds lived.[28] A significant new emphasis on interactions between Muslim and non-Muslim women came in the nineteenth century with the work of Nana Asma'u, mentioned earlier.[29] As the daughter of Shehu Usman 'dan Fodio, the jihadi leader who fought to reform Islamic practice in the Hausa emirates and founded the Sokoto Caliphate, Nana Asma'u was elite but not like urban Hausa royalty. Asma'u was a prolific poet, biographer, and, most significant, educator and exhorter of women to renounce non-Islamic practices such as *bori* (often translated as spirit possession).[30] Her reputation was made and popularized through her activism to reform women's practice of Islam. The political urgency of reformism allowed this elite woman to redraw the map of women's movements through her interaction with non-Muslim women and to justify pious Muslim women's mobility as a necessity for the flowering of Islam.

The new kind of Muslim womanhood was sown first in the small ascetic community of Degel, where the family of Usman 'dan Fodio lived apart from the rest of the world with a group of other nomadic Fulani families. The community was remote, being far even from other nomadic encampments. Manual labor was required of all community members,[31] but this labor was intended for subsistence, not accumulation. Asma'u's work was a part of her training as a woman in the scholarly community of the Fulbe. This community lived with insecurity, however, as pressure mounted from "settled" neighbors like the Hausa. Increasing taxation, cattle, and slave raids, and a growing animosity between rural-based and urban-based Muslim scholars and traders, threatened the Fulbe way of life.[32] 'dan Fodio placed increasing emphasis on the need for Fulbe girls and women to dress carefully as a protective measure in public spaces. This prescription was not necessarily a stringent interpretation of Islamic gender norms, or even exclusively religiously motivated, but a necessity to maintain "social presence" within an environment of increasing insecurity stemming from migration and political repression.[33]

With the success of the jihad and the establishment of the new caliphate's capital at Sokoto, Asma'u moved as a young bride of sixteen to the new town, where her status and stature surely acquired new meaning against an altogether novel set of circumstances. Urban elite women, as Kano's example showed, lived with a high degree of socioeconomic stratification, non-Muslim and Muslim living together as masters and servants, with a high price placed on spatial boundaries to mark differences within an enclosed household or urban enclave.[34] Asma'u was not so much an elite woman as she was a Muslim reformist seeking to adapt the idealism of the rural ascetic world into the Hausa cities; her worldview did not prioritize the boundaries of the city but rather saw them as spaces of activism to reform behavior and beliefs. Asma'u wrote to publicize the teachings of her father and her brother Caliph Muhammad Bello and composed poems warning against specific behaviors among women such as drumming except to call public meetings, performing communal labor, and serving during wartime. She also sermonized against the use of spirit possession (bori) for seeking rain, and jealousy.[35] Asma'u further promoted greater mobility for women and "purdahlessness" as not only acceptable but pious in the performance of religious duty to improve society.

The jihadists sought to reconstruct prevailing notions of shame (Hausa, *kunya*), which circumscribed social intercourse. 'dan Fodio disliked the Hausa practice of parental avoidance of speaking the name of their firstborn, which was part of the general avoidance between parents and their firstborn child, often leading to the firstborn being sent to the home of relatives to be fostered (*riko*).[36] 'dan Fodio's opposition, perhaps a rejection of cultural "superstition," made clear that prescriptions governing avoidance and social separation were surmountable, particularly in the interest of maintaining the domestic sphere as a moral community. The intimacy between himself and his children did, in fact, foster the inheritance of religious leadership from mothers and fathers to sons and daughters. Asma'u focused on the shame of women, arguing at once its limits and its necessity from the Islamic perspective. She viewed seclusion as not mandatory or religiously prescribed, nor a sign of socioeconomic status, but rather a mark of pious election.

In "Sufi Women," a poem Asma'u composed in 1837, the various activities of venerable pious girls and women are celebrated.[37] The list of activities that made women noteworthy includes domestic roles as wife, mother, and daughter as well as recluse, preacher, provider of horses for jihad, scholar, resolver of disputes, and seer of "male and female jinns." Even when the Prophet's daughter Fatimah, who preached on the mosque steps in Medina, which was the model community for Sokoto, tried to stop her own activities, Asma'u reminded her readers that the Prophet Muhammad himself encouraged her to continue her calling, describing her as noble because of her work. Significantly, on the issue of women's seclusion, Asma'u may have disagreed with her own brother, the caliph Muhammad Bello. Bello had to defend an attack from a scholar of the Borno Empire on Lake Chad, a Muslim stronghold that had refused allegiance to Sokoto, because women were allowed to join men at the caliph's meetings.[38] Bello hardened against women's participation as he faced more critics and challengers, including the members of the Tijaniyya Sufi order that competed with the Qadiriyya order to which 'dan Fodio's family belonged. Amid sectarian and political conflicts, Asma'u's religious agenda began to lose its more modest tone. She took a more authoritative and admonitory tone toward women's behavior in the poem "A Warning, II"; food and education as a religious obligation were reasons for women to move freely in public, albeit in "modest dress."[39] The admonition seems directed equally toward men and women in its depiction of women's movement for education as an obligation, not a choice.

Asma'u founded women's associations, known as *'yan taru*, which made the issue of women's movement in the public sphere more prominent. Intended initially as a collective of women undertaking pilgrimage to local shrines of Sufi leaders, 'yan taru were led by female literati known as *jajis*. The leaders were often postmenopausal women and their younger female followers. The leader wore a men's hat and magenta cloth as her caravan moved through villages singing songs, carrying alms of grain, and camping out in the open. The costume resembled the earlier precedent used by bori women, ostensibly building on and co-opting earlier precedent but perhaps seeking to blend in with the bori women in order to garner safe passage.[40]

These organizations, which lasted into the 1960s, have been described as "educational efforts" linking rural women within Islam. The links were vertical, however, for the 'yan taru clearly represented a model of "faith-based development," as the women took butter, cloth, and grain relief to less fortunate women.[41] Less fortunate did not necessarily mean poorer; it meant those who were less educated in Islam, or who had been defeated militarily, or even those who were unsuccessful in the use of other means, such as bori, in supplications for rain or other desired outcomes. In her poem "A Prayer for Rain," Asma'u asks Allah to answer their many requests made for rain.[42] Islam provided, whereas bori and gambling were effort and money misspent. Asma'u's strategy was intended not to stigmatize these practices but to demonstrate their futility. She strove to emphasize a lack of shame in women's move away from bori practices, or in full conversion to Islam. Joining the new club could be an aspiration, one that could enhance economic power. 'yan taru made alms distribution into a public women's effort, cementing the role of unmarried girls and older women as agents of the redistributive economic agenda of the jihad. Restricting their movements was tantamount to opposing Islamic duty.

Women's mobility had become a priority of Islamic reform, a measure of a society's success in achieving greater moral heights. Charity and efforts to instruct women or even convert them were permissible activities for pious Muslim women to undertake toward non-Muslim women outside the domestic realm. Yet, by the late nineteenth and early twentieth centuries, women's seclusion became increasingly popular among Muslim women, including nonelite women, as a marker of respectability and social improvement.[43] The transition of many women from slavery to freedom—hastened by British abolition of slavery in 1901—appears to be a major reason for increasing emphasis on female seclusion, but other reasons, such as seclusion being an attainable form of respectability, also prevailed to popularize purdah.

These social changes had many impacts on non-Muslim women—as their cultural practices were increasingly forbidden by Muslim women, slaves (including women in the domestic realm) became more mobile while Muslim women increasingly secluded to be respectable. With the British abolition of slavery, the mobility of non-Muslim girls and women, who were the slaves of choice in the trans-Saharan trade, became a problem. Even the emancipators—the British—viewed them with suspicion, fearing the formation of an "undesirable class of unattached females."[44] To "enclose" these "freed" females, in 1908 the Sudan United Mission (SUM) opened a freed slaves home on the Benue River at the behest of the British colonial government, and the Sudan Interior Mission (SIM) station at Wushishi on the Niger also effectively functioned as a home for freed slave girls. While male freed slaves were taken as soldiers and porters in the West African Frontier Force and other colonial government sectors, girls flooded the Christian freed slave homes. Christian missionaries like J. Lowry Maxwell, who led the SUM's freed slave work from 1909, had little hope about the prospects for Christianity among freed slave girls, who numbered well over half of those in his care. He believed that they did not work hard enough and were easily seduced by town life.[45]

This agenda affected women's Christianity and gendered Christian-Muslim politics in critical ways. First, Christianity was at first a religion of slave girls and women, who fled their former masters and were mobile in a manner that threatened the social order and religious (especially Islamic) norms. Second, the missions responded by inculcating a womanhood that was not socially disruptive; indeed Christian women, marked as former slaves and suspected practitioners of "pagan rites," were often made invisible to improve the reputation of the already marginalized Christian faith. Christian Northern Nigerian women were, in a sense, from the beginning doubly marginalized by their conversion.

CHRISTIAN WOMEN'S QUIET REVOLUTION

Northern Nigerian women who converted to Christianity, even those who were "rescued" from slavery, faced many burdens by becoming members of the new and wholly marginal religious community. Adding to scrutiny and reformists' attention brought about by the jihad and the moral imperative of reformists like Nana Asma'u, new control came with the European and American Christian missionaries, who faced obstacles to their preaching in Northern Nigeria and who tried to minimize the position of women in the church, in deference to the will of the British and Muslim authorities.[46] The patriarchal expectations of British colonial authorities matched those of many Christian missionary leaders. Many examples can be found in records of church discipline in all denominations. The Evangelical Churches of West Africa, the indigenous church that grew out of the SIM, compiled notes from the colonial-era mission documents in 1979 and found the following rules:

1. A woman who wishes to stay with an adulterous husband should be rebuked (on the orders of the church elders). (Dec. 28, 1942)
2. More attention should be paid to adultery. Cases were cited where Christian women were indifferent to the unfaithfulness of their Christian husbands and had offered no objection to their loose living. In two cases the women had later become "harlots" themselves. (Oct. 20, 1943)

In response to pressing questions from Nigerian church elders about women's rights to leave or remarry in cases of adulterous husband, SIM's general director Guy Playfair clarified that "innocent" women had such rights, leaving open the suggestion that most women were not innocent.[47] Women were held responsible for their husbands' behavior and had to be the ones to take action in such cases, risking negative perceptions that they had broken up their families.

The church elders, who were largely male in the early Northern Nigerian churches, were surely somewhat fearful that the older women who came into the mission fold might bring some "traditional" powers into Christianity. Yangola, a woman who had had ten children and was a grandmother before she was freed from slavery and worked at the British government home for freed slaves home, had facial piercings and other markings that made her different from younger uninitiated girls; missionaries speculated that she was a practitioner of spirit possession. While they trusted her and believed her Christianity became strong, she was never given the opportunity to attend the mission school or do much more than cook or care for children.[48] Barbara Cooper, in her study of a Christian mission in neighboring French Niger, describes a similar *arna* (pagan) ex-slave woman, Tashibka, who was considered one of the strongest Christian believers yet also something of an embarrassment to Nigerien men—"a former slave, a medium of sorts, a 'traditional' illiterate person, a poverty-stricken dependent of the mission."[49]

We do get a sense of how Christian girls and women constructed new kinds of respectability in the circumscribed avenues they had, although not from their own writings. While we are still waiting to find firsthand written accounts of Christian girls and women in Northern Nigeria that date from the colonial period, we find that educated Christian young men wrote with concern about the situation of girls, particularly Christian girls with whom they were schooled, whom the missionaries saw as their peers and potential spouses.[50] These educated Christian girls represented a distinct contrast with the majority of girls and women in Northern Nigeria, argued John Mamman Garba, a convert from Islam to Christianity who attended the Anglican school at Wusasa outside Zaria City. Garba and Joseph Mohammed Sani, another Muslim boy who was brought to the Church Missionary Society (CMS) to study, noted the contradictory demands that Christian education and marriage imposed on girls in particular.[51] Joseph wrote that his first teachers in the infant school where he was placed were pupil-teachers; that is, "they were themselves pupils in Standard V or VI, and they had no intention of taking teaching as a profession, they were only teachers for a short time."[52] The older girls, who were sixteen or seventeen years old, were either finished with the highest class, Standard VI, or too old to matriculate into that class. They were waiting to marry. Of the two Hausa Christian girls in John Garba's class, one married the school headmaster, a graduate of the school, and the other married the senior nurse at the CMS Saint Bartholomew Hospital.[53]

Marriage continued to be a tortured issue for Christians and Muslims as Northern Nigerian society was changing. In 1949–50, anthropologist M. G. Smith conducted fieldwork on economic conditions in Zaria and described increasing openness of Hausa Muslim parents to giving their children choice:

> Hausa say that parents nowadays consult the wishes of their children, when arranging their first marriages, much more readily than they did in the past; in pre-British days, particularly among the upper classes, marriages were usually arranged over the heads of the young people concerned, and if there was a clash of will between a girl and her parents there were three possible solutions; either the girl threw herself down a well, either before or after the marriage, or if she could obtain the backing of her mother and her mother's kin she might persuade her parents to seek a divorce for her, or she might tafi dandi—"go out into the world," risking enslavement to seek her independence in a distant city as a karuwa (prostitute or courtesan).[54]

Significantly, social strictures around Muslim marriage among nonelites seemed to be loosening, while Christian and elite Muslim marriages were tightly controlled by adults. This unexpected commonality between Christian and Muslim matrimonial matchmaking probably had to do with education, as missionaries and wealthier Muslims saw girls educated outside the home as more difficult to "marry off." Education superintendent Leith-Ross concluded that girls and women in Ilorin saw western schools as making girls, rather, refuse marriage to men who were not clerks or somehow in the ambit of colonial or modern institutions. Her research suggests that perhaps western education itself led to earlier marriage as protection against loss of respectability.[55]

Garba, who became active in Northern Nigerian politics, was so concerned about the general situation of women in Northern Nigeria that he wrote news commentaries on the topics; his concern stemmed in part from his own struggles to manage the expectations of his Muslim family and his mentor Dr. Walter Miller, the founder of the CMS mission at Zaria. In the 1940s, when he studied at the London School of Economics, he brought the issue of women's welfare for discussion at a meeting of Nigerian students in London who had gathered to write a collective letter to the Nigerian representative to legislative meetings with the British colonial authorities. A heated debate on girls' education and purdah ensued, leading the chairman, Alhaji Isa Koto, to oppose discussing the issue as a political imperative: "If you are heading towards changing our traditions by revolutionary methods then count me out."[56]

These conflicts as well as the curtailment of opportunities made education become a valued expression of piety among Christian girls and women. But it is important to define education in the local context. Mission records show that African women seemed not to have been baptized until many years after service to the mission, suggesting either their disinterest in such rites or the disinterest of the missionaries with whom they worked to conduct the rites. This disengagement from the ritualism regularly associated with missions, particularly with the agendas of male missionaries, remained the case for Northern Nigerian Christian women, who put little emphasis on church attendance and public testimony. Rather, literacy and oratory exegesis of the Bible were much more highly valued as a practice among women.

For example, the 1918 influenza pandemic and a sleeping sickness outbreak the following year killed a large number of early Hausa Christian converts in Gimi, near Zaria. Without "formal training," as it were, Hausa women replaced male teachers and conducted the classes held at the Zaria mission; some women were even able to become students because many children died and missionaries realized a crisis was unfolding.[57] A few older girls and women became evangelists.

One-time CMS missionary and sister of Walter Miller, Ethel Miller, was instrumental in teaching Muslim and Christian women to read and write in the Roman script in Zaria and later Kano.[58] Accompanied by Hausa Christian converts, she visited homes and offered the instruction as a service. She also used her home as a refuge for runaway girls—usually fleeing unwanted or abusive spouses—who came to her, instead of staying with the Christian missions.[59] Some missionaries would pay bride price or other sums for such girls, thus delaying marriage for some years. She described herself as a revolutionary even before coming to Nigeria and fostered Christianity as a faith that needed no institutional structure. One of her publications, *Hausa Heroines* (1923), describes the lives of girls and women who lived in Gimi and other places, demonstrating very clearly her idea of revolutionary possibilities for women in Northern Nigeria.[60]

The book is not concerned with religious conversion or Muslim-Christian conflicts, as her later publications and many other mission works were. Rather, it focuses on female fortitude—Christian and Muslim—in a society dominated by men, with marriage the sole expectation for girls. In four of the five stories named for their protagonists, the girls or woman meet Ethel Miller after fleeing unwanted or abusive marriages. And in all of the vignettes, learning to read as a means of self-contentment is central. The character Diji, for example, comes to Miller as a Qur'anic student from a lettered family; the girl is married off early, owing to her dad's debts; she reads her books in secret even within the palace into which she is married. Aya arrives in Gimi after fleeing her negligent husband and decides to try not only learning to read Roman script but the other "strange views" of the whites that "have done more for her in a month than her husband did in a life time."[61] The next story finds Rakiya finding a new husband with whom she converts to Christianity, and together they read hymns in church, unlike other Muslim converts who separate on the basis of sex. Miller relates in the next story teaching the freed slave girl Hawa to read, and, though she understands little, the Book of Revelation remains a comfort to which she returns again and again, especially when she decides not to walk five miles to church and instead prays alone at home. Jimai, of all the characters, is the only one who is still looking for a husband at the end of the book, but Miller continues to treat her ulcer and teach her to read and sing hymns: "Sweetest name on mortal tongue, Jesus precious Jesus."[62]

Miller's "revolutionary" work, as she saw it, was to foster women's personal piety through biblical teaching, without any church body or leadership needed. The fact that many women whom Miller mentored were not Christian was, in and of itself, testimony to the power of Christian words and deeds, unbound from institutions and rules that lay so heavily upon women in Northern Nigeria. Evangelical Christianity inspired a portable, personal, and private relationship between oneself and God, a relationship that even overshadowed marriage.

Indeed, for many Christian Northern Nigerian women, deepening this relationship with God meant delaying marriage, and education became the valorous path that justified that delay, a connection between education and later marriage that Sylvia Leith-Ross seemed to predict years before more schools opened after World War II. The life story of Mary Lar, who grew up in the Jos Plateau region, illustrates this well.[63] Mary's mother and father were early converts of the SUM, but even they did not want to challenge the norm that girls were not educated beyond gaining the ability to read the Bible in Hausa. Mary persisted in school, eventually marrying in her early twenties to Solomon Lar, who went on to become governor of Plateau State. She has had a distinguished career in education continuing today, along with many Christian Northern Nigerian women, and one of Mary's unique contributions has been to nomadic education in a part of Nigeria that has witnessed episodic conflict between nomadic and sedentary communities, Muslim and Christian.[64] She has also fought for the recognition of women evangelists through forums such as the World Congress on Evangelism, an issue that continues to be debated in Northern Nigeria but pushed vigorously by churchwomen.[65] Educational work for women like Mary serves as a public manifestation of a personal relationship with God.

CONCLUSION

Coming back to the Chibok girls and other Boko Haram abductees who have narrated their experiences, I argue that it is no coincidence that girl students might respond to Boko Haram's marriage proposals and forced conversions in the way they have. Christians' resistance to their girls marrying Muslims (or "pagans") goes back to the mission days, when white missionaries included these types of marriage on their list of punishable offenses. Today, unmarried Christian females in school possess a layered identity—cultivated in stories from church, elders, and peers—that represents a minority religious community's past struggles and futurist hopes. This identity, when attacked, has withstood and grown stronger in some quarters.

Whereas once non-Muslim girls and women were valued only for their labor as slaves in Muslim households and Muslim women were seen as pious religious agents, now a competition has arisen over female piety, social progress, and respectability. This competition gives a more nuanced meaning to Boko Haram's war on education. Western education is forbidden but especially so for anyone who wants to claim she is pious. Yet this view stands in fundamental conflict with the belief of Northern Nigerian Christian women, for whom the ability to read, write, and teach has brought some measure of independence they have been struggling to achieve for a long time.

NOTES

1. Matthew Adeiza and Philip Howard, "Social Media and Soft Power Politics in Africa: Lessons from #BringBackOurGirls and Kenya's #SomeoneTellCNN," in *The Routledge Handbook of Soft Power*, ed. Naren Chitty, Li Ji, and Gary D. Rawnsley (New York: Routledge, 2016), 219–31; Tricia Adaobi Nwaubani, "#BringBackOurGirls Was a Mistake," PRI's *World Commentary*, March 16, 2017. https://www.pri.org/stories/2017-03-16/bringbackourgirls-was-mistake; Hilary Matfess. "Paved with Good Intentions: Three Years Later, a Look at the #BringBackOurGirls Catch-22," *Daily Beast*, April 14, 2017; http://www.thedailybeast.com/three-years-later-a-look-at-the-bringbackourgirls-catch-22.
2. *Stolen Daughters: Kidnapped by Boko Haram*, dir. Gemma Atwal, produced by BCC and HBO, released October 22, 2018. English transcription from the film's producers.
3. Adaobi Tricia Nwaubani, "Chibok Diaries: Chronicling a Boko Haram Kidnapping," *BBC World News Africa*, October 22, 2017, accessed July 20, 2024, https://www.bbc.com/news/world-africa-41570252.
4. Adaobi Tricia Nwaubani, "Diaries Offer Hope to Chibok Bride in Captivity," Reuters, September 28, 2017, accessed November 20, 2019, http://news.trust.org/item/20170928170739-dc4cu/.
5. Nwaubani, "Chibok Diaries."
6. Nwaubani, "Chibok Diaries."
7. Ruth MacLean, "Boko Haram Kept One Dapchi Girl," *Guardian* (online), March 24, 2018, https://www.theguardian.com/world/2018/mar/24/boko-haram-kept-one-dapchi-nigeria-girl-who-refused-to-deny-her-christianity
8. MacLean, "Boko Haram Kept One Dapchi Girl."
9. Nwaubani, "Chibok Diaries."
10. Elizabeth Isichei, ed., *Varieties of Christian Experience in* Nigeria (London: Macmillan, 1982); Kathleen McGarvey, *Muslim and Christian Women in Dialogue: The Case of Northern* Nigeria (Bern, Switzerland: Peter Lang 2009); Shobana Shankar, *Who Shall Enter Paradise? Christian Origins in Muslim Northern Nigeria, c. 1890–1975* (Athens: Ohio University Press, 2014), especially chap. 5. In addition to these scholarly works, a recent news article on Hausa-speaking Christian women's church groups in the *Guardian* is a notable exception, a product of better-quality reporting on African affairs undertaken by Africa-based journalists. Eromo Egbejule, "The Nigerian Women in a Sisterhood of Millions," *Guardian*, June 19, 2024, accessed July 20, 2024, https://www.theguardian.com/global-development/article/2024/jun/19/fellowship-married-women-church-groups-northern-nigeria-conflict.
11. A recent examination by one of the foremost scholars of Nana Asma'u's writings, Beverly Mack, provides a good review of Asma'u's inspiration for a tradition of Northern

Nigerian Muslim women's writing, but there is a large literature that cannot all be cited here. Beverly Mack, "Nana Asma'u: A Model for Literate Women Muslims." In *The Routledge Companion to Black Women's Cultural Histories*, ed. Janell Hodgson (New York: Routledge, 2021), 100–108. Solagberu nicely places Asma'u's writings in a wider context of other Muslim women authors. Abdur-Razzaq Mustapha Balogun Solagberu, Nana Asma'u," *Islamic Studies* 60, no. 4 (2021): 399–410. See also Alaine S. Hutson, "The Development of Women's Authority in the Kano Tijaniyya, 1894–1963," *Africa Today* (1999): 43–64; Jean Boyd and Beverly Mack, *One Woman's Jihad: Nana Asma'u, Scholar and Scribe* (Bloomington: Indiana University Press, 2000); Jean Boyd, "Distance Learning from Purdah in Nineteenth-Century Northern Nigeria: The Work of Asma'u Fodiyo," *Journal of African Cultural Studies* 14, no 1 (June 2001): 7–22; Mary Wren Bivins, *Telling Stories, Making Histories: Women, Words, and Islam in Nineteenth-Century Hausaland and the Sokoto Caliphate* (Portsmouth, NH: Heinemann, 2007).

12. *Sharia Implementation in Northern Nigeria, 1999–2006, A Sourcebook; Comparative Perspectives on Shariah in Northern Nigeria*, comp. and ed. Philip Ostien (Ibadan: Spectrum Books, 2007).

13. Fatima L. Adamu, "Gender, Hisba and the Enforcement of Morality in Northern Nigeria," *Africa* 78, no. 1 (2008): 136–52. See also Alaine Hutson, "Gender, Mobility, and Sharia," *ISIM* Newsletter 11 (2002): 16.

14. Adamu, "Gender, Hisba and the Enforcement of Morality," 150.

15. Lydia Polgreen, "Nigeria Turns from Harsher Side of Islamic Law," *New York Times*, December 1, 2007, accessed July 20, 2024, https://www.nytimes.com/2007/12/01/world/africa/01shariah.html.

16. Edward Harris, "In Nigeria's North, A Compromise between Islamic Law, Secular Culture," *Washington Post*, April 15, 2007, accessed July 20, 2024, http://www.washingtonpost.com/wp-dyn/content/article/2007/04/14/AR2007041401279_2.html.

17. Author personal communication with Professor Mustapha Ismail, Kano, Nigeria, December 12, 2019.

18. E. P. T. Crampton, *Christianity in Northern Nigeria* (Zaria, Nigeria: Gaskiya, 1976); Toyin Falola, *Violence in Nigeria: The Crisis of Religious and Secular Ideologies* (Rochester, NY: University of Rochester Press, 1998); Andrew E. Barnes, *Making Headway: The Introduction of Western Civilization in Colonial Northern Nigeria* (Rochester, NY: University of Rochester Press, 2009); Shankar, *Who Shall Enter Paradise?*

19. Shankar, *Who Shall Enter Paradise?*; Moses E. Ochonu, *Colonialism by Proxy: Hausa Imperial agents and Middle Belt Consciousness in Nigeria* (Bloomington: Indiana University Press, 2014); Niels Kastfelt, *Religion and Politics in Nigeria: A Study in Middle Belt Christianity* (New York: British Academic Press, 1994); Jan Harm Boer, *Christianity and Islam under Colonialism in Northern Nigeria* (Jos: Christian Council of Nigeria, 1988).

20. Shobana Shankar, "Race, Ethnicity, and Assimilation: The Influence of American Anthropology on Christian-Muslim relations in British Northern Nigeria," *Social Sciences and Missions* 29, no. 1–2 (2016): 37–65.

21. Valerie M. Hudson and Hilary Matfess, "In Plain Sight: The Neglected Linkage between Brideprice and Violent Conflict," *International Security* 42, no. 1 (2017): 7–40.

22. Insa Nolte, Olukoya Ogen, and Rebecca Jones, *Beyond Religious Tolerance: Muslim, Christian and Traditionalist Encounters in an African Town* (Oxford: James Currey, 2017).

23. Dana Robert, "World Christianity as a Women's Movement," *International Bulletin of Missionary Research* 30, no. 4 (2006): 180–88.

24. Sylvia Leith-Ross papers, April 30, 1929, Rhodes House Library, MSS Afr.s.1520, Oxford, UK.

25. Sylvia Leith-Ross papers, April 30, 1929.

26. Margery Perham, Notes on Katsina, 1931–32, Rhodes House Library, MSS Perham Box 46/7 [file 7], Oxford, UK.

27. Margery Perham, Notes on Katsina, 1931–32.

28. Heidi Nast, "Islam, Gender, and Slavery in West Africa c. 1500: A Spatial Archaeology of the Kano Palace, Northern Nigeria," *Annals of the Association of American Geographers* 86, no. 1 (1996): 44–77.

29. Jean Boyd and Beverly Mack, *One Woman's Jihad: Nana Asma'u, Scholar and Scribe* (Bloomington: Indiana University Press, 2000), 91; Jean Boyd, "Distance Learning from Purdah in Nineteenth-Century Northern Nigeria: The Work of Asma'u Fodiyo," *Journal of African Cultural Studies* 14, no 1 (June. 2001): 7–22.

30. Sue O'Brien, "Spirit Possession and Muslim Practice Northern Nigeria," unpublished manuscript.

31. Boyd and Mack, *One Woman's Jihad.*

32. Jean Boyd and Murray Last, "The Role of Women as 'Agents Religieux' in Sokoto." *Canadian Journal of African Studies / La Revue canadienne des études africaines* 19, no. 2 (1985): 283–300, 289; Murray Last, "The Nature of Knowledge in Muslim Northern Nigeria, 1457–2007," in *The Trans-Saharan Book Trade: Manuscript Culture, Arabic Literacy and Intellectual History in Muslim Africa*, ed. Graziano Krätli and Ghislaine Lydon (Leiden, Netherlands: Brill, 2011), 174–211.

33. McGarvey, *Muslim and Christian Women in Dialogue*, 49.

34. Nast, "Islam, Gender, and Slavery."

35. Boyd and Mack, *One Woman's Jihad*, 41.

36. Boyd and Mack, *One Woman's Jihad*, 45.

37. Boyd and Mack, *One Woman's Jihad*, 45.

38. Boyd and Last, "Agents Religieux," 286.

39. Boyd and Mack, *One Woman's Jihad*, 167.

40. Boyd and Last, "Agents Religieux," 289.

41. Interestingly, Jean Boyd, the chief historian of women in Sokoto, used the term *gajiyyayu* in an unpublished paper but not in subsequent published works. This word relates to the root "to tire" but means, more specifically, those who are fatigued, not equal to the task. One often hears women speaking Hausa to use the term to mean defeated. "An Interim Report on the Yan-Taru Movement in the 20th c. with an Account of its Origins," by Jean Boyd, April 2–3, 1984, SOAS Special Collections, University of London, 5.

42. Jean Boyd and Beverly Mack, *Collected Works of Nana Asma'u, Daughter of Usman 'dan Fodio (1793–1864)* (Lansing: Michigan State University Press, 1997).

43. Mary Smith, *Baba of Karo: A Woman of the Moslem Hausa* (New York: Praeger, 1964).

44. Quoted in Paul Lovejoy, "Concubinage and the Status of Women Slaves in Early Colonial Northern Nigeria," *Journal of African History* 29, no. 2 (1988): 249.

45. J. Lowry Maxwell, June 26, 1911, Rhodes House Library, MS.AFr.S.1112, vol. 5, Oxford, U.K.

46. Shankar, *Who Shall Enter Paradise?*, esp. chap. 5.

47. Extracts from field letters concerning church discipline, April 18, 1979, ECWA (box), SIM International Archives, Fort Mill, South Carolina.

48. Letter to Rev. Wenger from Guy Playfair, February 12, 1943, File SIM-ECWA Polygamy 1943–5 EM-1 (1A), SIM International Archives, Fort Mill.

49. Barbara Cooper, *Evangelicals Christians in the Muslim Sahel* (Bloomington: Indiana University Press, 2006), 190–911.

50. I discuss the difficulties of Christian marriage among converts from Islam in Northern Nigeria in chap. 5 of *Who Shall Enter Paradise?*

51. Shankar, *Who Shall Enter Paradise?*, chap. 5.

52. Sani, "An Essay on My Education," unpublished essay in author's possession, 8.

53. John Mamman Garba, *The Time Has Come* (Ibadan: Spectrum, 1989), 53.

54. Smith, *Baba of Karo*, 51.

55. Leith-Ross, Report on Women's Education, Ilorin Province, April 30, 1929.

56. Garba, *Time Has Come*, 128.

57. Wusasa women elders, group interview by Shobana Shankar, Wusasa, Nigeria, August 5, 2001.

58. Extracts from diary of Walter Miller, August 4 (no year), University of Birmingham Library Special Collections, CMS/ACC237 F1; extracts from Ethel Miller, 1907, CMS/ACC237 F3.

59. Ethel Miller, *Change Here for Kano* (Zaria, Nigeria: Gaskiya Corporation, 1959), 24.

60. Shankar, *Who Shall Enter Paradise?*, chap. 5.

61. Ethel Miller, *Hausa Heroines* (Zaria, Nigeria: Gaskiya Corporation, 1923), 10.

62. Miller, *Hausa Heroines*, 33.

63. Mary Lar, *Ambassador for Christ: Mary Lar's Reflections on Nigeria, Past and Present* (London: Kingsway Publishers, 1997); Olabisi Chukwidile, "Lar, Mary Nwandor," *Dictionary of African Christian Biography,* http://www.dacb.org/stories/nigeria/lar_marynanwor.html.

64. Mary Lar, *Ambassador for Christ: Mary Lar's Reflections on Nigeria, Past and Present* (London: Kingsway Publishers, 1997); Olabisi Chukwidile, "Lar, Mary Nwandor," *Dictionary of African Christian Biography,* http://www.dacb.org/stories/nigeria/lar_marynanwor.html.

65. Shankar, *Who Shall Enter Paradise?*; Adam Higazi, "Social Mobilization and Collective Violence: Vigilantes and Militias in the Lowlands of Plateau State, Central Nigeria," *Africa* 78, no. 1 (2008): 107–35.

CHAPTER 8

Weddings Are Not a Sexy Affair!

Youth Sexuality, Embodiment, and Moral Imaginaries in a Neo-Pentecostal Church in Kenya

Damaris Seleina Parsitau

KENYAN YOUTH BETWEEN THE STATE AND RELIGION

Kenya, East Africa's biggest economy, is a youthful country with nearly 29 percent of its overall population of nearly 50 million people between the ages of fifteen and twenty-four years, by definition a "youth bulge."[1] Despite the economy seemingly doing well, it has not been able to adequately absorb youth into the job market. According to the Department of International Development (DFID) report, with nearly 500,000 to 800,000 young people entering the job market each year, Kenya's economy has not been able to provide the necessary amount of employment opportunities.[2]

For these reasons, many Kenyan youth live in an environment where the dominant issues they grapple with include, but are not limited to, inequalities, corruption, uncertain, and skewed distribution of resources such as employment (where there is a tendency by government to give most public jobs older political cronies) and many others.[3] In general, the majority of Kenyan youth are unable to access the center of power, and this has led to a sense of exclusion and marginalization. Youth live in and experience the effects of this uncertainty in a context of imbalanced resources amid a growing economy, leading to a restlessness for some among this important constituency.

A recent Kenyan Youth Survey Report commissioned by Aga Khan East African Institute,[4] for example, shows some of the salient issues facing youth, namely, unemployment and poverty, lack of access to capital, and lack of recognition and participation in governance and decision making, especially in national leadership. Youth in Kenya are particularly challenged by unequal opportunities, economic marginalization, unemployment, and social problems such as poverty, HIV / AIDS, drugs and substance abuse, and crime and violence.[5] Youth are further perceived as perpetrators of violence and crime, especially during electioneering periods, as witnessed in the 2007–08, 2013, and 2017 elections. Many youth are vulnerable to ethnic and political manipulation.[6]

Faith plays a strong role in the lives of many people in Africa, including youth. Kenyan youth cite religion and spirituality as very important to them. According to a 2016 Kenyan Youth Survey commissioned by the Aga Khan University of East Africa, 85 percent of Kenyan youth indicated faith as being very important to them, while 60 percent ranked family as important in their lives.[7] The same survey reported that 81 percent of Christians suggested that religion is very important to them. Youth also reported religion as the most trusted institution in the country followed by family.

However, Kenyan youth are exploring their religious beliefs in a context marked by social, political, and economic challenges. In the survey cited earlier, youth reported unemployment as their top concern (standing at 63 percent). The study also found that youth are vulnerable to bribery, with 35 percent reporting that they would readily take bribes and 40 percent reporting that they would vote for a candidate who would bribe them.[8] This is the paradox of Christianity in Kenya: many cite religion as deeply important, yet corruption ranks highly even among Christians.[9]

Religion- and faith-based organizations in Africa not only are important agents of social transformation but also play critical roles in the religious formation of young people.[10] For this reason, and given the central position of youth in modern-day Kenya, youth empowerment broadly conceptualized has become a subject of intense interest.[11] There is an urgent need for faith-based organizations to address the youth question and put it at the center of the national discourses and narrative, where Kenyan youth can thrive. This focus is critical given that youth need both institutions of training to help them acquire skills and acumen, and necessary abilities that will allow them to innovate outside of the state. It is in this context that I examine the roles of Pentecostal Christianity in the lives of Kenyan youth. In particular, I examine how the MRH helps youth to navigate intimacy and sexuality.

PENTECOSTALISM, GENDER, AND YOUTH SEXUALITY IN AFRICA

Over the last four decades, Pentecostalism has emerged as one of the most influential religious movements on the African continent.[12] Pentecostal Christianity and Charismatic churches continue to play significant roles in the construction and deconstruction of gendered and youth sexuality as well as other forms of intimacy.[13] Its impact is being felt in all areas of life, from politics,[14] to media, to women and youth (dis)empowerment,[15] gender and power,[16] sex and bodies, and marriage and intimacies, as well as sexual citizenship.[17] According to Sitna Quiroz, one of the most recent and emerging themes of African Pentecostalism is not only "how it is shaping new models of relationships among men and women but also how it is reproducing and reconstructing new forms of intimacy, gender, bodies, sexuality and reproduction in modern African societies."[18] "Consequently, the moral dilemmas arising from these tensions are key to understanding how Pentecostal churches shape the moral self and moral trajectories of intimate relationships in Africa and, more important, how they navigate sexual citizenship in their congregations and society at large."[19]

These churches carry out important social functions that the state has neglected.[20] They are, for example, involved in addressing HIV / AIDS,[21] building and running hospitals and health centers, establishing universities, promoting cooperative societies, and carrying out welfare services that provide housing for children and aging populations.[22] This kind of work, sometimes called the "social gospel,"[23] makes the churches much more than simply religious spaces. At the same time, Pentecostal churches and the "men and women of God" who constitute these churches are equally influential in the national and public spheres, especially in politics. The African church leaders—or the so-called prophets, bishops, apostles, and overseers—benignly referred to as "Men of God,"[24] are increasingly becoming powerful beyond the social and political sphere.[25] They are also having tremendous influence on women and youth constituencies and are impacting how they navigate their personal and sexual lives.[26]

Their teachings are also having a wide reach that is not limited to their Sunday morning and midweek services. Many have TV and radio programs, audiotapes and books, church magazines, websites, and social media pages; they communicate through YouTube in order to reach a wide audience beyond their congregations.[27] They are also influential voices on gender and youth issues. Some of these churches like to focus on particular themes in a bid to carve out a niche for themselves. Some focus of the health and wealth gospel, others on deliverance, and others on prophecy and healing, while still others focus on personal intimacy and sexuality. Yet, one of the most unexplored themes of African Pentecostalism is not only how it is shaping new models of relationships among youth populations but also, to quote Quiroz again, "how it is reproducing and reconstructing new forms of intimacy, gender, sexuality and reproduction in modern African societies."[28]

It is in this area that Pentecostal Christianity in Africa has played a significant role in shaping new patterns of intimacy in interpersonal relationships. Indeed it has been argued that in their efforts to transform society according to a Pentecostal ethos, Pentecostal churches have contributed to reshaping ideas of personhood, gender relations, and emotions that are compatible with a neoliberal ethic and aspirations that resonate with the modern ideals of intimacy.[29] In so doing, these churches provide new eschatological, spiritual, and moral narratives to reinterpret and predict world events and establish new forms of authority that regulate subjectivities and affects. All these efforts have informed and shaped the ways in which born-again converts navigate their intimate lives in both public and private spheres and assimilate notions of romantic love.

People in churches are encouraged to speak openly about matters of sexuality. Moreover, teachings on sexuality in these churches contribute to a moral revaluation of social conditions that in African contexts tend to be stigmatized, such as singlehood, infertility, and the bearing of children outside the marital bond.[30] Yet the position of many religious organizations is to continue to perpetuate teachings about youth sexuality that are at odds with the lived realities of the majority of African youth. This chapter examines youth and gendered sexuality in the context of a Neo-Pentecostal church in Kenya in an attempt to understand how youth navigate their intimate lives in a contested religious space.

ETHNOGRAPHIC SETTING, QUESTIONS, AND RESEARCH METHODOLOGY

In this study I explore the constructions of gendered and youth sexuality and the negotiation of intimate relationships, including love and courtship, notions of sexual sin / immorality, purity culture, and weddings and marriages in Kenya's Ministry of Repentance and Holiness (MRH). In particular, I examine how this ministry constructs notions of sexual purity and erotic geographies in order to consider the influences of certain Pentecostal discourses on youth and the way that moral imaginaries and gendered sexuality are constructed and deconstructed. I examine how the self-proclaimed prophet David Owuor and the MRH shape, challenge, and transform gendered and youth sexuality in the context of tremendous social changes brought about my modernization and globalization.

This study draws on ethnographic research carried out in Kenya since 2010 when I began researching on this church. During this period I interviewed around thirty-five youth, some church members and some ex-members (mainly university students) who belong to the MRH University Students Outreach group, to understand how they navigate sexuality and other forms of intimate relationships in both church settings and private spheres. My concern was to understand how Kenyan youth perceive not just their sexual and intimate lives but also their agency in religious terms, as it is through faith and fellowship that they negotiate associational life.

In this ministry youth have their own groups for Bible study, fellowship, and outreach that aim to keep them busy to divert them from having intimate relationships on campus and in private environments, especially in public universities, where there are now established student unions that help them navigate their spiritual as well as campus life. I interviewed female and male members of the church, focusing on student members of the University Students Outreach (USO) group in order to understand their views and conceptualization of sex, sexuality, intimacies, sexual purity, and holiness and how they navigate this contested terrain. I also interviewed student leaders and directly observed how they carry on with their religious lives on campus. I wanted to gather extensive data and knowledge of varied voices of youth members to conceptualize their worldviews and agency in respect to youth, sexuality, sexual purity, and moral regeneration in the MRH against the backdrop of contemporary Kenyan society.

I also utilized participant observations in the MRH—reflecting on both services, crusades, and live TV programs—as well as conducting semistructured interviews with youth leaders and congregants. I held extensive informal discussions in churches, homes, and university campuses with followers of the MRH and those from other faiths or no faith backgrounds at all. I followed their social media posts and WhatsApp groups; reviewed hundreds of text messages; and reviewed YouTube videos,[31] as well as Kenyan media publications,[32] and TV interviews about the MRH. Coupled with these materials are research and a review of contemporary literature on African Pentecostalism undertaken over ten years of working with Kenyan Pentecostalism. The study draws equally from content analysis of sermons, teachings, and belief practices of the MRH.

I posed many questions to young people, including members and nonmembers of MRH. What attracts a section of Kenyan youth, especially university students, to a church that strictly controls their intimate lives and personal choices? What makes purity messages attractive to the young and old? Why do young women submit to teachings that severely control their intimate lives and enforce strict dress codes, courtship, and compulsory HIV and pregnancy testing? Why would they want to wed in a certain way? This study explores these and many other questions by examining the practices related to youth sexuality, gendered geographies, dress codes, and the covering up of women's bodies as locales for sexual sins as well as the approach to wedding ceremonies in the MRH. Finally, I conclude with an analysis of sexual and gendered geographies in the MRH.

SINFUL BODIES, SACRED ECOLOGIES! YOUTH SEXUALITY IN THE MINISTRY OF REPENTANCE AND HOLINESS BETWEEN CONTROL AND PERSONAL AGENCY

Self-proclaimed prophet David Owuor is both powerful and influential. He has a large following locally and internationally.[33] In terms of his authority, Prophet Owuor stands out compared to other Pentecostal clergy in Kenya. I begin to explore Prophet Owuor and the MRH in this section.

First, Prophet Owuor has tremendous influence over a wide range of political, social, and moral issues, including marriage and choice of partner, intimacy, sex, singlehood, and funeral rites.[34] He also levies his influence on his follower's manners and mores, such as consumer behavior, for example, the choice of movies his followers watch and what radio channels they listen to. He has sway on how his members, both young and old, males and females, but especially females, present themselves in society. He also influences youth sexuality and intimate relationships, women's bodies, dress choices, behavior, morals, and social mores. He depicts himself as the moral policeman and one whose word is final.[35]

Prophet Owuor holds extreme views about sex and sexuality, as attested by hundreds of sermons he preaches on his pet subject. According to him, "sex is a very bad sin." It is the worst sin anyone could ever commit against God and his / her own body. Nearly all of his sermons are linked to notions of sin and death. His favorite sermons are titled "sexual purity in the church," "death is the penalty of sin," "sexual sins turns you into a rotten loaf of bread," and "sexual sin leads to separation from God."[36] In this ministry, Prophet Owuor considers "sexual sin" or "sins of immorality" premarital and extramarital sex, infidelity, homosexuality, lesbianism, and all other intimate relationships for single persons, particularly women who are divorced or never married, even widowed persons and all other intimate relationships, which are all loosely referred to as sexual sins or sins of immorality. These so-called sins take center stage as reflected in a series of highly sexualized and highly publicized sermons and church discourses that are preached and promoted in the MRH. Here, sexual sin, exclusively understood as sex outside of marriage (which is strictly understood within its heteronormative sense), is categorized as "a grievous sin" that attracts the "wrath of a vengeful God."

In the MRH, notions of sexual purity, holiness, repentance, holy thoughts, holy dressing, holy speaking, "the wedding of the lamb," holy bodies, and born-again bodies—as well as notions of righteousness, cleanliness, and rapture—not only receive primary focus but are also presented as the ideal traits for members of this ministry to adopt. These are also imaged as models of behavior and the prerequisites to enter the anticipated Kingdom of God. For these reasons, terms and phrases such as "sexual sin" or "sins of immorality" are central messages of Prophet Owuor's theology, sermons, teaching, and modes of worship.[37] These notions are also linked to the state of the nation of Kenya as well as the spiritual well-being of believers.[38] Female members are taught to stay holy and to learn to "cover up for the one" (which means dressing holy and waiting to get a spouse) and to say "if he loves me then he must take me to the altar" (which means that there is no dating or premarital sex until the wedding day). Moreover, weddings are not sexy affairs.[39]

Pentecostal Christianity, one of the most significant forces that influence the belief systems of African people, shapes and defines the deepest values of its adherents. This is because religion heavily impacts issues of sexual (im)morality.[40] The sexual (im)morality espoused by this church perpetuates gender hierarchies and sexual geographies, thereby depriving certain groups of their full citizenship in church and society. In his sermons, issues of masculinity, gender, patriarchy, and femininity come together. Prophet Owuor presents himself as the paragon of morality in the country, dictating sexual mores, control over bodies, and pleasure.

The prophet preaches and promotes an extreme form of purity culture and a sexualized view of women's bodies that puts such bodies directly at the center of an erotic economy. The sexual purity gospel espoused by Owuor is akin to the Evangelical purity culture popularized in Evangelical circles in the United States in the 1970s, 1980s, and 1990s. In this purity culture men and boys were imaged as sexually weak, and women and girls were supposed to be the beholders of sexual purity. Those of the female gender are also responsible if men fail to observe sexual purity and for the sexual thoughts and feelings of boys and grown men. Men and boys are easily aroused by the site of women's flesh, church members taught.[41]

Women must therefore keep male sexual desires at check by covering up and dressing holy, lest they provoke men who cannot keep their sexual urges in check. Because they are held responsible for men's actions, women and girls in Prophet Owuor's church have to, through their attire, embody and enflesh holiness so that they can enter the anticipated Kingdom of God. For the same reasons, Owuor prescribes a dress code for his female followers that explicitly forbids the wearing of sleeveless tops, hemlines at or above the knee, slit skirts that expose the knees and thighs, open shoes, bare legs, and the use of makeup.[42]

Women dress in heavy curtain-like materials that flow from the neck to the tips of the toes even in hot weather. Every part of their bodies is covered except for the face. Women are further urged to adopt certain manners and practices that are deemed appropriate for a holy religious life. When speaking about women's bodies and dress, Owuor often quotes biblical verses such as Hebrews 12:14, "Make efforts to be holy, for without holiness, no one will see the Lord!," and 1 Corinthians 6:19, "Do you not know that your bodies are temples of the Holy Spirit, who is in you, whom you have received from God?" Applying these verses to his female followers while speaking at a prayer rally, Owuor said: "When you cover your body, you are saying: I respect and honour my body which is the temple of the Lord. So make sure you do not defile the house of the Holy Spirit by dressing indecently."[43]

In a series of sermons preached by Owuor titled "Purity in the Church" and "How God Looks at Sexual Sin," women are frequently depicted as prostitutes and temptresses.[44] They are viewed as the chief cause of "men's sexual sins," and their "lack of sexual control" and the reason why men will not enter the anticipated Kingdom of God. Owuor often evokes biblical passages (or paraphrases of Scripture) like Proverbs 6:24–26: "Keep yourself away from the immoral woman and from the smooth tongue of the wayward wife. Do not lust in your heart after her beauty or let her captivate you with her eyes. For the prostitute reduces you to a loaf of bread and the adulteress preys upon your very life."[45] According to Owuor, "The Bible says that based on the way a woman is dressed, she can be called a prostitute. There is no such a verse in the bible. This is how God looks at sexual sin, he rumbles. Look, men are affected by what they see. Some women dress to get the attention of the pastor." Prophet Owuor's preaching makes fluent transitions from the biblical text to the contemporary context and back again, reinforcing negative images of women as adulterers and prostitutes and as dangerous and even potentially deathly sources of temptation. I have heard Prophet Owuor telling women not to moisturize their bodies with Vaseline. Such teachings influence how women dress and comport themselves in the MRH. Here teachings on sexual purity are so highly emphasized that even young widows and widowers are not allowed to remarry because it is considered sexual sin, while youth are encouraged to marry fast so as not to fall into sexual sin. Prolonged courtship is discouraged, and the church takes care of the wedding costs for young couples in an effort to avoid sexual sin.

The purity culture espoused by Owuor emphasizes how women need to be good Christians by protecting men from the threat women pose.[46] This message suggests that women's bodies and female sexuality are a threat to Christendom and men. Therefore, it is women's and girls' responsibilities to dress in a holy and acceptable manner. They must also sit right, talk right, and compose themselves so as not to tempt men. If they do not, then they risk being called prostitutes and impure harlots. As such, gender and sexuality are deeply intertwined in the MRH.

In the MRH women's bodies are depicted as a locus for impurity, lust, sin, and temptation. Through the teachings of this church holiness is promoted as the means through which Kenya will truly be a Christian nation devoted to God and obey God's commandments. The burden (of proof) appears to be primarily on women to achieve this moral and spiritual ideal.[47] Of course, from a gender or feminist perspective, it is easy to see in the MRH's teachings the workings of patriarchy, with women's bodies being made sites of surveillance, regulation, control, and power. Indeed, Owuor's project of moral regeneration echoes wider patterns in colonial and postcolonial Africa, in which women's bodies in particular have become symbolic sites of contestation over authenticity, decency, and purity. As South African feminist scholar Desiree Lewis points out: "The centrality of patriarchy in the control of women's bodies as evident in the policing of women's gender roles in many African countries requires a highly visible and explicit performance of prescribed gendered behaviour."[48] Owuor's sermons on female bodies are not just disturbing but also sexist and aim to control women's intimate lives. Ironically, Prophet Owuor's ministry has been embroiled in sexual scandals, and his own personal life has been the subject of controversy, including rape allegations against him being raised in the United States, as well as violence against his spouse. On his own admission, he has also fathered a child in Israel and abandoned both the mother and son in unclear circumstances. It appears that the prophet's own personal life is less than perfect or even "pure."[49]

Recently one of Owuor's close associates was expelled from his ministry, and the altar (the name for a church in the MRH) was burned down because the associate of Owuor sexually molested three female followers, whom he used to invite to his house for "prayer and anointing with oil." He did more than just "anoint" the women; he had sex with them. Three of these women gave harrowing testimonies of sexual abuse in the hands of a pastor of a church,[50] where 95 percent of the sermons preached are about sex. In many of his sermons Prophet Owuor promotes an extreme form of purity culture and sexualization of female bodies that is ultimately harmful to women and girls. But it is not just that such men of God promote a sexualized view of women as well as a harmful purity culture. They also continue to perpetuate beliefs and teachings that put the lives of women and youth in danger.

In a series of long sermons titled "Purity in the Church," Owuor describes purity as the bedrock of God's salvation for humanity.

> The fall of the church is because of the blatant flaunting of the laws of purity among believers in today's body of Christ. Spiritual purity can be defined as a state of lack of impurity. Spiritual impurity on the other hand is denoted by the complete embodiment of the confederacy of all evil forces of corruption and defilement that today run this dark world. Adherence to righteousness as the standard for Christian living is the only road to salvation. Spiritual impurity presents itself in the same old vices of immorality, deception, falsehood, false prophets, false apostles, witchcraft, pornography, homosexuality and the gospel of prosperity, shame and death, a cocktail of challenges. Because of the eminent vulnerability to sin that the church often presents, the Lord in his infinite wisdom has always placed upon her, a restriction that prohibits excessive indulgence with this dark world. When one observes the present-day Christians going to church immorally dressed and the pews being largely populated with virtually undelivered Christians, then you can't help but wail for her because of the contemptuous ignorance on the virtue of spiritual purity. Only genuine repentance can save the church.[51]

He continues in a series of sermons titled the "Penalty of Sexual Sin."

> Sin began to gradually creep into the church of Christ. Holiness took backbench as defilement paraded the front rows of pulpit. It beamed as the unspeakable tolerable in the otherwise holy house of the lord. And with the onset of modernity and post modernity in the church, every sin seems acceptable. Defilement entered the worship teams

and the congregation in the forms of homosexuality, masturbation, open gay and lesbianism, prostitution, the wearing of tight trousers by women that show their anatomies, tight skirts with long slits, deception, slutty dressing and fleshy immoral dancing during worship.

In the same sermon, he said:

> It is obvious that sexual sin escalated in church even as books were written about great televangelists in sexual scandals. Even inside the priesthood pastors can now openly confess to falling into the otherwise easily avoidable sexual sin of the day. Open day homosexuality is now reigning in the church including on global Christian television where gays homosexuals and lesbians cannot be rebuked. Shockingly, they now publicly share views expressing the position on the bible. As though this was not enough, the present day church has taken this to a new high by openly and publicly anointing open gay and homosexuals as pastors and bishops. To add salt onto the injury, there is raging debate that is currently threatening to split the church of Christ onto whether this abomination of sexuality be included in worship practices or thrown out, while this is going on, other Christians are busy attending movies of immorality driven by Hollywood.

In another sermon, he states: "The pulpit was not spared either as pastors become blind to the large crimson elephant in the house. This huge abomination of sin the servants of the lord have today claimed that they could not see. On their part, the pastors began to preach an inflated corrupt gospel of prosperity which exalts money and earthly wealth over and above the most important holiness of the lord." In these sermons Owuor seeks to control the narrative on sex and sexuality in the church as well as regulate his followers' sexual conduct. He covers a wide range of issues that touch on the sexual and intimate lives of people, including what he calls sexual immorality, immoral dressing, abortion, and pollution of the houses of worship by false prophets (read Pentecostal clergy) and same-sex relationships. In so doing, he images himself as the paragon of sexual purity and an antisex pastor who attempts to establish new forms of authority that regulate people's subjectivities. He also seeks to have a wide influence on these issues and control the narrative on sexual citizenship. For example, he has control over the kind of music played and listened to by his followers. Here gospel music is categorized into dirty, unholy, and holy music.

According to Prophet Owuor:

> The playing of ndombolo dance (a kind of dance from Central Africa) in the church is a form of occult worship in Kenyan churches and the dressing of worship dance troupes in T-shirts exposing their navels, playing of rap music, the perming and frying of male worship leaders' hair, including the punching and putting a shiny ring on the nose and at times earrings, these things could not go without catching the negative attention of the Lord. These things defile the altar of the Lord.[52]

For these reasons worldly dancing and gospel music used in other Pentecostal churches in Kenya are not acceptable in this church. Instead what is recommended is a different kind of music and worship that the MRH has evolved over the years. In fact it is through these differences that members of the MRH worship distinguish the church from other Pentecostal congregations. A rigorous, exuberant, and lively type of worship and dance—the sort of music where bodies swing in worship—is not accepted because the MRH deems it erotic and sinful. Members are also supposed to raise hands in worship in a still manner that is seen to be holy and pleasing to God.

Contemporary gospel music is also not acceptable, and youth are discouraged from dancing to such sinful music because it does not glorify God. Members must also not listen to such music on their handsets, computers, or even radio. The church only recommends a radio station for gospel music from the Jesus Is Lord Radio Station, which is affiliated with the MRH. The kind of music that is played in all meetings of the MRH has a distinct pattern and rhyme. It is played "slowly," and those who participate are not supposed to dance. Alongside this radio station, members are also encouraged to listen to the sermons and teachings of the prophet.

The young people as well as the general lay congregants are also forbidden from watching movies, which are deemed to propagate violence, horror, nudity, pornography, and other sexually explicit material. They are discouraged from watching any movie or TV programs that do not add value to their spiritual lives. Young children are not allowed to watch cartoons or wear T-shirts with their favorite characters, because they are considered satanic. Young women are forbidden from wearing jeans and pants, because they are deemed inappropriate. Programs that tend to promote "foolish and sexual jokes and ungodliness" must also be avoided at all costs. Members are also forbidden from watching secular movies or television programs that are not spiritual, as these media are thought to corrupt their bodies, minds, and moral values. They are discouraged from social media, particularly Facebook and Twitter (now X), even though Prophet Owuor hires bots to tweet thousands of tweets whenever there is a scandal about his church. These sorts of militarized Twitter bots attack and insult anyone who has criticized the prophet, leading to a sort of militarization of his followers.

There are church-approved programs exclusively from the MRH that members are allowed to watch. These include the prophet's preaching, faith healing meetings, and prophecies, both the fulfilled and yet to be fulfilled, and teachings provided through a YouTube channel, the ministry's website, and Amazon Prime TV, as well as an MRH program available through the Kenya Television Service (KTS TV). Thus, only materials from the prophet are to be taken in because he is the only true and "Mightiest Prophet of God" according to his followers, who have been taught that all other prophets are false, liars, and cons. At the same time the prophet's followers are encouraged to fellowship only with fellow church members and are encouraged to avoid being "yoked with nonbelievers" who in the understanding of members include all those who proclaim to be born-again Christians of other Christian denominations. This has created significant tensions within the families of church members, with his movement accused of creating an exclusive movement that is completely detached from the rest of the country and communities to which Owuor's followers belong.

It seems to us therefore that Prophet Owuor has created an exclusive community of born-again members whom he controls, dictating their mores, behavior, and other ways of life. This exclusion has a significant impact on how people from the ministry relate with friends and family and communities. Nonmembers of the MRH I interviewed suggested that members of the MRH have become distant from neighbors, colleagues, families, and communities. Even university students avoid social interactions with other students outside of the classroom.

For example, members of two university-based groups affiliated with the MRH, the MRH University of Students Outreach (USO), and the Kenya Students Fellowship (KSF) do not participate in joint Christian Students' activities such as the University Thanksgiving Services, interdenominational services that are common practices in Kenya's public universities, Prayer *kasha's* (overnight prayer vigils), Christian Students open-air crusades, or other evangelistic events and outreach programs. Instead, they are encouraged to hold parallel religious activities distinctly controlled and managed by the MRH leadership. All USO members must abide by the MRH set of principles.[53] From this discussion, it is clear that Prophet Owuor has a strong hold on his members' personal choices and liberties and attempts to discipline their sexual and personal lives.

His impact on youth sexuality and intimate relations beyond his followers is even more significant. Prophet Owuor has sought to influence youth sexual and moral behavior by focusing largely on youth in institutions of higher learning, particularly colleges and public universities. Using his teachings and notions of sin and moral reformation and regeneration, he has worked not just to create "youth church" in all the altars but also to establish parallel student unions in institutions of higher learning. A significant number of the discourses in the student movements focus on youth sexuality and female bodies as the locus of sexual sin.

In the following section, I consider teachings on youth sexuality in the MRH and how born-again youth navigate intimate relationships and related topics, including dating, courtship, premarital counseling, sex, marriage, HIV, infertility, and other such themes. I argue that these teachings not only aim to produce "a moral generation" but that they also inspire the youth to break free from sex and attain a kind of rapture from a sinful past so as to enter the Kingdom of God. Further, I show how this ministry, through its teachings, beliefs and practices, seeks to influence the sexual lives of youth, personal choices, and intimate relationships. I explore the diverse ways in which this self-declared prophet and his teachings shape, challenge, and transform the sexualities of his followers, particularly that of his youth followers.

THE CHURCH NEGLECT OF YOUTH MINISTRY: PERSPECTIVES FROM PROPHET OWUOR OF THE MRH

Prophet Owuor teaches that Kenyan Christian churches have neglected youth, who are an integral part of the society. In a long sermon titled "The First Fruit: The Youth and the Church,"[54] he argues that the youth church has been neglected (by the church) and that this rampant neglect has "as a matter of facts created a vacuum in the hearts of the young believers, thereby causing them to look for other means of satisfying their void." However, various churches have elaborate youth programs that specifically cater to the needs of the youth, making the prophet's claim that churches have neglected the Kenyan youth a little shaky.

Owuor's observations serve as a building block for him to establish a youth movement and ministry modeled after his own distinct beliefs and teachings on youth sexuality, in which sex features prominently. In a long, winding sermon, Owuor delves into his own understanding of the status of the youth in Kenyan Christian churches as well as his interventions to bring the youth on board in the church. This is what he had to say:

Most of what goes on in the youth churches today demonstrates a complete departure from spiritual understandings, knowledge and wisdom. That is the reason sexual sin, rap music, reggae, music, rock music, ndombolo, drug addiction, alcoholism, pornography, immorality, dirty language, slutty dressing, filthy dancing, name it, can persist among the Christian youth. It is also a reflection of the fall of the church and misinformation that prevails among their pastors. What today's youth pastors have known, is that there is a vast difference between spiritual wisdom and the knowledge that they are imparting into the youth. What is being downloaded on the youth today include the excesses of this world that have now become a youth fad in the church. Also the aping of any form of new age dancing that seems to establish in the youth church today, among others.[55]

Consequently, he explains, "When God's word becomes interwoven into the very fabric of the lives of today's Christian youth, that is when their lives will be transformed, and revival set in. Absurdly, a closer look at the youth church today reveals a conspicuous absence of the word of God and his corresponding wisdom, in what the youth think, say and do. Therefore, young men and women should learn to be self-controlled, sound in faith and in endurance and purity." Prophet Owuor, it seems to me, maps his teachings on youth on his sex and sexual purity ideologies, beliefs, and teachings. Owuor has aimed to influence youth spirituality through character formation, discipline, and righteousness in which sexual purity is never far away from his mind. In this, as well as many other sermons and teachings on the youth, Owuor riles against peer pressure, abortion, alcohol and drug abuse, "slutty dressing" and sinful music, HIV / AIDS, homosexuality, pornography, and prostitution, among many others alleged vices.

Consider this sermon:

Most youth churches have turned out to be sexual sin clubs at which sexual sin is committed in the parking lots and church compounds, during overnight prayer vigils. Equally, pastors have chosen for themselves some girls in the church for sexual sin, lust and defilement. Pornography is likewise too great a sin inside today's youth church. Even at the university level, the Christian union that ought to be the example of Christ in that community do routinely observe Friday night movie sessions in which sexual sin is the agenda. Only God can save the youth from the sin that has encroached in today's church.[56]

Because of the supposed fall of the Christian Church, and youth in the church in particular, Owuor set out to establish the alternative and parallel Christian youth movements (i.e., the USO) as noted.

DIVINE TARGETS: THE MINISTRY OF REPENTANCE AND HOLINESS FOCUS ON YOUTH MINISTRY

In his mission to influence youth morality, sexuality, and intimate lives, Prophet Owuor established USO parallel student movements in institutions of higher learning that take on the name of the university at which they are based. For example, the Egerton University (EU) chapter is called EU (USO), while Kenyatta University (KU) is called KU (USO). USO was launched in in 2008 and officially registered in 2012 as a student union movement. USO participates in prayer and peace rallies for peace building and engages with communities to preach national healing and cohesion.

The members of this organization frequently meet in their respective university chapters for prayer fellowships and other spiritual activities. Egerton University, for example, has a vibrant USO chapter, with nearly 200 students who are mostly male. The Egerton University USO chapter members meet every Thursday evening for two hours to pray and fellowship with one another. They also have weekly devotional times during most lunch hour breaks, where they pray and engage in fellowship and Bible study. Every Tuesday evening members meet for Bible study at designated student hostel rooms of USO members, where they read and discuss Bible verses. Similarly, on Monday evenings they carry out what is called outreach evangelism in which they preach and try to convert other students. On Sundays they attend church services at nearby altars.

In mid-April 2017, under the umbrella group Kenya Students Fellowship (KSF), an organization that brings together all USO chapters, USO held their National Thanksgiving Night Prayer vigils at Egerton University's Kilimo Hall. Such revival meetings can be organized regionally, subregionally, or sometimes as a group of altars in designated regions coming together to carry out joint spiritual activities. Each altar has an active youth church, led by members from the group and a designated youth pastor. Youth pastors in the various altars organize fellowships and revival meetings, particularly during breaks from school and national public holidays.

Thus by establishing a parallel student movement in universities and colleges, Prophet Owuor has ensured that he has significant influence over a huge youth constituency that he seeks to control and impact through his teachings. The USO movement provides him with a forum to continue to map his antisex gospel in a bid to influence youth intimate and sexual lives. He has even sought to have such movements recognized by university management, although many have resisted his efforts.

Although universities recognize various interfaith groups such as the long-standing Christian unions, which consist of interdenominational and interfaith groups, the USO movement has tended toward a more exclusive approach that does not recognize other associations as valid Christian communities. This exclusive and antagonistic stance toward long-established interdenominational groups makes it hard for university boards to recognize and approve USO chapters. Nevertheless, the USO chapters still carry on with their religious activities irrespective of the fact that they are not officially recognized. Next, I examine further how the MRH engages youth sexuality through its teachings and practices.

REDEEMING A SINFUL AND LOST GENERATION: MRH AND YOUTH SEXUALITY IN KENYA

After planting USO chapters in most institutions of higher learning, David Owuor moved to ensure his control and influence over youth sexuality through his quest to produce moral regimes and gendered geographies among this constituency. Sexual purity is at the center of the MRH's teachings and discourses. Members are taught to stay pure from sexual immorality, which the church frames as "a very bad sin punishable by death" and separation from God. Consequently, as mentioned, members of the church are called upon to be sexually pure in all aspects of their lives, and women are encouraged to dress holy. Members and especially young people are encouraged to have accountability partners and mentors to keep them in check regarding purity. The MRH focuses on five areas that are transforming youth sexuality and intimate relationships in significant ways: (1) absolute abstinence before marriage and marital fidelity; (2) mandatory HIV testing; (3) mandatory pregnancy testing; (4) courtship, premarital counseling, and restrictions on how youth should be married; and (5) drugs and substance abuse training.

KEEPING HOLY DISTANCE AND ABSTAINING UNTIL THE WEDDING NIGHT

The MRH position and teachings about sex before and outside marriage is that it is sinful, wrong, immoral, and plain evil. It is termed as "fornication," "a very bad sin" that attracts the wrath of God and as something that grieves the heart of God and the Holy Spirit. According to the teachings of Prophet Owuor, God will heavily punish sexual sin and it may even lead to death. As already said, sex is central to his preaching, as lucidly demonstrated in the following sermons on sexual sin in Christian churches, which he preached in one of the crusades attended by this author. In this highly sexualized sermon, titled "Overcoming Sexual Sin" and based on Deuteronomy 22:22–24, Prophet Owuor had this to say:

> Today I will speak about the gravity and the weight of sexual sin in your Christian life and how God looks at sexual sin so that you can begin to re-evaluate yourself Vis-a Vis sexual sin and how it has enslaved the church. He goes ahead to speak about the keys in the bible to break the chains of sexual immorality and lust. You see, the enemy brings a chain of events that creates sexual lust and defile you and bind you and render you useless before the lord.

He continues: "This is one area that has made the church fall. Sexual sin has become embedded into the lives of Christians, and the church of Christ. Sexual sin is embedded in the pulpit, the altar of the lord. It has also spread out and brought death in the church. It has made the lord not even to be able to use anyone. Sexual sin is a highway that leads to the grave." In this way youth are taught to stay away from sex before marriage. In fact the church position in respect to sex before marriage is zero tolerance. Consequently, as discussed earlier, youth are advised to keep busy at all times through engagements in spiritual activities so that they can eschew immoral thoughts and temptations. For example, they are advised to diligently engage in studies and socioeconomic activities such as seeking employment and working. For these reasons, there is no dating and intimacy outside of marriage in the MRH. Youth are also taught and counseled on how to navigate relationships between young men and women in the event that one of the male youths wants to get married. In addition to teaching a great deal on the subject of sex and relationships, the MRH provides young people with spiritual tools to reflect on their sexuality.

At annual youth conferences, as well as in frequent seminars in altars that now dot much of the country, youth are taught and empowered to navigate sexuality and intimate relations. For example, in a youth conference held December 14–16, 2017, at the Flamingo Altar in Nakuru County in the Rift Valley Province, and whose theme was Empower Youth Church,[57] hundreds of youth were trained on various issues that affect them. Information gleaned from interviews with two youth leaders who attended the training suggests that teachings focused on the following themes: dealing with habits like drinking alcohol, smoking cigarettes and other harmful substances, and eating habits as well as sexual addiction. Youth were encouraged to adopt healthy habits that are in line with their Christian lives. The youth were also trained on career paths, choices, and development. This could be an important opportunity for students in high schools and colleges who grapple with issues of career choices, unemployment, and career development. Yet, the overarching goal of the ministry in this sort of career development workshop is to help youth keep busy and avoid idleness.

More important, the conference focused on youth sexuality. Here, male youth are taught and given the tools to deal with sex and sexuality as well as how to relate with young women. They are taught how to start serious relationships leading to marriage. In the MRH, all relationships must lead to marriage. In fact, dating is discouraged in the MRH. There are various well-defined steps or stages that have been formulated by the church to help youth navigate relationships that should lead to marriage, the only space where sexual intimacy is acceptable. So how do youth navigate relationships in MRH?

When a young man likes a young woman from the ministry, he could directly approach the woman and tell her about his intentions. The other option is that he can go to his pastor and inform him about his intentions for the woman. In the case of the former, the couple usually agree to "see each other" and then inform the pastors of their specific altars. If the young man is shy about approaching the young woman, he can inform the pastor first and then the couple are urged to pray about the relationships in order to determine if it is God's will. Meanwhile, the pastor carries out a background check on the woman, her family, her spiritual life, and character; where she worships and if someone else has proposed to her. The pastor also checks on issues such as young woman's maturity and compatibility issues and whether the woman wants to get married. Members of the MRH are discouraged from dating anyone outside of the church. The man proposes when the pastor is satisfied with what is said. When the woman accepts, the pastor immediately begins to take them through a period of premarital counseling as well as courtship. But not before mandatory HIV testing is undertaken.

While most youth accept these teachings uncritically, some have been less satisfied and left the MRH. My interviews with youth revealed a life of extreme control and constraints, as well as the tensions it has generated for many who have to navigate between sexual desires and church teachings and regulations in a context where other youth have the freedom to live out their lives the way they want.

MANDATORY HIV TESTING

The MRH has a policy of compulsory HIV testing for would-be couples as well as a compulsory pregnancy testing for women prior to their wedding day. Once a couple has accepted to get married, they immediately begin rigorous premarital counseling sessions with a designated pastor. Here they are taught about marriage and the place of sex in the union. But they must first undergo mandatory HIV testing. This controversial practice is a nonnegotiable church policy. Only couples who are HIV free are allowed to get married. Discordant couples are not allowed to get married. Those who remain HIV positive cannot be allowed to get married so as not to infect the healthy party. The ministry is silent on whether couples in which both members HIV positive can get married. In this ministry, HIV is regarded as a serious disease and death sentence.

This disturbing practice is not only an MRH practice but one that is a mandatory policy for would-be couples in a majority of Pentecostal churches in Kenya.[58] Many Pentecostal churches refuse to marry couples unless they have undergone an HIV exam with negative testing results. Most churches claim that clergy cannot preside over short-lived marriages, only to be called within a short time to perform funeral rites when the couple succumbs to the virus. Such logic is not only faulty and discriminative against persons living with HIV / AIDS but continues to perpetuate stigma. Such churches are not attuned to the fact that antiretroviral drugs offer survivors a high quality of life that includes both longevity and good health.

Mandatory HIV testing in Christian churches draws tremendous criticism from HIV / AIDS human rights activists, academics, researchers, media, health practitioners, and society in general. Critics argue that mandatory HIV testing is not only discriminatory but, as noted, also continues to perpetuate stigma about HIV and AIDS. Such teachings and practices confine HIV / AIDS to issues of sex; obscure and gloss over the complexities of sexuality; and totally ignore the social, cultural, economic, and political issues that continue to fuel the spread of HIV / AIDS.

Mandatory HIV testing has drawn significant controversies in Kenya in recent times. Pentecostal clergy argue that this practice is part of their church constitutions and cannot be changed. For example, most Pentecostal churches' constitutions require that couples getting married undergo a mandatory HIV test before they are allowed to get married. In November 2018 a senior pastor of a church in Nakuru declined to officiate a young couple's wedding at the last minute because he wanted the couple to undergo HIV and pregnancy testing despite the couple having already done so.[59] The pastor argued in his defense that the results of the medical test were not clear and that he was following "God's word" and that his actions were not subject to discussion.

In a move that attracted widespread outrage, a public debate ensued about the role of pastors in people's intimate lives and how powerful and inconsiderate some clergy can be in exercising power over their followers. More relevant to the points of this essay is how Pentecostal theologies of sex and purity continue to perpetuate stigma around HIV and AIDS. While nearly all the Pentecostal churches I have studied have mandatory HIV testing for would-be couples, the practice stands in opposition to human rights and fails to accord dignity to persons living with HIV / AIDS. Further, it is a criminal offense under section 13, subsection 4, of the HIV and AIDS Prevention and Control Act in the Kenyan Constitution (2010).[60]

Pentecostal clergy have generated significant controversy around the HIV / AIDS epidemic. Many African countries have been heavily impacted by it, yet Pentecostal clergy continue to fuel stigma through their teachings and practices. At the same time, the HIV / AIDS epidemic has not only led to the emergence of thousands of healing ministries but has also attracted thousands of people to such churches in search of healing. The sheer desperation and need for solace, support, and hope and the anxieties around the disease have driven many into these "healing ministries," led by "healing prophets" who have proliferated in huge numbers across the African continent.

Self-proclaimed Prophet Owuor claims to heal HIV / AIDS. There are many testimonies of people who had HIV "deleted" from their blood. The MRH church also believes that God heals HIV, and Prophet Owuor has publicly paraded a number of people whom he claims to have been healed of HIV / AIDS. Their names are printed in magazines, and they are invited to give testimonies about how God healed them through his "Mighty Prophet," as Owuor is called by his followers. Many of these testimonies are backed by medical professionals who are also members of the MRH. They publicly issue such individuals with clean bills of health accompanied by medical certificates showing their former HIV positive status and their current HIV-negative status. This practice has raised serious controversies and ethical concerns in Kenya among medical practitioners and the general populace.

The moralization of HIV / AIDS as a sexually transmitted disease easily glosses over the real factors that perpetuate the spread of HIV / AIDS, which include poverty, violence against women, violent masculinities, rape, unequal gender relations, and the inability of women to negotiate safe sex from their spouses. At the same time, an HIV-negative status has never stopped the spread of the infection. Many men and women get married with HIV-negative test results but contract the disease later on due to marital infidelity or medical accidents.

In her study of HIV and intimate relationships in Tanzania, Melissa Browning,[61] a leading American theologian and expert in this field, speaks about "risky marriage," referring to a situation where marital and other intimate relationships put women at severe risk and in both serious danger of contracting HIV as well as suffering from domestic and sexual violence. In the context of women infected with HIV and AIDS, Browning argues that women's bodies have become sites not just of pain and promise but also where Christian moralization of the infection takes place. Women's bodies are the focal point upon which the daily struggle for human flourishing and well-being takes place. Nowhere is this more urgent than in the lived experiences of women living with AIDS.

The conversations that I had with many women explains not only their anxieties and fears about HIV / AIDS but also why messages and notions of holiness, holy ways of dressing, sexual purity, and marital fidelity both resonate with them and evoke admiration and submission to the promoter of such teachings.[62]

Pentecostal prophets like David Owuor have also used the HIV pandemic to entrench moral arguments around appropriate sexual behavior. Those I interviewed suggest that messages of sexual purity and abstinence and faithfulness in marriage also frown on condom use in the context of marriage, regardless of the realities of married people's sexual lives. This anti-condom stance is problematic on many levels.

While the central argument of Browning's thesis is that marriage is a risky factor based on testimonies and narratives of women survivors of the pandemic, it is easy to see the link between anxieties about marital infidelity and its relationship with faith. This could be applied to the Kenyan context, where women in our informal and formal conversations indicated that they feel safer single and as born-again Christians because church and faith are safe spaces for them. As one single mother and member of the MRH explained to me during an informal conversation about the proliferation of single motherhood in Kenya:

I love being single because I am in control of my life including my sex life. I don't have to go to bed worried that my husband or boyfriend cheated on me last night. I don't go to bed thinking that I don't know where he slept last night and who he slept with. I am not worried that someone will bring death into my bed. HIV to me is death and many women have been infected with HIV and other diseases on their marital beds. I don't have to worry about that. Let me worry about money issues but not death on my bed. I pity married women. They suffer in silence. And when they get a cough or skin rashes, they go, oh my God! Death has been brought to me. For me being lonely is better than being married and scared to death about my HIV status.[63]

Yet the response of Pentecostal Christianity in Africa to the HIV / AIDS pandemic cannot be divorced from the larger global HIV / AIDS policy and financing (PEPFAR [US President's Emergency Plan for AIDS Relief]). More important is the moralization of a global policy and public health challenge that cannot simply be explained through narrow spiritual lenses. A key area in which Pentecostal churches have had a negative impact in sub-Saharan Africa is in the area of gender, youth and sexualities, and women's health and reproductive rights (e.g., abortion and sexuality education, the moralization of HIV / AIDS, rallying homophobia, reinforcing violence against women). One of the key issues where it has attracted significant focus is the manner in which Pentecostal churches navigate HIV / AIDS on the African continent.

There have been concerns about the treatment and prevention of HIV, as well as how Pentecostal Christians have played an active role in teaching their congregations how to manage their marital and sexual lives. Much focus has been placed on how they carried out premarital counseling as well as mandatory HIV testing for couples intending to get married and how theologies of abstinence for the unmarried and fidelity for the married have been navigated and constructed.[64] And while evidence elsewhere suggests that involvement in a faith-based community may in itself be protective against a range of negative health behaviors, this positive aspect must be tempered with the need to give youth full and honest information about sexual and reproductive health. Sadly, some Pentecostal churches such as the MRH have continued to promote messages that are at odds with contemporary times and the lived realities of African and Kenyan youth. In particular, their sermons on zero abstinence, sexual purity, and morality that are linked to notions of eschatology, demons, heaven, and hell come into conflict with those who want youth to have tools and skills to make informed choices in the areas of sexuality and reproductive health.

MANDATORY PREGNANCY TESTING

As already noted, young women planning to get married in the MRH must accept to undergo a mandatory pregnancy test beforehand. The logic is to ensure that a woman marries while "sexually pure" and that she and her fiancé have not been having sex during courtship, something that is frowned upon in this church. Mandatory pregnancy testing, a common practice in many Pentecostal churches in Kenya, must be understood within the strict sexual purity culture espoused by Pentecostal clergy across the African continent.[65] It is important to note that the focus on moral and purity sanctions espoused by Prophet Owuor is directed at women's bodies. In this church, morality and sexual purity teachings are almost exclusively geared toward women's bodies, sexuality, reproductive rights, and dignity. It is interesting that while a woman is expected to go through a pregnancy test, the man is not subjected to virginity testing given that the woman, if found to be pregnant, did not impregnate herself.

There is also strict control of women's intimate lives and reproductive choices, including birth control technologies as well as abortion, which the church calls murder. The church further frowns on teenage pregnancy and abortion. However, it does not provide women with the skills to navigate even their married sexual lives, and women are blamed when they find themselves in a difficult situation. Prophet Owuor preaches about abortion as murder and a rampant national concern. He promotes a kind of sexism laced with his patriarchal ideologies that is specifically applied to women's bodies.

The sexism in the MRH as well as in many Pentecostal churches in Africa is an extension of attempts of patriarchal control of women's bodies and sexuality. Here women do not control their bodies. Instead, their sexual lives are policed and objectified. They are the subject of moral and patriarchal imaginaries, and many are denied bodily integrity and agency. From a feminist standpoint, it is safe to say that MRH and Prophet Owuor denigrate women's bodies. As Deidre Crumbley aptly observes of African American women in a Storefront Sanctified Church, "women's bodies are regarded as unmanageable and frequently impure and are relegated to the peripheries of society."[66] As has been shown in the MRH, women's flesh is seen as dangerous and pleasure is seen as sinful.

PREMARITAL COUNSELING

Premarital and postmarital counseling is a huge part of the MHR. All pastors and heads of altars are trained counselors. There are also marriage counselors stationed in all altars across the country. All couples must undergo a rigorous period of premarital counseling during a controlled courtship. This rigorous process can take up to six months, followed by a wedding in about a year or a year and a half's time and no longer. During courtship and premarital counseling couples are guided on the role of sex in marriage, the number of children to have, how to navigate infertility, and general questions pertaining to marriage. Prospective couples can ask a wide range of questions. In addition, young men also go through several sessions of premarital counseling with a male pastor, while the young women also do the same with a female pastor. The reason given for this is to encourage openness with the pastor. After the premarital counseling has been concluded to the satisfaction of all parties, and all legal requirements are met such as announcing the wedding in the altars for three consecutive Sundays, then the wedding planning can proceed.

During courtship, parental consent is sought by the couple with the help of a pastor. Cultural issues such as dowry and bride wealth that can arise during courtship and premarital counseling are discussed and resolved. The church mediates for youth couples in the event that parents raise issues with the relationship. In this case, the church acts as a mediator between parents and the couple. After both the mandatory HIV and pregnancy testing have been undertaken, and the couple are found to be HIV negative and the pregnancy test results are acceptable to the pastors, wedding preparations begin. Courtship is carried out according to the teachings of the MRH and must be done within the dictates of the confines of the holiness and purity culture as espoused by Prophet Owuor and his retinue of youth pastors. Courtship is a commitment that should precede engagements and marriage ideally between young men and women of the same denomination who are both pure and holy (i.e., they must be committed born-again Christians who have abstained from "sexual sin" since getting saved).

Cross-church unions are not allowed. During courtship the couple's behavior and mannerisms must reflect the morality and holiness taught by the church. This is another area in which the church seeks to control youth sexuality. Young men and women are encouraged to shun all manner of "indecent behaviors," which means absolute abstinence. Anything likely to hint at sexual immorality must be avoided at all costs. Young men and women are therefore called upon to relate with to another in absolute sexual purity and must observe total abstinence. In this ministry, fondling, holding of hands, hugging, kissing, and any other form of touch that may be considered foreplay are strictly forbidden.

All relationships must also be geared toward marriage, and, if marriage is not envisioned, then the relationship must not continue. Couples are also discouraged from engaging in activities that would tempt them into sexual immorality or sexual sin. All relationships must also be carried out with the consent of a "mentor(s)," usually a pastor who guides the couple through the relationship and courtship period. This step requires mentors to walk with couples throughout the relationship journey. Extramarital sex, just as premarital sex, is categorized as one of the worst sins a person can commit. This is the only sin that is committed against the body, which is the Temple of the Lord, according to the MRH's teachings. The couples must therefore learn to "keep holy distance" by ensuring that they only meet under the watchful eyes and full consent of their mentors. They should not pay each other visits at home or in their hostels if they are students except in the company of other "brethren" so as to avoid sexual temptations.

WEDDINGS AS NOT SEXY AFFAIRS: MARRIAGE AS RAPTURES AND ESCHATOLOGICAL MOTIFS IN MRH

Weddings are special occasions in the MRH to commence marriage life. All MRH weddings must take place in a designated altar or an open place and must be presided over by a licensed MRH pastor. The church has to officiate the wedding, and in most cases many weddings take place on Saturday. The groom, the bride, and bridesmaids must dress in a holy manner. The wedding gown must be made in such a way that the bride is covered with no body parts exposed. Wedding gowns that reveal the body are not accepted, because weddings, in the eyes of the church, are not a sexy affair. In this church women are exclusively forbidden from wearing inappropriate clothing or comporting themselves in any way deemed inappropriate, including how they dress on their wedding day.

The couple's wedding must be like a shadow of the "wedding of the lamb of God"—Jesus Christ is going to come soon and take the church away, according to MRH teachings. For these reasons, MRH weddings are different from other Christian weddings. It is the practice that the bride arrives first in the church before the groom. The significance of order is that the bride signifies the church, or the body of Christ, that waits in anticipation for the "coming of Jesus Christ" (the groom), "the lamb of God," who will come to take the bridge / church home during the rapture. Every wedding therefore should serve as a reminder that Jesus Christ is coming again to rapture the church. Such an occasion must therefore signify holiness and purity so that it is ready for this event. Thus weddings signify the "Second coming of the Lord."

The wedding night should be the first time the couple should have so-called holy sex—in this case the woman's virginity should be "raptured" on the wedding night just as Christ would come to rapture the church from a sinful world. Christ is coming to rapture the church, and only those who have remained pure and holy will be raptured as the groom / Jesus Christ raptures the bride-church on the wedding night. The significance of the wedding of the lamb has implications for Pentecostal intimacies and women's intimate citizenships. Here women bodies are linked to eschatological beliefs. The prophet also uses his authority to map his teachings onto women's bodies, trafficking in women's emotions by linking female bodies and notions of sex and sin to apocalyptic beliefs about heaven and hell as well as the second coming of Christ and the Kingdom of God. In so doing Prophet Owuor not only seeks to impose his own notions of sex and sin on his female followers, but he also places a heavy burden on them insofar as they are the reason that others would fail to enter into the anticipated Kingdom of God.

After the weddings, the couple can then proceed to a honeymoon and start their lives. But the policing of women's sexual lives does not end there. During prolonged fasts, which are common in this ministry, both women and men are expected to abstain from sex. At the same time couples are discouraged from having sex for a week before they attend frequent prayer meetings where the prophet will be speaking. This has created huge strains in families, especially where the partners are not members of this ministry. Husbands have complained publicly that their wives who follow the prophet in his many crusades neglect to give their husbands their conjugal rights during such times. This breeds resentment toward the church.

From the aforementioned discussion, it is clear that the MRH is deeply involved in the lives of youth and seeks to have intense influence over how they navigate their sexual lives and intimate relationships. Yet, this control of youth sexuality has drawn criticism from nonmembers of the church as well as the general public. This should not come as a surprise, insofar as many Pentecostal churches have always sought to control youth sexuality in a bid to produce moral regimes of their youthful constituencies. Many have left this church, citing its conservative and strict teachings on sex and marriage, which they think are out of touch with both their desires and feelings. This dissatisfaction raises questions of how sustainable these teachings are. The teachings of this church on sexuality are not only potentially unsustainable but also far removed from the reality of youth and sexuality in modern-day Kenya.

The MRH and its founder not only attempt to police, control, and direct the sexual lives of Kenyan youth in an era when a significant majority of this demographic determine their sex lives and personal choices irrespective of such teachings. This policing of youth sexuality puts enormous pressure on young people's emotional and mental health. What Kenyan youth need is real empowerment in sex education for them to be able to make informed choices. This moral panic appears to be increasing as Pentecostal clergy continue to grow their power and influence in the public sphere. The emphasis on sexual purity, the promotion of total abstinence before the wedding night, can be understood through the lens of the extreme purity culture espoused by Prophet Owuor and his ministry of "Repentance and Holiness."

The control of women bodies and intimate lives permeates all facets of life, like marital choices, as well as their reproductive health rights and choices. In ministry of Prophet Owuor, women's bodies are not just the sites of sexual sin and impurity but also the reason men will not get into the anticipated Kingdom of God. In such hegemonic tendencies, the submission of women through cultural and biblical scripts are mostly advanced by male pastors. Pentecostal clergy and society have contributed to the oppression of women by subjecting them in ways that they become mere sexual desires of men or laboratories to manufacture babies. When they are not objects of desire and their wombs are not factories to manufacture babies,[67] then they are the reason why men can't keep their trousers zipped and ultimately miss entering the anticipated Kingdom of God. The autonomy of women's bodies is taken away. The church and the purity culture dictate what a woman ought to do, including how she weds. Yet, the control of women's bodies and attire not only signifies inequitable power relations but also follows wider patterns of denigration of women's bodies in African Pentecostalism.

YOUTH SPIRITUALITY, SEXUAL PURITY BETWEEN DESIRE AND CONTROL

Religious leaders such as Owuor are extremely influential and vocal on social and moral issues and have not only used that influence to assert their position on sexual citizenship but have also helped entrench and legitimize those working with sexual surveillance systems to police young people, especially women. By heavily taming and controlling youth and women's sexual desires among his followers and the larger Kenyan public, Owuor has simultaneously navigated a heavily contested territory with some measure of success (judging by the number of women who are ardent followers of the prophet) and put himself at the center of the erotic economy. His notions of sin play a critical role in constructing youth and gendered sexuality and the manner in which members of his ministry experience sex and sexuality, ultimately giving this self-proclaimed prophet control over their bodies, how they dress, and how they conduct themselves. It also determines how women will be perceived by men and determine if they will be called "saved holy sisters" or "prostitutes."

However, in a bid to understand how the central teachings of the church in respect to youth sexuality is helping youth to navigate intimate relationships, we received interesting and some varied responses. Our research and observations of young people's intimate and sexual behavior in the MRH showed ambivalence that makes it difficult to tell if teachings on morality, sexual purity, and moral regeneration are really sustainable for youth in the MRH. Maintaining the demands of being born again or holy is a huge challenge for many youth, especially those in public universities in which intimate relationships are commonplace. While a number of youth we interviewed explained that they coped very well with such stringent demands to stay pure and holy, others suggested just how hard it is. As one ex-student told me in an interview:

> I can't live out the rest of my life like this. I have feelings! My body wants sex and love. But this prophet's teachings are extreme and borders on obsession. I don't know why he hates sex so much. He is telling us sex is a bad sin but he has had sex and sired a child and divorced his wife and enjoyed his youth. Then he comes here to tell me not to have sex. No way will I give him power over my life. If I wanted to be celibate, I would have become a Catholic nun. But I am not a nun so he can go preach to whoever wants to be controlled.[68]

Other students I spoke with felt that the prophet's teachings on total abstinence and sexual purity helped them navigate their sexualities in consideration of the HIV / AIDS pandemic and sexually transmitted infections (STIs). For these students it seems that the fear of getting infected with HIV and other STIs was a motivating factor for joining this ministry. One student suggested that he joined the church because it challenged him to be different. Others suggested it offered them identity, a pan-African orientation, and traditional family values such as monogamy and marital fidelity. For example, they explained that they were attracted by the born-again message and embraced it, that it is a deep and heavy message, that the pastoral relationship provided by clergy helped guide them in their spiritual and academic lives. One interviewee told me that he had learned to develop a mental shift in his thinking, explaining: "We are taught to be different and challenge each other, promote intellectual wellbeing, social wellbeing-visit the sick in hospitals, fellowships, prayers, evangelism, group discussions, teach the word of God." Asked how male interviewees navigated relationships with young women, the answers were varied. Many said they study together and connect in fellowships. When we asked about relating to young women at church, one respondent said that their beauty is appreciated but must be approached in a holy manner. "When I like a girl and I want to marry her, I tell my pastor and we begin counseling. We don't hug girls around. We must keep holy distance. We avoid sins." When asked to describe what bad sins are, many gave a cocktail of sins that include abortion, premarital sex, getting pregnant outside wedlock, homosexuality and promiscuous behavior, and HIV / AIDS among many others. Youth are taught that they must hold back their emotions and feelings so as not to fall into sins of immorality.

Youth in the MRH must wait for the appropriate time to be intimate. Young men who were asked if they would marry young women who are not virgins answered yes and explained that there is no judgment in the ministry for those who lived in sin before they joined the church. This is what a respondent named Kevin said during such discussions: "There is no judgement of one's past before they came to know Christ or join the ministry. And Yes I can marry an impure girl because the blood of Jesus cleanses all sins. Even I had a past before I got born again."[69] Youth from outside this ministry do not regard such teachings uncritically. Some youth I spoke with suggested that they could never allow anyone to dictate how they live out their lives, especially their sex lives. Some suggested that it would be challenging for the majority of youth to stay within the strict constraints set by the church or what is considered appropriate behavior in a world in which most youth follow another pattern. Others scoffed on such teachings, calling the ministry a cult that is misleading vulnerable people. "As for me, my body and what I do with it is my choice. There is no way I can allow some deluded self-proclaimed prophet to dictate what I should do to my body."

REPENTANCE AND HOLINESS:
A NEW GENERATION AND NEW FUTURE

This essay has examined how the MRH is navigating youth and gendered sexualities in contemporary Kenya. It has been argued that the MRH continues to promote conservative and stringent views and beliefs about sex and sexuality that are at odds with the lived realities of the Kenyan youth, particularly college students. As suggested above, the MRH's obsessive concern with youth and gendered bodies, especially women's bodies, and the covering of female bodies is more than just the moralization of youth sexuality but is also suggestive of Prophet David Owuor's dominance and attempt to control youth sexuality as well as mapping his own teachings on youthful bodies in a bid to assert his spiritual power and patriarchal ideals on Kenyan youth. The involvement of the MRH in the moral regeneration of Kenyan youth—especially in respect to teachings on holiness, sexual purity, abstinence, and morality—is significant and points to a specific need to control young people's intimate choices. The message of holiness and repentance is linked further to the notion of a moral regeneration, which is at the core of this ministry. The idea is uncritically embraced by a portion of young people in public universities. It is premised on the belief that the country needs to raise a new generation of leaders, rooted in a renewed concept of repentance and holiness. Repentance and holiness have value in the theology of this ministry, which can only be reached through true repentance and living a holy life.

CONCLUSION

Pentecostal clergy in Africa, and particularly in Kenya, are extremely influential and vocal on a wide range of social, political, economic, and cultural issues. Prophet David Owuor has used his spiritual power, voice, and platforms to assert his position on sexual purity to youth and female constituencies, including having a say on how youth and particularly women live out their intimate and sexual lives and the way they dress; comport themselves; and how, whom, and when to marry. He also asserts his position on the nation's morality; condemns sex, abortion, lesbianism, homosexuality, and women's reproductive rights; discriminates against women living with HIV / AIDS; and maps his extreme views onto women's bodies, gender equality, rights, sexuality, reproduction, bodily autonomy, and citizenship. This prophet promotes an extreme form of purity culture that blames sex for the state of the nation of Kenya that is riddled with corruption, ethnic bigotry, and many others that this antisex prophet sees through narrow prisms of sexual sin that leads to death. Yet, while Pentecostal churches and the MRH in particular attempt to help youth navigate sexuality using spiritual recourses, they are not sustainable. Despite the country undergoing remarkable social changes, the churches in Kenya still attempt to discipline people's personal lives and choices especially in the area of sexualities. More important, this is about the role of faith-based organizations in the lives of Kenyan youth and how they help to navigate questions of belonging, identity formation, socialization, and sexual citizenship.

NOTES

1. 2019 Kenya Population and Housing Census, https://www.knbs.or.ke/wp-content /uploads/2023/09/2019-Kenya-population-and-Housing-Census-Analytical-Report -on-Youth-and-Adolescents.pdf.
2. UK Department of International Development.
3. Parsitau, "Engaging Youth for a Culture of Peace and Security in Kenya."
4. Ismailimail.
5. Ismailimail. See also David Aduda, "Most Youth Prefer Self Employment, New Survey Shows," *Nation* (Kenya edition), January 15, 2016, http://www.nation.co.ke /news/Most-youth-prefer-self-employment-new-survey-shows/-/1056/3035216/ -/2brum0/-/index.html.
6. Aduda, "Most Youth Prefer Self Employment."
7. Parsitau, "Engaging Youth for a Culture of Peace and Security in Kenya."
8. Ismailimail.
9. Transparency International Kenya.
10. Parsitau, "Engaging Youth for a Culture of Peace and Security in Kenya."
11. Parsitau, "Engaging Youth for a Culture of Peace and Security in Kenya."
12. Freeman; Gifford, "African Christianity"; Kalu.
13. Quiroz, 1–16; Chammah; van Klinken and Obadare; Parsitau and van Klinken.
14. Afolayan, 159–79; Parsitau, "Soft Tongue, Powerful Voice, Huge Influence," 159–79.
15. Parsitau, "Engaging Youth for a Culture of Peace and Security in Kenya"; Parsitau, "Soft Tongue, Powerful Voice, Huge Influence," 159–79.
16. Parsitau, "Soft Tongue, Powerful Voice, Huge Influence," 159–79; Freeman; Gifford, *Christianity, Politics and Public Life in Kenya*; Gifford, *African Christianity*; Kalu *Pentecostalism.*
17. Quiroz, 1–16; Parsitau, "Keep Holy Distance and Abstain till He Comes," 45–64; van Klinken, 65–81; van Klinken and Chitando.
18. Quiroz, 102.
19. Parsitau, "Keep Holy Distance and Abstain till He Comes," 45–64.
20. Freeman; Gifford, "Christianity, Politics and Public Life in Kenya"; Browning, "HIV / AIDS Prevention and Sexed Bodies."
21. Parsitau, "Keep Holy Distance and Abstain till He Comes," 45–64; Browning, "HIV / AIDS Prevention and Sexed Bodies," 27–46; Adogame, 475–84; Epstein; van Klinken and Obadare.
22. Quiroz, 1–16.
23. Freeman; Gifford, *Christianity, Politics and Public Life in Kenya.*
24. Lindhardt, 252–72.
25. Obadare.

26. Obadare; Parsitau and Van Klinken; Parsitau, "Embodying Holiness," 181–201; Parsitau, "Prophets, Power, Authority and the Kenyan State," 233–56.
27. Obadare.
28. Quiroz, 1–16.
29. Quiroz.
30. Parsitau, "Praying for Husbands!"
31. Many of these sermons can be accessed at https://www.highwayofholiness.us/overcoming-sexual-sin/; they are also published in Owuor's church magazine, *Repentance and Holiness Magazine.*
32. For example, https://nation.africa/news/Baffling-transformation-of-David-Owuor-lifestyle/1056-4920624-uuqu58/index.html; https://www.standardmedia.co.ke/nairobi/article/2001315307/lawyer-s-family-accuses-prophet-owuor-of-brainwashing-her.
33. Parsitau, "Prophets, Power, Authority and the Kenyan State," 233–56.
34. Parsitau and Van Klinken; Parsitau, "Embodying Holiness," 181–201; Parsitau, "Prophets, Power, Authority and the Kenyan State," 233–56.
35. Parsitau, "Body Shaming in Prophet Owuor's Misogynistic Ministry."
36. Owuor, "Overcoming Sexual Sin."
37. Owuor, "Overcoming Sexual Sin."
38. Parsitau and Van Klinken.
39. Excerpts of interviews with youth in the MRH at Egerton University, 2016.
40. Quiroz, 1–16; see also Obadare.
41. Parsitau, "Body Shaming in Prophet Owuor's Misogynistic Ministry."
42. Parsitau, "Embodying Holiness," 181–201.
43. Parsitau and Van Klinken.
44. Owuor, "Overcoming Sexual Sin."
45. Owuor, "Overcoming Sexual Sin."
46. Parsitau, "Body Shaming in Prophet Owuor's Misogynistic Ministry."
47. Parsitau, "Body Shaming in Prophet Owuor's Misogynistic Ministry."
48. Lewis, 104–9.
49. Odongo.
50. Odongo.
51. This quotation comes from one sermon in a series titled "Purity in the Church; Overcoming Sexual Sins, and How God Looks at Sexual Sins!" All these sermons are printed in church magazines and uploaded on the websites and YouTube. Parsitau, "Body Shaming in Prophet Owuor's Misogynistic Ministry."
52. Owuor, "Overcoming Sexual Sin."
53. This information is based on dozens of interviews with members of the USO organizations between 2012 and 2018; see also "The First Fruit: The Youth and the Church," sermon published in *Repentance and Holiness Magazines* 4 (2009).
54. This information is based on dozens of interviews with members of the USO organizations between 2012 and 2018; for quotation, see "The First Fruit."
55. This information is based on dozens of interviews with members of the USO organizations between 2012 and 2018; for quotation, see "The First Fruit."
56. This information is based on dozens of interviews with members of the USO organizations between 2012 and 2018; for quotation, see "The First Fruit."
57. Empower Youth Church Conference, December 14–15, 2017, Nakuru Town.
58. Parsitau, "Keep Holy Distance and Abstain till He Comes," 45–64.

59. Kennedy Gachuhi, "Kenyans React to Pastor Who Refused to Officiate Nuptials over Medical Report," *Standard*, 2019, https://www.standardmedia.co.ke/rift-valley/article/2001301682/kenyans-react-to-pastor-who-refused-to-officiate-nuptials.
60. Opondo.
61. Browning, *Risky Marriage*.
62. Parsitau and Van Klinken.
63. Parsitau and Van Klinken, 12.
64. Parsitau, "Keep Holy Distance and Abstain till He Comes," 45–64.
65. Parsitau, "Violent Theologies."
66. Crumbley.
67. Mate, 549–68.
68. Interviews with Jessica (not her real name) at Egerton University, December 2017.
69. Interviews with Kevin, a youth leader of the MRH student movement, December 2017.

BIBLIOGRAPHY

Afe, O. Adogame. "HIV / AIDs Support in African Pentecostalism: The Case of the Redeemed Christian Church of God." *Journal of Health Psychology* 12, no. 3 (2007): 475–84.

Afolayan, Adesina et al. "Pentecostalism and Politics in Africa." In *Pentecostalism and Politics in Africa*. African Histories and Modernities Series. Gewerbestrasse, Switzerland: Palgrave Macmillan, 2018, 159–79.

Browning, Melissa. "HIV / AIDS Prevention and Sexed Bodies: Rethinking Abstinence and Sexed Bodies in the Light of the African AIDS Pandemic." *Theology and Sexuality* 15, no. 1 (2009): 27–46.

Browning, Melissa. *Risky Marriage: HIV and Intimate Relationships in Tanzania*. Plymouth: UK Lexington, 2014.

Chammah, J. Kaunda. *Gender, Sexualities and Spiritualities in African Pentecostalism*. Cham, Switzerland: Palgrave Macmillan, 2020.

Crumbley, Deidre. *The Spirit, Structure and the Flesh: Gendered Experiences in African Instituted Churches among the Yoruba of Nigeria*. Madison: Wisconsin University Press, 2010.

Epstein, Helen. "God and the Fight against AIDS!" *New York Review of Books* 52, no. 7 (2005).

Freeman, D. *The Pentecostalism and Development: Churches, NGO and Social Change in Africa*. Hampshire, UK: Van Leer Jerusalem Institute, and Palgrave Macmillan, 2012.

Gifford, P. *African Christianity: Its Public Role in Uganda and Other African Countries*. Kampala: Fountain Publishers, 1999.

———. *Christianity, Politics and Public Life in Kenya*. London: Hurst & Co., 2009.

Ismailimail. "Aga Khan University's Findings: East Africa Youth Survey Results." August 8, 2015. Ismailimail (blog). https://ismailimail.wordpress.com/2015/08/08/aga-khan-universitys-findings-east-africa-youth-survey-results/comment-page-1/.

Kalu, Ogbu. *African Pentecostalism: An Introduction*. Oxford: Oxford University Press, 2008.

Lewis, Desiree. "Rethinking Nationalism in Relation to Foucault's History of Sexuality and Adrienne Rich's 'Compulsory Heterosexuality and Lesbian Existence.'" *Sexualities* 11, no. 1–2 (2008): 104–9.

Lindhardt, Martin. "Men of God: Pentecostalism in Urban Tanzania." *Religion* 45, no. 2 (2015): 252–72.

Mate, Rekopantswe. "Wombs as God's Laboratories: Pentecostal Discourses of Femininity in Zimbabwe." *Africa* 72, no. 4 (2002): 549–68.

Obadare, Ebenezer. "The Pastor as Sexual Object." Opinion Nigeria. 2017. http://www .opinionnigeria.com/the-pastor-as-sexual-object-by-ebenezer-obadare/#sthash.LP2j1G4r .xog1gmYl.dpbs.

Odongo, David. "Prophet Owuor's Biography." 2014. Accessed August 2, 2024. https:// www.standardmedia.co.ke/entertainment/city-news/article/2000114584/prophet -owuors-biography.

Opondo, F. A. National Aids Control Council, "Management of Research Protocols, September 2007, http://guidelines.health.go.ke:8000/media/guidelines_for_mgt_of _research_protocols.pdf.

Owuor, David. Owuor, "The First Fruit: The Youth and the Church." Sermon. *Repentance and Holiness Magazines* 4 (2009).

———. "Overcoming Sexual Sin." Sermon transcript. Accessed June 4, 2024. https://www .highwayofholiness.us/overcoming-sexual-sin/.

Parsitau, D. S. "Engaging Youth for a Culture of Peace and Security in Kenya: The Role of Faith Based / Inspired Organizations and other Non-State Actors." Chap. 13 in *Themes in Religion and Human Security in Africa*, edited by Joram Tarusarira and Ezra Chitando. London: Taylor and Francis Group, 2020. https://www.routledge.com /Themes-in-Religion-and-Human-Security-in-Africa/Tarusarira-Chitando/p/book /9781003017080.

Parsitau, Damaris. "Keep Holy Distance and Abstain till He Comes: Interrogating a Pentecostal Church's Engagements with HIV / AIDS and the Youth in Kenya." *Africa Today* 56, no. 1 (2009): 45–64.

Parsitau, D. S. "Body Shaming in Prophet Owuor's Misogynistic Ministry." Elephant (website). 2019. https://www.theelephant.info/features/2019/11/21/body-shaming-in -prophet-owuors-misogynistic-ministry/.

———. "Embodying Holiness: Gender, Sex and Bodies in a Neo-Pentecostal Church in Kenya-Body Talk and Cultural Identity in the African World." In *Body Talk and Cultural Identity in the African World*, edited by Augustine Agwuele, 181–201. London: Equinox, 2015.

———. "Praying for Husbands! Single Women Negotiating Faith and Patriarchy in Contemporary Kenya." In *The Palgrave Handbook of African Social Ethics*, edited by N. Wariboko and F. Toyin. London and New York: Palgrave Macmillan.

———. "Prophets, Power, Authority and the Kenyan State: Prophet David Owuor of the National Repentance and Holiness Ministry." In *Religious Freedom and Religious Pluralism in Africa: Prospects and Limitations*, edited by Pieter Coertzen, Christian M. Green, and Len Hansen, 233–256. Stellenbosch, South Africa: SUN Media, 2016.

———. "Soft Tongue, Powerful Voice, Huge Influence: The Dynamics of Gender, Soft Power and Political Influence in Faith Evangelistic Ministries in Kenya." In *African Histories and Modernities Series: Pentecostalism and Politics in Africa*, edited by A. Afolayan, 159–79. Gewerbestrasse, Switzerland: Macmillan, 2018.

———. Violent Theologies, Women's Bodies and the 'Church Business' in Kenya." Elephant (website). 2019. Accessed July 19, 2024. https://www.theelephant.info/features/2019 /10/31/violent-theologies-womens-bodies-and-church-business-in-kenya/.

Parsitau, D. S., and Adriaan van Klinken. "Pentecostal Intimacies! Women and Intimate Citizenship in the Ministry of Repentance and Holiness in Kenya." *Citizenship Studies Journal* 1.22 no. 16 (2018): 586–602.

Quiroz, Sitna. "The Dilemmas of Monogamy: Pleasure, Discipline and the Pentecostal Moral Self in the Republic of Benin." *Religions* 7, no. 8 (2016): 102.

Transparency International Kenya. "Corruption Perceptions Index 2019." January 23, 2020. https://tikenya.org/2020/01/23/corruption-perceptions-index-2019/.

UK Department for International Development (DFID), "Youth Development in Kenya: Literature Review," 2017. https://www.britishcouncil.co.ke/sites/default/files/ng _kenya_youth_employment_in_kenya.pdf.

van Klinken, Adriaan. "A Kenyan Queer Prophet: Binyavanga Wainaina's Public Contestation of Pentecostalism and Homophobia." In *Christianity and Controversies over Homosexuality in Contemporary Africa*, edited by Ezra Chitando and Adriaan van Klinken, 65–81. Abingdon, UK: Routledge, 2016.

van Klinken, Adriaan, and Ezra Chitando, eds. *Public Religion and the Politics of Homosexuality in Africa*. Abingdon, UK: Routledge, 2016.

van Klinken, Adriaan, and Ebenezer Obadare, eds. *Christianity, Sexuality and Citizenship in Africa*. Abingdon, UK: Routledge, Taylor and Francis Group, 2018. https://www .routledge.com/Christianity-Sexuality-and-Citizenship-in-Africa/Klinken-Obadare/p /book/9780367141523.

"A Mightier Power"

Women and Gender Construction in the
African Challenge, 1951–1961

Andrew E. Barnes

They say that man is mighty,
He governs Land and Sea
He wields a mighty scepter
O'er lesser powers that be
But a mightier power and stronger,
Man from his throne has hurled,
For the hand that rocks the cradle
Is the hand that rules the world.

W. R. Wallace quoted from the "Women's Page"
African Challenge, January 1953[1]

1

In this chapter my plan is to review some articles published in the Christian magazine the *African Challenge*, from the magazine's inaugural issue in July 1951 to about a decade later. The articles under consideration all had a female readership in mind. Almost all of them were written by women. They spoke to the question of the future of Christian women in an anticipated soon-to-be-independent set of African nations. They outlined the expectations Christian women should have of themselves as citizens of those nation-states, then suggested some paths Christian women might follow to meet those expectations. Most broadly and importantly, the articles talk about the personas Christian women needed to assume relative to the changing world in which God had placed them. These personas shaped the expectations Christian women should aspire to meet.

The *African Challenge* was a monthly news magazine published by the Sudan Interior Mission (SIM). The SIM was a North Atlantic (Canadian / American / British) mission founded in Toronto, Canada, during the 1890s. At some unknown point before the period under discussion, the SIM became associated with the reverend Billy Graham and his missionary organization. From its foundation, the SIM had always looked to journalism as a way to communicate its message, and over the decades the SIM published a wide array of periodicals aimed at different but overlapping Christian readerships.[2] In 1948 the SIM began to publish a monthly magazine, the *West African Christian*, aimed at the African Christian communities created through the agency of its missionary endeavors in West Africa. The *African Challenge*, which targeted a broader audience of Christians of African descent, both across Africa, and across the Atlantic, replaced the *West African Christian* in 1951.

From the beginning the *African Challenge* was edited, with oversight by missionaries, by African Christians. Photographs of the editors published in the magazine feature a changing array of younger, thirty-something, African males, though significantly, no African females. Because of its African editorship, the magazine is presented here as having value for the historical investigation of the African Christian consciousness that emerged during the mid-twentieth century in the wake of the policies of "euthanasia of mission" pursued by some missionary organizations. By the 1950s the SIM was engaged in moving many of its church activities and the physical plants that provided venues for these activities over to African control via the African-headed coalition of churches the Evangelical Churches of West Africa (ECWA), formed from the African Christian communities founded by SIM missionaries. The publication of the *African Challenge* can be considered as part of this initiative.

From this perspective, the editorial concerns and journalistic content of the magazine may be explored for what they reveal about what the first generations of Africans who "inherited the kingdom"—that is, those who took over offices and decisions previously the preserve of missionaries—did with the lived religion they inherited. The African Christians who edited the *African Challenge*, the African Christians who published in the magazine, did not see themselves as breaking away from the SIM and its teachings. They saw themselves as carrying on SIM values and traditions. Thus, the *African Challenge* and its contents provide some helpful illustrations of the continuities and discontinuities that could occur as mission Christianity gave way to indigenous Christianity in twentieth-century Africa.

Accepting that discontinuities did happen, the concern here is actually with the continuities. The contents of the *African Challenge* are best appreciated for the sense they give of what African Christians saw as worthwhile in the faith passed on to them by their "missionary forefathers." One goal of this chapter is to demonstrate that the nature and character of the continuities between what missionaries believed and practiced and what African Christians believed and practiced can be and should be better understood. Dismissing as flawed past arguments about how Christianity facilitated the "colonization" of the African mind, a subject that demands further and deeper historical investigation is the positive image of Christianity in the African mind during the colonial era, when Christianity was most closely identified not just with European missionaries but with European colonizers. It is simple enough to say that for a significant subset of Africans during this era, the benefits of mission Christianity outweighed its costs but that assessment only prompts the further question of what the perceived benefits versus what the perceived costs were.

To make this same point in a manner more directly concerned with the Christianization of African women, there is a corpus of scholarship on the introduction in Africa of Western ideas of domesticity and domestic science, the latter involving systematic training in home management, nutrition and food preparation, and hygiene and sanitation. Lead by the pioneering research of Jean Allman and Nancy Rose Hunt, this scholarship has sought to show how the promotion of domesticity and education in domestic science served the purposes of colonial authorities and European missions. One criticism that can be made about this scholarship is that while it does an outstanding job of showing the rewards and benefits governments and missions saw themselves as gaining from the introduction of ideas of Western domesticity, it ignores the rewards and benefits African women saw themselves as gaining from the embrace of ideas of Western domesticity.[3] Christian women missionaries were the primary teachers of domestic science, and Christian mission schools were the primary venues where domestic science was taught. While it is true that where there were Muslim populations—and colonial governments made special efforts to teach Muslim girls in all-Muslim (but missionary-staffed) schools—the point remains that conversancy with Western notions of domesticity was first and foremost an attribute of feminine Christianity. How this attribute played out in the lives of African Christian women remains to be investigated. The discussion presented here of the debates triggered by Western notions of domesticity in the *African Challenge* may be considered a preliminary step toward such investigation.

The period 1945 to 1960, from the end of World War II to the beginnings of the African Independence era, was a liminal time in African history. Whatever determination shared among Europeans that African colonies must be maintained at whatever cost was matched by an awareness among Africans that there were routes Africans could collectively follow to free themselves from colonial rule. During these fifteen years a multitude of discourses opened up, between Africans and between Africans and Europeans, about what a postcolonial Africa would look like and about the steps required to get to that era. Africans, confident that the future belong to them, talked more openly about what they wanted to take from Europeans and European civilization than they would later, during the Independence era, when such conversation could be characterized as reactionary and nostalgia for colonialism.

Across the pages of the *African Challenge* through the 1950s, African Christians eagerly debated the positions and authority they would claim, as the Africans most familiar with the modern civilization of the West, once the Europeans left. One debate that took up a surprising amount of space in the magazine had to do with the role of African Christian women in the coming era of Independence. The *African Challenge* had a male editorship but also, it turned out, a large female readership. Some of the content aimed at women came from the news services. But another part was produced by local Christian women writers hired by the editors to write for a target audience. The content penned by these women writers did not only pursue the agenda the male editors intended. Women writers advocated ideas of Christian womanhood that did not overtly clash with the official editorial line, yet at least it seemed to some men, did subversively challenge it.

This subversiveness represented continuity as well. Going back to the 1920s, the collaborative efforts of governments and missions to implement the recommendations of the Phelps Stokes Education Commission reports had prompted women missionaries to question the conclusion of those reports that the primary way African women could contribute to the Christian development of Africa was as mothers. In the same way that the African men who edited the *African Challenge* were the heirs of the male missionaries who had guided the SIM during the 1920s and 1930s, the African women writing in the magazine were the heirs of the women missionaries who educated them during those earlier decades, and just like their "missionary foremothers," these women were committed to celebrating a more expansive idea of Christian womanhood.

The debate among Christians about how and where African Christian women would fit in postcolonial African society was multidimensional and suffused with various types of tension. The SIM had communicated mixed signals about the profile of Christian woman. These mixed signals continued to be sent by the editors of the *African Challenge*. The SIM, as did many other missions, taught its African adherents that Christian women were supposed to structure their lives around the fulfilment of their obligations as wives and mothers. In the wake of the Phelps Stokes Education Commissions reports and recommendations, missions had turned their attentions to the provision of social services and the training of Africans to facilitate such provision. In addition to being wives and mothers, Christian women were invited to train as social service providers. The opportunities for African women were much more limited than the opportunities for African men. Still, on the other side of their primary school education, African women could and did aspire to careers as nurses, teachers, and social welfare workers.[4]

The SIM was a faith mission, and faith missions demanded that all their adherents—men, women, and children—accept as Christians the duty to evangelize the non-Christians with whom they came into contact. The expectation was for women, even mothers, to do some proselytization. Women nurses, teachers, and social welfare workers were expected to evangelize their patients, students, and clients. The SIM put before African women at least three different evangelical personas. Women could proselytize in their persona as wives, or in their persona as mothers, or in their persona as workers outside the home. The SIM took for granted that while all three placed different demands on a woman's time and energy, all three could still be reconciled together in an active life of telling others about God's mercy. Married mothers could gain professional competence and use this competence outside the home to save souls.

The African males who edited the *African Challenge* followed the SIM's lead. The women who published in the *African Challenge* perceived things a bit differently, however. Some embraced and advocated the idea that feminine evangelism could be best pursued by mothers and wives. Others, though, celebrated as God's providence the professional and vocational achievements that allowed Christian women to pursue the age-old (European) Christian tradition of evangelization through poor relief. Typically, articles promoting both these perspectives were published in the same issue, on the same page of the magazine, leaving readers perplexed about the message being communicated. One constant among male readers of the magazine, however, seemed to have been resentment over all the attention given to women. Over the 1950s this tension seems to have built to a crisis point. In the months previous to July 1959, the *African Challenge* had run a series of articles by an African Christian woman explaining to other African Christian women the special ministry as wives and mothers granted to them by God. The author lauded the husband of the young women she used as her protagonist for his willingness to help his wife. At the end of the series, the *African Challenge* surveyed its male readers as to whether it was in fact healthy, modern, and Christian for husbands to help their wives with the latter's special ministry. The response to the query was negative overall, with one of the male respondents dismissing the idea as "crazy." Further, from July 1959, the issue where the survey was published, to February 1961, a period of eighteen months, the *African Challenge* published no further articles written from a women's perspective. There were other reasons for this hiatus in content by women for women, but the argument below will be that the direction in which content for women went after the freeze suggests that the magazine was trying to step away from the gender tensions that had beset its pages over the previous decade.

2

To better understand the debate in the *African Challenge* over Christian women and their future in Africa, it is helpful to characterize the magazine via some short descriptions of its makeup and the directions in which its content went. For the period under discussion the magazine was sixteen pages long (later it expanded to twenty-four pages), with two columns of text standard but with those two columns sometimes further divided into two. On the model of the American picture magazines *Look* and *Life*, many pages were dedicated to photographs. At least four pages of each issue were taken up with advertisements—the Africanization of the presentation of Western commodities in the advertisements would be worth a study in itself. Another four pages were typically reserved for things like letters to the editor, calendars, lists of daily Scripture readings for the month, group photos of Bible reader clubs, contests, and quizzes. Only about half the pages in a given issue were devoted to feature articles. This was not a lot of space. Many articles needed to be serialized over four to six issues. This arrangement of content worked, however, because the magazine was geared toward a subscription audience versus a newsstand one.

The magazine's Christian orientation should be acknowledged first. Stories about personal salvation, stories about successful proselytizing, stories about triumphing over Satan's lures were what Christians wanted to read, and such stories made up most of the feature articles published in the magazine. The fact that the SIM had other local journals across the globe meant that the *African Challenge* had plenty of such stories upon which to draw. For example, the magazine ran an excerpt from the autobiography of Madame Chiang Kai-shek, where she talked about her long life as a Christian. Readers voiced their appreciation of the article in the letters to the editor, and Madame Chiang Kai-shek wrote back thanking them in turn.[5] The SIM was a conservative mission, concerned with the threats posed to the spiritual life of its African adherents by the creeping materialism of the modern world. The editorials and opinion pieces in the *African Challenge* reflected this sensibility. So, for example, the magazine published an exposé that condemned cinemas and the films they presented as Satanic temptations. The magazine received a number of letters to the editor from young Africans who renounced their previous lives as moviegoers. The magazine ran similar exposes about polygamy, about "problem women," or prostitutes; and about "juju," or traditional healing. These pieces likewise garnered testimonials sent to the editors by young men who through reading the exposés recognized the evil of their past ways. Most issues of the *African Challenge* provided a selection of advice and guidance articles and columns, giving Christians pointers on the spiritual approach to life's problems. Worth mentioning here was the magazine's connection with the Billy Graham Crusade. Graham's smiling face is featured more than the visage of any other individual in the magazine during the period under study. Graham's Christian radio station, ELWA, broadcasting across Africa from Liberia, was advertised in every issue. In the later fifties, an African American protégé of Graham, Reverend Howard Jones, who broadcast across Africa via ELWA a weekly sermon from his home church in Cleveland, was regularly featured in the magazine.

The *African Challenge* also saw itself as a news magazine with a commitment to offering news of interest to its readers. A monthly one-to-two-page spread, "NEWS" ("North, East, West, South"), culled from the international news services short, paragraph-long news items from around the world. During the early years of the magazine's existence these news items had a Western, conservative political bias. There were a number of stories decrying the worldwide advance of Communism and the Communist oppression of Christians. There was a noteworthy identification in the magazine with Israel, as opposed to Arab countries, and with Jews as people of the book. By the close of the 1950s the fear of Communism was becoming submerged in enthusiasm for the anticipated end of European colonial rule and the establishment of African nation-states. The conservatism did not disappear, but there was an openness to thinking about a variety of strategies for future economic and social development, an openness mostly articulated in the context of stories about Kwame Nkrumah and Ghana. In the late 1950s Nkrumah served as a kind of favorite son for the magazine's readership. He usurped this position from African leaders such as President William Tubman from Liberia and Emperor Haile Selassie of Ethiopia, who had been more popular earlier in the decade. Leaving personalities aside, there was a noteworthy tendency in articles concerned about Africa's future development to look east toward Asia for models to potentially replicate, as opposed to north to Europe or west to the New World.

The *African Challenge* embraced Western modernity almost as fervently as it embraced Christianity. It would be fair to say that for readers of the magazine, Western modernity was transcendent in what they understood as Christianity. This is a little-known and little-appreciated fact about African-Christian evangelicals, though an extremely important one. The Christianization of Africa that readers of the magazine wanted to effect was simultaneously the modernization of Africa according to the Western paradigm. This generalization should be qualified by two caveats. First is that for readers of the magazine, Western modernity did not include all aspects and attributes of Western civilization. Western modernity was more closely associated with what is talked about today as STEM (Science, Technology, Engineering and Mathematics), and the liberal, technology-driven capitalist society that has been the outcome of the pursuit of STEM. It would be hard to find any magazine published anywhere that celebrated more the Whiggish technological triumphalism of the mid-twentieth century. In the 1960s this triumphalism would take the form of a two-page centerfold piece in every issue devoted to offering an entry-level introduction to some science or technology or industry, and for one stretch of time during that decade the magazine also ran in every issue "how to pass" articles on the General Certificate of Education (GCE) examinations annually administered in Africa by the British government. During the 1950s the magazine more modestly feted anything and everything related to Western-style schools and learning: there were a number of "back to school" issues, and one of the ongoing debates in the magazine was whether it was better to go overseas to school in Britain or to North America.

It bears repeating that this embrace represented no "colonization of the African mind."[6] The second caveat is that the writers and readers of the magazine were, as Christians, extremely wary of falling into what they identified as European and American patterns of consumption. Evangelical Christians saw their embrace of Western modernity as creating a self-identity they could use to claim precedence for themselves over local Muslim peoples. Yet the *African Challenge* framed the Christianity it promoted as both an antidote to the noxious materialism and sensualism of Western civilization, and as a passageway back to the virtuous traditional values of African societies that had been corroded by the European colonizers' imposition in conquered territories of their own decadent morality. Admittedly, there seems a good deal of contradiction between the magazine's simultaneous glorification of the good life offered as a reward for the acquisition of marketable Western intellectual skills and the idealization of the purity of African life before Europeans came along to offer those skills. But such observations do not take into consideration the power the readers of the *African Challenge* perceived Christianity to possess to counteract the worldliness of European culture. If the magazine and its readers are to be criticized for disingenuousness, probably it is fairest to censure them for promoting an African variant of the "Western science / Eastern essence" equation that framed the efforts at assimilating Western ways that took place in late nineteenth-century Asian countries, with "African Christianity" replacing "Eastern essence" in the equation.

African Christians were searching for role models for life as inhabitants of modern Western civilization. On the social and political level, Asian states seemed the best states to emulate. On the personal level the writers and readers of the *African Challenge* continued an older African tradition of looking to the New World, especially the United States, for guides. In the last decades of the nineteenth century, a Christian Black Atlantic evolved, with Christian peoples of African descent crisscrossing the Atlantic Ocean from Africa, Europe, North America, and South America—all committed to the Ethiopianist project of the Christian evangelization of the African continent by peoples of African descent. African American missionaries from the United States had been particularly active in the project, and it was during this time that African American schools of higher learning became a welcoming destination for African students. The growing influence of African Americans on Africans was not viewed positively by European colonizers or, for that matter, European missionaries. The first decades of the twentieth century saw a concerted effort on the part of Europeans to shut down connections across the Christian Black Atlantic, an effort that culminated in the Le Zoute missionary conference in 1926, when colonial governments and European missions agreed to work together to deny African American missions access to Africa. It was once thought that the Le Zoute conference signaled the end of the Christian Black Atlantic, but the pages of the *African Challenge* are some of the best evidence that this did not happen.[7]

Thanks in large measure to Edward W. Blyden, nineteenth-century Christian Africans had viewed African Americans as "Africans in America," the import being that despite centuries of life in the New World, African Americans had retained their African identity. In the *African Challenge*, African Americans kept this connotation as cousins several times removed. These American cousins were invoked as proof that people of African descent who assimilated what Max Weber called "the Protestant Ethic" could and were achieving more and greater honors as participants in Western civilization. There were few African Americans with any international recognition during the 1950s who did not have their photograph published in the magazine. Yet photographs of African American celebrities were not the true measure of the investment of the *African Challenge* in the Black Atlantic connection. More revealing were the many stories about ordinary African American Christians offered as role models for living an evangelical life. To supply one brief set of examples, the June 1952 issue offered "The Remarkable Story of an American Negro," the story of the life and teachings of Charles Albert Tindley, "The Prince of Coloured Preachers."[8] The January 1953 issue provided an article about Mrs. Hattie P. Smith of Chester, Pennsylvania, who, concerned for women too old or disabled to attend church regularly, established a "Community Bible Class" in her home.[9] In an article entitled "She Gave God Her Voice," published in February 1955, Madame Lillian Jones explained how she gave up her promising career as an opera singer to travel across the western parts of the United States and Canada singing gospel songs as a form of praise ministry aimed at the working classes.[10] Another article from 1955, this time from the August issue, told the story of the "Big City Samaritan," Raymond Lilly, who, touched by the Christian advice of a fellow worker, gave up a carefree life as a steelworker to become the first African American chaplain at Chicago Cook County Hospital, "the largest charity institution of its kind on the North American continent."[11]

The affinity with African Americans expressed in the magazine was balanced by a collective eagerness to affirm a British identity. Billy Graham took honors as the male most often pictured in the *African Challenge*. The woman who claimed that distinction was Queen Elizabeth II of Great Britain. Her Royal Highness also had the distinction of appearing on more issue covers, seven, than any other individual during the decade. In keeping with the magazine's championing of Christian motherhood, one photograph, in the February 1956 issue, featured the queen, her husband, and two children with the caption "The World's Busiest Mother."[12] Beyond the queen, visits by other British royals to Africa always merited at least a photograph of the event, as did most events where an African was honored by dignitaries in

Britain. It was still the 1950s, and the writers and readers of the *African Challenge* still thought of themselves as subjects of the British Crown. It seemed to be taken for granted that future independent African states would follow the settler colony model of integration into the British Commonwealth. As the African subjects with the greatest amount of exposure to European culture and civilization, the Christians who read the magazine anticipated futures where they in their turn would be photographed with a British royal.

3

The advancement in the *African Challenge* of Christian motherhood as a form of evangelism needs to be appreciated as one front in a three-front war pursued by Christians in Africa. The greatest of the three fronts was the battle of Christian missions, Christian churches, and Christian communities to institute monogamous marriage as a normative institution. A second front, aimed at men, attempted to delegitimize polygamy and sex outside of monogamous unions. The third front targeted Christian women and sought to enlist them as wives and mothers in the other two engagements. Christian missions brought the sanctification of monogamous union with them from the North Atlantic world, but the particular understanding of Christian motherhood being promoted in the 1950s is traceable back to the ideas of Thomas Jesse Jones and the Phelps Stokes Education Commission reports from the 1920s. Jones identified as two of the four "essentials" of civilized life the individual and collective pursuit of sanitation and hygiene, and the institutionalization of Christian matriarchy as the building block of modern society. These two ideas fused to become the ideal of Christian motherhood being taught to African girls during the later decades of the colonial era. Another thing that Jones did was convince colonial governments and Christian missions to use mission schools (as opposed to government schools) as the chief vehicles for the education of Africans. In terms of the larger, three-front war, by the time the first issue of the *African Challenge* was published, two generations of African students had been taught to believe that Western-style family life was the platform upon which Western modernity had been constructed and thus a primary goal of Africa's social development.[13]

Though there is not room for discussion in this chapter, it helps to know that in the pages of the *African Challenge* Christian ideals of family life and masculinity were pursued with fervor equal to, if not greater than, the Christian ideal of femininity. All three were approached as forms of social discipline that needed to be inculcated, individual by individual. The assumption was that Christians had already been inculcated. Thus, it was part of the Christians' ministry as evangelists to inculcate others. To focus only on women, and the problems they posed for the editors of the *African Challenge*, beyond motherhood, it is worth noting that there were other ideals of Christian femininity. Women writers wanted to write articles that serviced these ideals. Women readers wanted to read these articles. The task of the magazine was to come up with an appealing balance between the different types of articles women wanted to read. And, as it turned out, the task included doing this in ways that men did not find either alienating or threatening.

One aspect of the challenge was to include this coverage on one page or less per issue. Two pages of text were dedicated to articles for women in the first issue of the *African Challenge*. This decreased to one page in subsequent issues through the end of 1956. From 1956 onward, articles and items were randomly placed through the content portion of the magazine. However, the one-page rule could not always be maintained. There were some issues with no discernible content aimed at women. There were other issues where content aimed at women blossomed to two or more pages. The October 1956 issue was almost entirely devoted to content aimed at women, though not much of it is identified as having been written by women. The November 1958 issue was exceptional in presenting four lengthy contributions by women authors. For most of 1951 and 1952, the page for content for women was labeled "Mother's Page." Starting at the end of 1952, the page was relabeled "Women's Page." At the end of 1956 the "Women's Page" disappeared. By the late 1950s most content aimed at women was offered under a byline. In earlier years, however, many articles were anonymous. Most of the articles published on the "Mother's Page" the first year were written by a woman named Belle Taylor or another woman writing under the pseudonym "Motherlore."

A key characteristic of the early contributions to the magazine was the call for feminine evangelism to start in the home and then spread abroad. Advocacy of domestic evangelism could be understated and centered on home life as expressed by Belle Taylor:

> What we call "Women's World" is really a subtle one. It seems nothing yet it is everything. It appears little but it is grand. Its possibilities are prodigious. I wonder if we realize just how great. Go up a mountain overlooking any city. Stay there until nightfall, and watch the lights begin to appear. Draw upon your imagination and look within those thousands of houses, homes and families, and remember that the guiding hand in most belongs to a woman.[14]

This type of maternal activism built upon sentimentalism and almost always was pictured as cumulative and long term in its impact. Two stories capture a sense of the ideal. In one, entitled "Working Christianity," a voice came to the mind of a "busy mother" while she was scrubbing away at the washboard, saying that God had chosen her to convert the heart of the man painting the house of one of her neighbors. She answered back that she could not leave her chores. The voice answered back that she could sing while she did her chores. So as she hung the wash on the wash line, she began to sing, "What a friend we have in Jesus." Later that day the painter came to her fence and commented that her singing reminded him of how his mother use to sing while she worked. They chatted, and she invited the painter to come to the Gospel service her family attended. He did and later joined the church.[15] The second story, "I Carried With Me a Picture," was set in the United States. A young man along with four of his friends left their homes in "Western Pennsylvania" to look for work in the "great Northwest." His four friends came back home much the worse for the experience. The young man, however, came back stronger and healthier. To the question of what had saved him from the fate of his friends, he answered that he had carried a picture with him. To the question of whether the picture was of "some young maiden," he responded by telling the story of his last morning at home with his father and mother. As usual, after breakfast his father had insisted on family prayer and had opened the family Bible to do this. But his father had been too caught up with emotion to conduct the prayer. So his father had passed the Bible over to his mother, who finished the prayer. As the young man concluded his story, the picture he had carried with him was "the vision of my last morning in the atmosphere of a godly home and the remembrance of my precious mother's prayer."[16]

Maternal activism could be quiet and homebound, or it could be provocative and committed to changing the world outside the home, as articulated in the columns penned by Motherlore. Motherlore called Christian women to the task of changing child-rearing practices in the society around them. As explained by Motherlore, in a world dominated by men motherhood was the one inalienable right God had granted to women. Further, "Mother-love," the urge of women to protect and nurture the children to whom they gave birth, was an instinct that transcended any social or cultural restraint that could be validly placed on a mother's actions.[17] In one early article Motherlore sets up the dilemma facing one young African missionary wife, Binam, pregnant and about to give birth in a village where she and her husband were proselytizing, yet fearing for her fate and that of her baby in the hands of the old women who served as midwives out in the bush: "Before her arose the memory of her dearly loved friend Gimbaya. She had seen her held up by four old grannies, while another had cut, cut, cut. The knife had not been clean. They were cutting, they said, an obstruction preventing birth. The ground had looked as if an animal had been slaughtered. Poor little Gimbaya had died."[18] Motherlore never explained how Binam resolved her dilemma. Rather, she went on to do two things. First, she delegitimized traditional teachings about childbearing: "Just because a woman has had several children does not make her competent to advise others. She may have given her own children such improper care that several of them may have died and others may have been sickly. Well over half of the deaths amongst the babies in Africa are due to wrong advice given by other women, ignorant assistance in times of emergency and improper care of the mother."[19] Second, she argued that women should look at childbearing and childrearing as menfolk looked upon establishing and running a business, which was to not be bogged down by keeping to tradition but involved looking for the best methods available in order to ensure success. As Motherlore concluded, over the previous two years, well over 2 million babies had died across Africa, and the majority of these deaths were traceable to the ignorance of new mothers to the new scientific ways available to raise children. Presuming as she did that the source of the problem was the feminine culture that existed in Africa, Motherlore went on to dismiss the capacity of governments and missions to make the situation better. Rather, as she proclaimed, "Africa's literate mothers ALONE hold the key to unlock the hearts of Africa's motherhood." By literate she of course meant Christian. She was placing the onus of the transformation of feminine culture, of the salvation of African mothers and children in the hands of Christian mothers. As she suggested, there existed in every African Christian community several women awoke to "the pitiful ignorance of many young mothers." She invited these women to band together and purchase from the nearest Christian bookstore "how to" books on childrearing. The women should then take it upon themselves to collect local young mothers together and instruct the latter in the knowledge contained in the books. To those skeptical about the effectiveness of this type of ministry, she responded that if a critical mass of women followed her advice, then "a great cycle of acceptable and fruitful instruction will be permeating our womanhood."[20]

Motherlore could not keep her instincts toward feminist activism focused on issues related to motherhood, however. In July 1952, the *African Challenge* published on the "Mother's Page," with no attribution, a manifesto that declared in part:

> While Africa rapidly approaches its goal of full political emancipation, its women for the most part remain firmly bound by the chains

of superstition, fear and custom. Women continue to groan under their burdens and their hearts bleed because of man's shameful abuse of them. . . . But mothers, wives, women, a light is shining in a dark place. The fight for freedom and liberty—for your glorious emancipation—has already begun. The Challenge calls YOU to rise from your graveyard of a living death, to demand for yourselves and your sex, that to which you, as women, are entitled.[21]

The publication of this manifesto caused some commotion. The piece had no byline, yet its prose very much resembled that in Motherlore's writings. After the manifesto, in fact, the byline "Motherlore" was never used again in the magazine, though several latter-published pieces sounded some of the same themes and were written in the same style as affected by Motherlore. These pieces sported the byline "by a Contributor." The designation "Mothers' Page" disappeared from the magazine after the publication of the manifesto as well. For the next four months, there were few articles focused on issues of concern to women. Such a page did reappear in December, however. It was now designated the "Women's Page," with most of its space taken up with a theological reflection entitled "The Gospel According to the Virgin Mary." Yet, while Motherlore never again spoke as an identifiable voice in the magazine, her idea of Christian mothers as evangelical activists continued to influence the magazine's discourse about Christian femininity, mostly in the direction of reifying Western science and medicine as the new and improved, "Christian" approach to raising children.[22]

January 1953 brought a new strategy for writing aimed at the Christian woman audience. A new byline appeared, again a pseudonym, in this case "Iyolade," the name of the highest-ranking woman title holder in the Yoruba hierarchy of titles. Iyolade offered short thought pieces and advice on the subject of living life as a Christian woman. Another new addition included articles about Christian women acting as activists *outside* their personas as mothers. The initial story of this type—about the women at the Zagun Christian Church in Nigeria who banded together to place a new roof on their church and help pay bride price so that some local girls could get married—can be considered as representative. Also worth mentioning again is the story about the African American woman, Mrs. Hattie P. Smith, who founded a Bible reading class for her church community, which was on the same page. By the end of 1953, yet another new series appeared on the "Women's Page." Short reports about women and their achievements were summarized in paragraph format, culled together in the same style as the monthly "NEWS" segment, and then published as "Women in the News," on an occasional basis.

Most significant for the shaping of the message the magazine strove to convey to women, however, was the inauguration in February 1953 of a new series "Women of the Bible," which ran monthly off and on for the next three years. The series featured stories from both the Old Testament and the New Testament retold to frame some problem facing contemporary African women. Many of these stories sought to reinforce notions of Christian mothers and wives as homebound. The story of Lemech and Zillah was used to address the problems facing women in polygamous marriages.[23] Then there was Keturah, who comforted Abraham in his old age, who provided guidance for second wives in general and young wives of old widowers in particular.[24] The story of Leah, the unattractive sister of Rachel who served as ancestor to the family line of the Virgin Mary, was offered as proof that God did not always reward physically beautiful people with the prize.[25] The child-rearing lessons to be gleaned from the story of Moses were considered so great that his story was told from two perspectives. The May 1954 issue published the story from the perspective of Jochebed, his birth mother.[26] The July 1954 issue told the story from the perspective of Thermutis, the Egyptian princess who adopted him.[27] Finally, Claudia Procula, who counseled her husband, Pontius Pilate, not to condemn Jesus of Nazareth, was cited as biblical precedence for the admonition that husbands should listen to the advice of their wives.[28]

Yet there were many women from the Bible who provided examples of women serving the Lord outside the home, outside of motherhood and wifedom. There were Shiphrah and Puah, who had for 3,000 years supplied midwives with examples of members of their profession who correctly feared God.[29] Lydia from the New Testament was celebrated as the first Christian businesswoman.[30] Lydia could be compared with Rhoda, who worked for people like Lydia. Rhoda was the servant girl who guarded the door of the mansion where her mistress was hosting a fateful meeting of Christians in the days before the Crucifixion. Rhoda was offered as an example to all the African shopgirls who seemed indifferent to the affairs of their employers.[31] Last, there was the example of Deborah, "fighter for God," who rose to be the ruler of the Israelites.[32]

The "Women of the Bible" series contributed to the mixed message being communicated on the Women's Page, where stories of what to do when your baby begins to teethe occupied space next to stories about the activities and achievements of Christian women of color in the New World, Africa, and Asia. Women readers were being offered too many interesting and inspiring examples of women outside the household. This prompted the editors of the magazine to take a stand. In August 1954 an unsigned opinion piece entitled "Woman's Great Career" was published. The piece was nominally a response to a letter to the editor asking about the Bible's teaching on whether women should be confined to housework. The conclusion of the piece, based upon the biblical exegesis it performed, was that "Scriptures imply that motherhood and homemaking is a full-time job. The ideal woman is pictured (in the Scriptures) as a mother and wife in the home." The author conceded that sometimes women worked outside the home because their husbands did not sufficiently provide for them. But the author went on to argue that such women could probably save more money by staying at home than they could make by going out to work. The author also acknowledged that Africa needed more professionally trained women. The author argued that professional women who planned their outside work in such a fashion that they gave priority to their husbands and children were doing things right. Those women who did not plan their outside work toward this goal brought suffering to their families. The author went further and added that "it is an established fact that child delinquency and divorces have been on the increase since women have left home-making and have gone into the professional and working world." As the author concluded, "Happiness is the essence of a well-formed life. A mother should not undertake any career which endangers this happiness. Material things cannot take its place."[33]

At the end of the opinion piece the editors inserted a query to the readers: "What do you think is more important to the development of Africa— more women in the professions and civil service, or more women to build up a better generation of healthy bodies, minds and characters through their children?"[34] Readers were invited to send in their opinions. The results of the query must have been desultory. The findings were only presented five months later, in January of the next year, and only one No and one Yes letter were printed. The No letter cited childcare as the chief reason women should not be trained for the professions. The primary reason listed in the Yes letter for training women for the professions was that it would bring honor to the name of the women's fathers.[35]

During 1955 the editors of the *African Challenge* made a good faith effort at using the Women's Page to promote the ideal of the Christian woman as mothers and homemakers. "Women in the News" columns were not published during the year. With three exceptions—a photograph of India's Madame Vijaya Lakshmi Pandit, who became the first woman to preside over a meeting of the United Nations,[36] a short article about a young girl who partially overcame paralysis to build a youth ministry in an orthopedic hospital,[37] and a longer piece about Christian African women weavers[38]—there were no stories about Christian women working outside the home printed on the page. But this strategy only created cognitive dissonance, as these types of stories were printed elsewhere in the magazine. The February 1955 issue published the story about Lillian Jones, the opera singer turned evangelist, discussed earlier in this chapter, on one page, and on the following page provided the picture of a young African woman working as a disc jockey for the Nigerian Broadcasting Company.[39] In July 1955 one page featured the story of Dr. Hilda Lazarus, an Indian Christian lay leader and surgeon fighting off the efforts of Communists to corrupt the minds of Indian Christians.[40] Last, the December issue announced in the "NEWS" section the passing of the African American educator Mary McLeod Bethune. A photograph of Bethune being received by Mamie Eisenhower, wife of the sitting American president, accompanied the announcement, in order to communicate her stature to those who did not know it.[41]

The cognitive dissonance was apparently too much. By 1956 "Women in the News" and other stories about women working outside the home were back on the Women's Page. The magazine did other things that signaled the backing away from the glorification of domesticity that had preoccupied it in 1955. February 1956 saw the publication of the story of "The Lady of Kakata," Ellen Moore of Liberia, who after training as a nurse in the United States, returned to Liberia to open her own maternal and child welfare center. As the photograph of Moore with a baby doll in her hand lecturing a group of reluctant pregnant women suggests, Moore was doing exactly what Motherlore had advocated Christian mothers do but as a single professional woman. The February issue was notable also for the photograph celebrating Queen Elizabeth as "the World Busiest Mother," the queen obviously serving as an example of a mother working outside the home. The queen's photograph was on the Women's Page. On that page as well was a photograph of Dr. Abimbola Akerele Awoliyi, "West Africa's First Lady Doctor," who, as the caption read, "had been an inspiration to other women who have followed in her footsteps."[42] During the middle months of 1956, Iyolade's columns on the Women's Page, which for almost four years had served to promote the idea of domestic maternal activism first articulated by Belle Taylor, were discontinued. Later in 1956 the Women's Page itself was unceremoniously discontinued. The content of the last Women's Page was emblematic of the future. Domestic evangelism was no longer the measure or the focus of the feminine activity being spotlighted in the magazine. The largest portion of the page was given over to the "Women of the Bible" installment, which presented the seductress Delilah as the antitype to a Christian wife. Another portion of the page was taken up by a photograph and caption of Althea

Gibson receiving her trophy as the winner of the Women's Doubles Championship at Wimbledon that year. Another portion of the page was taken up with a picture of the Nigerian Women's Track team, who had won the championship at the recent Inter-Colonial games.[43]

From the beginning the *African Challenge* had solicited copy from readers, typically by sponsoring writing contests for which readers sent in articles in response to a given prompt. The authors who won these contests had their articles with their bylines and their photographs printed in the magazine. Perhaps it was the case that women did not submit entries to these contests, but there were few articles published by women before 1957. Starting in 1957 this changed, as the *African Challenge* pursued a new strategy to retain women readers. Almost every issue had at least one article written by a woman author. Most of these articles were either testimonials about escaping past sinful practices or advice columns about how to avoid future sinful practices. The authors of the articles were typically African women. There were a number of feature articles by Asian women, though, such as the piece by Madame Chiang Kai-shek noted earlier, and "Women in Public Life," an article by Madame Rajkumari Amrit Kaur, minister of health in India.[44] Articles by European women about African women were also published. The serialized story "The Joys of Aleshi," written by the English woman Olive Garbutt, narrativized the life of a young African Christian woman constantly beaten by her husband and regularly rejected by her own people because of her faith. Eventually she ran away and discovered a vocation as a midwife. There is an edifying photograph accompanying the conclusion of the story of a mature smiling Aleshi, now a senior midwife, weighing a baby on a scale.[45] No doubt inadvertently, "The Joys of Aleshi" made a powerful case for the Christian life women could have outside of marriage.

A favorite practice of the *African Challenge* was to invite readers to debate some issue. A September 1954 article had first broached the subject of Christian women and fashion. Under the title "Does Style Corrupt Morals?," next to a photograph of a young African woman attired in the fashion of a young Queen Elizabeth II, Iyolade had made the case that dressing "moderately" was the way to avoid the moral corruption evangelical Christians associated with being fashion conscious. The magazine returned to the topic in the July 1957 issue with the first debate explicitly set up between women: "Which Is Better—Modern or Traditional Dress?" "Modern dress" was Western attire. "Traditional dress" was "Native" attire. The case argued for Modern dress was that it was smart and fashionable, easy to wear in public versus cumbersome and liable to come loose like African attire. The case argued for Traditional dress was that it was fast to put on, and the woman "did not have to worry about her size. She can eat all she wants."[46] The magazine editors evidently felt themselves open to second-guessing having run this piece, so they followed it on the next page with an opinion piece by a male writer who admonished Christian women to "Beware of the evil of fashion!"[47]

Still, the progress the editors of the *African Challenge*, and by extension the SIM as publisher, made in regard to recognizing and responding to the interests of women readers should be acknowledged. In just five years the *African Challenge* went from segregating content aimed as women to one page, to mainstreaming such content throughout the magazine; from a paternalistic (maternalistic?) preaching down to women readers, to granting women the same voice in articulating their faith that male readers had been granted from the start. The editors continued to recognize as part of the magazine's mission, however, the promotion of Western ideas of domesticity as a vehicle of evangelism. Every Christian needed an opportunity to evangelize, and going back to those first articles by Belle Taylor there was a conviction at the magazine that women staying in the home, in the act of being mothers, in the act of being wives, could facilitate a long-term, slow-acting, but still effective ministry. So the magazine set about reintroducing that element to its content directed toward women. Different from the past, however, the magazine sought to do this by hiring women experts on domesticity. The missiological path forward was not through teaching young mothers out in the villages to change their child-rearing practices but by teaching Christian women how to set better examples.

There has been much written on the development of European expertise about Africa in the Western academy across the twentieth century.[48] There is need for more research on the African experts who informed those experts. There is also need for further research on how Africans came to frame the concept of expertise and the use of experts in intra-African discourse. For example, in the November 1958 issue of the *African Challenge*, which published four articles by women, all four of the women authors held degrees from institutions of higher learning. They wrote out of their personas as Christian women seeking to show other Christian women how to be better Christians. But they also wrote as experts passing on their knowledge and experience to mass audiences. The contributions of two of these women authors illustrate the new approach being taken by the magazine. Both contributions were serialized over a number of issues, back to back, with the November 1958 issue offering the last installment of the first contribution and the first installment of the second contribution. Together the two contributions spread out over a year of issues, from July 1958 to June 1959. Intentionally or unintentionally the magazine re-created a de facto "Women's Page," this one dedicated to Christian homemaking.

The first contribution, "Science in the Kitchen," was written by Miss Ruth Omosunlola Williams, who was listed as a woman education officer working out of the Nigerian Education Department in Ibadan. She had spent three years in Britain getting a degree in domestic science. She was better known in West Africa for her *Cookery Book*, the first cookbook published in English on Nigerian cuisine. As Williams announced in her introduction to the first installment, "We need better kitchens, better cooking, better foods, and surely a healthier Nigeria." With those goals in mind, over five installments she offered Christian women ideas on how to refashion a traditional cooking area into a kitchen up to Western standards.[49]

The second contribution was by Mrs. Adeola Adegbite, MA, a well-known personality on the Nigerian Broadcasting Company radio station. Her seven-part series, "What Every Woman Ought to Know," was adapted from her radio program. The format of Mrs. Adegbite's series merits some mention. The series was framed as a dialogue with two male interlocuters, one a "U.S.A trained doctor" and the other a "U.K. trained lawyer," both arriving back in Nigeria at the same time from their studies abroad. They became friends and met together from time to time to lament the backwardness of their homeland in comparison to the Western lands where they had trained. One "bright little star" they discovered while standing outside conversing one day was a clean, neatly dressed little girl they both concluded would be a great little representative to the rest of the world of what an African can be. The little girl was lost and after learning her address, the two men took her home. The series is all about the family the two men encountered when they took the child home. In particular it is about the child's mother, presented by Adegbite as a model that other Christian women should emulate. The family was not wealthy—the father was a third-class clerk and the mother a primary school teacher. The family did not live in a flat with Western conveniences; they had to share cooking and laundry and bathing facilities with other families. But thanks to the mother, they lived a happy, sanitary, comfortable Western-style life together. After giving various examples of how the mother's faith and domestic science skills helped her attend to the needs of her family, Adegbite let the readers in on the "big secret" behind the mother's success—her husband helped around the house! It was her husband's Christian willingness to make childcare and housework part of his daily regime that allowed the mother to become a role model.

4

It is clear that almost from the beginning there were men who took exception to the magazine's glorification of motherhood as the primary duty of Christian women. In an opinion piece published in the March 1952 issue of the *African Challenge*, under the title "MARRIAGE . . . Is It Meant Solely for Childbearing?," an irate reader complained that "most women in this country think that marriage is meant for child bearing and nothing more." For this reader a wife's chief duty was to support and comfort her husband. As the reader went on, "the woman must be industrious and always do her utmost to lighten the work of her husband and avoid making him miserable by unnecessary complaints and teasing."[50] Ironically, Motherlore's last byline in the magazine, in the May 1952 issue, was a response to a letter from a woman who wrote that the opinion being offered in the piece in question could have only been written by a man, because it was only men who were obsessed with having many, many children. She then went on to lament that although she had given birth to two healthy children, her husband still condemned her for not having more and accused her of being barren before the neighbors. Motherlore's rather out-of-character response was to counsel the woman to exercise the patience of Hannah in the Bible, who accepted her barrenness yet continued to pray to God until she was rewarded with her son Samuel.[51]

As mentioned above, the *African Challenge* spent most of 1955 trying to affirm the idea that the home was an evangelical frontier where God meant women to labor. This effort angered some men who begrudged the space the magazine gave to women and their concerns. A letter to the editor printed in the August 1955 issue, presumably meant to be representative, asked why there was no Men's Page to go along with the Women's Page, because "it is unkind to leave us men and boys without any help." The editorial response was to jokingly dismiss the request with the comment that while it was true that women had their own page, men had the rest of the magazine.[52] This notion did not seem to mollify men, and the following January, the magazine inaugurated a new series "Ways of a Man," which ended, however, after only three installments. Whatever feelings of being ignored male readers had probably only increased as articles by and of concern to women seemed to claim more and more content space.

At the end of the fifth installment of Mrs. Adegbite's seven-part series "What every woman ought to know," the *African Challenge* posted an invitation: "What do you husbands think of this? What are YOUR ideas of a husband's duties? Write in to let us know." The responses to the query were available for publication the issue immediately following the conclusion of the series. The format of the page with the survey results merits mention. The *African Challenge* made effective use of comic-book-style animation in almost every issue to render some Bible story more accessible. The use of cartoon drawings in the magazine thus was not unusual. What was uncommon was the use of cartoon drawings as marginalia, such as was the fashion with medieval European manuscripts. At the top of the page, overshadowing the title "SHOULD HUSBANDS HELP THEIR WIVES?" there was a drawing of an African woman, dressed in traditional attire, with a wooden club in her hand, standing over a half-naked man scrubbing the floor. At the bottom of the page, there is a drawing of a muscle-bound African man dragging by the hair, caveman style, an African woman dressed in modern attire. Even before one reads the contents of the page, it is clear that the issue at hand, at least for the men who edited and read the magazine, was who should win the battle of the sexes. And in the responses selected for publication, very clearly the battle is understood as being fought between husbands with traditional values and educated African women with modern views.

There are five responses on the page: two by men labeled "husband," two by men labeled "bachelor," and one by a man labeled "Librarian." One bachelor, under the title "Husband is Master," argued that "education is like a knife. It can be used for good or for bad. To a proud woman, education is certainly a danger to happiness." Under "Crazy Idea," one husband asked, "Why should I spend most of my time in the office and then go home to do domestic duties for my wife?" He did accept, though, that he should help his wife with some of the domestic duties like chopping wood. The other bachelor offered a moderate contrary position, which was summed up with the title "Woman not a Servant." Why should a wife do all the domestic duties, he asked, "while the husband sits on a comfortable chair?" "Why do we drive the white man's car, he asked rhetorically, pointing to one attribute of Western culture all Africans would recognize as an improvement. He then placed men sharing housework under that rubric. "Equality of women," he concluded, "although Western, is certainly most desirable." The other husband in the survey also advanced a moderate case. Under the title "Give and Take," he insisted that while "the husband is the head of the family . . . the husband is not always right." "A spirit of give and take must prevail for the smooth running of the home," he concluded. The Librarian's response broke the tie. The Librarian's response took up twice the space as did the other responses, a reflection perhaps that his views best represented those of the editors. Under the title "Makes Wives Lazy," he argued that while in the West husbands helping their wives around the house made sense, since only the wealthy could afford servants, in Africa servants were easy to come by. "Mrs. Adegbite's proposition," he concluded, "is a philosophical ideal," which in application would be like the "casting of pearl before swine."[53]

The most definitive sign that Mrs. Adegbite's series sparked conflict in the magazine's editorial offices was the fact that articles about women and their concerns once again disappear from the magazine, this time for the next eighteen months. There were contributing factors to this development. The eighteen months in question were the highpoint of the decolonization of the African continent. Across Africa, European states withdrew their claims of sovereignty, and newly formed African-states came into existence. Nation building was perceived by men at that time as a masculine affair, and this view was certainly reflected in the *African Challenge* as its editors selected topics and articles that focused on the male decision making going into state formation.

Yet when content directed at women did come back, that content was always filtered through male control. An article published in February 1961 without a byline, but obviously put together by staff reporters, answered the question "If you are a teacher" with a number of ways primary school teachers, pictured as exclusively female, could fold Christian evangelism into their lesson plans.[54] An article published in September 1961, "How To Rear Children in This Modern Age," involved an interview conducted by an *African Challenge* reporter with an unidentified "progressive mother-teacher" who taught in a large urban school.[55] Last, an article published in November 1961, "How to choose your VOCATION," featured a woman student nurse talking about how she discovered that she could best serve God as a nurse.[56] These articles support the conclusion that the new strategy of the magazine was to promote evangelization by women through their persona as social service providers. An article the March 1961 issue illustrated the new strategy for allowing women to testify about their faith. "Why I Left My Fiancé: As Told to a Challenge Staff Writer" told the story of an educated young woman who gave up on marriage with the man of her dreams because he was an "unbeliever."[57] None of the above articles was written by a woman, though in all four cases they could have been told as first-person narratives, as they probably would have been a few years before. An article in the February 1961 issue, with a byline by a woman author, actually reinforces the above conclusion. Mrs. J. T. Ayorinde, BSc, president of the Baptist Women's Union of Africa, offered an opinion piece on "The Place of Women in the Church." The piece provided a survey of the role of women in organized religion dating back to ancient times. There was no commentary on the role of women in present churches. She did offer a list of things women could do in the present, and the list did include opening preaching stations and creating missionary organizations for young people, but the point was that these were things that were to be done in existing churches, under male direction.[58] To be fair, the magazine did continue to publish articles by women about women, but on a very irregular basis and rarely in the first-person singular. And the types of health and hygiene advice proffered on the Women's Page by women authors in previous years were now proffered by senior male experts. Educated women were being invited to find happiness but under male supervision.

To sum up, gender tensions of the sort that historians of the West typically associate with the 1970s and 1980s can be seen in evangelical circles in West Africa during the 1950s. The tensions were triggered by the push among evangelical Christians to identify ways in which Christian women could extend the domestic sphere in evangelical ways. The debate that ensued was never simply two sided. There were different groups of women with different sets of notions about how women could best serve as evangelists. And there were always men who felt that the debates taking place between these women had no value, that the place of the Christian woman was at home preparing her husband's evening meal. Other men simply resented the space the *African Challenge* magazine granted to women and their concerns. In the end, realizing the contention that women and their evangelism generated, the magazine's editors opted to take the topic off the table, shelving, for at least the early years of the Independence era, the question of Christian women and their role in the new nations.

NOTES

1. *African Challenge*, January 1953, 4.
2. For a sense of the broad array of periodicals the SIM published over time, visit the SIM website: http://archives.sim.org/.
3. See Nancy Rose Hunt, "'Le Bebe en Brousse': European Women, African Birth Spacing and Colonial Intervention in Breast Feeding in the Belgian Congo," *International Journal of African Historical Studies* 21, no. 3 (1988): 401–32; Hunt, "Domesticity and Colonialism in Belgian Africa: Usumbura's Foyer Social, 1946–1960," *Signs* 15, no. 3 (1990): 447–74; Jean Allman, "Making Mothers: Missionaries, Medical Officers and Women's Work in Colonial Asante, 1924–1945." *History Workshop Journal* 38, no. 1 (1994): 23–47; Karen Tranberg Hansen, ed., *African Encounters with Domesticity* (Rutgers, NJ: Rutgers University Press, 1992).
4. Andrew E. Barnes, "'Making Good Wives and Mothers': The African Education Group and Missionary Reactions to the Phelps Stokes Reports," *Studies in World Christianity* 21, no. 1 (2015): 66–85; Barnes, "Christianity and Vocational Education," in *The*

Palgrave Handbook on African Education and Indigenous Knowledge, ed. Toyin Falola and Jamaine Abidogun (2020).

5. See *African Challenge,* "Letters to the Editor," July 1957.

6. See Jean Comaroff and John L. Comaroff, *Of Revelation and Revolution,* vol. 1, *Christianity, Colonialism, and Consciousness in South Africa* (Chicago: University of Chicago Press, 2008); John L. Comaroff and Jean Comaroff, *Of Revelation and Revolution,* vol. 2, *The Dialectics of Modernity on a South African Frontier* (Chicago: University of Chicago Press, 2009).

7. See Andrew E. Barnes, *Global Christianity and the Black Atlantic: Tuskegee, Colonialism and the Shaping of African Industrial Education* (Waco, TX: Baylor University Press, 2017).

8. *African Challenge,* June 1952, 7.

9. *African Challenge,* January 1953, 4.

10. *African Challenge,* February 1955, 6.

11. *African Challenge,* August 1955, 7.

12. *African Challenge,* August 1951, 7.

13. See Sean Morrow, " 'No Girl Leaves the School Unmarried': Mabel Shaw and the Education of Girls at Mbereshi, Northern Rhodesia, 1915–1940," *International Journal of African Historical Studies* 19, no. 4 (1986): 601–35; Julia Allen, "Mabel Shaw's Theology in the Context of Her Work as a Christian Missionary Teacher in Northern Rhodesia 1915–1940," *Feminist Theology* 16 (2008): 194–210; Rebecca Hughes, "Africans in the British Missionary Imagination, 1910–1965" (PhD diss., University of Washington, Seattle, 2010), 152–76; Elizabeth E. Prevost, "Troubled Traditions: Female Adaptive Education in British Colonial Africa," *Journal of Imperial and Commonwealth History* 45, no. 3 (2017): 475–505.

14. *African Challenge,* August 1951, 7.

15. *African Challenge,* August 1951, 7.

16. *African Challenge,* November 1951, 7.

17. *African Challenge,* August 1951, 7.

18. *African Challenge,* October 1951, 7.

19. *African Challenge,* October 1951, 7.

20. *African Challenge,* November 1951, 7.

21. *African Challenge,* July 1952, 7.

22. See, for example, "Why DEATH Takes Our Babies," *African Challenge,* January 1954, 7.

23. *African Challenge,* March 1953, 7.

24. *African Challenge,* June 1953, 7.

25. *African Challenge,* September 1953, 7.

26. *African Challenge,* May 1954, 7.

27. *African Challenge,* July 1954, 7.

28. *African Challenge,* October 1954, 11.

29. *African Challenge,* April 1954, 7.

30. *African Challenge,* June 1956.

31. *African Challenge,* November 1954, 11.

32. *African Challenge,* August 1956.

33. *African Challenge,* August 1954, 7.

34. *African Challenge,* August 1954, 7.

35. *African Challenge,* January 1955, 7.

36. *African Challenge*, May 1955, 11.
37. *African Challenge*, July 1955, 11.
38. *African Challenge*, October 1955, 11.
39. *African Challenge*, February 1955, 6–7.
40. *African Challenge*, July 1955, 4.
41. *African Challenge*, November 1955, 4.
42. *African Challenge*, February 1956, 7, 11.
43. *African Challenge*, November 1956, 11.
44. *African Challenge*, March 1958, 7.
45. *African Challenge*, January 1958, 10; February 1958, 13.
46. *African Challenge*, July 1957, 10.
47. *African Challenge*, July 1957, 11.
48. See Douglas Rimmer and A. H. M. Kirk-Greene, *The British Intellectual Engagement with Africa in the Twentieth Century* (Houndmills, UK, New York: Macmillan Press; St. Martin's Press in Association the Royal African Society, 2000); Joseph M. Hodge, *Triumph of the Experts: Agrarian Doctrines of Development and the Legacies of British Colonialism* (Athens: Ohio University Press, 2007); Helen Tilley, *Africa as a Living Laboratory: Empire, Development and the Problem of Scientific Knowledge, 1870–1950* (Chicago: University of Chicago Press, 2011); Patrick Harries and David Maxwell, eds., *The Spiritual in the Secular: Missionaries and Knowledge about Africa*, Studies in the History of Christian Missions (Grand Rapids, MI: W.B. Eerdmans Pub., 2012).
49. *African Challenge*, June–November 1958.
50. *African Challenge*, March 1952, 14.
51. *African Challenge*, May 1952, 12.
52. *African Challenge*, August 1955, 3.
53. *African Challenge*, July 1957, 6.
54. *African Challenge*, February 1961, 8, 14.
55. *African Challenge*, September 1961, 10.
56. *African Challenge*, November 1961, 7.
57. *African Challenge*, March 1961, 7.
58. *African Challenge*, February 1961, 11.

PART III

African Traditional Religion and Interfaith Relations

CHAPTER 10

Awakening the Market

Small Pentecostal Genres and Religious Accommodation in Kinshasa

Katrien Pype

A GROWING RELIGIOUS DIVERSITY

Starting around 2004, several incidents occurred on Marché Kato, a smaller market (*wenze*) located in the south of Kinshasa's central market (*nzando monene*). Leaders of the mosque adjacent to Marché Kato recurrently complained about the interference of the gospel music and biblical instructions on Friday afternoons. The Pentecostal market radio studio had just been set up with generous funding from a consortium run by the Canadian embassy and several local nongovernmental organizations (NGOs). These entities invested heavily in consciousness raising in the runup to the first democratic elections of Democratic Republic of the Congo's (DR Congo's) postcolonial history (in 2006), and homed in on the market crowd to communicate their messages on a large scale. Because the quarrels with representatives of the local Muslim community persisted, the head of the market (*chef de marché*), a state representative, was called in. After carefully listening to the grievances of the Muslim representatives and the rebuttal by Pastor Victor, the coordinator of a network of eight Pentecostal market radios, a decision was made in favor of the Pentecostal radio station. After all, DR Congo is a secular state that endorses freedom of religion, and the market is a public space, so the chef de marché reminded all parties. Yet, the dust did not settle. In the following years, Pastor

Victor remarked: "the Muslims changed strategy." Around 2005 and again in 2006, they offered money to buy the radio station. Papa Victor and the *animateurs* (radio hosts) perceived this as a strategy to eliminate the Pentecostals from the market square altogether. This could be a valid interpretation of the events, since "Islam is not an evangelizing religion. We do not use mass media to convert souls," so the chef de marché of another marketplace, the Marché de Liberté, himself a Muslim, told me during an interview in 2014. The Muslim community was not at all interested in taking over the market radio, even though since around 2010 the Islamic community also buys airtime on local television channels and broadcasts prayers and religious debates on RTNC: the public radio and television station. Pastor Victor refused to sell his market radio, because it would mean "offering souls to Islam," so he told me. The conflict, which has abated since, is archived as an episode in the spiritual battle that Kinshasa's Pentecostal communities are engaged in. From the Muslim perspective, this incident dealt more with the respect for the Friday afternoon prayers than with an effort to block Christian evangelization.

This ethnographic material raises questions about Pentecostal publics, religious cohabitation, and sonic presence. In this chapter, I will focus on Pentecostal genres performed in the market space, a thick religiously plural environment, as the vignette has shown. I will look at the ways in which Pentecostal evangelizers (animateurs, a subcategory of the evangelizing ministry in Pentecostal churches) negotiate their public presence in terms of form and style, how they navigate the religious plural market space, and how this navigation is expressed discursively. I will study different forms of textual mediation and the ways in which Pentecostal publics are construed. My main argument is that part of the Pentecostal accommodation is the conscious selection of evangelizing genres that fit the performance context. Animateurs choose evangelizing genres in terms of the performance space. The innovative aspect of this chapter is the social significance of what I call "small Pentecostal genres," seemingly banal discursive forms that may escape the scholar's analytic gaze because they are less dramatic and formalized than the more common genres such as sermons, gospel songs, and testimonies.[1]

The material for this chapter was collected through ethnographic research on technology and the city (2014–19). I visited public and private big and small markets (nzando, wenze) in Kinshasa and hung out with the Pentecostal animateurs, both in the market space, such as in their churches, and in their private lives. I have been studying Kinshasa's Pentecostal popular culture since 2003, and I draw also on insights gained during previous research visits.

In the first part of this chapter, I describe Kinshasa's Pentecostal world among an increasingly diversifying urban religious field. The second part situates Pentecostal-Charismatic Popular Culture within this dense urban space. In particular, I argue that not only genres such as evangelizing songs and serials, but also smaller genres such as calls for fuel and quizzes, produce Pentecostal publics, which may consist of members identifying as members of other religious communities. This discussion will be followed by an exploration of Kinshasa's markets within the Pentecostal imagination. The final parts analyze the social work of binding, bonding, and differentiating that the small evangelizing genres performed in Kinshasa's markets set forth. In the conclusion, I return to the "accommodating" work of small genres and the social significance of fragmentation in Pentecostal thinking and practice.

RELIGIOUS PLURALISM IN KINSHASA

The opening vignette indexes two significant transformations that Kinshasa's religious landscape has undergone in the last twenty years. First, just like everywhere in sub-Saharan Africa, Pentecostal-Charismatic Christianity has grown and has taken on a very public presence. The second significant transformation is the gradual expansion of the Islamic community (mainly Sunni Islam) in the city. "Pentecostal-Charismatic Christianity" itself is an umbrella word indicating a heterogenous group of churches and networks of Christians who cultivate a bodily engagement with the Holy Spirit and biblical teachings. "Touch," and the other senses,[2] are key in becoming a *mukristu* (Pentecostal Christian).

The dominant strand in Kinshasa are the so-called *églises de réveil* (Churches of the Awakening, also called "born-again Christianity"). Members call themselves *nouveau nés* (born-agains) or *bato ya sika* (new persons). These churches communicate an ideology of spiritual warfare and cultivate public witnessing of the Holy Spirit's miraculous interventions. They combine the prosperity gospel with a deliverance narrative. The latter dominates. Evangelization happens on the street, on market squares, in public transportation, and on mass media via electronic ministries (on radio, television, and the internet).[3] Other Pentecostal-Charismatic groups in Kinshasa are, for example, the so-called Branhamist churches;[4] these have a more ambiguous stance toward electronic ministries.

Notwithstanding internal differentiation among Kinshasa's Pentecostal community, the third wave of Pentecostal Christianity has produced a genuine celebrity culture, with churches that attract thousands of believers, and pastors (Lingala singular *pasta*) whose spiritual and private lives are widely discussed in households, in gossip, and on media platforms. The most successful Pentecostal pastors have become "big men," integrating various models of masculinity (the fighter, the rich businessman, the teacher, the traveler, and the spiritual stronghold).[5] In Kinshasa, Pentecostals' Other in general is first and foremost *bakoko* (tradition) and its animist beliefs; to a lesser extent, the *missioni* (the mainline Catholic and Protestant religions); and, then, Islam.

As noted, the second significant transformation is the increased presence of Islam in Kinshasa. Many Kinois hold that former rebel and president Laurent Kabila (1997–2001), himself a Muslim, brought Islam to Kinshasa when he and his troops marched into the city and overthrew Mobutu in 1997. Even though Islam was practiced in Kinshasa before that time, it remained very much a religion of *bapaya* (literally "guests," meaning foreigners), such as the West African migrant community living in the municipality of Barumbu, and of expats, especially Lebanese commercial migrants. There were only a handful of mosques in Kinshasa around 2000, yet the number has steadily increased, and nowadays there are mosques in almost all of Kinshasa's twenty-four municipalities. In 2003 the Muslim community set up the Islamic Community in Congo (COMICO; Communauté Islamique en R.D. Congo), through which the Muslim community is represented in public debates and in state affairs. Ever since I began fieldwork in Kinshasa (in 2003), rumors have been circulating about Middle Eastern militant groups such as Hezbollah doing money laundering in Kinshasa; time and again, when we would pass on Boulevard 30 June (Kinshasa's main boulevard), friends reminded me, usually with fierce conviction, that high-level buildings such as the Congo Future tower and Soficom are financed by Hezbollah militants. Similar rumors are told about the owners of some of Kinshasa's Lebanese-owned fast-food restaurants. Yet, these suspicions do not incite sit-ins, nor refusal to enter these buildings, and they certainly do not cause Kinois to stop consuming their products.[6] Political rumors are told about jihadists arriving via the north in DR Congo and gradually making their way to Kinshasa. These stories express a critique on the inadequacy of the postcolonial state apparatus to monitor mobility around the country's borders and should not be mistaken for a manifestation of anti-Islamic sentiment.

Despite these two changes, Catholic, Protestant, and Kimbanguist Christianity remain dominant in the city.[7] A large set of smaller religious traditions is present as well: Church of Jesus Christ of the Latter-Day Saints, the Baha'i community, Judaism, Hinduism, Le Message du Graal, a range of animistic beliefs such as Mpeve ya Nlongo, Tokoism, Tata Gonda communities, and the Japanese Sekai Kyûseikyô (Church of World Messianity).[8] Of all these religions, Pentecostal-Charismatic Christianity is by far most present in the public sphere, though the Catholic Church continues to exercise much influence on national politics.

DR Congo observes religious freedom, and every citizen is de jure allowed to express and practice his or her own beliefs. Also on an interpersonal level, there is much tolerance toward people from other faiths. Many households are heterogeneous in terms of religious affiliation, and people adhering to different religious groups live together peacefully. Furthermore, it is fully accepted that someone moves from one religion to another in their spiritual journey. After all, so many Kinois, including Pentecostal Christians, hold that "salvation is individual" and one's religion "a matter between him and his god" (*ye na nzambe na ye*). The same tolerance structures daily life on the market. When a Christian market vendor needs to run an errand themselves, they can easily ask their Muslim neighbor to sell on their behalf if a customer would arrive, and vice versa. I was also told by Muslim vendors that the Christian radio broadcasts in the market space are instructive to Muslims as well. "The Koran after all does not deny the Bible," said a recently converted Muslim ambulant vendor of soft ice-cream.

Humor is one major lubricant in these peaceful interreligious relationships. Kinois can joke about a relative, neighbor, or friend as having become "too Christian," being "too involved in deliverance discourse," or suddenly not drinking any alcohol anymore, and now being able to dream of "having four wives, as the Koran prescribes," as I would hear recurrently. On May 25, when the Kimbanguist community celebrates the birthday of Salomon Dialungana, dubbing it as their "Christmas," anyone meeting up with the cheerful Kimbanguist groups that parade through town, jokingly ask "whether it is snowing in Nkamba," the sacred space of the Kimbanguists. These jokes are pragmatic strategies of cohabitation in a religiously plural society, and they hardly ever go beyond discursive challenging. All in all, it is rare that conflicts between Kinois occur because of religious difference.

The foregoing observations are in line with a new analytical lens in Africanist scholarship, where the study of religious pluralism in sub-Saharan Africa has moved from the study of incorporation of African cultural materials, and thus focusing on the interaction between local religious beliefs and a religion of the colonizer, to questions of coexistence and "the multiple ways in which people engage with religions other than their own."[9] These various forms of cohabitation range from conflict and intolerance,[10] to religious tolerance, which may lead to new forms of community and institutions. Studying radio evangelization on Kinshasa's markets through this lens of religious cohabitation and accommodation offers us a new, exciting insight into public religion.

PENTECOSTAL PUBLICS

One of the major transformations in sub-Saharan Africa since the mid-1990s is the emergence of a Pentecostal-Charismatic Popular Culture, which even has become a distinct analytical field in African studies.[11] More than any other denomination, Pentecostal Christianity relies strongly on popular culture forms such as songs, dance, and fiction in order to attract new souls and to support the converted in their everyday religiosity. Popular culture is more than a mere space of representation of Pentecostal beliefs; it is a technology through which one can become a Christian and be nourished by spiritual powers. As such, popular culture is critical to the expansion and consolidation of Pentecostal-Charismatic communities.

All in all, popular culture and mass media play an ambiguous role in the coexistence between various religious communities. At times, Pentecostal media are accused of inciting religious conflict.[12] Starting in the early 1990s, Pentecostal print and electronic media production in sub-Saharan Africa became infused with an "aesthetics of violence."[13] Unsurprisingly, much research has been devoted to the aesthetics and representational strategies of African Pentecostal cultural products such as in films, television serials, video tapes, websites, radio shows, and smartphone apps.[14] Yet, less attention has been given to smaller genres in Pentecostals' evangelization campaigns (such as shouts of complicity, quizzes, and riddles) that are less dramatic and sometimes even do not evoke the spiritual battle between the Holy Spirit and the Devil. Even though these "softer" genres of evangelization may not be as spectacular as the films that use special effects to expose witchcraft and sorcery (*kindoki*) and reveal miracles, such small genres are part and parcel of Pentecostals' "aesthetics of persuasion,"[15] aimed at binding audiences to the Pentecostal community. These smaller genres display forms of Pentecostal accommodation and should be interpreted in terms of the pragmatics of Pentecostal evangelization, meaning evangelizers' constant adaptation in order to ensure a peaceful relationship with other institutions and communities while trying to persuade their audiences to convert to Pentecostal Christianity.

I have arrived at these insights after having observed the wide array of genres that Kinshasa's radio hosts mobilize in order to animate the market population. Some genres, such as the prayers and *mateya* (instructions, predications),[16] are also practiced in church settings and during prayer camps. Yet, smaller genres such as quizzes, dilemma tales, and shouts appear as well. These genres are informal and more participatory and thus can be called "popular." The texts of quizzes, dilemmas, requests for fuel, and so on do not necessarily evidence the familiar Pentecostal "aesthetics of violence," though they take up most airtime on the market radio. These smaller genres may be apprehended as part of "banal Pentecostalization," with a nod to Michael Billig's notion of "banal nationalism,"[17] referring to everyday representations of Pentecostal faith, producing a shared sense of belonging among the Christian community. I will show that these small forms are embedded in a strategy of evangelical nudging, that is, softly exposing moral predicaments and suggesting that Pentecostal Christianity saves. Scholarly attention to these soft strategies of evangelization is meaningful, not only because these take up more time of the overall evangelization praxis but also because they are more likely to be exercised in religiously heterogeneous spaces.

In all of this milieu, sound, especially aural presence, plays a key role in Pentecostal evangelization. Gospel songs, Christian dance, and other sensuous forms are part of the wide array of evangelizing techniques.[18] Maybe unsurprisingly, then, there is a growing scholarly record documenting how sound both in Kinshasa (as the opening vignette illustrates) and elsewhere in sub-Saharan Africa is a matter of struggle between various religious communities.[19] Various explanations have been put forward for this conflict. First of all, sound and spoken words, but also melodies and rhythms, constitute lifeworlds, and activate spiritual powers. Through the pronunciation of the name of Jesus, for example, spiritual efficacy is expected, and Christians experience the material environment as purified from non-Christian immaterial presence. Second, and relevant for this chapter, is that these struggles also express competition over people's attention. Captivating attention—the practice of trying to orient someone's mind and body toward a particular object, event, or text—is central in any evangelizing effort. This struggle for attention and, consequently engagement and attachment, inspires the architecture of Pentecostal religious gatherings (when a sound blaster on the church walls is turned toward the street), the dramatization of sermons, and the establishment of a distinct field of cultural expressivity: Pentecostal popular culture.

The competition over people's attention is integral to the effort to establish Pentecostal publics. Following Warner's definition of "publics,"[20] I consider "Pentecostal publics" as a space of discourse organized by Pentecostal discourse. "Publics" are formed through rhetorical address and the context of reception.[21] This formation demands the existence of myriad publics, which emerge when new forms of address are expressed and when these discourses are interpreted, given meaning to, and acted upon. Bringing this understanding of multiple publics closer to the study of Pentecostal popular culture entails that every Pentecostal genre produces its own Pentecostal public.[22] A gospel song generates its own public as much as an evangelizing television serial does, and digitally shared excerpts of sermons do.

Such attention to the variegated Pentecostal publics that discourse can establish, and to the ways in which people engage with these texts, helps us to gain deeper insights in lived evangelical Christianity, as well in Pentecostal practice, which, as Simon Coleman has argued,[23] is always fragmentary. Pentecostal Christianity always proposes a choice (you are with God or not) and presents the world as divided (others are either Christians, or they are not).

The lens on "publics" also dissolves the taken-for-granted tie between Pentecostal communities and Pentecostal-Charismatic Popular Culture: people who do not identify as Pentecostals can become part of Pentecostal publics if they are singing along to a gospel song or commenting on a digital clip that documents a Pentecostal sermon.

Furthermore, the study of Pentecostal publics allows us to explore the less spectacular yet still meaningful ways in which evangelizers establish relationships with nonbelievers and believers. After all, Muslim vendors on Kinshasa's markets readily interpret the mateya (lessons, sermons) as instructions about everyday life, and they filter out the references toward Christian spirituality, just like Catholics and Kimbanguist market vendors appreciate the Christian sonic presence that the Pentecostal market radio affords but tend to deliberately ignore the messages about spiritual warfare. They may consume the mateya and other Pentecostal genres for their entertaining, social, and moral messages, rather than for the immediate spiritual effects on their souls.[24]

MARKETS AND THE PENTECOSTAL IMAGINATION

Every morning, Pastor Zeza (pseudonym), who works for Pastor Victor and animates on the Marché Kato, picks up the radio equipment in the main church in Yolo (about six kilometers away from the market). Every evening, he returns to the church to deposit the equipment, and sometimes he participates in additional training sessions, or he joins the prayer groups for *intercession* (praying on behalf of others). He also briefs his patron, Pastor Victor, who hardly has time to visit the market radio studios.[25] Pastor Victor counts on the power of the market population to assess the performance of his animateurs. After all, the market is a perfect testing ground for a pastor's abilities. Promising pastors manage to consolidate ties with followers on the market, who then can literally follow the pastor to a church space, once he has the means either to rent a space for a few hours or to buy a plot and build a church.[26]

Markets occupy a central position in the study of African Pentecostalism, urban sociality, and popular culture for various reasons. First, Pentecostal pastors are keen to address market publics. And a closer look at the individual careers of Pentecostal pastors reveals that markets occupy a foundational role in the construction of a pastor's authority and following. For many Pentecostal pastors, the market is the starting point of their religious career. Most evangelizers who engage in ambulant evangelization have just had their calling and roam around in the streets, on the markets, and in public transport as they have not yet gathered a following around them, nor can they yet rent a location for a few hours a day where they would organize prayer cults and sermons. Most pastors' ambition is to set up their own church compound; yet this requires a significant amount of spiritual, social, and economic capital, which can be accumulated quickly through market evangelization.[27]

Surely, not only lack (of experience, of funds, of flock) pushes pastors to the market. The marketspace constitutes a space of freedom and experimentation: market evangelizers do not need approval from the head of the church, nor from another church structure for their market initiatives. They can operate beyond the control of church leaders. Market animateurs do need to work hard for the attention of the market dwellers. While visitors in the church have entered the sacred premise exactly because of religious intentions, the opposite is the case for market dwellers. Usually these are *passagers*—passersby, people on the move—and they do not visit the market for religious purposes.

An additional pull toward market evangelization is the market's foundational role in urban sociality. Kinshasa itself is said to have grown at the crossroads of market exchange between riverine peoples. Yet, apart from being the space of urban origins, millions of Kinshasa's households rely literally on markets for physical reproduction. If a market like the Central Market hosts more than 20,000 vendors for the 100 square meters of the buildings on the market space,[28] then that means that this market alone allows 20,000 families to live. If that same market gets more than 100,000 visitors on a busy day, then it means that within the span of a week, the whole city virtually has visited the market.

The markets also have another symbolic meaning for Kinois life: the "health" of the market spaces determines the overall mood in the city. The atmosphere at Kinshasa's Central Market, for example, is often apprehended as a state of the security in the city itself. When panic emerges in the Central Market—for example, due to riots by soldiers and shooting incidents—people seek refuge outside the market, literally fleeing the space. This information spreads rapidly throughout the city, leading to a sense of alertness all around. Upheaval, chaos, and unrest in the Central Market are often interpreted as part of a larger, more general social problem. "The country is unsafe" (*le pays n'est pas bon*), one then often hears, and such a slogan literally pushes people to limit their movement around town and to stay at home. This importance of the market for urban life is not limited to the Central Market. The activities in smaller markets are also inherently tied to urban social and political tensions. For example, during "dead city days" (which are days of political protest, organized by opposition parties), the smaller markets are also closed. Sales at the market are also indicative of the overall urban economy, even the national economy. If "money circulates not easily," then "the country is not doing well" (le pays n'est pas bon; see above).[29]

Markets are often considered to be the origin of information and rumors. These rumors then spread via the moving bodies in public transport and the streets into people's homes. As such, language and stories travel from markets in a ripple movement. The market is the space from which quite literally urban virality originates.

The market's symbolic meaning for the city's reproduction goes even deeper: the market is the space of women. Women are at the heart of this society-regenerating space. As symbolically and economically, the market (and its smaller markets) comprises the regenerative spaces of the city; it is a powerful space to spread the gospel in this world. Evangelizing the market of African cities equals "awakening" the womb of the city.[30]

Within the Pentecostal imagination itself as well, the market appears as an attractive space for evangelization because of the various market activities and social encounters. This can be broken down in five reasons. First and foremost, the market is a space where words are used to seduce. Words are turned into value and money exchange.[31] The market thus appears as a space of barter, quarrels, deceit, and manipulation. Second, according to Birgit Meyer,[32] it is exactly the global nature of the marketspace that inspires the Pentecostals' inclination to diabolize the market: it is a place "from which globally circulated products pass into private homes."[33] As such, the Pentecostal imagination, which represents commodities in the market as animated, is a reaction to "global economic, political, social, cultural, and religious processes."[34] This focus on consumption and religion in the context of globalization then explains the production of fear regarding "strange things going on in the market which would not meet the eye but which might have very severe consequences 'in the physical.' "[35]

Third, this attention to potentially demonic activity on the market is keenly connected to the "female" identity of the market space. As a predominantly female space populated with successful female traders,[36] such as in Kinshasa, the Nanas Benz (also the topic of an evangelizing television serial), market life generates suspicions about spiritual sacrifices these women have carried out in exchange for material success. These suspicions are not "new"; rather, Pentecostal interpretations about the market build further on existing imaginaries of market spaces as spiritually ambiguous locations. Regarding the Onitsha market (Nigeria), Bastian writes that "Onitsha's markets [. . .] sometimes were believed to go beyond the boundaries of appropriate heat into dangerous overheatedness."[37]

Fourth, and a matter of concern for most Pentecostals, markets favor a constant confluence of individuals. Markets are considered to be a space that is risky and unsafe because of the excess of mobility and anonymity. Kinois Pentecostals imagine life as a path (*nzela*), and encounters with others (even strangers) are conceptualized as "crossing roads." In this conceptualization, "strangers" as such do not exist. There is no Lingala word for "stranger." People either use "guests" (mainly used for expats) or "passersby," people with whom one crosses paths and whose influence can divert one from God's chosen path for you. In Kinois sociality, the market is one of many "hotspots," such as the public *phonie* cabin, the body of a prostitute, and the street. Markets constitute "crossroads," where "human beings and all kinds of energies cross paths."[38] Kabata Kabamba and Kabale Ntumba, writing about local markets situated between cities and villages in the Kananga region, remind us that "the market needs to be sacralized in order to avoid it becoming a space where malicious people complete their murderous transactions, and so that those who frequent it can be protected from nuisances."[39] The reference to nuisance is telling here, as it suggests the possibility of negative, asocial interaction at the crossroads.[40] Markets, as loci of crowds, produce an unclear multitude of numerous passersby. This multitude creates chaos (*mubulu*), excess, and opens opportunities for antisocial behavior such as theft, cheating, physical violence—enacted by passengers—anonymous others. But the market space is risky also for Pentecostals, mainly because the temporarily crossings with others may have consequences on a spiritual level. It is in this regard that one needs to understand Kinois' tolerance of bus evangelizers. When mounting a bus heading to the Central Market, at any time of the day, one meets ambulant Pentecostal preachers praying and communicating their message to anyone on the bus. These evangelizers usually do not have to pay a bus fee, as the majority of Kinshasa's inhabitants are Christians and value the presence and words of pastors to protect the passengers. Even if not all passengers on the bus would identify as Pentecostal Christians, hardly anyone takes offense at this unsolicited preaching; most people understand that they are headed toward spiritually unsafe territory and seize on the spiritual protection that is made available to them.

Finally, Kinshasa's markets—as cacophonic spaces of sound, smell, and objects—are spaces of seeming disorder, chaos, immorality, and all kinds of risk. In the Pentecostal imagination in Kinshasa, and elsewhere in sub-Saharan Africa, there is a spiritual connection between material disorder and evil.[41] It is a space of "loose morals," where quarrels easily erupt, where vulgar, and often irrational language is used in order to outdo someone else, where all kinds of moral transgressions (among others crossdressing) are perceived.[42] Market visitors do not wander around in the market space; rather they move quickly, hasten to arrive at the table where they need to buy wares. In that rush, bodies bump into one another; people need to navigate wares spread out on the ground, often in front of market stalls, and have to pass through narrow corridors, which sometimes only allow one person at a time to move. This is due to new tables that have been added. Sounds are coming in from all sides. These can be from vendors shouting and trying to attract clients or from transistor radios on the small tables broadcasting Congolese music. Visitors may be distracted by quarrels between vendors and clients, or vendors and suppliers, or market dwellers and thieves. The disorder in design and sound is complemented by the presence of food waste, plastic, cardboard, and other rubbish that lie on the ground and are only removed after 5 P.M., once the market has closed. Unsurprisingly then, markets appear in African Pentecostal popular culture as loci of evil:[43] they are spaces where demonic sacrifices occur and that are spiritually hazardous. For example, encounters in the market figure as significant plot twists of evangelizing films in Accra and television serials in Kinshasa.[44]

"SMALL" PENTECOSTAL GENRES

This section will look into the discursive genres that the Pentecostal animateurs mobilize. Above all, they understand the market public as a community to instruct, to transfer *bwanya ya nzambe* (wisdom from God), Christian knowledge. Therefore, the most important genre is the mateya (formal teachings). However, for the purpose of this chapter, I am more interested in the other Pentecostal genres that are mobilized on the market and that can be called popular because they are "defined by the relationship between performers and audience."[45] Examples are calls for fuel, quizzes (e.g. "at what age did Jesus die?"), shouts of complicity, and dilemmas (also called *question-réponse*, question-answer plays). The social significance of these small genres cannot be underestimated, even if the evangelizers themselves do not consider them as genres at all. During fieldwork, the market animateurs did not understand I was paying so much attention to these calls for fuel and the quizzes, which they seemed embarrassed about. They preferred to talk about the more conventional Pentecostal genres like the sermons and prayers. The calls for fuel provoked shame, as they illustrated that the church was not rich enough to provide for the basic sonic infrastructure. Further, one of the animateurs even argued that these calls for fuel actually are not becoming for a man of God, who should be focusing on spreading the gospel. Moreover, the quizzes were considered merely for killing time, in order to retain the market population's attention. However, exactly these banal discursive actions make up most of the radio broadcasting time on the market and have several socially and religiously performative effects.

In particular, these smaller genres contribute to a reconfiguration of the market population in other ways than gospel music, predication, and collective prayers do, which are also performed in church. Yet, in the church spaces, the public attends in order to be instructed, inspired, and healed. Market publics are heterogeneous by design, and Pentecostal animateurs perform various small genres that fracture the market public and that emphasize the boundaries between Pentecostal market vendors, customers and staff, versus others in ways that are unnecessary in church. Other popular evangelizing genres, such as the dilemmas, occupy a moral middle: they are at once intended to entertain the market public and, as I will show, nudge the public toward Christian ethics.

Calls for Fuel

In one of my first conversations with Papa Victor, he argued, much to my surprise, that "the power of our [market] radios is the predication and the *collectes*." "Collectes" means the money collection that happens twice a day: once in the morning, to collect funds for the fuel for electricity generators, and once at the end of the day, to pay for the animateurs' transport fees. Collectes are taken from the Christian vendors with tables on the market, as well as their customers, and other Christian visitors and passersby.

These calls are very explicit and can range from (a) asking for a gift to (b) requesting a kind of payment ("You have come on our path, you have listened to us"). Money, then, is said to compensate for the spiritual work that the animateurs carry out for the Christians on the market. Pleas can also include (c) tests of solidarity, reminding that people need to assist one another, including the animateurs ("give us fuel; god will set you free from your suffering, when he sees how you are helping us"). Finally, (d) these calls sometimes are formulated as an obligation to keep the Christian word present on the market space.

Although the call for fuel may seem banal, it often makes up more than two hours of the radio broadcasting, during which time prayers and mateya only seem to interrupt the calls for fuel (rather than the other way around). Calls for fuel constitute thus a hybrid genre.

Just like in church calls for the tithe, animateurs' calls for fuel are inclusive. There is an emphasis that everybody can contribute—"even if it is only with 100F or with 200FC."[46] These calls signal a circuit of money, intentions, words, affect, and spiritual powers on the market. Enticing about this circuit is that it appears as a closed environment; there is a direct return: "give, and I will make sure that god will give too," so the animateurs promise.

These requests for gifts for fuel as well as the gifts themselves are "thick," laden with social and spiritual significance. First, these collectes are embedded within a Christian ideology of sowing and donating money. Through donating to the animateurs, one accumulates spiritual capital. Second, the collectes constitute the building blocks of the market radio: without the transport fees the animateurs are not able to travel to the market, without the fuel they are not able to broadcast their religious messages. In this way Christian market vendors materialize the Christianization of their area on the market. Without the Christian songs, predications, and quizzes, the market is a multireligious space. With an operating Pentecostal market radio, the radio sounds produce a Christian acoustic field that dominates the market space. The donations for fuel contribute to the "awakening" of the market, and from there on, with its ripple effect, partake in the evangelization of the city as a whole. Third, the calls for fuel are technologies of connection: those who donate publicly confirm their Christian identity. The gesture of accepting an envelope (to be filled with the collecte), or the act of walking toward the studio with some paper money hidden in the fist, are public performances of Christian identity.

Shouts of Complicity

Apart from calling out for fuel, other discursive performances occur as well through which born-again Christians set themselves apart from others on the market. Especially shouts (*cris*) for cheering and applauding stand out. These shouts can vary, for example, from *nzambe ya…* (god from …), to which people need to answer *likolo* (above, heaven); to the shout *lipata moke* (one small cloud), to which people respond with *eeee*" (yes). Other types of shouts can be called motivational, for example, *na nzambe tokolonga* (with god, we will win), to which people answer *eee* or *ya solo* (indeed); to *bana ya nzambe prêt* (are god's children ready [for the fight]?), to which the appropriate answer is eeee, *toza* (yes, we are [ready]).

These shouts can be performed when the animateur walks around the market tables and asks the vendors for money; or during mateya (instructions), to vie for people's attention; and during dead moments, for example, when waiting for people to come to the market radio studio with answers to the questions in the quiz, and so on.

It is meaningful that Papa Victor called these shouts *des cris de complicité*, shouts of complicity, and that they were a part of the training for the market radio evangelizers. While similar shouts constitute a common gesture within the church meetings, in the market context these almost phatic expressions gain a specific social significance. These become discursive practices through which Christians signal to one another their shared religious orientation. As such, the heterogenous market public becomes fractured, and responding is a powerful gesture of Christian belonging.

When one of the street children who often took a nap in the radio studio on Marché Kato joined the shouts, Pastor Zeza always smiled. Although the street child did not identify as a Pentecostal, and certainly did not behave like a Christian as he sometimes smoked weed on the verandah of the radio studio, Pastor Zeza interpreted his almost tacit responses as hopeful. Indeed, applause and cheering—even if these gestures seem small, and are easily dismissed as banal—are actually "meaning-doing."[47] These everyday cultural performances are critical to the processes of Christian life at the market because they allow Kinshasa's Pentecostals to confirm and establish ties with a select segment of the market community. It is in and through these small genres that the market public gets fractured, yet under the seduction of answering questions, and engaging in the animation of the cheering and applauding, sometimes a non-Christian aligns discursively.

The Social Significance of Small Performances

These discursive genres and the accompanying gestures happen in public but only engage particular individuals. They set in motion a Pentecostal system of thought and action that deliberately performs attachment and detachment at the same time.

Regarding the market, the animateurs take on a double role: on the one hand they are clearly anchored, through the microphone line with the radio studio, and thus posit themselves as separate from the market population. On the other hand, at the beginning and at closing of the market, they abandon the radio studio, and wander the marketspace, when distributing the envelopes to collect money for fuel, picking them up, and taking a break from broadcasting. In these instances, the animateurs move into the crowds, literally dissolving the distance between the public and themselves, and perform accessibility and closeness.[48]

"Small" genres set forth a proximity between the animateurs and (parts of) the market population. This intimacy, discursively produced, vouches for the continuing popularity of Christian radio broadcasts. This is a big difference from followers' engagement with the pastors in church, who usually arrive in big jeeps, guarded by various small boys and for whom people have to queue for hours to potentially meet. Sometimes the followers even make appointments to see pastors, only to be received by the pastor's assistant or to be asked to return the next day. The market animateurs are invariably ambitious young men who want to move up in the Pentecostal hierarchy and who deem the market the perfect place to start. They are open to any complaint from a member of their public, and they often express concern for or worry about their audience's suffering, from the smallest boy on the market to the wealthiest female trader.

"Small genres" are, very much like "small media,"[49] "powerful means of establishing communicative space" in media environments dominated by control and censorship. While Christian discourse is by no means curtailed in Kinshasa's marketplaces, there is nevertheless an awareness of the presence of religious others and of the necessity not to offend them. "Small genres," then, are, just like "small media," of the utmost productivity in such an environment and function as expressive devices in the formation of group identity and solidarity.[50] Yet, in contrast to "bigger" genres, small genres are often transitory, and, for example, one can expect that as soon as the electricity provision on the markets becomes more stable, or when Pastor Zeza's church contributes for the generator, that the genre of the calls for fuel will disappear.

Probably the most significant social outcome of these small genres is that they provoke "small acts":[51] the donors cannot contribute large amounts of Congolese francs, nor can the market women spend much time in church, yet they can cheer and applaud, as well as fill an envelope with "merely" 200 Congolese francs, or offer a plate with some fufu and vegetables to the radio host. Central to the logics of small acts is, so Chua argues, "the insistence that many individual contributions, however tiny, can cumulatively make a big difference."[52] Through these "small" practices, donors construe their Christian persona and contribute to the sonic presence of their faith on the market.

On the level of the pastors' careers, these small genres can make an enormous difference. The closeness of these pastors to the market population strengthens their position as influential storytellers. When I queried Pastor Victor about the selection and training of his animateurs, he mentioned that his animateurs needed to be "above all good Christians, and they need to preach well." He relied to a huge extent on the market population itself to assess whether a newly recruited radio preacher was someone without any skill or talent (an *animateur ya pamba*) or a "real one" (*moto ya nzambe*, a man of God), claiming a particular Pentecostal authenticity. This assessment would translate in the market's response on the calls for fuel. If for several days on end, an animateur would arrive in the church in the evening, complaining about the lack of funds for fuel and transport, then pastor Victor interpreted this as a signal that the market population did not appreciate the animateur's interventions. The audience participation on which these Pentecostal small genres rely thus not only has consequences for the success of the evangelization campaign but also can make or break an (aspiring) pastor's career.

DILEMMAS, OR QUESTION-ANSWER PLAYS

While the shouts and the calls for fuel fractured the market public in a Christian community versus a non-Christian group, the genre of the *dilemme* (also called question-réponse, question-answer) unites the market audience into one moral public. As I will show, this genre occupies the "moral middle," insofar as it allows an unresolved moral ambiguity. Dilemma performances on Kinshasa's markets cultivate open-endedness, though are part of an evangelizing strategy that we can qualify as nudging. I will first illustrate this with a description of a dilemme performance in Kinshasa's second-largest market, the Marché de Liberté (Freedom Market), in Ndjili (from August 24, 2014).

Around 1 P.M., animateur Jeancy (pseudonym) takes the microphone and positions himself about one and a half meters outside of the shabby radio studio made of sheet metal plates. This studio, close to tables of women vending stationary, works with only four loudspeakers, so the reach of the pastor's voice is limited. Only two meters away is a tiny crossroad in the market, where anyone who wants to access the pavilions with food, or who wants to return to the paved parts of the market, or looks for the main entrance, needs to pass. Jeancy's yelling and shouting are passionate, maybe because of his small moving radius due to the short microphone cable. Before long, a small group of people, initially mainly children, has gathered around him, curious to follow the spectacle. Jeancy manages to halt them briefly in a space defined by movement and transiting. Gradually, as more and more adults join the group, the crowd grows bigger and bigger.

In just fifteen minutes, Jeancy recounts the story. There are intermittent repetitions of the main plotlines so that listeners who may just have arrived can easily chip in. There is also a lot of joking and entertainment going on, which attracts attention. All in all, this dilemme performance will last about one hour and a half. Most time of the performance is devoted to answers by the market dwellers sharing their take on the situation.

> Let me tell you a story of pain and suffering [*lisolo ya mpasi*]; it is also a story of *mawa* [sorrow] and of miracles. There was an orphaned girl, without father or mother. She grew up like a bird, *ndeke ndeke* [on her own]. This story will give you pain. Especially the way in which she grew up, even when she was a small girl, she began to take care of herself [*kodébrouiller*] the way in which we here in Kinshasa, even when a small girl begins to grow up, she will have to fend for herself. She met a boy, who visited her from time to time. He was from the same neighborhood as our orphan. She took him to the house of her *bayaya* [elder brothers, assuming that she introduced him formally as her partner]. But what happens these days? What do young men do these days? When they visited her *bayaya*, listen to his French—"je suis, je serais, je dois" [look who I am, and all the plans I have]—and his Lingala: "naza na mbongo, naza prêt" ["I have money, I am ready," suggesting he will formally marry her]. When the boyfriend asked her uncle to help him organizing the marriage, the uncle refused, saying that he had too many other things to deal with. Look, *bandeko* [brothers and sisters]; look at these problems. This is suffering. The boy made her immediately pregnant. Her belly began to swell. When she visited the boy, she told him, "she is not seeing [her menstruation] anymore." He jokingly asked her whether she had become blind. "Can't your eyes see anymore? What is wrong?" So, this orphaned girl was pregnant, and the boy just left her like that. *Bien aimés* (beloved ones), misfortune never happens in isolation.

As the story unfolds, the pregnant orphan is chased away by her own relatives and by those of the boy. Jeancy details the small jobs the girl undertakes on the market, such as selling paper handkerchiefs. When the girl arrives in the hospital to give birth, she narrates her suffering to the medical doctor. Although Jeancy does not label him as such, the doctor becomes the hero of the story. Feeling pity (mawa), the doctor offers her one of the flats in the hospital, where she can stay as long as she pleases. And so, life goes on. The girl and her baby daughter are well cared for in the hospital. The doctor pays for all expenses, accommodation, education, and subsistence included. At several occurrences, Jeancy mentions that it is the doctor who *abokoli* the baby girl, "made her grow up." Then, many years later, the daughter meets a man, who unlike her father, is "correct" (*aza logique*). Jeancy narrates that this boy does not make any promises like "I will marry you" but rather begins preparing the marriage and starts talking to his own relatives. One day, the man asks his "fiancée": "to whom should I give the money [*mbongo ya libala*, the bride price]? Your mother, the doctor, or the man who made your mother pregnant? whose family?" At this point, Jeancy invites the crowd to take the microphone: "Come here and talk in the microphone. To whom should they give the bride price?"

For about more than an hour, people shared their opinions. Some women argued that the money should be offered to the girl's mother; for others, the doctor merited the symbolic gesture as a kind of compensation for the *charge* (burden) he had taken on; while still others deemed that the money should go to the "blood." Several people gave more nuanced responses; for example, according to an elderly man, *la veste* (jacket), an item on the list for the customary marriage (this list groups money and commodities), should go to the father but the money to the mother. During the answers, people often narrated their own, similar experiences, thus signaling that many identified with the dramatic events.

During these discussions, Jeancy sometimes pushed for more clarification, for example, commenting on another old man: "Oh you say that the father, who only spent 5 seconds with the girl, should receive the money, while the doctor, who has paid during 23 years for the girl, will not receive anything? really?" Or, at other instances, Jeancy made statements that seemingly countered the Pentecostal message, like "blood remains blood, after all" (*makila eza makila*), after a woman had warned people that the matrimony may be cursed if the biological father did not get the money. And, when one woman shouted through the microphone, "Does love come from heaven or from the earth?" and added that "pregnancy is spiritual" (*zemi eza ya molimo*), Jeancy only asked her whether she prayed. He never told the crowd whether their answer was right or wrong. Rather, he let the public discuss among themselves.

It was only near the end that some soft directives toward a Christian framing were made. When Jeancy felt that the performance had to end, he invited three more people to come and answer "according to God's word" (*selon logique ya liloba ya nzambe*). And, when repeating the question to whom the bride price should be transmitted, he added "the church?" as a potential receiver, thus suggesting that the orphan had become a member of a Christian community.

The topic was clearly very popular, and many more people continued the debate longer than Jeancy initially had in mind. One man reminded that "author's rights" (*droits d'auteur*) exist, euphemistically speaking for the biological father, but at the same time, he argued that "one needs to be grateful to the person who has made sure that the girl's road opened" (*nzela afungwami*). Other people took up Jeancy's nudge toward a Christian framing and responded that "according to the Bible," the biological father should not receive anything, but anyway, the matrimony will be one of suffering. A miller, fully covered in white cassava dust, seized the opportunity to recount his own story, of how he married a single mother. Their customary wedding ceremonies dictated that he not only marry the mother but also the child. He paid a double bride price. Furthermore, when the daughter got married seventeen years later, he initiated a meeting between the son-in-law and the girl's biological relatives so that "the child's route would not be blocked" (*mpo akopesa mwana nzela*). Someone else was firmer and argued, with a confident and clear voice, that "the solution is in Jesus's name. Full stop. Amen" (*solution eza na kombo ya yesu—un point un trait. Amen*"), though without providing a clear answer to Jeancy's initial question.

The final contribution came from a market vendor who passionately talked about divine justice. "People should not so quickly dismiss the biological father's involvement," so he shouted with a hoarse voice through the microphone. He reminded the bystanders about the story of Moses, "who may have been raised by the pharaohs, but in the end, Moïse returned to his own people." Jeancy did not comment on this reference to the Old Testament, which Pentecostals hardly attribute any validity, but closed the performance by thanking the crowd, because "all of those who have intervened, they have given us some knowledge [*connaissance*]; may God in heaven bless you all." At this point, Jeancy returned to the radio studio and played a CD of Soeur L'Or Mbongo, a Kinois gospel singer.

This description of one *dilemme* performance is representative of the various *dilemme* events that I attended. Another storyline is about a husband who travels to neighboring Angola to find his luck over there, leaving behind his wife in Kinshasa. For years, he does not call; nor does he send her any money. From time to time, his wife hears through the grapevine that her husband has married another woman in Angola. So, after several years, when a man with a steady job, without children, and with prospects for a life in Europe courts her, she agrees with the marriage. Fearing that her married status will hinder this new *nzela* (route), she hides that she is already customarily married to another, absent, husband. Yet, as the husband to be prepares to visit her relatives, the absent husband returns from Angola, though without any money. He takes back his wife from his relatives' house, where she has stayed during his absence, as he wants to set up house again with his wife. What should this woman do? Another dilemma narrative recounts the experience of a *bonne* (household help), who remains home alone with her male boss after the latter's wife has traveled to Dubai. Upon her return, the bonne observes how this woman changes her behavior, humiliates her husband, and lacks respect for her in-laws. Through eavesdropping, the bonne learns that the wife visits a wealthy lover in Dubai. Around the same time, the husband makes sexual advances to the household help. What should the bonne do?

Apart from a lack of immediate references to the spiritual battle between the Holy Spirit and demonic agents, two more characteristics of the Pentecostal dilemme genre stand out: (a) The genre plays with the public's familiarity with the dramatized events, and thus mobilizes unity beyond the various religious affiliations of the crowd. (b) The moral frame and the animateur's authoritative voice are absent; members in the crowd are requested to think along the *logic* of the Bible for themselves. Both characteristics will be discussed more deeply in the next section.

Beyond Religious Difference

I consider the fact that the market animateurs refrain from emphasizing religious difference within the dilemma genre as significant. Despite the fact that they obviously speak from a Christian positionality, the evangelizing agenda of their performance is obscured. Throughout the performance, Jeancy does not mention spirits, nor the Holy Spirit, nor any demons. As such, distance with practitioners of other faiths is dissolved. This distance differs from, for example, the evangelizing television serials produced in Kinshasa,[53] and Pentecostal films in Accra,[54] where, even though most of the storyline is devoted to an exposé of the workings of diabolic others, and the moral instructions only become clear at the end of the storyline, there is nevertheless a Pentecostal framing.[55] These genres are often criticized for "initiating" their publics in demonic cults, and pastors expressed concern regarding the moral consequences for the audiences if they missed the moralizing closure due to power cuts or due to other kinds of interruption.

Jeancy made use of every possible method to include as many people as possible in the market in the conversation. He used street slang, referred to collective knowledge, sometimes also acted as if he did not know a word, and asked people in the market to help him out. There was much joking and mild teasing going on. As mentioned, at several points in the story telling, he quickly summarized the story in a few lines so that new visitors could quickly get into the performance. Further, everybody could take the microphone and narrate their own opinions and experiences without an initial vetting of the contributor's identity or the appropriateness of her words. This format contrasts with the politics of speaking in the church setting, where even for public witnessing, the speaker will have first discussed the content with the pastor or with one of his assistants.[56]

Another characteristic of the dilemme performances is the choice for familiar protagonists: all protagonists have an intimate connection with the market space. The young girl of the first narrative chooses the market to sell her handkerchiefs; household help visit markets to buy food for the household where they work several times a week; and many Kinois women know men—either their husbands, brothers, or sons—who migrate for economic reasons to other regions and disappear for years.

Betrayal is invariably part of the plotline. Sometimes this deception occurs outside of Kinshasa, for example, in Angola or Dubai, yet these "elsewheres" are also very familiar to the market public. Apart from China and South Africa, Dubai and Angola are prime destinations of Kinshasa's economic migrants. Every Kinois has a relative, friend, or neighbor who has gone to these places, and these destinations figure prominently in ambitious plans of traders who have not yet been able to travel. The locations of the dilemma narratives thus occupy an important position within the economic imagination of Kinois. Yet, what should be places of progress and mobility suddenly appear as places of cheating, lies, adultery, and other forms of immoral behavior. In the dilemme tales, those who have stayed behind, like the husband whose wife cheats on him in Dubai, or the wife whose husband spent years in Angola, are duped. The market space, which is commonly taken for granted as a dangerous space (see above), becomes here a space of morally correct people. The market dwellers (the vendor of the handkerchiefs, the vendor whose husband is abroad, and the bonne, a typical market customer) are stripped from their ambiguous or ambivalent morality. Rather, they are presented as victims, with choices to make.

All of the above (using familiar protagonists, rendering the audience as moral people, situating the stories within familiar locations) are "techniques of immediacy" that producers of African popular art readily mobilize.[57] These approaches generate an "aesthetic of immediate impact"[58] on the audiences. Through these performances, a commonness, a shared experience of suffering (*mpasi*), and an awareness of living with untrustworthy others gain prominence among the market dwellers.

Absent Moral Frame—Cultivation of Choice

Fundamental to the dilemme genre is the confrontation with a choice. It is not a coincidence that the dilemma is so important on the market; the market is by definition a space of choice. The narrative starts with bad news, a loss, betrayal, or departure. Then comes a period of sacrifice, and coping. Yet, the turning point in the narrative comes when a "good person" appears on the scene, and seems to *fungola nzela*—to open the road for the suffering subject. At this point, with a brighter future on the horizon, the painful past reappears and seems to have tied (in an Africanist spiritual sense) the subject. The choice the protagonist is faced with is about cutting the ties,[59] and choosing for oneself, or about remaining tied to previous obligations, and forsaking new opportunities. It can be argued that a genre such as dilemme gives the Christian herself a sense of autonomy and self-governance. The fundamental line is that every new, bright future comes with a loss. Ties need to be cut—with the disrespectful husband, with the cheating boss, with the irresponsible father, and so on.

Onlookers and listeners are left reflecting on the various nzela that have been proposed and can turn to the Bible or to the animateur if they wish so. Yet, it is the market dwellers themselves who have brought knowledge (connaissance) to the public, so Jeancy mentions when closing the performance. This expansiveness contrasts with the space of the church, where not only leadership and authority but also knowledge are embodied by the pastor who physically occupies the center stage: the pastor is often placed on a platform, and the public's spatial organization is so arranged that the followers' attention goes to the *pasteur* and his words. Testimony to that hierarchy is the additional loudspeakers, the translator in the church, and the set-up of the chairs facing the pastor. All these arrangements invite people to enter in a more passive, receptive mode than the market audience.

Significant is that the dilemma as the animateur recounted it remains open ended.[60] No information about the doctor's religious identity is made. The connection between the Christian God and the sudden gift of the doctor needs to be clear to the audience. Yet, the fact that this is not mentioned either allows for some confusion and slippage or makes it a story that does not immediately scare off practitioners of other religions.

The moral ambiguity is a characteristic of "African dilemma tales." Bascom wrote that dilemma tales often have no answers, because their importance is more in the fact that "dilemma tales lead to argumentation and debates."[61] Yet, the "moral middle" of the dilemme genre is unique for Pentecostal-Charismatic Popular Culture. Well-known Pentecostal genres—such as predications, evangelizing TV shows, and gospel music—are usually very explicit, even graphic, regarding moral lessons.

Nevertheless, I see two "Pentecostal" principles at play in this soft evangelizing. First, Jeancy counts on the Christian responders to do the persuasive work. Nudging the interlocutors to "answer according to the Bible" signifies a transfer of the persuasive labor from the evangelizing animateur to other market dwellers, of whom some may be Christians and others not. They are literally invited to participate in the spiritual battle by contributing to soft evangelization practices. Furthermore, the firmness and conviction that emanate from Christian responders are in line with the Christian ethical stance that doubts, anxiety, and uncertainty are unbecoming of a Christian. This nature explains the label of "question-answer" that evangelizing animateurs also use to talk about the dilemme performances: for a Christian, these stories do not present any "choice," or dilemma. Rather, there is only one clear answer for a Christian: the bride price will be given to the doctor, the woman would marry the wealthy man and abandon her first husband, and the maid will leave that household.

Second, the unresolved dilemma tales resonate with Pentecostals' emphasis on "active choice."[62] Simon Coleman, studying Swedish so-called prosperity Pentecostals, describes an "active cultivation of 'dilemmas' or 'breakdowns' as part of [Pentecostal's] dispositional makeup," and becoming born-again means "to enter a whole new range of ethical choices."[63] Kinshasa's market animateurs know that their public is heterogeneous and that most of the crowd members are not (yet) born-again Christians. The step of conversion follows a change in consciousness, a decision consciously made by the convert. The dilemme genre familiarizes potential converts with the Christian disposition of choosing and cutting ties.

CONCLUDING THOUGHTS

In conclusion, most relevant for this volume on the relationship between evangelical Christianity and the transformation of Africa has been the attention to the emergence of Pentecostal publics, the role of so-called small genres therein, the fragmentation of Christian communities, and religious accommodation. I have put forward that the transformation of African societies through evangelization is dialectically related to the emergence of Pentecostal-Charismatic Popular Culture, which in its diversity of styles and genres can speak to numerous publics. Some of these genres engage in aggressive evangelization, while others, what I call "small" genres, are softer, and subtly orient audiences toward a Pentecostal ethos. The shouts of complicity, quizzes, calls for fuel, and dilemma tales that I have studied here are key to a Pentecostal-Charismatic Popular Culture. These genres are unofficial, are noncanonical, and only gain significance within the everyday workings of the market.

Probably the most significant contribution of this chapter is that Pentecostal publics are not homogeneous social entities; rather, Pentecostal publics are organized around texts. As texts, they group people merely because of the attention they devote to the text. If Pentecostal publics come about through Pentecostal texts, then one cannot assume that all members of these publics identify as Pentecostals themselves. Rather, some of these Pentecostal texts reach audiences beyond the Pentecostal community, for example, when a text travels outside the church, or when an evangelizing leaflet is picked up by a random pedestrian.

More than the more conventional Pentecostal genres, small genres harbor potentiality of conversion. While sermons, gospel songs, and dramatizations in film speak to big emotions of horror, shock, amazement, and wonder, the small genres are more incisive because they speak to less dramatic affects, even to the extent that the animateurs themselves did not consider some of these study worthy, yet, therefore, the messages communicated through the small genres may insinuate themselves more easily into the members of the public. Despite their seeming banality, these genres constitute easy ways to reach out to non-Christian publics. This phenomenon relates to the core argument of this chapter, which is about the constitution and configuration of Pentecostal publics.

The ethnography of market evangelization has shown how smaller genres may have another significance for non-Pentecostals than they have for Pentecostals, yet a significance is acknowledged by these non-Pentecostals.

Although the observation may seem banal in itself, it is fully in line with the very evangelizing mission of Pentecostal Christianity: it is not against but totally part of the ambition of Pentecostal popular culture to reach out to people who are not yet Pentecostals. This confirms again Pentecostalism's fragmentary nature, as posited firmly by Coleman.[64] Pentecostal-Charismatic Christianity cultivates fragmentation and thrives on difference, distinction, and heterogeneity. And here we come full circle. Kinshasa's markets provide the perfect feeding ground for Pentecostalism, as it introduces new others, and provides new opportunities to reach out to these others, and to integrate them in Pentecostal publics. Most of the members of the Pentecostal publics are not Pentecostal Christians (yet). Therefore, more scholarly attention to these "small genres" is required if we want to understand how African societies and individuals' lives are transformed by evangelical Christianity.

The diversification of Pentecostal publics provides insights into the pragmatics of evangelization, which can be termed "Pentecostal accommodation." This chapter has analyzed two levels of Pentecostal accommodation. First, much—and maybe most—of the proselytization occurs beyond the church space, in spaces where people spend most of their time and very often where they dwell with other intentions and goals than listening to predications and sermons. Small genres such as the shouts of complicity and the calls for fuel may seem banal, yet, as the analysis has shown, they are part of the more insidious forms of binding and bonding people to animateurs and their messages. The shouts of complicity and the calls for fuel fragment the market population, and mainly address the already converted. The dilemma tales, by contrast, aim at capturing the attention and participation of as many market dwellers as possible. In order to enhance the inclusivity of this public, the animateur carefully avoids demonizing other religions. Rather, jokes, repetition, seemingly non-Pentecostal statements, questions for clarification, and above all nudging toward biblical orientations are rhetorical devices of the dilemma tales.

Second, evangelical pragmatism is also inspired by an assessment of the environment, both the market environment and the generic context. In the plural space of the market, Pentecostal animateurs tend to avoid offending other religious believers, censure their broadcasts and performances, and choose for genres of evangelical nudging such as dilemma tales. Obviously, the generic context adds the moral frame. The dilemma tales are one among the many small genres and instructive genres (such as the *mateya*), prayers, and gospel music that the animateurs broadcast from the radio studio. It is the overall embedment of the dilemma genre within a series of Pentecostal genres that supports its evangelizing character.

ACKNOWLEDGMENTS

Fieldwork for this research was funded by an FWO (Fonds voor Weten-schappeljk Onderzoek) ERC (European Research Council) Runner Up fellowship (FWO G.A005.14N). I would like to thank Liana Chua and Héritier Mesa for feedback on an earlier version of this chapter, and to the participants at the 5th CongoResearchNetwork (CRN) conference in Milan (September 2022), and the "Sacred Texts, Profane Images" colloquium at the University of Calabria (June 2024).

NOTES

1. All the genres performed on the market are in a mixture of Lingala and kiKinois (street slang, combining French, Lingala, kiKongo, and some neologisms based on English, and various forms of global culture). These genres are part of an oral culture and address an illiterate and semiliterate crowd.
2. Meyer, *Aesthetic Formations.*
3. The Congolese Churches of the Awakening grouped themselves in 1997 and became officially recognized as a religion in DR Congo in 2002.
4. Pype, "Branhamist Kindoki," 115–44.
5. Pype, "Fighting Boys, Strong Men and Gorillas," 258.
6. So far, no social research has been carried out on the Islamic communities in Kinshasa, most probably because it is still a minority religion.
7. On Kimbanguist Christianity, see Kaninda-Muana; Mélice, 59–80; Ndongala Maduku.
8. Lambertz.
9. Nolte, Ogen, and Jones, 4; see also Soares, 1–16.
10. Smith and Hackett.
11. Ogbu Kalu, 103–62; Pype, "The Liveliness of Pentecostal-Charismatic Popular Culture in Africa," 345–78.
12. See Hackett, "Charismatic / Pentecostal Appropriation of Media Technologies in Nigeria and Ghana," 270; Smith and Hackett, *Displacing the State.*
13. Hackett, "Charismatic / Pentecostal Appropriation," 263.
14. Pype, *The Making of the Pentecostal Melodrama*; Meyer, *Sensational Movies*; Grätz, "'Paroles de vie,'" 161–88; Hackett, "The New Virtual (Inter)Face of African Pentecostalism," 496–503; Taru, 153–73.
15. Meyer, "Aesthetics of Persuasion," 741–63.
16. *Mateya* often vividly describe the spiritual battle and its consequences for believers and nonbelievers.
17. Billig.
18. Meyer, *Aesthetic Formations*; Pype, "Dancing for God or for the Devil," 296–318.
19. Van Dijk, 97–117; De Witte, 690–709; Parsitau, 55–72.
20. Warner, 413.
21. Warner, 414.
22. Even if, recently, scholars have begun to explore the emergence of various Pentecostal publics, when they talk about plurality, it seems a consequence of the cultivation

of style, the production of spiritual kinship, or the mobilization of technologies rather than the outcome of textual performativity and mediation. E.g., Englund.

23. Coleman, 275–300.

24. A similar differentiation of the imagined publics is also operational in the production of evangelizing television serials. The producers argue that depending on the spectator's spiritual condition, the television serial either entertains, provides moral instructions, or feeds the viewer's soul. Pype, *The Making of the Pentecostal Melodrama*, 161.

25. Apart from running the church in Yolo, Pastor Victor is also a gospel musician, and records CDs with his vocals. Pastor Victor has amassed a large group of followers, and in the last five years he has been invited to Christian crusades in Dallas, Texas, and in Australia, each time by Congolese diaspora communities.

26. I did not encounter female pastors in the market space either.

27. Karen Lauterbach mentions how a female pastor in Kumasi, Ghana, resorts to the radio market "in order for her to function and perform as a pastor" because she hardly has access to the church space. Lauterbach, 136. In Kinshasa, all market animateurs are male.

28. The press document designed by a collective of architects renovating the Central Market also mention 20,000 vendors. Think Tank Architecture Sogema, 7. I want to thank Héritier Mesa for pointing me to these numbers, Sogema's press document, and Flouriot's work (personal communication January 2024): Flouriot, 36.

29. Thanks to Héritier Mesa for pointing out the "mirror" function of the market regarding the national economy (personal communication, January 2024).

30. Interpreting the discursive work of market animateurs as a form of "awakening" the market and thus the city resonates with Bastian's observation about the cosmological work of markets in Igbo-land (Nigeria): "the work of constructing and reconstructing the (not always material) everyday worlds that Igbo-speaking peoples inhabit" (Bastian, 111.

31. Pype, "On Interference and Hotspots," 229–60.

32. Meyer, "Commodities and the Power of Prayer," 751–76.

33. Meyer, "Commodities and the Power of Prayer," 752.

34. Meyer, "Commodities and the Power of Prayer," 752.

35. Meyer, "Commodities and the Power of Prayer," 763.

36. Meyer, "Commodities and the Power of Prayer," 764.

37. Bastian, 113.

38. Kabamba and Ntumba, 96; translated by the author.

39. Kabamba and Ntumba, 96.

40. see Pype, "On Interference," 253. A similar observation was made by Filip De Boeck, who considered the market as a microcosm of the urban environment: "It is experienced as a potentially dangerous and contaminating place where strangers skillfully intrude into one's life." De Boeck, 168.

41. Pype, *Making the Pentecostal Melodrama*, 39–40.

42. Thanks to Héritier Mesa for pressing on the various kinds of transgressions in the market space (personal communication, January 2024).

43. Somewhat along these lines, in her study of the history of popular culture in Africa, Karin Barber argues that the market is the space for renewal of popular culture. Probably best known are the Onitsha pamphlets (Nigeria) and their counterparts in other African cities, which were sold in the 1950s and 1960s and narrated moral dilemmas

and life stories of unmarried young men and women trying to find matrimonial stability, though enticed by urban seduction and pleasures, and falling on untrustworthy potential lovers. Barber, 168.

44. Meyer, *Sensational Movies*; Pype, *The Making of the Pentecostal Melodrama*.

45. Barber, 47.

46. In 2014 100 Congolese francs equaled 0.1 USD.

47. Covington-Ward, 231.

48. The animateurs' closeness to the market women also allows these women to assess the animateur's authority. During fieldwork, female vendors would constantly tell me how Pastor Zeza was a courageous man, a real Christian, and if I had a spiritual need, he would certainly be able to intervene.

49. Spitulnik, 181.

50. Spitulnik, 181.

51. Chua, 7–11.

52. Chua, 8.

53. Pype, *The Making of the Pentecostal Melodrama*.

54. Meyer, *Sensational Movies*.

55. The case is different from dubbed Nigerian films in Kinshasa, where dubbers already from the onset engage in moralizing language. See Pype, "Religion, Migration and Media Aesthetics."

56. Usually, the pastor or his assistants advise the speaker to silence certain parts of their story or emphasize other parts. For example, Kinshasa's pastors tell Christians not to mention abortion in the witnessing narratives, as this is considered a crime according to the Congolese Constitution. In the early 2000s policemen and soldiers awaited churchgoers to arrest them based on the crimes publicly confessed in church. Now, pastors and assistants want to protect their followers, and censor personal narratives.

57. Barber, "Popular Arts," 48.

58. Barber, "Popular Arts," 48.

59. Meyer, "Commodities and the Power of Prayer," 751–76.

60. George Olusola Ajibade describes a similar ambiguous poetry of Sàngo worshippers, a "traditionalist" religion in Nigeria (Ede), who thus relate with (compete with, dialogue with) Christianity and Islam. In Sàngo poetry, the other religions are explicitly mentioned, in contrast to the evangelizing dilemme plays in Kinshasa. Olusola Ajibade, 75–94.

61. Bascom, 12.

62. Coleman, 280.

63. Coleman, 280.

64. Coleman.

BIBLIOGRAPHY

Barber, Karin. *A History of African Popular Culture*. Cambridge: Cambridge University Press, 2017.

———. "Popular Arts in Africa." *African Studies Review* 30, no. 3 (1987): 1–78.

Bascom, William. *African Dilemma Tales*. The Hague / Chicago: De Gruyter, 2011.

Bastian, Misty L. *The World as Marketplace: Historical, Cosmological, and Popular Constructions of the Onitsha Market System*. PhD dissertation, Department of Anthropology, University of Chicago, 1998.

Billig, Michael. *Banal Nationalism*. London: Sage, 1995.

Chua, Liana. "Small Acts and Personal Politics: On Helping to Save the Orangutan via Social Media." *Anthropology Today* 34, no. 3 (2018): 7–11.

Coleman, Simon. "Borderlands. Ethics, Ethnography, and 'Repugnant' Christianity." *Hau: Journal of Ethnographic Theory* 5, no. 2 (2015): 275–300.

Covington-Ward, Yolanda. *Gesture and Power: Religion, Nationalism, and Everyday Performance in Congo*. Durham, NC: Duke University Press, 2016.

De Boeck, Filip. "On Being Shege in Kinshasa: Children, the Occult and the Street." In *Reinventing Order in the Congo: How People Respond to State Failure in Kinshasa*, edited by Theodore Trefon, 155–73. London: Zed Books, 2004.

De Witte, Marleen. "Accra's Sounds and Sacred Spaces." *International Journal of Urban and Regional Research* 32, no. 3 (2008): 690–709.

Englund, Harri. *Christianity and Public Culture in Africa*. Cambridge: Cambridge University Press, 2011.

Flouriot, Jean. "Kinshasa 2005: Trente ans après la publication de l'Atlas de Kinshasa." *Les Cahiers d'Outre-Mer* 261 (January–March 2013), accessed March 19, 2024. http:// journals.openedition.org/com/6770; https://doi.org/10.4000/com.6770.

Grätz, Tilo. "'Paroles de vie": Christian Radio Producers in the Republic of Benin." *Journal of African Media Studies* 3, no. 2 (2011): 161–88.

Hackett, Rosalind I. J. "Charismatic / Pentecostal Appropriation of Media Technologies in Nigeria and Ghana." *Journal of Religion in Africa* 18, no. 3 (1998), 258–77.

———. "The New Virtual (Inter)Face of African Pentecostalism." *Society* 46, no. 6 (2009): 496–503.

Kabamba, Kabata, and Kabale Ntumba, K. "Marchés ruraux et relations ville-campagne dans l'arrière-pays immédiat de Kananga (Congo)." *Bulletin de la Société Géographique* no. 36 (1999): 93–101.

Kalu, Ogbu. *African Pentecostalism: An Introduction*. Oxford: Oxford University Press, 2008.

Lambertz, Peter. *Seekers and Things: Spiritual Movements and Aesthetic Difference in Kinshasa*. Oxford: Berghahn Books, 2019.

Lauterbach, Karen. *Christianity, Wealth, and Spiritual Power in Ghana*. Cham, Switzerland: Palgrave / MacMillan, 2017.

Mélice, Anne. "Le kimbanguisme et le pouvoir en RDC entre apolitisme et conception théologico-politique." *Civilisations* 58, no. 2 (2009): 59–80.

Meyer, Birgit. "Aesthetics of Persuasion: Global Christianity and Pentecostalism's Sensational Forms." *South Atlantic Quarterly* 109, no. 4 (2010): 741–63.

———. "Commodities and the Power of Prayer: Pentecostalist Attitudes towards Consumption in Contemporary Ghana." *Development and Change* 29, no. 4 (1998): 751–76.

———." 'Make a Complete Break with the Past': Memory and Post-colonial Modernity in Ghanaian Pentecostalist Discourse." *Journal of Religion in Africa* 28, no. 3 (1998): 316–49.

———. *Sensational Movies Video, Vision, and Christianity in Ghana*. Berkeley: University of California Press, 2015.

Meyer, Birgit, ed. *Aesthetic Formations. Religion, Media, and the Question of Community*. New York: Palgrave Macmillan, 2009.

Mukanya Kaninda-Muana, Jean-Bruno. 2008. *Église catholique et pouvoir au Congo / Zaïre*. Paris: Harmattan.

Ndongala Maduku, Ignace. *Autoritarismes étatiques et régulation religieuse du politique en République démocratique du Congo: Analyse discursive de la parole épiscopale catholique sur les élections (1990–2015)*. PhD dissertation, Faculté des arts et des sciences: Institute d'études religieuses, Université de Montréal, 2006.

Nolte, Insa, Olukoya Ogen, and Rebecca Jones, eds. *Beyond Religious Tolerance: Muslim, Christian and Traditionalist Encounters in an African Town*. Suffolk, UK, and Rochester, NY: James Currey, 2017.

Olusola Ajibade, George. 2017. "Sàngó's Thunder: Poetic Challenges to Islam and Christianity." In *Beyond Religious Tolerance: Muslim, Christian and Traditionalist Encounters in an African Town*, edited by Insa Nolte, Olukoya Ogen, and Rebecca Jones, 75–94. Suffolk, UK, and Rochester, NY: James Currey, 2017.

Parsitau, Damaris. S. "Sounds of Change and Reform: The Appropriation of Gospel Music and Dance in Political Discourses in Kenya." *Studies in World Christianity* 14, no. 1 (2008): 55–72.

Pype, Katrien. "Branhamist Kindoki: Ethnographic Notes on Connectivity, Technology and Urban Witchcraft in Contemporary Kinshasa." Chap. 5 in *Pentecostalism and Witchcraft: Spiritual Warfare in Africa and Melanesia*, edited by Knut Rio, Michelle MacCarthy, and Ruy Blanes. Cham, Switzerland: Palgrave Macmillan, 2017.

———. "Dancing for God or for the Devil: Pentecostal Discourse on Popular Dance in Kinshasa." *Journal of Religion in Africa* no. 3–4 (2006): 296–318.

———. "Fighting Boys, Strong Men and Gorillas: Notes on the Imagination of Masculinities in Kinshasa." *Africa: Journal of the International African Institute* 77, no. 2 (2017): 250–71.

———"The Liveliness of Pentecostal-Charismatic Popular Culture in Africa." Chap. 14 in *Pentecostalism in Africa: Presence and Impact of Pneumatic Christianity in Postcolonial Societies*, edited by Martin Lindhardt. Leiden, Netherlands: Brill, 2015.

———. *The Making of the Pentecostal Melodrama: Religion, Media, and Gender in Kinshasa*. New York: Berghahn Books, 2012.

———. "On Interference and Hotspots: Ethnographic Explorations of Rural-Urban Connectivity in and around Kinshasa's Phonie Cabins." *Mededelingen der Zittingen van de Koninklijke Academie voor Overzeese Wetenschappen* 62, no. 2 (2016): 229–60.

———. "Religion, Migration and Media Aesthetics: Notes on the Circulation and Reception of Nigerian Films in Kinshasa." Chap. 9 in *Global Nollywood: The Transnational Dimensions of an African Video Film Industry*, edited by Matthias Krings and Onookome Okome. Bloomington: Indiana University Press, 2013.

Smith, James H., and Rosalind I. J. Hackett, eds. *Displacing the State: Religion and Conflict in Neoliberal Africa*. Notre Dame, IN: University of Notre Dame Press, 2017.

Soares, Benjamin. "Introduction: Muslim-Christian Encounters in Africa." In *Muslim-Christian Encounters in Africa*, edited by Benjamin Soares, edited by B. Soares, 1–16. Leiden, Netherlands: Brill, 2006.

Spitulnik, Debra. "Alternative Small Media and Communicative Spaces." In *Media and Democracy in Africa*, edited by Goran Hyden, Michael Leslie, and Folu F. Ogundimu, 177–205. New Brunswick, NJ: Transaction, 2002.

Taru, Josiah. "Mobile Applications and Religious Processes among Pentecostal Charismatic Christians in Zimbabwe." In *Anthropological Perspectives on the Religious Uses of Mobile Apps*, edited by Jacqueline H. Fewkes, 153–73. London: Palgrave MacMillan, 2019.

Think Tank Architecture Sogema. "Grand Marché Central: Reconstruction du grand marché central de Kinshasa (République Démocratique du Congo)." Press document. November 2023.

Van Dijk, Rijk. 2001. "Witchcraft and Scepticism by Proxy: Pentecostalism and Laughter in Urban Malawi." In *Magical Interpretations, Material Realities: Modernity, Witchcraft and the Occult in Postcolonial Africa*, edited by Henrietta Moore and Todd Sanders, 97–117. London: Routledge, 2001.

Warner, Michael. "Publics and Counterpublics (abbreviated Version)." *Quarterly Journal of Speech* 88, no. 4 (2002): 413–25.

CHAPTER 11

"Let Us Offer Thanks for the Nation of Ghana"

Indigenous Harvest Festival as a Civil Ceremony of Thanksgiving

Mariam Goshadze

I. INTRODUCTION

In August 2016 I attended a Thanksgiving event at the Presbyterian Church of Ghana in Osu, one of the central neighborhoods in Accra. The event— "Remembering the Living Dead: A Christian Response to the Offering of Kpokpoi to the Departed"—was organized in celebration of *Hɔmɔwɔ*, the harvest festival of the Ga people. Reverend Dr. Philip Laryea, one of the most prominent Ga scholars of religion, was invited for the occasion to deliver a lecture on revisiting "the past traditional values" and salvaging tradition. The assorted audience boasted both Ga and non-Ga members of the Ebenezer Presbyterian Church. The space was decorated with a large colorful poster commemorating the occasion; photographers, journalists, and cameramen had already positioned themselves strategically to document the occasion without interruptions. Prominent visitors were seated to the right of the speaker's platform; to its left, the church choir was preparing to launch the event with a musical introduction. The prized guest of honor was the paramount chief of Osu traditional area, where the ceremony was taking place. In his short address, Nii Kinka Dowuona VI professed his dedication to bridging the gap between "tradition" and "god," referring to the long-standing schism between traditional religion and Christianity.

The Thanksgiving initiative was first organized by the Christian Council of Ghana (CCG) in culmination of the 2015 Hɔmɔwɔ season. This annual festival reaffirms the bonds between the living and the deceased members of the Ga community.[1] The Ga have allegedly occupied the territory of present-day Accra since the early sixteenth century. In line with Ghana's customary law introduced during the British colonial control as a means to facilitate regional distribution of authority between various indigenous communities in the country, the Ga are the rightful owners and guardians of Accra's lands. Unlike other groups in Ghana, the Ga are not centralized; rather, they are separated into six individual townships, each with its own hierarchy of traditional leadership. Even so, regardless of their township affiliation, all Ga are believed to be part of the same group with a shared language, history, and practices. Hɔmɔwɔ is the prime Ga celebration common to all townships; in the words of Marion Kilson, it is "the quintessential celebration of Ga ethnic identity," and the only Ga harvest ceremony that belongs to all Ga people.[2] Preparations for Hɔmɔwɔ include a one-month period of quiet called *ŋmaadumɔ*, which marks the ritual planting of millet by the *wulomɛi*, the Ga priests, to mark the commencement of the planting season.[3] In common parlance, the custom is known as "the ban on drumming and noise-making" or, more recently, as "the ban on noise." *Ŋmaadumɔ* can be recognized as a type of sonic fast, imposed on both Ga and non-Ga citizens, for the sake of fostering a comfortable environment for *jemawɔji*—the Ga deities who visit around this time to facilitate a smooth harvest season. At the present time, the Ga traditional lands constitute all of Accra proper, which means that throughout the months of May and June, the city's tourist hubs, entertainment venues, and religious groups are obliged to be sonically reticent.

The "ban on drumming and noise-making" escalated into a matter of national concern in the late 1990s. Amid rapid Pentecostalization of Accra, inflow of labor migrants who had no affiliation with the autochthonous Ga, and liberalization of media, the Ga authority in the city was significantly unsettled. These developments deteriorated interfaith relations between the Ga "traditionalists" and the ill-disposed Pentecostal / Charismatic congregations, triggering a ripple effect of resistance among the former. When members of Pentecostal / Charismatic congregations refused to temper their sonically spirited worship sessions in the late 1990s, the friction culminated in violent physical confrontations and assaults on the straying churches.[4] The state responded immediately by resurrecting the 1995 noise-abatement bylaw and mobilizing the Nuisance Control Task Force, a special interinstitutional body at the helm of regulating urban sonic ambience. The newly imposed aural control was publicized as a remedy for the pressing problem of noise pollution in the city, yet in practice the task force, which underwent certain organizational changes throughout the years, continues to operate exclusively within the ban.

Although the state-mediated conflict resolution initiative is interesting in its own terms, in this chapter I would like to focus on a peace-building venture launched by the Christian Council of Ghana in the aftermath of the tensions. The joint Hɔmɔwɔ-Thanksgiving event briefly addressed in the opening has been held in select mainline churches since 2015. Publicized as a bold interfaith enterprise geared toward communal harmony and national advancement, the initiative has received generous attention in the media. While it professes sympathy toward the spirit of reconciliation, I suggest that the venture has ambivalent implications. On the one hand, it champions acceptance of the "meaning" behind traditional celebrations, fosters enhanced comprehension of traditional knowledge, and seeks to bolster communal harmony. On the other hand, however, by rendering traditional practices "safe" for Christian or secular consumption, it disengages them from Ga religious cosmology and places them in the category of "culture," an enterprise that lays bare the skewed epistemological chain of command in Ghana.

II. RUPTURE AND CONTINUITY

Because the focus of this volume is the trajectory of Evangelical Christianity in Africa, it is crucial to outline where an interfaith initiative that seeks to celebrate a traditional festival in the name of inclusivity fits into the Evangelical interfaith practice more broadly. Since the 1990s, born-again Evangelical denominations essentially have stolen the spotlight in Ghana,[5] and in Africa at large.[6] Pronounced as the long-awaited harbinger of non-Western Christianity in Africa,[7] as a "vitalistic" movement,[8] or simply as "more responsive to contemporary needs in Africa,"[9] these born-again denominations maintain an ambiguous relationship with traditional beliefs. On the one hand, they romanticize rupture with the past life believed to be fraught with misbelief and sin; on the other hand, their very identity is defined by how it contrasts with traditional religion, often conceptualized as "culture," which inadvertently marks them as "Africanized." Here, my interpretation of "Africanization" aligns with Birgit Meyer's argument that it denotes both positive and negative incorporation of indigenous elements in the process of identity building.[10] The patent antitraditionality of Pentecostal / Charismatic churches derives, first and foremost, from their acknowledgment of spiritual forces that operate within a shared ontological frame.[11] This framework, of course, provides no reason to disregard the detrimental effects of "othering" that Pentecostal / Charismatic Christianity engages in, an exercise that consumes everything "cultural" broadly defined—traditional music, language, dance, and clothing.

While a shortage of constructive dialogue with traditional religion was also a notable feature of the so-called mission of mainline Evangelical churches that came earlier, they did not outwardly reject the traditional worldview and instead targeted select features, such as libation pouring, ancestor veneration, and ritual sacrifice. The rest was labeled as "culture" and judged to be worthy of preservation. The second half of the twentieth century witnessed an increased tolerance toward indigenous cosmology on the part of mainline churches. This shift can be ascribed to majority-African leadership in the post-independence period, as well as major competition from African Initiated Churches that not only condoned but also celebrated African spirituality.

Regrettably, the honeymoon stage between Christianity and traditional religion met its end with the rise of Pentecostal / Charismatic churches. Against the backdrop of continuous verbal attacks on traditional practice by leaders of born-again denominations, their active denouncement of culture as "fetish," and abrupt Pentecostalization of all forms of public discourse, some hardline Ga "traditionalists" interpreted the late 1990s sonic transgressions as a full-fledged Christian onslaught on their lifeworld. The lumping together of all Christian churches in an "us" against "them" discourse was made possible by a simultaneous process of Charismatization that occurred in the mainline denominations. An unparalleled prominence of Pentecostal / Charismatic churches throughout the past decades and the ensuing erosion of interest in the older churches on the part of the youth prompted mainline churches to develop survival strategies that emulated some of the Charismatic modus operandi, such as exuberant worship, Christocentrism, emphasis on healing, speaking in tongues, and deliverance.[12] Although the majority of the Ga continued to distinguish between the more "respectful" mainline churches and the "insolent" Pentecostal / Charismatic transgressors, the 2010s interfaith initiatives launched by some of the Christian Council of Ghana should be seen as a gamble to stitch back the tattered interfaith trust.

III. "THIS FESTIVAL IS ABOUT PROBLEM-SOLVING"

The Hɔmɔwɔ-Thanksgiving initiative was the brainchild of Reverend Dr. Kwabena Opuni-Frimpong, who at the time was the general secretary of the Christian Council of Ghana. The council was born in 1929 as a venture to create official representation for the mainline churches in the country, especially when engaging with other religious bodies or the state. As proclaimed on its official website, the mission of the Christian Council is "to contribute to achieving Justice, Unity, Reconciliation and Integrity of Creation among various sectors of Ghanaian society and provide a forum for joint action on issues of common interest."[13] Today, the council services more than thirty churches, including the classical Evangelical denominations such as the Methodist Church of Ghana, Evangelical Presbyterian Church, Ghana Baptist Convention, Evangelical Lutheran Church, and others. Its annual meetings are designed to identify and negotiate a shared position in regard to national and local issues, as well as to coordinate interdenominational and interreligious collaboration programs.

In the aftermath of the first Hɔmɔwɔ-Thanksgiving event in 2015, I had a meeting with Reverend Opuni-Frimpong at the headquarters of the Christian Council in Osu. My goal was to understand how the contentious traditional festival would be stomached within the bounds of Christian cosmology. Opuni-Frimpong is a charismatic individual with an extensive knowledge of traditional religion and a distinctive vision of its role in contemporary Ghana. As a fellow academic, he welcomed my inquiries, allowing our heated exchange to go way over the allotted time. He insisted that rather than downplaying the theological foundation of the festival, Ghanaians ought to integrate its wisdom into their daily lives. "The festival is about solving problems," he said calmly. "Now there are modern problems—unemployment is a problem, these are modern day challenges that must be solved in order to have meaningful *Hɔmɔwɔ*."[14] Opuni-Frimpong was alluding to a narrative that links the origins of the festival to the Ga victory over a terrible famine experienced upon settling the territory of present-day Accra. Since then, the Ga community has gathered annually to offer thanks to deities for delivering their ancestors from imminent death and to celebrate yet another prosperous and peaceful year.

Since the primary aspiration behind the Thanksgiving initiative was to mend the deteriorating interfaith relations between the mainline churches and the Ga community, the organizing committee set out on a quest for viable past models of similar collaboration. As it turns out, variations on the theme of Thanksgiving have existed as early as the nineteenth century, yet they were publicized as Christian ceremonies unrelated to Hɔmɔwɔ and dedicated to expressing gratitude to god for a bountiful yield following the harvest season. Although these services established no direct connection with Hɔmɔwɔ, they invariably coincided with the festival calendar, even though the latter falls on different dates every year.

I did my own research about the past Thanksgiving ventures in the National Archives of Ghana and found that even at the time, some were puzzled at the conjunction of the two events. Bothered by the potential entanglement of Christianity with traditional religion, the *Gold Coast Leader* reporter inquired in 1912: "One thing I wish to point out is, that the annual Harvest Festival of the Wesleyan Church here always falls on the very Sunday as the Homowo. I do not see how these can coincide as the Harvest is of a Christian origin and not fetish: how can the two festivities then come in together, when the one is Christian and the other fetish?"[15] A few years later, another journalist, this time from the *Gold Coast Nation*, shared his concerns over the permissibility of the "duplicate-festival," suggesting that efforts to "raise funds for chapel and other building or repairs, or to support the poor members of the church" were destined to fail in securing acceptance of god.[16] Even these precursors of Hɔmɔwɔ-Thanksgiving ceremony, however, had their apologists who attempted to disengage Hɔmɔwɔ from its religious connotations, suggesting that it had "very little to do with Custom."[17]

Interdenominational Thanksgiving services persevered throughout the twentieth century with little engagement with Hɔmɔwɔ festival. The *Daily Graphic* routinely reported on these observances at various mainline churches in and around Accra, packaging them as special services dedicated to the harvest season. There were, nonetheless, individual instances when a mainline church would expressly organize a Thanksgiving service to close the Hɔmɔwɔ season. This activity happened exclusively in the traditional section of the Ga *akutsɛi* (quarters), where both the congregation and church leadership were members of the Ga community. We know, for instance, that the politically engaged and prominent *mantsɛ* (chief) of the Ga Mashi traditional area, Nii Amugi II, read the first lesson at an interdenominational Thanksgiving service at the Wesley Church in Accra to round off the festival. The *Daily Graphic* reported that in a sermon delivered for the occasion, Reverend Stephens urged the Ga community "to enhance their tradition and culture and develop a spirit of unity, love and harmony," a formulation that continues to resonate with the state-led discourse on "national culture."[18]

"Cultural Enhancement" and "modernization" are prominent objectives of current state policy on tradition, following the belief that the latter needs to be refined in order to become adequate in the modern context. In this framework, the "revamped" Hɔmɔwɔ is almost invariably written into the discourse of "progress." It is no coincidence that since 2014, the Ministry of Culture has been holding Homofest, an undertaking that unifies Hɔmɔwɔ celebrations across Ga townships and combines them with other annual festivals observed in greater Accra. Akin to the Hɔmɔwɔ-Thanksgiving ceremony, the concept behind Homofest is to come together in celebrating the common past and culture. Unlike the initiative of the Christian Council, Homofest was primarily designed to increase Ghana's allure as a tourist destination. As stated in a news article on 2018 Homofest activities, "it is to encourage business development and promotion through sponsorship, create value for happiness through entertainment and pleasure, forge tourism partnerships with neighboring sister countries in a bid to promote multi-destination tours."[19]

As it happens, Opuni-Frimpong's presentation of Hɔmɔwɔ-Thanksgiving ceremony—most notably, the impetus to tap into the collective consciousness in order to solve national challenges—reverberated with the dominant "culture with progress" paradigm. With a convincing timbre in his voice, Opuni-Frimpong elaborated his vision in the course of our discussion: "They are saying that if you want to attract the blessing of the unknown, the god, the ancestors, we must go through it in their terms, and we must have a moment of silence. . . . Which makes sense if you want to solve the problem!"[20] Indeed, as he spoke those words, accentuating the urgency of reflection for transitioning to a problem-solving mode, his proposition made sense to me. When I further interrogated whether this approach meant making the festival national in character, Opuni-Frimpong concurred that Ghana needed a collective Hɔmɔwɔ to engender the right mind space for solving national problems like unemployment, the energy crisis, lack of discipline, corruption, and economic hurdles. This is no doubt a commendable disposition on the part of the former head of a countrywide Christian ecumenical body. In practice, however, Hɔmɔwɔ-Thanksgiving was and continues to be an exclusively mainline Christian initiative rather than a national endeavor and continues to be observed only by a handful of churches.

This brings us to the second motivating factor in advocating for Hɔmɔwɔ-Thanksgiving. In our conversations, the organizers explicitly articulated their aspiration to bring the "traditionalists" closer to Christian faith. Although the immediate plan is to consistently hold the program in parallel to the traditional celebrations, Opuni-Frimpong indirectly communicated the ultimate expectation to absorb "the idea, the wisdom, the intellectual weight" of the festival, just as the Christmas holiday of today recasts pre-Christian celebrations and beliefs.[21] The head of interfaith relations at the Christian Council, Abraham Opoku-Baffour, was more explicit about the sought-after "side effects" of the Thanksgiving venture. Although he recognized that healing of interfaith wounds was the primary concern, he acknowledged that the fundamental aspiration was to bring traditional people closer to the church. "Perhaps there are some who want to become Christians and they are not, so we have our own evangelistic agenda behind this," he told me as we were sitting in his office at the Christian Council headquarters.[22] As evangelism is a significant component of Christian faith, it is only natural that in their perfect world Christian leaders in Ghana would seek more than merely peaceful coexistence. It is curious, however, that this aspiration does not come up in public statements made by the CCG and the participating churches regarding the intents of the Hɔmɔwɔ-Thanksgiving venture.

Irrespective of the motivation, permissibility of joint church services continues to be a delicate subject for many mainline Christians. Roots of the argument go back to the theological preoccupation with the corruption of absolute truth as embodied by Christianity. While the Protestant Reformation unsettled the notion of a single source of truth, anxieties over acceptable deviations come to the surface when synergy with indigenous religion is on the table.[23] The CCG generously shared with me the Hɔmɔwɔ-Thanksgiving invitation it annually sends to various Christian actors. Curiously, the letter is almost apologetic in its rationalization of Christian involvement in traditional practices:

> Our involvement in the Homowo celebrations, among others, is premised on Colossians 1:15–20. We believe that if all things were created by Christ, through Him, and for Him, then we the Christians in the Ga state must join in the celebrations with the message that it is our God the Jehovah Jireh who provides for us abundantly.
>
> Moreover, the Church Service will promote peaceful coexistence between the church and the Ga Traditional Councils.[24]

As the letter shows, the conviction behind the initiative is that it is Jehovah who provides for humanity, both in spiritual and material terms, and hence, offering gratitude in its name is nothing to regard with contempt. This interpretation builds on the premise that Christian theological epistemology takes precedent over the Ga cosmology, enabling the organizers to be guided by their own exposition of abundant harvest, concurrently looking the other way in regard to the eminent role played by the Ga deities and ancestors in securing communal prosperity. In other words, theological validation of

Hɔmɔwɔ-Thanksgiving demands an alternative interpretation of the story behind the festival. "They know of one god but they tell us that god can be reached through *jemawɔji* [deities]," reasoned Daniel Lankai Lawson, the second minister of Osu Presbyterian Church in 2017. "Now we are saying that, okay, that same god that we are referring to, the scripture says that he can be reached through Jesus Christ. So, if we want to celebrate *Hɔmɔwɔ*, you want to do that through *jemawɔji*, we want to do it through Jesus Christ."[25] Although interfaith dialogue is a noble cause, the insistence of mainline Christians that the Ga ancestors were simply misguided in their belief in deities can be viewed as yet another instance of winners rewriting history. A press release published by the CCG in 2015 resonates with this disposition by proposing that the Hɔmɔwɔ-Thanksgiving service was designed "to offer Ga indigenes and residents who are Christians, and their leaders the opportunity to thank God for the year and also commit the coming years into the hands of God as it seeks for God's prosperity and abundance in the land."[26] The porous nature of traditional faith, particularly its openness to synchronous worship across religious boundaries, primed many mainline churches not to be threatened by the Ga rendering of "Africanized Christianity." Abraham Opoku-Baffour told me stories about Ga Christians from royal families who continue sprinkling the Hɔmɔwɔ ritual meal of *kpokpoi* while also attending the church.[27] There is no doubt that the late 1990s discourse on Hɔmɔwɔ lent itself to the ease with which traditional rites and beliefs were molded to Christian or Muslim contexts. Deeply impacted by the intermittent national policy of "culturalization" throughout the twentieth century, devotees of the Ga traditional religion chose to downplay religious language in favor of the more flexible "cultural" label. The reality of overlapping religious loyalties impelled leaders of mainline churches to allow exceptions or deviations from what was previously considered unbiblical. For instance, the Presbyterian Church in Akropong recently sanctioned a traditional chief to take communion. From a Christian perspective, such concessions bolster coexistence and increase the likelihood that Christianity will prevail.

Elsewhere I expressed my concern about the long-term impact of Christianization on the Ga cosmology—especially the risk of condensing Ga deities into the collective "god" and trivializing their overall role in Hɔmɔwɔ.[28] Returning to the same subject in the present chapter, I have come to appreciate interfaith benefits of the initiative, most notably the eagerness to "understand rather than condemn," which comes as a welcome gesture in response to the clashes of the late 1990s and truly resonates with the disposition of many mainline churches. It is also crucial to acknowledge that the initiative was discussed with the chief of Osu from the outset, who welcomed the idea partly as a means to build peace with the Osu Presbyterian Church, whose high-ranking officials had previously spoken negatively about the "traditionalists" as "idol-worshippers." As a matter of fact, the Ga traditional community at large positively received the proposal due to its reconciliatory fervor.

Regrettably, the CCG efforts have not been successful in ameliorating interfaith politics of Pentecostal / Charismatic churches. My inquiries with various Pentecostal / Charismatic denominations around Accra revealed their reluctance to be engaged with "traditionalists" combined with presumed futility of such endeavors. Sensing their hostility, mainline churches are less likely to extend invitations to "hybrid" religious events akin to Hɔmɔwɔ-Thanksgiving to the representatives of born-again denominations, which of course rubs salt in the wound of already tense relations with the Ga community. The overwhelming majority Pentecostal / Charismatic Christians do not believe in the benefits of compromise implicit in the soft-handed approach. A conversation I had with the leader of Victory Bible Church International was by far the most memorable exemplification of this mood. When I asked why his branch did not offer special Hɔmɔwɔ-Thanksgiving functions, he was almost puzzled by the absurdity of the inquiry: "You see, . . . we are Charismatics and I ask myself, to what effect? If it has effect, then I should have seen this effect. So, you see that it is just like coexistence, but not really changing their philosophy because to change culture, it is something beyond man. I don't think that meeting is having any effect on *Hɔmɔwɔ* and whether it has changed their thinking."[29] The majority of Pentecostal / Charismatic leaders find the efforts to hold joint initiatives futile, since they believe that cosmetic modifications cannot erase deeply rooted beliefs. From their perspective, a carrot is too soft of a motivation to harness change, and hence only strict state policies against poverty can fight the "mediocrity" that, in the words of one of my interlocutors, feeds "the culture of darkness."

IV. THE FOOD OF LIFE: JESUS OR MILLET?

Held with varying fervor since 2014, the Hɔmɔwɔ-Thanksgiving program normally includes a series of events at select mainline churches. Its highlight is the special Hɔmɔwɔ service dedicated to expounding the value of the festival beyond its traditional theological implications. In fact, the 2019 Hɔmɔwɔ lecture title, "Sparks of Divine Revelation: Ga Folklore and Tradition as Witnesses to God's Faithfulness," directly engaged with the notion of clandestine Christianity camouflaged with traditional beliefs. As an illustration of events that are typical to the program, the 2015 ceremony included an Hɔmɔwɔ-themed Bible quiz and what-do-you-know, praise and worship, prayer bazaar, and crusade.[30] These happenings are evocative of Pentecostal / Charismatic terminology and format, a clear sign of mass Charismatization of mainline churches.

The Hɔmɔwɔ-themed lectures delivered at the closing service function as the centerpiece of the program, as they are geared toward teaching Christians about the benefits of the festival and the ideology behind it. "We want to see how best we can Christianize some of the things they do," reasoned Andrew Odonkor, the district minister of Osu Presbyterian Church, who as a Ga man believes that traditional rituals should not be abandoned but rather celebrated in the Christian context.[31] The lectures function as an icebreaker for many Ga Christians, who either refrain from engaging in traditional rituals or do so with a sense of self-reproach. I heard from the organizers that Philip Laryea, who traditionally delivers the crowning lecture, is frequently approached by Ga Christians after the ceremony. They confess that until that day they had been weary of partaking in Hɔmɔwɔ festivities, even refusing to consume the "idol food."[32] It is analogous demonization of Hɔmɔwɔ that organizers of the Thanksgiving initiative reproach. They propose to look at the festival as the celebration of deliverance and subsequent abundance following the times of crisis. "And who gave us the abundance?" asks Abraham Opoku-Baffour in the name of all Christians. "It's god. So, why can't we celebrate with them?"[33]

Before discussing the nuts and bolts of the 2016 Hɔmɔwɔ lecture that I had the pleasure to attend, it is instructive to consider the 2019 lecture theme. It should be reiterated that Philip Laryea has been delivering all Hɔmɔwɔ-Thanksgiving lectures so far. Laryea has dedicated his academic career to melding Ga indigenous customs with the Christian faith. Embodying strong devotion to both Christianity and his Ga background, he believes that rescripting tradition is a matter of personal urgency. In 2011 he published a monograph that fleshes out his Christian take on Hɔmɔwɔ, titled *Yesu Hɔmɔwɔ Nuŋtsɔ* (Jesus, the Hɔmɔwɔ Lord). The book epitomizes the position of many Ga Christians who fully comprehend the exigency of conserving "cultural values" inherent in the Ga cosmology but are weary of contravening the basic tenets of Christian faith. Laryea's tactic for overlaying Hɔmɔwɔ with Christian garb is to identify the cardinal concern behind the celebration, which he maintains is human aspiration to live a long life— hence, the appeal for food, water, fertility, longevity, health, and peace.

The 2018 *Hɔmɔwɔ* lecture corresponds to the themes advanced in Laryea's book. The title, "Yesu Anokwale Wala Ŋmaa [Jesus, the True Food of

Life]: The Significance of Ŋmaadumɔ for the Christian Faith," builds on the dual meaning of the Ga word *ŋmaa*, which broadly stands for the food that humans eat and, more narrowly, for the millet planted before the festival.[34] Laryea argues that in the contemporary context, the planted millet signifies long life, progress, and development. "From my point of view, there is nothing wrong with the Gas seeking these things," he writes. "My belief as a Christian tells me that the life we seek is in Jesus."[35] To corroborate this point, he cites John 10:10 and 1 John 5:11–12 from the scriptures and maintains that the knowledge that life is vested in Jesus evaded Ga ancestors, but it surely can be grasped with time.

Laryea also recognizes the possible link between the Harvest-Thanksgiving holiday celebrated by some Christian congregations and Hɔmɔwɔ festival. He introduces the former as Ŋmaakpamɔ, or "Harvesting of the millet" in Ga language. He believes that conceptual similarities between the two holidays, as well as the shared idea of *ŋmaa* as the source of life, occasion the identification of Hɔmɔwɔ with the god's testament.[36] In fact, Laryea demonstrates that Christian hymns often refer to Jesus as *ŋmaa wala*, or "the food of life." Consider this excerpt from a song addressed to Jesus:

> Bo, anɔkwale wala ŋmaa, [You, true life food]
> Hii wɔŋɔɔ, ni efiŋ wɔ kwraa! [Stay with us, and we will not be in need
> forever!]

Recognizing these parallels, Philip Laryea and other organizers of Hɔmɔwɔ-Thanksgiving are convinced that it would be a grave mistake to banish Hɔmɔwɔ enthusiasts from Christian ceremonies.

V. SECULARIZED ANCESTORS

The formula that Laryea utilized in his 2016 lecture to harmoniously bring his devotion to Ga "culture" and Christianity together was to frame the Hɔmɔwɔ-Thanksgiving function as ancestor commemoration. Save for the introductory pronouncement of the service as "an act of Christian worship of god and in no sense a compromise to traditional customs," contents of the lecture were in alignment with any generic, secular homage to the founding fathers of the community. Laryea explained that the act of feeding ancestors with the ritual food of kpokpoi is performed exclusively as a sign of respect and in no way suggests that the dead can impact the realm of the living. This seems to be a prominent disposition among other Ga scholars who identify as Christians. In an essay written in 1939, E. A. Ammah made a case for Christians to attend Hɔmɔwɔ because it is "never celebrated in honor of the dead" who are "simply remembered" and "asked to join the living in the participation of the feast."[37] In another article, he further elaborated on the role of Ga ancestors: "We do not worship them, we remember them on public and private occasions. If we do not pour libation for them, nothing will happen. Before we eat, we put some food down for them; we remember that in the past he or she was eating with us. We think that the essence of the food is enjoyed by the ancestors even though the practical thing is still on the ground."[38] While the overall role of the deceased in Hɔmɔwɔ remains ambivalent from these pronouncements, one claim is constant: ancestors are never worshipped. At the lecture, Laryea maintained that the relationship between ancestors—the so-called living dead—and the living could be transported to the Christian context as long as the latter are remembered as indispensable in the process of community building. He made sure to note that ancestors could only be remembered as departed relatives and not in the slightest as potent beings in the lives of the living. "It appears that the power and authority that the ancestors held in the past do not exist any longer," Laryea maintained. "Otherwise, how do we explain the near breakdown of our traditional societies?" He passionately chronicled undeniable signs of dwindling deference to ancestors: "Such a thing could not be imagined in the past, that anyone could sell the sleeping places of their ancestors, let alone desecrate their tombs, because people are looking for jewelry or something of value, or worse still, remove coffins and resell them, or crush the remains, the bones, and use the powdery substance to smell [snort] dangerous drugs like cocaine."[39] Laryea contended that the only way to maintain the idea of ancestor reverence in a modern nation was to look at ancestors as prominent members of society who exercised selfless devotion to the community. He drew attention to the fact that commemoration of prominent Ga individuals on the plaques of Osu Presbyterian Chapel did not denote their post-mortem potency but rather their dedication to the progress of the nation.

Acceptance of ancestors in the Christian context can be traced back to prioritization of refined interfaith relations by mainline denominations from the mid-twentieth century onward. Already in 1955 the Christian Council of the Gold Coast organized a Conference on Christianity and African Culture, where African regard for ancestors was made intelligible in the framework of the Fifth Commandment: "honor thy father and thy mother."[40] A few years later, in 1962, the First International Congress of Africanists in Accra brought together the Ghana Presbyterian Church, the Methodist Church, and the Evangelical Presbyterian Church. Reverence for ancestors and their services was the key point on the agenda, yet it was strictly set apart from "worship." Much like Hɔmɔwɔ-Thanksgiving coordinators, members of the conference claimed that adoption of African "culture" would not threaten Christian values.[41] On the contrary, echoing some of the issues raised by Philip Laryea in his 2016 lecture, ancestors were presented as worthy role models for the younger generation.

Recasting ancestor veneration in a secular light by representing it as a cultural attribute might as well prove to be a fruitful method of bolstering communal commitment among the youth. Even so, it would be enlightening both in the context of this article, and Christian interfaith approach more broadly, to outline the original role of ancestors in the pantheon of African Traditional Religion (ATR). Scholars are united in their conviction that ancestors represent a defining feature of ATR;[42] in fact, ancestral spirits are usually listed among the four primary elements that differentiate it from other faith systems, together with the supreme deity, other deities, and potent objects.[43] While there is a disagreement in regard to the actual relationship between humans and ancestors, it is generally recognized that rites performed for ancestors are religious acts,[44] and that the human-ancestor association is unbroken and reciprocal.[45] Bolaji Idowu even argues that although ancestors are on a lower footing than deities, they "receive veneration that may become so intense as to verge on worship or even become worship."[46] In his 2018 lecture Philip Laryea stressed the urgency of incorporating cultural values in celebrating Ghanaian national identity: "We need to salvage as much as we can from our past cultures," he contended.[47] While "culturalizaiton" of Hɔmɔwɔ makes it possible to frame its worth in broader national and worldly terms, the short exposition of ATR above serves to remind us that secular recasting of Hɔmɔwɔ significantly downplays the original function of ancestors in the Ga cosmology.

VI. CONCLUSION: FREEING "CULTURE" FROM THE RELIGIOUS CONTENT

What initially drew my attention to the Hɔmɔwɔ-Thanksgiving venture was the "culture with progress" branding, promotion, and coverage it received both within mainline Christian discourse and public media. I wondered whether the enterprise was yet another clandestine instrument for reasserting Christian monopoly over Accra in the aftermath of the Ga pushback against Pentecostal / Charismatic ascendance and patent command over Accra's soundscape. Initially, I thought that interviews with representatives of mainline denominations confirmed my speculations, due to the lack of refrain in divulging the aspiration to fully "Christianize" Hɔmɔwɔ in the future. Yet with time I came to appreciate the ambivalent import of the initiative. On the one hand, there is an implicit conviction that elements of traditional religion can be unfastened from their matrix of associations, purged of threatening and outdated elements, and refined to become suitable for the modern Ghanaian nation-state. On the other hand, I came to discern and appreciate the true commitment of Hɔmɔwɔ-Thanksgiving organizers to building bridges rather than fighting wars. My investigation ultimately brought me to the conclusion that the central objective of the venture, from the perspective of its main actors, is to bring the community together around their shared allegiance to national welfare and "progress," regardless of their religious background. However, the case study also brought to the forefront the long history of prioritization of certain "regimes of truth" over others deeply ingrained in the Ghanaian public discourse.[48]

Words articulated by the Osu Presbyterian minister Andrew Odonkor during our long discussion were illustrative of the ultimate equivocacy of the Hɔmɔwɔ-Thanksgiving endeavor: "The Christians are thinking, 'How can we still celebrate *Hɔmɔwɔ* as a traditional festival in a Christian context?' That is what we are working on now. It is not only about *Hɔmɔwɔ* but also about other traditional rites, which have been Christianized now—like child naming. Because there are good things in those celebrations, they do not need to be abandoned, but they need to be celebrated in Christian context." As mentioned above, it is the emancipation from religious context that calls for consideration—the expectation that indigenous practices can be forged into instruments of social solidarity. The story of "expanding" the breadth Hɔmɔwɔ is not entirely straightforward, because the audience can only inflate at the expense of the festival's deflating ritual and spiritual depth. The ease with which both state and mainline Christian actors talk about doing away with "religious" elements in traditional celebrations cannot be disassociated from the epistemological framework wherein traditional religion belongs to the realm of "culture," a likely target for bricolage, while Christianity and Islam are part of the sacrosanct domain of "religion." Ghana's 1994 Constitution bolsters these distinctions by placing traditional religion under the auspices of the customary law, further reinforcing the entrenchment of traditional practices and beliefs in the discourse on "culture."

Notwithstanding its manifestation—as Hɔmɔwɔ proper, Hɔmɔwɔ-Thanksgiving, or Homofest—the festival has become increasingly concerned with addressing "developmental issues," a trend that is consistent with national and regional patterns. On its part, the CCG initiative, with its penchant for secularizing rather than demonizing certain elements of traditional religion, seems to correspond to the more recent mainline Christian focus on cohabitation in Ghana and Africa at large. In her investigation of missionization in the Catholic Church, Kathleen J. Martin posits that "incorporation of native images and symbols" in the Catholic ritual repository is a contemporary alternative to proselytization formerly performed via vilification and othering." Indeed, "suggesting and maintaining the appearance of similarity and integration" is an integral part of the Hɔmɔwɔ-Thanksgiving concept.[49] On an ideological level, this modus operandi embraces "ideas" and "philosophy" in traditional religion, and in practice it singles out "developmental potential" as the barometer of worth. Speaking in the context of Yoruba religion, John Peel argues that secularization, which involves working with "a highly reified concept of culture," is yet another means of rendering traditional religion "safe" and disarming it as a potential competitor.[50] Consequently, along with the discourse of goodwill and cohabitation, *Hɔmɔwɔ*-Thanksgiving also communicates the lower standing of traditional epistemology in the public discourse.

NOTES

1. Ammah; Fosu; Kilson; Lokko.
2. Kilson, 92–93.
3. Amartey; Field; Laryea.
4. Amanor; Arthur; Asante; Atiemo; Dijk; de Witte.
5. Asamoah-Gyadu, *African Charismatics*; Gifford, *Ghana's New Christianity*; Sackey.
6. Anderson; Corten and Marshall-Fratani; Gifford, *African Christianity*; Kalu; Marshall; Meyer.
7. Asamoah-Gyadu "Get up"; Kalu.
8. Dovlo.
9. Omenyo, "Charismatic Churches in Ghana and Contextualization," 264.
10. Meyer.
11. Gifford, *Ghana's New Christianity*.
12. Omenyo, "From the Fringes to the Centre; Sackey.
13. Christian Council of Ghana, "Vision and Mission."
14. Kwabena Opuni-Frimpong, interview, August 3, 2015.
15. *Gold Coast Leader*, September 21, 1912.
16. Kwor Tarpim, "The Harvest Festival or (The Harvest Thanks-giving Service)," *Gold Coast Nation*, September 29, 1917.
17. *Gold Coast Independent*, August 17, 1918.
18. "Nii Amugi Attends Service," *Daily Graphic*, September 26, 1972.

19. "Ministry of Tourism to launch Ghana Carnival and Homofest," *Ghana Business News*, April 20, 2018, accessed November 2, 2019, https://www.ghanabusinessnews.com /2018/04/20/ministry-of-tourism-to-launch-ghana-carnival-and-homofest/.
20. Interview, August 3, 2015.
21. Interview, August 3, 2015.
22. Abraham Opoku-Baffour, interview, September 15, 2017.
23. Van der Veer 1994, 197.
24. Christian Council of Ghana, "Invitation to Osu Homowo Thanksgiving Church Service."
25. Interview, September 15, 2017.
26. Christian Council of Ghana, "CCG Proposes Homowo Thanksgiving Church Service for Ga Traditional Council."
27. Interview, September 15, 2017. The meal is sprinkled on / around special areas during the festival procession—shrines, sacred spots, entrances, etc.
28. Goshadze.
29. Cornelius Adja Cofie, interview, March 7, 2018.
30. Peace FM Online.
31. Interview, August 9, 2016.
32. Abraham Opoku-Baffour, interview, September 15, 2017.
33. Interview, September 15, 2017.
34. Laryea, *Yesu Hɔmɔwɔ Nuŋtsɔ*, 86.
35. Laryea, *Yesu Hɔmɔwɔ Nuŋtsɔ*, 29.
36. Laryea, *Yesu Hɔmɔwɔ Nuŋtsɔ*, 31.
37. Ammah, 408.
38. Ammah, 102.
39. Laryea, "Remembering the Living Dead."
40. "Christianity and African Culture," 65.
41. Parsons, 2–3.
42. Asare-Opoku; Zahan.
43. Parrinder; Rattray; Idowu.
44. Asare-Opoku.
45. Zahan, 12.
46. Idowu, 186.
47. Kodjo.
48. Foucault.
49. Martin, 25.
50. Peel, 222.

BIBLIOGRAPHY

Adams, Kodjo. "Incorporate Traditional Values into Christian Worship." *Ghana News Agency*, August 16, 2018. https://www.ghanabusinessnews.com/2018/08/17/incorporate -traditional-values-into-christian-worship-rev-laryea/?.

Amanor, Kwabena J. D. "Pentecostal and Charismatic Churches in Ghana and the African Culture: Confrontation or Compromise?" *Journal of Pentecostal Theology* 18 (2009): 123–40.

Amartey, A. A. *Omanye Aba*. Accra: Bureau of Ghana Languages, 1991.

Ammah, E.A. *Kings, Priests and Kinsmen: Essays on Ga Culture and Society*, edited by Marion Kilson. Accra: Sub-Saharan Publishers, 2016.

Anderson, Allan. *An Introduction to Pentecostalism: Global Charismatic Christianity*. Cambridge: Cambridge University Press, 2004.

Arthur, Justice Anquandah. *The Politics of Religious Sound: Conflict and the Negotiation of Religious Diversity in Ghana*. Berlin: LIT Verlag, 2017.

Asamoah-Gyadu, Kwabena. *African Charismatics: Current Developments within Independent Indigenous Pentecostalism in Ghana*. Leiden, Netherlands: Brill, 2005.

———. "Get up . . . Take the Child . . . Escape to Egypt": Transformation of Christianity into a Non-Western Religion in Africa." *International Review of Mission* 100, no. 2 (2011): 337–54.

Asante, Richard. "Ethnicity, Religion, and Conflict in Ghana: The Roots of Ga Nativism." *Ghana Studies* 14 (2011): 81–133.

Asare-Opoku, Kofi. *West African Traditional Religion*. Accra: FEP International, 1978.

Atiemo, Abamfo. "Fighting for the Rights of the Gods: Tradition, Religious Rights, and the Modern Nation-State in Africa." *Studies in World Christianity and Interreligious Relations* 48 (2014): 233–47.

Christian Council of Ghana. "CCG Proposes Homowo Thanksgiving Church Service for Ga Traditional Council." 2016. Accessed March 12, 2017. http://www .christiancouncilofghana.org/Archive/CCG%20proposes%20Homowo. . . . . .php.

———. "Invitation to Osu Homowo Thanksgiving Church Service." CCG/GS/15/08/225. 2015.

———. "Vision and Mission." N.d. Accessed November 4, 2019. http://www .christiancouncilofghana.org/Pages/Vision.php.

"Christianity and African Culture." Report of Proceedings of a Conference under Auspices of the Christian Council of Gold Coast. Accra: Christian Council of the Gold Coast, 1955.

Corten, André, and Ruth Marshall-Fratani, eds. *Between Babel and Pentecost: Transnational Pentecostalism in Africa and Latin-America*. Bloomington: Indiana University Press, 2001.

Dijk, Rijk van. "Contesting Silence: The Ban on Drumming and the Musical Politics of Pentecostalism in Ghana." *Ghana Studies* 4 (2001): 31–64.

Dovlo, Elom. "The Church in Africa and Religious Pluralism: The Challenge of New Religious Movements and Charismatic Churches." *Exchange* 27, no. 1 (1998): 52–69.

Field, Margaret. *Religion and Medicine of the Ga People*. London: Oxford University Press, 1937.

Fosu, Kwaku Amoako-Attah. *Festivals in Ghana*. Kumasi, Ghana: Centre for National Culture, 1999.

Foucault, Michel. *Power / Knowledge: Selected Interviews and Other Writings 1972–1977*. New York: Pantheon, 1980.

Gifford, Paul. *African Christianity: Its Public Role*. London: Hurst and Company, 1998.

———. *Ghana's New Christianity: Pentecostalism in a Globalising African Economy*. London: Hurst and Company, 2004.

Goshadze, Mariam. "When the Deities Visit for *Hɔmɔwɔ*: Translating Religion in the Language of the Secular." *Journal of the American Academy of Religion* 87, no. 1 (2019): 191–224.

Idowu, Bolaji. *African Traditional Religion: A Definition.* Maryknoll (Order): Orbis Books, 1973.

Kalu, Ogbu. *African Pentecostalism: An Introduction.* Oxford: Oxford University Press, 2008.

Kilson, Marion. *Dancing with the Gods: Essays in Ga Ritual.* Lanham, MD: University Press of America, 2013.

Laryea, Philip Tetteh. "Remembering the Living Dead: A Christian Response to the Offering of Kpokpoi to the Departed." Lecture transcript. August 2016, Accra.

———. *Yesu Hɔmɔwɔ Nuŋtsɔ.* Akropong-Akuapem. Ghana: Regnum Africa, 2011.

Lokko, Sophia D. "Hunger-Hooting Festival in Ghana." *Drama Review* 25, no. 4 (1981): 43–50.

Marshall, Ruth. *Political Spiritualties: The Pentecostal Revolution in Nigeria.* Chicago: University of Chicago Press, 2009.

Martin, Kathleen. J. "Resistance and Change: Visual Culture, Missionization and Appropriation." In *Indigenous Symbols and Practices in the Catholic Church: Visual Culture, Missionization and Appropriation,* edited by Kathleen J. Martin, 9–38. Farnham, UK: Ashgate Publishing, 2013.

Meyer, Birgit. "Christianity in Africa: From African Independent to Pentecostal-Charismatic Churches." *Annual Review of Anthropology* 33 (2004): 447–74.

Omenyo, Cephas. "Charismatic Churches in Ghana and Contextualization." *Exchange* 31, no. 3 (2002): 252–77.

———. "From the Fringes to the Centre: Pentecostalization of the Mainline Churches in Ghana." *Exchange* 34, no. 1 (2005): 39–60.

Parrinder, Geoffrey. *African Traditional Religion.* Westport, CT: Greenwood Press, 1976 [ca. 1962].

Parsons, Robert Thomas. *Some Problems in the Integration of Christianity and African Culture in Ghana, 1918–1955.* Accra: University of Ghana, 1962.

Peace FM Online. "CCG to Celebrate Homowo with Ga Traditional Councils." July 19, 2015. Accessed November 15, 2019. http://www.peacefmonline.com/pages/local/religion/201507/248311.php?storyid=100&.

Peel, John D. Y. *Christianity, Islam and Oriṣa-Religion: Three Traditions in Comparison and Interaction.* Oakland: University of California Press, 2016.

Rattray, Robert Sutherland. *Ashanti.* New York: Negro University Press, 1969.

Sackey, Brigid M. "Charismatics, Independents, and Missions: Church Proliferation in Ghana." *Culture and Religion* 2, no. 1 (2001): 41–59.

Van der Veer, Peter. *Religious Nationalism: Hindus and Muslims in India.* Berkeley, CA: University of California Press, 1994.

de Witte, Marleen. "Accra's Sounds and Sacred Spaces." *International Journal of Urban and Regional Research* 32, no. 3 (2008): 690–709.

Zahan, Dominique. "Some Reflections on African Spirituality." In *African Spirituality: Forms, Meanings, and Expressions,* edited by Jacob K. Olupona, 3–26. New York: Crossroad Publishing, 2009.

CHAPTER 12

"I Am a Witch for Jesus!"

Confronting Ritual Praxis, Symbolic Violence, and Trauma in African Evangelical Pentecostalism

Afe Adogame

INTRODUCTION

In December 2011, a controversial YouTube video clip went viral, evoking prolonged virtual public discourse, outrage, and vexed commentaries. This resulted when Bishop David Oyedepo, the general overseer of the evangelical Pentecostal megachurch Living Faith Church Worldwide (LFCW), aka Winners Chapel International, slapped a teenage female congregant publicly, during an "altar call" at a deliverance ritual service for her unprecedented public affirmation "I am a Witch for Jesus" while kneeling at the apex of the rostrum. Without availing the female congregant an opportunity to substantiate what she meant by the phrase, Bishop Oyedepo slapped the girl abruptly. The bishop took umbrage at the female congregant's reiteration of the claim, an indignation accompanied with his brisk proclamation: "Jesus has no witches. If you do not want to repent of your sins I will release you to go to the bottom of hell." During a subsequent church worship service, Oyedepo claimed that the girl came privately to apologize to him. Not even the bishop's verbal defense of his action could pacify a livid, enraged public who, through social media, accused him of humiliation, abuse, and individual rights violation. Ikhide Ikheloa, who addressed an online petition to the Nigerian government, wrote, "Pastor David Oyedepo's abusive conduct has outraged millions of people all over the world. The government of Nigeria owes the Nigerian people basic protections from the likes of Pastor Oyedepo. Children see the church as a sanctuary. Pastor Oyedepo must be held accountable for his abominable conduct. If you believe that a child must be free from physical, verbal and emotional abuse please send a strong message by signing this petition."[1]

It was against this backdrop that human and child rights activists and a cross-section of the virtual public rose to denounce Oyedepo's singular action and his defense of it as rash, unjust, and counterintuitive. The media canvased accusations of criminal rights violation and demanded justice. Social media and the press even reported litigation instituted against the bishop by some human rights lawyers.[2] Although the author has verified none of these incidents independently, the raging controversy over social media and the tabloid undoubtedly had a backlash, an adverse impact on Bishop Oyedepo's public prestige and repute. This singular incident gives some insight into contested discourses of evil and witchcraft and into LFCW's theological imagination of benevolent and malevolent spiritual cosmologies. Oyedepo disavows any compatibility between Jesus as a benevolent being and witchcraft personified as a malevolent spiritual entity. Such religious imagery that derives from both biblical worldviews and Indigenous African cosmologies conveys African evangelical Pentecostal churches' spiritual maps of the cosmos and epistemologies of the sacred.

Generally, religious ethnography in Africa has paid little critical attention to religious idioms and aspects of the ritual dimension that are associated with incidences of ritual abuse, verbal terror, and symbolic violence. These actions, often unleashed by some religious entrepreneurs on adherents / clientele, sometimes infringe on the followers' human and individual rights and pose dire health consequences and challenges. The rest of the chapter will briefly unpack the historiography on religion, crime, and deviant behavior, drawing upon some theoretical currents, perspectives, and existing lacunae. I shall demonstrate the expediency of research attention in grasping and contextualizing the complex intersection between religion and crime, in this case exploring recent contentious ritual actions of some African evangelical Pentecostals. Thus, this chapter will focus on instances of ritual acts and symbolic idioms with a proclivity for abuse, the attendant trauma adherents and clientele face, and their personal narratives (testimonies). The essay will also focus on the public discourses of approval / disapproval that accompany such ritual actions and verbal expressions. Using case examples from southern Africa, I point to how such ritualism could benefit from critical analysis by engaging moral panic theory and social / spiritual capital theory. First, I present a brief preface of the LFCW, its belief in supramundane entities, and ritual emphasis on spiritual warfare as a backdrop to situating the deliverance ritual incident above in proper religiocultural context.

JESUS HAS NO WITCHES!: WRESTLING SPIRITUAL TERRORISM IN THE WINNERS CHAPEL

David Oyedepo, a trained architect, founded the LFCW in the early 1980s in Kaduna, the commercial nerve center of northern Nigeria and a city with a predominantly Muslim presence. In 1981 Oyedepo claimed to have received a divine mandate to start a church ministry: "Now the hour has come to liberate the world from all oppressions of the Devil through the preaching of the word of faith, and I am sending you to undertake this task."[3] It is stated that the mandate for ministry was a direct revelation, "in an 18-hour vision" to Oyedepo from the Lord Himself. Thus, during this visionary experience, "a commission was received from the Lord to liberate mankind in all facets of human existence, to restore broken destinies, to bring healing to the infirmed." Oyedepo started the LFCW as a house fellowship (cell) and with fewer than fifty members in Kaduna. Within six months, the church claims that the membership rose exponentially to 500. It relocated from Kaduna to Ota, Ogun State, to a large expanse of land now called Canaanland, which represents its international headquarters. The church has more than 5,000 branches in Nigeria; at least 1,000 branches and thirty-six missions in twenty-eight other African countries; and numerous branches in Europe, North America, and beyond.

Belief in the stark reality and existence of evil and witchcraft is rife among LFCW members and held by majority Africans, although it is hardly an African trademark, as some observers would imagine.[4] The discourse on evil, demonology, witches, and witchcraft is a global phenomenon that carries an exotic fascination. The idea of an evil entity—a witch—fondly evokes a sense of the mysterious, a malevolent spiritual agent or a malign person. Historically, witch-hunting was a prevalent feature of western societies and of medieval Christian Europe. Historical perspectives from the ancient world to contemporary paganism, Wicca, and neo witchcraft movements exemplify the fluidity of notions about witchcraft. The reinvention of witchcraft as history, religion, fiction, fantasy, and metaphor has been of scholarly interest. While conceptions of evil, witches, and witchcraft may be valorized and deconstructed as fairy tales and fiction in some contexts, they nevertheless continue to resonate within African religious sensibilities.

In most African societies and the African diaspora, conceptions of evil and witchcraft remain a robust reality confronting perceptions of modernity, although the meanings, etiologies, and modalities of combating them are fluid, diverse, and contested. How do we comprehend resilient epistemologies of evil and witchcraft from Indigenous religious traditions to African Christianities? One main thrust of African evangelical Pentecostal religiosity is the belief in the stark reality and existence of evil and witchcraft as well as in the preponderance of deliverance and healing rituals to combat them. Thus, the epistemology and negotiation of spiritual warfare make ample ritual sense. There is an observable resilience in the belief in, and ritual attitude toward, incorporeal, superhuman entities that church members perceive as inherently evil. This rapprochement with Indigenous cosmologies and ritual praxis distinguishes this conviction within global Pentecostalism and accounts largely for its horizontal and vertical mobility.

One basic feature that reveals affinity and continuity between African Pentecostal worldviews and Indigenous cosmologies is the belief in indiscernible spiritual forces. Linked to this is the tenacity with which they embody ritual enactments. Members believe that a multiplicity of supramundane entities populate the physical cosmos. However, a remarkable change is in the constitution of this spiritual repertoire, agencies, and strategies through which they authenticate ritual enactments. Most African Pentecostals share a similar mentality in their belief tradition, employing an Indigenous hermeneutic of spiritual power but casting it within new conceptual frames of reference. The bedrock of Pentecostal belief is the preeminence of benevolent powers: God, Jesus Christ, the Holy Spirit, and Angels. Within the Indigenous worldview, people propitiate benevolent powers, the Supreme Being, Divinities, and Ancestors through divination, ritual prayer, and sacrifice in order to ward off malevolent forces. Through elaborate rituals, they seek benevolent power, favor, healing, security, and prosperity. This cosmological tradition has continued in most evangelical Pentecostal churches, although the medium and object have changed. Benevolent powers within the Indigenous worldview radically translate as malevolent forces in the new Pentecostal rhetoric and imagination. Pentecostals argue that the Bible clearly portrays human life as lived in a context of perpetual warfare between the kingdoms of God and Satan. The appropriation of metaphoric language and imagery of warfare is rife in the Bible, pointing to the expediency of warfare on the part of God's forces to defeat the enemy: evil, Satan, and demonic forces. Most African evangelical Pentecostals are critical of European mission churches, as they claim, for having been blinded by a Western worldview that ignores this facet of biblical teaching and social concern.

The texture of spiritual terrorism ventilated in African Pentecostal churches demonstrates domesticity of Christianity tailored toward existential preoccupations and challenges that many Africans confront in their everyday lives. Thus, prayer, healing, and deliverance rituals in LFCW are packaged and deployed to engage spiritual terrorist attacks against sickness, unemployment, social insecurity, death, emotional stress, hunger, poverty, singleness, barrenness, and virtually all life's vicissitudes. As members frequently testify during church services, deliverance, and healing rituals, they link most existential problems to the Devil / Satan / the evil eye. It is these enigmatic circumstances, consciously located within Satan's portfolio, that serve as stimuli of attraction and conversion to these churches. People throng to these spaces of worship, imagining the churches capability in dealing with the Devil in the spiritual battles they confront daily.

Thus, most African Pentecostals are preoccupied with waging war against Satan and its cohorts. They claim to achieve this mainly through elaborate prayer rites, rituals of healing, deliverance, fasting, anointing, spiritual baptism, and night vigil services. Bishop Oyedepo invokes the fact that life can feel like a battle and insists that victory is the gift of God.[5] He remarks that being engaged in a struggle is a sign that one is living the Christian life. The biblical warfare motif provides humans with ample instruments with which to thwart the "evil eye" and the enemy's plans. The Devil is constantly active and very crafty in his attempts to thwart the aspirations of the Christian believer. There is therefore a need to invoke the promised help of the Holy Spirit and discover the immunity from pain that is the rightful experience of the people of God. Such a message illustrates what Oyedepo and the LFCW have come to represent for members / clientele. Similar rhetoric and mental imaginaries of evil are commonplace in most evangelical Pentecostal churches in Africa. Their liturgical tradition is thus a highly expressive action characterized by a heavy dose of rituals enacted to resolve individual and collective existential problems. In this vein, the LFCW, representing one of Africa's fastest-growing evangelical Pentecostal churches, is making a significant mark in global Christian circles through imaginaries of evil and witchcraft and ritual emphasis on deliverance, healing, and spiritual warfare.

This brief explication of LFCW's demonology and deliverance rhetoric foregrounds the pervasiveness and continuum of local epistemologies of spiritual constitution and agency in African evangelical Pentecostal ritual cosmology, thus accounting for their popularity and swelling clientele in Africa and the African diaspora. I shall demonstrate in the section "Doing

Things in God's Name: Religion and Crime within African Religious Landscapes" how this quest for sustaining social harmony, cosmic balance, and human flourishing is coterminous with the allure of evangelical Pentecostal entrepreneurs and ritual landscapes. Ensuing in the process is the tendency, sometimes, for members, clients' vulnerability, and exposure to crime-related attitudes, behavior, and practices at the behest of unsuspecting aberrant leadership.

THEORIZING RELIGION AND CRIME

Research on religion and crime remains a novel, burgeoning area of study in the purview of sociology of religion and criminology. In the last few decades, both fields advanced a variety of theories to explain attitudes and behaviors. Researchers sought mainly to grasp whether being more or less religious has anything to do with why people do or do not break the law. Travis Hirschi and Rodney Stark's (1969) landmark *Hellfire and Delinquency* pioneered empirical scholarship into the relationship between religion and crime and concluded that religious commitment among youth was unrelated to measures of delinquency. Both found no difference between frequent church attendees and those who did not attend church frequently and their propensities for engaging in criminal behavior.[6] Neither did they see any major distinctions between inclinations to engage in criminal behavior relative to students who believed in the Devil and life after death, and those who did not believe in an afterlife or supernatural cosmos. In sum, they suggested that religion has a minimal impact on criminal offending and that the religion-crime relationship is specious. This pioneering work generated a stir among scholars, spawning considerable debate. However, Stark reconceptualized *Hellfire and Delinquency* by developing a theory of religious contexts in which he contended that sustaining religion through interaction and fostering a collective consensus on the importance and value of religion promote conformity to societal norms and reinforce religion as a structural safeguard against crime.[7]

This initial theorizing produced the moral communities hypothesis and was consequential in a plethora of studies seeking to untangle the nexus between religion and crime, and exploring how religious groups, regions, and nations may heighten the influence of personal religious beliefs on attitudes and behaviors. "Stark's hypothesis predicted religion would successfully deter delinquency in moral communities only. Conversely, little or no effect of religiosity would be expected for individuals residing in largely secularized communities. . . . This moral communities' thesis provided an important theoretical framework for understanding why some studies of delinquency yielded an inverse relationship between religious commitment and delinquency, and other studies failed to generate such inverse relationship."[8] Byron R. Johnson and Sung Joon Jang noted further, "Though the moral communities' thesis remains a perspective of interest, scholars have approached the religion-crime nexus from a number of different methodological as well as theoretical perspectives and by doing so have helped to clarify the role of religion." Mostly, empirical findings suggest an inverse relationship between religion and crime, although conclusions are sometimes ambiguous and conflicting. Melvina Sumter demonstrated that though this relationship between religion and crime is popularized as inverse, such a relationship within criminological and sociological scholarship remains conversational, given divergent conceptions / conceptualizations of religion.[9] As Cullen opines, "The Hellfire approach got the research agenda on religion and crime off on the wrong foot—or at least off on only one foot."[10]

Some recent, important studies and reviews that charted historiographical maps in research on religion and crime deserve terse mention. For instance, Johnson and colleagues vividly demonstrated that religion is associated with less crime.[11] The latter's meta-analysis of sixty studies published between 1969 and 1998 concluded that religious beliefs and behaviors exert a moderate negative impact on individuals' criminal behavior. In the same vein, the Johnson's systematic review of the religiosity and delinquency literature, which analyzed forty studies published between 1985 and 1997, opined that religion measures are usually inversely related to deviance with a higher proportion of more rigorous studies finding this relationship.[12]

Another related research focus on the interconnectedness between religion, substance use, and recovery resulted in similar conclusions that religion negatively affected these behaviors. Andre Weaver, Kevin Flannelly, and Adrienne Strock reviewed twenty-nine studies published between 1990 and 2003 on the relationship between religion and adolescent tobacco use and found that the majority included at least one significant positive relationship between them.[13] Dale Chitwood, Michael Weiss, and Carl Leukefeld established a positive, though complex, relationship between religiosity and reduced risk of substance use in their systematic review of 105 studies published between 1997 and 2006.[14] Jerf Yeung, Yuk-Chung Chan, and Boris Lee employed a meta-analysis on twenty-two studies published between 1995 and 2007.[15] They concluded mainly that religion is usually associated with less youth involvement with substance use such as alcohol, cigarette, marijuana, and other illicit drugs. Johnson and Jang also conducted a comprehensive review of 270 articles between 1944 and 2010, exploring the efficacy of the "faith factor" in both reducing crime and promoting pro-social behavior.[16] They discussed how various dimensions of religiousness explain crime and delinquency (directly or indirectly) and contribute to criminological theories and research. Their findings suggest that "the vast majority of the studies report prosocial effects of religion and religious involvement on various measures of crime and delinquency."[17]

Besides these examples of meta-analyses with a focus on the relationship between religion, crime, deviance, substance use, and abuse, scholars have continued to offer new theoretical and methodological perspectives for grasping this correlation. Again, a few examples will suffice here. K. Sadique and P. Stanislas used an interdisciplinary approach to studying crime and responses to crime through a religious / faith-based lens. They interrogated religion as a motivating factor, as well as a means to prevent, reduce, and respond to crime and disorder.[18] R. Durrant and Z. Poppelwell provided a critical theoretical perspective to grasping how religion influences criminal and antisocial behavior, punishment, and the law; intergroup conflict and peacemaking; and the rehabilitation of offenders.[19] They contend that to understand religion's complex relations to both prosocial and antisocial behavior requires a recognition of the evolutionary origins of religion and how both genetic and cultural evolutionary processes have shaped religion in ways that influence various aspects of human behavior and the development of social institutions. Amy Adamczyk, Joshua Freilich, and Chunrye Kim provided theoretical and empirical insights demonstrating the methodological limitations in current research and the rich theoretical potential in research on religion and crime.[20] This rich, mixed-methods systematic review of empirically based journal articles, published between 2004 and 2014, illuminated what religion brings to the study of crime and what crime in turns brings to the study of religion. This extensive essay helps to grasp "how scholars are currently studying the link between religion and crime, what they are finding, and how to improve further research. . . . The results highlight the most popular theoretical perspectives, which include religious contextual effects, social control, and social learning, as well as the least popular ones."[21]

In another review of literature, Sumter et al. delineated the iterations of religion in conjunction with the theoretical underpinning of religion and crime, underscoring how certain aspects of religion reduce participation in criminal activity in two broad ways.[22] First, they demonstrated that religion seems to operate at a microlevel, underscoring how religious beliefs are associated with self-control. They observed that researchers have typically examined the ways in which internalized attitudes, beliefs, ideologies, and values have the ability to influence the behavior of the individual.[23] Second, they illuminated how researchers explore the social control aspects of religion, in particular, how factors such as the level of participation and social support from such participation reduce criminal activity. In examining religion as a form of social control, they observed that social scientists typically point to the ways in which being a member of a religious community may exert influence over decisions and behaviors people engage in.[24] Thus, gleaning from these extant studies, Sumter and colleagues did a comprehensive assemblage of the most salient self-control and social control aspects of religion that mitigate participation in criminal activity. They underscore the process in which religion functions as a safeguard for individuals against the allure of criminal / deviant behavior and address the role of social control and self-control as potential mediators to the religion-crime nexus. Sumter et al. noted that despite the findings, available research remains limited in accurately accounting for the role of self-control, social control, and religion in influencing criminal / deviant propensities.[25]

A review of a few decades of empirical scholarship indicate that sociologists nurture the belief that religious attachment or participation suppresses criminal behavior or at least tends to have a deterring influence on crime-related attitudes and behaviors. However, there is scarcity of research about when and how religious leaders commit crimes and violence (symbolic / verbal / physical) against some of their followers. The nature of the religious phenomenon calls for transdisciplinary, multidisciplinary research—scholars of religion, sociologists of religion, criminologists, psychologists, theologians, and so on. There is rich theoretical potential in work on religion and crime. Adamczyk, Freilich, and Kim show that criminology has understudied religion compared to other factors such as the peer crime relationship, reentry issues, gangs and crime, self- / social control, and economics and crime.[26] They aptly noted that "one key theoretical issue is that crime and religion could have a reciprocal relationship. The literature until now, has perhaps surprisingly, almost completely ignored this possibility." Similarly, "the leading criminology textbooks have tended to overlook the role of religion in understanding the etiology of crime, a criminology of religion and crime."[27] Cullen observed that religion remains ignored paradoxically as a cause of crime. Religion is a multifaceted experience that potentially affects the onset, persistence, and desistance of crime across the life course. Thus, the study of religion should be an integral part of the criminological enterprise and a vibrant subfield.[28]

Thus, there are noticeable drawbacks in current scholarship on religion and crime. First, extant scholarship on religion and crime, particularly in North America, has been too quantitatively driven, thus making less space for qualitative-focused research perspectives to enrich the discourse further. As Adamczyk, Freilich, and Kim aptly noted, "Additionally, for understanding recent research on religion and crime, it is important to include qualitative studies that do not have effect sizes and are not typically part of traditional meta-analyses."[29] They contend that with a systematic review, both quantitative and qualitative studies can be included in the same analysis, such as a mixed method systematic review, which they utilized successfully, and that their results are consistent, reliable, and inclusive of recent findings from qualitative and quantitative studies. Second, most of these studies seem to have overriding assumptions on how religion influences crime while neglecting the inverse connection of how crime affects religion. This tendency to equate religion with less crime, or as a panacea for crime or deviant behavior, is rather simplistic and one sided. In such considerations, a nuanced concept of religion is essential, achieved by unpacking its complex ambivalence in terms of its functional and dysfunctional iterations.

Religion as a multidimensional and ambivalent phenomenon exerts profound control over members of society. Nonetheless, scholars have mostly prioritized the functional dimension of religion while undermining its dysfunctional potentials at the same time. This inherent ambivalence of religion warrants probing into how religious beliefs and rituals can be potentially harmless but also harmful and prone to crime simultaneously. How does religion induce criminal practice, or endorse or condone criminal or deviant behavior? Does religion—"the god effect"—provide justification and an opportunity for committing crime? What happens when religious leaders have the tendency or behave in ways that are delinquent, deviant, and criminal? How should adherents / members of religious institutions who repose much trust in their leaders react or respond? What makes adherents / members accept or refrain from contesting pronouncements, practices, and instructions that they might consider problematic? What about the victims and survivors of sexual crime, abuse, or deviant behavior?

Ninian Smart's concept of religion encompasses seven "dimensions" in what he described as "a general account of religion."[30] Here, Smart first describes six dimensions: the "Ritual," "Mythological," "Doctrinal," "Ethical," "Social," and "Experiential."[31] Smart introduced a seventh "material" dimension and expanded the titles of the other dimensions: "the Practical and Ritual," "the Experiential and Emotional," "the Narrative or Mythic," "the Doctrinal and Philosophical," "the Ethical and Legal," "the Social and

Institutional," and, finally, "the Material and Artistic dimension."[32] The experiential and emotional dimension is obviously the core of Smart's analysis, indicating that the experience of the invisible world was the hallmark of religion. These various dimensions, I would argue, are especially helpful in understanding the relationship between religion and crime.

A vast number of studies investigated whether religion influenced crime and ignored the possibility of crime or deviant attitudes influencing religious beliefs and practices. Crime and religion could have a reciprocal relationship, that is, a bidirectional relationship—religion influencing crime and vice versa[33]—or criminal behaviors could shape religion.[34] As Johnson and Jang observed, "While none of these theories focus on religion as a key cause or correlate of crime, they all offer explanations of the religion-crime relationship by identifying processes, by which religiosity is expected to decrease the probability of crime."[35] Thus, the effect on crime "explained" by nonreligious variables might be partly religious, though not detected because of model misspecification. This is a reminder that causation is both an empirical and theoretical issue.[36] Adamczyk and his colleagues' call is very germane:

> It is time for the religion and crime literature to likewise fully engage the possibility of reciprocal relationships between outcomes and key predictor variables. Relatedly, future research should consider how precisely religion (i.e. the causal mechanisms) influences criminal behavior. It is likely that religious attributes have varying impact on criminal activity depending upon the context and the processes that unfold. . . . Our findings also show that a lot more could be done to study religion and crime in terms of better data, and theoretical sophistication.[37]

Religion may promote conformity through fear or social cohesion. The impact of religious beliefs and narratives on the process of desistance, or not, for people convicted of sexual offenses is important. The religious narratives constructed by adherents or followers can be both protective and risky in relation to criminogenic factors.[38] A careful description of criminal activity is the cornerstone of contemporary criminological theory.[39] Criminologists would need to expand the domain of causes and outcomes they study. They should be interested in religion not only because it may be useful in explaining why people do or do not commit crimes but also because religion may be helpful in understanding why people engage in prosocial activities. "It is important to understand how religiousness keeps individuals from engaging in criminal behavior, but also significant is isolating the effects, if any, of faith-motivated individuals, groups and organizations in fostering prosocial activities because prosocial behaviors decrease the probability of antisocial behaviors including crime."[40]

Terrorism scholars have long highlighted the importance of religion.[41] It is important, then, to study how religious mechanisms might relate positively to terrorism while simultaneously acting to inhibit regular criminal activity.[42] Research that probes the extent to which religiosity relates to crime, deviance, and delinquency has proliferated to include studies of the nature, extent, practice, and the impact of faith and faith-based programs in prisons and other correctional contexts.[43] Also, Kent Kerley's *Religion and Crime: Theory, Research, and Practice* contains sixteen rich, comprehensive, and contemporary studies of religion and crime comprising review studies, quantitative and qualitative studies, legal studies, and some case studies.[44] Perhaps, we should also pay attention to how religion could serve as a pedestal or canopy for deviant behavior, sex crimes, and religion-related hate crimes.[45] C. P. Scheitle and M. Hansmann present a rich overview of religion-related hate crime trends and patterns as seen from both police-report-based data and victim-report-based data, thus calling social scientists to pay attention to issues of religious discrimination, prejudice, violence, and religion-related hostilities, and how hate crimes could be motivated by a religion bias.

There seems to be a parallel development: binaries of focus and interpretation between scholars of religion and sociologists of religion on the one hand; and criminologists' or psychologists' approach to religion, crime, and deviant behavior. Scholars and sociologists of religion mostly focus on the functional, upside of religion in mitigating crime, abuse, and deviant behavior; while criminologists and others are more concerned with the dysfunctional, downside of religion. In order to have a holistic perspective of the relationship between religion and crime, a complementarity of scholarship that illuminates the ambivalent characteristics that shape such an intricate relationship is appropriate. Scholars of religion and sociologists of religion should consider how religion could be both a crime stopper and a crime enabler; harmless and harmful; a deterrence and a catalyst. Thus, attention should be toward the criminology of religion, the criminogenic character of religion, and the religionization of crime. The religious economy of crime works side by side with religion-influenced crime, religion-induced crime, and the religious rituals with crime propensity and proclivity. I shall demonstrate with an instance of the downside of religion how religion correlates to crime and deviant behavior.

HOLY SEX! RELIGION AND THE GLOBALIZATION
OF CRIME AND DEVIANCY

Findlay aptly remarked, "On a contracting world stage, crime is a major player in globalization and is becoming as much a feature of the emergent globalized culture as are other forms of consumerism."[46] Crime is as much a force for globalization as globalization is a force for crime. "Crime is a social phenomenon involving people, places and institutions. Crime can neither exist nor make sense without its particular social context."[47] In other words, we can understand crime more effectively as relationships that develop along with the dynamics of its selected context. Clergy sexual abuse has a history that is perhaps as long as the Roman Catholic Church (RCC). The RCC's official documents showed that the Catholic Church did not only carry a century-old history of child clerical sexual abuse but also repeatedly condemns it by successive papal authorities, organizational laws, and institutional management mechanisms.[48] For centuries, clergy misconduct of this sort was a carefully guarded secret, hidden and ignored by church officials.[49]

Faisal Rashid and Ian Barron have demonstrated, through a historical analysis, that debates in international forums and in mainstream media on the role, responsibility, liability, and response of ecclesiastical authorities of the RCC toward clerical Child Sexual Abuse (cCSA) fail to take into account both the historical roots and awareness of the problem and the historic organizational laws developed over the centuries.[50] They traced reported cCSA back to the first century and critically examined the organizational laws and institutional policies developed by the RCC to address clerical sexual misconduct up to the end of the nineteenth century. The church developed a culture of secrecy using clandestine organizational management models and institutional laws prescribed in 1568, 1622, 1741, 1866, 1922, and 1962, which aimed to manage clerical child sexual abuse. For many centuries, the Catholic Church focused on the perpetrators, the sinners, and the possibility of forgiveness. The solution was confession, conversion, penance, absolution, and forgiveness. Because of the seal of confession, the abuse remained secret. No measures capable of solving the problem were taken, and bishops aware of the abuse chose fraternal correction or a pastoral approach.[51] Thus, discourses on clerical sexual abuse hinge on sin as a cause of abuse and explanations that moral decay contaminates the clergy, the "rotten apple" explanation.[52]

A storm of news coverage about Catholic priests who had sexually abused young people and an entrenched pattern of Catholic bishops who concealed the perpetrators to save the church's "face" came into greater limelight from the late 1970s and beginning of the 1980s. With increasing media focus on clerical sexual abuse, offending priests also became characterized as pedophiles, men suffering from a pathology, in need of care, not punishment.[53] While there were earlier cases, the 1984 high-profile case of Father Gilbert Gauthe in the Roman Catholic Diocese of Lafayette, Louisiana, and the subsequent cover-up by his bishop, Gerard Frey, perhaps mark the start of the contemporary clergy sexual abuse scandal, the abominable realm of child molestation by men of the cloth and the unconscionable responses of the church. Thus, Father Gauthe became the first Catholic priest in the United States to face a widely publicized criminal trial for child sexual abuse. He pleaded guilty to thirty-nine counts of sex crimes against children.[54] The church implemented policies in 1985 to attempt to address the problem of child sexual abuse by priests. In the 1990s a new discourse that looked at systemic causes within the cultural realm became dominant.[55] The next pivotal year in the abuse crisis was 1993, when, after another series of high-profile abuse cases, the church formed the Bishops' Ad Hoc Committee on Sexual Abuse and published a two-part report called *Restoring Trust* the following year.[56] In 2002 the high-profile case of Father John Geoghan, a priest in the Boston Archdiocese, marks a watershed in the clerical sex crime scandal and brought the history of problems of child sexual abuse by priests to global attention. The accusation was that he abused more than 130 children within three decades. He was defrocked, convicted of indecent child assault, and imprisoned. A fellow inmate murdered him during incarceration. Most unsettling about this case was that church authorities knew of his history of abusive behavior but retained him in ministry.

Scanty empirical research on child sexual abuse by clergy was undertaken prior to this most celebrated case. In June 2002 the full body of Catholic bishops of the United States in their general meeting in Dallas approved the Charter for the Protection of Children and Young People. The charter created a National Review Board with assigned responsibility to oversee the completion of the study of the causes and context of the crisis. Consequently, the board engaged the John Jay College of Criminal Justice of the City University of New York to conduct research, summarize the collected data, and issue a summary report of findings to the United States Conference of Catholic Bishops. The research team presented two reports based on investigations of the sexual abuse of minors by Catholic priests and using quantitative and qualitative perspectives. The first study by Terry et al., *The Nature and Scope of Sexual Abuse of Minors by Catholic Priests in the United States, 1950–2002*, focused on the description and extent of the problem.[57] The report provided information about what happened, including the number of abuse incidents, the distribution of offenses geographically and over time, the characteristics of the priests against whom allegations were made and the minors they abused, the Catholic Church's response to the allegations, and the financial impact of the abuse incidents. The second study, *The Causes and Context of Sexual abuse of Minors by Catholic Priests in the United States, 1950–2010*, outlines the results of an empirically based study of the causes and context of the phenomenon.[58] By integrating research from sociocultural, psychological, situational, and organizational perspectives, the study sought to understand why the sexual abuse of minors by Catholic priests occurred as it did. As Terry et al concluded: "No single 'cause' of sexual abuse of minors by Catholic priests is identified as a result of our research. Social and cultural changes in the 1960s and 1970s manifested in increased levels of deviant behavior in the general society and also among priests of the Catholic Church in the United States. Organizational, psychological, and situational factors contributed to the vulnerability of individual priests in this period of normative change."[59] These studies provide a framework for understanding not only the sexual abuse of minors by Catholic priests but sexual victimization of children in any institution. Following the watershed incident of 2002, a number of consultations and conferences took place.[60] The interdisciplinary *Journal of Child Sexual Abuse* provides an essential interface for researchers, academicians, attorneys, clinicians, and practitioners. The journal has given ample space, as some of the literature cited in this section indicate, for increased networking in the sexual abuse field and a devoted research focus on child and adolescent victims of sexual abuse or incest, adult survivors of childhood sexual abuse or incest, and sexual abuse or incest offenders since the journals' inception.

Karen Terry and J. Tallon provide a comprehensive overview of major academic works on child sexual abuse in the general population, with one aim being to compare the prevalence of child sexual abuse in the Catholic Church with its prevalence in other institutions and organizations.[61] The authors found that there is little or no empirical data on the prevalence of sexual abuse within organizations other than the Catholic Church, thus making it difficult to compare child sexual abuse in the Catholic Church with its occurrence in other groups, including the general population. Relying on two sources of empirical literature—the general psychological writing on priest sex abuse and the psychoanalytic literature on child sexual abuse—K. A. Dale and J. L. Alpert reviewed the history of child sexual abuse in the church, the recent events that brought this tragedy into societal consciousness, and the efforts by the church to conceal the abuse.[62] They demonstrated how both sources of literature sought explanation for priests' child sexual abuse within the church's structure and culture rather than viewing the priest as a "typical" sex predator. In fact, Dale and Alpert argued that the guilty priests are child predators who differ little from other child predators.

Terry presents the results of the "Stained Glass: The Nature and Scope of Child Sexual Abuse in the Catholic Church."[63] Findings show that 4,392 priests had allegations of abuse—preyed on young boys in a half-dozen Boston-area parishes for decades, 10,667 victims made allegations, and the church paid $572.5 million for legal and treatment fees and more than $1.3 billion in compensation to the victims. The *Boston Globe* Spotlight Investigation extensively documents investigation of clergy sex abuse, thus implicating and indicting the Catholic Church.[64] T. G. Plante and K. L. McChesney explored the problem of clergy sexual abuse and the bishops' response to it through a variety of disciplines and perspectives.[65] Bohm et al. provided a systematic literature review on child sexual abuse in the context of the Roman Catholic Church between 1981 and 2013.[66] In a review article, Terry aptly demonstrated that child sexual abuse by Catholic priests is a global issue.[67] He warned that reports of abuse that proliferated in the United States in 2002 could give the appearance that it was an American phenomenon. By 2010, revelations of abuse had occurred in countries around the world, leading to public inquiries and commissions that investigated the crises in other western and English-speaking countries.

Vicencio Ballano attempts to bring the sociological perspective to the center stage of the debate on the causes of clerical sexual abuse in the RCC.[68] He utilized social disorganization theory on crime and deviance as the overall theoretical framework, with some perspectives from social organization, social network, and social capital, and secondary literature and qualitative data. The author examined the "diocesan's clergy's social interaction, mutual support, and social control system in the hierarchical community; the connection between mandated clerical celibacy and clerical sexual abuse; and the implication of the laity's lack of empowerment and ecclesiastical authority to monitor and sanction clerical behavior." Ballano argued that beyond clericalism and psychological causes of clerical sexual abuse, sexual misconduct by the Catholic clergy in the RCC has social roots and global dimensions, which require a structural investigation into the loopholes in the social interaction and control systems in the Catholic hierarchy as a clerical community.[69]

At the same time, clerical-collar crimes or priest sexual abuse is hardly peculiar to the RCC in the United States and other European countries. Rather, it is a phenomenon prevalent in other Christian churches and in virtually all religious traditions globally.[70] Ballano provides a snapshot of the structural and global scope of clerical sexual abuse. Although the sexual abuse scandal involving priests first exploded in the United States, reports, stories, and investigations of clerical sexual abuse persist throughout the world, including in Europe, Asia, Latin America, and Africa.[71] Thus, we can hardly consider clerical sexual abuse incidents as isolated cases. A 2017 study released by the Sexual Abuse Royal Commission showed that 7 percent of all Catholic priests were alleged perpetrators of cCSA, and the average age of victims was a preteen. It also showed that 4,444 people reported incidents of cCSA to ninety-three Catholic Church authorities from January 1980 to February 2015.[72] It is a growing global pattern in the RCC. Pope Francis himself acknowledged the global dimension of clerical sexual abuse in a Sexual Abuse Summit held in Rome in February 2019.[73] Rape committed by priests and bishops against nuns is also a serious form of CSA in the Catholic hierarchy. Priests and bishops abused nuns "as sex slaves." "The clerical abuse of nuns was a global issue and particularly prevalent in Africa, Asia, and Latin America. The Vatican received reports of priests abusing nuns in Africa in the 1990s."[74]

Deviant sexual behavior is also not unique to the Catholic Church, nor is it a recent problem as we have shown above. While clergy from various denominations (Baptist, Episcopal, Jewish, Lutheran, Presbyterian, etc.) have been accused or convicted of child sexual abuse, the RCC dominated cases in which individual offenders were accused of molesting from several to over 100 children apiece during their tenure as religious professionals.[75] Philip Jenkins argued that the concept of "normal" sexual behavior is a socially constructed reality,[76] and behavior that is defined as "deviant" has varied across religions, cultures, nations, and states. In addition, these definitions change over time, adapting to the prevailing social norms. Sexual mores were largely defined by the Catholic Church beginning in the Middle Ages, at which time homosexuality and other sexual behavior not resulting in procreation became criminalized.[77]

Clerical sexual abuse and child / youth sex crimes have remained a highly publicized phenomenon in both institutionalized and noninstitutionalized contexts in recent times. This development has heightened societal but also academic discourse on sexual abuse of children, youth, and women. Clergy-perpetrated sexual abuse during childhood represents a tragic betrayal of trust that inflicts damage on the survivor, the family, and the parish community. This pernicious form of child sexual abuse occurs in the context of institutional credibility and righteousness, whereby the abusers often use God and religious conditioning to silence the victims.[78] In the Catholic tradition, for example, a priest or bishop is described as an alter Christus, "another Christ" in carrying out religious duties.[79] The nature and context of the abuse committed by respected leaders, "anointed men of God," within their religious institutions create barriers to understanding the full impact of pain, grief, suffering, and trauma on the self-identity of victims and survivors. For the victim who has a religious faith, besides the psychological consequences suffered, the victim's faith may also become traumatized. Thus, we need to unpack the psychological consequences of sexual abuse as well as the potential consequences on the victims' faith, highlighting the search for meaning and the effect of sexual abuse on an individual's relation to God.[80] In the next section, I shall demonstrate the prevalence and proliferation of clergy-perpetrated abuses and crime-prone rituals among some evangelical Pentecostal churches within Africa's contemporary religious landscape.

DOING THINGS IN GOD'S NAME: RELIGION AND CRIME WITHIN AFRICAN RELIGIOUS LANDSCAPES

In the last several decades, sub-Saharan Africa has continued to witness remarkable resurgence, resilience, and expansion of its religious landscape, especially through its triple religious heritage of Christianity, Islam, and the Indigenous religious traditions. Several commentators now eulogize a perceptive shift in the center of gravity of Christianity from the Northern to the Southern Hemispheres, where sub-Saharan Africa is increasingly assuming a role as major hub and as player in the demographic expansion of Christianity. The public visibility and mobility of African Christianities are perhaps most noticeable within the evangelical Pentecostal churches. Thus, what makes religious institutions such as new African Christianities tick is that they remain a dynamic, growing force in public life in Africa and its diaspora. African Christianities, particularly evangelical Pentecostal churches, play a distinctive role within specific local-global contexts as those constituencies such as governments, trade unions, and blue-collar workplaces that previously generated trust and sustained broad social networks have deteriorated. It is within such a context that we interrogate how and to what extent African Christianities generate religious and social capital amid social and cultural flux.[81]

At the same time, academic researchers, more than ever before, are paying attention to religion, to the extent in which religious adherents, practices, and organizations are gaining increasing visibility. However, scholars have paid scant attention to the interconnectedness of religion and crime.

The proliferation and globalization of what some characterize as "exotic," "bogus," or "quackery" religion (Christianity) deserve further scholarly scrutiny. Scholars need to investigate how the increasing religious innovation, creativity, competition, and commodification of religion are partly associated with a kind of religious gullibility and the somewhat fetishization of healing and miracles. Media seem to have uncovered these developments far more robustly than have scholars of religion, sociologists, and criminologists in Africa. These media stories, mostly sensationalized, are usually not subject to rigorous scrutiny and research. James Beckford aptly summarized the tendency of the mass media to caricature new religious movements as threatening, strange, exploitative, and provocative.[82] Biased presentations of a generalizing nature are sometimes rooted in cultural stereotypes, commercial pressures, and armchair journalism. Public images, particularly in the media (social media), are controversial and suspect in some respects. Popular media portray movements' activities, especially in the face of internal conflicts, fraud, scandals, or matters the public consider problematic. Even where such accounts appear balanced, the exotic and conflictual aspects often predominate. Thus, if we are to grasp this new religious phenomenon, it behooves scholars to engage in more nuanced studies that will embrace qualitative (ethnography) and quantitative approaches in illuminating the complex, inverse relationship between religion and crime. Below, I shall highlight and briefly assess the few extant works in Africa and demonstrate the theoretical and methodological potentialities of transdisciplinary, multidisciplinary research on the nature of this evolving religious phenomenon. Global studies on religion and crime have so far focused on the functional role of religion in mitigating crime and deviant behavior. Similar research in Africa is perhaps at its infancy. In fact, as I shall demonstrate, none of the few existing literature related to religion and crime has engaged ethnography or qualitative or quantitative research as the basis. There has been a strong reliance on mass media, the press, social media, government documents, and church websites. Useful as these sources could be, there is the need for analysis to draw from concrete data gathered through fieldwork research.

So, while African scholars of religion, sociologists of religion, and criminologists might chart this new course of investigation, I would mention the urgency to reconsider the dysfunctionality of religion and the inverse relationship between religion and crime at the same time as exploring the functional, upsides of this relatedness. In this regard, I propose a theoretical focus on religion as a primary correlate of crime, a potential cause of crime, or a religious objectification of crime and deviant behavior. Transdisciplinary, multidisciplinary research involving qualitative and quantitative studies will enhance the theoretical and methodological understanding of religion, crime, and deviance; of religion and psychology such as the psychoanalytic approaches to ritual; of delinquency, crime, faith, religion, and spirituality; of religion, power, and morality; and of ritual, crime, and the body. It will also open new vistas in grasping religion, self-control, and social control; religion, risk taking, and conflict / violence; poverty, sociopolitical crises, and occult economies; and materiality of ritual and religion—to mention only a few.

Scholars must not treat the relationship between religion, crime, and deviancy ahistorically. The complexity of this intermix may also have to do with hegemony and power, especially in relation to the colonial / missionary encounter, and gender dynamics, for instance. To historicize the links between religion and crime in the African context might warrant a retrospective gaze at the horrendous iconoclasm of European missionaries against Indigenous religions, such as the forceful assemblage and burning of Indigenous religious paraphernalia. Such religious-influenced crimes, symbolic violence, and demonization processes were to ensure religious swapping from the Indigenous religions into Christianity. Power has become contested regarding who has the right to define religion or the authenticity of ritual practices. Religion, crime, and deviant behavior relate to the vulnerability of the female gender and the politics of the body. Why are women mostly at the receiving end of sexual abuse and crime-prone rituals orchestrated by religious leaders? Does the fact that women dominate the membership of most evangelical Pentecostal churches make them more responsive and susceptible to religion-related crimes, abuses, and deviant behaviors? Are women more attractive to spirituality and thus receptive to religious gullibility? Investigators should pay attention to the social and cultural settings within which these churches are emerging and within which such ritual performances occur. Such ritual practices with deviant behavior and crime propensities do not happen in a social, cultural vacuum. Rather, such acts reflect and embody social mores and religocultural practices within the specific milieu.

One controversial issue that went viral in social media and the tabloids, from 2014, is that involving some evangelical Pentecostal pastors and prophets and the ritual disposition appropriating material objects and their contentious claims of miracles in many sub-Saharan African countries, including South Africa, Nigeria, Ghana, Uganda, and Zimbabwe. In southern Africa, the most prominent outliers within the evangelical Pentecostal churches and leaders who came under public and government scrutiny include Rabboni Centre Ministries, led by Pastor Daniel Lesego; End Time Disciples

Ministries, led by Prophet Penuel Mnguni; Mount Zion General Assembly (MZGA), led by Pastor Lethebo Rabalago; and Incredible Happenings Church, led by Pastor Paseka Motsoeneng. We have, for instance, Prophet Temitope Balogun (TB) Joshua, founder of Synagogue Church of All Nations, and Prophet Chukwuemeka Odumeje, also known as Indaboski, as founder of Mountain of Holy Ghost Intervention and Deliverance Ministry Inc., in Nigeria; Prophet Daniel Obinim, founder of International God's Way Church, in Ghana; and Pastor Paul William Muwanguzi, in Uganda—to name a few. A simple online search of any of these religious figures will yield robust results and sobering experience of exotic headline stories and YouTube video clips.

Space will not allow for a detailed treatment of any of these narratives here; thus I will only mention a few of the most controversial topics and ritual acts. In fact, some of the few existing works mentioned below focused on some of these churches. Reports had it that Pastor Lesego commanded his congregation to go outside the church building and eat grass, as it would allegedly bring congregants closer to God. At other times, he asked some of his followers to drink petrol, which he claimed to have miraculously turned into fruit juice. There is a report that he asked his congregation during church services to lie down, and then stepped on and walked through them while preaching. Prophet Mnguni claimed to have turned rocks into bread, and live rats and snakes into chocolate before feeding his congregation with the items. Pastor Rabalago reportedly sprayed his congregants with an insecticide, Doom, to demonstrate his healing powers of ailments. Pastor Motsoeneng also lay claims to special powers to heal infertility in women by stepping on their stomachs. During an Easter church service in 2016, he allegedly offered pictures of himself as visiting heaven. Pastor Muwanguzi, famously known as Kiwedde, of Masaka, Uganda, received public censure when a YouTube video went viral of him flogging members of his congregation for not attending church service. Prophet Daniel Obinim, also known as Angel Obinim, came under public scrutiny in 2014, when a television broadcast showed him stepping on the belly of a pregnant woman during a church deliverance ritual. Thus, social media, YouTube video clips, and tabloids are replete with a litany of controversial stories and debates. This new religious phenomenon deserves rigorous scholarly attention in order to grasp what is really taking place within these settings. Ethnographic work can help open new vistas of understanding the belief systems and ritual traditions of these churches; what attracts followers to these religious leaders; and their theologies, hierarchical, and organizational structures, but also, most important, this research can uncover how members themselves respond to the perceptibly controversial ritual practices, potentially criminal acts, and abuse, and in that case negotiate incidences of victimhood.

Against the backdrop of public outcry on controversial news reports and media articles about some pastors, government and religious authorities in South Africa launched an investigative study, "The Commercialisation of Religion and Abuse of People's Belief Systems," under the mandate of the Commission for the Promotion and Protection of the Rights of Cultural, Religious and Linguistic Communities.[83] More than eighty-five randomly sampled religious leaders and institutions, including the ones mentioned above, received summons to appear before the Commercial, Religious and Linguistic (CRL) Rights Commission, under the provision of the CRL Rights Act 19 of 2002. The hearings took place across the country in all nine provinces, between November 2015 and March 2016. The constitutional mandate of the CRL Rights Commission (2017) Inquiry was to

> i) investigate and understand further issues surrounding the commercialisation of religion and traditional healing; ii) identify the causes underlying the commercialisation of religion and traditional healing; iii) understand the deep societal thinking that makes some members of our society vulnerable and gullible on views expressed and actions during religious ceremonies; iv) assess the religious framework and its relevance to deal with the prevailing religious challenges; v) formulate findings and recommendations that address the status quo on commercialized religion and traditional healing; vi) investigate the spread of religious institutions in the country; vii) enquire about the various miraculous claims that are made by religious leaders and traditional healers regarding the powers to heal and create miracles; and viii) realize what form of legal framework regulates the religious and traditional sectors currently.[84]

The most dominant motive of this inquiry was investigating the commercialization of religion, and incidences of ritual abuse, crime, and deviant behavior. The findings and recommendations of the CRL Rights Commission pertain to the regulation of the "Religious Sector," an amendment to the Promotion and Protection of the Rights of Cultural, Religious and Linguistic Communities Act No. 19 of 2002 (CRL Act) legislation. As the CRL remarked,

> This will assist all religious institutions to create an environment where they, and not the State, can effectively regulate themselves,

and hold people who bring religion into disrepute accountable, as per their various religious systems. This proposed amendment to the CRL Act will ensure that freedom of religion is not only protected but it is also guaranteed in the country and that the religious sector is given space and capacity to resolve its challenges and make all relevant recommendations to the Commission.[85]

The CRL Rights Commission acknowledges freedom to worship and freedom of association as inalienable rights enshrined in the Constitution of the Republic of South Africa (RSA), section 15(1) and 18 respectively. Nevertheless, they did not escape to mention that "facts presented, explicitly and by implication, during the hearings led to the conclusion that religious freedom has been interpreted, enacted, and exercised in ways, which cannot pass the 'reasonable man / person' or 'objective observer' test."[86] The imperative about exploitation and therefore financial matters led the CRL Rights Commission to infer that there were financial issues, which were unlikely to pass stringent tests and were not legally aboveboard. While the commission recommended that some organs of the state handle issues of exploitation and finance by the institutions, the CRL raised a serious concern that because of their exploitation of fear or other reasons, some religious leaders gave the impression that they were above the law and that no process would affect them. They would simply contravene any legal framework put in place.[87] While this inquiry aimed at protecting and promoting religious freedom and curbing apparent and prevalent abuses and malpractices, the very composition of the CRL Commission—its modus operandi, deliberations, observations, conclusions, and recommendations—met with a mixture of relief, cautious optimism, distrust, disaffection, and criticism.

Besides the proliferation of media stories on this phenomenon in southern Africa, academic attention was perhaps first drawn by the theologian Tinyiko Maluleke, through a short essay on the "prophet syndrome": in a tabloid and a journal article.[88] In the first essay, "The Prophet Syndrome: Let Them Eat Grass," he contrasts Prophet Lesego Daniel and Prophet Paseka Motsoeneng and their perceived miracle genres.[89] His title choice is perhaps analogous and mimics J. Tonda's *The Prophet's Syndrome* in the settings of conventional medicine and "traditional therapies" in the Congo.[90] Maluleke introduced both prophets in his "The Prophet Syndrome":

This year, prophet Lesego Daniel has given us at least two depraved miracles, now posted on YouTube to horrify doubters into faith. In one, Daniel instructs his sample congregants of mainly young black women to eat grass; in another, he serves them a bottle of petrol to drink. There is a triumphal smirk on his face and a disdainful tone in his hypnotic voice as he makes fun of his grass-eating followers. Prophet Paseka Motsoeneng, otherwise known as Pastor Mboro (which means penis in Shona)[,] performs his own genre of miracles in Katlehong township outside Alberton. His "miracles" seem to centre on women's reproductive organs and private parts. Some of his healing rituals reportedly require Motsoeneng to put his foot, literally, upon many a "demon-possessed woman." In his spare time, Motsoeneng is often seen driving around the townships in an expensive luxury car, flanked by bodyguards.[91]

In the analysis of the "wealthy" prophets, he also referred to Temitope Balogun (TB) Joshua, a Nigerian prophet and founder of Synagogue Church of All Nations, and the tragic incident of the multistorey guesthouse collapse with several fatalities including eighty-four South Africans at his church international headquarters in Lagos. Maluleke posed a rhetorical question: But why do people patronize these modern-day prophets? Although evidence of any empirical data and the basis of analysis were not immediately apparent, Maluleke through a rather normative approach presented a critical theological extrapolation that was somewhat convincing. He posited "possible theological and psychological explanations for this peculiar behavior" but argued, "the socioeconomic rationale of these collective actions must be prioritized." The anecdotal evidence and generalizations usually adduced by commentators to explain followers' appeal to prophets, useful as they may be, would need to derive from ethnographic data. Maluleke seemed to address the question of what endears people to these prophets by pointing to religious gullibility, feigned charisma, poverty, greed, corruption, socioeconomic crises, and the indiscriminate quest and hope for miracles.

Maluleke admitted that the answer to the question of why people patronize these modern-day prophets is a complex one. At the heart of it, he argued, is a toxic model of leadership. While these "men of god" may be the most dramatic examples, they are also part of a large and growing guild of leaders who display the same warped values in various sectors of society.[92] Maluleke contrasted the situation of prophets and followers in these Charismatic churches to what transpires with politicians and citizenry within the local context of South Africa, producing a kind of sociopolitical critique. He remarked that these churches, through their beliefs and practices, not only reproduce prevailing social stratifications, but they also affirm and reinforce them in ways that are contrary to the Constitution. "We may sneer at pastors like Mnguni, Daniel and Motsoeneng—but corporate and political leaders are doing the same thing in other ways. The levels of inequality and poverty in our society are ripe conditions for toxic leaders to thrive."[93] Maluleke concluded, "Were Jesus to return today, he would find a country not only battling with the triple challenges of poverty, unemployment and inequality, but also with the challenges of corruption, bad religion and toxic leadership." He goes on to say, "I suggest that all of these are at play in the bizarre practices of a few Charismatic church groups and their leaders, such as the 'snake pastor' phenomenon that has raged in our media in the second half of 2015."[94]

While Maluleke's approach seemed a pragmatic theological critique, M. S. Kgatle, K. T. Resane, and T. D. Mashau were overtly normative and theologically prescriptive in many respects.[95] Kgatle reflected theologically on what he calls "the unusual practices within some neo-Pentecostal churches in South Africa," focusing on four case examples, namely,[96] Rabboni Centre Ministries, led by Pastor Daniel Lesego; End Time Disciples Ministries, led by Prophet Penuel Mnguni; Mount Zion General Assembly (MZGA), led by Pastor Lethebo Rabalago; and Incredible Happenings Church, led by Pastor Paseka Motsoeneng. Kgatle highlights the possible theological, psychological, and socioeconomic explanations for such practices and concludes that the socioeconomic factors are the main explanation for the support of these unusual practices. The conclusions, which hardly derive from any evident ethnographic data and analyses, along with the lack of rationale or basis for evaluation and recommendations, bear marks of theological normativity. Resane employed the biblical narrative of Daniel and Nebuchadnezzar (Daniel 4) as a metaphor for understanding "dangerous practices" observed in some new Charismatic churches in South Africa and justifies government intervention through the CRL as a way of protecting citizens from ensuing harmful effects of these practices.[97] Mashau and Kgatle proposed the African Christian Theology of Ubuntu as an alternative to what they called the culture of greed in prosperity gospel.[98] With a rather pejorative stance and a contested definition of prosperity theology, the authors prescribed, "African Christianity will be able to stand against any form of the gospel that seeks to promote the spirit of consumerism and idolisation of material and physical health as the ideal that must be pursued."[99]

Two recent academic works that provide some theoretical richness and depth to the phenomenon of prophets and controversial rituals within some African evangelical Pentecostal churches are the essays by Lee Scharnick-Udemans and Federico Settler.[100] Although both articles show hardly any ethnographic evidence from which their theorizing draw, the former points to the neglect of gender perspectives as a blind spot in the discourse of religion, media, and culture. Using the example of the CRL in South Africa, the essay makes a persuasive case "for theorizing the study of gender, religion and the media outside of the epistemological and contextual frame of Western sensibilities and motivates instead for a feminist intersectional lens to avoid the double bind of sexism and racism."[101] The author demonstrated vividly that the media's framing of the topic—the rise of unorthodox and exploitative religious practices—for newsworthiness achieved two results. First, it played a critical role in bringing the issue to the attention of the public and state authorities. Second, it framed the gender implications of these "stories" as secondary to the more sensational and entertaining spectacles of the religious leaders and to the economics of the exploitation.[102]

Scharnick-Udemans highlighted the intersections of power and authority in relation to race politics and the defining power of religion. In this case, the media reporting and the CRL, in response to the rise of the so-called unorthodox and exploitative, failed to treat the Charismatic Black pastors at the center of the controversies as religious leaders in their own right. This perspective also resulted in their female constituencies' depiction as gullible victims of fraudsters and as insincere religious believers with their own stories ignored. She aptly concluded that the simple caricaturizing of the pastors / prophets as nouveau riche and zealous evangelicals denies them of agency. This depiction, coupled with the utter disregard of women's voices and experiences, undermines the religious legitimacy of the churches, their leaders and followers. As she noted, "A focus on the experience of women also requires scrutiny of the possibilities and limitations of individual agency in its many variances."[103] Maluleke's remark on the victimization of women also alludes to the complexity of this gender power dynamics: "The god of Lesego Daniel of Rabboni Ministries in Garankuwa asked young women and a few young men to eat grass. And they did. The same god later desired members to partake in the drinking of petrol, and again the young women took the lead. Patriarchy is in charge in the church as it is in society. . . . The gospel according to these pastors appears to teach that the way to salvation is via humiliation and indignity."[104]

Settler provided a useful theoretical lens on the materiality of religion, in grasping the public discourse on prophets and their ritual emphasis, with respect to contestations of the "embodied," what constitutes religion, and "things," the appropriation of everyday ritual objects.[105] He drew attention to public criticism about the events and CRL reports to demonstrate that much of the legal and theological debates frame the use of everyday things for religious purposes, or religious objects for social improvement. Settler contended that the sale of prayer towels, blessed water, and oils, or the use of grass, fridges, snakes, and heavenly pictures all predate the public debates about religious freedom and exploitation of people's beliefs.[106] In historicizing the events and contestations over the use of everyday objects and animals in religious rituals in southern Africa, he suggested that such conditions, forces, and relations are so historically entangled with racial schemas that taxonomies of the sacred are invariably contested over what objects or things come to be regarded as sacred and religious, or not. Settler argued that "the material turn in religion also marks the shift from institutional religion to the everyday religion—mundane routines and practices related to religion or religious beliefs enacted in the course of everyday life."[107]

The religious phenomenon of diagnosis and remedy, using everyday artifacts or plants, is not new within the broader religious context of South Africa. What people consider as new are Christian churches who use the material and the embodied reception as the locus of their religious work and practices, and through which they contest and assert boundaries over what counts as sacred.[108] Settler homed in on the point that contestations over sacred things and their embodied reception draw on race and gender. Thus, he concluded, "the religious activation of everyday things is disruptive but productive; provocative but deliberative; and ultimately decolonial—in that it disrupts the knowledge and power matrix in religion—and postcolonial, because it draws on available, though contested, imperial taxonomies, archives, and artefacts to assert new meaning."[109]

Three recent dissertations are worthy of mention, in spite of their limited scope and grasp. S. B. Khanyile's sociological work explored how the social media such as Facebook represent the church performances and practices of "controversial" South Africa neo-Pentecostal church End Time Disciples Ministries, led by Prophet Penuel.[110] Utilizing a multimodal critical discourse analysis, the study analyzed online representations of church performance but also sought to understand how audiences decode, interpret, and consume messages and representational exhibitions. S. Pondani's was a rather normative work that investigated the phenomenon of healing and power dynamics in neo-Pentecostal South African churches, demonstrating how what was called "Prophets of Doom" resorts to "dangerous healing practices" that endanger the lives of congregants desperate for miracles.[111] Schmidt's is a dissertation on the regulation of religion in the Rainbow Nation, exploring how possible limits to rights related to the freedom of religion are socially negotiated and religious practices politicized.[112]

I have briefly sketched above a few attempts at grasping the phenomenon of evangelical Pentecostal prophets / pastors and controversial rituals in sub-Saharan Africa through theological, sociological, and feminist intersectional lenses. These works share a commonality; none of them derived from or were based on rigorous ethnographic work on the development in these churches. Nonetheless, in spite of the normative theological approach by some of the scholars, each of these works brings some theoretical, conceptual, or methodological insight to understanding the intricate relationship between religion, and crime and deviant behavior. Future research must go beyond anecdotal evidence and raise crucial questions that illuminate not only the complexities of religion, crime, and deviant behavior in these churches but also how members or followers navigate these experiences and behavior in their everyday ritual lives. More interdisciplinary approaches with mixed methods, embracing qualitative and quantitative approaches, are needed to unpack the nexus between religion and crime, the upsides and downsides of religion, how religion could be both a crime stopper and a crime enabler depending on the operationalizing or instrumentalizing agency. As context also matters, we must historicize these incidents and situate them within the specific social context of occurrence, as well as contrasted with global impact.

In the last two sections of this chapter, I shall shed some light, albeit briefly, on how moral panic theory and social capital theory may contribute to the theoretical and methodological grasp of the phenomenon. I suggest a caveat that such theorization would only make concrete sense as frames for interpreting and analyzing ethnographic data gathered from these churches and the society within which they exist and operate.

RELIGION, CRIME, AND MORAL PANIC

Moral panic (moral panics) as a theory is widely employed to delineate the intense feelings expressed as people engage the public sphere with regard to a given issue that appears to threaten the social order. The media, the government and its agencies, and mainstream religions all play significant roles in creating moral panics by evoking "unambiguously unfavorable feelings" in the public, which reiterate "the phobia and hatred" toward a particular group.[113] Philip Jenkins argued that all concepts of sex offenders and offenses are subject to social, political, and ideological influences and that no particular view of offenders represents an unchanging objective reality.[114] He examined the various groups (including mass media) who have been active in promoting particular constructions of the emerging problem; the impact of public attitudes on judicial and legislative responses to these crimes; and the ways in which demographic change, gender politics, and morality campaigns have shaped public opinion. Moral panic theory draws attention to the reaction of the public to what is assumed to be a deviant act.[115] It also accentuates the role that the agents of social control play in order to magnify or even manufacture deviance. Moral panics cannot be widely spread without mass media. The role of social media, YouTube videos, and the press is crucial in the criminalization process and in generating moral panic. Thus, mass media is one of the strongest tools for creating moral panics. How reliable are these sources, especially when we consider fake social media and YouTube videos that are products of fabrication? What methodological challenges do these media pose to academic research?

Furthermore, moral panics could not be created or sustained without the "stable patterned structure of politics, mass media, crime control, professions and organized religion."[116] Mass media is the primary source of information for the public with regard to deviance and social issues, and it may play the following roles in the creation of moral panics: it may set the agenda, transmit images, become the claim maker by breaking the silence and creating moral panics.[117] Thus, social media, press, mainstream churches, and theologians serve as moral entrepreneurs or moral crusaders who initiate moral crusades in order to influence and change the public outlook concerning the somewhat criminal, deviant dimensions of rituals in some evangelical Pentecostal churches. From our discussion above, the social media, the CRL Rights Commission in South Africa, mainstream churches, and theologians play the role of moral crusaders or moral entrepreneurs. It is within these interpretations that we can understand the pastors / prophets as one of the main "folk devils" of the moral panic creation in African religious landscapes. Thus, pastors / prophets as "folk devils" are deviant stereotypes identified as the "enemy" in the face of outsiders, although their followers and members portray them momentarily as saints, anointed men of God who should never be criticized. In this case, deviant stereotypes (pastors / prophets) and their followers or members are vulnerable figures. Moral panic is not about the deviant stereotype (pastor / prophet); the moral panic is in fact the pastor or prophet.

The moral panic theory explains the moral entrepreneurs' exploitation of the social media to manufacture moral panics. To this end, social media and the press, for example, use or even invent images and themes that portray these pastors / prophets as devilish, deviant, and criminal and their members and followers as docile, brainwashed, hypnotized, and manipulated. "The degree of success of moral entrepreneurs in manufacturing a moral panic depends on five conditions: their ability in deployment of power, the presence of the apparent threat in an issue that they can crusade, the ability to make the public aware of a particular issue, the nature of resistance they face, and finally the ability to present an 'acceptable' and clear solution concerning the issue."[118] We can understand the resistance and defense on the part of the church pastors and members before the CRL Rights Commission against the backdrop of responses to scapegoating and the repercussion of the creation of moral panic. Morality and power dynamics shape how moral crusaders generate moral panic. Michel Foucault's structural analysis of power links his objectification of crime and the criminal.[119] From the new tactics of power, there emerge two lines of objectification of crime and of the criminal. A Foucauldian conceptualization of power refers to the various forms of domination and subordination that operate whenever and wherever social relations exist. Foucault's alternative perspective of power places emphasis on the exercise of power through relationships of communication, goal-oriented activities, and imbalanced relationships rather than on the agency of the individual. Foucault states an ethnographic approach is best for its study.[120]

CRIME, MORAL PANIC, AND SOCIAL CAPITAL

The social, cultural, or spiritual capital theory is, in my view, useful in grasping the interrelatedness between religion, on the one hand, and crime and deviant behavior, on the other hand, especially against the backdrop of their upsides and downsides. The central idea of "social capital" is that social networks are a valuable asset.[121] Social capital refers to connections among individuals—social networks and the norms of reciprocity and trustworthiness that arise from them. Attendance at religious events is associated with increased volunteering. Religious beliefs can influence the meaning of volunteering in people's lives. Churches act as communication networks that foster religious and civic volunteerism. People are more likely to give money and time, even to secular efforts, if they are church members. Thus, religious communities as strategic actors are involved in processes of social, cultural, and spiritual capital formation. Religious communities such as the evangelical Pentecostal churches founded and led by the pastors / prophets constitute a significant resource in associational life. They generate new forms of community that provide a means of (dis)empowerment and social mobility in Africa. The churches establish continuities with the past as well as locate themselves as part of the processes of African modernity.[122]

Pierre Bourdieu (1986) distinguished three forms of capital: economic capital, cultural capital, and social capital. He defined social capital as "the aggregate of the actual or potential resources which are linked to possession of a durable network of more or less institutionalised relationships of mutual acquaintance and recognition."[123] Robert Putnam contrasted bonding social capital and bridging social capital.[124] Bourdieu defined cultural capital acts as a social relation within a system of exchange that includes the accumulated cultural knowledge that confers power and status. He located a set of cultural experiences, values, beliefs, norms, attitudes, and experiences as representing a form of cultural capital that equips people for their life in society. Religious (spiritual) capital is the amalgamation of the norms, values, languages, and social practices that sustain and transform the religious groups in relation to the specific contexts in which they find themselves. Religious capital, mainly a sociological concept, is the investment an individual makes into his or her religious faith. The investment is the time and physical work involved with the religious faith, as well as the personal investment in ideology, doctrine, and practice. The concept of religious capital is similar to the more general concept of social capital because it is a resource based on relationships that individuals and faith groups can access for their personal well-being but can also "donate" as a gift to the wider community. Therefore, both religious capital and social capital include investments and participation in networks and activities. The impact and influence of social networks on continued participation within religious communities are large indeed.

While the upsides of social capital are good to think with, we must not fail to capture the downsides of social capital. The advocates of the concept of social and religious capital often overemphasize its benefits in a way that understates its negative dimensions. As we have shown above, some scholars often prioritize functional dimensions of religion over and against its dysfunctional attributes. Some examples of social capital include churches, mosques, fraternal organizations, internet networks, and other groups that create exclusionary but also inclusionary social capital and their attendant positive and negative effects. Alejandro Portes identified four negative consequences of social capital: exclusion of outsiders, excess claims on group members, restrictions on individual freedom, and downward leveling norms.[125] He contended that these consequences and the unequal nature of access to social capital need balancing against the optimistic view if social capital is to be useful as a tool for societal analysis and transformation. All these groups can help build and break societies because of their bridging/bonding behavior.[126] If the amount of human interaction increases, people are more likely to help one another and later become more politically, religiously, and socially involved.

Xavier Briggs discussed two faces of social capital: social capital as an individual good and social capital as a collective good.[127] He suggested that the dark side of social capital, especially the potential for exclusion, is very evident in social capital as a collective good, a resource possessed by a social system that helps the system as a whole to solve problems. For instance, community norms can be tied to religious beliefs and symbols, and to ethnicity, in ways that exclude or imagine others. Bonding social networks can reinforce and deepen ethnic and religious distinctions and conflicts. Thus, there is high potential for exclusion in relation to social capital. M. G. Quibria explored the downside of social capital, identifying four potentially destructive dimensions of networks, norms, and reciprocities, especially focusing on urban and ethnic communities.[128] First, social capital that opens up opportunities for the members of the network—which is often based on ethnicity, religion, language, and profession—can at the same time constitute an enormous barrier to entry for others outside the network. Second, while a close-knit group can be a source of economic dynamism for its membership, it can also dilute personal incentives to work hard, as in the case of a community that is substantially supported by welfare. Third, group membership of the community can enforce strict conformity when it infringes on individual freedoms and can thus create pressure for submission to mediocrity. Fourth, network and group coordination can often lead to the establishment of negative norms and values that are self-reinforcing. How do religious beliefs help in normalizing ritual abuse and deviant behavior? To what extent do truth and trustworthiness facilitate followers and members' accommodation and receptivity toward ritual abuse and deviant behavior of their leaders, pastors, or prophets? How do we interpret the politics of the body at the intersection of religion and crime within the evangelical Pentecostal ritual world?

I contend that social capital theorizing might proffer answers to these questions, following qualitative or quantitative data and analysis. There is an intricate relationship between religious commitment, participation, and volunteerism. These resources generated within the religious groups as social and religious capital produce viable reservoirs for mobilizing members either to facilitate order or disorder. Religious entrepreneurs often exploit these resources to the advantage of some and the disadvantage of others. The display of charisma and the routinization of charisma closely connect with empowerment and disempowerment. Thus, incidences of ritual abuse, verbal terror, and symbolic violence within sacred spaces such as evangelical Pentecostal churches described in this chapter also help to illuminate the relationship between religion, crime, and deviant behavior but also trauma.

NOTES

1. See Ikheloa's online petition; "Bishop David Oyedepo Slaps to Conquer," YouTube video; John T. Didymus, "Bishop Oyedepo Boasts about Slapping Teenage Girl," *Digital Journal*, December 22, 2011, http://www.digitaljournal.com/article/316550.
2. See "Bishop Oyedepo Faces N2bn Suit for Slapping Church Member," *Premium Times*, https://www.premiumtimesng.com/news/4740-bishop_david_oyedepo_n2bn_suit _for_slapping_church_member.html. "Bishop Oyedepo's Slapping Case Goes To Appeal Court," *Sahara Reporters*, New York, September 8, 2012, http://saharareporters .com/2012/09/08/bishop-oyedepos-slapping-case-goes-appeal-court; and "Bishop Oyedepo Wins in N2billion Exorcism Slap Case as Judge Strikes Out Suit," *Premium Times*, Tuesday, July 7, 2020, https://www.premiumtimesng.com/news/93443-bishop _oyedepo_wins_in_exorcism_slap_case.html.
3. Oyedepo; see also LFCW website for "The Mandate."
4. Adogame and Kuponu, 306–30.
5. Oyedepo.
6. Hirschi and Stark, 202.
7. Stark.
8. Johnson and Jang, 118.
9. Sumter.
10. Cullen, 154.
11. Johnson et al.; Baier and Wright.
12. Johnson.
13. Weaver, Flannelly, and Strock.
14. Chitwood, Weiss, and Leukefeld.
15. Yeung, Chan, and Lee.
16. Johnson and Jang.
17. Johnson and Jang, 120.
18. Sadique and Stanislas, 2.
19. Durrant and Poppelwell.
20. Adamczyk, Freilich, and Kim.
21. Adamczyk, Freilich, and Kim, 193–94.
22. Sumter.
23. Sumter et al., 5.
24. Sumter et al., 7.
25. Sumter et al., 3.
26. Adamczyk, Freilich, and Kim, 217.
27. Cullen, 158.
28. Cullen, 158.
29. Adamczyk, Freilich, and Kim, 195.
30. Smart, *Religious Experience of Mankind*, 31.
31. Smart, *Religious Experience of Mankind*, 15–25.

32. Smart, *The World's Religions*, 12–21.

33. Heaton.

34. Camp et al.

35. Johnson and Jang, 122.

36. Johnson and Jang, 127.

37. Adamczyk, Freilich, and Kim, 218.

38. Micklethwaite, Blagden, and Winder.

39. Piquero et al.

40. Johnson and Jang, 117.

41. Juergensmeyer; Stern; Hewitt and Kelly-Moore.

42. Adamczyk, Freilich, and Kim, 218.

43. Johnson; Kerley, *Religious Faith in Correctional Contexts*; Kerley, *Current Studies in the Sociology of Religion*; Kerley, *Finding Freedom in Confinement*; Kerley, *Religion and Crime*.

44. Kerley, *Religion and Crime*.

45. Scheitle and Hansmann.

46. Findlay, 2.

47. Findlay, 6.

48. Ballano, 2.

49. Wilbourn; Isely.

50. Rashid and Barron.

51. Demasure.

52. White and Terry.

53. Doyle; Demasure.

54. Berry, "The Tragedy of Gilbert Gauthe. Part I," *Times of Acadiana*, May 23, 1985; Berry, *Lead Us Not into Temptation*; Jon Nordheimer, "Sex Charges against Priest Embroil Louisiana Parents," *New York Times*, June 20, 1985; Kohn.

55. Burkett and Bruni; Berry, *Lead Us Not into Temptation*; Terry, "Child Sexual Abuse within the Catholic Church."

56. Bishop's Ad Hoc Committee.

57. Terry et al., *The Nature and Scope of Sexual Abuse of Minors by Catholic Priests in the United States, 1950–2002* (2004).

58. Terry et al. *The Causes and Context of Sexual abuse of Minors by Catholic Priests in the United States, 1950–2010*.

59. Terry et al., *The Causes and Context of Sexual Abuse of Minors by Catholic Priests in the United States*, 2.

60. Hanson et al, *Sexual Abuse in the Catholic Church*.

61. Terry and Tallon.

62. Dale and Alpert.

63. Terry, "Stained Glass."

64. The Boston Globe Spotlight Investigation *Abuse in the Catholic Church*, Boston Globe, 2004, accessed July 15, 2020, http://archive.boston.com/globe/spotlight/abuse /index.shtml.

65. Plante and McChesney.

66. Bohm et al.

67. Terry, "Child Sexual Abuse within the Catholic Church."

68. Ballano.

69. Ballano, 1.

70. Guerzoni.

71. Ballano, 2–4.

72. E. Blackwell, "7 Percent of all Catholic Priests Were Alleged Sex Abuse Perpetrators: Royal Commission," *Huffpost News*, June 2, 2017.

73. Ballano, 5; Formicola, *Papal Policies on Clerical Sexual Abuse*; Formicola, "The Politics of Clerical Sexual Abuse"; Formicola, *Clerical Sexual Abuse*.

74. Buncombe; Christopher Lamb, "Pope Intent on Tackling Sexual Abuse of Nuns by Clergy," *Tablet: The International Catholic News Weekly*, February 5, 2019; Inés San Martín, "Editor of Vatican Women's Magazine Aims to Shatter Silence on Abused Nuns," *Crux: Taking the Catholic Purse*, February 16, 2019, accessed March 16, 2020. https://cruxnow.com/vatican/2019/02/editor-of-vatican-womens-magazine-aims-to-shatter-silence-on-abused-nuns.

75. Isely, 278; Berry, *Lead Us Not into Tempatation*.

76. Jenkins.

77. Mondimore.

78. Easton, Leone-Sheehan, and O'Leary; Farrell and Taylor.

79. Guido, 255.

80. Rudolfsson.

81. Adogame, 101–22.

82. Beckford.

83. CRL Commission.

84. CRL Commission, 6.

85. CRL Commission, 4.

86. CRL Commission, 50.

87. CRL Commission, 51.

88. T. S. Maluleke, "The Prophet Syndrome: Let Them Eat Grass," *Mail and Guardian*, October 23, 2014; Maluleke, "Between Pretoria and George Goch Hostel."

89. Maluleke, "The Prophet Syndrome."

90. Tonda.

91. Maluleke, "The Prophet Syndrome."

92. Maluleke, "Between Pretoria and George Goch Hostel," 39.

93. Maluleke, "Between Pretoria and George Goch Hostel," 39.

94. Maluleke, "Between Pretoria and George Goch Hostel," 36.

95. M. S. Kgatle; Resane, 1–17; Mashau and Kgatle, a1901.

96. Kgatle.

97. Resane.

98. Mashau and Kgatle.

99. Mashau and Kgatle, 7.

100. Scharnick-Udemans; Settler.

101. Scharnick-Udemans, 146.

102. Scharnick-Udemans, 154.

103. Scharnick-Udemans, 158.

104. Maluleke, "The Prophet Syndrome," 29.

105. Settler.

106. Settler, 38.

107. Settler, 42.

108. Settler, 45.

109. Settler, 49.
110. Khanyile.
111. S. Pondani.
112. Schmidt.
113. Cohen, 37.
114. Jenkins.
115. Moinipour, 190.
116. Cohen, 44.
117. Moinipour, 192.
118. Ben-Yehuda, 496.
119. Foucault, *Discipline and Punish*, 101–2.
120. Foucault, "The Subject and Power."
121. Field, 12.
122. Adogame, 101–22.
123. Bourdieu, "The Field of Cultural Production or the Economic World Reversed," 249.
124. Putnam.
125. Portes.
126. Putnam.
127. Briggs.
128. Quibria.

BIBLIOGRAPHY

Adamczyk, Amy, Joshua D. Freilich, and Chunrye Kim. "Religion and Crime: A Systematic Review and Assessment of Next Steps." *Sociology of Religion: A Quarterly Review* 78, no. 2 (2017): 192–232.

Adogame, Afe. *The African Christian Diaspora: New Currents and Emerging Trends in World Christianity*. London: Bloomsbury Academic, 2013.

Adogame, Afe, and Selome Kuponu. "Spiritual Terrorism beyond Borders: African Pentecostalism, Cultural Synthesis within Local-Global Space." In *Unpacking the New: Critical Perspectives on Cultural Syncretization in Africa and Beyond*, edited by A. Adogame, M. Echtler, and U. Vierke. Vienna: Lit Verlag, 2008, 306–30.

Baier, Colin J., and Bradley R. E. Wright. "If You Love Me, Keep My Commandments": A Meta-analysis of the Effect of Religion on Crime. *Journal of Research in Crime and Delinquency* 38 (2001): 3–21.

Ballano, Vicencio O. *Sociological Perspectives on Clerical Sexual Abuse in the Catholic Hierarchy: An Exploratory Structural Analysis of Social Disorganization*. Singapore: Springer, 2019.

Beckford, James A. *Cult Controversies: The Societal Response to the New Religious Movements*. London: Tavistock, 1985.

Ben-Yehuda, N. "The Sociology of Moral Panics: Toward a New Synthesis." *Sociological Quarterly* 27 (1986): 499–507.

Berry, Jason. *Lead Us Not into Temptation: Catholic Priests and the Sexual Abuse of Children*. New York: Doubleday, 1992.

Bishop's Ad Hoc Committee. *Restoring Trust: A Pastoral Response to Sexual Abuse*. Vol. 1. Washington, DC: National Conference of Catholic Bishops, 1994.

"Bishop David Oyedepo Slaps to Conquer." YouTube video. https://www.youtube.com /watch?v=-XfvOUUYf-8.

Bohm, Bettina et al. "Child Sexual Abuse in the Context of the Roman Catholic Church: A Review of Literature from 1981–2013." *Journal of Child Sexual Abuse* 23, no. 6 (2014): 635–56.

Bourdieu, Pierre. "The Field of Cultural Production or the Economic World Reversed." *Poetics* 12, no. 4–5 (1983): 311–56.

Briggs, Xavier. "Social Capital: Easy Beauty or Meaningful Resource?" *Journal of the American Planning Association* 70, no. 2 (2004): 145–49.

Buncombe, A. "Pope Admits Sexual Abuse of Nuns by Priests in Catholic Church for First Time." *Independent*, 2019. Accessed March 16, 2020. https://www.independent.co .uk/news/world/europe/pope-francis-nuns-sexual-abuse-catholic-church-priests -scandal-bishops-a8765031.html.

Burkett, E., and F. Bruni. *A Gospel of Shame: Children, Sexual Abuse, and the Catholic Church.* New York: Viking Books, 1993.

Camp, Scott D., Jody Klein-Saffran, Okyun Kwon, Dawn M. Daggett, and Victoria Joseph. "An Exploration into Participation in a Faith-Based Prison Program." *Criminology and Public Policy* 5, no. 3 (2006): 529–50.

Chitwood, Dale D., Michael L. Weiss, and Carl G. Leukefeld. "A Systematic Review of Recent Literature on Religiosity and Substance Use." *Journal of Drug Issues* 38, no. 3 (2008): 653–88.

Cohen, Stanley. *Folk Devils and Moral Panics: The Creation of the Mods and Rockers.* London: MacGibbon and Kee, 1972.

CRL Commission. *Report of the Hearings on the Commercialisation of Religion and Abuse of People's Belief Systems.* Johannesburg: CRL Rights Commission, 2017.

Cullen, Francis T. "Toward a Criminology of Religion: Comment on Johnson and Jang." In *Contemporary Issues in Criminological Theory and Research: The Role of Social Institutions,* edited by R. Rosenfeld, K. Quinet, and C. Garcia. Boston: Wadsworth, Cengage Learning, 2012, 151–71.

Dale, K. A., and J. L. Alpert. "Hiding behind the Cloth: Child Sexual Abuse and the Catholic Church." *Journal of Child Sexual Abuse* 16, no. 3 (2007): 59–74.

Demasure, K. "The Politics of Meaning: Societal Discourses on the Sexual Abuse of Children and Their Influence on the Catholic Church." In *Reforming Practical Theology: The Politics of Body and Space* 1. Vol. 1, edited by A. Vähäkangas, S. Angel, and K. H. Johansen (Tübingen: International Academy of Practical Theology, 2019), 20–28.

Doyle, Thomas. "Clericalism, Enabler of Clergy Sexual Abuse." *Pastoral Psychology* 54, no. 3 (2006): 189–213.

Durrant, R., and Z. Poppelwell. *Religion, Crime and Punishment: An Evolutionary Perspective.* London: Palgrave Macmillan, 2017.

Easton, S. D., D. M. Leone-Sheehan, and P. J. O'Leary. " 'I Will Never Know the Person Who I Could Have Become': Perceived Changes in Self-Identity Among Adult Survivors of Clergy-Perpetrated Sexual Abuse." *Journal of Interpersonal Violence* 34 / 6 (2016): 1–24.

Farrell, D. P., and Taylor, M. "Silenced by God: An Examination of Unique Characteristics within Sexual Abuse by Clergy." *Counselling Psychology Review* 15, no. 1 (2000): 22–31.

Field, J. *Social Capital.* Routledge: London, 2003.

Findlay, M., *The Globalisation of Crime: Understanding Transitional Relationships in Context.* Cambridge: Cambridge University Press, 1999.

Formicola, Jo Renee. *Clerical Sexual Abuse: How the Crisis Changed US Catholic Church-State Relations*. Palgrave Macmillan, 2014.

———. *Papal Policies on Clerical Sexual Abuse: God Weeps*. New York: Peter Lang, 2019.

———. "The Politics of Clerical Sexual Abuse," *Religions* 7, no. 1 (2016): 1–13.

Foucault, M. *Discipline and Punish: The Birth of the Prison*. New York: Vintage Books, 1995.

———. "The Subject and Power." In *Power: Essential Works of Foucault 1954–1984*, edited by P. Rabinow. New York: New York University Press, 1994, 326–48.

Guerzoni, M. A. "A Situational Crime Prevention Analysis of Anglican Clergy's Child Protective Practices." *Child Abuse and Neglect* 77 (2018): 85–98.

Guido, J. J. "A Unique Betrayal: Clergy Sexual Abuse in the Context of the Catholic Religious Tradition." *Journal of Child Sexual Abuse* 17 (2008): 255–69.

Hanson, Karl R. et al. *Sexual Abuse in the Catholic Church: Scientific and Legal Perspectives*. 2004. Proceedings of the conference "Abuse of Children and Young People by Catholic Priests and Religious," April 2–5, 2003. Vatican City: Libreria Editrice Vaticana.

Heaton, Paul. 2006. "Does Religion Really Reduce Crime?" *Journal of Law and Economics* 49, no. 1 (2006): 147–72.

Hewitt, C., and J. Kelly-Moore. "Foreign Fighters in Iraq: A Cross-National Analysis of Jihadis." *Terrorism and Political Violence* 21, no. 2 (2009): 211–20.

Hirschi, Travis, and Rodney Stark. "Hellfire and Delinquency." *Social Problems* 17, no. 2 (1969): 202–13.

Ikheloa, Ikhide. "Investigate the Abuse of a Young Girl Slapped by Pastor David Oyedepo." Online petition to the federal government of Nigeria. https://www.change.org/p/the-nigerian-government-investigate-the-abuse-of-a-young-girl-slapped-by-pastor-david-oyedepo.

Isely, Paul J. "Child Sexual Abuse and the Catholic Church: An Historical and Contemporary Review." *Pastoral Psychology* 45, no. 4 (1997): 277–99.

Jenkins, Philip. *Moral Panic: Changing Concepts of the Child Molester in Modern America*. New Haven, CT: Yale University Press, 1998.

Johnson, Byron R. *More God, Less Crime: Why Faith Matters and How It Could Matter More*. West Conshohocken, PA: Templeton Press, 2012.

Johnson, Byron R., Spencer De Li, David B. Larson, and M. McCullough. "A Systematic Review of the Religiosity and Delinquency Literature." *Journal of Contemporary Criminal Justice* 16 (2000): 32–52.

Johnson, Byron R., and Sung Joon Jang. "Crime and Religion: Assessing the Role of the Faith Factor." In *Contemporary Issues in Criminological Theory and Research: The Role of Social Institutions*, edited by Richard Rosenfeld, Kenna Quinet, and Crystal Garci. Boston: Wadsworth, Cengage Learning, 2012, 117–49.

Juergensmeyer, M. *Terror in the Mind of God: The Global Rise of Religious Violence*. Berkeley: University of California Press, 2000.

Kerley, Kent R. *Current Studies in the Sociology of Religion*. Basle, Switzerland: MDPI, 2015.

———. *Finding Freedom in Confinement: The Role of Religion in Prison Life*. Santa Barbara, CA: Praeger, 2018.

———. *Religious Faith in Correctional Contexts*. Boulder, CO: First Forum Press / Lynne Rienner Publishers, 2014.

Kerley, Kent R., ed. *Religion and Crime: Theory, Research, and Practice*. Basle, Switzerland: MDPI, 2018.

Kgatle, M.S. "The Unusual Practices within Some Neo-Pentecostal Churches in South Africa: Reflections and Recommendations." *HTS Teologiese Studies / Theological Studies*73, no. 3 (2017): a4656. https://doi.org/10.4102/hts.v73i3.4656.

Khanyile, S. B. "The Virtualization of the Church: New Media Representations of Neo-Pentecostal Performance(s) in South Africa." MA dissertation, University of the Witwatersrand, Johannesburg, 2016.

Kohn, David. "The Church on Trial: Part I. Rage in Louisiana." *CBSN*, June 11, 2002. Accessed July 15, 2020. https://www.cbsnews.com/news/the-church-on-trial-part-1-11-06-2002/.

———. "Between Pretoria and George Goch Hostel: God in South Africa in 2015." *New Agenda: South African Journal of Social and Economic Policy* 59 (2015): 35–39.

"Mandate," the. LFCW website. Accessed May 15, 2019. http://faithtabernacle.org.ng/about.

Mashau, T. D., and M. S. Kgatle. "Prosperity Gospel and the Culture of Greed in Post-colonial Africa: Constructing an Alternative African Christian Theology of Ubuntu." *Verbum et Ecclesia* 40, no. 1 (2019): a1901. https://doi.org/10.4102/ve.v40i1.1901.

Micklethwaite, D., N. Blagden, and B. Winder. "Understanding the Experiences of Religious Perpetrators of Sexual Abuse." *Sexual Crime, Religion and Spirituality* (2019): 71–114. https://doi.org/10.1007/978-3-030-26040-8_5.

Moinipour, S. "Moral Panic and Power: The Means of Legitimisation of Religious Intolerance and Human Rights Violation against the Bahá'ís in Iran." *Religion and Human Rights* 13 (2018): 179–212.

Mondimore, F. M. *A Natural History of Homosexuality*. Baltimore: Johns Hopkins University Press, 1996.

Oyedepo, David. O. *Winning Invisible Battles*. Ota, Nigeria: Dominion Publishing House, 2006.

Piquero, A. R., N. Piquero, K. J. Terry, T. Youstin, and M. Nobles. "Uncollaring the Criminal: Understanding Criminal Careers of Criminal Clerics." *Criminal Justice and Behavior* 35, no. 5 (2008): 583–99.

Plante, T. G., and K. L. McChesney, eds. *Abnormal Psychology. Sexual Abuse in the Catholic Church: A Decade of Crisis, 2002–2012*. Santa Barbara, CA: Praeger / ABC-CLIO, 2011.

Pondani, S. "'Prophets of Doom': The Phenomenon of Healing and Power Dynamics in Neo-Pentecostal African Churches. MA dissertation, Stellenbosch University, Western Cape, South Africa, 2019.

Portes, A. "Social Capital: Its Origins and Applications in Modern Sociology." *Annual Review of Sociology* 24 (1998): 1–24.

Putnam, R. *Bowling Alone: The Collapse and Revival of American Community*. New York: Simon and Schuster, 2000.

Quibria, M. G. "The Puzzle of Social Capital: A Critical Review." *Asian Development Review* 20, no. 2 (2003): 19–39.

Rashid, Faisal, and Ian Barron. "The Roman Catholic Church: A Centuries Old History of Awareness of Clerical Child Sexual Abuse (from the First to the 19th Century)." *Journal of Child Sexual Abuse* 27, no. 7 (2018): 778–92.

Resane, K. T. "'And They Shall Make You Eat Grass like Oxen' (Daniel 4:24): Reflections on Recent Practices in some New Charismatic Churches." *Pharos Journal of Theology* 98 (2017): 1–17.

Rudolfsson, Lisa. "Religious Victims of Sexual Abuse." In *Sexual Crime, Religion and Spirituality*, edited by B. Winder, N. Blagden, K. Hocken, R. Lievesley, H. Elliott, and P. Banyard. London: Palgrave Macmillan, 163–94.

Sadique, K., and P. Stanislas. *Religion, Faith, and Crime. Theories, Identities and Issues.* London: Palgrave Macmillan, 2016.

Scharnick-Udemans, Lee. "Gender Perspectives and African Scholarship: Blind Spots in the Field of Religion, Media, and Culture." *Journal of Gender and Religion in Africa* 23, no. 2 (2017): 145–63.

Scheitle, C. P., and M. Hansmann. "Religion-Related Hated Crimes: Data, Trends, and Limitations." *Journal for the Scientific Study of Religion* 55, no. 4 (2016): 859–73.

Schmidt, M. *Regulation of Religion in the Rainbow Nation: The Situatedness of Religious Groups in Post-apartheid South Africa.* BA thesis, University of Leipzig, Germany, 2019.

Settler, Federico G. "Race and Materiality in African Religious Contexts." *Journal for the Study of Religion* 31, no. 2 (2018): 36–56.

Smart, Ninian. *The World's Religions: Old Traditions and Modern Transformations.* Cambridge: Cambridge University Press, 1989.

———. *Religious Experience of Mankind.* New York: Charles Scribner's Sons, 1969.

Stark, Rodney. "Religion as Context: Hellfire and Delinquency One More Time." *Sociology of Religion* 57, no. 2 (1996): 163–73.

Stern, Jessica. *Terror in the Name of God: Why Religious Militants Kill.* New York: Harper Collins, 2003.

Sumter, Melvina. *Religiousness and Post-release Community Adjustment.* Doctoral dissertation, School of Criminology, Florida State University, Tallahassee, 1999.

Sumter, Melvina et al. "Religion and Crime Studies: Assessing What Has Been Learned." *Religions* 9, no. 193 (2018): 1–15.

Terry, Karen J. "Child Sexual Abuse within the Catholic Church: A Review of Global Perspectives." *International Journal of Comparative and Applied Criminal Justice* 39, no. 2 (2015): 139–54.

Terry, Karen J., et al. *The Causes and Context of Sexual abuse of Minors by Catholic Priests in the United States, 1950–2010.* Washington, DC: United States Conference of Bishops, 2011.

———. "Stained Glass: The Nature and Scope of Child Sexual Abuse in the Catholic Church." *Criminal Justice and Behavior* 35, no. 5 (2008): 549–69.

Terry, Karen J., and J. Tallon. *Child Sexual Abuse: A Review of the Literature.* New York: John Jay College of Criminal Justice, 2004.

Tonda, J. "The Prophet's Syndrome: African Medicines and Identity Precarities." *Cahiers d'Études africaines* 161, no. 1 (2001): 139–62.

Weaver, Andrew J., Kevin J. Flannelly, and Adrienne L. Strock. "A Review of Research on the Effects of Religion on Adolescent Tobacco Use Published between 1990 and 2003." *Adolescence* 40, no. 160 (2004): 761–76.

White, M. D., and K. J. Terry. "Child Sexual Abuse in the Catholic Church: Revisiting the Rotten Apples Explanation." *Criminal Justice and Behavior* 35, no. 5 (2008): 658–78.

Wilbourn, Beth. "Suffer the Children: Catholic Church Liability for the Sexual Abuse Acts of Priests," *Review of Litigation* 15, no. 1 (1995): 251–66.

Yeung, Jerf W. K., Yuk-Chung Chan, and Boris L. K. Lee. "Youth Religiosity and Substance Use: A Meta-analysis from 1995 to 2007." *Psychological Reports* 105, no. 1 (2009): 255–66.

PART IV

Global/Transnational Christianity and Mission

CHAPTER 13

Some Thoughts on Evangelical Christianity in Africa and the Diaspora

Jacob K. Olupona

EVANGELICAL CHRISTIANITY
IN AFRICA AND THE DIASPORA

In the early nineties, I embarked on the study of African religious communities in the United States. I coined the phrase "reverse mission" to describe African Christian Missionaries in their new homes as immigrants in the United States. I have, since then, moved my research home to African nation-states, particularly Nigeria and in the diaspora among African Evangelical communities. This is not only because of the lacuna I found in the literature on contemporary Christianity in Africa but also because of the lack of clarity on the historiography of Christianity in Africa and the overemphasis on the modern Pentecostal-Charismatic movements. The missing link was the variegated evangelical tapestry noticeable in African Christian identities in both the past and the present. For the purpose of this chapter, I shall focus on African Evangelical church identity in Africa, the United States, and Europe.

African Evangelical identities exhibit many features and traits that cannot fully be listed here. My primary concern will be to assess how immigrant evangelicals respond, engage, and perform in the public spaces of their new home. To this end, I will pose the following theoretical questions:

1. How do African Evangelicals perceive of themselves as actors in the public domain, and how does that affect their role as stakeholders

in the discourse of belongingness, citizenship, and identity and the performance of their civic duties?

2. How do they relate to questions surrounding the law as it intersects with their immigration status and role as immigrants (whatever that might mean)?

3. How do these churches supersede their role as civil society as they engage politically and interact with the public space and participate in the democratization process both at home and in their new communities?

In the African context I am concerned with the African Evangelical identity of many who are classified or labeled as belonging to Pentecostal-Charismatic churches. I refer to them as African Evangelicals because of their alignment with mainline Christian denominations, that is, the old European and American missionary churches, such as the Anglican, Methodist, and Baptist churches, which encompass Protestant Christian evangelicalism broadly defined. It thus sets them apart from Evangelicals in the West and in the Global North.

It is also important to note that it is now an acceptable fact that evangelicalism is a complex phenomenon and term, whose meaning varies from place to place. In the African immigrant context, I refer to it as a phenomenon that embraces different forms of Protestant Christianity and that prioritizes the following features: the literal interpretation of the Bible, believing in personal conversion, also known as the "born-again" phenomenon, and engagement in the special mission of rigorous evangelization of so-called pagans and nominal Christians. They also exhibit social conservatism particularly as it relates to gender and sexuality. And while glossolalia may be common among some forms of evangelical Christianity, it is not an indicator of Evangelicalism on the whole. Based on my most recent research as well as previous work that I have done on African immigrant populations, I have often argued that while all Pentecostals and Charismatics are Evangelicals, not all Evangelicals are Pentecostal / Charismatic. I refer to the fact that different forms and manifestations of Evangelicalism neither share an origin nor do they necessarily share its ingredients and manifestations.

While Pentecostalism is a practice that espouses Christianity's dominance over other religions, it has gained prominence at a cost. Often, it has done so by creation of increasing sectarian distinctions, thereby encouraging the religious equivalent of xenophobia. This has opened a renewed public space, surely, but it is often a space in which certain Christian values and symbols are privileged to the detriment of others—frequently resulting in intolerance, symbolic, and actual violence and human rights violations. The "renewed public space" must interrogate how civilians participate in both political and religious contexts, pointing to Christian involvement in politics or Christians' role in community and civic organizations.

The word "Evangelical" and the terminology around evangelicalism continue to provoke much debate. However, my use of the term is to denote how these forms of Protestant Christianity exhibit evangelical traits—thus emphasizing their connectedness despite doctrinal difference. The Evangelicalism I am speaking about is evident in several African churches, which have evolved from small and local congregations to achieving megachurch status in a brief amount of time. These include churches such as the Deeper Life Church and the Redeemed Christian Church of God (RCCG), both founded in Nigeria, which are not only transnational but global in reach, having representation in every nook and cranny of the world. The founding leaders of most of these churches are still alive and well and intimately involved in the daily running of these movements, thereby surpassing the Weberian charisma thesis on the eventual demise of charismatically led organizations.[1] The transnational and global presence of African Evangelicals grants them a unique status in the Christian world. Not considered an ordinary Southern church, they are gradually changing the religious contours of Europe, the United States, and other parts of the African continent. The impact of their presence is being felt most deeply in the context of their interactions with the public sphere.

AFRICAN CHURCHES AND CIVIL SOCIETY

A central role of the church in the new African nation-states was the role of civil society. The immigration of the African Christian church does not follow clear-cut demographic and religious patterns. Perhaps the earliest to come, after the Independent African Churches, were the orthodox churches from Ethiopia. The first group came as a result of the massive migration of Ethiopians to the United States following the civil wars in their country. The Independent African Churches came to the United States in trickles, with churches being established by individuals, especially students who had traveled to the United States for education.

The establishment of African churches in the United States reflects patterns of African migration to the United States, which has increased considerably over the last fifty years. With economic and political resources affording travel, African, educated elites previously schooled in Europe or in the United States formed the vanguard of emigrants. These learned refugees and exiles often founded African religious institutions. In more recent years, the US Immigration and Naturalization Service (INS), in a Diversity Immigrant Visa Green Card Lottery system, created an opportunity for a second wave of less-educated African immigrants. Africans immigrate to the United States for myriad reasons, but whatever they may be, those immigrants who have religious affiliations in their home countries usually find religious communities to join. There are at least small African immigrant communities in every metropolitan community in the United States. At times these communities are new to the old immigrants, and at others connections may have already been established before coming. Today, the new African diaspora in the United States represents many religions currently practiced by Africans.

Sociopolitical and economic shifts, however, have challenged the church to reconsider its position with regard to politics. For example, pastors from the Christian Council of Zambia drafted letters to then president Kenneth Kaunda that called for the government to address poverty, economic woes, and political system that allowed only one party.[2] Examples such as these bring to the foreground the role of the church in developing agency among the civil society. Religion can provide platforms for advocacy just as easily as it can provide vocabularies for violence. While we might not provide a full explication of the importance of African Christian immigrants, we must point to the fact that they are making waves in the Americas, Europe, and the United States. African immigrant religious groups are important sites for investigating civic engagement and other interactions within the public space. For Africans in the United States, it seems, religion, race, and nationality form a complicated choreography. Religion provides a rhythm for ethical exchange with their non-African counterparts, and public life becomes the stage upon which immigrants articulate their transnational dance.

Today, several Nigerian churches and pastors play a leading role in the religious life of Europe and the United States, as they claim to be "taking the Gospel back" to these countries. Considering that Nigeria boasts the largest Anglican, Catholic, Baptist, and Pentecostal congregations, it is no surprise that in the past decade Nigerian Evangelicals have had an immense impact on the global face of Christianity.

AFRICAN EVANGELICAL CHURCH INFLUENCE ON POLITICAL SPACES IN EUROPE

The best example of this trend is Pastor Sunday Adelaja, whose Embassy of the Blessed Kingdom (based in Kiev, Ukraine) is the largest Protestant religious congregation in Europe.[3] In 1986, in the dying years of the Soviet Union, Adelaja won a scholarship to study journalism at the Belarus State University in Minsk. Shortly before leaving Nigeria he had been converted by a televangelist, William F. Kumuyi, a former professor of mathematics. As a student in Minsk, he led an African Christian students' fellowship. He remained in the country after graduating and founded the Word of Faith Church in 1989. He subsequently moved to Kiev, the capital of Ukraine, where in 1994 he founded a church that became known as the Embassy of the Blessed Kingdom of God for all nations. Within a decade the church became the largest congregation in eastern Europe, with more than 25,000 members.[4] The success of the church can be ascribed to Sunday Adelaja's charismatic personality and his extensive itinerant, print, and media ministry aimed at world evangelization. The church is actively involved in community service, offering assistance and shelter to the poor, alcoholics, and drug addicts.

There are a number of levels on which the story of Rev. Adelaja is fascinating. First, there is the irony of Adelaja's ejection from the Soviet Union. Marx's famous designation of religion as the "opiate of the people" is greatly challenged by the story of Adelaja. Communist Russia, supposedly of and for the people, found the peasant agency that Adelaja stirred to be threatening. This paradox would be more humorous if it did not underlie the tragic circumstances of many people who found their religious lives suppressed under the Soviet system. However, of greater interest for the purposes here is the fact that the most dynamic and powerful religious leader in the Ukraine is a Nigerian. Ukraine's megachurch is African in origin. It is not too much to say that Adelaja's missionary work has permanently altered the religious and political landscape of Eastern Europe, instilling African religious sensibilities in a region that had previously been a religious vacuum. Adelaja is credited as the person who determined the outcome of the Kiev mayoral election.

THE AFRICAN EVANGELICAL CHURCH
AND CHURCH-STATE POWER STRUGGLE

Another prominent Nigerian pastor abroad is Matthew Ashimolowo, the senior pastor and founder of Kingsway International Christian Centre (KICC) in London. Forbes estimated Ashimolowo's net worth to be between 6 and 10 million pounds, which is a testimony to the influence of his mission, which includes the daily *Winning Ways* program aired on Premier Radio (London) as well as other television and media presences.[5] Ashimolowo's political influence prompted his confrontation with the British government, which is not used to such a powerful presence of religious institutions. The government remained hands off until Ashimolowo decided to build a megachurch at a very visible space at the center of London. Alarmed by this development, the British government quickly frustrated his efforts to control his growing influence among the British public. Ultimately, they accused him of embezzlement and fraud, eventually driving him back to Nigeria. This encounter led to government disruption and to the installation of increased regulation over African Evangelical church presence in the United Kingdom. Later, other African immigrant church leaders, such as Kenyan archbishop Gilbert Deya, were also casualties of newly imposed church regulation. Deya was involved in a scandal related to managing church funds and extortion of congregants and was extradited back to Kenya soon after to face child-trafficking charges. His church in Peckham, Southeast London, is reported to have had an income of 652,000 pounds for the fiscal year ending 2015.

African immigrant religion must be situated within the broader context of the cultural and religious pluralism of the United States and its relationship to law and the state. Immigrants, many of whom have just escaped dire circumstances, suddenly find themselves in exile, having escaped one kind of oppression only to find themselves at the mercy of another. As a professor of African studies, I am regularly called upon to work with lawyers and officials for immigration and asylum services. Cases range from those fleeing the Boko Haram insurgency in northeastern Nigeria, to those who claim they have escaped from ritual killings and female genital cutting of their daughters. However, with the resources of religious communities that have adopted them, their integration into American society takes on a less traumatic character. In turn, their new home congregations are making meaningful contributions to the American religious and cultural mosaic. As African immigrants are a distinct and growing group, we expect to see them progressively exercising their expertise and rights to demand the fair distribution and allocation of community resources.

If this discussion of African immigrant religion has seemed to take us afield, it remains for me to make my point clearer: in a world of increasing globalization, we must expand our focus in order to recognize these satellite religious expressions as part and parcel of the African religious experience in toto. If, in our world of increasingly hyphenated and hybrid identities, it has become more challenging to say what African Evangelical Christianity is, it has become perhaps even more challenging to say for certain what it is not. Once we look, we find manifestations of it everywhere.

POLITICS, PRAYER, AND POWER

Religious scholars also need to make prayer the subject of scientific analysis and examine the religious and social significance of prayer in contemporary Africa as well as its meaning and function in both private and public spheres. Through prayer the public presence of religion is significantly felt in Africa. It is important that we probe into how prayer performances are not just embodied expressions of faith but also signifiers of how various religious communities foster human striving and construct identity. Various faith communities deploy prayer as a method for shaping individual, group, and national identities according to their definitions of human virtue. Although it is true that these varying constructions of identity often fuel intra- and interreligious conflicts, I am interested in how prayer also paradoxically attempts to resolve it. Our work as social scientists should address how prayer serves as both a powerful marker of personal, communal, and national identity, and as a conduit for political and hegemonic claims in the African state's private and public spheres.

The question of the politics of prayer at a global level can be seen in relation to evangelical Christianity in America. During the 2008 US presidential election, Republican vice-presidential candidate Sarah Palin was embroiled in a prayer controversy due to her association with a visiting Kenyan Pentecostal preacher. The press described the preacher as a "witch doctor." In the midst of the controversy, the *Boston Herald* newspaper asked me to provide an expert opinion.[6] I explained that the confusion arose because the visiting Kenyan pastor led the congregation in an African prayer against witchcraft in an American church setting. Who could have thought that an African prayer would become an issue in American elections? The same prayer, delivered in the preacher's Kenyan context, would not have raised any major objections.

Within immigrant African Evangelical churches, there are diverse expressions of identity. Pastors range from those who would rather not be associated with anything African to others who argue for the growth of a culturally based African church in America. The evangelical mission, Nigerian Aladura churches, and even Pentecostal-Charismatic churches are found all over the United States. In reality there is a great deal of fluidity, as church leaders and members express the complex identities of their transnational lives. In any one church, ethnic cell groups may coexist with prominent markers of Pan-African identity and with symbols of global internationalism. Negotiating two identities—that of the homeland and the new country—is a more complex phenomenon than this dichotomy suggests.

EVANGELICALS AND THE MORAL ORDER

The general belief is that American evangelicals are the drivers of moral temperature in Africa, and, consequently, the American state in particular has moved to take measures against what they consider to be liberal American positions on morality on the continent. While I have no objection to this line of thought, it would be interesting to look at the issue from the other side. Are African Evangelicals also influencing the American political and religious landscape?

An intriguing case is that of Jasper Akinola, an Anglican archbishop who took over after the second primate of the Nigerian Anglican Church, Joseph Abiodun Adetiloye. It was said that Akinola was a rich man in charge of considerable resources in operating the church, which can explain why he was appointed as a bishop at the time when the church was becoming aware of how much the Anglican Church, once regarded as a state church, had succumbed to Pentecostal evangelical ethos. Akinola was concerned with two things. First, he wanted to make sure that the presence of the Nigerian Anglican Church was felt throughout the country. He thus embarked on establishing more missionary dioceses in different parts of Nigeria to the point that many of the parishes I used to know in the southwest had become the seats of Anglican bishops. Second, because most of his ministry took place in the north, he was deeply attentive to Muslim-Christian encounters. The third notable aspect about Akinola's career was his involvement in the Global Anglican Communion, namely, in the controversy surrounding the ordination of a noncelibate gay man, Gene Robinson, as a bishop of the diocese of New Hampshire of the Episcopal Church of the United States of America (ECUSA). In association with American evangelicals, Akinola launched a severe attack on the ECUSA in 2005, demanding its expulsion from the Anglican Communion. To this end, the Nigerian Anglican delegation was the largest at the Lambeth Conference of the Anglican Church during that year. The delegation's success in lobbying against the recognition of the American Episcopalian bishop in New Hampshire marked the start of this crisis in the Anglican Church, which still continues. Perhaps one of the problems was that the Nigerian evangelical churches, particularly those located in Africa, were very much concerned with the question of sexuality, rejecting nonheterosexual relationships on terms that they were unbiblical and immoral. Nigerian evangelicals championed this trend on a global scale. Akinola began to reach out to other like-minded Evangelicals in Africa and other countries, forming a separate ecumenical association opposed to the

Church of England, which led the group to hold successive meetings in Jerusalem rather than Lambeth. By the time he retired, Akinola had significantly transformed the Anglican Church.

The United Methodist Church (UMC) is currently facing the same dilemma after the 2019 special session of its general conference failed to pass the vote on the amendment of the clauses in the Book of Discipline relating to human sexuality. In an effort to strengthen church unity, the UMC urged global conferences to sign on to the new vision, allowing for more inclusivity and tolerance within the denomination. Africans were quickly dubbed the "sin-eaters" for this decision and their conservative stance, which they viewed as being a traditionally biblical one.

This affair raises several important questions regarding the response, involvement, and relational positioning and negotiation of identity among African Evangelical immigrants. In regard to the latter, I wish only to highlight one significant contributing factor here, focusing on the case of Nigerian immigrant congregations. Nigerian immigrants in the United States depend on both interpersonal and transnational relationships to help maintain a sense of home. Because Nigerian immigrants seek belonging in the just-mentioned congregations, they tend to create local communities that serve to ease the feeling of being strangers in a new land. However, the way these new spaces are imagined is more complex than one might think. The way Nigerian evangelical immigrants positioned themselves in regard to the decision of the General Conference of the UMC cannot be reduced to *only* interpersonal communal connections among Nigerians in the United States and from home. For many members of Nigerian immigrant churches, their transnational relationships are not merely bidirectional—between Nigeria and the United States—but rather comprise a web of transnational networks that span the entire world. What we find, in reality, are religious communities engaged in reverse missions that construct new ideological, epistemic, spatial, and temporal configurations and include places as far as Asia, South America, and Europe.

However, while we can locate the development of polycentric identities among certain African immigrant populations, many evangelical congregations endeavor to preserve a strong commitment to their "parent" church back home. This phenomenon is exemplified by the Redeemed Christian Church of God congregations. Though the church is based in Nigeria and holds its annual worldwide convention at the Redemption Camp on the outskirts of Lagos, it also holds an annual convention in the United States at the RCCG's American headquarters in Texas. The Redemption Camp in

Lagos functions as a mini-Mecca, imbuing the Texas headquarters with an authority it would otherwise lack.

RELIGION AND THE POLITICAL SPHERE

The Nigerian immigrant evangelical communities have also played a central role in shaping political expression, especially through the explicit or implied messages conveyed by leaders and through informal community gatherings (such as in conversation after a service), which often serve as forums for political discussion and debate. I recall the instance of former president George W. Bush's reelection bid in Atlanta. An African pastor preaching the Sunday before the election spoke about the "burning bush." The pastor expressed an ambivalent attitude toward President Bush. Whether speaking for or against Bush's reelection, the pastor left the congregation to make up their own minds from his nuanced sermon. In the same vein, the most recent presidential election also witnessed an African response to the American electoral process. Certainly, many Africans voted in support of Secretary Hilary Clinton, following the general interests of America electing a female president. However, and surprisingly, a considerable number of Africans voted for President Donald Trump. I explore some of the reasons for this below.

The political choices and activity of African Evangelical immigrants were different for several reasons. First, Nigerian Christian Evangelicals (who constitute the majority of African Christians in the United States) were overwhelmingly opposed to Hilary Clinton on somewhat ideologically based grounds. The current Democratic National Convention seems to be at odds with the majority African view on same-sex marriage. After discussions with some African leaders, it is clear that African Evangelical Christians often argue that not only are the Democrats too liberal but in addition they had formulated policies that Africans considered to be morally abhorrent to African Evangelical Christian values. They also tend to blame President Obama, the first Black president, for some of these policies concerning same-sex marriage and a pro-LGBTQ stance, which they consider to be anti-African. Some African immigrants do not appreciate the way American politicians try to promote their own moral stances in Africa while being highly critical of African norms. At this juncture, we should recall that Nigerians at home and Africans on the continent—regardless of whether they tend to lean more left or right—have supported government policies against homosexuality and the rights of gays and lesbians. This position was reflected in a recent conversation I had with a visiting Nigerian pastor at Harvard University. I expressed the uncertainty of the contemporary situation in Nigeria with regard to the state of immigrants and the Muslim ban. "Since my twenty five-year sojourn in America, I have never seen anything like this before," I shared. He angrily retorted that his view differs strongly from my sentiments. "America is a God-given country, the light of the world; God has raised a man to correct the ills of the past and restore America to its rightful place among the nations of the world." In this respect, there is a meeting of minds between some American and African Evangelicals, which also translates politically regarding the issue of Israel. Mostly, though, they agree on the stance of many Republicans on homosexuality, and other issues about sex and marriage that have been inculcated through policy, such as the transgender bathroom debate. For this reason, many African immigrants voted Republican in the last election in support of the pervasive Islamophobia and moral intolerance that they perceive were not upheld during the Obama era.

Second, the African immigrant church position on the state of Israel may at first seem to ally with the general American Evangelical view, religiously inspired by the Zionist position that perceives Jerusalem as the holy city of the Bible to be defended at all costs. The difference is that African Christians are not quite as familiar with Israeli-Palestinian conflict matters. They hardly know that there are Palestinians who are also Christians, like the members of St. George's Cathedral, Jerusalem, where I worshipped during my sabbatical leave at the Hebrew university of Jerusalem in 2011. Most Africans are less astute about the Israel-Palestine issue and are more interested in the status of Jerusalem as a so-called Christian city. The largest number of Christian pilgrims to Jerusalem to date are Nigerians and Ethiopians. Perhaps one of the unforgettable events highlighting this phenomenon was the pilgrimage of former president Goodluck Jonathan to Israel prior to his campaign bid for a second term. In his entourage were high-profile evangelical church leaders. He would later describe the visit as "necessary for him to seek the face of God [in Israel]" before he declared his candidacy for reelection. A unique example of the interaction with evangelical ideology and the state is the case of Ethiopian evangelical underground churches under the Derg junta, a provisional socialist military government between 1974 and 1987. Religious scholar Tibebe Eshete argues that evangelical Christians during this period went the route of "self-preservation and fought for [their] integrity and independence by creating an autonomous space, [within the public sphere]."[7] Evangelical Christians, Eshete notes, "established a sphere of existence beyond the authority of a state . . . [and] maintained a degree of coherence and social sanity in a period marred with civil strife and political discord that eroded relational capital among citizens of Ethiopian society."[8]

CONCLUSION

The emerging presence, power, and influence of African immigrant religious communities within the United States and Europe are gradually changing the American and European religious landscape. From magnificent churches to modest storefront churches, African Christians have created distinct identities and continue to perpetuate their cultural values. The impressive and ever-expanding variety of these congregations indicates a growing and formidable trend in the Euro-American religious field. Already we have seen a number of major cities such as Washington, DC, Atlanta, New York, London, Paris, Amsterdam, and Hamburg begin to undergo a fundamental religious transformation. Unlike earlier waves of immigration, these new immigrants retain an ability to utilize modern technologies of communication and travel, which serve to both expand and strengthen these communities. As a consequence, we see a reformation and adaptation of the Euro-American locale into a cohesion that retains a non-Western memory within a Western environment. In effect, we can observe the resiliency, adaptation, and even expansion of the traditions of African Christianity utilizing a transglobal paradigm. On the other hand, in African nation-states the public presence of evangelicals has made significant impact on the political, social, and cultural activities of the continent.

NOTES

1. Max Weber, *Economy and Society*, ed. Guenther Roth and Claus Wittich (New York: Bedminster Press, 1968).
2. Tom Mirambo, "Zambia's President Fence-Sits as Churches and Marxists Duel," *Christianity Today* (Pre-1986), April 10, 1981, 68, https://www.christianitytoday.com/ct/1981/april-10/zambias-president-fence-sits-as-churches-and-marxists-duel.html.
3. Asamoah-Gyadu, J. Kwabena. 2006. "African Initiated Christianity in Eastern Europe: Church of the 'Embassy of God' in Ukraine," *International Bulletin of Mission Research* 30 (2): 73–75, https://doi.org/10.1177/239693930603000205.
4. Anonymous, September 30, 2007.
5. "The Five Richest Pastors in Nigeria," by Mfonobong Nsehe, *Forbes*, June 7, 2011, https://www.forbes.com/sites/mfonobongnsehe/2011/06/07/the-five-richest-pastors-in-nigeria/.
6. Fargen, Jessica. 2008. "Sarah Palin 'Witchcraft' Flap All Smoke and No Fire. McClatchy—Tribune Business News," Washington: Tribune Content Agency LLC, https://www.bostonherald.com/2008/09/26/sarah-palin-witchcraft-flap-all-smoke-and-no-fire/.
7. Tibebe Eshete, *The Evangelical Movement in Ethiopia: Resistance and Resilience* (Waco, TX: Baylor University Press, 2009), 277.
8. Eshete, *The Evangelical Movement in Ethiopia*, 277–78.

CHAPTER 14

African Evangelical Politics in Global Perspective

Paul Freston

While evangelical Christians have become more and more prominent in African politics since the closing decades of the twentieth century, the politicization of evangelicalism is not, of course, an exclusively African phenomenon. The case of the United States immediately springs to mind, but what can we say about evangelical politics in Africa from a more global perspective? The most fruitful comparison would seem to be not so much with traditionally Protestant contexts such as the United States and northern Europe, nor with contexts where Christians as a whole struggle to find political space (as in much of Asia and the heavily Muslim areas of Africa), but with Latin America. Sub-Saharan Africa and Latin America share impressive evangelical growth, dating from the second half of the twentieth century, in political contexts that have ranged from dictatorships to more or less consolidated democracies, and in economic contexts that, while on the whole somewhat wealthier in the latter region, are not hugely different. Such an intercontinental South-South comparison may in some ways be more illuminating than the more customary comparison with the United States, with its globally unique mix of immense wealth and power, Protestant heritage, long-standing democratic institutions, and large contemporary politicized evangelicalism.

Africa and Latin America are the two major continents of the new heartland of evangelical religious dynamism and political involvement. Outside the United States, three countries are probably tied for having the largest number of evangelical Christians: Brazil, Nigeria, and China. But whereas Chinese evangelicals are as yet restricted in their political activity, their African and Latin American co-religionists, most of whom are politically freer, have been able to exercise growing influence. Nigeria and Brazil exemplify this: besides being regional powers, they are in many ways the leading cases of evangelical political involvement in the Global South. They also have the two largest populations of African descent in the world and can both make a good claim to being the global capital of Pentecostal Christianity. In fact, in Nigeria and in Brazil, Pentecostalism has changed the very nature of the religious field, both by its numerical growth and by its influence (in imitation or in countermobilization) on other religious actors. In Latin America, Pentecostal denominations are now much more important than historical Protestant ones. While this is not true to the same extent in Africa, the Pentecostalization of historical churches is perhaps even further advanced.

One other common factor is that the spread of evangelical Christianity in Africa and Latin America, unlike rapid processes of religious change in some other parts of the world, is due to conversion and not to international migratory movements. This clearly has political implications: a new religion that is largely located among immigrants and their descendants will generally face greater barriers to mainstream political engagement, in contrast to conversion movements among the established local population, even if (as often in Latin America) tilting heavily toward its lower socioeconomic echelons.

Mention of sociological characteristics reminds us that evangelical religion holds different positions in the society and religious field of each country. Hence there exists the need to multiply in-depth country studies, in order to move beyond conspiracy theories on the one hand (about the influence of the American religious right), and general theories about the potential of evangelical religion based on historical analogies on the other hand. In the study of any religion's relationship to politics, we are always navigating between the extremes of contextualism (all religious traditions are epiphenomenal, and the social context is always decisive) and essentialism (the weight of a religious tradition is always decisive, and the political consequences can be "read off" from the doctrine, as in "Protestantism is essentially democratic" or "Islam is incompatible with democracy"). In reality, religious traditions are never univocal or immutable; there is always diversity and evolution, but each tradition changes within a certain sociologic, subject to constraints and prevailing tendencies.

Thus, when studying evangelicals (or other religious confessions), it is important to remember that their political action cannot be deduced directly from their theology. Theology is just one influence among many others that have to be potentially taken into account. In the space between religious doctrine and political practice, several factors intervene. First are factors from within the evangelical world itself: its size; social composition; rhythm of growth, stagnation, or decline; its structures and internal conflicts; the existence or absence of international connections. Second, factors from the broader religious field, that is, the position of evangelicalism vis-à-vis other confessions, and the nature of those confessions. And last are factors from the national sociopolitical context: the degree of religious freedom; how evangelicalism relates to concepts of national identity, and its degree of legitimacy in relation to the national myths; the party and electoral systems.

The two most basic observations about evangelical politics globally are that, first, it varies a great deal, leading to many different, and even contradictory, forms of politics; and, second, its political impact is always smaller than one might expect or fear. Evangelicalism is divided organizationally, socially and theologically . . . and therefore politically as well. In addition, in the Global South it is generally a faith of "the people." It often does not have long-standing cultural and educational traditions, nor a heritage of theological reflection on politics. It tends to be inexperienced but supremely confident in its capacities and prospects.

Because of some of these characteristics, it has attracted some controversial ideas regarding its political impact in the Global South. It is often seen, for example, as an extension of American soft power, conflating American and godly interests. However, the scanty data available regarding the attitudes of ordinary evangelicals in the Global South relativize that perception. A 2006 survey by the Pew Forum (on Pentecostalism in the United States and in three African, three Asian, and three Latin American countries) asked whether respondents favored "the US-led efforts to fight terrorism." Everywhere, Pentecostals were similar to the national average, except (rather predictably) in half-Christian and half-Muslim Nigeria. Only there was the reaction of Pentecostals (71 percent favorable) similar to that of American Pentecostals (72 percent). But in Latin America and South Africa, it was only around one-third favorable; and in the Latin American cases, Pentecostals were actually slightly less favorable than their general populations.[1]

Another idea regarding the political implications of global evangelicalism is through a comparison with Islamic radicalism. Since Islam and evangelicalism are the most popular religions among the disadvantaged in many regions of the world, some analysts consider that the latter might also carry a terrorist potential.[2] Again, the data do not, as yet, hint at an evangelical version of religiously justified geopolitical violence. Not that evangelicals have never been involved in violence; one can mention attacks (or retaliations) by Christians against Muslims in Nigeria and in the Central African Republic.[3] In the 1980s the Pentecostal military dictator Efrain Ríos Montt terrorized

Guatemala and later faced accusations of genocide against the indigenous population.[4] In Brazil there have been a growing number of cases of invasion by Pentecostals of temples associated with the Afro-Brazilian religions, not to mention the daily verbal violence of the demonizing discourse they direct against those and other religions. But the 2006 Pew data paint a more encouraging picture. When asked whether religious freedom should apply to all religions, Global Southern Pentecostals respond as positively as the general populations of their countries. And the comparison with Islam is dubious for other reasons. Notwithstanding some recent, more theocratic, trends, Pentecostalism has a very different relationship to the state, to territory, and to the use of force. It sees itself as a return to primitive Christianity, and the Christianity of the first centuries was distant from political power and the use of force, as well as indifferent to questions of territory (being a voluntary and transnational community). Even though some contemporary Pentecostals seem very susceptible to the "temptations" of power, force, and territoriality, the idealization of those origins and the normativity attributed to the New Testament writings (all of which date from the period of political impotence) constitute a brake on such ambitions. There is no concept of the honor of a sacred community or defense of a sacred territory. And Pentecostalism's insistence on a discourse of "winning" is opposed to the discourse of victimhood that generally undergirds political violence.

Perhaps the biggest challenge to this "primitivist" tendency to territorial indifference comes from the recent rise in global southern evangelicalism (and above all in Africa and Latin America) of Christian Zionism (CZ): geopolitical activism by Christians in favor of the state of Israel, not just its right to exist but also to expand, including attempts to influence the foreign policy of one's own nation-state. While owing a lot to endogenous initiatives, it also reflects efforts by external actors, both Western CZ organizations and the Israeli government.

An example of the latter was the invitation to Israeli prime minister Benjamin Netanyahu to address the Economic Community of West African States (ECOWAS) summit in Liberia in 2017. In exchange for Israeli development assistance in areas such as agriculture, high-tech, and security, Netanyahu asked for African votes in the UN Security Council and General Assembly, and bodies such as United Nations Educational, Scientific and Cultural Organization (UNESCO) and the UN Human Rights Council. He knew that Israel has, for many in the Global South, an attraction that goes beyond standard calculations of development benefits.[5] We read, for instance, how a former Nigerian government minister criticized the decision of the country's acting president not to meet Netanyahu at the ECOWAS summit: "To have snubbed and insulted the Jewish state was . . . reprehensible and deeply repugnant. . . . Nigeria is not a Muslim country, but rather a . . . multi-religious . . . secular state in which over 90 million Christians . . . adore the great nation of Israel." This boycott will mark the beginning of the end for this government, he said.[6] We hear, also, of a sign seen on the desk of one African president by an Israeli diplomat: "Genesis 12:3" (the text says: "I will bless those who bless you, and whoever curses you I will curse; and all the peoples on earth will be blessed through you"). As the director of the Knesset Christian Allies Caucus says: "Faith-based diplomacy has opened up endless possibilities for cooperation with African countries at the highest level of government. It is no coincidence the vast majority of African heads of state involved in the Israeli government's new diplomatic push are Bible-believing Christians."[7]

In Latin America, the rise of Christian Zionism is exemplified by the fact that Guatemala, when under an evangelical president, became the first country to imitate President Trump and move its embassy to Jerusalem. And in Brazil, the strong evangelical support for winning presidential candidate Jair Bolsonaro in 2018 led him to immediately declare he would do the same—a decision that was not implemented due to strong opposition from military and commercial sectors. Netanyahu made the first ever visit to Latin America by an Israeli prime minister in 2017 and was one of the few heads of government to attend Bolsonaro's inauguration.

Most of this Christian Zionism is a relatively recent phenomenon. The 2006 Pew study asked whether respondents sympathized more with Israel or the Palestinians. In all ten countries, Pentecostals were above their national average in sympathy for Israel. American (60 percent) and Filipino (67 percent) Pentecostals sympathized very strongly with Israel, considerably above their national averages. Nigerian, Kenyan, Guatemalan, and Indian Pentecostals were over 40 percent, but their co-religionists in Brazil, Chile, South Africa, and South Korea were below 40 percent. Of course, "sympathy" for Israel does not necessarily indicate Christian Zionism, but the other three replies do seem to preclude it (sympathy for the Palestinians, both or neither). Only 18 percent of American Pentecostals came in those categories, versus 56 percent of Pentecostals in Chile, followed by five other countries between 52 percent and 46 percent. Once again, Nigeria (32 percent) and the Philippines (25 percent) were the only southern countries whose Pentecostals mirrored their American brethren. Judging from that survey, it seemed that the globalization of evangelicalism had increased global support for CZ only up to a very limited point. For whatever reasons, that position seems to have changed considerably in the last few years.

Another idea regarding global Pentecostalism is that it will promote a wave of "new Christendoms" in Africa and Latin America.[8] Its internal divisions make this inherently difficult. Nevertheless, Pentecostalism is frequently attracted to the dream of converting the ruler, or of electing one of its own, as the solution to national problems. There is little understanding of politics as a system; instead, there is a "messianic" hope in an evangelical president (or in a "Cyrus," a nonevangelical who nevertheless does God's bidding) and in the possibility of "the people of God" exercising power without ambiguities.

It is significant that a generation after independence, with churches growing rapidly in the context of corrupt states and weakened economies, "Christian nationalism" emerges in Africa. Zambia under President Frederick Chiluba was the template: an attempted "Christianization" of the nation by declaration, which ended up provoking the founding of Christian parties as a critique of the superficiality of this process.[9] In much of sub-Saharan Africa, Christianity has become almost an obligatory idiom of politics. The Pew survey of 2006 found a difference between Africa and Latin America in this respect: when respondents were asked whether government should make their country a Christian country or whether there should be separation of church and state, Pentecostals preferred a "Christian country" in Nigeria (58–35) and South Africa (45–37). Elsewhere, they rejected the idea, notably, in Chile (23–62) and Brazil (32–50). However, everywhere except Chile Pentecostals were more favorable to the idea than were other religious believers.

This difference may not be so marked now. Before the populist wave in Brazil, Joanildo Burity had concluded that there was nothing in Pentecostal political attitudes to suggest an aspiration to impose a political project over the whole of society or to set up a fundamentalist regime. In fact, the Pentecostals turned out to be rather like many of their opponents: minority groups in a pluralist society who were using hegemonic strategies to uphold their perceived rights. But with the election of Bolsonaro, there has been a tendency to try to portray the evangelicals (who refer to themselves as "the people of God") as effective proxies for the Brazilian people,[10] encouraged by the religious ambiguity of Bolsonaro himself, the first "pan-Christian president" of Brazil.[11]

Apart from my own *Evangelicals and Politics in Asia, Africa and Latin America* (2001) and *Protestant Political Parties: A Global Survey* (2004), the main (albeit now-dated) comparative work on evangelicals and politics in both Africa and Latin America is *Imaginaires politiques et pentecôtismes: Afrique/Amérique latine*, edited by André Corten and André Mary (2000).

Corten and Mary affirm two generic characteristics of Pentecostalism: it "opposes the power of the Holy Spirit to the world of 'diabolical' spirits," and it "feeds identitarian mobilizations."[12] Thus, Pentecostalism "contributes to the globalization of an imaginary of the forces of evil, presenting itself as capable of manipulating these forces."[13] The authors contrast Latin America, "where, in many countries, the elite controls democratic institutions which supposedly function in terms of public space," with Africa, where corruption and the "politics of the belly" are often evoked in terms of the control of "invisible forces."[14]

Their thesis is that Pentecostal discourse gets its power from its ability to mobilize both these imaginaries, that of the public space and of the invisible forces, and to invent a new syntax that disturbs the "syntax of the sayable." As Ruth Marshall says in her contribution to the book, "the Pentecostal 'project' of remoralising the public sphere is not understood in terms of debate or negotiation with the other groups or associations. . . . Rather, Pentecostals want to colonise it completely." Thus, say Corten and Mary, Pentecostals engage "with the public scene . . . under the banner of 'moralization' of public space. But this 'moralization' . . . cannot be seen as a political program"; rather, it is "a space of annihilation of the representation of the political."[15]

Here (although Corten and Mary do not say as much), we encounter an understandable, but limiting, phenomenon: the problem of a social analysis that is both simplistic and self-serving, in the sense that it maintains one's own centrality in the solution. An emphasis on a critique of corruption in public life makes sense because it is a political issue that can be portrayed in moral terms (thus easing any fears about an excessive politicization of the faith) and, moreover, one in which Pentecostalism can claim a "comparative advantage" in the solution (whether through the transformation of individuals, and/or through spiritual warfare against "the spirit of corruption"). The leaders of a traditionally apolitical faith, if they decide to enter politics, will tend to do so by defining the key problems and solutions in a way that retains their own importance and competence, rather than in a way that leaves them at a disadvantage and dependent on others who have the expertise they lack (whether laypeople within the church or total outsiders to the faith).

We can see this approach to maintaining church leaders' centrality working itself out even in Richard Burgess's account of recent attempts by up-market Nigerian Pentecostal leaders at nation building through values-based education, enterprise, and good governance.[16] Whereas the old holiness Pentecostalism was apolitical, and the newer prosperity gospel tried an enchanted approach to politics (exorcising the demons of the political realm and emphasizing supernaturalist recipes for personal prosperity), some younger pastors are now shifting to an emphasis on hard work, entrepreneurial skills, and social responsibility in the use of wealth and also on the development of transformational leaders and citizens shaped by Christian values, challenging the rampant patrimonialism of Nigerian public life.

It is hard not to see this new emphasis as an improvement on its apolitical holiness and "enchanted" prosperity gospel predecessors. But closer examination reveals considerable doses of naivete, messianism, and presumption. There is a lack of appreciation for the complexity of reforming public life, for the need to interact with the social sciences, and with the rich history of Christian thought and experience across the globe and the centuries. And the definition of the "Christian values" to be applied in public life seems to be prematurely decided by the American provenance of many of the ideas taught in the new institutions that these enterprising pastors are creating.

One also detects the influence of Nigeria's most successful missionary abroad: Sunday Adelaja. Adelaja has created one of the largest churches in Europe, the God's Embassy Church in Kiev, and is one of the very few African preachers to have had success among white Europeans.[17] He encourages social and political engagement as a charismatic duty to "destroy the evil that reigns in this world, to liberate every person from the curse and spiritual slavery." "Through domination of the spiritual world," he asserts, "the church will dominate the physical world." "We want our Christianity to transform medicine, the military, politics, sports, education, even entertainment."[18]

In 2008 he published a book and launched a movement called Church-Shift, intended to teach the lessons of his experience in Ukraine and "how to change the culture." The thrust of Adelaja's book is that he has achieved prominence in Ukraine through "applying kingdom principles.... These principles are to be embraced by people everywhere." They include the fact that the mission of believers is not only "to save nations" but also "to rule nations." The evidence for this claim is a 2003 protest to get land for the church in Kiev; "our unprecedented protest changed the mind-set of an entire country." Adelaja believes that his church "played a leading role in toppling the corrupt powers": its members participated in the 2004 demonstrations against electoral fraud and donated food, clothing, and tents to the demonstrators. "I am now the deliverer of a nation," he concludes.[19]

It is true that, as Catherine Wanner estimates, about 4,000 members of God's Embassy protested daily during the Orange Revolution of 2004, swelling the ranks of the hundreds of thousands of Ukrainians who did the same. It is also true that Adelaja's participation was later recognized by the leader of the Orange Revolution, Viktor Yushchenko. And his strategy of spiritual solutions to social ills, and proselytizing entrepreneurs to put godly people into public office,[20] can have a real impact, notwithstanding its evident limitations.

Nevertheless, Adelaja's book lacks any interaction with the centuries-old wealth of Christian reflection on such matters. It suffers from the Johnny-come-lately syndrome that assumes that something that we have just thought of must never have been thought of or implemented by anyone before. As a result, there are no lessons to learn, just a vision to share, principles to be embraced by everybody. The special conditions of Ukraine are not put into any perspective, and therefore the possibility of repetition elsewhere is not evaluated; in addition, Adelaja makes mind-boggling claims for his own political role ("the deliverer of a nation") on the mere basis of having led a public protest to obtain a concession for the church and then encouraging his members' participation in the vast movement of the Orange Revolution. It thus remains to be seen whether the "transformational leadership" approach in Nigeria, heavily influenced by Adelaja, can avoid repetition of these limitations.

Two other authors on the emblematic African case of Nigeria, Marshall and Ebenezer Obadare, along with Kevin O'Neill's work on Guatemala, need to be mentioned before tracing some comparisons and contrasts with the emblematic Latin American case, Brazil. Marshall says Pentecostalism ruptures with traditional politics and is difficult to reconcile with more classical forms of representation and action. Its practices are "impossible to recognize from . . . secular vocabularies." Pentecostalism constructs "a universe where words and things have agency"; it is "a national revival . . . to reclaim from the devil what he illegally holds in his control." Marshall talks of a born-again vision of citizenship in which the moral government of the self is linked to the power to influence the conduct of others and for which, in the words of one leader, "prayer—militant, strategic and aggressive—must be our weapon." But alas for Nigerian Pentecostalism, "Islam's competing theocratic project violently excludes the possibility of national conversion."[21]

Kevin O'Neill is perhaps the author on Latin America who comes closest to Marshall's approach. Writing on Guatemala, which is generally considered to have the highest percentage of evangelicals anywhere in Latin America and has had three evangelical presidents, O'Neill says Pentecostalism repositions the meaning of politics to include prayer itself. In his view, we need to reconsider how we understand political action, since non-Western populations (and Guatemala has the highest percentage of indigenous people in the Latin American region) blend spheres of life that Western modernity has separated. He focuses on what he styles "Christian citizenship," a strongly Pentecostalized concept of prayer based on notions of "spiritual warfare" against invisible demonic forces. O'Neill criticizes scholars such as me for "linger[ing] at the level of political parties and candidates" and for doing little to "reveal what Christians do at the everyday level in the name of democracy."[22]

In reply to O'Neill, I would say this is a useful corrective and complement to other approaches but not enough on its own. While the attempt to understand this sort of Pentecostal politics in its own terms, sympathetically, is praiseworthy, at the end of the day politics has to do with certain ineluctable realities. We must consider the formal mechanisms of political participation, especially because, when the founder of El Shaddai, the church that O'Neill studies, runs for president of Guatemala he does not make use of spiritual warfare explanations but develops mainstream conservative rationales. And when he loses badly, he berates his own flock for "ultimately los[ing] contact with reason" by thinking the good Christian citizen need only pray.[23]

Perhaps the idea of Pentecostalism fundamentally rewriting the script in relation to politics is more useful when looking at it operating in certain contexts but less so in others. It may be least useful at the extremes: in contexts where it is quite small numerically and has little political legitimacy, such as Russia; and in contexts where it has become very large and has a real chance of achieving power, such as in some Central American countries. Whatever the implicit desire to rewrite the rules of the political game, in practice it fails because the project is ultimately self-limiting. Central American societies are probably the most Pentecostalized in the world, but precisely there "normal politics" ends up reinforced, vis-à-vis the erstwhile Pentecostal aspirations to completely redesign the political game in terms of spiritual warfare.

Ebenezer Obadare, in his 2018 book appropriately titled *Pentecostal Republic*, points strongly in the direction of that self-limitation and the incapacity to ultimately rewrite the rules of politics. The title refers to post-1999 Nigeria, in which the dawn of democratic rule coincided, he says, with the triumph of Christianity over Islam as a political force and the simultaneous triumph of Pentecostalism as the dominant expression of Christianity. The emergent power of Pentecostalism operates in two ways: in the rising political influence of pastors and in the popular tendency to view sociopolitical problems in spiritual terms, what Obadare calls the ascendancy of a paradigm of enchantment, making Nigeria in fact an "enchanted democracy."[24] These two factors are mutually reinforcing: the influence of Pentecostal ideas on ubiquitous evil and of the need for spiritual warfare to overcome economic and political problems bolsters the social power of the leading pastors, the "theocratic class" that astutely manages this discourse.[25] This relationship is entirely consistent with what we said above, about defining political problems and solutions in a way that maintains one's own centrality and competence.

Obadare concludes that while Pentecostalism has *affected* the sociopolitical order in Nigeria, it has largely shied away from *challenging* it. In fact, "it is not altogether clear what Pentecostalism's theory of politics is, or indeed whether it has any"[26] (beyond, perhaps, the naive and self-serving ones we have already mentioned). He warns correctly (if Brazil is anything to go by) that if more of the leading pastors embrace party politics as candidates, they will lose much of the social prestige that they currently enjoy. Finally, he characterizes the Nigerian case as a cautionary tale of "what happens to weak political institutions when they fall under the sway of powerful religious forces"—all the more so because Nigerian Pentecostalism has become the ideological kin of Islamism in its attitude to state power.[27]

I would make two suggestions for building on Obadare's fine book. First, there is the need to foreground more the key figures of the Pentecostal elite who, as he says, are prone to personal and political differences. And second, it is worth considering the use of Brazil as a comparative case for illuminating, from a different angle, the present and possible future of Nigeria. Not only are the two continents, and these two countries particularly, suggestively comparable, but also Brazilian democracy is somewhat older, and, partly due to that, its Pentecostal political involvement is also slightly older.

Brazil is a cautionary tale for Nigeria, since its Pentecostal participation in public life has reinforced rather than weakened corruption. However, this condition is related to some extent to its unique evangelical electoral corporatism.

Brazil is unique in its successful evangelical electoral corporatism, that is, the practice of several huge Pentecostal denominations in presenting "official" candidates in elections and in convincing many of their members to vote for these candidates. What makes this Pentecostal political corporatism possible is above all the Brazilian electoral system (proportional representation with open lists) and the party system (fragmented, volatile, and not very ideological). Its success has been impressive in proportional elections for parliaments at all levels (federal deputy, state deputy, and city councilor), in which the votes of one denomination may be sufficient to elect someone. But it does not function in majoritarian elections for president, state governors, and mayors, in which larger electoral coalitions are necessary and the returns for the sponsoring church more doubtful. The model of "official" candidates is linked, entirely disproportionately, to cases of involvement of evangelical politicians in political scandals.

We thus see the importance of the electoral system in constraining evangelical politics. Another fundamental factor is the composition of the religious field and the relative position of evangelicals within it. Here, the singularity is Nigerian rather than Brazilian. Nigeria's religious situation makes it globally unique in terms of evangelical politics and accentuates aspects only dimly perceived elsewhere. Christianity in Nigeria (including Pentecostalism as its now dominant manifestation) is affected by the unique situation of virtual parity between the two great monotheisms, as well as by historic Muslim political predominance from Independence until almost the end of the twentieth century.

The massive presence of Islam in Nigeria is a double-edged sword: while it constitutes an irreducible obstacle both to Pentecostal Church growth and its political aspirations (unlike in Latin America or indeed in many parts of Africa), it also "authorizes," in reaction, certain Pentecostal political postures that might be harder to legitimize elsewhere. Nigeria's "Islamized Pentecostalism" does not have to "manufacture" enemies and can be more blatant in its attempts to take over state institutions.

Or, rather than (or in addition to) an Islamized Pentecostalism, should we think in terms of a "Pentecostalism unbound," largely free from secular constraints and even from the constraints of non-Pentecostal Christian institutions? Obadare's "theocratic class" of leading pastors is precisely benefitting from the hollowing out of many institutions from the 1980s onward, largely due to structural adjustment policies, which left an intellectual and social void that these pastors have been able to partially occupy. It helps, of course, that some of them are themselves university teachers; in fact, the Pew survey of 2006 discovered that Pentecostals in Nigeria are more highly educated than other Christians and Muslims; 38 percent of them have at least some college education, and this has undoubtedly helped the process of "elite insertion" of the leading pastors that Obadare portrays. This situation contrasts with the social condition of Pentecostals in most of Latin America and has important political corollaries. Guatemala may be the closest Latin American parallel; but in Brazil, it is lower-middle or lower-class Pentecostal leaders of large denominations that have predominated in political engagement.

Obadare mentions other feathers in the cap of the Pentecostal theocratic class: the fact that their prevailing social image is of moral uprightness (an image long since lost in Brazil) and the common assumption that real power is ultimately spiritual. Marshall talks of the "explicit staging of the problem of moral uncertainty and mastery in an uncertain world" as central to Pentecostalism everywhere.[28] That assessment may be true, but it comes with a differential "purchase" in different social contexts. Stephen Ellis and Gerrie Ter Haar comment that "in Africa . . . unlike in Europe or North America . . . [there is a belief that] access to the spiritual world is a vital resource in . . . political in-fighting."[29] Brazil, as in so many other ways, culturally straddles the regions they mention, which gives a certain footing to such concepts but nothing as securely as in Nigeria. In addition, there has not been in Brazil anything like the same diminution of secular poles of authority.

An illustration of this difference can be seen in the case of the Brazilian Pentecostal who has come closest to the presidency (albeit by an atypical route), Marina Silva. A globally respected Black environmentalist from the Amazon region, she overcame childhood poverty and illness to become educated and politicized in the Base Communities of the Catholic Church, rising to senator of the main left-wing party, the Partido dos Trabalhadores (PT), and then to minister of the environment in the Lula government. Dissatisfied with its handling of the Amazon, she broke with the party and ran for president in 2010 with the Green Party, and in 2014 with the Socialist Party. In the latter case, she was ahead in the polls only a few weeks before the first round of the election. But the fact that she had converted from a Catholicism influenced by Liberation Theology to Pentecostalism in 1997 was seen as politically problematic by sectors of the electorate, the media, and the intelligentsia. By some, she was characterized as "fundamentalist," by others, as easily influenced by leading Pentecostal public figures widely seen as fundamentalist and therefore as threats to the secular state. It was not enough that she was herself discreet in the electoral use of her Pentecostal identity; she still seemed to be obliged, as her biographer said, "to prove that her religious worldview will not lead the country backwards socially or intellectually."[30] Her very sincerity of religious conviction worked against her; even though everything she said could be matched by comments from other candidates, the concern of many electors was precisely with her sincere beliefs. In Brazil, the fundamentalist (or saintly person regarded as susceptible to fundamentalist pressure) is more worrying than the hypocrite. Marina certainly did not do enough to clarify the divisions within the Pentecostal world and distance herself from compromising associations. In the end, her campaign fell well short of getting into the run-off.[31]

Pentecostalism worldwide suffers many limitations on its political influence. In many places, one such limitation is *social*: a predominantly lower-class composition, lack of educational opportunities, lack of a tradition of reflection on politics, absence of links with the elite. In these cases,

Pentecostals are arriving at new levels of public visibility, almost totally unprepared (but excessively confident in their own capacities). Another frequent limitation in many countries is *ideological*: a legitimacy deficit due to a disadvantageous relationship to national identity. And everywhere, there is the *organizational* limitation: the divisions of the Pentecostal world. But is there also a *theological* limitation?

I have referred to the triumphalism that believes the "people of God" should be governing. But Islamist currents in the Middle East, who also believe in the rule of the true believers, have internal debates between short-term strategies focused on taking power and long-term strategies focused on recruitment of students and professionals and penetration of key positions in society. Brazilian Pentecostalism has no such debates; instead, it has the recurrent hope in an illusory shortcut to the conquest of influence.

It is true that new political actors, especially when they emerge from underprivileged sectors traditionally distant from politics, need time to negotiate a learning curve. But in Brazil, after thirty-five years of major Pentecostal political involvement and few signs of negotiating such a curve, one might start to wonder whether Pentecostalism has some inherent difficulties in learning certain lessons at the political level. Is it because Pentecostalism's pragmatism and intense self-belief discourage perseverance in apprenticeships in political activism? Is it because, as Alexis de Tocqueville says, the New Testament lacks the idea of moral citizenship and creates a political void,[32] which means Pentecostalism's "primitivist" concept of a return to origins (which in Christianity's case were times of powerlessness) does not produce clear-cut political proposals or the consensus for effective action? Pentecostalism has little experience in teasing out sociopolitical implications from the Christian scriptures. In addition, rapid growth in the Global South places market pressures on church leaders that are unfavorable to ethical reflection.

Theologically, Pentecostalism is formed around the universal and unincarnate Spirit, obviating the need for translation and cultural adaptation. The Spirit's initial universalist thrust, overcoming all sorts of social barriers (as in the impressively multiracial earliest days of Pentecostalism in the United States and South Africa), gets clawed back over time, hampered by its difficulty in recognizing the hardness and durability of cultures and structures. It can be an immensely attractive reforming and creative power, but it easily becomes imprisoned in a default unrealism that seeks to eliminate lengthy learning curves through various types of spiritual short-circuiting.

Over time, both primitivist Christianity's oscillation between, on the one hand, default apoliticism and unrealistic forms of involvement and, on the other, third-person Christianity's deficiencies in ethics and culture, which make a learning-curve difficult to negotiate, can lead to a disastrous self-undermining of Pentecostalism's public image. One sees that process already at work in Brazil and some other Latin American countries; it remains to be seen whether Nigeria and other African countries are heading in the same direction.

NOTES

1. Pew Forum on Religion and Public Life.
2. Davie, Heelas, and Woodhead, 13.
3. On the case of Nigeria, see Freston, *Evangelicals and Politics in Asia, Africa and Latin America*, 181–90.
4. On the case of Ríos Montt, see Freston, *Evangelicals and Politics*, 266–73.
5. Conor Gaffey, "Who Are Israel's Allies—and Enemies—in Africa?" *Newsweek*, June 5, 2017, http://www.newsweek.com/benjamin-netanyahu-israel-enemies-and-allies -africa-620733.
6. "Not Meeting Israeli's Netanyahu at ECOWAS Summit Marks Beginning of the End for Buhari/Osinbajo Govt," *Vanguard*, June 6, 2017, https://www.vanguardngr.com /2017/06/not-meeting-israelis-netanyahu-ecowas-summit-marks-beginning-end -buhariosinbajo-govt/.
7. Yosef I. Abramowitz, "Why Was the Landmark Africa-Israel Summit Shelved?", *Jerusalem Post*, September 12, 2017, www.jpost.com/Israel-News/The-story-behind-the -delayed-Africa-Israel-Summit-504793.
8. Jenkins.
9. Freston, *Protestant Political Parties*.
10. Burity, 83–107.
11. Freston, "Bolsonaro, populismo, os evangélicos e América Latina," 372.
12. Corten and Mary, 17.
13. Corten and Mary, 21.
14. Corten and Mary, 28.
15. Corten and Mary, 23.
16. Burgess.
17. Freston, "Reverse Mission."
18. Cited in J. Kwabena Asamoah-Gyadu, 306.
19. Adelaja, xxvi–xxvii, 8, 120.
20. Wanner.
21. Marshall, quotes from 3, 4, 1, 1, 215 respectively.
22. O'Neill, 216.
23. O'Neill, 204.
24. Obadare, 15.
25. Obadare, 23.
26. Obadare, 166.
27. Obadare, 35.
28. Marshall, 9.

29. Ellis and Ter Haar, 188.
30. César, 173.
31. Freston, "Marina Silva."
32. Siedentop, 134.

BIBLIOGRAPHY

Adelaja, Sunday. *ChurchShift*. Lake Mary, FL: Charisma House, 2008.

Asamoah-Gyadu, J. Kwabena. "An African Pentecostal on Mission in Eastern Europe: The Church of the 'Embassy of God' in the Ukraine." *Pneuma: The Journal of the Society for Pentecostal Studies* 27, no. 2 (2005): 297–321.

Burgess, Richard. *Nigerian Pentecostalism and Development*. London: Routledge, 2020.

Burity, Joanildo. "Conservative Wave, Religion and the Secular State in Post-impeachment Brazil." *International Journal of Latin American Religions* 4, no. 1 (2020): 83–107.

César, Marília de Camargo. *Marina: A vida por uma causa*. São Paulo: Mundo Cristão, 2010.

Corten, André, and André Mary, eds. "Introduction." In *Imaginaires politiques et pentecôtisme: Afrique / Amérique latine*. Paris: Karthala, 2000, 11–33.

Davie, Grace, Paul Heelas, and Linda Woodhead, eds. *Predicting Religion*. Aldershot, UK: Ashgate, 2003.

Ellis, Stephen, and Gerrie Ter Haar. "Religion and Politics in Sub-Saharan Africa," *Journal of Modern African Studies* 36 (1998): 175–201.

Freston, Paul. "Bolsonaro, populismo, os evangélicos e América Latina." In *Novo ativismo político no Brasil: Os evangélicos do século XXI*, edited by José Luiz Pérez Guadalupe and Brenda Carranza. Rio de Janeiro: Konrad Adenauer Stiftung, 2020, 371–91.

———. *Evangelicals and Politics in Asia, Africa and Latin America*. Cambridge: Cambridge University Press, 2001.

———. "Marina Silva: A Brazilian Case Study in Religion, Politics and Human Rights." In *Church, Cosmovision, and Environment: Religion and Social Conflict in Latin America*, edited by Evan Berry and Robert Albro. New York: Routledge, 2018, 75–95.

———. *Protestant Political Parties: A Global Survey*. Aldershot, UK: Ashgate, 2004.

———. "Reverse Mission: A Discourse in Search of Reality?" *PentecoStudies* 9, no. 2 (2010): 153–74.

Jenkins, Philip. *The Next Christendom: The Coming of Global Christianity*. New York: Oxford University Press, 2002.

Marshall, Ruth. *Political Spiritualities: The Pentecostal Revolution in Nigeria*. Chicago: University of Chicago Press, 2009.

O'Neill, Kevin. *City of God: Christian Citizenship in Postwar Guatemala*. Berkeley: University of California Press, 2009.

Obadare, Ebenezer. *Pentecostal Republic: Religion and the Struggle for State Power in Nigeria*. London: Zed Books, 2018.

Pew Forum on Religion and Public Life. *Spirit and Power: A 10-Country Survey of Pentecostals*. Washington, DC: Pew Research Center, 2006.

Siedentop, Larry. *Tocqueville*. Oxford University Press, 1994.

Wanner, Catherine. *Communities of the Converted: Ukrainians and Global Evangelism*. Ithaca, NY: Cornell University Press, 2007.

CHAPTER 15

"Africa . . . Leads the Way"

Kwame Bediako's Understanding of the Remaking of Christian Theology

Tim Hartman

Kwame Bediako understood Western Christianity to have been fatally wounded by the elimination of religious difference during Christendom.[1] "When the context of religious pluralism is succeeded," he wrote, by "a Christendom from which all possible alternatives are presumed eliminated, not only from the context, but from theological existence too, [then] the theological enterprise ceases to need to make Christian decisions. Because no other kinds of decisions are conceivable, the character of theology itself becomes changed."[2] In Bediako's analysis, Western theology failed by eradicating religious pluralism, which eliminated theological alternatives.[3] Bediako repeatedly referred to Christendom as a "disaster,"[4] and was certain that "Africa has not produced and is not likely to produce, a new Christendom."[5] Instead, African Christianity—an understanding of the Christian faith within a religiously pluralistic environment—can offer hope and guidance to Christians stuck within a Christendom mindset.

For Bediako, Western Christianity cannot continue to operate on a Christendom-era model; there must be a "re-making" of Christian theology to address the contemporary challenges presented by religious pluralism. Bediako described the problem, and the need for Western Christianity to ask new questions: "theology cannot be done, studied and taught in quite the same way in which it has been in the Western European tradition, where the challenge of pluralism was virtually unknown or else was minimal for a very long time. It also means that the intellectual framework as well as the kind of questions that will be posed, will differ from those that have characterized the Western European tradition in theology."[6] Since the experience of African Christianity has always included religious pluralism, both in the form of traditional religions and Islam, Bediako believed that Africa can help the West in the remaking of its theology. In the process, the complex character of Christianity itself will be revealed and explored. Bediako believed that "African theologians [had] recaptured the character of Christian thought as Christian intellectual activity on the frontier with the non-Christian world, and as essentially *communicative* and *missionary*."[7] For Bediako, the gift of African Christianity to the Western world is to point toward the true Christian faith, an authentic understanding of Christian identity that was not corrupted by Christendom.

As a self-described "African evangelical Christian of the twentieth century,"[8] Bediako believed that authentic Christian faith emerged from the primary encounter of individuals with the Scriptures. He was convinced that everyone should be able to read the Bible in his or her mother tongue, and he followed fellow Ghanaian theologian J. S. Pobee's belief that "African theologies should be in the vernacular."[9] Bediako employed Pobee's insights on engaging traditional African religions as he developed his own understanding of Jesus as the Supreme Ancestor.[10] For Bediako, "the practice of evangelical Christian apologetics becomes also an exercise in spirituality, one in which we affirm a commitment to the ultimacy of Jesus Christ."[11]

Bediako's core understandings of the Gospel as infinitely translatable and Christianity as indigenous to Africa are based on upon insights from Lamin Sanneh. Bediako cited Sanneh over seventy-five times in his works.[12] For Bediako, as for Sanneh, the Gospel is beyond the West. The exponential growth of the Christian faith worldwide has challenged the prevailing Western understanding of the Christian faith. While Christianity had been receding in the West (both in terms of influence and numbers of adherents), Christianity had been growing exponentially in the Global South. In 1910, 66 percent of Christians worldwide lived in Europe and North America. In 2010, 61 percent of Christians lived in the Global South (63 percent of Africans are Christians).[13] While the number of Christians worldwide has quadrupled over the last century to 2.2 billion, the proportion of the world's population that is Christian has remained constant at about one-third. Yet, in a dramatic change few saw coming, there are now nearly twice as many Christians in the Global South as in the Global North.[14] The demographic shifts within world Christianity require theological shifts in traditional (Western) theological understandings: a shift worldwide from Christendom to post-Christendom.[15]

Bediako strongly argued for an intellectual shift away from treating Western thought as the center, the reference point, for Christian theological reflection. Importantly, Bediako did not simply want to replace the former center of Christian thought in the West with a new center. The presence of a vibrant and growing African Christianity demonstrates that there can be no single definition of Christianity today. Since Christianity does not radiate from a single geographic center but multiple centers, a single meaning or message of Christianity is not possible.

Bediako followed Sanneh's insights by pursuing what the shift *away* from Christendom is a shift *toward*. Since the European Renaissance and the Protestant Reformations of the sixteenth century, the contexts of belief and the content of those beliefs have changed dramatically. The task of Christian theology has changed as well. No longer is it simply to articulate the mysteries of God for those who already believe among a culture of fellow believers. In this sense, theology had been faith-seeking-understanding. Rather, the task of contemporary theological reflection worldwide is to articulate (or translate) human understandings of divine revelation in particular contexts. Identifying this shift has helped to create the field of world Christianity through a more polycentric understanding of the faith by undermining European claims to possess the center of the Christian faith.

WORLD CHRISTIANITY, NOT GLOBAL!

The diversity of expressions of the Christian faith worldwide led Bediako to assert that "it becomes less helpful to speak of a 'global Christianity' whereby, presuming a contest for 'global' hegemony, the new centres of Christian vitality are represented as 'the next Christendom'—a relocation of power from Western churches, and therefore a global threat to the West."[16] Bediako, while aware of power dynamics, did not primarily think about the Christian faith in terms of power. The growth of Christianity in Africa and the Global South did not come at the expense of or take anything away from Christianity in the Global North; the growth of the Christian faith is not a zero-sum game. For Bediako, there are multiple centers leading to multiple Christianities. Not only is there "no *one* centre from which Christianity radiates," he claimed, but "it was never intended to be so."[17] The implication is that there are multiple centers for Christianity, not just one and certainly not just one in the West.[18]

Rather, it is more helpful and more accurate, as Bediako wrote, "to recognise the emergence of a 'world Christianity,' the result of diverse indigenous responses to the Christian faith in various regions of the world, the emergence of a positive polycentrism, in which the many centers have an opportunity to learn from each other."[19] Bediako much preferred the language "world Christianity" to that of global Christianity." To him, world Christianity emphasized indigenous responses to the Christian faith, a more bottom-up understanding, while global Christianity was more hegemonic and too concerned with issues of power within the Christian faith around the world. The learning opportunities between different cultures and contexts are a significant implication of the positive polycentricism of contemporary world Christianity.

Bediako criticized Philip Jenkins for referring to Christianity in the Global South as "a very exotic beast indeed, intriguing, exciting, and a little frightening."[20] The underlying impetus for Bediako's harsh critiques of Jenkins's *The Next Christendom* concerned the latter's fear that the rise of global Christianity was a threat to the West and the geopolitical order.[21] Bediako read Jenkins as painting "a frightening scenario that he does little to dispel" where the Christian South is ostracized by the increasingly secular North, which prides itself on being rational and tolerant.[22] Further, Bediako attacked Jenkins's search for "a new Christendom, a new 'power block.' "[23] In Bediako's view, Jenkins desired to understand the new emergence of Christianity in the southern continents "in terms of world geopolitics."[24] Jenkins's approach fueled polarizations and minimized the African significance "because it [did] not fit his geopolitical perspective."[25] Bediako acknowledged that in Jenkins's subsequent work he dropped the "frightening aspect" of the rise of global Christianity but that the exotic and intriguing descriptors remained.[26] Jenkins's core problem, according to Bediako, was that the former's analysis assumed a dichotomy between the Global North and South that was defined by the economic and political realities of late capitalism.[27] Jenkins's analysis relied on a colonial paradigm, an assumption that Bediako wholly rejected.

POSTCOLONIAL THEOLOGY IS TOO COLONIAL

Bediako's commitment to the local and the indigenous in theological reflection also caused him to be skeptical of the movement toward postcolonial theology, arguing, "In positioning oneself as postcolonial, one is handicapped to understand one's indigenous heritage."[28] He did not want to lose the insights of the "primal imagination"[29] from the precolonial period through a too hasty jump to the postcolonial. Bediako's understanding of the term "post-colonial" is primarily historical, consistent with the use of the hyphen, rather than theoretical.[30] Though Bediako's project is consistent with the postcolonial thread of pushing back against colonizing powers and influences, he insisted that "the nature and the significance of African Christian life reach[es] beyond the Western colonial connection. This means that the post-colonial paradigm can be restrictive and, when used exclusively, can be distorting."[31] To shape an African Christian identity, he looked to the twin heritage of African Christianity in precolonial Africa and pre-Christendom Christianity. As such he sought "a larger intellectual framework than post-coloniality for describing, analyzing and interpreting African Christian history, life, and thought. . . . the Christian faith in Africa is not ultimately determined by Western paradigms of interpretation."[32] For Bediako and his interests in African Christianity, the colonial period brought the Bible—translated into African mother tongues—and the name of God in Jesus Christ. Aside from these—not insignificant—contributions, the colonial period need not impact African Christianity any more than it already has.

Bediako was more interested in theology that is indigenous and pre-colonial and that emerges from Christianity as an African religion, rather than postcolonial, defined as a response to Western culture and theological concepts. In these ways, Bediako sought to be post-postcolonial by moving toward an indigenous African Christian identity that was neither shaped, nor defined, by European colonial history and ideas.[33] He rejected the secularity of modern Western thought and its skepticism of the transcendent and religious phenomena. By the end of the twentieth century, he was quite clear that "Christianity has now entered a post-Western phase."[34] In fact, he understood "the post-colonial crisis in mission" to be a part of "the dying stages of Western ethnocentrism."[35] As long as the churches in Europe and North America remained unaware or unwilling to engage the shift of the center of gravity, they perceived a crisis surrounding their historically self-appointed roles as sending churches and the peoples of the Global South as receiving churches.

Bediako preferred the term "post-missionary" to "post-colonial." The growth of the Christian faith radically altered the demographics of the Christian faith worldwide and calls for similar changes in mindset. He wanted to stress the African role in the growth of the Christian faith as well as what Africans have to offer to the world. "The experience of African Christianity," he wrote, vindicated "the transcendent as a specifically religious phenomenon and experience, [that] need not be surrendered in a culturally and religiously plural world."[36] In this sense for Bediako, "the African experience may have anticipated some aspects of post-modernity!"[37] by valuing the spiritual over the material and experience over rationality.

CHRISTENDOM ASKED WRONG QUESTIONS, GAVE WRONG ANSWERS

In the twentieth century, according to Bediako, "The missionaries were completely unaware that there could be other 'Christianities' than the form they knew. This problem persists right up to our day."[38] Thus, not only were the missionaries mistaken for presuming their understanding of Christianity was the only possibility, but Western Christianity has not learned any different in the ensuing hundred years. Christianity is not a Western religion, rather a non-Western one: "This is not to say that Christianity has ceased to exist in the West, but simply that the faith and its expression are no longer determined by dominant Western cultural and social norms."[39] Yet, "the sheer number of African Christians makes it difficult to ignore what African theologians say and write."[40] Even still, his real concern lay with the future of the church worldwide as a result of "the increasing intellectual stiffening of African Christian conviction."[41]

Contemporary theological reflection—in the spirit of Lamin Sanneh—lies in collaboration and dialogue between theologians from contexts all around the world. Truly, as Sanneh wrote and Bediako would agree, "theology cannot go on subsisting on the legacy of rented pews."[42] Each new context and each new generation within that context must respond to and interpret the Gospel of Jesus Christ for themselves. Yet, these acts of interpretation and translation do not occur in isolation. Christians the world over can (and must) listen to one another as the biblical texts are interpreted in local contexts. This listening and call for collaboration are mandatory for Western theologians today. Bediako amplified Sanneh's insights by demonstrating that the work of translation is ongoing; the Gospel is dynamic, not fixed; and the Christian faith does not belong to the West, or even to Africa, but is shared by all. The future of constructive theology lies not in North America, in Europe, or among white peoples. Instead, the future of constructive Christian theology lies in collaborations across cultural, ethnic, economic, and gender lines.

REMAKING OF THEOLOGY: "AFRICA . . . LEADS THE WAY"

The implications of this shift were clear to Bediako. The demographic changes necessitated theological changes: "It may well require a more active partnership with Third World churches to effect the rescue of Western churches from their captivity to culture."[43] While the theology of European Christians may remain important to themselves, it will only serve as a historical footnote to the theologies written in the developing world.[44] The intellectual adjustment then "requires nothing less than the complete rethinking of the Church history syllabus."[45] The focus now should be on the ongoing developments of the church in the Global South, not the fossilized remains of European churches and theologies. This shift provides an opportunity for the developing world to help the West, not that the former colonial powers deserve to be helped by those whom they oppressed.

"In the remaking of theology in our time," Bediako wrote, "the Christian churches and scholars of Africa, and also of the other Christian heartlands in Latin America, Asia and the Pacific, are called upon to lead the way."[46] The change in role for African Christian theologians—from the earliest stages of seeking an African Christian identity, to now leading the way for the remaking of Christian theology worldwide—transformed Bediako's understanding of the African theologian's task. African Christian theological scholarship "is no longer merely for Africa. It is for the world, which means that it cannot narrow its focus on Africa for its inspiration. . . . African theological scholarship can ill afford any short cuts, and it must resist the temptation to succumb to them."[47] Bediako's goal was for the depth and particularity of African theological scholarship serving to influence theological reflection worldwide. The sources of African theology lay in Africa—not outside of the continent, not in Europe, or elsewhere. Bediako expressed his point passionately: "The point here is the need for African, Asian and Latin American Christian scholars and theologians to also learn to do fundamental theological work and not merely content themselves with quoting the results of other people's work. We have little choice!"[48] The growth of African Christianity and the concurrent process of globalization (and reverse globalization)[49] have offered a new role to Africans within the worldwide Christian community. For the next era in Christian history, African theologians will lead, and others will follow.

African theologians have been deeply invested in the type of future toward which Africans are leading. Emmanuel Katongole, of Uganda, hopes for a future that is "qualitatively different from the present."[50] He desires a future "characterized not simply by the numerical growth of the Christian population, nor merely by an abstract concern for African Christian identity, but also by such mundane concerns"[51] as define the lives of many Africans. South African Tinyiko Maluleke believes that African theologies must take note of the poor of Africa, who are "already creating alternative structures to a global economy that excludes them,"[52] and will do the same theologically and ecclesiastically if they are excluded. More than Bediako's concern about "responding to the charge of African intellectuals who say that Christianity can never become an adequate frame of reference for the full expression of African ideals of life,"[53] (according to Maluleke) it is in discerning "Africa's ability to provide answers to its inhabitants' most vexing questions that we find a clue to its deepest intellectual critique of Christianity."[54] Bediako's understanding of African Christian thought has attempted to respond to both intellectual critiques: from non-Christian African intellectuals, such as Okot p'Bitek and Ali Mazrui, and also from the lives of everyday Africans affected by poverty and injustice.

UNIVERSALIZING IN REVERSE . . . UNIVERSALIZING IN PRINCIPLE VERSUS PRACTICE!

For Bediako, the considerable intellectual adjustment of a non-Western Christianity and the processes of reverse globalization led to a *universalizing in reverse*. The shift to a non-Western Christianity also leads "a reverse process to the prevailing Western-driven globalization . . . [a] process of globalization 'from below.' "[55] Particularly through migration, African immigrants are leaving Africa yet bringing their African Christianity with them to the West.[56] Since the Gospel is universal and applies everywhere, it can be translated from Greek and Hebrew and understood in Africa, as God speaks in every tongue. In this way, the universal Gospel can be translated into particular, contextualized theologies. The Gospel is universal; theology is contextual. Then, once understood in Africa, the implications for the meaning of Christianity worldwide can be universalized as a non-Western religion.

Bediako used Revelation 7:9 to justify the universal applicability of the Christian faith,[57] claiming that "though Christianity has always been universal in principle it can be seen to have become universal in practice only in recent history in fact. Now this, of course, is a fact that is not only unique among the world's religions, it is a new feature for the Christian faith itself. One must not underestimate, therefore, what the outworking of a global, Christian identity might involve."[58] Bediako later moved beyond only trying to establish and articulate an African Christian identity and toward "a global, Christian identity." Yet, it must be noted, that even a global, Christian identity is not abstract, somehow apart from its host culture. Instead, as always, this universalizing from the bottom up, or at least from Africa to the world, *must* be particular.

A THEOLOGICAL REORIENTATION

New theologies needed to emerge from Africa because new theological answers were needed to contemporary questions, and the West was incapable of offering any helpful insights.[59] According to Bediako, "It is obvious that the kind of theological re-orientation that is needed cannot be done in the West, nor by Western churches and institutions. The reason is evident: the West is now not the major theatre of Christian interaction. Indeed, Western culture is becoming increasingly hostile to that interaction. The work has to be done in the major theatres of Christian interaction."[60] Africa, Asia, and Latin America are the locations of exponential growth of the Christian faith. These locales offer the greatest possibility for new theological insights.

African theology is not merely interested in different content. "African theology was, in fact, charting a new course in theological method."[61] The new method concerns identity, questions of "old" and "new," continuity and discontinuity, African and Christian. One result of the changed method is that it "forced the theologian to become the *locus* of this struggle for integration through a dialogue, which, if it was to be authentic, was bound to become personal and so infinitely more intense."[62] Bediako's own theology demonstrated his claim of the theologian's struggle for integration as the locus for theological reflection. His major themes of identity, translatability, history, mother-tongue Scriptures, and contextual theology were all deeply personal.

The theologian herself became a central site of theological reflection. The deeply contextual African theology of identity refused to separate theologians from their theologies. Bediako described the work of African theologians in the same manner that he also described the work of early Greco-Roman theologians, as "apologia pro vita sua" (a defense of one's life).[63] Bediako further explained why the path of African theologies differed from the prior, Western, approaches: "African theology in the last half century has not developed categories or rubrics of systematic or dogmatic theology. . . . Instead, African Christian thought has followed a sense of direction of its own, and sought its own responses to its own questions."[64] The focus on African identity continually drives African theologians back into local African communities. An African understanding of Christianity freed Bediako from his captivity to Western culture. His hope was that by articulating his understanding of Christianity in Africa, his fellow Africans would be freed also.

The spread of the Christian faith through the Scriptures translated into vernacular languages has encouraged everyday Christians—not just educated pastors and church leaders—to actively engage the Scriptures with their spiritual questions. For his part, Bediako saw "African academic theology as being challenged to be in close contact with the vernacular apprehension of the Christian faith and with its roots in the continuing realities of the traditional primal world-view."[65] In spite of Bediako's insistence on universality in theological reflection, he believed that the starting point for academic theology was "spontaneous or grassroots theology."[66] Focusing on grassroots theologies prevented academic theology from becoming "detached from the community of faith . . . [as an insular] conversation . . . among the guild of scholars."[67] Thus, academic theologians are not under any burden to construct a theology out of nothing but, rather, "academic theology has the important role of understanding, clarifying and demonstrating the *universal* and *academic* significance of the grassroots theology in the interest of the wider missionary task of encountering the world with the Gospel."[68]

For Bediako, the "laboratory for the world" offering by African Christian thought presents a way forward to Christian theological reflection worldwide.[69] By simultaneously appealing to pre-Christendom theological understandings and postmissionary expressions of Christianity, African Christian thought and lived African Christianities can lead the way toward the remaking of Christian theology away from Western-centric norms and toward vernacular Christian understandings.

NOTES

1. Kwame Bediako (1945–2008) was a Ghanaian theologian who published two monographs and over seventy-five articles and book chapters. He was the founding director of the Akrofi-Christaller Institute for Theology, Mission, and Culture in Akropong-Akuapem, Ghana; see acighana.org. For more on Bediako, see Tim Hartman, *Theology after Colonization: Bediako, Barth, and the Future of Theological Reflection* (Notre Dame, IN: University of Notre Dame Press, 2020); Sara Fretheim, *Kwame Bediako and African Christian Scholarship: Emerging Religious Discourse in Twentieth-Century Ghana* (Eugene, OR: Pickwick Publications, 2018); and Bernhard Dinkelaker, *How Is Jesus Christ Lord? Reading Kwame Bediako from a Postcolonial and Intercontextual Perspective* (Berne, Switzerland: Peter Lang, 2017).

2. Kwame Bediako, *Christianity in Africa: The Renewal of a Non-Western Religion* (Edinburgh: Edinburgh University Press, 1995), 257.

3. Bediako, *Christianity in Africa*, 257.

4. See Kwame Bediako, "Africa and Christianity on the Threshold of the Third Millennium: The Religious Dimension," *African Affairs* 99 (2000): 316.

5. Bediako, *Christianity in Africa*, 249. Of no minor significance, here, is that Bediako published these words eight years *prior* to Philip Jenkins, *The Next Christendom: The Coming of Global Christianity* (New York: Oxford, 2002).

6. Kwame Bediako, *Theology and Identity: The Impact of Culture on Christian Thought in the Second Century and Modern Africa* (Oxford: Regnum, 1992), 434.

7. Kwame Bediako, "African Christian Thought," in *Oxford Companion to Christian Thought*, ed. A. Hastings and A. Mason (Oxford: Oxford University Press, 2000), 10; original emphasis.

8. Bediako, "How Is Jesus Christ Lord? Evangelical Christian Apologetics amid African Religious Pluralism," in *Jesus and the Gospel in Africa* (Maryknoll, NY: Orbis, 2000), 34.

9. J. S. Pobee, *Toward an African Theology* (Nashville: Abingdon, 1979), 23; quoted by Bediako in *Christianity in Africa*, 72.

10. See Bediako, "Jesus in African Culture," in *Jesus and the Gospel in Africa* (Maryknoll, NY: Orbis, 2000), 23. See also Pobee, *Toward an African Theology*, 46, 48, and 94.

11. Bediako, "How Is Jesus Christ Lord?," 44.

12. When Bediako pursued his PhD at the University of Aberdeen from 1978 to 1983, Sanneh was a young professor in the Department of Religious Studies. Andrew Walls was the department chair and Bediako's supervisor. Most often, Bediako cited Sanneh, "The Horizontal and the Vertical in Mission: An African Perspective" *International Bulletin of Missionary Research* 7, no. 4 (1983): 166; Lamin Sanneh, *Piety and Power: Muslims and Christians in West Africa* (Maryknoll, NY: Orbis, 1996), x; Lamin Sanneh, *West African Christianity: The Religious Impact* (Maryknoll, NY: Orbis, 1983), 250; or Lamin Sanneh, *Translating the Message: The Missionary Impact on Culture* (Maryknoll, NY: Orbis Press, 1989), 1.

13. Pew Research Center, "Global Christianity: A Report on the Size and Distribution of the World's Christian Population," December 19, 2011, www.pewforum. org/2011/12/19/ global-christianity-exec/.

14. The rapid growth of Christianity in Africa began to receive scholarly attention in the 1970s. David Barrett first identified the shift in "centre of gravity" in 1970. "By AD 2000," he wrote, "the centre of gravity of the Christian world will have shifted markedly southwards, from Europe and North America to the developing continents of Africa and South America." David Barrett, "AD 2000: 350 Million Christians in Africa," *International Review of Mission* 59, no. 233 (January 1970): 49–50. Shortly thereafter, British church historian Andrew Walls expanded and interpreted Barrett's observation, republished in Andrew F. Walls, *The Missionary Movement in Christian History: Studies in the Transmission of Faith* (Maryknoll, NY: Orbis Books, 1996), 6.

15. See Lamin Sanneh, *Disciples of All Nations* (New York: Oxford University Press, 2007) and Lamin Sanneh and Joel A. Carpenter, eds., *The Changing Face of Christianity: Africa, the West, and the World* (New York: Oxford University Press, 2005).

16. Kwame Bediako, "Conclusion: The Emergence of World Christianity and the Remaking of Theology," *Understanding World Christianity: The Vision and Work of Andrew F. Walls*, ed. William R. Burrows, Mark R. Gornik, and Janice A. McLean (Maryknoll, NY: Orbis, 2011), 248.

17. Bediako, *Christianity in Africa*, 164; original emphasis.

18. Kwame Bediako, "New Paradigms on Ecumenical Co-operation: An African Perspective," *International Review of Mission* (July 1992): 376. See also Bediako, *Christianity in Africa*, 164, 167, 169.

19. Bediako, "Conclusion," 248.

20. Kwame Bediako, "'Whose Religion Is Christianity?': Reflections on Opportunities and Challenges for Christian Theological Scholarship as Public Discourse: The African Dimension," *Journal of African Christian Thought* 9, no. 2 (2006): 47n4; citing Jenkins, *The Next Christendom*, 220.

21. For Bediako's earliest critique of Jenkins, see his 2003 Stone Lecture at Princeton Theological Seminary," published as Kwame Bediako, "'Ethiopia Shall Soon Stretch Out Her Hands to God' (Ps. 68:31). African Christians Living the Faith: A Turning Point in Christian History," in *A New Day Dawning: African Christians Living the Gospel. Essays in Honour of Dr. J.J. (Hans) Visser*, ed. Kwame Bediako, Mechteld Jansen, Jan van Butselaar,

and Aart Verburg (Zoetermeer, Netherlands: Boekencentrum, 2004), 30–40, esp. 32–38.

22. Kwame Bediako, "A New Era in Christian History—African Christianity as Representative Christianity: Some Implications for Theological Education and Scholarship." *Journal of African Christian Thought* 9, no. 1 (2006): 7n9. Bediako is referring to Jenkins, *The Next Christendom*, 161–62.

23. Bediako, "A New Era," 3.

24. Bediako, "A New Era," 3.

25. Bediako, "A New Era," 4. See also James Ferguson, who describes Africa as "an inconvenient case" for globalization theorists, since it does not fit the storyline for either proponents or opponents of globalization. Instead, "the recent history of Africa does pose a profound challenge to ideas of global economic and political convergence." James Ferguson, *Global Shadows: Africa in the Neoliberal World Order* (Durham, NC: Duke University Press, 2006), 26, 28.

26. Kwame Bediako, "'Why Has the Summer Ended and We Are Not Saved?': Encountering the Real Challenge of Christian Engagement in Primal Contexts." *Journal of African Christian Thought* 11, no. 2 (2008): 5. See Philip Jenkins, *The New Faces of Christianity: Believing the Bible in the Global South* (New York: Oxford University Press, 2006).

27. See Bediako, "Whose Religion Is Christianity?," 47n4.

28. Bediako, "Whose Religion Is Christianity?," 48.

29. Bediako insisted on the integrity of "the primal imagination" in his understanding of Christianity. *Christianity in Africa*, 92. He borrowed the term from C. G. Baëta's *Christianity in Tropical Africa* (Oxford: Oxford University Press, 1968). For Bediako, primal imagination was understood as an outlook of "a spiritual universe which was both simple and complex, and yet . . . able to [be] embraced as a totality." *Christianity in Africa*, 92. Further, the maintenance of the primal imagination must derive from African traditional religions; it cannot be imposed from without. "A starting point for appreciating the primal imagination," Bediako wrote, "must be in primal religions themselves." *Christianity in Africa*, 93. Bediako sees the primal imagination as the core of what is distinctive about African Christianity. The term "primal" had no pejorative meaning whatsoever for him.

30. For more on the use of the historical use of the hyphen in "post-colonial," see Bill Ashcroft, Gareth Griffiths, and Helen Tiffin, *The Empire Writes Back: Theory and Practice in Post-colonial Literatures*, 2nd ed. (Routledge, 2002), esp. 193–222.

31. Bediako, "Whose Religion Is Christianity?," 46.

32. Bediako, "Whose Religion Is Christianity?," 47.

33. For an opposing interpretation, see Tinyiko Maluleke, who believed that Bediako's understanding of African Christianity was "too thickly clouded by the mist of colonialism." Tinyiko Maluleke, "Black and African Theologies in the New World Order: A Time to Drink from Our Own Wells." *Journal of Theology for Southern Africa* 96 (November 1996): 8.

34. Bediako, "Whose Religion Is Christianity?," 47.

35. Bediako, *Christianity in Africa*, 131.

36. Kwame Bediako, "A Half Century of African Christian Thought: Pointers to Theology and Theological Education in the Next Half Century," *Journal of African Christian Thought* 3, no. 1 (2000): 8.

37. Bediako, "A Half Century," 8.

38. Kwame Bediako, "Biblical Christologies in the Context of African Traditional Religion," in *Sharing Jesus in the Two-Thirds World*, ed. Vinay Samuel and Chris Sugden (Grand Rapids, MI: Eerdmans, 1984), 121.

39. Kwame Bediako, " 'In the Bible . . .': Why the World Needs Africa," *AICMAR Bulletin* 6, 36.

40. Kwame Bediako, "Review of *African Theology en Route*," in *Journal of Religion in Africa* 11, no. 2 (1980): 159.

41. Bediako, "Review of *African Theology en Route*," 159.

42. Lamin Sanneh, *Whose Religion is Christianity?: The Gospel Beyond the West* (Grand Rapids, MI: Eerdmans, 2003), 58.

43. Kwame Bediako, "The Willowbank Consultation, January 1978—A Personal Reflection," *Themelios* 5, no. 2 (January 1980): 32.

44. Walls, *Missionary Movement*, 10.

45. Bediako, *Christianity in Africa*, 207. Bediako is quoting Andrew Walls here. Perhaps Bediako was also thinking of John Mbiti's famous quotation that Western Christians know more about the heretics of the second and third centuries than about contemporary Christians living in the developing world. See Bediako, *Christianity in Africa*, 154ff. Mbiti wrote, "It is utterly scandalous for so many scholars in older Christendom to know so much about Christian movements in the second and third centuries, when so few of them know so little about Christian movements in areas of the younger churches. We feel deeply affronted and wonder whether it is more meaningful theologically to have academic fellowship with heretics long dead than with the living brethren of the church today in the so-called Third World." John Mbiti, "Theological Impotence and the Universality of the Church," in *Mission Trends 3: Third World Theologies*, ed. Gerald Anderson and Thomas Stransky (Grand Rapids, MI: Eerdmans, 1976), 17.

46. Kwame Bediako, "The Emergence of World Christianity and the Remaking of Theology," *Journal of African Christian Thought* 12, no. 2 (2009): 54.

47. Bediako, "The Emergence of World Christianity," 54.

48. Bediako, "In the Bible . . . ," 48.

49. "Reverse globalization" is the term given to the movement of peoples and ideas from the so-called developing, or Third, World to the so-called developed, or First, World.

50. Emmanuel Katongole, *A Future for Africa: Critical Essays in Christian Social Imagination* (Scranton, PA: University of Scranton Press, 2005), 156.

51. Katongole, *A Future for Africa*, 156.

52. Maluleke, "Black and African Theologies in the New World Order," 18.

53. Maluleke, "Black and African Theologies in the New World Order," 6.

54. Maluleke, "Black and African Theologies in the New World Order," 16.

55. Bediako, "Africa and Christianity on the Threshold of the Third Millennium," 314.

56. See Mark Gornik, *Word Made Global: Stories of African Christianity in New York City* (Grand Rapids, MI: Eerdmans, 2011); Jacob K. Olupona and Regina Gemignani, *African Immigrant Religions in America* (New York: New York University Press, 2007); Afe Adogame, *The African Christian Diaspora: New Currents and Emerging Trends in World Christianity* (New York: Bloomsbury Academic, 2013); Afe Adogame, ed., *The Public Face of African New Religious Movements in Diaspora* (New York: Routledge, 2016); and Soong-Chan Rah, *The Next Evangelicalism: Freeing the Church from Western Cultural Captivity* (Grand Rapids, MI: InterVarsity Press, 2009). In postcolonial poetry, Louise Bennett has described this phenomenon in her 1966 poem "Colonization in Reverse." Louise Bennett, *Selected Poems* (Kingston: Sangster's Book Stores, 1982), 107.

57. Revelation 7:9: "After this I looked, and there was a great multitude that no one could count, from every nation, from all tribes and peoples and languages, standing before the throne and before the Lamb, robed in white, with palm branches in their hands."

58. Kwame Bediako, "Reading Signs of the Kingdom," Stone Lecture #1, Princeton Theological Seminary, October 20, 2003, Princeton, NJ.

59. See "if it is true that the new configuration of the Christian world has taken Christian theology into areas of life where Western theology has no answers because it has no questions, then it is evident that Western theology may not be of much help to us either.... Western Christian theology may have little with which to help Africa and why, rather, the world and the West in particular, may need to learn from Africa and from African experience." Bediako, "In the Bible," 44.

60. Bediako, "In the Bible ...," 47.

61. Bediako, "A Half Century," 6.

62. Bediako, "A Half Century," 7; original emphasis.

63. Bediako, "A Half Century," 7. For more on the usage of this description, see Fretheim, *Kwame Bediako and African Christian Scholarship*, 129–32.

64. Bediako, "A Half Century," 7.

65. Bediako, *Christianity in Africa*, 86. In order to investigate the relationship between academic and grassroots theologies, Bediako turned to Afua Kuma, an "illiterate Christian woman ... theologian from rural Ghana whose prayers and praises of Jesus remind us that, in the final analysis, the whole of our Christian calling is to worship Jesus the Lord." See Kwame Bediako, "Cry Jesus!," in *Jesus and the Gospel in Africa* (Maryknoll, NY: Orbis, 2000), 9, 18. For more on Afua Kuma, see Afua Kuma, *Jesus of the Deep Forest*, trans. Jon Kirby (Accra: Asempa Publishers, 1981). Also see Philip Laryea, "Mother Tongue Theology: Reflections on Images of Jesus in the Poetry of Afua Kuma" *Journal of African Christian Thought* 3, no. 1 (2000): 50–60; Mercy Amba Oduyoye, "Jesus Christ," in *The Cambridge Companion to Feminist Theology*, ed. Susan Frank Parsons (Cambridge: Cambridge University Press, 2002); and Richard Fox Young, "Clearing a Path through *Jesus of the Deep Forest:* Intercultural Perspectives on Christian Praise and Public Witness in Afua Kuma's Akan Oral Epic," *Theology Today* 70, no. 1 (2013): 38–45.

66. Bediako, *Jesus and the Gospel*, 17.

67. Bediako, *Jesus and the Gospel*, 17–18.

68. Bediako, *Jesus and the Gospel*, 18; original emphasis.

69. Bediako, *Christianity in Africa*, 252.

CHAPTER 16

Evangelical Transformation and Transnationalism in Africa

Stephen Offutt

INTRODUCTION

Tremendous diversity exists among the vast numbers of African evangelicals. Images of Pentecostals dancing in open air markets, high church leaders wearing liturgical garb, women from conservative sects in head coverings, the sparse décor of the ascetic Reformed churches, and the overhead shots of sprawling independent megachurch campuses all tell part of the story. Behind such images are a range of worship styles, religious practices, sets of doctrines, and approaches to ordering community. The differences are magnified and multiplied by evangelicalism's intersection with the various ethnic cultures that exist across Africa and even within nation-states.

African evangelicals nonetheless share a common DNA. I argue that the building blocks of the African evangelical DNA include transnational networks (shared social structures) and an understanding and template of mission (shared cultural content). Evangelicalism's transnational networks knit together national, continental, and global communities of faith. They also undergird evangelical mission, increasingly referred to as transformation, which looks surprisingly similar across the continent. These building blocks of evangelical identity are cobbled together differently in different corners of Africa. But, as this chapter shows, it consistently results in efforts to build social institutions, engage in spiritual activities, and create grassroots social change.

To elucidate these essential elements of evangelicalism, I draw on five case studies from around the continent. I organize the case studies into three categories: mission denominations, indigenous Pentecostal and charismatic organizations, and nongovernmental organizations (NGOs) and their local partners. These categories do not capture the entirety of African evangelicalism. Evangelicals who are not represented include traditional "mainline" denominations like the Anglican and Reformed Churches. Neither do independent megachurches feature in this account, many of which have a prosperity gospel orientation. But the three categories presented here provide several advantages. They are central nodes in the global evangelical movement. They provide historical depth in telling the story of African evangelicalism. And they bear witness to both the extensive transnational ties and the central evangelical agenda of transformation, both of which are the main focus of this argument.

Identifying Evangelicals

Who, among African Christian groups, should be considered evangelical? This is a tricky question that requires a flexible methodology. It must have the ability to recognize that certain faith traditions and denominations may opt into the evangelical community in some African countries and out of it in others. It also must reckon with the fact that the term "evangelical" is a common reference point for Christian subgroups in some African locations but less used in others. I present a set of identity filters that meet these criteria: (1) self-identity as an evangelical, (2) agreement by other evangelicals that the individual or group belongs, (3) active participation in evangelical networks, and (4) a general fit of established definitions of evangelicalism. With regard to the latter, David Bebbington argues that evangelicalism's defining characteristics include an emphasis on conversion or a need for change in one's life, an active bent toward sharing their faith with others, a high regard for the Bible, and an emphasis on Christ's atoning work on the cross.[1] Although somewhat dated, this definition still captures evangelicalism's most basic characteristics.

Identifying evangelical communities in this way helps to sift through socioreligious complexities. Consider the case of South Africa, where the evangelical community consists of Christian groups with diverse doctrines and religious practices. The Pentecostal Assemblies of God denomination and the decidedly non-Pentecostal Baptists, for example, agree that they share an evangelical identity. As a result they are willing to collaborate in projects at municipal and national levels. Likewise, traditional or mainline denominations and independent churches who sometimes articulate a prosperity gospel message can find common ground in the midst of difference. An Anglican, for example, may rail against the "prosperity light" Rhema Bible Church but will concede (sometimes glumly) that conservative Anglicans are co-religionists with Rhema members. This is a key indication that while differences remain, the resulting contentiousness is understood as "insider" evangelical bickering.[2]

Conversely, the approach also shows where the fault lines are among African Christian groups. The findings in some cases run against commonly perceived notions. It is not useful, for example, to talk about Pentecostals as a single faith community in South Africa, because there is a decisive split between African Independent Churches (AICs), all of which are Pentecostal, and evangelical Pentecostals. A member of the Apostolic Faith Mission (AFM), an evangelical denomination that emerged from the 1906 Azusa Street revival, even speaks of the need to evangelize members of the Zion Christian Church (ZCC) and the Shembe movement. This is true despite the fact that the ZCC came out of the AFM in the early twentieth century.[3]

Evangelical identity is reinforced by formal religious networks. The Assemblies of God, the Baptist denomination, the Anglican Church, and Rhema Bible Church are all members of the Evangelical Association of South Africa (TEASA). All four groups generally fit Bebbington's definition of evangelicalism. Conversely, neither the ZCC nor the Shembe movement have pursued membership in TEASA, and assigning Bebbington's definition to their religious beliefs and activities is more problematic. One begins to see, then, the logic and reality of the evangelical community in South Africa and who is part of it, and who is not.

Mission as Transformation

Evangelical mission, or the way the movement engages with society, has increasingly taken on the moniker of "transformation." Of course the term is not only used by evangelicals. It has become popular in the wider international development sector, with groups of various stripes hoping to "transform" communities, countries, social structures, and so on. But "transformation" holds a particularly meaningful place in the evangelical lexicon. It references the spiritual and social activities in which evangelicals believe God has asked them to participate. How this came to be, and the significance of transformation as a concept, needs a brief explanation.

The evangelical intelligentsia and global evangelical leadership began working on a theology and theory in the 1970s that explained how their evangelistic and church-planting activities could and should connect with social work. By 1983, when a key conference was held by the World Evangelical Fellowship in Wheaton, Illinois, they had developed basic principles that could be used to solve this puzzle and began to use the term "transformation" to reference these ideas. Conference participants founded a journal called *Transformation: An International Journal of Holistic Mission Studies*, which is housed at the Oxford Centre for Mission Studies. This remains an important evangelical publishing outlet that explores how issues of faith intersect with themes such as poverty, the environment, and inequality.[4] The journal has served as both a spur and a guide to action for evangelical mission and development organizations.

Arguably the most influential academic in creating this narrative was South African David Bosch (1929–92). Bosch was born into a nationalist Afrikaner family. As a student at the University of Pretoria, he began to question the apartheid system. This intellectual misgiving matured into full dissent as he pursued his doctoral work in Switzerland. Upon completion of his degree, he returned to South Africa to serve as a missionary to the Transkei for the Dutch Reformed Church. It was the Dutch Reformed Church that created the theology of apartheid; Bosch chose to work against the apartheid system from within. This strategy met with success: in 1982, 123 pastors and theologians signed an open letter to the church that Bosch promoted and that publicly condemned apartheid.[5] In the midst of such work Bosch also grew in his reputation as a scholar. In 1991 he published a book called *Transforming Mission: Paradigm Shifts in Theology of Mission*. This is considered a magnum opus of Christian mission. In 1999 two books that Bosch influenced, and which were an outgrowth of the 1983 Wheaton conference that Bosch attended, were published. *Mission as Transformation* expanded the missiological understanding of transformation.[6] *Walking with the Poor* articulated the idea of transformation as it can be applied by Christian community development organizations.[7] This set of literature, along with numerous derivative publications, has impacted how evangelicals do outreach around the world, not least in Africa.

Evangelicalism's transformation literature argues that the end goal of mission should be shalom. The most direct translation for "shalom," a Hebrew word, is peace. But shalom is a broad concept that implies wholeness and completeness, including in the areas of relationships, health, safety, and prosperity. God, evangelical scholars argue, is interested in restoring broken relationships in multiple spheres of life, including with God, oneself, others in the community, and the environment.[8] Evangelicals apply this theological stance through a wide range of ministry activities, including addressing the brokenness of extreme poverty through education, microfinance initiatives, water and sanitation projects, and preventative health programs. Most evangelical organizations state that where possible, local churches should be the locus of such activities. Transformation carries with it a spirituality that can include miraculous healings and divinely inspired dreams and visions. Transformation seeks a seamless integration of material, ecclesial, and spiritual elements.

Quite a number of African evangelicals have never heard of Bosch and are not aware of the intellectual history behind the term "transformation." But the term has outpaced the literature about it, and evangelicals not involved in these conversations nonetheless reference transformation and engage in these kinds of activities. The net result is that this general package of beliefs and activities has come to typify significant swaths of the global and African evangelical movement.

Although the concept of transformation was not articulated until the late twentieth century, it has continuity with centuries-long Christian activity in Africa. Many (but not all) early missionaries organically integrated efforts at church planting and addressing human need. They created healthcare institutions, helped to increased literacy, or contributed to other core elements of human flourishing.[9] There has nonetheless been a sector of evangelical churches, both in the West and in Africa, that have been inward looking and uninterested in social outreach. For these churches, the ideas promoted by the theology of transformation provides a justification and explanation of mission that has a more holistic orientation.

CASE STUDIES

I present the case studies in this section in roughly historical order. First, I present two mission denominations: Evangelical Churches Winning All (ECWA) in Nigeria and Africa Gospel Church (AGF) in Kenya. Second, I present indigenous African organizations in the Pentecostal / charismatic streams: CAPRO, a Pentecostal Nigerian missionary organization, and Faith Ministries, a Zimbabwean charismatic association of churches. Finally, I discuss an NGO / church partnership in Democratic Republic of Congo (DRC), where World Vision is partnering with Evangelical Covenant churches. All of these cases are heavily networked transnationally, and all of them expend significant resources and energy engaging in transformational activities.

MISSION DENOMINATIONS: ECWA AND AGC

Early evangelical incursions onto the continent came through mission organizations. These organizations arrived in different waves. Several originated in England in the late 1700s, such as the Baptist Missionary Society (1792), the London Missionary Society (1795), and Oxford's Church Mission Society (1799). A North American wave of organizations came a century later, including the Sudan Interior Mission (SIM) (1893), the African Inland Mission (1895), and the World Gospel Mission (1910). All of these organizations had confessional positions, including Anglican, Baptist, Reformed, and Wesleyan. But they also fit the evangelical ethos of the day.

As with many such organizations, the SIM and the World Gospel Mission (WGM) nurtured African-led church movements: Evangelical Churches Winning All and the Africa Gospel Church, respectively. ECWA, founded in Nigeria in 1954, currently has roughly 6,000 churches and 7 million members. The AGC, founded in Kenya in 1961, has roughly 2,000 churches. Both denominations have complete autonomy from the organizations from which they sprang, but cordial relationships between denominations and mission organizations continue.

ECWA and AGC Transformational Activities: Building Institutions to Promote Human Flourishing

ECWA and AGC have created institutions designed to foster human flourishing. ECWA oversees more than 200 primary and secondary schools, four teaching colleges, a microfinance bank, a major agricultural initiative, 110 health clinics, and multiple television and radio stations.[10] Such institutions are intended to enable ECWA to carry out its transformational mission, and they have brought ECWA into nonprofit and marketplace spaces in society. ECWA has also become a financially robust denomination, with a roughly $40 million annual budget.

ECWA's institutions are important to the central and northern regions of Nigeria, as well as to neighboring countries. ECWA began its agricultural extension program in 1978. Few such services were available in the region at that time, and the program positively impacted crop yields, which in turn enriched people's diets, in Nigeria and in parts of Burkina Faso, Chad, and Cameroon. The program grew such that ECWA decided to break off parts of the enterprise and make them businesses, including a regional feed mill and a chick distribution program. In the health sector, ECWA has established clinics in remote places where no other healthcare services exist. ECWA's hospitals are in urban centers in the central and northern regions of Nigeria. The denomination runs the only eye hospital in the city of Kano. In Jos, ECWA officials report that Muslims go to their hospital rather than government hospitals outside the city because of the quality of service, security concerns, and proximity. In the education sector, schools run by ECWA also significantly impact northern Nigeria. Bingham University, for example, was founded by ECWA in 2005. Located in the city of Karu (near Abuja), it is one of just six private universities in Nigeria's northern region. The goal of the university is to integrate faith with "secular" disciplines. It offers undergraduate and master's programs related to technology, health sciences, social sciences, law, and education.[11] Bingham is gaining a reputation for providing a dependable educational environment in a region where state university schedules are disrupted by labor disputes and other issues.

In Kenya, the AGC's institutions seek to address health, education, and economic issues. Tenwek Hospital is one of the AGC's signature institutions. Its origins predate the AGC: a land grant was awarded to WGM by the government in 1935; it gradually built medical facilities on this site. By 1959 Tenwek had formally become a hospital. The AGC has assumed joint governance for Tenwek, whose website states that it is the "medical ministry of the African Gospel Church in collaboration with the World Gospel Mission."[12] Tenwek currently serves as a teaching hospital and offers a wide range of medical services. These include an intensive care unit, the capacity to perform heart surgery and other complicated surgical procedures, a pediatric wing and eye and dental services. Tenwek appears on several lists of the best hospitals in Kenya. It is ranked eleventh in the country overall, for example, by the independent Ranking Web of Hospitals.[13] Leading members of Kenya's national political and business community choose to be treated at Tenwek, which is an indication of its reputation and stature in a country that does not have sufficient institutional capacity to address much of its population's medical needs.

Tenwek's Community Health and Development arm takes a participatory approach to community development. The programs it runs include HIV / AIDS programs, water and sanitation projects, efforts to increase food security, and outreach to women in prostitution.[14] These programs target impoverished rural areas in Masai and Turkana as well as other communities.

The Kenya Highlands University (KHU) is another AGC institution. The university began as an informal Bible school that became the Kenya Highlands Bible College. A school of nursing was added to the Bible program. The need for government accreditation later changed the makeup of the school, and additional programs in education, counseling, and computer training were added. The number of Bible and theology students dropped, causing the original intention of the school to suffer. But other programs, such as a master's in philosophy and religion, have grown. Many current AGC church leaders have been trained at KHU, and it remains an important part of the denomination.

The AGC also runs an infant rescue facility called the African Gospel Church Baby Centre. The center emerged in the mid-2000s in partnership with WGM. It receives babies on referrals from hospitals and police and from parents who are unable to care for their child. Sometimes babies arrive who were abandoned in public toilets and have already suffered permanent disabilities. The center thus has a wing for disabled babies in addition to a larger area for generally healthy babies. International and local personnel staff the center. They care for the children and seek families to adopt them. Kenyan families are preferred, but the center also facilitates international adoptions. The Kenyan government's stance on international adoptions has made the latter option more difficult.

ECWA and AGC Transnational / Transcultural Imports

SIM provides ECWA's most important transnational / transcultural network. The two groups' Nigerian headquarters remain housed in the same building. SIM has assumed a supporting role, identifying and helping to respond to areas of need that exist within ECWA. SIM posts these needs to its donor and support base. For example, there are expatriate faculty members in ECWA's seminaries and universities. SIM recruits such faculty, making clear that they won't earn a salary. Rather, they must raise their own support from North America and elsewhere. The same kind of dynamic exists for expatriate medical staff. In one example, the SIM Nigeria director recruited a medical team from Australia to see how they might reach internally displaced peoples in northern Nigeria with medical services. In the process, SIM provided motivation for ECWA to reach out to victims of Boko Haram. The leadership of ECWA maintains the ability to decide its own trajectory, but it is often receptive to ideas and suggestions from SIM that are consistent with ECWA's mission and vision.

ECWA maintains other transcultural ties that draw resources for transformational initiatives. Sometimes these are initiated by SIM but are then maintained by ECWA. Calvary Church in Lancaster, Pennsylvania, for example, financially supports one of ECWA's seminaries in Nigeria. Churches from across North America as well as from the UK and Europe send short-term mission teams to ECWA churches in Nigeria. These teams often help to establish church to church partnerships that last for years and sometimes for decades. More professionally, ECWA draws funds for its People Oriented Development (POD) of ECWA both from private donations and from government and nongovernment sources. They have developed such relationships with entities around the world, including in Australia, Canada, Germany, Israel, the Netherlands, New Zealand, and South Korea. These kinds of relationships are usually handled by denominational representatives and have a different feel from the more grassroots church partnerships. But both types of transnational networks are important components of ECWA's outreach efforts.

Like the ECWA / SIM relationship, WGM serves as the AGC's most important transnational / transcultural network. Funding from WGM supports western missionaries in Kenya, a part of Tenwek's budget, and various other projects in which AGC shares joint ownership. WGM and AGC maintain clear organizational distinctions; AGC leadership is completely Kenyan. But the mission and vision of one organization continue to strongly overlap with those of the other, allowing close partnership across cultures to continue.

Other western church and mission networks connect to the AGC from the United States, the United Kingdom, Germany, and elsewhere. For example, some AGC pastors are very involved in the Kenya chapter of the Global Leadership Network, a church network based in South Barrington, Illinois. The network is active in 135 countries.[15] Numerous smaller western mission and Christian development organizations, as well as individual churches, send mission teams and other resources to assist with AGC ministries.

The AGC also has connections to nonwestern countries. Pastors and missionaries from a Japanese organization, the Immanuel General Mission (IGM), for example, have helped with funding and personnel to start at least two AGC churches in Kenya. One of these was the Immanuel AGC in Nairobi, which is currently the largest AGC church. The IGM has also sent nurses to Tenwek from Japan. Likewise, churches in India have sent professors to work with the AGC; O. E. Joseph, for example, served in the Kenya Highlands Bible College. In sum, the AGC has developed partnerships with like-minded organizations in many parts of the world.

ECWA and AGC Migration-Based Transnational Relationships

Nigeria and Kenya have both experienced heavy emigration. There are an estimated 17 million Nigerians living abroad;[16] Kenya has roughly 3 million citizens living outside the country.[17] This has allowed ECWA and AGC to build extensive migration-based transnational networks, the implications of which are felt both in the countries of origin and in the migrants' host countries.

ECWA churches have sprung up in Atlanta, Brooklyn, Chicago, Louisville, Memphis, and Washington, DC. ECWA USA has been formed from such churches, with its own executive council and website.[18] The leadership of the ECWA USA District is installed by the executive of ECWA from Nigeria. ECWA USA leaders travel to Jos, Nigeria, every April to attend the ECWA General Church Council, thus maintaining close contact with the denominational leadership in Nigeria. A symbol of ECWA USA's tight linkage to Nigeria is that sermons in the churches in the United States follow the theme of the year that is established in Nigeria. ECWA USA also financially supports ECWA's work in Nigeria. Each US-based congregation is encouraged to send 25 percent of their tithes and offerings back to Nigeria. Although this level of remittance is not always, and perhaps not often, achieved, funds from US-based churches are used to support ECWA's transformational efforts in Nigeria.

AGC members who find themselves living outside Kenya stay connected to the AGC in a variety of ways. In the United States, for example, the AGC tasked a national liaison to help keep people connected. The liaison hosts reunions for AGC members who travel from across the United States to attend. An AGC official from Kenya sometimes flies in to speak at the event. The reunion is designed to facilitate discussions about how the Kenyan diaspora can get plugged into AGC initiatives in Kenya and receive updates on the ministries they support.

Kenyans' global mobility has strong implications for religious organizations back home. Some AGC members increase their earning power when they emigrate. They then send their tithe to their congregations of origin. This transaction is made easier by the fact that Kenya has one of the continent's most advanced mobile banking systems. Emigrants can wire money back home through Wave or other applications. AGC emigrants also mobilize short-term mission teams and return to Kenya for ministry purposes. Even when AGC members of the Kenyan diaspora are not visiting Kenya, they communicate with their co-religionists back home through Facebook, WhatsApp, email, Skype, and phone calls. The AGC's transformational initiatives thus often incorporate emigrant participation and contributions of various types.

ECWA and AGC Transnational Exports

Transnational ties are not only about incoming resources. ECWA and the AGC are actively engaged in exporting religion as well. ECWA has roughly

3,000 Nigerian missionaries in eighteen countries, including the Gambia, Senegal, Togo, Israel, and the United Kingdom. ECWA missionaries are largely supported by funds raised by Nigerians in Nigeria. Their missionaries are not always from Nigeria, a fact that has created interesting transnational dynamics. In one example, ECWA recruited a Kenyan, brought him to Nigeria to be trained, then sent him back to Kenya, financially supported from Nigeria. This is a practice that ECWA has repeated with citizens from Togo and elsewhere.

The AGC also exports religion. Kenyan AGC missionaries have, for example, started churches in Uganda, Rwanda, Tanzania, South Sudan, and Democratic Republic of Congo. AGC leaders often look for people within their denomination who believe they have a spiritual call to be a missionary. They then provide the training and resources they need to realize their goal. The AGC's affluent, urban congregations are particularly involved in mobilizing and equipping missionaries. In all, the AGC has more than fifty missionaries serving within and outside of Kenya.

INDIGENOUS PENTECOSTAL/CHARISMATIC ORGANIZATIONS: CAPRO AND FAITH MINISTRIES

Evangelical groups that did not originate in the West or from western actors have sprung up across Africa. They have been founded by Africans and are headquartered in Africa. Such groups create significant social and religious change on the continent; they also develop ties and export religious people, goods, and messages across the globe.

In this section I introduce two such groups. One is a Nigerian missionary organization network; the other is a network of charismatic churches in Zimbabwe. Both organizations were founded in the 1970s. They carry the same basic Gospel message as the mission denominations, but they are younger and there are important differences in the way they think about spirituality and transformation. There are also differences between charismatics and Pentecostals and between these two specific cases, but their shared characteristics place them in the same cohort within the broader evangelical community.

Calvary Ministries (CAPRO)—Nigeria

Calvary Ministries (known as CAPRO because its original name was Calvary Productions) is such an organization. It was founded in 1975 by university students from southern regions of Nigeria who were highly committed to their faith and who were posted to the country's remote northern regions as part of Nigeria's compulsory National Youth Service Corps program. They encountered an Islamic presence there and were not able to share their faith in the ways they were used to doing in Nigeria's southern regions. CAPRO was thus founded as a way to facilitate such efforts. Serving with CAPRO meant extending their time in these impoverished areas beyond what the government required. To do so, CAPRO missionaries often had to forego potential earnings and experience poverty themselves.[19] This remains common practice among CAPRO missionaries, which the organization currently describes as having "extreme devotion to Jesus, extreme commitment to the Word of God, extreme passion for the lost, extreme sacrifice for the missions mandate and extreme commitment to honouring the Bride of Christ."[20]

CAPRO's culture is grounded in classical Pentecostalism, or the kind of Pentecostalism described by David Martin and Brigitte Berger.[21] Such authors highlight Pentecostalism's emphasis on virtues such as honesty, frugality, and diligence, as well as abstention from drugs, alcohol, and womanizing. This more ascetic (but still spiritually active) approach to the faith is different from some Word of Faith or prosperity gospel emphases and doctrines. For most of CAPRO's history it has striven to keep its institution separate from prominent Word of Faith actors in the Nigerian context, although ties to such actors may be starting to emerge.

CAPRO has grown rapidly since the 1970s. It currently has around 750 missionaries in the field and many other volunteers. The annual budget of the organization is roughly $9.2 million. CAPRO has a presence on multiple continents: it is working in thirty-seven countries,[22] with a particular interest in North Africa and the Middle East.[23] CAPRO continues to grow: in 2019 CAPRO's Nigeria-based website (CAPRO also has US- and UK-based websites) listed new opportunities to serve in northern Nigeria, Rwanda, India, and China, among other locations. CAPRO recruits evangelists, pastors, teachers, and medical professionals to help in in its work.[24] People with these and other professional skills help the organization pursue its approach to transforming communities.

Faith Ministries—Zimbabwe

Faith Ministries in Harare, Zimbabwe, is part of the global charismatic movement. Its origins can be traced to 1976, when its founder, Alistair Geddes, a white Rhodesian who was originally from Scotland, began speaking in tongues. His traditional Methodist Church believed such activities to be taboo and so removed Geddes from the congregation. But Geddes soon found other Rhodesians who were having similar religious experiences. The group grew into a charismatic congregation—a trajectory shared by numerous other churches springing out of traditional denominations at that time.

Faith Ministries began as an exclusively white church but quickly decided to remake itself into a multicultural congregation. The leadership began inviting Black Zimbabweans from the community to join them and, more important, worked with the University of Rhodesia to invite Black university students into their congregation. Discipling young adults became a focal point for their ministry.

The 1980 political transition from colonial Rhodesia to independent Zimbabwe further impacted Faith Ministries' composition. White members began to emigrate, including Geddes, who left for the United States in 1982. At the time the congregation was still 80–90 percent white, but Geddes named Ngwiza Mnkandla, a rising young Ndebele leader, as his successor. This change hastened the departure of older and middle-aged white members of the congregation, and the church became a primarily Black (largely Shona) congregation.

A time of rapid growth ensued. At the time Mnkandla took over, Faith Ministries had one congregation of about 300 adults. There are now more than seventy congregations in Zimbabwe and about five internationally. The movement has approximately 10,000 adults. Faith Ministries has a number of strong congregations in the more affluent suburban areas, but the majority of its churches are found in poorer urban areas. Still, the church has gained a reputation of having an upper-class membership. Young Black professionals and university students remain important to Faith Ministries' identity, but the actual membership has diversified in both age and economic status.

Transformational Activities of CAPRO and Faith Ministries

CAPRO employs strategies of evangelism and discipleship to create transformation. Part of CAPRO's mission is to "reach 'unreached' people groups"[25] with the biblical message that Christ died for the sins of all. This is why the organization began with missions to northern Nigeria and has maintained a strong focus on northern Africa and the Middle East. Like Faith Ministries, the term "discipleship" is emphasized in CAPRO's programs. To this end, CAPRO has created mission training schools in Nigeria, Togo, Kenya, and elsewhere.[26] The organization also has an organic approach to discipleship, as missionaries live in communities with this purpose in mind. Chinyereugo Adeliyi, a CAPRO missionary, stated that "CAPRO sees discipleship as integral to everything we are doing. Spending time with the converts on the farm is discipleship, eating with them, Bible study, literacy class, church service *etc.* . . . That is why the missionaries are resident, we intentionally want them to see every part of the way we live."[27]

CAPRO believes evangelism and discipleship help to make the presence and love of God known in communities and that this is the true motor of transformation. Spiritual encounters with Christ, CAPRO argues, change how people treat one another. They do so in part by changing behavior patterns, replacing harmful ones with other behaviors that are edifying and empowering. Stories from CAPRO's ministry include men who become Christians. They stop spending their earnings on alcohol and channel their resources toward better care for their children. Another CAPRO account tells of a young woman who tried to guard against her children dying at birth by sacrificing livestock, one of her few material assets, to the gods. When she became a Christian she kept her livestock and instead trusted fellow believers to take her to the hospital to give birth. CAPRO argues, based on this example and others, that assumptions about the transcendent shape behavior. Conversion changes those assumptions and thus increases social well-being.

Spiritual activity can also be seen in the lives of CAPRO missionaries. Dreams, visions, and miracles are common and expected components of their ministries. One CAPRO missionary was reportedly delivered by God from lions that he happened upon while searching for "unreached" people groups in northern Nigeria. Experiences like these are, to CAPRO's way of thinking, evidence that the Holy Spirit is the central actor in the transformation process. Evangelism and discipleship are important in part because these are the activities that draw people into more dynamic relationship with the Holy Spirit.

CAPRO focuses on the spiritual side of transformation but also engages material poverty in various ways. CAPRO works in remote regions where basic human needs are great. They thus dig wells, start schools, and create community health centers. There is some concern that not all the institutions that CAPRO starts and then hands over to local leadership, including churches, survive.[28] But many do have a lasting impact. Adeliyi points to Rumana Gbagyi, a village in the state of Kaduna.[29] CAPRO has engaged in numerous community development projects there, and residents have nicknamed the village "small London" because of the resulting transformation. CAPRO points to numerous other villages in northern Nigeria that have also benefited from such projects.

Faith Ministries believes that individual and community change occurs principally through discipleship and church planting. Its mission statement references "discipleship through relationships." This approach includes an emphasis on discipling, or mentoring, people who take leadership roles in various parts of society. Such people, should, according to Faith Ministries' way of thinking, create positive change throughout society. Faith Ministries has pursued variations of this idea ever since its early partnership with the University of Rhodesia. The church's primary transnational connections have been aimed at facilitating and deepening this kind of approach.

Like CAPRO, Faith Ministries' transformational activities have an overtly spiritual element. Its meetings include a time in which leaders lay hands on people and pray. This practice commonly results in people falling down because they are "slain in the spirit." Exorcisms can also be conducted during these times. As Dwight Mutonono, a member of the Faith Ministries International Council, puts it: "God's miraculous intervention is expected and invited; and meetings hear testimonies of God working in that way."[30] Some of Faith Ministries' church planting efforts utilize crusades, during which miracles and exorcisms also occur.

In the 1990s a new opportunity arose for Mnkandla; he was invited to be the head of Zambuko Trust, a faith-based microfinance organization. Zambuko Trust makes financial services available to the poor with the hope of creating "lasting solutions [for] the basic needs of families."[31] Zambuko was founded through a partnership of Zimbabwean Christian businesspeople and Opportunity International (OI), a faith-based microfinance institution headquartered in Chicago. It quickly became one of Zimbabwe's leading microfinance organizations, garnering visits and mentions by well-known international leaders.

Mnkandla maintained the position of senior pastor at Faith Ministries while leading Zambuko Trust. According to Mutonono, who handled the day-to-day operations of the church during this time, there were discussions among Faith Ministries members about whether such a close tie to Zambuko might pull the church away from its core commitments to discipleship, evangelism, and church planting. Mnkandla, however, was able to navigate these concerns. He used Zambuko as a way to broaden Faith Ministries' understanding of mission and service. Faith Ministries subsequently started programs such as a prison ministry and an outreach to widows and orphans, including helping with school fees and other living expenses. This trajectory also led Faith Ministries to deliver emergency supplies to affected areas of Mozambique after it was ravaged by Cyclone Idai in 2019.

CAPRO and Faith Ministries—Transnational Networks

CAPRO was created by Nigerians to minister to other Nigerians, but it is now a Nigeria-based transnational organization. The international office remains in Lagos; this is where policy decisions are made. But CAPRO now has a multinational workforce (a majority of employees are still Nigerian) that draws on transnational resources and has a global reach.

Nigerians living in the West help to shape CAPRO's identity. In the United Kingdom, CAPRO gears some of its ministry toward the Nigerian immigrant community. It has held events about missions in the diaspora and uses language about the "global harvest," which signals an interest to take global migration patterns into account when understanding missions. It has formed chapters in major cities across the United Kingdom.[32] CAPRO also tries to mobilize Nigerians in the West to finance personnel and programming in resource-scarce regions of the world. CAPRO actively recruits short-term mission teams and prayer groups. It also seeks to tap the financial resources of the Nigerian diaspora, including those who have reached senior executive positions in their companies. CAPRO's trustees include, for example, the CEO of an oil and gas consultancy and the chief medical physicist at a cancer center.[33]

CAPRO also builds transcultural partnerships with churches and organizations. As one CAPRO missionary explained, "We don't go pursuing churches because they are black or white or red or yellow." Rather, CAPRO is looking for churches that think about missions in the ways that CAPRO thinks about missions. As a result, an ethnically diverse set of churches in the United States now partner with and financially support CAPRO's work. They have had, for example, a relationship with Christian Life Center, a multiracial but primarily African American congregation in Chicago, for over two decades. CAPRO also partners and draws support from western mission and Christian development organizations such as Tearfund, the United Kingdom's largest evangelical relief and development organization. CAPRO can leverage such partnerships to dramatically increase the scope and reach of its programming.

Faith Ministries is an independent group, but it seeks to develop relationships within the global charismatic movement. In the early 1980s the church joined a network spearheaded by American leader Bob Mumford, who saw a need to create discipleship and accountability structures for charismatic churches. Mnkandla, influenced by Dave Richards and Barney Coombs from the United Kingdom, gravitated to this kind of thinking. Mumford's "shepherding movement" helped to shape Faith Ministries' identity. Faith Ministries also joined Salt and Light Ministries, part of the Restoration movement in the United Kingdom. Over time Faith Ministries has become a leading member of this network, which includes churches in the Nordic area (Norway, Sweden and Finland), United States, Kenya, and India.

Discipling a Whole Nation (DAWN), a church-planting movement that originated in the United States, is a third transnational charismatic network in which Faith Ministries has vigorously participated. DAWN provided Faith Ministries with educational resources and ways of thinking that channeled its church-planting energies in the 1990s and 2000s. Most of these churches are in Zimbabwe, but Faith Ministries has churches in South Africa, Botswana, and the United Kingdom. Faith Ministries is no longer quite as active in DAWN's networks, but it remains committed to principles of church planting and discipleship.

Zimbuko Trust, as part of OI's global network, has also been a source of transnational ties. Larry Reed, an American who led OI's side of the partnership with Zambuko, invited Mnkandla to be the speaker at OI's annual global conference. OI's partner institution in Russia was impressed with Mnkandla's presentation and asked him to speak again at OI's next Eastern Europe regional conference.[34] Mnkandla formed deep friendships around the globe through OI's networks and through other similarly minded organizations. These connections have deepened and expanded in the ensuing decades.

CAPRO's and Faith Ministries' Mission Networks in Africa and Beyond

CAPRO's missionaries can be found throughout West Africa and in many eastern and southern African countries, as well as in the Middle East and Asia. CAPRO believes the process of placing a missionary in a given country is guided by the Holy Spirit. To the outsider, the process may appear to be haphazard. One of CAPRO's staff members, for example, may have a vision for a particular country. He or she will then go to the leadership and say, "God wants me in this place." The leadership responds by encouraging the individual to continue to pray, and they begin to see if they can raise support. The CAPRO member explained that "we have done it [this way] over and over again. It just works."

CAPRO missionaries in the field maintain strong lines of communication with other CAPRO personnel around the world. Prayers are shared daily through a confidential WhatsApp forum. Adeliyi shared examples of messages that appear in the forum:[35] "Brethren, this morning, a man just walked in. We don't know him, we think we are being monitored. Could you pray?" Two days later a message could come in saying, "Our fears proved right. We have been summoned to the police. Could you pray?" Not all messages are as sensitive. Another message may read, "Our sister who has been battling with cancer finally went to be with the Lord. Can we pray?" Such communications keeps the CAPRO community closely connected.

As in other case studies, emigration is part of Faith Ministries' contemporary story. Zimbabwe's political and economic turbulence has caused a quarter of all Zimbabweans to leave the country.[36] Faith Ministries' members are no more or less likely to emigrate than other Zimbabweans, so it is fair to assume that about a quarter of its members have also emigrated. Members who do so are usually encouraged to find fellowship in other charismatic churches in their new homes rather than planting new Faith Ministries churches. Still, Zimbabwean emigrants have planted Faith Ministries congregations in the United Kingdom and elsewhere. In these cases, Faith Ministries' leadership encourages the new plants to move quickly beyond an exclusively Zimbabwean membership. It is not clear how successful they have been in this endeavor to date. But as Faith Ministries grows beyond Zimbabwe, it hopes to have a transcultural makeup.

NGOS AND PARTNERING CHURCHES

NGOs are financially the most powerful organizational vehicle that evangelicals use to pursue transformation. The scope of NGO activity around the globe is enormous. Although finding exact measurements is difficult, the US NGO sector's total income is estimated to be about $29 billion.[37] Faith-based actors, most of whom are Christian, make up one-third to one-half of the sector.[38] The Accord Network, which is an evangelical network of about 100 US faith-based organizations, estimates that their members channel over $4.4 billion a year and employ over 110,000 people around the world.[39] Accord Network members are more engaged in Africa than in any other continent.[40] Although the total amount of money spent by evangelical NGOs in Africa per year is not known, these related numbers make clear that evangelical NGOs have significantly more resources at their disposal than those of other evangelical actors. Any discussion of evangelicals and social change in Africa must acknowledge the powerful role played by NGOs, both internationally and locally.

Most evangelical NGOs partner with local congregations. In a recent survey of Accord Network members, 89 percent of all responding organizations suggested that local churches help poverty efforts. This call to action indicates "a strong belief and adherence to the transformational development message that good development is church-centered development."[41] NGOs have developed various ways of pursuing church partnerships: they may work through the church in the community, they may consider the community as the primary partner but keep the church involved, or they may try to achieve scale by partnering with denominations at the regional level. The latter approach is used in the case study below.

The Evangelical Covenant Church / World Vision Partnership in Democratic Republic of Congo

The Evangelical Covenant Church (ECC) is a small denomination in the United States. Swedish immigrants who were part of a Pietist movement within the Swedish Lutheran Church began planting churches in the north-central United States in the 1860s. They formalized the denomination in 1885, calling it the Swedish Evangelical Covenant Church.[42] The denomination later sought a multicultural identity and so removed the term "Swedish" from its name.

The ECC sent its first missionaries to the northern part of Democratic Republic of Congo (DRC) in the mid-1930s. At one point roughly 100 ECC missionaries were working in the area, and the ECC has maintained a particularly close relationship to the region. Perhaps the most well-known twentieth-century missionary was Paul Carlson, an ECC doctor and missionary. In 1964 at the age of thirty-six, Carlson was killed in the midst of political turbulence. This became an international incident; Carlson was referred to as a martyr by mainstream media and appeared on the covers of *Time* and *Life* magazines.[43] The ECC created a foundation in his name, whose purpose is to facilitate medical and economic development in the region he served.[44]

It was also in the 1960s, in the years after Congo won its independence from Belgium, that the ECC began to transition formal leadership in the Congo from missionaries to local leaders. The ECC transferred property ownership to the Covenant Church of Congo (CEUM), which by then was organizationally and legally separate from the ECC. Properties that were transferred included medical and educational facilities as well as local church properties. The CEUM now oversees the premier hospital in the region (financially supported by the Paul Carlson Partnership and other ECC entities), two nursing schools (one college level and one high school level), about 1,500 elementary or secondary schools, and roughly 2,000 congregations. The CEUM, the Catholic Church, and the Evangelical Free Church are the three largest Christian traditions in the region. The CEUM now has roughly twice as many members than the ECC in the United States, which is also still growing.

World Vision is the world's largest Christian NGO. It was founded by American Robert Pierce and Korean Kyung-Chik Han in Korea in 1950; its original intent was to care for orphans.[45] World Vision currently works in nearly 100 countries and has an annual budget of roughly $2.75 billion.[46] World Vision's programs continue to prioritize children, but this emphasis is now embedded in a wide range of relief, development, and advocacy strategies. In regions where there is a Christian population, it seeks to empower churches and partner with local congregations.

World Vision started its work in DRC in 1984. It originally engaged only in emergency relief. In 1998 World Vision Congo began sustainable community development programming, and it currently claims to be "working towards the measurable, sustainable well-being of 5,311,208 children and their communities."[47] World Vision Congo runs education, economic, health, and water, sanitation, and hygiene (WASH) programs and is engaged in four different regions of the country.

ECC and World Vision began to partner in the Congo in 2012. The ECC's then president, Gary Walter, and other ECC administrators met with World Vision's then president, Richard Stearns, in 2010. The CEUM began some community development initiatives but felt an NGO partnership could make it more effective. World Vision was not at that time working in DRC's northwest region. At the 2010 meeting, Stearns agreed to establish an Area Development Program in the area in partnership with the CEUM. To generate some of the funding for the partnership, the ECC promoted World Vision's child sponsorship program in its North American churches.

Transnational Ties

The ECC / World Vision partnership has created a new set of transnational ties. Members of ECC churches have committed to roughly 10,000 child sponsorships through World Vision since 2010, 6,500 of which are still active. In 2019, ECC sponsorships accounted for over 50 percent of World

Vision's annual project budget (not including the WASH program), or roughly $970,000. Local churches in the United States remain energized by the partnership. The ECC congregation in Naperville, Illinois, for example, responded warmly to the initial push for child sponsorships in 2012. Church members signed up for eighty sponsorships in the first few weeks. The pastor at the time, Scot Gillan, stated that "it was a move of God to say your [congregation's] focus needs to be Congo."[48] The church took a team to DRC in 2013, which created personal ties between members of the Naperville church and members of CEUM churches. A CEUM official subsequently visited Naperville, which now counts among its own membership several people of Congolese descent. Meanwhile, World Vision's child sponsorship system continues to link sponsors in the church to the children they sponsor in DRC. Numerous other ECC churches in the United States have developed similar ties through the program.

If a partnership is brokered in the United States by two American organizations, is it fair to consider the resulting programs a manifestation of African evangelicalism? To the extent that it is not, problems have emerged. Officials in the ECC characterize at least some of their interaction with the CEUM as being colored with the problem of dependency. But reality is more complex than just one dynamic; the CEUM is a mature denomination with active leadership. The CEUM brokered a separate partnership with World Vision to give its main hospital access to running water for the first time. With respect to the day-to-day operations, the CEUM is the actual partnering entity for World Vision.

For its part, World Vision has long struggled with dependency issues around the world. It has taken some steps to mitigate the problem. National World Vision offices are legally distinct from the United States offices: for example, World Vision Kenya and World Vision Congo are both their own legal entities. Most personnel hired by World Vision Congo are Congolese. But funding flows still create an uneven global power dynamic. World Vision continues to experiment with ways to address this, including by flipping its child sponsorship approach. World Vision now goes to North American churches and asks people who would like to sponsor a child to fill out the paperwork and get their photo taken. Staff then take the photos to, in this case, DRC, where they host a "choosing party," and children choose the people they wish to have as a sponsor. This initiative has reversed the policy of displaying children's photos from developing countries in western churches so that future sponsors could make a choice. The strategy is too new to be fully evaluated, but there are indications that it is having a positive, if limited, effect.

Transformational Activities

The development initiative continues amid the dilemmas and challenges questions raised above. The scale of the initiative is significant: in addition to the nearly $2 million annual budget for economic development, mother and child survival, community development, and child protection, the WASH project was on a three-year budget cycle from 2018 to 2020 of over $3 million. The project focused on the remote city of Gemena, where there previously was no municipal water system, no paved roads, no electricity, little in the way of financial services, and, outside of the CEUM's institutions, almost no health services.

In such a context, the partnership has resulted in measurable social change. The project's initial major push was access to clean water. By the end of 2019, roughly 60,000 people had gained access to clean water, primarily through digging two new wells and capping springs in the area. The recipients of these improvements equate to close to 50 percent of the population of Gemena. The project has also expanded the capacity of the city's education system: three new schools in Gemena have been built; they are serving about 4,000 students. To improve the local economy, over 700 farmers are being trained in agricultural techniques designed to improve crop yields and increase environmental sustainability. World Vision also introduced animal husbandry programs and is training business groups in how to create a local value chain business model for their products. In the area of health, over 200,000 immunizations have been administered to children, and nutrition centers have been established to address symptoms and results of hunger.[49] One of World Vision's more innovative programs is intended to help children increase their own resilience. To do so, they organize what they call child parliaments, where children learn how to debate issues of importance to them and advocate more effectively for their own safety. World Vision attempts to make the resulting change sustainable by building in mechanisms by which skills and knowledge are transferred to community members over the life of the projects.

World Vision invites CEUM churches to participate in their community programs and also gears some of their programming toward local congregations directly. These include activities that strengthen or create Sunday schools, "Good News Clubs," and Bible camps. Money is budgeted to facilitate the provision of Bibles and Bible study curriculum. The project also includes efforts to mobilize faith leaders to advocate for ideas initiated by World Vision. They are being trained to help protect children and provide family counseling. The project also advocates for faith leaders to discourage "harmful practices such as early marriage" and to support interfaith forums that focus on child protection. The project thus not only creates measurable change of economic indicators but also introduces at least the possibility of cultural change through and within partnering congregations.

CONCLUSION

The image of African evangelicalism that emerges from these case studies is one that is heavily transnationally networked and highly invested in creating social change throughout the continent. When these transnational networks get examined more closely, certain characteristics begin to emerge. Likewise, social change that evangelicals hope to create becomes clearer. Both are critical to African evangelical identity more generally.

Transnational Networks

Some aspects of African evangelicalism's transnational networks are not surprising. First, African evangelicals are more heavily networked with the West than with other regions of the world. Second, considerable resources flow from the West to be used by African evangelicals. These include monetary resources as well as short-term mission teams, religious curriculum, and goods intended to reduce human need. Related to this dynamic is the fact that discussions about dependency on the West are still relevant for at least some African evangelicals. Third, denominations and mission organizations are particularly useful in creating and sustaining transnational networks over time. All of these dynamics have been shown to be true in other studies; they surface again in the case studies presented above.

Other elements of transnational networks have been less discussed. African evangelicals, for example, send missionaries to other locations. Students of global Christianity and missiology have been aware for several decades that Global South actors are sending missionaries of their own. However, the fact that groups in the first four cases in this study send missionaries indicates that it is no longer exceptional; it may now be a taken-for-granted element of African evangelical activity. A related finding has to do with the nonwestern transnational connections of African evangelicals. These case studies show connections to the Middle East and parts of Asia, including Israel, India, and South Korea. The AGC is networked with Japan; some of CAPRO's connections are in Muslim-majority countries. Little is known about how African evangelical networks are impacting such regions or about how such networks are helping to shape African evangelicals. But it is increasingly evident that they are important.

The case studies in this chapter also show that there is enough breadth in this sector of global civil society that despite common points of reference, networks have not become clogged up with too many actors inhabiting the same relational space. The mission denominations have likely known about each other since almost their inception. But the two groups have developed different sets of support networks in the West and do not appear to be in direct competition for resources. Neither ECWA nor the AGC operates in the networks that Faith Ministries has tapped into, which are different again from those of CAPRO, and finally of the CEUM. These distinct pathways point to the diversity of African evangelicals' histories, experiences, styles of expressing the faith, and ways of approaching transnational relationships.

Transformational Activities in Africa

African evangelicals draw from a common basket of activities when they engage society. The case studies reveal spiritual initiatives such as evangelism, church planting, prayer, faith healings, and other types of miracles. They also show the creation of social institutions such as schools, health facilities, nonprofits, and microbusinesses. Such institutions enable African evangelicals to engage in a wide range of activities, such as responding to humanitarian crises, promoting agricultural work, and digging wells. This collection of spiritual initiatives, institution building, and social programming is what constitutes the evangelical approach to transformation.

Some evangelical groups draw more from one category of activities than others. Stories of prayer, miracles, and evangelism are particularly evident in the narratives of CAPRO and Faith Ministries. These groups argue that Pentecostal and charismatic beliefs and practices can replace elements in traditional religious systems that have negative effects on human flourishing. They also report that spiritual interactions lead to physical healings and other positive life outcomes.

Other evangelical groups appear to emphasize institution building over spiritual initiatives. ECWA, the AGC, CEUM, and World Vision Congo have earned a place in the history of their countries for the role they have played in community and economic development. These evangelicals create organizations that in turn provide solutions in a wide range of areas, including healthcare, agricultural output, basic literacy, and advanced education. Their current social impact fits Woodberry's description of how early conversionary Protestant missionaries reshaped society.[50]

Such emphases do not imply that groups practice one set of transformational activities to the exclusion of other sets. Although highly spiritually active, CAPRO and Faith Ministries also build institutions and run poverty alleviation programs. Practical approaches to helping the poor have a more instinctive quality for these groups—they may be "led by the Spirit" to respond to a natural disaster or to start a literacy program. But such leadings occur frequently enough that they are an important part of their faith communities and identities. The notion that such groups only engage in otherworldly activities is, quite simply, empirically problematic.

Conversely, ECWA and the AGC engage in spiritual transformation. ECWA is a non-Pentecostal denomination, but some of its pastors report that they perform exorcisms and that the people for whom they pray sometimes experience miraculous healings. ECWA has a "prayer renewal ministry department" that oversees formal initiatives in these areas. In the AGC, prayer, fasting, and meditation have always been part of denominational practice. Some AGC congregants report receiving visions and dreams. The AGC also believes in the existence of demon possession, and members pray for those under such influences but are less explicit in practicing exorcisms than some of their Pentecostal counterparts. ECWA and the AGC may prioritize narratives of how God is using them to create sustainable solutions to social problems, but they do so within the context of a spiritually dynamic worldview.

The five grouped case studies in this chapter demonstrate the transnational connectedness, the creative power, and the particular approach African evangelicals take to social transformation. Together, the actors in these cases have planted tens of thousands of churches, thousands of elementary and secondary schools, and hundreds of health facilities, and they have engaged in scores of economic empowerment schemes. Millions of dollars flow through these organizations every year, and most or all of these organizations continue to grow. Their spiritual vitality is having an impact on African worldviews and culture. Shared social structures and cultural content run across these cases, providing strong evidence that African evangelicals are major social, cultural, and economic change agents on the continent. We should pay more attention to their impact.

NOTES

1. Bebbington.
2. Offutt.
3. Offutt.
4. Tizon.
5. Livingston.

6. Samuel and Sugden.

7. Myers.

8. Myers.

9. Woodberry.

10. ECWA USA website, accessed December 2, 2019. https://www.ecwausa.org/.

11. Bingham University website, accessed December 2, 2019. http://binghamuni.edu.ng /v2/.

12. Tenwek Hospital, "A Brief History."

13. Ranking Web of Hospitals.

14. Tenwek Hospital, "Community Health and Development."

15. Global Leadership Network.

16. Melody Fidelis, "17 million Nigerians Living Abroad, Says Government," *Guardian*, October 20, 2017, accessed February 11, 2020, https://www.pressreader.com/nigeria /the-guardian-nigeria/20171020/281994672729062.

17. Heuler.

18. ECWA USA website, accessed December 2, 2019, https://www.ecwausa.org/.

19. Jakada.

20. CAPRO Nigeria.

21. Martin; Berger.

22. CAPRO UK.

23. CAPRO USA.

24. CAPRO Nigeria

25. CAPRO USA.

26. Jakada.

27. Chinyereugo Adeliyi, personal interview, 2019.

28. Jakada.

29. Chinyereugo Adeliyi, personal interview, 2019.

30. Dwight Mutonono, personal interview, 2019.

31. Zambuko Trust.

32. CAPRO UK.

33. CAPRO USA; CAPRO UK.

34. Larry Reed, person communication, January 22, 2020.

35. Chinyereugo Adeliyi, personal interview, 2019.

36. Bloomberg, "A Quarter of Zimbabwe's Population Has Emigrated," *Business Tech*, August 4, 2019, accessed January 10, 2010, https://businesstech.co.za/news/business /333063/a-quarter-of-zimbabwes-population-has-emigrated-and-more-will-follow -analyst/.

37. Schnable.

38. McCleary.

39. Accord Network.

40. Offutt and Reynolds.

41. Offutt and Reynolds, 13.

42. The Evangelical Covenant Church.

43. Hamilton.

44. Paul Carlson Partnership website, accessed January 11, 2020. https://www.paulcarlson.org/

45. Swartz.

46. World Vision.
47. World Vision Congo.
48. Scott Gillan, personal interview, 2019.
49. The Evangelical Church and World Vision.
50. Woodberry.

BIBLIOGRAPHY

Accord Network. "Convening the Body of Christ to Serve the Poor with Excellence." 2020. Accessed January 14, 2020. https://www.accordnetwork.org/.

Bebbington, David. W. *Evangelicalism in Modern Britain: A History from the 1730s to the 1980s.* Boston: Unwin Hyman, 1989.

Berger, Brigitte, ed. *The Culture of Entrepreneurship.* San Francisco: ICS Press, 1991.

Bosch, David. *Transforming Mission: Paradigm Shifts in Theology of Mission.* Maryknoll, NY: Orbis Books, 1991.

CAPRO Nigeria. "Calvary Ministries: CAPRO—Our Story." 2019. Accessed December 9, 2019. http://capromissions.org/

CAPRO UK. "Welcome to CAPRO UK." 2020. Accessed January 17, 2020. https://capro .global/.

CAPRO USA. "Who We Are." 2019. Accessed December 9, 2019. https://caprousa.org/.

The Evangelical Church and World Vision. "Covenant Kids Congo: The Impact of Sponsorship." 2019. Accessed April 25, 2019. https://covchurch.org/covenantkidscongo.

The Evangelical Covenant Church. "Covenant Foundations." Website. Copyrighted in 2018. Accessed January 13, 2020. https://covchurch.org/history/foundations/.

Global Leadership Network. "Global Leadership Network." 2019. Accessed December 3, 2019. https://globalleadership.org/who-we-are/.

Hamilton, Joan O'Connell. "Who Was Paul Carlson?" Published by Stanford Alumni Association, Stanford University. 1991. Reprinted by the Paul Carlson Partnership with permission. Accessed January 11, 2020. https://www.paulcarlson.org/aboutus/paulcarlson/.

Heuler, Hilary. "Kenyans Abroad Concerned about Diaspora Policy." Voice of America. February 3, 2015. Accessed November 12, 2019. https://www.voanews.com/africa /kenyans-abroad-concerned-about-diaspora-policy.

Jakada, Yakubu Tanko. "Nigerian Indigenous Mission Agencies and the Evangelization of West Africa: A Case Study of Calvary Ministries (CAPRO), Nigeria." MA thesis, Nigerian Baptist Theological Seminary, Ogbomoso, Nigeria, 2006.

Livingston, Ken. "The Legacy of David J. Bosch." *International Bulletin of Missionary Research* 23, no. 1 (1999): 26–32.

Martin, David. *Tongues of Fire: The Explosion of Protestantism in Latin America.* Oxford: Basil Blackwell, 1990.

McCleary, Rachel. *Global Compassion: Private Voluntary Organizations and U.S. Policy Since 1939.* New York: Oxford University Press, 2009.

Myers, Bryant. *Walking with the Poor: Principles and Practices of Transformational Development.* New York: Orbis Books, 1999.

Offutt, Stephen. *New Centers of Global Evangelicalism in Latin America and Africa.* New York: Cambridge University Press, 2015.

Offutt, Stephen, and Amy Reynolds. 2019. "Christian Ideas of Development: Understanding the Current Theories, Networks, and Priorities of Accord Organizations." *Christian Relief, Development and Advocacy Journal* 1, no. 1 (2019): 1–14.

Ranking Web of Hospitals. "Kenya." 2019. Accessed December 13, 2019. https://hospitals.webometrics.info/en/Africa/Kenya%20.

Samuel, Vinay, and Chris Sugden, eds. *Mission as Transformation: A Theology of the Whole Gospel*. Eugene, OR: Wipf and Stock Publishers, 1999.

Schnable, Allison. "Frames, Modes of Action, Networks: What Religion Affords Grassroots NGOs." Presentation at the Annual Conference of the Social Scientific Study of Religion, 2014, Indianapolis.

Swartz, David. *Facing West: American Evangelicals in an Age of World Christianity*. New York: Oxford University Press, 2020.

Tenwek Hospital. "A Brief History." 2019. Accessed December 14, 2019. https://www.tenwekhosp.org/about-us/.

———. "Community Health and Development." 2019. Accessed December 19, 2019. http://www.tenwekhosp.org/medical-outreach/community-health-development/.

Tizon, Al. *Transformation after Lausanne: Radical Evangelical Mission in Global-Local Perspective*. Eugene, OR: Wipf and Stock Publishers, 2008.

Woodberry, Robert. "The Missionary Roots of Liberal Democracy." *American Political Science Review* 106, no. 2 (2012): 244–74.

World Vision. "World Vision Partnership Update 2018." Accessed January 17, 2020. https://www.wvi.org/sites/default/files/2019-10/WV-2018-Partnership-Update_FINAL%20270919.pdf.

World Vision Congo. "Congo." 2020. Accessed January 13, 2020. https://www.wvi.org/congo.

Zambuko Trust. "Who We Are." 2019. http://www.zambukotrust.co.zw/.

ABOUT THE CONTRIBUTORS

JACOB K. OLUPONA is a professor of African and African American Studies, Harvard University, and a professor of African Religion, Harvard Divinity School. Prior to Harvard he was a professor at the University of California Davis (1991–2006). In addition to serving on the editorial boards of several influential journals, Olupona was the president of the African Association for the Study of Religion and served on the Board of Trustees and Executive Council of the American Academy of Religion (AAR). In 2008 he was awarded the highest distinction Nigeria bestows on her scholars, the Nigerian National Order of Merit (NNOM), and he was inducted as a Fellow of the Nigerian Academy of Letters (FNAL) in 2015. His book *City of 201 Gods: Ile Ife in Time, Space and the Imagination* (University of California Press, 2011) received the Harvard University's Cabot Fellowship for distinguished faculty scholarship. In 2018 he received the Martin E. Marty Award for the Public Understanding of Religion from the American Academy of Religion and in 2023 was inducted into the American Academy of Arts and Sciences.

ESTHER E. ACOLATSE is a professor of pastoral theology and world Christianity at Garrett Evangelical Theological Seminary. She works at the intersection of psychology and Christian thought in intercultural perspective. Her recent publications include *For Freedom or Bondage: A Critique of African Pastoral Practice* (Eerdmans) and *Powers, Principalities, and the Spirit: Biblical Realism in Africa and the West* (Eerdmans). She previously taught at Duke University Divinity School and Knox College at the University of Toronto.

AFE ADOGAME, the Maxwell M. Upson Professor of Religion and Society, is a leading scholar of the African diaspora. He earned a PhD in history of religions from the University of Bayreuth in Germany and has served as associate professor of World Christianity and religious studies, and director international at the School of Divinity, New College, at the University of Edinburgh in Scotland. His teaching and research interests are broad but tend to focus on interrogating new dynamics of religious experiences and expressions in Africa and the African diaspora, with a particular focus on African Christianities and new indigenous religious movements; and on the interconnectedness between religion and migration, globalization, politics, economy, media, and civil society.

ANDREW E. BARNES is a professor of history and faculty head of the School of Historical, Philosophical, and Religious Studies at Arizona State University. Barnes is the author of three monographs: *The Social Dimension of Piety: Associative Life and Religious Change in the Penitent Confraternities of Marseille 1499–1792* (Paulist Press, 1994); *Making Headway: The Introduction of Western Civilization in Colonial Northern Nigeria* (University of Rochester Press, 2009); *Global Christianity and the Black Atlantic: Tuskegee, Colonialism and the Shaping of African Industrial Education* (Baylor University Press, 2017), as well as forty research journal articles and scholarly book chapters. He is presently editing *The Palgrave Handbook of the History of Christianity in Africa from Apostolic Times to the Present*, while working on a study of the evolution of Ethiopianism among Christians of African descent across the Atlantic, 1780–1930.

REV. DR. BLAIR D. BERTRAND is a senior lecturer at Zomba Theological University (Zomba, Malawi) where he also serves as the director of research and educational quality assurance. In addition, Bertrand continues as an instructor at Tyndale University (Toronto, Ontario). Ordained in the Presbyterian Church in Canada, Bertrand brings to his work in practical theology an exploration of the intersection of theology and lived experience. Recently his writing has included a book he coauthored with Andrew Root, *When Church Stops Working* (Brazos Press, 2023), and articles or presentations on exorcism in the Reformed tradition, decolonizing education in Malawi, and a theological account of artificial intelligence.

YOLANDA COVINGTON-WARD is the department chair and a professor in the W.E.B. Du Bois Department of Afro-American Studies at the University of Massachusetts at Amherst. She is former president of the Association for Africanist Anthropology and an Advisory Board member of the Association for the Study of the Worldwide African Diaspora (ASWAD). She received her MA and PhD degrees in Cultural Anthropology from the University of Michigan and a BA in Afro-American Studies from Brown University. Her research focuses on embodiment, identity, religion, performance, and politics, emphasizing the agency and creativity of people of African descent in transforming the worlds around them. Her first book, *Gesture and Power: Religion, Nationalism, and Everyday Performance in Congo* (Duke University Press, 2016), was awarded the 2016 Amaury Talbot Award for African Anthropology from the Royal Anthropological Institute and the 2017 Elliott P. Skinner Book Award from the Association for Africanist Anthropology. Her second book project, *Transformation through Migration: Community, Conflict, and Identity in the Liberian Diaspora*, is currently under contract at the University of Pennsylvania Press. She has also coedited two volumes, *Embodying Black Religions in Africa and Its Diasporas* (Duke University Press, 2021) and *African Performance Arts and Political Acts* (University of Michigan Press, 2021). She has received a number of prestigious fellowships and awards including but not limited to the Ford Postdoctoral Fellowship, the Andrew W. Mellon Fellowship, a grant from the National Science Foundation, and the Teshome H. Gabriel Award for Distinguished Research and Scholarship in African Studies. She is also a former Fulbright fellow.

TIBEBE ESHETE is a scholar of African history and religion, who taught at Michigan State University. He is the author of *Jijiga: The History of a Strategic Town in the Horn of Africa* (Tsehai Publishers), *My Journey: The Deranged Life and Divine Grace*, and *The Evangelical Movement in Ethiopia: Resistance and Resilience* (Baylor University Press).

PAUL FRESTON is a sociologist of religion, and one of the world's most celebrated and accomplished scholars on Latin American religions, global Evangelicalism, and Christian-based politics. He is the Centre for International Governance Innovation (CIGI) Chair in Religion and Politics in Global Context at the Balsillie School of International Affairs and Wilfrid Laurier University. He is also professor of sociology on the postgraduate program in social science at the Universidade Federal de São Carlos, Brazil. His research has focused on, among other things, religion and democratization, the growth of Pentecostalism in the Global South, and questions of religion and globalization. His books include *Evangelicals and Politics in Asia, Africa and Latin America* (Cambridge University Press, 2001), *Protestant Political Parties: a Global Survey* (Ashgate, 2004), and *Evangelical Christianity and Democracy in Latin America* (Oxford University Press, 2008).

MARIAM GOSHADZE is a scholar of religious studies with geographical area of expertise in Accra, Ghana. Her research is at the crossroads of urban anthropology, sonic studies, sensory anthropology, and historical analysis. She is currently a professor of religion at the University of Leipzig, Germany.

TIM HARTMAN is an associate professor of theology at Columbia Theological Seminary. He holds a BA in history from Stanford University, a MDiv from Princeton Theological Seminary, and an MA in religious studies, and a PhD in theology, ethics, and culture from the University of Virginia. He is the author of two books: *Theology after Colonization: Kwame Bediako, Karl Barth, and the Future of Theological Reflection* (University of Notre Dame Press, 2020) and *Kwame Bediako: African Theology for a World Christianity* (Fortress Press, 2022; Langham Publications, 2021). He has published essays in *Modern Theology, Black Theology, Stellenbosch Theological Journal,* and *Cross Currents,* and his scholarly interests include contemporary Christian theologies worldwide; Christology; Lived Theology (the interrelationship between religious beliefs and practices); African theologies; Election / Predestination; antiracist theologies; ecclesiology; postcolonial mission; and the work of Karl Barth, Kwame Bediako, Dietrich Bonhoeffer, and James Cone.

STEPHEN OFFUTT is the author of multiple books and articles, including *Blood Entanglements: Evangelicals and Gangs in El Salvador* (Oxford University Press, 2023) and *New Centers of Global Evangelicalism in Latin America and Africa* (Cambridge University Press, 2015). He is a coauthor of *Religion and Poverty: Monotheistic Responses around the Globe* (Routledge, 2024) and a cofounder of the journal *Christian Relief, Development & Advocacy* (*CRDA*). Offutt received his BA in political science (Wheaton College), his MA in international relations (SAIS–Johns Hopkins University), and his PhD in sociology (Boston University).

DAMARIS SELEINA PARSITAU is the director of the Nagel Institute for the Study of World Christianity at Calvin University. She is also an associate professor of religion and gender studies, and the president of the African Association for the Study of Religion in Africa and Its Diaspora (AASR) 2020–25. In 2018–19, she served as a research associate and visiting professor at the Women Studies in Religion Program (WSRP) at the Harvard Divinity School, where she taught for one academic year. Dr. Parsitau was also the immediate former Kenya country director of the British Institute in East Africa (BIEA). In 2017 the Brookings Institution in Washington, DC, appointed her as an Echidna Global Scholar in Girls Education, and she spent a year working and studying policy-oriented research. Dr. Parsitau is also a professor extraordinaire at the University of South Africa and the University of the Western Cape respectively. She has equally held visiting research fellowships at the University of Cambridge and Edinburgh University in

Scotland. Her fields of teaching and research expertise and interests include World Christianity, African Pentecostal / Evangelical Christianity, and their intersections with gender, politics, civic engagement, and public life. Dr. Parsitau is highly published in peer-reviewed journal articles, book chapters, monographs, opinion pieces, and policy blogs and briefs.

DEREK R. PETERSON is Ali Mazrui Professor of History and African Studies at the University of Michigan. His second book, *Ethnic Patriotism and the East African Revival: History of Dissent* (Cambridge University Press, 2012), won "best book" prizes from the African Studies Association and the American Historical Association. In 2017 Peterson was awarded a MacArthur "Genius" fellowship. His newest book, *A Popular History of Idi Amin's Uganda*, is forthcoming from Yale University Press.

KATRIEN PYPE is a cultural anthropologist, working at KU Leuven, who has been carrying out ethnographic research on Kinshasa's religious media since 2003. Katrien explores how cultural expressivity and media technologies shape religious subjectivities. Her monograph, *The Making of the Pentecostal Melodrama: Religion, Media, and Gender in Kinshasa* (Berghahn Books, 2012), is an ethnography of the production of evangelizing television serials. She has also published numerous book chapters and articles, in scientific journals such as *Journal of Religion in Africa, Africa: Journal of the International Africa Institute, Journal of the Royal Anthropological Institute, Studies in World Christianity*, and *Journal of Pentecostal-Charismatic Christianity*.

SHOBANA SHANKAR is professor of history at Stony Brook, State University of New York. Her research focuses on colonial and postcolonial West Africa and Africa-South Asia networks and covers themes related to religious encounter, racial politics, humanitarianism, women and gender, history of health and disease, intellectual history, and critical development studies. She is the author of many articles and two books, *An Uneasy Embrace: Africa, India and the Spectre of Race* (Hurst / Oxford, 2021) and *Who Shall Enter Paradise? Christian Origins in Muslim Northern Nigeria, 1890–1975* (Ohio University Press, 2014), and coeditor of two edited collections on religion and globalization and on the Sudan Interior Mission (SIM) in Sudanic Africa. Her work has been supported by the Wilson Center, Goethe University, Council for American Overseas Research Centers, and others. She is founder and coeditor of the book series African Religions, Social Realities, published by Ohio University Press.

DR. NIMI WARIBOKO is the Walter G. Muelder Professor of Social Ethics at Boston University. His transdisciplinary oeuvre combines social sciences, philosophy, radical theology, literary, and cultural studies in order to create new ideas and theories, disrupt conventional wisdom, and promote human flourishing. The six pillars of his scholarship are (1) economic ethics, (2) Christian social ethics, (3) African social traditions / political theology, (4) Pentecostal studies, (5) philosophical theology, and (6) literary studies. He is the author of *Transcripts of the Sacred: Beautiful, Monstrous, Ridiculous* (Indiana University Press, 2023).